A WORD INDEX TO JAMES JOYCE'S

DUBLINERS

A WORD INDEX TO JAMES JOYCE'S

DUBLINERS

Edited by

GARY LANE

Programmed by

ROLAND DEDEKIND

60173

HASKELL HOUSE PUBLISHERS LTD.

Publishers of Scarce Scholarly Books

NEW YORK ■ 1972

Iublished by Haskell House Publishers, Ltd.
280 Lafayette Street, New York, N.Y. 10012

Copyright © 1971 by Haskell House Publishers, Ltd.

International Standard Book Number: 0-8383-1384-1

Library of Congress Catalog Card Number: 71-183760

Printed and Bound in the United States of America

This Concordance is compiled from
DUBLINERS by James Joyce
Originally published by B.W. Huebsch, Inc. in 1916
And copyright © 1967 by the Estate of James Joyce
Reprinted by permission of THE VIKING PRESS, INC.

PREFACE

The scholar of Joyce, accustomed to patterns of language extraordinarily rich and complex, will scarcely ask the reason for this book, but it is perhaps pertinent to note that an inquiry into the unity of *Dubliners* was its origin. I have not yet concluded that inquiry, but this index has been extremely helpful in tracing the symbols about which Joyce formed his first major work; it should prove similarly useful in any intensive study of *Dubliners*. With its completion, too, one can now trace a word throughout the major work of Joyce, for, with indices to *A Portrait of the Artist as a Young Man, Ulysses, Finnegans Wake,* and the poetry already available, this book completes the tabulation of Joyce's word use.

After nearly four months of part-time work on programming, card punching, and proofreading, the index was compiled in about twelve minutes on an IBM 360 computer. It includes each word and number in *Dubliners*—the words on pages 1-251, the numbers on page 252—and lists in addition, on pages 253-263, the components of Joyce's many hyphenated words. Following each entry is its frequency of occurence, but where that frequency is greater than ninety-nine, I have supposed the word to be unlikely to interest and suppressed the listing of its locations. Certain words—"hall-door" and "halldoor," "pierglass" and "pier-glass" are examples—appear sometimes hyphenated, sometimes merely compounded, but this is because Joyce did not always write them the same way.

With the publisher's kind permission, this index is keyed to the definitive 1968 Viking Press edition of *Dubliners*. Entries are followed by the title of the story in which they appear, the page number, and the line. The abbreviated story titles and their full forms are as follows:

SISTR	The Sisters	PARTS	Counterparts
ENCTR	An Encounter	CLAY	Clay
ARABY	Araby	PNFUL	A Painful Case
EVELN	Eveline	IVY D	Ivy Day in the Committee Room
RACE	After the Race		
GALNT	Two Gallants	MOTHR	A Mother
HOUSE	The Boarding House	GRACE	Grace
LITTL	A Little Cloud	DEAD	The Dead

A number of people helped make this book possible. My colleague Roland Dedekind tackled and solved an intricate problem in programming while sustaining his full-time role as Registrar of Muhlenberg College and Assistant Professor of Mathematics. Michael Boldissar's crew in our Luther J. Deck Computer Center, Mary Schellhamer and Jean Weidner, taught me key punching. Leonard Dimmick and Mike Filipos of Bethlehem Steel Corporation's Corporate Data Processing generously gave us use of their IBM 360, while Robert Vogelsinger, a systems engineer with Bethlehem Steel, took a personal interest in the project, helping us to debug and print out our program. Finally, I must acknowledge the cheerful and cheering help of my wife Carmen, who took time out of her busy graduate student's career to read aloud, slowly and with punctuation, the whole of *Dubliners* to me.

GARY LANE

```
A (1586)
ABACK (1) ........................................ DEAD   211/15
ABANDONED (1) .................................... MOTHR  140/27
ABBOT (1) ........................................ ARABY   29/12
ABHORRED (1) ..................................... PNFUL  108/14
ABJECT (1) ....................................... PARTS   92/08
ABLE (6) ......................................... GALNT   52/10
    GALNT   58/10    HOUSE   61/02    LITTL   73/19  CLAY   100/04
    DEAD   195/33
ABOUT (129)
ABOVE (18) ....................................... SISTR   14/11
    ARABY   30/03    EVELN   37/12    RACE    42/16  RACE    45/24
    HOUSE   61/17    HOUSE   68/23    LITTL   75/06  PNFUL  107/15
    IVY D  125/12    GRACE  166/19    GRACE  172/11  GRACE  173/13
    DEAD   177/32    DEAD   179/10    DEAD   186/16  DEAD   188/17
    DEAD   209/12
ABROAD (3) ....................................... ENCTR   21/07
    LITTL   78/15    DEAD   203/02
ABRUPT (2) ....................................... GRACE  170/28
    DEAD   196/08
ABRUPTLY (5) ..................................... ENCTR   27/33
    MOTHR  149/09    DEAD   187/24    DEAD   210/33  DEAD   216/30
ABSENCE (2) ...................................... PNFUL  113/22
    GRACE  154/29
ABSENT (1) ....................................... DEAD   204/04
ABSENT-MINDEDNESS (1) ............................ PARTS   89/14
ABSOLVE (1) ...................................... SISTR   11/30
ABSTINENT (1) .................................... LITTL   80/18
ABSTRACT (1) ..................................... MOTHR  141/25
ABSTRACTED (2) ................................... PARTS   91/04
    DEAD   217/08
ABU (1) .......................................... MOTHR  136/01
ABUNDANCE (1) .................................... DEAD   209/08
ABUSE (1) ........................................ PARTS   91/08
ABUSED (1) ....................................... HOUSE   64/27
ACADEMY (3) ...................................... MOTHR  137/21
    DEAD   176/10    DEAD   186/02
ACCENT (12) ...................................... ENCTR   26/02
    ENCTR   28/07    LITTL   70/04    LITTL   77/01  PARTS   86/03
    PARTS   92/19    PARTS   95/22    PARTS   97/33  MOTHR  139/18
    GRACE  151/20    GRACE  161/02    DEAD   183/23
ACCENTS (2) ...................................... ARABY   35/07
    GRACE  154/31
ACCEPTED (3) ..................................... GRACE  156/21
    GRACE  169/04    DEAD   185/25
ACCIDENT (11) .................................... PNFUL  110/12
    PNFUL  114/23    PNFUL  114/33    PNFUL  115/07  GRACE  152/07
    GRACE  152/08    GRACE  152/34    GRACE  153/20  GRACE  155/03
    GRACE  157/32    GRACE  158/09
ACCIDENTS (1) .................................... PNFUL  115/13
ACCLAMATION (1) .................................. DEAD   205/32
ACCOMMODATION (1) ................................ GRACE  172/05
ACCOMPANIED (2) .................................. ARABY   31/01
    PARTS   89/06
ACCOMPANIMENT (1) ................................ GRACE  156/02
ACCOMPANIMENTS (2) ............................... HOUSE   62/26
    MOTHR  149/16
ACCOMPANIST (5) .................................. MOTHR  138/09
    MOTHR  138/16    MOTHR  145/31    MOTHR  147/06  MOTHR  149/17
ACCOMPLISHMENTS (2) .............................. RACE    46/01
    MOTHR  136/15
ACCORD (2) ....................................... DEAD   217/10
```

```
          DEAD    217/32
ACCORDANCE (1) .................................. PNFUL  115/08
ACCORDING (3) ................................... PNFUL  107/18
     MOTHR 141/05      DEAD   197/02
ACCORDINGLY (1) ................................. PARTS   95/33
ACCOUNT (6) ..................................... HOUSE   68/13
     LITTL   81/23    CLAY   104/30    IVY D 127/04    MOTHR 145/06
     GRACE 166/32
ACCOUNTANT (1) .................................. GRACE  174/14
ACCOUNTS (4) .................................... GRACE  174/24
     GRACE 174/26    GRACE 174/29    GRACE 174/31
ACCURATELY (1) .................................. GRACE  174/17
ACCUSED (1) ..................................... CLAY   103/29
ACCUSTOMED (1) .................................. CLAY   100/18
ACHED. (1) ...................................... PARTS   90/30
ACHIEVED (1) .................................... GALNT   50/25
ACHING (1) ...................................... PARTS   92/24
ACKNOWLEDGED (2) ................................ RACE    42/14
     GALNT   51/16
ACQUAINTANCE (2) ................................ SISTR   13/28
     LITTL   75/27
ACQUAINTANCES (1) ............................... RACE    43/30
ACQUIESCENCE (1) ................................ DEAD   193/16
ACRES (1) ....................................... DEAD   202/12
ACROBAT (1) ..................................... PARTS   94/20
ACROSS (23) ..................................... ENCTR   26/34
     ENCTR   28/05    ENCTR   28/10    GALNT   52/09    GALNT   55/11
     GALNT   58/11    GALNT   60/11    LITTL   74/30    IVY D 124/15
     MOTHR 146/26    GRACE 153/33    GRACE 161/16    GRACE 171/15
     DEAD   184/24    DEAD   191/21    DEAD   191/30    DEAD   193/17
     DEAD   197/23    DEAD   198/25    DEAD   213/02    DEAD   214/25
     DEAD   218/16    DEAD   219/15
ACT (2) ......................................... LITTL   81/04
     LITTL   82/05
ACTING (3) ...................................... RACE    47/25
     DEAD   206/01    DEAD   220/02
ACTION (1) ...................................... PNFUL  114/21
ACTIVE (2) ...................................... GALNT   59/08
     GRACE 155/32
ACTIVELY (1) .................................... DEAD   178/14
ACTOR (1) ....................................... IVY D 125/23
ACTS (2) ........................................ SISTR   13/12
     PNFUL 108/24
ACTUATED (1) .................................... DEAD   203/19
ACUTE (1) ....................................... HOUSE   65/29
ACUTELY (1) ..................................... LITTL   80/23
ADA (2) ......................................... PARTS   97/15
     PARTS   97/15
ADAM (1) ........................................ DEAD   176/15
ADAPTED (1) ..................................... GRACE  173/31
ADDED (12) ...................................... SISTR   11/07
     ENCTR   25/12    GALNT   50/12    GALNT   52/30    GALNT   53/07
     PARTS   91/17    IVY D 127/04    IVY D 132/30    GRACE 163/06
     DEAD   195/08    DEAD   206/14    DEAD   216/05
ADDING (1) ...................................... ENCTR   25/01
ADDRESS (10) .................................... LITTL   79/04
     PARTS   89/24    IVY D 121/01    IVY D 122/02    IVY D 122/05
     IVY D 122/16    IVY D 131/25    GRACE 151/21    GRACE 154/09
     DEAD   209/02
ADDRESSED (2) ................................... ARABY   31/30
     GRACE 168/18
ADDRESSING (2) .................................. IVY D 121/22
```

```
        IVY D 126/04
ADIEUS (1) ....................................... DEAD    209/23
ADMIRE (2) ....................................... LITTL    73/06
        IVY D 132/15
ADMIRED (3) ...................................... RACE     46/12
    PARTS  95/18    MOTHR 136/14
ADMIRING (2) ..................................... ENCTR    21/31
    DEAD  180/22
ADMIRINGLY (1) ................................... PARTS    95/16
ADMIT (4) ........................................ PARTS    93/28
    GRACE 161/26    GRACE 163/05    GRACE 174/28
ADMITTED (2) ..................................... IVY D   124/27
    MOTHR 140/06
ADORATION (1) .................................... ARABY    31/17
ADORNED (1) ...................................... CLAY    101/33
ADROITNESS (1) ................................... GALNT    50/18
ADVANCE (3) ...................................... RACE     43/05
    PARTS  90/32    PARTS  91/01
ADVANCED (2) ..................................... RACE     43/15
    DEAD  206/24
ADVANCING (2) .................................... IVY D   120/25
    DEAD  192/29
ADVANTAGE (3) .................................... HOUSE    64/31
    IVY D 131/21    MOTHR 137/26
ADVENTURE (6) .................................... ENCTR    24/11
    RACE   48/07    GALNT  57/29    LITTL  80/18    PNFUL 110/24
    DEAD  215/17
ADVENTURELESS (1) ................................ PNFUL   109/16
ADVENTURES (3) ................................... ENCTR    20/06
    ENCTR  21/05    ENCTR  21/05
ADVERTING (1) .................................... DEAD    191/22
ADVERTISEMENT (2) ................................ EVELN    37/25
    PNFUL 108/09
ADVERTISEMENTS (2) ............................... SISTR    12/28
    GRACE 158/22
ADVICE (5) ....................................... GALNT    54/01
    MOTHR 138/25    GRACE 152/02    DEAD  208/31    DEAD    211/32
ADVISE (1) ....................................... ENCTR    20/29
ADVISED (2) ...................................... MOTHR   138/14
    MOTHR 141/01
ADVISING (1) ..................................... MOTHR   138/26
AFFAIR (10) ...................................... ARABY    32/21
    EVELN  39/17    HOUSE  63/20    HOUSE  65/03    HOUSE    65/12
    HOUSE  65/31    HOUSE  65/34    HOUSE  66/18    LITTL    72/28
    DEAD  175/13
AFFAIRS (2) ...................................... GALNT    51/31
    PARTS  87/26
AFFECTED (1) ..................................... SISTR    17/32
AFFECTION (3) .................................... CLAY    101/32
    DEAD  203/31    DEAD  205/13
AFFECTIONATE (2) ................................. ENCTR    27/30
    DEAD  213/13
AFFECTIONS (1) ................................... DEAD    204/08
AFFIRMED (1) ..................................... GALNT    52/22
AFFORDED (1) ..................................... HOUSE    65/32
AFFRONT (1) ...................................... GRACE   160/29
AFORESAID (1) .................................... DEAD    203/07
AFRAID (12) ...................................... ENCTR    20/05
    ENCTR  21/17    ENCTR  25/18    ARABY  33/26    GALNT    51/07
    IVY D 124/28    MOTHR 138/30    MOTHR 138/30    MOTHR   146/04
    DEAD  176/27    DEAD  195/22    DEAD  202/16
AFTER (115)
```

```
AFTERNOON  (1) ......................................  GALNT   50/16
AFTERWARDS  (7) .....................................  SISTR   13/31
        EVELN   36/06    RACE    43/23    PNFUL 110/04    PNFUL 114/01
        MOTHR 137/20    DEAD    195/11
AGAIN  (115)
AGAINST  (40) .......................................  SISTR   16/04
        SISTR   17/01    ARABY   32/15    ARABY   33/11    ARABY   35/28
        EVELN   36/02    EVELN   39/33    GALNT   50/20    GALNT   58/07
        GALNT   59/05    HOUSE   66/33    HOUSE   68/27    LITTL   71/14
        LITTL   73/09    LITTL   74/26    LITTL   83/22    PARTS   95/21
        PARTS   97/08    PNFUL 112/31    IVY D 118/10    IVY D 121/03
        MOTHR 145/02    GRACE 161/11    GRACE 169/12    GRACE 169/33
        DEAD    179/03    DEAD    194/12    DEAD    202/06    DEAD    209/16
        DEAD    210/07    DEAD    213/03    DEAD    213/14    DEAD    215/26
        DEAD    215/31    DEAD    216/14    DEAD    217/17    DEAD    220/21
        DEAD    220/22    DEAD    221/17    DEAD    223/25
AGE  (15) ...........................................  SISTR   10/34
        ENCTR   25/28    ENCTR   25/32    RACE    43/13    HOUSE   64/28
        IVY D 120/10    IVY D 129/15    MOTHR 136/13    MOTHR 137/19
        GRACE 155/32    GRACE 157/30    GRACE 167/06    DEAD    203/23
        DEAD    203/28    DEAD    223/08
AGED  (2) ...........................................  SISTR   12/08
        PNFUL 113/23
AGENCIES  (1) .......................................  GRACE 163/19
AGENT  (4) ..........................................  HOUSE   62/17
        IVY D 119/15    GRACE 158/24    GRACE 172/26
AGES  (1) ...........................................  LITTL   71/15
AGILE  (1) ..........................................  GRACE 152/11
AGING  (1) ..........................................  LITTL   75/01
AGITATED  (2) .......................................  ENCTR   25/18
        MOTHR 146/04
AGITATION  (4) ......................................  ENCTR   27/33
        HOUSE   66/34    LITTL   74/16    DEAD    190/05
AGO  (11) ...........................................  ENCTR   25/03
        EVELN   37/02    EVELN   38/33    LITTL   78/34    LITTL   82/12
        CLAY    106/14    PNFUL 115/02    DEAD    176/06    DEAD    194/07
        DEAD    218/28    DEAD    218/30
AGONY  (1) ..........................................  LITTL   82/27
AGREE  (1) ..........................................  MOTHR 148/01
AGREEABLE  (1) ......................................  GRACE 169/05
AGREEABLY  (1) ......................................  CLAY    103/10
AGREED  (9) .........................................  RACE    43/34
        HOUSE   65/16    LITTL   80/01    LITTL   80/02    PARTS   96/01
        CLAY    103/07    PNFUL 112/06    MOTHR 141/22    GRACE 153/01
AH  (18) ............................................  SISTR   15/12
        SISTR   16/01    SISTR   16/17    SISTR   16/22    SISTR   16/28
        ENCTR   25/11    LITTL   75/26    LITTL   76/23    LITTL   77/25
        LITTL   78/25    PARTS   96/23    IVY D 119/27    IVY D 124/25
        IVY D 128/33    MOTHR 142/14    GRACE 159/07    GRACE 164/34
        GRACE 165/16
AID  (3) ............................................  ENCTR   28/11
        PARTS   94/06    IVY D 124/04
AIM  (1) ............................................  GRACE 167/07
AIMLESSLY  (1) ......................................  ENCTR   27/03
AIR  (40) ...........................................  ENCTR   22/04
        ARABY   29/08    ARABY   30/05    ARABY   33/01    ARABY   33/23
        EVELN   40/01    EVELN   40/06    RACE    45/07    GALNT   49/02
        GALNT   49/07    GALNT   54/16    GALNT   55/22    GALNT   56/04
        GALNT   56/19    GALNT   57/19    LITTL   70/03    LITTL   71/28
        PARTS   89/13    PARTS   98/20    CLAY    105/11    CLAY    105/12
        PNFUL 113/13    PNFUL 116/06    GRACE 151/01    GRACE 156/28
        GRACE 159/05    GRACE 163/22    DEAD    177/19    DEAD    193/03
```

```
      DEAD   200/26     DEAD   202/09     DEAD   202/28     DEAD   206/03
      DEAD   210/02     DEAD   210/22     DEAD   211/34     DEAD   212/14
      DEAD   213/02     DEAD   213/25     DEAD   223/04
AIRING  (1) ....................................... DEAD   179/16
AIRS  (1) ......................................... MOTHR  147/17
AISLES  (1) ....................................... GRACE  172/05
ALACOQUE  (1) ..................................... EVELN   37/14
ALARM  (2) ........................................ HOUSE   68/29
      CLAY   101/26
ALARMED  (4) ...................................... LITTL   72/11
      LITTL   84/27     MOTHR  141/03     GRACE  151/04
ALAS  (1) ......................................... IVY D  134/23
ALCOVE  (1) ....................................... PNFUL  107/12
ALDERMAN  (2) ..................................... IVY D  127/11
      IVY D  127/13
ALE  (3) .......................................... GALNT   57/05
      DEAD   197/02     DEAD   197/24
ALERT  (2) ........................................ RACE    46/26
      PNFUL  108/22
ALIGHT  (1) ....................................... LITTL   72/08
ALIGHTED  (1) ..................................... RACE    45/16
ALIKE  (1) ........................................ GALNT   54/12
ALIVE  (6) ........................................ EVELN   37/01
      EVELN   39/29     LITTL   81/26     IVY D  122/15     DEAD   177/11
      DEAD   203/12
ALL  (256)
ALLAN  (1) ........................................ EVELN   39/11
ALLEN  (1) ........................................ DEAD   223/29
ALLEY  (1) ........................................ PARTS   92/33
ALLEYNE  (26) ..................................... PARTS   86/07
      PARTS   86/17     PARTS   87/03     PARTS   87/06     PARTS   87/24
      PARTS   87/26     PARTS   87/31     PARTS   87/33     PARTS   88/09
      PARTS   89/15     PARTS   89/23     PARTS   89/32     PARTS   90/02
      PARTS   90/06     PARTS   90/10     PARTS   90/11     PARTS   91/05
      PARTS   91/08     PARTS   91/17     PARTS   91/28     PARTS   92/08
      PARTS   92/11     PARTS   92/14     PARTS   92/17     PARTS   92/18
      PARTS   94/02
ALLEYNE'S  (2) .................................... PARTS   87/02
      PARTS   89/34
ALLEYS  (1) ....................................... PNFUL  117/03
ALLOW  (6) ........................................ SISTR   12/18
      MOTHR  149/17     GRACE  154/07 _   GRACE  167/17     DEAD   185/34
      DEAD   195/29
ALLOWED  (12) ..................................... ARABY   35/28
      GALNT   56/19     HOUSE   63/04     HOUSE   64/25     LITTL   75/20
      PARTS   89/20     PARTS   93/04     PNFUL  109/13     PNFUL  111/19
      PNFUL  117/29     GRACE  167/21     DEAD   201/27
ALLS  (1) ......................................... GRACE  154/34
ALL'S  (2) ........................................ GRACE  159/07
      GRACE  160/07
ALLUDED  (2) ...................................... RACE    43/20
      PNFUL  110/06
ALLUDING  (5) ..................................... SISTR   11/19
      ENCTR   26/11     IVY D  125/13     IVY D  133/28     DEAD   192/20
ALLUSION  (3) ..................................... HOUSE   68/12
      PNFUL  110/08     DEAD   194/33
ALLUSIONS  (2) .................................... HOUSE   64/14
      LITTL   74/06
ALMIGHTY  (1) ..................................... IVY D  125/19
ALMOND  (1) ....................................... CLAY   102/21
ALMONDS  (2) ...................................... DEAD   196/26
      DEAD   201/22
```

ALMOST (14) .... ENCTR 20/04

ENCTR 27/30	RACE 42/18	HOUSE 65/32	HOUSE 68/12
HOUSE 68/29	PARTS 91/21	PNFUL 110/30	PNFUL 113/13
GRACE 172/03	DEAD 178/31	DEAD 181/30	DEAD 188/10
DEAD 196/11			

ALMS (1) .... PNFUL 108/28

ALONE (14) .... ENCTR 21/02

ARABY 32/05	ARABY 34/21	GALNT 56/17	HOUSE 67/14
PARTS 92/04	PNFUL 111/16	PNFUL 116/31	PNFUL 117/34
GRACE 172/16	DEAD 192/04	DEAD 213/15	DEAD 214/10
DEAD 214/12			

ALONG (50) .... SISTR 12/27

SISTR 13/30	ENCTR 21/15	ENCTR 21/29	ENCTR 22/15
ENCTR 22/19	ENCTR 22/20	ENCTR 24/20	EVELN 36/05
RACE 45/09	RACE 46/30	GALNT 50/29	GALNT 50/30
GALNT 53/03	GALNT 53/18	GALNT 54/06	GALNT 55/20
GALNT 56/19	GALNT 56/22	GALNT 57/30	GALNT 58/15
GALNT 59/01	LITTL 71/10	LITTL 73/14	LITTL 74/33
PARTS 97/11	CLAY 103/11	PNFUL 107/06	PNFUL 113/07
PNFUL 116/21	PNFUL 117/02	PNFUL 117/10	PNFUL 117/21
MOTHR 145/18	GRACE 172/05	DEAD 175/05	DEAD 186/11
DEAD 192/04	DEAD 208/25	DEAD 209/05	DEAD 209/22
DEAD 213/08	DEAD 213/19	DEAD 213/31	DEAD 214/21
DEAD 215/32	DEAD 216/20	DEAD 219/23	DEAD 222/25
DEAD 223/05			

ALOUD (2) .... PARTS 90/25

PNFUL 113/17			

ALPHY (6) .... CLAY 100/10

CLAY 100/20	CLAY 102/08	CLAY 103/18	CLAY 104/24
CLAY 104/28			

ALREADY (8) .... ARABY 33/02

GALNT 55/04	PARTS 93/13	CLAY 101/05	MOTHR 142/17
DEAD 189/08	DEAD 191/33	DEAD 195/16	

ALSO (30) .... SISTR 12/05

SISTR 15/05	RACE 43/08	RACE 43/18	RACE 44/02
RACE 45/28	GALNT 54/11	HOUSE 62/22	HOUSE 62/27
HOUSE 64/15	CLAY 106/10	PNFUL 108/19	PNFUL 114/32
GRACE 151/24	GRACE 158/08	GRACE 168/09	GRACE 173/17
DEAD 175/07	DEAD 176/13	DEAD 179/25	DEAD 182/34
DEAD 190/22	DEAD 192/31	DEAD 195/08	DEAD 197/18
DEAD 200/20	DEAD 204/14	DEAD 209/27	DEAD 209/31
DEAD 220/15			

ALTAR (3) .... SISTR 14/28

MOTHR 137/10	GRACE 172/14		

ALTARS (1) .... GRACE 165/32

ALTER (1) .... MOTHR 140/33

ALTERNATELY (2) .... SISTR 13/25

PNFUL 116/23			

ALTOGETHER (3) .... RACE 44/09

HOUSE 67/01	DEAD 202/02		

ALWAYS (53) .... SISTR 9/10

SISTR 11/02	SISTR 12/16	SISTR 12/24	SISTR 13/11
SISTR 17/16	ENCTR 24/29	ENCTR 28/11	ARABY 30/22
ARABY 30/29	EVELN 37/26	EVELN 38/09	EVELN 38/11
EVELN 38/12	EVELN 39/07	RACE 44/10	GALNT 50/19
GALNT 51/24	GALNT 51/28	GALNT 53/21	HOUSE 62/20
HOUSE 62/20	HOUSE 64/15	LITTL 71/12	LITTL 71/21
LITTL 72/11	LITTL 72/30	LITTL 75/12	LITTL 75/14
PARTS 87/08	PARTS 87/13	CLAY 99/12	CLAY 99/13
CLAY 99/14	CLAY 99/18	CLAY 100/29	CLAY 102/09
PNFUL 108/03	PNFUL 110/14	PNFUL 114/24	IVY D 121/21
IVY D 123/28	GRACE 154/04	GRACE 156/22	GRACE 166/01

```
        DEAD    175/13     DEAD    176/30     DEAD    182/14     DEAD    186/26
        DEAD    197/20     DEAD    204/02     DEAD    204/06     DEAD    218/20
AM  (17) ...............................................     SISTR     9/08
        SISTR   10/34      HOUSE    62/30     HOUSE    66/30     HOUSE    66/30
        HOUSE   67/23      LITTL    78/11     LITTL    81/29     DEAD    177/12
        DEAD    194/02     DEAD    195/22     DEAD    196/15     DEAD    202/16
        DEAD    203/06     DEAD    216/25     DEAD    218/14     DEAD    218/28
AMATEUR  (1)· ..........................................     MOTHR   147/19
AMBITION  (1) .........................................     IVY D   135/11
AMBULANCE  (1) ........................................     PNFUL   114/13
AMEN  (1) ..............................................     DEAD    207/30
AMERICA  (1) ..........................................     RACE     47/32
AMERICAN  (5) .........................................     ENCTR    20/08
        RACE    47/05      MOTHR   144/29     GRACE   169/24     DEAD    196/32
AMERICAN'S  (1) .......................................     RACE     47/21
AMIABILITY  (1) .......................................     ARABY    32/23
AMIABLE  (2) ..........................................     HOUSE    68/26
        PARTS   91/27
AMIABLY  (3) ..........................................     GALNT    54/33
        MOTHR   144/02     DEAD    198/12
AMID  (14) ............................................     SISTR    14/17
        ARABY   31/05      EVELN    41/11     RACE     44/22     RACE     47/08
        LITTL   77/04      PARTS    89/30     CLAY    105/10     IVY D   133/33
        MOTHR   136/15     GRACE   162/10     DEAD    198/04     DEAD    208/12
        DEAD    209/23
AMIDST  (1) ...........................................     PNFUL   110/34
AMN'T  (1) ............................................     IVY D   120/13
AMONG  (12) ...........................................     ENCTR    20/01
        ARABY   29/10      ARABY    34/17     EVELN    40/22     CLAY    102/12
        MOTHR   139/23     MOTHR   143/34     DEAD    192/21     DEAD    203/02
        DEAD    203/06     DEAD    203/12     DEAD    204/07
AMUSE  (2) ............................................     GALNT    56/30
        PARTS   92/19
AMUSED  (3) ...........................................     SISTR    13/07
        ENCTR   23/29      GALNT    49/13      .
AMY  (1) ..............................................     DEAD    187/33
AN  (186)
'AN  (1) ..............................................     GRACE   153/21
ANALOGY  (1) ..........................................     IVY D   132/22
ANCESTRAL  (2) ........................................     CLAY    106/09
        DEAD    207/32
ANCIENT  (1) ..........................................     SISTR    12/22
AND  (2230)
ANDRE  (2) ............................................     RACE     43/01
        RACE    47/03
ANEW  (1) .............................................     LITTL    84/24
ANGELICAL  (1) ........................................     PNFUL   111/25
ANGER  (7) ............................................     SISTR    11/17
        ARABY   35/34      LITTL    84/17     PARTS    96/09     PARTS    96/32
        MOTHR   141/10     DEAD    218/33
ANGERED  (1) ..........................................     DEAD    181/09
ANGLE  (1) ............................................     GALNT    56/06
ANGRILY  (2) ..........................................     MOTHR   148/26
        DEAD    219/02
ANGRY  (6) ............................................     SISTR    11/18
        PARTS   95/27      MOTHR   140/23     MOTHR   148/32     MOTHR   149/19
        GRACE   170/22
ANGUISH  (2) ..........................................     ARABY    35/33
        EVELN   41/11
ANIMAL  (2) ...........................................     EVELN    41/15
        RACE    45/12
ANIMATEDLY  (2) .......................................     MOTHR   145/28
```

```
                 DEAD   193/15
ANIMATION (1) ...................................... DEAD   196/15
ANKLES (1) ........................................ ENCTR   28/03
ANNIE (4) ......................................... LITTL   82/14
     LITTL   83/01    LITTL   83/21    LITTL   85/03
ANNIE'S (2) ....................................... LITTL   82/09
     LITTL   82/23
ANNIHILATE (1) .................................... ARABY   32/14
ANNIVERSARY (1) ................................... IVY D  132/28
ANNOUNCED (3) ..................................... IVY D  134/02
     GRACE 166/11    DEAD   181/33
ANNOY (1) ......................................... DEAD   212/16
ANNOYANCE (1) ..................................... DEAD   217/07
ANNOYED (5) ....................................... SISTR   12/30
     PARTS   92/13    CLAY   102/24    DEAD   212/17  DEAD   217/09
ANNUAL (1) ........................................ DEAD   175/13
ANOINTED (1) ...................................... SISTR   15/20
ANOTHER (42) ...................................... SISTR   18/05
     ARABY   29/06    EVELN   38/27    EVELN   39/28  RACE    46/34
     GALNT   49/18    GALNT   51/24    GALNT   54/03  GALNT   58/33
     GALNT   59/15    GALNT   59/21    HOUSE   62/14  HOUSE   62/15
     HOUSE   67/34    LITTL   78/01    LITTL   79/28  LITTL   80/10
     PARTS   87/14    PARTS   87/18    PARTS   93/30  PARTS   94/26
     PARTS   95/04    PNFUL  112/09    PNFUL  116/18  IVY D  126/24
     IVY D  126/34    IVY D  129/13    IVY D  130/27  IVY D  133/09
     IVY D  133/12    MOTHR  138/01    MOTHR  138/02  MOTHR  140/10
     MOTHR  148/03    GRACE  153/15    DEAD   175/05  DEAD   183/17
     DEAD   198/12    DEAD   204/27    DEAD   205/23  DEAD   208/25
     DEAD   219/33
ANOTHER'S (1) ..................................... GRACE  164/21
ANSWER (19) ....................................... SISTR   13/20
     ENCTR   28/09    ARABY   31/31    RACE    44/11  RACE    44/19
     RACE    45/12    GALNT   52/12    GALNT   55/11  GALNT   56/28
     CLAY   104/06    CLAY   104/08    MOTHR  149/04  DEAD   185/17
     DEAD   189/33    DEAD   190/04    DEAD   211/01  DEAD   218/08
     DEAD   218/12    DEAD   220/19
ANSWERED (30) ..................................... ENCTR   24/33
     ENCTR   25/23    ENCTR   26/25    ARABY   31/32  ARABY   32/22
     ARABY   32/30    EVELN   40/28    GALNT   55/07  LITTL   83/10
     PARTS   91/05    PARTS   91/09    PARTS   95/18  MOTHR  142/08
     GRACE  152/19    GRACE  153/21    GRACE  158/28  GRACE  160/25
     DEAD   177/29    DEAD   178/03    DEAD   185/10  DEAD   187/29
     DEAD   190/02    DEAD   190/20    DEAD   190/28  DEAD   198/27
     DEAD   198/34    DEAD   213/29    DEAD   216/25  DEAD   219/04
     DEAD   220/18
ANSWERING (3) ..................................... GALNT   60/21
     PARTS   89/19    GRACE  152/06
ANSWERS (3) ....................................... HOUSE   64/11
     LITTL   82/15    DEAD   176/23
'AN'T (2) ......................................... GRACE  152/30
     GRACE  153/21
ANTICIPATION (1) .................................. PARTS   91/07
ANTIENT (4) ....................................... MOTHR  138/10
     MOTHR  139/07    MOTHR  141/29    DEAD   176/11
ANTIQUE (1) ....................................... SISTR   13/33
ANXIETY (1) ....................................... GALNT   60/12
ANXIOUS (3) ....................................... GALNT   55/23
     HOUSE   65/23    DEAD   181/19
ANXIOUSLY (1) ..................................... DEAD   184/17
ANY (57) .......................................... SISTR   15/31
     SISTR   16/23    SISTR   16/27    ENCTR   20/25  ENCTR   23/25
     ENCTR   24/13    ENCTR   27/13    ARABY   32/25  ARABY   33/21
```

ARABY 34/26	EVELN 38/13	EVELN 38/18	GALNT 50/20
GALNT 51/28	HOUSE 68/16	HOUSE 68/28	LITTL 75/01
LITTL 75/24	LITTL 78/01	LITTL 79/12	LITTL 80/15
LITTL 82/16	PARTS 90/10	PARTS 91/14	PARTS 94/09
PARTS 97/27	CLAY 100/15	CLAY 101/11	CLAY 103/27
PNFUL 109/09	PNFUL 110/24	PNFUL 110/25	PNFUL 115/29
IVY D 121/21	IVY D 127/01	IVY D 127/06	IVY D 128/22
IVY D 131/23	IVY D 132/29	MOTHR 140/12	MOTHR 142/01
MOTHR 142/05	MOTHR 148/26	GRACE 160/29	GRACE 161/06
GRACE 170/26	DEAD 175/16	DEAD 176/28	DEAD 186/05
DEAD 192/14	DEAD 192/15	DEAD 198/32	DEAD 199/23
DEAD 204/11	DEAD 213/07	DEAD 216/04	DEAD 223/13

ANYBODY (2) .... SISTR 13/14
RACE 44/12
ANYHOW (4) .... IVY D 128/34
IVY D 133/19   DEAD 206/32   DEAD 208/09
ANYONE (10) .... HOUSE 62/34
CLAY 100/28   PNFUL 110/21   PNFUL 115/14   PNFUL 116/33
IVY D 121/20   IVY D 123/02   DEAD 176/01   DEAD 194/15
DEAD 198/07
ANYTHING (24) .... SISTR 16/02
ENCTR 25/04   ENCTR 27/29   ARABY 35/15   EVELN 39/18
HOUSE 68/33   LITTL 84/14   LITTL 85/13   PARTS 92/21
CLAY 104/21   PNFUL 108/14   IVY D 123/15   IVY D 124/09
MOTHR 142/05   MOTHR 142/30   MOTHR 144/11   MOTHR 144/20
MOTHR 147/29   GRACE 161/01   DEAD 183/05   DEAD 183/16
DEAD 197/14   DEAD 199/26   DEAD 203/04
ANYWAY (6) .... EVELN 37/20
HOUSE 67/15   IVY D 121/14   IVY D 122/10   IVY D 129/04
MOTHR 144/16
ANYWHERE (4) .... SISTR 18/01
SISTR 18/02   LITTL 76/09   PARTS 92/29
A.P. (1) .... LITTL 80/08
APACHE (1) .... ENCTR 20/23
APART (3) .... HOUSE 61/12
LITTL 74/27   GRACE 167/09
APOLLINARIS (3) .... PARTS 94/22
PARTS 94/24   PARTS 95/25
APOLOGETIC (1) .... IVY D 131/08
APOLOGISE (2) .... PARTS 91/33
PARTS 92/02
APOLOGISED (1) .... GRACE 156/33
APOLOGY (2) .... PARTS 92/08
DEAD 216/03
APPARENTLY (1) .... PNFUL 114/11
APPEAL (2) .... LITTL 74/03
DEAD 194/11
APPEALED (4) .... MOTHR 145/06
MOTHR 146/14   MOTHR 148/15   MOTHR 148/16
APPEAR (4) .... GALNT 57/21
LITTL 74/23   LITTL 82/29   DEAD 209/29
APPEARANCE (5) .... GALNT 55/23
PARTS 90/02   PARTS 95/12   IVY D 125/30   DEAD 179/27
APPEARED (7) .... GALNT 54/28
LITTL 75/07   PNFUL 115/18   IVY D 125/23   MOTHR 141/17
MOTHR 142/22   DEAD 188/06
APPEARING (1) .... GRACE 173/13
APPLAUDED (3) .... MOTHR 147/17,
MOTHR 147/20   DEAD 193/07
APPLAUDING (1) .... DEAD 193/14
APPLAUSE (6) .... PARTS 96/20
IVY D 135/23   DEAD 187/13   DEAD 192/31   DEAD 193/08

```
            DEAD   204/18
APPLE (4) ................................................. PNFUL  108/12
       DEAD   179/30    DEAD   197/19    DEAD   197/20
APPLES (3) ............................................... CLAY   102/18
       DEAD   196/32    DEAD   201/22
APPLE-TREE (1) ........................................... ARABY   29/15
APPLYING (1) ............................................. HOUSE   67/22
APPOINTED (1) ............................................ RACE    43/06
APPOINTMENT (2) .......................................... GALNT   51/01
       PNFUL  110/13
APPRECIABLE (1) .......................................... MOTHR  137/25
APPRECIATED (2) .......................................... MOTHR  141/25
       GRACE  166/31
APPRECIATION (1) ......................................... GALNT   54/04
APPRECIATIVE (1) ......................................... DEAD   183/28
APPREHEND (1) ............................................ DEAD   223/18
APPREHENSIVELY (1) ....................................... LITTL   72/14
APPROACH (1) ............................................. MOTHR  149/15
APPROACHED (5) ........................................... SISTR   12/05
       SISTR   17/22    GALNT   55/14    GALNT   55/21    DEAD   223/17
APPROACHING (2) .......................................... ENCTR   22/06
       ENCTR   24/18
APPROPRIATENESS (1) ...................................... GRACE  157/31
APPROVAL (2) ............................................. PARTS   91/17
       MOTHR  149/33
APPROVED (2) ............................................. MOTHR  149/11
       GRACE  158/06
APPROVING (1) ............................................ PNFUL  116/02
APPROVINGLY (1) .......................................... GALNT   55/31
ARAB'S (1) ............................................... ARABY   34/10
ARABY (3) ................................................ ARABY   29/ T
       ARABY   31/32    ARABY   32/18
ARAMBURO (1) ............................................. DEAD   199/06
ARAN (1) ................................................. DEAD   188/33
ARC (2) .................................................. GRACE  154/17
       GRACE  154/18
ARCH (2) ................................................. LITTL   71/26
       GRACE  166/17
ARCHBISHOPS (2) .......................................... GRACE  169/11
       GRACE  169/29
ARCHLY (1) ............................................... DEAD   206/10
ARDENTLY (1) ............................................. LITTL   74/14
ARDOUR (1) ............................................... DEAD   217/11
ARE (71) ................................................. SISTR   11/14
       SISTR   16/02    ENCTR   25/11    ARABY   34/01    EVELN   37/28
       GALNT   53/26    GALNT   54/29    HOUSE   66/23    HOUSE   66/24
       LITTL   74/28    LITTL   75/18    LITTL   77/22    LITTL   78/25
       LITTL   81/29    LITTL   83/16    LITTL   83/31    PARTS   88/03
       PARTS   97/23    PARTS   97/31    CLAY    99/16    PNFUL  111/29
       IVY D  120/22    IVY D  120/24    IVY D  121/21    IVY D  125/05
       IVY D  125/08    IVY D  126/18    IVY D  129/15    IVY D  132/10
       IVY D  133/03    MOTHR  138/34    MOTHR  139/33    MOTHR  140/04
       MOTHR  140/05    MOTHR  143/05    GRACE  150/17    GRACE  161/22
       GRACE  163/32    GRACE  168/14    GRACE  169/23    GRACE  173/22
       DEAD   181/01    DEAD   181/03    DEAD   181/31    DEAD   182/26
       DEAD   189/05    DEAD   195/05    DEAD   195/06    DEAD   195/06
       DEAD   195/08    DEAD   195/08    DEAD   195/30    DEAD   199/18
       DEAD   199/20    DEAD   201/21    DEAD   202/17    DEAD   202/22
       DEAD   203/21    DEAD   203/29    DEAD   204/02    DEAD   204/12
       DEAD   204/13    DEAD   204/21    DEAD   205/17    DEAD   205/18
       DEAD   205/19    DEAD   205/28    DEAD   205/29    DEAD   205/30
       DEAD   217/26    DEAD   218/07
```

AREA (3) .... GALNT   59/33
    GRACE 167/04   DEAD   213/01
AREAS (1) .... ARABY   30/14
AREN'T (2) .... DEAD   187/34
    DEAD   206/31
ARGUING (4) .... MOTHR 136/06
    MOTHR 149/12   GRACE 169/32   GRACE 169/33
ARGUMENTATIVELY (1) .... IVY D 132/13
ARISE (1) .... LITTL   73/17
ARM (19) .... GALNT   50/34
    LITTL   77/18   PARTS   95/16   PARTS   98/11   IVY D 128/21
    GRACE 152/22   GRACE 152/24   GRACE 156/07   GRACE 156/09
    GRACE 170/31   DEAD   189/07   DEAD   192/30   DEAD   202/28
    DEAD   213/05   DEAD   215/06   DEAD   215/08   DEAD   215/14
    DEAD   218/05   DEAD   218/08
ARM-CHAIR (3) .... SISTR   12/13
    SISTR   14/33   HOUSE   64/03
ARMED (1) .... GALNT   50/23
ARMS (19) .... EVELN   40/21
    EVELN   40/21   RACE   47/17   HOUSE   66/29   HOUSE   68/08
    LITTL   82/09   LITTL   82/19   LITTL   84/09   LITTL   84/16
    LITTL   84/22   LITTL   85/15   PARTS   95/34   PARTS   96/17
    CLAY   101/04   GRACE 155/22   DEAD   215/24   DEAD   215/25
    DEAD   218/16   DEAD   218/24
AROMA (2) .... PARTS   90/05
    MOTHR 144/34
AROMATIC (1) .... RACE   46/31
AROSE (3) .... ARABY   30/10
    HOUSE   67/11   PNFUL 109/15
AROUND (4) .... GALNT   52/15
    IVY D 124/34   DEAD   192/25   DEAD   202/24
AROUSED (1) .... RACE   46/24
ARRANGED (11) .... ENCTR   19/04
    ENCTR   21/14   ENCTR   22/30   LITTL   79/28   CLAY   102/04
    CLAY   104/32   PNFUL 107/17   MOTHR 136/08   MOTHR 147/19
    DEAD   187/19   DEAD   189/08
ARRANGEMENTS (1) .... ENCTR   21/23
ARRANGING (6) .... SISTR   10/03
    SISTR   16/09   MOTHR 136/03   MOTHR 140/03   GRACE 162/28
    DEAD   179/06
ARRAY (1) .... GRACE 173/21
ARRAYED (3) .... DEAD   182/32
    DEAD   193/02   DEAD   222/28
ARRIVAL (1) .... PNFUL 114/12
ARRIVED (5) .... PNFUL 114/10
    PNFUL 114/34   MOTHR 139/06   MOTHR 141/29   MOTHR 143/32
ARRIVING (2) .... MOTHR 142/16
    GRACE 159/22
ARROWROOT (1) .... PNFUL 108/33
ARTERIES (1) .... DEAD   213/31
ARTICLE (2) .... PNFUL 107/08
    DEAD   216/06
ARTICLES (1) .... GRACE 154/03
ARTISTE (5) .... HOUSE   62/22
    HOUSE   68/14   PARTS   94/21   MOTHR 142/22   MOTHR 142/23
ARTISTES (12) .... HOUSE   62/06
    HOUSE   62/24   HOUSE   68/11   MOTHR 138/19   MOTHR 138/20
    MOTHR 139/23   MOTHR 140/04   MOTHR 140/06   MOTHR 142/16
    MOTHR 145/01   MOTHR 147/31   MOTHR 148/14
ARTS (1) .... PNFUL 111/14
AS (370)
ASCEND (2) .... HOUSE   67/34

PNFUL 111/25
ASCENDED (1) .... IVY D 118/05
ASCENT (1) .... DEAD 215/22
ASHAMED (4) .... ENCTR 28/08
    DEAD 187/34   DEAD 188/01   DEAD 188/03
ASHEN-GREY (1) .... ENCTR 24/25
ASHPIT (1) .... ENCTR 21/28
ASHPITS (1) .... ARABY 30/10
ASIDE (6) .... GALNT 53/31
    MOTHR 139/34   MOTHR 149/17   DEAD 182/04   DEAD 183/07
    DEAD 185/22
ASK (22) .... EVELN 38/17
    LITTL 77/30   PARTS 87/08   PARTS 90/32   CLAY 104/21
    CLAY 106/17   PNFUL 110/17   PNFUL 113/04   IVY D 124/23
    IVY D 125/06   IVY D 126/27   IVY D 128/25   IVY D 128/28
    IVY D 132/07   MOTHR 145/29   MOTHR 149/03   GRACE 174/23
    DEAD 175/11   DEAD 176/33   DEAD 181/26   DEAD 181/30
    DEAD 202/19
ASKED (125)
ASKER (1) .... DEAD 190/18
ASKING (6) .... SISTR 13/08
    HOUSE 63/03   PNFUL 112/01   MOTHR 141/11   MOTHR 148/34
    GRACE 154/26
ASKS (1) .... ENCTR 26/28
ASLEEP (4) .... SISTR 11/18
    SISTR 15/26   SISTR 16/05   DEAD 222/03
ASPEN (1) .... MOTHR 147/05
ASPIRATED (1) .... GALNT 52/02
ASSAILED (1) .... DEAD 220/01
ASSEMBLE (1) .... MOTHR 137/31
ASSEMBLED (1) .... CLAY 106/06
ASSEMBLY (1) .... GRACE 172/07
ASSENT (3) .... SISTR 15/13
    GRACE 161/23   DEAD 203/13
ASSERT (1) .... LITTL 80/30
ASSISTANT (2) .... PNFUL 114/15
    MOTHR 136/01
ASSISTED (1) .... PNFUL 110/32
ASSOCIATED (1) .... GALNT 50/26
ASSOCIATION (1) .... GRACE 157/21
ASSUMED (5) .... ENCTR 20/21
    MOTHR 149/05   GRACE 161/02   GRACE 162/09   DEAD 183/23
ASSUMING (2) .... HOUSE 64/26
    PARTS 89/13
ASSURANCE (1) .... GRACE 173/26
ASSURE (1) .... DEAD 195/24
ASTONISHED (3) .... LITTL 78/24
    GRACE 166/19   DEAD 201/03
ASTONISHING (2) .... GRACE 168/25
    GRACE 168/28
ASTONISHMENT (1) .... DEAD 218/17
ASTON'S (1) .... DEAD 188/15
ASTOUNDED (1) .... PARTS 91/26
ASTRAKHAN (2) .... PNFUL 110/02
    DEAD 206/20
ASTUTENESS (1) .... GRACE 157/20
ASUNDER (1) .... CLAY 101/19
AT (495)
ATALANTAS (1) .... LITTL 72/11
ATE (6) .... ENCTR 24/01
    GALNT 57/26   PNFUL 113/05   DEAD 200/18   DEAD 200/19
    DEAD 200/21

ATKINSON (1) .... IVY D 131/15
ATLANTIC (1) .... DEAD 189/01
ATMOSPHERE (1) .... GRACE 172/22
ATOM (1) .... LITTL 76/05
ATTACHED (3) .... PNFUL 111/25
    PNFUL 115/14   IVY D 127/01
ATTACK (1) .... MOTHR 148/33
ATTACKED (3) .... PNFUL 115/23
    PNFUL 116/04   DEAD 193/03
ATTACKING (1) .... PNFUL 116/05
ATTAIN (1) .... IVY D 135/12
ATTEMPT (2) .... DEAD 204/26
    DEAD 204/27
ATTEMPTING (2) .... PNFUL 113/25
    PNFUL 114/04
ATTEMPTS (1) .... HOUSE 65/24
ATTEND (2) .... PARTS 87/12
    DEAD 175/06
ATTENDANCES (1) .... PNFUL 111/03
ATTENDED (3) .... HOUSE 66/12
    CLAY 102/14   MOTHR 140/18
ATTENTION (5) .... PNFUL 110/06
    GRACE 172/24   DEAD 185/23   DEAD 192/28   DEAD 202/20
ATTENTIVE (3) .... GRACE 173/18
    DEAD 190/22   DEAD 206/10
ATTENTIVELY (2) .... PNFUL 112/32
    IVY D 119/24
ATTITUDE (5) .... ENCTR 25/31
    DEAD 210/03   DEAD 210/06   DEAD 212/04   DEAD 213/07
ATTRACTED (1) .... DEAD 192/28
AUDIBLE (1) .... MOTHR 143/31
AUDIENCE (7) .... RACE 48/09
    MOTHR 138/22   MOTHR 140/20   MOTHR 146/04   MOTHR 146/14
    GRACE 171/30   DEAD 193/30
AUDITORIUM (2) .... MOTHR 143/13
    MOTHR 146/29
AUDITORS (1) .... IVY D 135/24
AUGHRIM (4) .... DEAD 212/10
    DEAD 212/12   DEAD 218/14   DEAD 219/05
AUGUST (1) .... GALNT 49/01
AUNGIER (1) .... IVY D 122/30
AUNT (125) .... DEAD 176/13
AUNTS (7) .... DEAD 176/13
    DEAD 179/21   DEAD 179/22   DEAD 180/23   DEAD 192/26
    DEAD 205/04   DEAD 220/02
AUNT'S (2) .... SISTR 14/09
    DEAD 222/22
AUTHOR (1) .... PARTS 91/26
AUTHORITATIVE (1) .... GRACE 151/27
AUTOBIOGRAPICAL (1) .... PNFUL 108/25
AUTUMN (2) .... LITTL 71/06
    PNFUL 112/04
AVENUE (4) .... EVELN 36/02
    EVELN 36/12   EVELN 39/22   EVELN 39/34
AVERAGE (1) .... LITTL 70/12
AVOIDED (1) .... DEAD 190/06
AWAKENED (2) .... ENCTR 20/33
    HOUSE 68/25
AWARD (2) .... LITTL 78/17
    DEAD 205/03
AWARDED (1) .... MOTHR 142/33
AWARE (4) .... HOUSE 64/19

LITTL	81/16	PARTS	91/21	GRACE	166/32		
AWAY (53)	....					SISTR	12/25
SISTR	12/27	SISTR	13/34	SISTR	14/32	ENCTR	23/08
ENCTR	23/11	ENCTR	26/21	ENCTR	26/31	ENCTR	27/18
ARABY	35/27	EVELN	37/05	EVELN	37/18	EVELN	37/23
EVELN	38/28	EVELN	40/07	RACE	48/22	HOUSE	63/08
HOUSE	63/10	HOUSE	65/34	HOUSE	66/07	HOUSE	67/34
LITTL	73/11	PARTS	90/21	CLAY	100/04	CLAY	101/23
CLAY	104/02	PNFUL	110/22	PNFUL	111/22	PNFUL	112/22
PNFUL	117/30	IVY D	124/03	IVY D	133/26	MOTHR	137/09
MOTHR	141/03	MOTHR	147/07	MCTHR	149/09	GRACE	150/05
GRACE	164/02	GRACE	170/18	DEAD	186/08	DEAD	187/16
DEAD	190/13	DEAD	194/09	DEAD	195/31	DEAD	196/09
DEAD	200/31	DEAD	203/15	DEAD	214/10	DEAD	215/17
DEAD	216/20	DEAD	217/05	DEAD	218/33	DEAD	219/23
AWFUL (1)	....					DEAD	180/15
AWFULLY (4)	....					EVELN	39/05
LITTL	79/24	LITTL	79/27	DEAD	184/06		
AWKWARD (6)	....					HOUSE	64/11
HOUSE	64/12	HOUSE	64/14	HOUSE	64/15	PNFUL	109/25
DEAD	219/20						
AWKWARDLY (1)	....					DEAD	189/14
AWOKE (3)	....					EVELN	41/02
LITTL	83/23	LITTL	84/07				
AY (6)	....					PARTS	87/18
IVY D	121/20	IVY D	125/18	IVY D	133/16	IVY D	133/16
IVY D	133/24						
AYRES (3)	....					EVELN	38/30
EVELN	39/15	EVELN	40/33				
B. (1)	....					PNFUL	114/22
BABE (1)	....					DEAD	210/26
BACHELOR (1)	....					LITTL	71/18
BACHELOR'S (1)	....					DEAD	188/14
BACK (92)	....					SISTR	14/22
SISTR	16/33	SISTR	17/14	ENCTR	19/04	ENCTR.	23/25
ENCTR	26/31	ARABY	29/08	ARABY	30/09	ARABY	31/20
ARABY	34/20	ARABY	35/22	EVELN	37/04	EVELN	38/34
EVELN	40/08	EVELN	41/01	RACE	44/11	RACE	48/02
GALNT	49/14	GALNT	51/05	GALNT	51/18	GALNT	55/09
GALNT	56/16	GALNT	57/21	GALNT	60/09	HOUSE	63/12
HOUSE	67/24	HOUSE	68/24	LITTL	71/21	LITTL	74/15
LITTL	74/26	LITTL	75/16	LITTL	79/17	LITTL	79/22
LITTL	82/32	LITTL	83/05	LITTL	84/06	LITTL	85/20
PARTS	86/09	PARTS	89/12	PARTS	91/21	PARTS	93/17
PARTS	94/12	PARTS	95/02	PARTS	95/05	PARTS	95/23
PARTS	97/04	PNFUL	117/27	IVY D	119/01	IVY D	120/02
IVY D	128/26	IVY D	129/08	IVY D	129/09	IVY D	129/19
IVY D	131/10	MOTHR	137/29	MOTHR	142/15	MOTHR	143/13
MOTHR	144/23	GRACE	156/26	GRACE	162/02	GRACE	162/05
GRACE	165/18	GRACE	165/21	GRACE	172/12	GRACE	173/19
DEAD	176/17	DEAD	176/23	DEAD	178/08	DEAD	180/01
DEAD	181/32	DEAD	182/29	DEAD	187/17	DEAD	191/21
DEAD	191/33	DEAD	194/28	DEAD	199/01	DEAD	199/04
DEAD	200/04	DEAD	201/33	DEAD	207/33	DEAD	208/03
DEAD	208/09	DEAD	208/21	DEAD	216/15	DEAD	217/03
DEAD	217/29	DEAD	218/25	DEAD	219/01	DEAD	220/06
DEAD	221/11	DEAD	221/18	DEAD	221/21		
BACKWARDS (2)	....					DEAD	184/33
DEAD	185/32						
BACON-FAT (1)	....					HOUSE	64/02

```
BACON-RIND (1) ...................................  HOUSE   64/02
BAD (24) ..........................................  SISTR   10/32
      SISTR  11/13    ARABY   32/33    ARABY   33/23  EVELN   37/01
      EVELN  38/16    RACE    43/24    HOUSE   61/09  LITTL   75/30
      LITTL  82/15    PARTS   92/07    CLAY   100/24  CLAY   104/10
      IVY D 128/33    IVY D  129/05    IVY D  131/24  IVY D  132/29
      GRACE 161/25    GRACE  163/23    GRACE  168/24  GRACE  171/08
      DEAD  185/08    DEAD   194/07    DEAD   217/05
BADE (5) ..........................................  ENCTR   24/32
      ENCTR  28/01    CLAY   105/33    PNFUL  112/10  DEAD   185/02
BADGE (1) .........................................  ENCTR   22/28
BADGES (1) ........................................  MOTHR  139/09
BADLY (2) .........................................  ENCTR   21/26
      GRACE 170/33
BAFFLED (1) .......................................  GALNT   60/24
BAG (7) ...........................................  ENCTR   23/19
      CLAY  102/16    CLAY   103/04    CLAY   103/18  CLAY   103/20
      CLAY  103/24    IVY D  133/04    -
BAGGAGES (1) ......................................  EVELN   40/25
BAGGOT (3) ........................................  GALNT   50/33
      GALNT  59/30    PNFUL  108/31
BAILIFFS (1) ......................................  IVY D  124/01
BAILIFF'S (1) .....................................  HOUSE   61/18
BALANCED (3) ......................................  MOTHR  145/23
      MOTHR 145/25    GRACE  156/09
BALBRIGGAN (1) ....................................  DEAD   186/33
BALCONY (2) .......................................  MOTHR  140/25
      DEAD  186/16
BALFE (1) .........................................  CLAY   106/15
BALL (2) ..........................................  GALNT   56/14
      MOTHR 139/29
BALLAD (1) ........................................  ARABY   31/08
BALLAST (2) .......................................  PARTS   94/14
      GRACE 153/17
BALLOONED (1) .....................................  HOUSE   63/28
BALLS (1) .........................................  LITTL   77/20
BALLSBRIDGE (1) ...................................  CLAY   100/04
BALUSTRADE (1) ....................................  GRACE  173/13
BAND (2) ..........................................  GALNT   52/28
      LITTL  73/14
BANDAGE (2) .......................................  CLAY   105/07
      CLAY  105/14
BANDED (1) ........................................  ENCTR   20/03
BANG (1) ..........................................  DEAD   209/16
BANGED (1) ........................................  PARTS   98/01
BANISH (1) ........................................  DEAD   190/25
BANISTER-RAIL (1) .................................  SISTR   14/11
BANISTERS (7) .....................................  HOUSE   69/02
      DEAD  175/11    DEAD   176/33    DEAD   181/29  DEAD   182/09
      DEAD  196/06    DEAD   209/30
BANK (11) .........................................  SISTR   14/06
      ENCTR  21/29    ENCTR   24/07    ENCTR   24/17  ENCTR   24/20
      RACE   45/15    LITTL   81/23    PNFUL  108/30  PNFUL  109/15
      PNFUL 112/23    GRACE  159/29
BANKNOTES (1) .....................................  MOTHR  146/32
BANSHEE (1) .......................................  GRACE  158/08
BANTAM (1) ........................................  HOUSE   65/10
BAPTISMAL (1) .....................................  GRACE  171/17
BAR (16) ..........................................  GALNT   50/21
      GALNT  57/03    LITTL   74/18    LITTL   74/21  PARTS   88/31
      PARTS  92/33    PARTS   94/15    GRACE  150/10  GRACE  150/12
      GRACE 151/11    GRACE  152/13    GRACE  152/32  GRACE  171/26
```

```
        GRACE  171/29      GRACE  171/31      DEAD   187/10
BARDS (1) ........................................... IVY D  134/21
BARE (3) ............................................ ARABY   34/21
      IVY D  121/01     DEAD   175/05
BAREHEADED (1) ...................................... IVY D  135/27
BARELY (1) .......................................... CLAY   102/03
BARGAIN (1) ......................................... LITTL   80/04
BARGAINING (1) ...................................... ARABY   31/04
BARGES (1) .......................................... ENCTR   23/08
BARITONE (8) ........................................ MOTHR  143/32
      MOTHR  144/26     MOTHR  146/02     MOTHR  146/21   MOTHR  146/23
      MOTHR  147/24     MOTHR  147/28     MOTHR  149/17
BARMAN (4) .......................................... LITTL   76/29
      LITTL   76/32     LITTL   80/33     PNFUL  115/28
BARMAN'S (1) ........................................ LITTL   76/26
BARMBRACK (1) ....................................... CLAY   101/07
BARMBRACKS (2) ...................................... CLAY    99/06
      CLAY    99/06
BAROMETER (1) ....................................... PARTS   91/02
BARRACKS (1) ........................................ PARTS   97/11
BARRELS (1) ......................................... ARABY   31/06
BARREN (1) .......................................... DEAD   224/01
BARRIER (1) ......................................... EVELN   41/13
BARS (1) ............................................ PARTS   89/29
BARTELL (15) ........................................ DEAD   184/09
      DEAD   198/18     DEAD   198/25     DEAD   198/27   DEAD   199/18
      DEAD   199/21     DEAD   199/30     DEAD   200/01   DEAD   201/25
      DEAD   206/30     DEAD   210/27     DEAD   211/02   DEAD   213/04
      DEAD   214/30     DEAD   215/01
BASE (2) ............................................ GALNT   53/17
      PNFUL  117/12
BASKET (4) .......................................... IVY D  128/17
      IVY D  128/20     IVY D  128/21     IVY D  128/29
BASS (8) ............................................ RACE    44/06
      GALNT   54/14     HOUSE   68/06     MOTHR  142/16   MOTHR  142/17
      MOTHR  142/20     MOTHR  147/24     DEAD   187/12
BATH (2) ............................................ SISTR   11/04
      HOUSE   67/07
BATHROOM (1) ........................................ DEAD   175/08
BATTALION (1) ....................................... GRACE  154/10
BATTER (1) .......................................... DEAD   176/03
BATTERED (1) ........................................ GRACE  152/03
BATTLE (2) .......................................... ENCTR   19/07
      ENCTR   19/08
BATTLES (1) ......................................... ENCTR   19/04
BAWLED (1) .......................................... PARTS   97/14
BAZAAR (9) .......................................... ARABY   31/33
      ARABY   32/20     ARABY   32/29     ARABY   33/26   ARABY   33/32
      ARABY   34/21     ARABY   34/27     ARABY   34/32   ARABY   35/27
BE (247)
BEADY (1) ........................................... SISTR   10/26
BEANNACHT (1) ....................................... DEAD   196/03
BEANS (1) ........................................... PNFUL  108/09
BEAR (2) ............................................ HOUSE   65/02
      MOTHR  139/20
BEARD (4) ........................................... HOUSE   65/26
      MOTHR  137/06     MOTHR  145/33     MOTHR  146/16
BEAT (5) ............................................ ENCTR   28/10
      PARTS   98/22     PARTS   98/24     IVY D  120/02   DEAD   205/22
BEATING (2) ......................................... ENCTR   19/14
      ENCTR   28/02
BEATS (1) ........................................... RACE    48/30
```

```
PEAUTIES  (1)  ....................................  RACE    46/16
BEAUTIFUL  (17)  ..................................  SISTR   15/17
    SISTR   15/27    ENCTR   20/10    ENCTR   26/07    RACE    47/23
    LITTL   76/16    LITTL   76/20    LITTL   76/21    LITTL   76/22
    DEAD   182/16    DEAD   190/21    DEAD   190/22    DEAD   191/23
    DEAD   191/23    DEAD   191/26    DEAD   200/06    DEAD   222/14
BEAUTIFULLY  (1)  .................................  DEAD   208/06
BEAUTY  (1)  ......................................  DEAD   222/13
BECAME  (11)  .....................................  ENCTR   21/03
    GALNT   50/15    GALNT   59/08    HOUSE   67/32    LITTL   71/13
    PARTS   94/25    PNFUL  110/31    PNFUL  116/32    MOTHR  143/31
    MOTHR  146/10    GRACE  156/31
BECAUSE  (44)  ....................................  SISTR   11/13
    SISTR   14/21    SISTR   15/06    ENCTR   21/04    ENCTR   22/27
    ENCTR   22/30    ENCTR   25/18    ARABY   29/14    ARABY   32/03
    EVELN   38/04    RACE    43/04    RACE    43/06    RACE    43/08
    RACE    43/09    HOUSE   64/14    HOUSE   64/15    LITTL   70/11
    LITTL   80/08    PARTS   93/01    PARTS   94/30    CLAY   100/09
    CLAY   101/19    CLAY   102/30    CLAY   105/25    PNFUL  107/01
    PNFUL  107/03    PNFUL  112/20    PNFUL  112/21    IVY D  121/17
    IVY D  125/26    IVY D  133/01    MOTHR  145/01    MOTHR  146/04
    MOTHR  148/18    GRACE  162/19    GRACE  166/21    GRACE  168/30
    DEAD   181/12    DEAD   198/28    DEAD   198/33    DEAD   199/16
    DEAD   200/17    DEAD   214/06    DEAD   217/05
BECKON  (1)  ......................................  SISTR   14/14
BECKONED  (1)  ....................................  SISTR   14/12
BECOME  (14)  .....................................  RACE    43/20
    HOUSE   64/19    LITTL   71/03    CLAY   100/18    PNFUL  110/06
    PNFUL  116/25    MOTHR  136/09    MOTHR  142/21    MOTHR  145/30
    MOTHR  146/21    GRACE  156/11    GRACE  158/25    GRACE  159/27
    DEAD   204/31
BECOMING  (3)  ....................................  EVELN   39/25
    IVY D  127/24    DEAD   223/06
BED  (21)  ........................................  SISTR   14/20
    SISTR   14/26    ARABY   34/01    HOUSE   66/25    HOUSE   67/05
    HOUSE   67/26    HOUSE   67/31    HOUSE   68/19    HOUSE   68/24
    PARTS   97/31    CLAY   101/28    CLAY   101/28    PNFUL  107/13
    GRACE  154/26    GRACE  156/20    GRACE  156/32    GRACE  170/11
    DEAD   196/18    DEAD   201/15    DEAD   218/15    DEAD   221/32
BED-CLOTHES  (1)  .................................  PNFUL  107/13
BED-RAIL  (2)  ....................................  HOUSE   68/27
    DEAD   218/16
BEDROOM  (5)  .....................................  ARABY   32/16
    CLAY   101/24    PNFUL  113/14    GRACE  156/28    GRACE  166/11
BEDS  (1)  ........................................  ARABY   31/24
BEDSTEAD  (1)  ....................................  PNFUL  107/09
BEEF  (3)  ........................................  PNFUL  112/28
    DEAD   196/21    DEAD   197/16
BEEF-TEA  (2)  ....................................  SISTR   16/27
    GRACE  156/20
BEEN  (144)
BEER  (6)  ........................................  GALNT   57/05
    GALNT   57/18    GALNT   57/26    GALNT   57/28    HOUSE   62/12
    PNFUL  108/33
BEESWAX  (1)  .....................................  DEAD   186/15
BEFORE  (101)
BEFOUL  (1)  ......................................  IVY D  135/03
BEG  (1)  .........................................  IVY D  126/15
BEGAN  (100)
BEGGARS  (1)  .....................................  PNFUL  108/29
BEGGED  (2)  ......................................  DEAD   186/06
    DEAD   198/01
```

```
BEGIN (8) ..............................................  GALNT   58/14
      HOUSE   64/24   LITTL   77/21   PARTS   90/27   MOTHR  141/31
      MOTHR  149/14   DEAD   198/09   DEAD   217/08
BEGINNERS (1) .........................................  DEAD   176/16
BEGINNING (14) ........................................  SISTR   13/28
      SISTR   17/26   ENCTR   22/02   ARABY   32/23   RACE    46/03
      HOUSE   66/16   LITTL   76/34   PARTS   92/20   PARTS   95/03
      IVY D  122/31   MOTHR  141/02   GRACE  156/11   DEAD   187/17
      DEAD   220/28
BEGINS (1) ............................................  IVY D  129/23
BEGONE (1) ............................................  LITTL   73/17
BEGUN (9) .............................................  EVELN   38/05
      EVELN   38/10   EVELN   39/09   RACE    43/15   PARTS   92/25
      CLAY   101/23   GRACE  159/25   DEAD   184/13   DEAD   223/24
BEHALF (2) ............................................  PNFUL  114/22
      GRACE  163/19
BEHAVED (1) ...........................................  MOTHR  140/20
BEHELD (1) ............................................  GALNT   57/30
BEHIND (31) ...........................................  SISTR   12/12
      SISTR   15/08   ENCTR   24/14   ARABY   29/09   ARABY   29/14
      ARABY   30/08   RACE    44/05   HOUSE   64/17   HOUSE   67/09
      LITTL   80/30   PARTS   94/28   PARTS   96/11   PARTS   98/09
      CLAY   102/23   CLAY   103/31   IVY D  127/29   MOTHR  139/14
      MOTHR  143/30   GRACE  162/01   GRACE  171/12   GRACE  172/16
      GRACE  172/17   DEAD   175/03   DEAD   178/21   DEAD   184/16
      DEAD   184/23   DEAD   192/14   DEAD   197/01   DEAD   206/24
      DEAD   211/02   DEAD   215/21
BEING (30) ............................................  SISTR    9/13
      SISTR   14/10   ENCTR   23/02   ENCTR   23/10   ARABY   29/01
      EVELN   37/10   EVELN   40/12   GALNT   52/31   HOUSE   62/17
      HOUSE   63/16   HOUSE   65/32   HOUSE   66/17   LITTL   70/12
      LITTL   71/15   LITTL   82/31   PARTS   94/32   CLAY   104/29
      PNFUL  117/15   IVY D  124/29   MOTHR  143/12   GRACE  152/11
      GRACE  158/01   GRACE  164/20   GRACE  167/09   DEAD   176/15
      DEAD   185/26   DEAD   187/05   DEAD   194/34   DEAD   201/28
      DEAD   220/21
BEIRNE (4) ............................................  MOTHR  142/03
      MOTHR  142/04   MOTHR  147/23   MOTHR  148/01
BELFAST (4) ...........................................  EVELN   36/09
      CLAY   100/08   CLAY   100/10   GRACE  156/16
BELFRY (1) ............................................  HOUSE   63/29
BELGIAN (1) ...........................................  RACE    42/12
BELGIUM (2) ...........................................  DEAD   189/13
      DEAD   189/15
BELIE (1) .............................................  GALNT   57/19
BELIEF (2) ............................................  GRACE  165/32
      GRACE  170/08
BELIEFS (1) ...........................................  GRACE  158/04
BELIEVE (15) ..........................................  ENCTR   25/24
      GALNT   52/32   LITTL   77/10   LITTL   80/12   LITTL   81/28
      IVY D  125/08   IVY D  126/30   IVY D  128/05   GRACE  158/08
      GRACE  163/24   GRACE  166/04   GRACE  166/06   GRACE  170/01
      DEAD   193/23   DEAD   203/21
BELIEVED (5) ..........................................  ARABY   34/07
      MOTHR  147/12   GRACE  154/01   GRACE  158/04   DEAD   176/19
BELIEVER (1) ..........................................  MOTHR  138/05
BELL (9) ..............................................  EVELN   41/04
      PARTS   86/01   CLAY   100/34   MOTHR  142/30   MOTHR  143/07
      MOTHR  145/30   MOTHR  147/04   MOTHR  148/04   DEAD   175/04
BELLE (1) .............................................  RACE    48/15
BELLS (2) .............................................  RACE    47/10
      HOUSE   64/20
```

BELL'S (1) .... MOTHR 146/03
BELONG (1) .... IVY D 131/23
BELONGED (2) .... DEAD 176/11
    DEAD 203/25
BELOW (6) .... ARABY 31/25
    ARABY 33/09   ARABY 33/15   GALNT 49/06   PNFUL 107/17
    DEAD 215/28
BELT (2) .... GALNT 55/25
    GALNT 55/26
BENCH (3) .... GRACE 172/16
    GRACE 172/17   GRACE 172/18
BENCHES (5) .... LITTL 71/08
    PNFUL 109/23   GRACE 172/10   GRACE 172/15   GRACE 173/17
BENDED (1) .... IVY D 125/19
BENDING (2) .... LITTL 84/17
    CLAY 103/11
BENEATH (5) .... HOUSE 63/29
    HOUSE 64/26   IVY D 131/03   MOTHR 145/08   DEAD 178/22
BENEFIT (2) .... IVY D 131/19
    IVY D 131/30
BENT (6) .... GALNT 55/18
    LITTL 75/08   PARTS 87/24   MOTHR 146/25   DEAD 193/10
    DEAD 209/01
BEQUEATHED (1) .... LITTL 71/15
BERGIN (2) .... DEAD 183/34
    DEAD 184/02
BERLIN (1) .... LITTL 78/17
BERNARD (5) .... PARTS 88/15
    PARTS 90/15   PARTS 90/26   PARTS 90/27   PARTS 90/27
BESIDE (26) .... ENCTR 22/07
    ENCTR 23/06   ENCTR 24/33   ENCTR 26/32   ARABY 34/22
    EVELN 37/13   EVELN 40/27   GALNT 55/20   GALNT 59/26
    HOUSE 67/14   PARTS 90/04   PARTS 91/18   PARTS 96/21
    CLAY 101/28   CLAY 105/32   PNFUL 109/17   PNFUL 109/27
    PNFUL 115/17   GRACE 151/23   GRACE 172/27   DEAD 186/17
    DEAD 196/21   DEAD 213/17   ·DEAD 222/31   DEAD 223/05
    DEAL 223/09
BESIDES (10) .... EVELN 37/01
    EVELN 38/09   RACE 43/10   RACE 44/12   HOUSE 63/07
    HOUSE 65/13   LITTL 74/05   DEAD 176/26   DEAD 181/20
    DEAD 195/05
BESSIE (1) .... DEAD 181/20
BEST (18) .... ARABY 29/14
    LITTL 79/03   PARTS 96/14   CLAY 101/27   CLAY 102/10
    PNFUL 116/29   IVY D 129/18   MOTHR 140/05   MOTHR 142/14
    GRACE 167/33   DEAD 176/19   DEAD 176/20   DEAD 181/18
    DEAD 197/22   DEAD 201/10   DEAD 205/02   DEAD 207/31
    DEAD 207/32
BET (1) .... LITTL 81/21
BETOKENED (1) .... PNFUL 108/14
BETRAY (1) .... ENCTR 27/33
BETRAYED (2) .... LITTL 81/17
    IVY D 134/29
BETRAYER (1) .... GALNT 53/17
BETTER (33) .... SISTR 15/12
    ENCTR 20/08   ENCTR 22/17   ENCTR 27/28   GALNT 58/08
    LITTL 74/11   LITTL 74/12   LITTL 74/29   LITTL 75/17
    LITTL 80/26   PARTS 89/22   CLAY 102/05   IVY D 118/11
    IVY D 121/20   IVY D 127/34   IVY D 129/04   IVY D 135/30
    MOTHR 137/08   MOTHR 139/28   MOTHR 140/18   MOTHR 141/21
    MOTHR 144/18   GRACE 161/28   DEAD 179/12   DEAD 193/13
    DEAD 195/10   DEAD 197/08   DEAD 199/22   DEAD 202/26

```
        DEAD   207/06     DEAD   208/26     DEAD   221/12     DEAD   223/06
BETTER-CLASS (1) .................................................. DEAD   176/12
BETWEEN (30) ...................................................... ENCTR   25/21
        ARABY   32/17     ARABY   32/26     RACE   43/26     RACE    48/20
        RACE    48/30     HOUSE   63/13     HOUSE  63/18     LITTL   75/07
        LITTL   80/23     LITTL   84/28     PARTS  87/09     PARTS   93/06
        PNFUL  110/10     PNFUL  112/19     PNFUL 112/21     PNFUL  113/01
        IVY D  121/18     IVY D  129/33     IVY D 132/23     MOTHR  138/23
        GRACE  158/20     GRACE  166/03     GRACE 166/33     GRACE  167/20
        DEAD   192/15     DEAD   196/21     DEAD  204/27     DEAD   207/08
        DEAD   218/04
BEVELLED (1) ...................................................... PARTS   94/11
BEWILDERED (1) .................................................... DEAD   209/12
BEWLEY'S (1) ...................................................... LITTL   82/14
BEYOND (7) ........................................................ ENCTR   23/09
        ARABY   33/20     EVELN   41/13     PNFUL 117/21     DEAD   203/29
        DEAD   204/29     DEAD   205/32
BICEPS (2) ........................................................ PARTS   95/31
        PARTS   95/34
BICYCLE-PUMP (1) ........................... ARABY   29/17
BID (1) ........................................................... LITTL   73/17
BIDDING (3) ....................................................... SISTR   15/04
        GALNT   58/33     DEAD   215/07
BIG (26) .......................................................... SISTR   13/26
        ENCTR   21/13     ENCTR   23/05     ENCTR 23/10     ENCTR   23/12
        ARABY   34/29     RACE    43/22     GALNT 55/30     GALNT   56/13
        HOUSE   62/03     PARTS   95/08     PARTS 97/08     CLAY    99/04
        CLAY    99/05     CLAY   100/34     CLAY 102/16     CLAY   103/17
        CLAY   103/19     IVY D  130/05     IVY D 131/19     GRACE  161/09
        GRACE  161/13     GRACE  161/14     DEAD  191/26     DEAD   191/26
        DEAD   219/10
BIGGEST (2) ....................................................... RACE    43/33
        GRACE  168/25
BILE (1) .......................................................... PNFUL  108/09
BILL (3) .......................................................... PNFUL  109/03
        PNFUL  113/06     GRACE  160/18
BILLIARD (1) ...................................................... GALNT   58/26
BILLS (3) ......................................................... RACE    43/29
        RACE    44/28     MOTHR  138/18
BILLY (1) ......................................................... DEAD   208/08
BILLY'S (1) ....................................................... DEAD   208/07
BIRD (1) .......................................................... DEAD   209/20
BIRDS (2) ......................................................... ENCTR   22/11
        DEAD   213/18
BIRTH (2) ......................................................... RACE    43/02
        LITTL   80/25
BIRTHDAY (1) ...................................................... DEAD   186/22
BISCUIT (3) ....................................................... GALNT   50/10
        GALNT   50/14     GALNT   51/15
BISCUIT-BARREL (1) ................................................ MOTHR  138/12
BISCUITS (4) ...................................................... ENCTR   23/34
        ENCTR   24/01     GALNT   57/10     PNFUL 108/33
BISHOPS (2) ....................................................... GRACE  169/12
        GRACE  169/28
BIT (17) .......................................................... GALNT   50/34
        GALNT   51/12     GALNT   52/16     GALNT 53/06     GALNT   53/22
        GALNT   58/26     HOUSE   65/17     LITTL 75/17     LITTL   76/08
        LITTL   77/31     LITTL   79/20     LITTL 81/08     LITTL   82/07
        PARTS   89/22     IVY D  123/09     IVY D 125/05     IVY D  132/17
BITE (1) .......................................................... GRACE  158/13
BITS (1) .......................................................... LITTL   77/20
BITTEN (2) ........................................................ GRACE  153/30
```

GRACE 158/11
BITTER (3) .... PARTS   91/11
    PARTS   95/06   DEAD   179/05
BITTERLY (1) .... GRACE 159/31
BITTERNESS (1) .... DEAD   178/09
BLACK (27) .... SISTR   10/26
    SISTR   12/17   SISTR   14/29   ENCTR   23/27   EVELN   38/20
    EVELN   40/27   GALNT   55/25   GALNT   55/28   GALNT   55/29
    PARTS   90/06   PNFUL 107/09   PNFUL 107/14   PNFUL 108/18
    IVY D 123/28   IVY D 125/24   IVY D 125/29   IVY D 126/09
    IVY D 126/31   IVY D 128/16   MOTHR 142/18   GRACE 154/12
    GRACE 172/07   DEAD   178/20   DEAD   197/03   DEAD   198/33
    DEAD   209/29   DEAD   222/30
BLACKENED (1) .... SISTR   12/23
BLACKTHORN (1) .... EVELN   36/16
BLACKWHITE (1) .... GRACE 154/05
BLADE (1) .... GRACE 157/20
BLAME (4) .... PNFUL 114/30
    PNFUL 115/09   PNFUL 115/14   PNFUL 116/29
BLANCMANGE (2) .... DEAD   196/24
    DEAD   200/13
BLANDLY (1) .... DEAD   181/33
BLANKETS (1) .... SISTR   11/22
BLANKLY (1) .... DEAD   196/09
BLAST (4) .... PARTS   86/08
    PARTS   90/24   IVY D 123/19   IVY D 130/18
BLATHERING (1) .... GRACE 170/18
BLEACHING (1) .... ENCTR   23/34
BLEAK (1) .... PNFUL 117/03
BLENDED (1) .... RACE   47/09
BLESSED (2) .... SISTR   14/32
    EVELN   37/14
BLEW (1) .... EVELN   40/31
BLIND (6) .... SISTR   9/06
    SISTR   14/17   ARABY   29/01   ARABY   29/04   ARABY   30/26
    GRACE 154/08
BLINDFOLD (1) .... CLAY   105/02
BLINDFOLDING (1) .... CLAY   105/06
BLINDS (1) .... DEAD   222/30
BLINKED (1) .... IVY D 118/07
BLINKING (2) .... DEAD   188/02
    DEAD   188/20
BLISS (1) .... LITTL   78/34
BLOCKS (1) .... DEAD   196/23
BLOND (1) .... HOUSE   68/11
BLOOD (12) .... ARABY   30/34
    HOUSE   67/09   CLAY   104/28   IVY D 125/17   IVY D 132/29
    GRACE 150/08   GRACE 151/03   GRACE 151/25   GRACE 153/03
    GRACE 153/29   DEAD   200/22   DEAD   213/08
BLOODY (4) .... GALNT   51/05
    HOUSE   68/17   GRACE 161/13   GRACE 161/14
BLOODY-MINDED (1) .... GRACE 157/33
BLOOMING (1) .... LITTL   81/07
BLOTCHES (1) .... IVY D 118/13
BLOUSE (5) .... GALNT   55/27
    LITTL   82/25   LITTL   83/01   LITTL   83/03   CLAY   101/29
BLOUSES (2) .... LITTL   82/30
    CLAY   101/03
BLOWING (4) .... HOUSE   63/27
    GRACE 153/18   DEAD   180/06   DEAD   222/32
BLOWN (2) .... HOUSE   67/06
    GRACE 153/30

```
BLUE (18) ..................................................... ENCTR  23/27
     RACE    42/08    RACE    42/12    RACE    45/12    GALNT  54/23
     GALNT   55/24    GALNT   55/33    GALNT   57/06    LITTL  82/25
     PNFUL  109/31    IVY D  118/07    IVY D  125/33    IVY D 130/04
     IVY D  130/06    MOTHR  139/09    MOTHR  143/18    DEAD  186/19
     DEAD   210/07
BLUISH (1) .................................................... LITTL  75/05
BLUNT (2) .................................................... GALNT  56/01
     DEAD   184/28
BLUNTLY (2) .................................................. GRACE 171/06
     DEAD   187/32
BLUSH (4) .................................................... LITTL  80/13
     LITTL   80/15    CLAY   102/25    DEAD   189/26
BLUSHED (2) .................................................. LITTL  79/01
     LITTL   79/13
BLUSHES (1) .................................................. LITTL  82/33
BLUSHING (3) ................................................. CLAY  105/04
     CLAY    99/17    DEAD   202/25
BLUSH-PINK (1) ............................................... MOTHR 138/32
BOA (1) ...................................................... GALNT  55/29
BOARD (3) .................................................... HOUSE  62/12
     CLAY    99/17    DEAD   202/25
BOARDING (5) ................................................. HOUSE  61/ T
     HOUSE   62/03    HOUSE   63/28    HOUSE   63/34    HOUSE  66/16
BOAST (1) .................................................... CLAY  106/08
BOASTED (2) .................................................. HOUSE  66/08
     DEAD   203/04
BOASTING (1) ................................................. PARTS  95/31
BOAT (4) ..................................................... EVELN  40/27
     EVELN   40/31    PNFUL  110/10    DEAD   214/24
BOB (6) ...................................................... ENCTR  22/18
     ENCTR   22/18    HOUSE   66/30    HOUSE   66/30    PARTS  92/27
     PARTS   92/27
BODICE (1) ................................................... DEAD  187/22
BODIES (2) ................................................... ARABY  30/06
     DEAD   183/13
BODILESS (1) ................................................. MOTHR 147/10
BODLEY (4) ................................................... PARTS  87/09
     PARTS   88/16    PARTS   90/15    PARTS   90/27
BODY (30) .................................................... SISTR  16/18
     ARABY   30/24    ARABY   31/18    EVELN   41/02    GALNT  49/18
     GALNT   51/17    GALNT   51/27    GALNT   55/26    GALNT  55/32
     PARTS   90/30    PARTS   92/24    PARTS   96/11    PARTS  97/11
     CLAY   101/19    CLAY   101/32    CLAY   101/33    PNFUL 108/24
     PNFUL  113/22    PNFUL  114/12    IVY D  125/25    MOTHR 143/19
     MOTHR  145/06    MOTHR  145/23    GRACE  163/32    GRACE 165/20
     DEAD   178/24    DEAD   215/12    DEAD   215/27    DEAD  217/17
     DEAD   218/05
BOG (1) ...................................................... DEAD  223/29
BOHEMIAN (3) ................................................. EVELN  39/03
     RACE    47/31    LITTL   76/30
BOILED (1) ................................................... DEAD  191/27
BOILERS (1) .................................................. CLAY   99/04
BOLD (2) ..................................................... GALNT  56/28
     LITTL   72/33
BOLDEST (1) .................................................. DEAD  183/14
BOLDLY (9) ................................................... ENCTR  20/03
     RACE    48/06    GALNT   54/30    LITTL   72/17    LITTL  76/19
     LITTL   80/34    DEAD   197/05    DEAD   202/31    DEAD  223/07
BONA-FIDE (1) ................................................ GRACE 159/24
BONAPARTE (1) ................................................ SISTR  13/04
BOND (2) ..................................................... PNFUL 112/07
```

```
                PNFUL  112/07
BONE  (1)  .......................................... DEAD   199/27
BONES  (1)  ......................................... GRACE  152/22
BONNET  (1)  ........................................ EVELN   39/31
BONY  (1)  .......................................... IVY D  118/07
BOOK  (9)  .......................................... ENCTR   25/09
        LITTL   73/33    LITTL   74/07    LITTL   83/26    LITTL   83/30
        GRACE  151/19    GRACE  154/27    GRACE  156/26    DEAD   186/28
BOOK-CASE  (1)  ..................................... PNFUL  107/11
BOOKED  (1)  ........................................ EVELN   40/33
BOOKS  (15)  ........................................ SISTR   13/17
        ENCTR   21/27    ENCTR   25/07    ARABY   29/11    ARABY   30/28
        LITTL   71/17    LITTL   71/22    PNFUL  107/16    PNFUL  110/27
        PNFUL  112/11    GRACE  174/16    GRACE  174/16    DEAD   188/09
        DEAD   188/12    DEAD   188/22
BOOKSELLERS  (1)  .'................................. DEAD   188/14
BOOKSHELF  (1)  ..................................... LITTL   71/20
BOOKWORM  (1)  ...................................... ENCTR   25/11
BOOSE  (3)  ......................................... LITTL   76/02
        IVY D  130/12    GRACE  158/30
BOOSING  (1)  ....................................... IVY D  119/30
BOOT  (1)  .......................................... DEAD   222/19
BOOTEES  (1)  ....................................... SISTR   11/34
BOOTMAKER  (1)  ..................................... MOTHR  137/04
BOOTS  (5)  ......................................... SISTR   14/23
        GALNT   55/13    PNFUL  116/15    IVY D  119/17    DEAD   181/04
BORDER  (2)  ........................................ ARABY   32/10
        ARABY   33/15
BORDERS  (1)  ....................................... GALNT   50/22
BORE  (5)  .......................................... ARABY   31/10
        PARTS   86/16    PNFUL  112/13    GRACE  166/25    DEAD   187/23
BORED  (2)  ......................................... ENCTR   25/06
        MOTHR  145/02
BORGIA  (1)  ........................................ DEAD   199/16
BORN  (2)  .......................................... SISTR   17/05
        GRACE  165/08
BORNE  (3)  ......................................... DEAD   193/08
        DEAD   206/22    DEAD   214/09
BORROWED  (1)  ...................................... LITTL   72/27
BOSOM  (5)  ......................................... ARABY   31/15
        GALNT   55/31    HOUSE   66/34    PNFUL  110/02    MOTHR  145/08
BOSS  (1)  .......................................... GRACE  161/20
BOSTOONS  (1)  ...................................... GRACE  160/32
BOTH  (17)  ......................................... SISTR   15/33
        ENCTR   24/06    EVELN   37/22    EVELN   41/08    HOUSE   64/11
        PARTS   89/19    PNFUL  114/25    MOTHR  137/17    MOTHR  143/15
        MOTHR  143/32    GRACE  166/04    DEAD   177/10    DEAD   179/32
        DEAD   181/05    DEAD   186/26    DEAD   193/18    DEAD   210/20
BOTHER  (2)  ........................................ CLAY   104/18
        DEAD   180/16
BOTTLE  (21)  ....................................... ENCTR   24/04
        GALNT   57/17    CLAY   104/18    PNFUL  108/11    PNFUL  108/33
        IVY D  123/28    IVY D  129/03    IVY D  129/13    IVY D  129/17
        IVY D  129/19    IVY D  129/27    IVY D  130/27    IVY D  130/30
        IVY D  130/33    IVY D  131/09    IVY D  131/10    IVY D  132/32
        IVY D  133/09    IVY D  133/12    IVY D  135/26    GRACE  169/01
BOTTLED  (1)  ....................................... DEAD   176/20
BOTTLE-GREEN  (1)  .................................. ENCTR   27/17
BOTTLES  (19)  ...................................... HOUSE   68/05
        PNFUL  115/27    IVY D  128/18    IVY D  128/19    IVY D  128/22
        IVY D  128/23    IVY D  128/25    IVY D  129/09    IVY D  129/25
        IVY D  130/20    IVY D  130/25    IVY D  135/25    MOTHR  145/20
```

```
        GRACE 162/10    DEAD    183/05    DEAD   197/01    DEAD   197/24
        DEAD  197/24    DEAD    213/23
BOTTOM (1) ........................................... LITTL   81/21
BOUGHT (10) .......................................... ENCTR   23/05
        ENCTR  23/34    ENCTR   24/04    EVELN  36/09    HOUSE  66/11
        LITTL  71/18    LITTL   83/20    CLAY  102/14    PNFUL 107/08
        MOTHR 138/31
BOUNDED (1) .......................................... GRACE 158/07
BOUNDING (2) ......................................... RACE   45/12
        DEAD  213/08
BOUQUET (1) .......................................... SISTR  12/03
BOUTS (1) ............................................ ENCTR  19/08
BOW (2) .....•........................................ PARTS  90/10
        PARTS  95/14
BOWED (8) ............................................ SISTR  14/10
        SISTR  15/13    PARTS   90/09    CLAY  103/09    CLAY  103/10
        IVY D 134/17    GRACE  157/23    DEAD  215/22
BOWING (1) ........................................... ARABY  32/06
BOWL (2) ............................................. GRACE 161/13
        DEAD  196/28
BOWLER (1) ........................................... IVY D 130/09
BOWLS (2) ............................................ GRACE 154/12
        GRACE 154/13
BOWS (2) ............................................. RACE   45/31
        DEAD  179/06
BOWSY (1) ............................................ IVY D 120/13
BOX (5) .............................................. SISTR  11/02
        ENCTR  27/14    IVY D 130/32    IVY D 132/33   DEAD  214/22
BOX-OFFICE (1) ....................................... MOTHR 139/22
BOY (46) ............................................. SISTR  12/04
        ENCTR  21/10 •  ENCTR   25/02    ENCTR  25/30   ENCTR  27/05
        ENCTR  27/12    ENCTR   27/21    ENCTR  27/23   ENCTR  27/25
        ENCTR  27/27    ARABY   32/31    ARABY  34/08   EVELN  39/10
        LITTL  75/21    LITTL   77/30    LITTL  79/16   LITTL  81/07
        LITTL  81/31    PARTS   97/06.   PARTS  97/18   PARTS  97/33
        PARTS  98/04    PARTS   98/12    PARTS  98/14   PARTS  98/19
        CLAY  103/18    IVY D  128/13    IVY D 128/16   IVY D 128/19
        IVY D 128/21    IVY D  128/27    IVY D 128/31   IVY D 129/08
        IVY D 129/10    IVY D  129/11    IVY D 129/12   IVY D 129/14
        IVY D 129/16    IVY D  129/17    MOTHR 142/19   GRACE 154/28
        GRACE 165/06    DEAD   219/04    DEAD  219/08   DEAD  219/30
        DEAD  221/03
BOYOS (1) ............................................ GRACE 163/31
BOYS (27) ............................................ ENCTR  20/27
        ENCTR  20/29    ENCTR   22/23    ENCTR  22/25   ENCTR  25/17
        ENCTR  25/17    ENCTR   25/33    ENCTR  27/07   ENCTR  27/09
        ENCTR  27/11    ARABY   29/03    ARABY  32/04   LITTL  73/03
        PARTS  91/01    PARTS   93/15    PARTS  93/30   PARTS  94/23
        PARTS  94/24    PARTS   96/28    CLAY  100/22   CLAY  102/09
        IVY D 122/24    IVY D  124/07    MOTHR 141/15   GRACE 156/24
        DEAD  194/23    DEAD   199/12
BOY'S (1) ............................................ SISTR  17/28
BRACELET (1) ......................................... ARABY  32/02
BRACING (1) .......................................... DEAD  200/26
BRAIDED (1) .......................................... DEAD  179/30
BRAIN (2) ............................................ GALNT  56/30
        DEAD  213/09
BRAINS (1) ........................................... DEAD  186/25
BRANCHES (2) ......................................... ENCTR  21/34
        DEAD  192/06
BRANDISHING (1) ...................................... ENCTR  22/22
BRANDY (2) ........................................... GRACE 151/26
```

```
         GRACE  151/28
BRASS  (2)  .......................................  PARTS    86/16
     PNFUL  108/07
BRAVE  (2)  .......................................  GALNT    50/20
     MOTHR  136/16
BRAVED  (1)  ......................................  DEAD    222/16
BRAVELY  (3)  .....................................  LITTL    73/23
     LITTL   83/24      DEAD   204/07
BRAVERY  (1)  .....................................  ENCTR    28/07
BRAVO  (1)  .......................................  LITTL    79/18
BRAZEN  (1)  ......................................  HOUSE    65/34
BREAD  (2)  .......................................  HOUSE    64/05
     HOUSE   64/06
BREAD-PUDDING  (1)  ...............................  HOUSE    64/06
BREAK  (8)  .......................................  SISTR    17/25
     ENCTR   21/09      GALNT   49/16      HOUSE   61/07    LITTL    84/28
     PNFUL  112/06      DEAD   206/19      DEAD   211/05
BREAKFAST  (4)  ...................................  SISTR    11/31
     HOUSE   63/34      HOUSE   64/04      GRACE  156/23
BREAKFAST-CUP  (1)  ...............................  DEAD    213/17
BREAKFAST-ROOM  (1)  ..............................  HOUSE    64/01
BREAKFAST-TIME  (1)  ..............................  GALNT    57/12
BREAKING  (1)  ....................................  DEAD    217/15
BREAKS  (1)  ......................................  IVY D  135/16
BREAK-UP  (1)  ....................................  CLAY   100/22
BREAST  (5)  ......................................  SISTR    18/12
     HOUSE   66/27      LITTL   84/29      DEAD   197/11    DEAD    197/12
BREATH  (9)  ......................................  SISTR    15/17
     RACE    47/29      HOUSE   67/03      LITTL   84/23    PARTS    86/08
     PNFUL  113/12      IVY D  129/28      MOTHR  143/33    DEAD    222/06
BREATHED  (1)  ....................................  GRACE  150/07
BREATHING  (2)  ...................................  GALNT    60/24
     PARTS   91/25
BREECHES  (1)  ....................................  GALNT    50/03
BREEZE  (1)  ......................................  HOUSE    63/27
BREVIARY  (1)  ....................................  SISTR    16/33
BREWERS  (1)  ...................................:.  GRACE  166/22
BRICK  (1)  .......................................  EVELN    36/11
BRICKLAYER  (1)  ..................................  IVY D  121/18
BRIDAL  (3)  ......................................  GRACE  156/05
     DEAD   193/02      DEAD   222/28
BRIDGE  (12)  .....................................  ENCTR    21/12
     ENCTR   21/27      ENCTR   21/31      ENCTR   22/02    ENCTR    22/07
     LITTL   73/12      LITTL   84/05      PARTS   96/31    CLAY   103/09
     PNFUL  116/08      DEAD   214/25      DEAD   214/27
BRIDGES  (1)  .....................................  PNFUL  114/25
BRIEF  (3)  .......................................  LITTL    80/21
     GRACE  157/22      DEAD   204/12                  `
BRIGHT  (10)  .....................................  EVELN    36/11
     GALNT   53/29      HOUSE   63/26      PARTS   95/15    CLAY    99/05
     IVY D  125/33      MOTHR  139/08      DEAD   178/19    DEAD    192/06
     DEAD   213/07
BRIGHTENED  (1)  ..................................  GALNT    53/04
BRILLIANT  (4)  ...................................  RACE     44/02
     LITTL   71/04      MOTHR  136/16      DEAD   217/30
BRIM  (2)  ........................................  IVY D  120/27
     GRACE  173/05
BRIMMING  (1)  ....................................  DEAD    217/31
BRING  (17)  ......................................  SISTR    16/32
     ENCTR   28/11      ARABY   32/12      GALNT   51/04    GALNT    53/26
     GALNT   57/11      GALNT   57/17      LITTL   74/31    LITTL    82/14
     PARTS   90/25      PARTS   96/04      CLAY   103/19    IVY D  119/28
```

```
          IVY D 123/09      MOTHR 141/09      MOTHR 144/16      GRACE 155/23
BRINGING (3) ....................................  .........  SISTR  16/26
     GALNT  49/10     GALNT  55/07
BRINGS (2) ......................................................  IVY D 124/15
     IVY D 135/17
BRISK (1) .......................................  DEAD   181/14
BRISKLY (1) .....................................  GALNT  59/01
BRISTLED (1) .................................... .  DEAD   182/25
BRITAIN (1) .....................................  SISTR  11/32
BRITON (4) ......................................  DEAD   188/05
     DEAD   188/09     DEAD   190/12     DEAD   190/29
BROAD (3) .......................................  GALNT  56/01
     GALNT  60/04     DEAD   218/19
BROADER (1) .....................................  DEAD   183/11
BROADLY (2) .....................................  PARTS  91/28
     DEAD   193/26
BROKE (9) .......................................  SISTR  17/26
     GALNT  59/22     LITTL  85/01     DEAD   180/21     DEAD   181/27
     DEAD   183/11     DEAD   195/31     DEAD   213/33     DEAD   218/15
BROKEN (9) ......................................  ARABY  31/22
     EVELN  37/12     HOUSE  64/05     HOUSE  64/06     HOUSE  68/12
     LITTL  79/33     MOTHR 148/25     GRACE 152/22     DEAD   201/29
BRONCHITIC (1) ..................................  DEAD   185/30
BRONZE (4) ......................................  EVELN  39/01
     MOTHR 142/33     DEAD   210/07     DEAD   212/02
BROOCH (1) ......................................  DEAD   187/22
BROOD (1) .......................................  DEAD   204/06
BROODED (1) .....................................  DEAD   212/31
BROTHER (8) .....................................  ENCTR  19/05
     ENCTR  21/14     ARABY  30/17     ARABY  30/22     ARABY  32/04
     CLAY   104/25     CLAY   104/28     DEAD   176/02
BROTHERS (3) ....................................  EVELN  36/13
     EVELN  37/02     IVY D 119/29
BROTHERS' (1) ...................................  ARABY  29/02
BROUGHT (43) ....................................  SISTR  11/09
     SISTR  15/01     SISTR  16/11     SISTR  18/05     ENCTR  21/20
     ENCTR  22/08     ENCTR  22/10     ENCTR  22/11     ARABY  30/07
     RACE   43/29     RACE   47/29     GALNT  51/02     GALNT  51/05
     GALNT  57/24     GALNT  59/04     LITTL  71/02     LITTL  73/01
     LITTL  73/24     LITTL  80/33     LITTL  82/25     LITTL  83/01
     PARTS  89/01     PARTS  96/07     PARTS  96/18     CLAY   100/09
     CLAY   103/22     PNFUL 109/05     PNFUL 114/01     IVY D 118/13
     MOTHR 137/27     MOTHR 138/11     MOTHR 138/12     MOTHR 142/02
     MOTHR 143/33     MOTHR 144/01     MOTHR 147/16     GRACE 152/33
     GRACE 153/27     GRACE 156/27     GRACE 166/28     DEAD   175/02
     DEAD   176/32     DEAD   191/24
BROW (3) ........................................  GALNT  54/02
     GRACE 154/31     DEAD   184/29
BROWN (23) ......................................  ENCTR  23/09
     ARABY  29/06     ARABY  30/29     EVELN  36/10     EVELN  40/25
     RACE   43/14     PARTS  95/19     CLAY   102/01     CLAY   102/32
     PNFUL 108/17     IVY D 120/26     MOTHR 137/06     MOTHR 138/32
     MOTHR 139/17     DEAD   186/19     DEAD   186/23     DEAD   187/21
     DEAD   196/17     DEAD   197/03     DEAD   200/15     DEAD   200/17
     DEAD   200/17     DEAD   213/05
BROWN-CLAD (1) ..................................  ARABY  33/13
BROWNE (48) .....................................  DEAD   182/21
     DEAD   182/24     DEAD   183/03     DEAD   183/15     DEAD   183/17
     DEAD   183/27     DEAD   185/04     DEAD   185/16     DEAD   185/17
     DEAD   185/22     DEAD   185/27     DEAD   192/28     DEAD   193/28
     DEAD   193/34     DEAD   194/03     DEAD   194/30     DEAD   194/32
     DEAD   195/09     DEAD   198/01     DEAD   198/31     DEAD   199/03
```

DEAD	199/20	DEAD	199/24	DEAD	200/03	DEAD	200/16
DEAD	200/29	DEAD	201/02	DEAD	201/07	DEAD	201/09
DEAD	201/12	DEAD	202/18	DEAD	203/34	DEAD	205/15
DEAD	206/07	DEAD	206/08	DEAD	206/17	DEAD	207/01
DEAD	207/06	DEAD	207/15	DEAD	208/29	DEAD	208/31
DEAD	208/33	DEAD	208/34	DEAD	209/03	DEAD	209/05
DEAD	209/12	DEAD	209/17	DEAD	217/05		

BROWNING (2) .... DEAD 179/09
    DEAD 192/10
BROWNING'S (1) .... DEAD 188/29
BROWS (7) .... GALNT 53/31
    GRACE 170/21   DEAD 181/09   DEAD 185/09   DEAD 187/31
    DEAD 190/09   DEAD 211/16
BRUNT (1) .... HOUSE 65/02
BRUSH (1) .... SISTR 12/25
BRUSHED (4) .... PARTS 95/21
    PARTS 97/08   DEAD 178/21   DEAD 210/31
BRUTAL (2) .... DEAD 217/11
    DEAD 217/16
BUCK (1) .... DEAD 185/20
BUCKINGHAM (1) .... ARABY 34/12
BUCKLE (1) .... GALNT 55/25
BUCKLED (1) .... ARABY 30/12
BUENOS (3) .... EVELN 38/29
    EVELN 39/15   EVELN 40/33
BUFF (1) .... PNFUL 113/09
BUFFER (1) .... PNFUL 114/06
BUILD (2) .... DEAD 179/26
    DEAD 184/25
BUILDING (3) .... ARABY 34/25
    MOTHR 141/33   DEAD 214/20
BUILT (4) .... EVELN 36/10
    RACE 42/15   PNFUL 107/07   GRACE 170/06
BULB (1) .... GALNT 51/24
BULGED (2) .... ENCTR 22/08
    PARTS 86/11
BULK (4) .... GALNT 55/12
    PARTS 86/10   PNFUL 107/18   GRACE 173/12
BULL (1) .... GRACE 170/22
BULLDOG (1) .... HOUSE 68/07
BULLIED (2) .... PARTS 97/16
    PARTS 97/17
BUMPER (1) .... MOTHR 140/28
BUMPKINS (1) .... GRACE 160/30
BUMPTIOUS (1) .... GRACE 164/10
BUNCH (1) .... GALNT 55/30
BUNCHES (1) .... DEAD 196/25
BUNDLED (1) .... RACE 48/24
BUNDLES (2) .... MOTHR 141/16
    DEAD 182/33
BUNS (1) .... ENCTR 23/06
BUNSEN (1) .... ENCTR 22/12
BURDEN (2) .... LITTL 71/15
    DEAD 215/23
BURIED (4) .... RACE 46/23
    DEAD 201/18   DEAD 221/28   DEAD 223/32
BURKE (10) .... MOTHR 144/27
    MOTHR 145/12   MOTHR 145/21   MOTHR 146/06   MOTHR 147/15
    MOTHR 147/25   MOTHR 148/01   MOTHR 149/33   GRACE 165/06
    GRACE 165/07
BURKE'S (2) .... PNFUL 108/32
    IVY D 123/06

BURLY (1) .... GALNT 51/17
BURNED (3) .... ARABY 35/33
    PNFUL 117/11   DEAD 220/07
BURNER (1) .... ENCTR 22/12
BURNING (1) .... DEAD 213/01
BURNS (1) .... DEAD 199/03
BURST (5) .... LITTL 84/30
    IVY D 135/22   MOTHR 146/30   DEAD 204/18   DEAD 213/16
BURSTING (1) .... LITTL 84/24
BUSHES (1) .... ARABY 29/16
BUSHY (1) .... GRACE 170/20
BUSINESS (28) .... ENCTR 21/33

EVELN 37/22	EVELN 38/08	RACE 45/04	RACE 45/06
HOUSE 61/09	HOUSE 62/02	HOUSE 63/11	HOUSE 66/03
LITTL 81/33	PARTS 93/08	CLAY 103/15	IVY D 121/09
IVY D 126/11	IVY D 131/21	MOTHR 144/14	MOTHR 144/15
MOTHR 144/17	MOTHR 144/17	MOTHR 149/06	GRACE 154/06
GRACE 164/27	GRACE 166/20	GRACE 171/24	GRACE 171/25
GRACE 171/31	GRACE 174/01	GRACE 174/12	

BUSINESSLIKE (1) .... GRACE 174/13
BUSTLE (2) .... LITTL 77/05
    DEAD 204/12
BUSTLING (1) .... IVY D 122/20
BUSY (1) .... RACE 45/13
BUT (351) .... RACE 43/16
BUTCHER (2) .... HOUSE 61/01
    HOUSE 62/02
BUTCHER'S (2) .... ENCTR 20/13
    HOUSE 61/04
BUTLER (5) .... ENCTR 22/12
    ENCTR 20/21   ENCTR 21/17   ENCTR 21/19   GRACE 165/29
BUTLER'S (1) .... HOUSE 64/07
BUTTER (1) .... IVY D 125/24
BUTTONED (2) .... MOTHR 140/30
    DEAD 211/30
BUTTONHOLED (1) .... DEAD 195/15
BUTTONING (1) .... GALNT 55/28
BUTTONS (4) .... ARABY 35/15
    IVY D 125/27   DEAD 177/18   DEAD 186/24
BUY (11) .... CLAY 102/17
    GALNT 52/28   CLAY 100/06   CLAY 102/16   PNFUL 115/05
    CLAY 102/19   CLAY 102/20   CLAY 102/25
    IVY D 123/27   DEAD 180/29
BUYERS (1) .... ARABY 34/14
BUYING (2) .... EVELN 38/18
    HOUSE 61/09
BY (218) .... IVY D 124/07
'BYE (3) .... IVY D 124/07
    IVY D 124/07   IVY D 124/12
BYGONES (2) .... IVY D 132/15
    IVY D 132/15
BYRNE'S (1) .... PARTS 93/21
BYRON'S (1) .... LITTL 83/28
BYSTANDER (1) .... ENCTR 23/22
BYSTANDERS (2) .... GRACE 151/23
    GRACE 152/02
BY-STREET (1) .... DEAD 188/16
BYWORD (2) .... GRACE 154/22
    DEAD 204/31

C (1) .... DEAD 199/11

C. (1) .... DEAD 187/29
CAB (15) .... MOTHR 149/22
    GRACE 152/10   DEAD 180/01   DEAD 180/05   DEAD 208/24
    DEAD 208/30   DEAD 208/33   DEAD 208/34   DEAD 209/04
    DEAD 209/22   DEAD 214/17   DEAD 214/23   DEAD 209/19
    DEAD 214/34   DEAD 215/07
CABBAGE (6) .... PNFUL 112/29
    PNFUL 113/02   GRACE 161/04   GRACE 161/14   GRACE 161/15
    GRACE 161/17
CABIN (4) .... RACE 47/24
    RACE 48/23   RACE 48/31   IVY D 134/15
CABMAN (6) .... DEAD 208/34
    DEAD 209/02   DEAD 209/12   DEAD 209/15   DEAD 209/19
    DEAD 209/21
CABS (2) .... LITTL 72/07
    DEAD 206/23 ·
CADENCE (1) .... DEAD 210/22
CADET (1) .... RACE 47/17
CAFE (1) .... ARABY 34/34
CAFES (1) .... LITTL 76/30
CAITIFF (1) .... IVY D 134/27
CAKE (1) .... CLAY 102/19
CAKES (4) .... CLAY 102/15
    CLAY 103/18   CLAY 103/20   CLAY 103/29
CAKESHOP (1) .... PNFUL 112/03
CAKE-SHOP (1) .... CLAY 102/12
CALCULATE (1) .... RACE 48/13
CALL (18) .... SISTR 17/34
    ENCTR 24/23   ENCTR 28/08   ARABY 30/16   ARABY 32/24
    ARABY 35/29   EVELN 36/17   EVELN 39/07   GALNT 50/13
    GALNT 52/17   IVY D 122/33   IVY D 126/30   DEAD 186/25
    DEAD 190/29   DEAD 198/08   DEAD 204/16   DEAD 210/09
    DEAD 214/12
CALLAN'S (1) .... PARTS 93/27
CALLED (41) .... ENCTR 23/28
    ENCTR 27/07   ENCTR 28/04   ARABY 32/18   EVELN 41/13
    EVELN 41/14   GALNT 55/05   GALNT 60/12   GALNT 60/14
    LITTL 70/10   LITTL 82/32   PARTS 86/02   PARTS 88/32
    PARTS 91/05   PARTS 95/29   PARTS 95/32   PNFUL 108/15
    PNFUL 116/17   IVY D 120/19   IVY D 124/11   IVY D 133/06
    MOTHR 136/05   MOTHR 138/24   MOTHR 139/34   MOTHR 141/03
    GRACE 151/24   GRACE 151/26   GRACE 152/13   GRACE 160/30
    GRACE 162/02   GRACE 162/07   GRACE 165/25   GRACE 174/03
    DEAD 177/06   DEAD 177/13   DEAD 178/33   DEAD 185/23
    DEAD 203/29   DEAD 212/10   DEAD 213/25   DEAD 215/34
CALLING (6) .... ENCTR 23/29
    HOUSE 66/04   HOUSE 69/01   PARTS 89/15   GRACE 154/01
    DEAD 175/11
CALM (4) .... GALNT 60/23
    LITTL 78/14   GRACE 163/22   DEAD 216/14
CALMED (1) .... GALNT 59/13
CALMER (1) .... LITTL 82/02
CALMLY (3) .... ENCTR 28/02
    LITTL 81/10   IVY D 135/10
CALVE (1) .... IVY D 130/13
CAMARADERIE (1) .... DEAD 204/15
CAMBRIDGE (3) .... RACE 43/27
    RACE 43/29   RACE 46/07
CAME (101)
CAMP (1) .... IVY D 124/22
CAMPANINI (1) .... DEAD 199/05
'CAMPBELL (1) .... MOTHR 146/22

CAN (33) .... SISTR   16/18
    ENCTR   25/11   GALNT   52/13   GALNT   53/26   GALNT   55/01
    HOUSE   64/34   LITTL   75/16   LITTL   79/22   LITTL   81/15
    LITTL   81/28   LITTL   82/03   PARTS   90/12   IVY D 124/29
    IVY D 126/17   IVY D 130/21   GRACE 152/22   GRACE 161/20
    GRACE 162/17   GRACE 162/21   GRACE 167/28   GRACE 168/12
    GRACE 171/06   DEAD   178/11   DEAD   181/23   DEAD   191/17
    DEAD   194/01   DEAD   195/26   DEAD   200/30   DEAD   202/19
    DEAD   205/20   DEAD   205/31   DEAD   219/09   DEAD   221/24
CANADA (1) .... EVELN   39/11
CANADIAN (1) .... RACE   43/01
CANAL (4) .... ENCTR   21/12
    ENCTR   21/29   GALNT   50/33   CLAY   103/09
CANDID (2) .... IVY D 124/21
    IVY D 126/07
CANDIDATE (2) .... IVY D 131/06
    IVY D 131/17
CANDIDLY (1) .... DEAD   201/02
CANDLE (10) .... HOUSE   67/06
    HOUSE   67/11   HOUSE   67/19   GRACE 171/19   GRACE 171/21
    DEAD   215/19   DEAD   215/28   DEAD   215/33   DEAD   216/05
    DEAD   216/07
CANDLE-LAMPS (1) .... RACE   46/08
CANDLELIGHT (1) .... IVY D 125/28
CANDLES (8) .... SISTR   9/06
    SISTR   9/06   SISTR   14/18   GRACE 171/17   GRACE 171/25
    GRACE 171/26   GRACE 171/29   GRACE 172/01
CANDLESTICK (1) .... IVY D 126/20
CANDLESTICKS (3) .... SISTR   16/11
    IVY D 120/31   IVY D 126/14
CANE (1) .... PNFUL 107/10
CANISTERS (1) .... GRACE 154/10
CANNOT (1) .... PNFUL 111/29
CANS (2) .... CLAY   101/06
    PNFUL 115/27
CAN'T (13) .... ARABY   32/01
    ARABY   34/04   GALNT   53/14   GALNT   53/32   GALNT   60/26
    LITTL   78/31   IVY D 124/01   IVY D 124/30   IVY D 132/18
    MOTHR 149/04   DEAD   180/10   DEAD   208/16   DEAD   211/12
CANVAS (1) .... ENCTR   21/31
CANVASS (2) .... IVY D 119/16
    IVY D 130/16
CANVASSER (3) .... IVY D 130/01
    IVY D 131/03   GRACE 158/22
CANVASSES (1) .... GRACE 172/10
CAP (11) .... ENCTR   22/29
    EVELN   38/33   GALNT   49/14   GALNT   56/03   GALNT   57/21
    LITTL   73/04   PARTS   88/26   PARTS   89/12   DEAD   192/06
    DEAD   202/11   DEAD   206/21
CAPABLE (1) .... GRACE 158/02
CAPE (1) .... DEAD   177/16
CAPEL (3) .... GALNT   58/15
    LITTL   72/21   LITTL   73/10
CAPERED (1) .... ENCTR   19/13
CAPITAL (5) .... RACE   45/03
    RACE   46/29   IVY D 131/28   IVY D 131/33   DEAD   200/22
CAPITALS (2) .... LITTL   78/16
    MOTHR 138/20
CAPS (1) .... ARABY   32/05
CAPTAIN (5) .... PNFUL 110/10
    PNFUL 110/18   PNFUL 114/31   PNFUL 115/11   DEAD   190/21
CAPTURE (1) .... IVY D 132/34

CAPTURING (1) .... DEAD 198/03
CAR (21) .... RACE 42/11
    RACE   42/12   RACE   42/15   RACE   43/01   RACE   44/03
    RACE   44/13   RACE   45/08   RACE   45/20   RACE   46/34
    RACE   47/01   RACE   47/08   GALNT   53/09   CLAY   102/02
    GRACE 153/11   GRACE 153/16   GRACE 153/23   GRACE 153/27
    GRACE 154/24   GRACE 155/25   GRACE 155/29   GRACE 158/31
CARAT (1) .... IVY D 124/29
CARAWAY (1) .... PARTS 89/02
CARD (4) .... SISTR 12/05
    SISTR   12/10   IVY D 119/22   IVY D 126/24
CARDBOARD (4) .... IVY D 118/01
    IVY D 118/10   IVY D 119/25   IVY D 119/32
CARDINAL (3) .... GRACE 169/16
    GRACE 169/20   GRACE 170/05
CARDINALS (2) .... GRACE 169/11
    GRACE 169/28
CARD-PARTY (1) .... LITTL 79/29
CARDS (9) .... RACE 47/21
    RACE   48/04   RACE   48/04 - RACE   48/12   RACE   48/24
    HOUSE 65/06   LITTL   81/32   IVY D 119/06   IVY D 119/09
CARE (7) .... ENCTR 24/34
    HOUSE 61/13   LITTL   70/15   GRACE 173/10   DEAD 192/26
    DEAD 195/34   DEAD 200/23
CAREER (2) .... ARABY 30/07
    MOTHR 147/27
CAREERED (1) .... GALNT 54/14
CAREERING (2) .... RACE 42/04
    RACE   45/09
CAREERS (1) .... DEAD 188/18
CAREFUL (5) .... PNFUL 111/10
    MOTHR 144/33   GRACE 155/01   DEAD 180/11   DEAD 211/33
CAREFULLY (4) .... GALNT 55/29
    MOTHR 141/21   DEAD 177/34   DEAD 211/18
CARELESSLY (2) .... MOTHR 139/17
    DEAD 198/27
CARES (1) .... DEAD 214/04
CARESS (2) .... DEAD 220/23
    DEAD 220/26
CARESSED (2) .... DEAD 220/15
    DEAD 220/27
CARESSES (1) .... HOUSE 67/03
CARESSING (1) .... DEAD 213/18
CARETAKER (2) .... IVY D 119/19
    DEAD 182/31
CARETAKER'S (2) .... DEAD 175/01
    DEAD 176/17
CARGO (1) .... RACE 44/03
CARMAN (2) .... GRACE 153/12
    GRACE 155/21
CARPETED (1) .... DEAD 215/21
CARRIAGE (5) .... ARABY 34/15
    ARABY 34/19   ARABY 34/21   DEAD 199/13   DEAD 215/11
CARRIAGES (1) .... SISTR 17/07
CARRIED (10) .... PNFUL 108/16
    PNFUL 116/27   IVY D 120/33   IVY D 131/i0   MOTHR 144/22
    GRACE 150/09   GRACE 151/08   GRACE 154/04   GRACE 156/08
    DEAD 197/23
CARRIER (1) .... DEAD 186/26
CARRY (3) .... ENCTR 19/06
    ENCTR 24/09   ARABY 31/03
CARRYING (4) .... PNFUL 108/29

```
                                                                        RACE    42/01
      PNFUL 115/27    IVY D 130/25    DEAD   184/19                      RACE    42/15
CARS (6) .............................................................  RACE    42/15
      RACE   42/04    RACE   42/08    RACE   42/08
      RACE   43/09
CARTS (1) ............................................................  ENCTR   23/03
CARUSO (2) ...........................................................  DEAD   199/22
      DEAD   199/26
CARVE (5) ............................................................  DEAD   190/34
      DEAD   191/01    DEAD   196/14    DEAD   196/16                    DEAD   197/28
CARVER (2) ...........................................................  DEAD   197/06
      DEAD   197/08
CARVING (1) ..........................................................  DEAD   197/31
CASE (20) ............................................................  ENCTR   26/28
      RACE   45/04    HOUSE  62/18    HOUSE  63/25                       LITTL   79/30
      PARTS  88/15    PARTS  89/23    PARTS  90/15                       PNFUL 107/ T
      PNFUL 113/20    PNFUL 114/29    PNFUL 115/10                       IVY D 132/20
      MOTHR 148/23    GRACE 157/12    GRACE 158/10                       GRACE 158/27
      GRACE 159/19    GRACE 160/11    GRACE 163/31
CASES (7) ............................................................  SISTR   10/09
      HOUSE  64/33    HOUSE  65/03    LITTL  78/11                       LITTL   78/11
      IVY D 132/23    GRACE 157/21
CASH (1) .............................................................  LITTL   81/28
CASHIER (7) ..........................................................  LITTL   82/32
      PARTS  87/32    PARTS  90/32    PARTS  90/33                       PARTS   92/04
      PARTS  92/05    PNFUL 108/30
CASSIDY (1) ..........................................................  DEAD   183/19
CAST (5) .............................................................  ARABY   32/19
      ARABY  33/13    LITTL  71/07    DEAD   179/05                      DEAD   223/01
CASTE (1) ............................................................  LITTL   78/19
      IVY D 125/11    GRACE 154/17    GRACE 160/33                       IVY D 125/08
CASUAL (4) ...........................................................  ARABY   30/32
      EVELN  37/16    HOUSE  67/03    GRACE 173/29
CASUALLY (1) .........................................................  GRACE 162/13
CAT (4) ..............................................................  ENCTR   24/05
      ENCTR  24/06    ENCTR  26/33    ENCTR  27/01
CATACOMBS (1) ........................................................  SISTR   13/04
CATAPULT (3) .........................................................  ENCTR   22/08
      ENCTR  22/23    ENCTR  24/12
CATCH (12) ...........................................................  RACE    44/09
      HOUSE  64/22    MOTHR 141/08    GRACE 161/04                       GRACE 161/16
      GRACE 161/17    DEAD   185/04    DEAD   190/16                     DEAD   193/19
      DEAD   210/01    DEAD   213/12    DEAD   214/23
CATCHING (4) .........................................................  ENCTR   26/33
      GALNT  55/26    LITTL  76/26    IVY D 133/06
CATECHISM (2) ........................................................  SISTR    9/12
      PNFUL 108/02
CATER (1) ............................................................  GRACE 164/07
CATHEDRA (3) .........................................................  GRACE 168/27
      GRACE 168/30    GRACE 169/31
CATHEDRAL (1) ........................................................  MOTHR 137/32
CATHERINE'S (1) ......................................................  SISTR   12/07
CATHOLIC (7) .........................................................  RACE    43/22
      HOUSE  65/14    LITTL  77/18    GRACE 157/08                       GRACE 158/06
      GRACE 170/30    GRACE 171/33
CATHOLICISM (1) ......................................................  GRACE 157/10
CATS (1) .............................................................  IVY D 133/04
CAUGHT (21) ..........................................................  ARABY   32/07
      ARABY  32/09    EVELN  40/26    RACE   47/01                       LITTL   70/17
      LITTL  72/10    LITTL  83/18    LITTL  84/28                       PARTS   98/13
      PNFUL 111/23    PNFUL 111/31    PNFUL 114/06                       IVY D 118/09
      IVY D 127/14    MOTHR 149/20    GRACE 158/31                       DEAD   180/07
```

	DEAD 191/26	DEAD 218/18	DEAD 220/05	DEAD 222/27

```
                DEAD    191/26      DEAD    218/18      DEAD    220/05      DEAD    222/27
CAUSE (3) ..................................................................... HOUSE   65/29
        MOTHR  139/12      DEAD    196/07
CAUSED (1) ................................................................... PNFUL  114/19
CAUSES (1) ................................................................... LITTL   72/16
CAUTIOUS (1) ................................................................. PNFUL  115/22
CAUTIOUSLY (3) ............................................................... GALNT   60/02
        LITTL   83/29      DEAD    223/05
CAVALIER (2) ................................................................. RACE    47/25
        HOUSE   64/13
CAVALIERS (1) ................................................................ LITTL   72/08
CAVERNOUS (1) ................................................................ SISTR   14/30
CEASED (7) ................................................................... PNFUL  116/24
        PNFUL  116/32      IVY D  135/24      DEAD    192/34      DEAD    193/14
        DEAD    201/28      DEAD    202/02
CEDARWOOD (1) ................................................................ PNFUL  108/11
CEILING (1) .................................................................. DEAD    177/31
CELEBRATED (1) ............................................................... GRACE  155/33
CELERY (4) ................................................................... DEAD    196/30
        DEAD    200/20      DEAD    200/21      DEAD    200/22
CELIBATE (2) ................................................................. HOUSE   67/02
        HOUSE   67/23
CELL (1) ..................................................................... LITTL   84/12
CELTIC (2) ................................................................... LITTL   74/04
        LITTL   74/09
CEMETERY (2) ................................................................. SISTR   16/13
        PNFUL  109/11
CENTER (1) ................................................................... DEAD    196/30
CENTRAL (2) .................................................................. ARABY   29/15
        DEAD    223/28
CENTRE (3) ................................................................... ENCTR   27/10
        ARABY   34/32      GALNT   55/26
CENTURIES (1) ................................................................ PNFUL  111/08
CENTURY (1) .................................................................. GRACE  157/28
CEOIL (1) .................................................................... MOTHR  142/32
CEREMONIES (1) ............................................................... SISTR   13/05
CERTAIN (20) ................................................................. SISTR   13/08
        SISTR   13/11      RACE    45/27      RACE    45/28      HOUSE   66/01
        HOUSE   66/16      LITTL   72/30      LITTL   78/31      PNFUL  109/02
        PNFUL  109/14      PNFUL  110/03      PNFUL  114/28      IVY D  125/12
        GRACE  154/19      GRACE  163/03      GRACE  166/25      GRACE  174/05
        DEAD    192/22      DEAD    202/27      DEAD    204/14
CERTAINLY (1) ................................................................ LITTL   83/10
CHAFED (1) ................................................................... ARABY   32/15
CHAFFED (1) .................................................................. PARTS   94/32
CHAIN (3) .................................................................... MOTHR  146/26
        DEAD    190/08      DEAD    190/10
CHAINS (2) ................................................................... GALNT   55/04
        GALNT   55/20
CHAIR (17) ................................................................... SISTR   14/34
        SISTR   16/34      SISTR   17/23      LITTL   84/21      PARTS   86/09
        PARTS   90/07      PARTS   95/21      IVY D  122/26      IVY D  122/28
        IVY D  126/02      GRACE  161/33      GRACE  167/04      DEAD    191/31
        DEAD    198/04      DEAD    201/33      DEAD    215/18      DEAD    222/18
CHAIRS (4) ................................................................... PARTS   97/32
        PNFUL  107/10      GRACE  156/29      DEAD    201/30
CHALICE (4) .................................................................. SISTR   14/28
        SISTR   17/26      SISTR   18/12      ARABY   31/10
CHALLENGE (1) ................................................................ GRACE  159/05
CHANCE (2) ................................................................... LITTL   80/28
        IVY D  127/06
CHANCES (1) .................................................................. HOUSE   62/15
```

CHANDELIER (2) .... DEAD 186/15
  DEAD 202/05
CHANDLER (41) .... LITTL 70/11
  LITTL 71/31 LITTL 72/24 LITTL 72/33 LITTL 73/07
  LITTL 74/07 LITTL 74/12 LITTL 74/12 LITTL 75/10
  LITTL 75/20 LITTL 75/23 LITTL 75/31 LITTL 76/03
  LITTL 76/10 LITTL 76/16 LITTL 76/25 LITTL 76/32
  LITTL 77/07 LITTL 77/15 LITTL 77/23 LITTL 77/27
  LITTL 78/24 LITTL 78/27 LITTL 79/01 LITTL 79/06
  LITTL 79/11 LITTL 79/13 LITTL 79/19 LITTL 79/34
  LITTL 80/04 LITTL 80/09 LITTL 80/13 LITTL 80/33
  LITTL 81/10 LITTL 81/14 LITTL 81/25 LITTL 82/08
  LITTL 82/12 LITTL 82/24 LITTL 85/09 LITTL 85/19
CHANDLER'S (1) .... LITTL 70/08
CHANGE (4) .... LITTL 82/31
  IVY D 120/01 GRACE 157/30 DEAD 189/18
CHANGED (8) .... ENCTR 25/02
  ARABY 35/21 LITTL 76/05 PARTS 96/17 CLAY 101/25
  CLAY 101/29 GRACE 160/08 GRACE 171/05
CHANGES (3) .... EVELN 37/04
  LITTL 71/02 DEAD 204/04
CHANGING (4) .... ENCTR 26/20
  GALNT 49/06 GALNT 56/05 MOTHR 143/28
CHANNEL (1) .... RACE 42/04
CHANTANT (1) .... ARABY 34/34
CHANTING (1) .... ARABY 31/07
CHAP (15) .... SISTR 10/21
  LITTL 76/31 LITTL 79/08 LITTL 79/24 LITTL 79/28
  IVY D 125/03 IVY D 129/34 IVY D 131/16 IVY D 132/04
  GRACE 159/12 GRACE 159/13 GRACE 160/09 GRACE 170/19
  DEAD 200/30 DEAD 217/02
CHAPEL (10) .... SISTR 16/09
  SISTR 16/12 SISTR 18/03 SISTR 18/04 PARTS 97/26
  PARTS 97/34 PARTS 97/34 IVY D 127/01 GRACE 156/04
  GRACE 166/01 •
CHAPELIZOD (4) .... PNFUL 107/01
  PNFUL 108/31 PNFUL 113/11 PNFUL 116/08
CHAPLAIN (1) .... IVY D 127/32
CHAPS (2) .... EVELN 39/19
  IVY D 130/16
CHARACTER (5) .... PNFUL 108/20
  PNFUL 111/22 GRACE 154/21 GRACE 164/20 GRACE 164/24
CHARGE (9) .... SISTR 16/13
  ENCTR 22/25 EVELN 38/24 RACE 46/34 LITTL 83/04
  CLAY 100/01 MOTHR 141/32 MOTHR 144/10 DEAD 188/16
CHARGES (1) .... DEAD 183/03
CHARITABLE (1) .... ARABY 29/17
CHARITY (1) .... GRACE 163/07
CHARLES (1) .... RACE 42/18
CHARLIE (1) .... PARTS 97/23
CHARM (2) .... GALNT 56/27
  LITTL 77/05
CHARMEUSE (1) .... MOTHR 138/32
CHARMING (1) .... RACE 44/01
CHASE (1) .... ENCTR 27/01
CHASED (2) .... ENCTR 22/22
  ENCTR 24/05
CHASTISING (1) .... ENCTR 27/08
CHAT (1) .... CLAY 103/03
CHATTING (2) .... MOTHR 143/15
  MOTHR 144/25
CHEAP (1) .... SISTR 17/09

CHEAPER (1) .... MOTHR 147/14
CHECK (3) .... SISTR 12/11
    PARTS   95/08   DEAD   215/27
CHEEK (6) .... EVELN 40/29
    LITTL   73/01   LITTL   81/18   PARTS   92/16   PNFUL 111/32
    MOTHR 141/11
CHEEKBONES (2) .... PNFUL 108/19
    IVY D 125/31
CHEEKS (7) .... ARABY 31/07
    GALNT   55/33   LITTL   85/19   MOTHR 144/23   GRACE 156/33
    DEAD   178/16   DEAD   212/06
CHEER (2) .... RACE   42/07
    RACE   42/13
CHEERFUL (2) .... IVY D 120/34
    DEAD   205/01
CHEERFULLY (4) .... ENCTR 23/29
    HOUSE   68/29   LITTL   75/26   IVY D 128/32
CHEERFULNESS (1) .... ENCTR 24/13
CHEERING (1) .... RACE   48/24
CHEERLESS (1) .... PNFUL 115/16
CHEESE (2) .... GALNT 51/06
    IVY D 125/30
CHEQUE (1) .... DEAD 188/10
CHERISH (1) .... DEAD 203/31
CHEST (1) .... DEAD 216/14
CHEVAL-GLASS (1) .... DEAD 218/18
CHEWED (2) .... ENCTR 24/19
    MOTHR 139/20
CHIEF (12) .... ENCTR 20/23
    PARTS   88/20   PARTS   88/24   PARTS   89/15   PARTS 89/19
    PARTS   90/17   PARTS   92/05   PARTS   92/07   PARTS 93/26
    IVY D 133/15   GRACE 172/32   DEAD   204/30
CHIEFTAIN (1) .... DEAD 198/22
CHILD (20) .... SISTR 11/19
    LITTL   79/14   LITTL   82/08   LITTL   82/19   LITTL 83/30
    LITTL   84/07   LITTL   84/15   LITTL   84/20   LITTL 84/22
    LITTL   84/27   LITTL   84/28   LITTL   85/01   LITTL 85/05
    LITTL   85/15   PNFUL 110/11   IVY D 126/04   DEAD 177/27
    DEAD   180/18   DEAD   194/12   DEAD   218/25
CHILDISH (1) .... LITTL 70/18
CHILDISHLY (1) .... LITTL 79/20
CHILDREN (36) .... SISTR 10/29
    SISTR   10/32   SISTR   11/11   SISTR   11/13   SISTR 11/14
    EVELN   36/09   EVELN   36/11   EVELN   38/23   EVELN 39/31
    HOUSE   61/13   LITTL   71/09   LITTL   71/29   PARTS 97/18
    PARTS   97/31   CLAY   100/14   CLAY   103/16   CLAY 103/20
    CLAY   103/27   CLAY   103/28   CLAY   104/13   CLAY 104/34
    CLAY   105/02   CLAY   105/23   CLAY   105/29   CLAY 105/33
    IVY D 119/28   IVY D 120/05   GRACE 154/27   GRACE 154/28
    GRACE 156/18   GRACE 158/18   GRACE 166/26   GRACE 173/22
    GRACE 173/23   DEAD   181/19   DEAD   214/03
CHILDREN'S (1) .... SISTR 11/34
CHILD'S (4) .... ARABY 32/26
    ARABY   32/27   LITTL   84/17   LITTL   85/21
CHILL (3) .... ENCTR 26/01
    LITTL   73/17   PARTS   92/25
CHILLED (1) .... DEAD 223/04
CHILLY (1) .... MOTHR 136/15
CHIN (5) .... PARTS 95/14
    CLAY   99/11   CLAY   101/14   CLAY   101/19   CLAY 105/09
CHINA (2) .... LITTL 82/21
    GRACE 154/12

CHIVALRY (1) .... ENCTR   22/24
CHOCOLATE (2) .... ENCTR   24/01
    GALNT   52/28
CHOCOLATES (2) .... DEAD   196/28
    DEAD   201/23
CHOICE (1) .... LITTL   76/13
CHOIR (3) .... DEAD   175/16
    DEAD   194/09   DEAD   194/15
CHOIRS (1) .... DEAD   194/22
CHOKED (1) .... PARTS   97/09
CHOKING (1) .... DEAD   221/31
CHOOSE (1) .... DEAD   204/27
CHOOSING (1) .... IVY D 131/05
CHOPS (2) .... IVY D 128/09
    IVY D 128/11
CHORDS (1) .... DEAD   209/33
CHORUS (3) .... RACE   47/17
    DEAD   198/09   DEAD   209/23
CHOSE (2) .... LITTL   72/16
    PNFUL 110/14
CHOSEN (2) .... LITTL   83/21
    DEAD   186/31
CHRIST (5) .... IVY D 125/19
    IVY D 132/09   GRACE 173/30   GRACE 174/01   GRACE 174/18
CHRISTIAN (3) .... ARABY   29/02
    IVY D 119/29   GRACE 160/20
CHRISTMAS (7) .... SISTR   11/23
    PNFUL 109/10   DEAD   194/16   DEAD   206/12   DEAD   211/26
    DEAD   211/27   DEAD   217/19
CHRISTMAS-CARD (1) .... DEAD   217/19
CHRISTMAS-TIME (3) .... DEAD   178/26
    DEAD   178/31   DEAD   178/31
CHRISTY (1) .... DEAD   181/12
CHRONICLES (1) .... ENCTR   21/02
CHUMMY (1) .... HOUSE   62/14
CHURCH (23) .... SISTR   12/07
    SISTR   13/11   SISTR   13/17   ARABY   34/31   EVELN   38/08
    HOUSE   63/30   HOUSE   63/32   HOUSE   64/20   PNFUL 109/08
    IVY D 127/01   GRACE 156/06   GRACE 157/09   GRACE 163/26
    GRACE 163/34   GRACE 164/05   GRACE 169/08   GRACE 169/31
    GRACE 170/05   GRACE 170/07   GRACE 172/02   GRACE 172/07
    DEAD   194/24   DEAD   201/01
CHURCHES (1) .... GRACE 167/07
CHURCHYARD (1) .... DEAD   223/32
CIGAR (4) .... LITTL   78/13
    LITTL   80/17   MOTHR 144/33   MOTHR 144/34
CIGAR-CASE (1) .... LITTL   78/05
CIGARETTE (9) .... GALNT   52/04
    GALNT   59/19   GALNT   59/22   IVY D 118/14   IVY D 119/04
    IVY D 119/23   IVY D 124/18   IVY D 126/23   IVY D 135/29
CIGARETTE-PAPERS (1) .... IVY D 125/02
CIGARETTES (2) .... GALNT   51/04
    GALNT   59/04
CIGARS (2) .... GALNT   51/06
    LITTL   78/06
CINDER (1) .... EVELN   36/06
CINDERS (4) .... IVY D 118/01
    IVY D 118/09   IVY D 122/12   GRACE 156/33
CIRCLE (7) .... ENCTR   27/10
    LITTL   74/03   MOTHR 136/15   GRACE 151/30   GRACE 154/22
    DEAD   202/28   DEAD   208/11
CIRCLED (2) .... SISTR   14/30

```
        GALNT   52/07
CIRCLES (1) .............................................. RACE    43/26
CIRCLING (1) ............................................. ENCTR   26/10
CIRCULAR (1) ............................................. GALNT   52/26
CIRCULATED (3) .......................................... ENCTR   20/12
        GALNT   49/02   MOTHR 143/12
CIRCUMSTANCES (4) ....................................... SISTR   13/08
        PNFUL 109/14    PNFUL 109/15    PNFUL 114/29
CIRCUS (1) .............................................. HOUSE   63/31
CITIES (1) .............................................. RACE    45/29
CITIZEN (2) ............................................. PNFUL 107/02
        IVY D 131/22
CITIZENS (1) ............................................ IVY D 131/29
CITIZENSHIP (1) ......................................... GRACE 160/28
CITY (29) ............................................... RACE    45/24
        RACE    46/29   GALNT   49/02   GALNT   58/15   GALNT   58/30
        HOUSE   62/07   HOUSE   66/02   LITTL   70/10   LITTL   72/14
        LITTL   76/23   LITTL   77/27   PARTS   94/13   PNFUL 107/02
        PNFUL 109/05    PNFUL 112/24    PNFUL 112/25    PNFUL 113/21
        PNFUL 114/15    IVY D 127/22    IVY D 127/24    IVY D 131/20
        MOTHR 142/19    GRACE 154/02    GRACE 158/26    GRACE 159/21
        GRACE 159/23    GRACE 160/28    GRACE 166/21    GRACE 172/26
CIVIC (1) ............................................... PNFUL 109/13
CIVIL (1) ............................................... MOTHR 149/04
CIVILISATION (1) ........................................ PNFUL 115/30
CLACKING (2) ............................................ EVELN   36/05
        DEAD  179/12
CLAIM (2) ............................................... DEAD  204/09
        DEAD  204/09
CLAMBERED (2) ........................................... ENCTR   22/07
        DEAD  208/30
CLAMOUR (1) ............................................. MOTHR 146/29
CLANCY (1) .............................................. DEAD  189/02
CLANGED (2) ............................................. EVELN   41/04
        DEAD  175/04
CLAP (1) ................................................ DEAD  193/16
CLAPPED (2) ............................................. RACE    48/02
        IVY D 135/23
CLAPPING (8) ............................................ RACE    47/34
        IVY D 135/23    MOTHR 146/01    MOTHR 146/14    MOTHR 146/31
        DEAD  182/01    DEAD  183/30    DEAD  187/15
CLASPED (2) ............................................. PARTS   98/20
        DEAD  191/15
CLASPING (2) ............................................ LITTL   85/15
        PARTS   96/03
CLASPS (1) .............................................. CLAY  100/08
CLASS (3) ............................................... ARABY   32/22
        GALNT   51/12   PNFUL 111/13
CLASSES (2) ............................................. IVY D 121/26
        GRACE 164/07
CLASSROOM (1) ........................................... ARABY   32/16
CLATTER (3) ............................................. PARTS   89/30
        DEAD  191/33    DEAD  200/09
CLATTERED (1) ........................................... CLAY  101/16
CLAY (3) ................................................ LITTL   84/12
        LITTL   84/13   CLAY   99/ T
CLEAN (2) ............................................... HOUSE   66/27
        PARTS   90/28
CLEAN-SHAVEN (3) ........................................ LITTL   75/04
        PARTS   87/03   IVY D 130/08
CLEAR (7) ............................................... PARTS   90/21
        PARTS   90/29   CLAY  100/12    CLAY  101/23    DEAD  193/02
```

```
          DEAD   193/25     DEAD   201/12
CLEARED (7) ........................................ RACE   48/04
     HOUSE  64/06     LITTL  74/24     PARTS  96/02   IVY D 134/05
     GRACE 151/22     DEAD  191/33
CLEARLY (1) ........................................ DEAD  210/17
CLEAVER (2) ........................................ HOUSE  61/10
     HOUSE  63/24
CLENCHING (1) ...................................... ARABY  33/24
CLERGYMAN (1) ...................................... IVY D 125/23
CLERGYMAN'S (1) .................................... IVY D 125/26
CLERK (15) ......................................... SISTR  18/03
     SISTR  18/04     HOUSE  62/16     PARTS  88/20   PARTS  88/24
     PARTS  89/15     PARTS  89/19     PARTS  90/17   PARTS  92/05
     PARTS  92/07     PARTS  93/02     PARTS  93/26   GRACE 156/16
     GRACE 158/21     GRACE 158/24
CLERKS (4) ......................................... HOUSE  62/07
     PARTS  91/06     PARTS  91/25     PARTS  92/04
CLERK'S (1) ........................................ GRACE 172/31
CLEVER (5) ......................................... LITTL  79/28
     PARTS  93/29     IVY D 125/03     IVY D 125/05   MOTHR 138/04
CLICKING (1) ....................................... PARTS  90/19
CLIENTS (3) ........................................ PARTS  86/13
     PARTS  89/17     PARTS  89/19
CLIMATE (1) ........................................ GRACE 156/21
CLIMAX (2) ......................................... DEAD  185/21
     DEAD  185/29
CLIMBING (1) ....................................... GALNT  56/15
CLINCH (1) ......................................... LITTL  80/04
CLINKED (1) ........................................ LITTL  75/28
CLIP (1) ........................................... GALNT  55/27
CLOAK (4) .......................................... MOTHR 149/20
     MOTHR 149/23     DEAD  195/15     DEAD  216/16
CLOAKS (1) ......................................... RACE   46/31
CLOCK (9) .......................................... ARABY  33/04
     ARABY  34/24     GALNT  50/31     GALNT  53/19   GALNT  58/34
     GALNT  59/17     HOUSE  64/18     PARTS  90/23   GRACE 153/17
CLOSE (12) ......................................... EVELN  40/05
     GALNT  49/10     GALNT  53/28     GALNT  55/17   GALNT  59/24
     PARTS  95/09     DEAD  183/32     DEAD  193/08   DEAD  205/06
     DEAD  206/05     DEAD  206/15     DEAD  213/25
CLOSED (19) ........................................ SISTR  16/16
     ARABY  34/27     ARABY  34/30     GALNT  52/12   GALNT  60/06
     LITTL  81/04     LITTL  82/17     LITTL  85/10   PARTS  95/01
     IVY D 118/09     MOTHR 147/18     GRACE 150/07   GRACE 151/02
     GRACE 151/07     DEAD  182/34     DEAD  196/34   DEAD  210/11
     DEAD  210/17     DEAD  210/33
CLOSELY (4) ........................................ SISTR  13/18
     LITTL  75/04     PNFUL 111/26     DEAD  215/14
CLOSER (1) ......................................... CLAY   99/07
CLOSING (3) ........................................ EVELN  40/13
     IVY D 124/09     GRACE 153/32
CLOTH (3) .......................................... SISTR  14/23
     PNFUL 108/02     DEAD  182/31
CLOTHE (1) ......................................... GRACE 160/32
CLOTHED (1) ........................................ PNFUL 107/13
CLOTHES (8) ........................................ GALNT  51/30
     IVY D 125/24     IVY D 130/04     MOTHR 141/32   GRACE 150/05
     GRACE 172/08     DEAD  176/08     DEAD  222/18
CLOTHES-RACK (1) ................................... PNFUL 107/10
CLOTHING (1) ....................................... GRACE 154/03
CLOTTED (1) ........................................ GRACE 153/29
CLOUD (2) .......................................... RACE   46/30
```

```
                LITTL    70/ T
CLOUDS (4) ...................................................... SISTR   12/20
        SISTR   14/06    ENCTR   24/14    LITTL   78/09
CLOWNISH (1) .................................................... DEAD   220/04
CLUB (2) ........................................................ ENCTR   22/29
        GALNT   54/07
CLUMPS (2) ...................................................... RACE    42/03
        RACE    42/06
CLUMSILY (1) .................................................... SISTR   14/22
CLUMSY (1) ...................................................... ENCTR   20/14
CLUTCH (1) ...................................................... IVY D  134/25
CLUTCHED (1) .................................................... EVELN   41/10
COACHMAN (1) .................................................... ARABY   30/11
COAL-(3) ........................................................ IVY D  123/09
        IVY D  123/31    GRACE  158/24
COALS (1) ....................................................... IVY D  118/03
COAL-SCUTTLE (1) ................................................ PNFUL  107/10
COARSE (1) ...................................................... DEAD   184/28
COAT (7) ........................................................ SISTR   12/21
        HOUSE   67/28    PARTS   98/13   - PNFUL  116/07    IVY D  119/24
        IVY D  122/13    GRACE  153/33
COATS (2) ....................................................... LITTL   73/15
        MOTHR  139/09
COCK-EYE (1) .................................................... IVY D  125/13
COCKS (1) ....................................................... IVY D  120/04
COCOTTES (1) .................................................... LITTL   77/21
CODE (1) ........................................................ GRACE  159/30
COFFEE (1) ...................................................... LITTL   82/14
COFFIN (5) ...................................................... SISTR   14/25
        SISTR   16/08    SISTR   18/11    DEAD   201/15    DEAD   201/16
COFFINED (1) .................................................... SISTR   14/18
COFFINS (1) ..................................................... DEAD   201/04
COIN (2) ........................................................ GALNT   60/30
        DEAD   178/25
COINS (2) ....................................................... ARABY   35/02
        PARTS   93/06
COLD (32) ....................................................... SISTR   11/04
        ARABY   30/05    ARABY   33/07    EVELN   40/29    HOUSE   67/15
        PARTS   94/13    PNFUL  112/04    PNFUL  112/05    PNFUL  113/03
        PNFUL  116/06    PNFUL  117/01    PNFUL  117/11    IVY D  119/21
        IVY D  122/21    IVY D  130/17    GRACE  153/19    GRACE  158/31
        DEAD   177/19    DEAD   180/05    DEAD   180/07    DEAD   192/02
        DEAD   206/06    DEAD   207/03    DEAD   208/22    DEAD   210/26
        DEAD   211/08    DEAD   211/32    DEAD   213/22    DEAD   213/24
        DEAD   213/25    DEAD   214/06    DEAD   220/08
COLDLY (5) ...................................................... HOUSE   68/06
        LITTL   83/09    LITTL   83/10    DEAD   191/17    DEAD   219/17
COLDS (1) ....................................................... DEAD   211/20
COLGAN (1) ...................................................... IVY D  121/16
COLGAN'S (2) .................................................... IVY D  121/17
        IVY D  124/22
COLLAPSE (1) .................................................... PNFUL  112/09
COLLAR (10) ..................................................... IVY D  120/28
        IVY D  122/13    IVY D  125/26    IVY D  125/26    IVY D  130/09
        GRACE  151/06    GRACE  153/33    DEAD   187/23    DEAD   206/20
        DEAD   207/32
COLLAR-BONE (1) ................................................. MOTHR  143/30
COLLARETTE (1) .................................................. GALNT   55/29
COLLARS (1) ..................................................... GRACE  172/08
COLLEAGUE (1) ................................................... GRACE  157/13
COLLEAGUES (1) .................................................. DEAD   204/14
COLLECT (1) ..................................................... HOUSE   64/04
```

```
COLLECTED (4) ...................................... ARABY   33/18
    RACE    45/16    HOUSE   64/07    GRACE 151/12
COLLECTING (1) ..................................... ENCTR   21/21
COLLECTION (1) ..................................... GRACE  163/05
COLLEGE (12) ....................................... SISTR   13/02
    ENCTR   20/25    ENCTR   21/18    RACE    43/22   GALNT   53/18
    GALNT   58/34    GALNT   59/17    GRACE  169/11   DEAD   188/12
    DEAD   209/14    DEAD   209/16    DEAD   209/20
COLONEL-LOOKING (1) ................................ CLAY   102/33
COLOUR (12) ........................................ ARABY   30/04
    LITTL   81/17    PARTS   88/32    IVY D  120/34   MOTHR  145/06
    MOTHR  148/32    GRACE  156/32    DEAD   178/15   DEAD   179/31
    DEAD   184/27    DEAD   193/10    DEAD   212/06
COLOURED (6) ....................................... ARABY   35/01
    EVELN   37/13    GALNT   49/04    CLAY   103/33   DEAD   178/12
    DEAD   187/31
COLOURLESS (1) ..................................... LITTL   75/08
COLOURS (2) ........................................ RACE    47/09
    DEAD   197/02
COLUMN (2) ......................................... DEAD   184/19
    DEAD   188/07
COMBED (1) ......................................... ARABY   30/12
COMBING-JACKET (1) ................................. HOUSE   67/07
COME (78) .......................................... ENCTR   22/15
    ARABY   33/20    ARABY   35/03    EVELN   39/01   EVELN   39/16
    EVELN   40/02    EVELN   41/05    EVELN   41/09   RACE    45/09
    GALNT   56/16    GALNT   58/11    GALNT   60/20   HOUSE   63/03
    HOUSE   69/05    LITTL   78/01    LITTL   78/29   LITTL   79/34
    LITTL   80/03    LITTL   81/02    LITTL   82/13   PARTS   87/01
    PARTS   89/11    PARTS   92/04    PARTS   93/31   PARTS   96/14
    CLAY   100/14    CLAY   101/01    CLAY   103/15   PNFUL  110/09
    PNFUL  117/27    IVY D  124/34    IVY D  125/22   IVY D  126/02
    IVY D  126/05    IVY D  126/10    IVY D  128/26   IVY D  130/12
    IVY D  132/04    IVY D  133/06    IVY D  133/06   MOTHR  138/22
    MOTHR  139/02    MOTHR  142/17    MOTHR  144/28   MOTHR  146/05
    GRACE  152/21    GRACE  155/02    GRACE  155/16   GRACE  155/19
    GRACE  166/16    GRACE  166/16    GRACE  168/11   DEAD   175/12
    DEAD   176/33    DEAD   181/24    DEAD   185/14   DEAD   186/07
    DEAD   187/17    DEAD   188/23    DEAD   188/26   DEAD   188/32
    DEAD   189/02    DEAD   189/03    DEAD   189/06   DEAD   190/17
    DEAD   194/28    DEAD   199/05    DEAD   200/31   DEAD   203/09
    DEAD   206/15    DEAD   211/01    DEAD   217/10   DEAD   217/22
    DEAD   217/32    DEAD   218/02    DEAD   220/29   DEAD   221/09
    DEAD   223/26
COME-ALL-YOU (1) ................................... ARABY   31/07
COMEDY (1) ......................................... PNFUL  116/27
COMES (6) .......................................... IVY D  122/03
    IVY D  124/06    IVY D  124/33    IVY D  132/10   DEAD   189/21
    DEAD   207/24
COMETTY (1) ........................................ MOTHR  141/12
COMFORT (4) ........................................ SISTR   15/31
    HOUSE   67/30    PARTS   92/24    DEAD   181/22
COMFORTABLE (1) .................................... DEAD   201/14
COMFORTABLY (1) .................................... DEAD   208/32
COMFORTED (1) ...................................... HOUSE   66/32
COMIC (3) .......................................... HOUSE   62/22
    MOTHR  138/22    GRACE  172/20
COMICAL (2) ........................................ GRACE  162/09
    DEAD   196/01
COMING (24) ........................................ SISTR   16/31
    EVELN   36/17    EVELN   40/10    GALNT   50/21   GALNT   55/09
    GALNT   56/09    GALNT   59/23    HOUSE   68/05   PARTS   89/29
```

```
        IVY D 119/13      IVY D 120/08      IVY D 128/11      IVY D 131/28
        MOTHR 141/26      GRACE 158/32      GRACE 159/01      GRACE 161/20
        DEAD  177/02      DEAD  189/02      DEAD  191/29      DEAD  191/30
        DEAD  194/02      DEAD  210/34      DEAD  220/21
COMMAND (1) ..........................................  GRACE 161/03
COMMERCE (1) .........................................  ENCTR  23/08
COMMERCIAL (2) .......................................  GRACE 153/34
        GRACE 173/01
COMMERCIALLY (1) .....................................  RACE   45/32
COMMISSION (3) .......................................  HOUSE  62/16
        LITTL  75/33      GRACE 158/24
COMMITTED (1) ........................................  DEAD  201/11
COMMITTEE (12) .......................................  IVY D 118/ T
        IVY D 119/18      MOTHR 140/02      MOTHR 140/07      MOTHR 140/27
        MOTHR 141/10      MOTHR 142/01      MOTHR 148/05      MOTHR 148/22
        MOTHR 148/24      MOTHR 148/26      MOTHR 149/11
COMMON (3) ...........................................  HOUSE  62/13
        CLAY  101/21  ·  DEAD  195/02
COMMONLY (1) .........................................  DEAD  207/17
COMMONPLACE (2) ......................................  EVELN  40/12
        PNFUL 115/23
COMMON-SENSE (1) .....................................  GRACE 165/04
COMMUNICANT (1) ......................................  ARABY  29/13
COMMUNING (1) ........................................  SISTR  16/29
COMMUNION (1) ........................................  PNFUL 109/09
COMPANIES (1) ........................................  DEAD  199/04
COMPANION (5) ........................................  RACE   44/01
        PNFUL 111/26      PNFUL 115/26      IVY D 119/26      DEAD  196/26
COMPANIONS (5) .......................................  ARABY  33/09
        GALNT  51/33      HOUSE  66/09      PNFUL 109/08      IVY D 131/02
COMPANION'S (3) ......................................  GALNT  49/12
        GALNT  50/01      GALNT  53/29
COMPANIONSHIP (1) ....................................  PNFUL 111/18
COMPANY (21) .........................................  ENCTR  23/18
        RACE   44/17      RACE   48/03      GALNT  50/22      PARTS  94/04
        PARTS  94/31      PARTS  95/10      PARTS  95/31      PARTS  95/34
        PNFUL 113/30      PNFUL 114/22      PNFUL 114/23      PNFUL 115/12
        MOTHR 143/34      GRACE 166/30      GRACE 170/10      GRACE 170/31
        DEAD  198/17      DEAD  198/20      DEAD  202/03      DEAD  205/07
COMPARED (2) .........................................  LITTL  77/28
        PARTS  96/01
COMPARING (1) ........................................  DEAD  219/33
COMPASSIONATELY (1) ..................................  DEAD  207/28
COMPELLED (1) ........................................  PNFUL 110/17
COMPETE (1) ..........................................  PNFUL 111/10
COMPETED (1) .........................................  MOTHR 142/31
COMPETITION (1) ......................................  LITTL  77/05
COMPETITORS (1) ......................................  RACE   44/19
COMPLACENT (1) .......................................  MOTHR 143/33
COMPLAIN (1) .........................................  PARTS  87/08
COMPLETE (2) .........................................  PARTS  88/25
        PNFUL 107/18
COMPLETELY (2) .......................................  ARABY  35/30
        GRACE 171/14
COMPLEX (1) ..........................................  SISTR  13/10
COMPLEXION (3) .......................................  PARTS  96/16
        GRACE 152/11      DEAD  177/25
COMPLICITY (1) .......................................  HOUSE  63/18
COMPLIMENT (4) .......................................  RACE   44/19
        GALNT  51/16      CLAY   99/18      DEAD  200/19
COMPLIMENTED (1) .....................................  GRACE 166/25
COMPLIMENTS (1) ......................................  DEAD  193/27
```

COMPOSE (1) .... PNFUL 108/26
COMPOSED (1) .... GALNT 60/23
COMPOSURE (1) .... LITTL 83/12
COMPROMISED (1) .... DEAD 197/30
CONCEAL (2) .... PNFUL 115/22
   GRACE 171/02
CONCEDED (1) .... PNFUL 109/12
CONCEIT (1) .... DEAD 191/11
CONCEIVED (2) .... RACE 46/09
   PNFUL 116/23
CONCERN (2) .... RACE 45/03
   GRACE 163/19
CONCERT (18) .... PNFUL 109/06
   PNFUL 110/04   MOTHR 138/10   MOTHR 139/01   MOTHR 139/07
   MOTHR 140/12   MOTHR 140/15   MOTHR 140/18   MOTHR 140/20
   MOTHR 140/26   MOTHR 141/28   MOTHR 141/29   MOTHR 141/31
   MOTHR 143/02   MOTHR 144/28   MOTHR 147/09   DEAD 176/10
   DEAD 176/11
CONCERTS (11) .... PNFUL 112/22
   MOTHR 136/04   MOTHR 138/09   MOTHR 138/16   MOTHR 139/05
   MOTHR 140/03   MOTHR 140/07   MOTHR 140/34   MOTHR 141/04
   MOTHR 141/07   MOTHR 145/01
CONCLAVE (1) .... GRACE 169/13
CONCRETE (1) .... EVELN 36/05
CONDEMNED (1) .... MOTHR 149/10
CONDENSED (1) .... PNFUL 113/13
CONDITION (1) .... GRACE 166/21
CONDUCT (4) .... MOTHR 140/23
   MOTHR 147/28   MOTHR 149/10   DEAD 208/16
CONFERENCE (1) .... DEAD 205/24
CONFESS (5) .... SISTR 11/24
   SISTR 11/26   GRACE 170/32   DEAD 203/27   DEAD 205/02
CONFESSED (1) .... GALNT 53/25
CONFESSION (2) .... HOUSE 65/29
   GRACE 171/25
CONFESSIONAL (2) .... SISTR 13/13
   PNFUL 112/03
CONFESSION-BOX (1) .... SISTR 18/07
CONFESSOR (1) .... PNFUL 110/31
CONFIDENCE (2) .... GRACE 162/25
   DEAD 203/15
CONFIDENTIALLY (1) .... DEAD 183/22
CONFIRMED (1) .... GRACE 170/14
CONFUSE (1) .... RACE 44/12
CONFUSED (12) .... ENCTR 20/32
   ENCTR 23/26   ARABY 31/17   ARABY 31/31   EVELN 39/07
   RACE 44/19   LITTL 74/19   LITTL 80/17   PARTS 89/25
   CLAY 103/32   PNFUL 109/32   DEAD 208/34
CONFUSEDLY (1) .... LITTL 79/19
CONFUSION (2) .... DEAD 197/25
   DEAD 209/02
CONGENIAL (1) .... RACE 46/22
CONGREGATION (3) .... GRACE 164/06
   GRACE 173/09   GRACE 173/16
CONNACHT (1) .... DEAD 189/04
CONNIVED (1) .... HOUSE 64/13
CONNUBIAL (1) .... LITTL 78/33
CONQUER (1) .... DEAD 216/30
CONQUEROR (1) .... GALNT 55/13
CONROY (17) .... DEAD 176/34
   DEAD 177/02   DEAD 177/08   DEAD 177/21   DEAD 179/34
   DEAD 180/14   DEAD 180/26   DEAD 181/05   DEAD 181/20

DEAD 182/13	DEAD 188/32	DEAD 195/17	DEAD 195/26
DEAD 196/01	DEAD 196/06	DEAD 197/14	DEAD 211/08

CONSCIENCE (1) .... GRACE 174/17
CONSCIENCES (1) .... ENCTR 20/33
CONSCIOUS (9) .... ARABY 29/05
    RACE 44/29   GALNT 52/31   PNFUL 110/25   MOTHR 145/07
    GRACE 154/28   GRACE 160/28   GRACE 171/29   DEAD 223/18
CONSCIOUSNESS (1) .... DEAD 219/33
CONSECUTIVELY (1) .... PNFUL 111/11
CONSENTED (3) .... EVELN 37/18
    MOTHR 149/16   GRACE 159/25
CONSERVATIVE (2) .... IVY D 131/03
    IVY D 131/17
CONSERVATIVES (2) .... IVY D 131/04
    IVY D 132/30
CONSERVATORY (2) .... CLAY 100/27
    CLAY 100/30
CONSIDER (2) .... MOTHR 148/24
    DEAD 204/34
CONSIDERABLE (1) .... GRACE 172/33
CONSIDERABLY (1) .... MOTHR 145/02
CONSIDERATELY (1) .... LITTL 79/31
CONSIDERATION (1) .... MOTHR 147/31
CONSIDERED (3) .... GALNT 50/17
    IVY D 131/02   GRACE 157/24
CONSIDERING (2) .... ENCTR 26/30
    LITTL 73/04
CONSIGNOR (1) .... PARTS 93/03
CONSISTED (1) .... SISTR 11/34
CONSOLE (2) .... MOTHR 136/18
    DEAD 223/02
CONSOLED (1) .... LITTL 71/23
CONSTABLE (12) .... PNFUL 114/14
    GRACE 151/11   GRACE 151/15   GRACE 151/24   GRACE 151/26
    GRACE 152/03   GRACE 152/09   GRACE 152/17   GRACE 152/18
    GRACE 152/19   GRACE 152/33   GRACE 160/19
CONSTABULARY (1) .... GRACE 154/17
CONSTANT (3) .... SISTR 12/21
    GALNT 49/15   HOUSE 63/30
CONSTANTINE (2) .... DEAD 186/29
    DEAD 186/32
CONSTANTLY (2) .... EVELN 40/14
    MOTHR 136/06
CONSTITUTION (1) .... ENCTR 20/02
CONSTRAINED (1) .... GRACE 166/21
CONSUME (1) .... IVY D 135/01
CONSUMPTION (1) .... DEAD 220/16
CONTAINED (2) .... SISTR 17/27
    ARABY 29/15
CONTAINING (3) .... PNFUL 108/27
    PNFUL 112/11   DEAD 196/33
CONTEMPT (1) .... MOTHR 139/31
CONTENT (3) .... HOUSE 65/02
    MOTHR 138/06   MOTHR 147/21
CONTENTED (1) .... GALNT 56/02
CONTENTEDLY (1) .... GRACE 167/26
CONTENTS (1) .... IVY D 129/19
CONTINENT (5) .... RACE 42/05
    LITTL 78/20   GRACE 164/15   DEAD 181/06   DEAD 181/07
CONTINENTALS (1) .... RACE 44/17
CONTINUALLY (2) .... SISTR 11/27
    MOTHR 138/23

CONTINUE (1) .... DEAD   205/11
CONTINUED (26) .... SISTR   10/18
    SISTR   17/02   ENCTR   24/26   ENCTR   26/16   ENCTR   27/19
    EVELN   39/32   GALNT   60/15   .LITTL 76/28   PARTS   88/14
    PARTS   91/11   IVY D 135/23   MOTHR 146/15   GRACE 155/12
    GRACE 165/17   GRACE 167/21   DEAD   177/14   DEAD   188/20
    DEAD   189/27   DEAD   194/14   DEAD   194/26   DEAD   204/01
    DEAD   204/24   DEAD   208/05   DEAD   217/03   DEAD   220/23
    DEAD   220/26
CONTINUING (2) .... IVY D 119/27
    GRACE 171/30
CONTRACT (13) .... PARTS   87/09
    PARTS   87/15   PARTS   88/10   PARTS   89/28   MOTHR 138/14
    MOTHR 140/33   MOTHR 140/34   MOTHR 141/05   MOTHR 144/12
    MOTHR 144/16   MOTHR 144/21   MOTHR 148/25   MOTHR 148/27
CONTRACTED (1) .... LITTL   84/26
CONTRACTS (1) .... RACE   43/19
CONTRADICTIONS (1) .... DEAD   209/07
CONTRALTO (3) .... MOTHR 143/16
    MOTHR 147/15   DEAD   198/20
CONTRAST (1) .... LITTL   80/23
CONTROL (4) .... RACE   44/18
    RACE   44/24   GALNT   56/20   DEAD   221/13
CONTUSIONS (1) .... PNFUL 114/17
CONVENIENT (1) .... GRACE 162/18
CONVENT (7) .... ARABY   32/04
    CLAY   105/25   MOTHR 136/10   MOTHR 137/20   DEAD   220/30
    DEAD   221/09   DEAD   221/28
CONVENTIONS (1) .... PNFUL 109/13
CONVERGED (1) .... ARABY   31/09
CONVERSATION (16) .... ARABY   35/07
    RACE   46/13   GALNT   51/33   GALNT   57/24   PARTS   95/28
    MOTHR 137/05   MOTHR 143/14   MOTHR 145/29   MOTHR 146/24
    GRACE 161/06   GRACE 163/21   GRACE 167/03   DEAD   198/15
    DEAD   201/28   DEAD   211/34   DEAD   214/18
CONVERSE (2) .... GALNT   55/15
    GALNT   58/17
CONVERSING (1) .... DEAD   192/01
CONVERTED (2) .... GRACE 157/08
    DEAD   175/08
CONVEX (1) .... DEAD   184/29
CONVEYED (1) .... GRACE 163/17
CONVICTION (1) .... RACE   47/22
CONVINCING (1) .... GALNT   52/30
CONVULSED (1) .... GALNT   49/18
CONVULSIVELY (1) .... LITTL   84/26
COOK (5) .... PARTS   98/04
    CLAY   99/03   CLAY   100/33   CLAY   101/05   CLAY   101/23
COOKED (1) .... PNFUL 113/04
COOL (6) .... ARABY   33/11
    HOUSE   68/22   HOUSE   68/27   PARTS   94/04   MOTHR 149/29
    DEAD   192/03
COOLLY (1) .... PARTS   93/16
COPIED (3) .... PARTS   87/15
    PARTS   88/10   PARTS   88/13
COPING (1) .... ENCTR   21/30
COPIOUS (1) .... SISTR   14/27
COPIOUSLY (1) .... IVY D 124/19
COPPER (1) .... GLAY   99/04
COPPERS (1) .... CLAY   100/12
COPY (13) .... ENCTR   20/14
    HOUSE   66/11   LITTL   75/13   PARTS   87/09   PARTS   87/31

PARTS	89/10	PARTS	89/22	PARTS	89/27	PARTS	90/20
PARTS	90/23	PARTS	91/10	PNFUL	108/01	IVY D	121/01

CORDIALLY (1) .... DEAD 215/05
CORK (3) .... IVY D 131/08
  IVY D 132/32   IVY D 135/26
CORKS (1) .... DEAD 197/27
CORKSCREW (7) .... CLAY 106/18
  IVY D 128/28   IVY D 129/08   IVY D 129/09   IVY D 129/20
  IVY D 130/21   IVY D 133/10
CORLESS'S (3) .... LITTL 72/03
  LITTL 74/15   LITTL 80/20
CORLEY (46) .... GALNT 50/28

GALNT	50/29	GALNT	51/10	GALNT	51/18	GALNT	52/05
GALNT	52/10	GALNT	52/12	GALNT	52/15	GALNT	52/21
GALNT	52/25	GALNT	52/34	GALNT	53/02	GALNT	53/11
GALNT	53/14	GALNT	53/15	GALNT	53/21	GALNT	53/24
GALNT	53/25	GALNT	53/30	GALNT	54/21	GALNT	54/26
GALNT	54/27	GALNT	54/33	GALNT	55/04	GALNT	55/07
GALNT	55/11	GALNT	56/04	GALNT	56/31	GALNT	58/19
GALNT	58/20	GALNT	59/02	GALNT	59/07	GALNT	59/08
GALNT	59/13	GALNT	59/14	GALNT	59/18	GALNT	59/26
GALNT	59/29	GALNT	59/34	GALNT	60/03	GALNT	60/06
GALNT	60/13	GALNT	60/14	GALNT	60/17	GALNT	60/22
GALNT	60/27						

CORLEY'S (6) .... GALNT 51/16
  GALNT 54/02   GALNT 56/12   GALNT 57/29   GALNT 57/31
  GALNT 59/12
CORNED (1) .... PNFUL 112/28
CORNER (33) .... SISTR 11/02

SISTR	14/34	SISTR	17/23	ARABY	30/14	RACE	46/33
GALNT	54/22	GALNT	55/09	GALNT	55/22	GALNT	56/34
GALNT	58/10	GALNT	58/16	GALNT	59/03	GALNT	59/20
GALNT	60/21	LITTL	73/02	LITTL	82/17	PARTS	88/29
PARTS	93/20	PARTS	94/11	PARTS	94/18	PARTS	96/30
IVY D	123/29	IVY D	127/20	MOTHR	137/32	MOTHR	140/25
MOTHR	143/27	MOTHR	147/23	MOTHR	148/03	GRACE	150/08
GRACE	155/14	DEAD	183/01	DEAD	190/14	DEAD	214/17

CORNERS (2) .... GALNT 49/16
  MOTHR 136/06
CORNFACTOR (1) .... DEAD 176/05
CORN-FACTOR'S (1) .... HOUSE 63/02
CORONER (3) .... PNFUL 113/21
  PNFUL 115/10   GRACE 158/26
CORPORATION (1) .... IVY D 121/20
CORPSE (2) .... SISTR 9/07
  SISTR 15/28
CORRESPONDENCE (4) .... PARTS 89/23
  PARTS 89/31   PARTS 90/08   PARTS 90/11
CORRIDOR (2) .... MOTHR 144/08
  DEAD 215/32
CORROBORATED (1) .... PNFUL 114/14
CORRUPTION (1) .... LITTL 78/15
COST (3) .... LITTL 82/26
  LITTL 82/27   MOTHR 138/33
COT (1) .... IVY D 134/15
COTTAGE (1) .... PNFUL 111/15
COTTAGES (1) .... ARABY 30/09
COTTER (11) .... SISTR 9/16

SISTR	10/16	SISTR	10/20	SISTR	10/25	SISTR	10/31
SISTR	10/32	SISTR	11/06	SISTR	11/08	SISTR	11/11
SISTR	11/13	SISTR	11/19				

COTTER'S (1) .... SISTR 13/30

COUCH (1) .... DEAD   216/12
COUGH (1) .... MOTHR 137/14
COUGHED (2) .... GALNT   60/03
    DEAD   201/31
COULD (133)
COULDN'T (21) .... SISTR   15/16

SISTR 18/01	SISTR 18/02	ENCTR 25/17	ENCTR 25/17
ARABY 33/21	LITTL 73/06	LITTL 84/14	LITTL 84/14
LITTL 85/13	PARTS 90/24	PARTS 92/23	IVY D 123/20
IVY D 124/30	IVY D 127/13	DEAD 195/21	DEAD 198/32
DEAD 211/09	DEAD 212/11	DEAD 212/12	DEAD 221/17

COUNCILLORS (1) .... GRACE 172/28
COUNSEL (2) .... HOUSE   63/15
    GRACE 174/06
COUNT (3) .... PARTS   95/28
    CLAY   106/08   MOTHR 146/25
COUNTED (5) .... HOUSE   65/06
    LITTL   84/27   PARTS   88/12   IVY D 128/20   MOTHR 146/33
COUNTER (13) .... LITTL   74/26
    LITTL   82/29   PARTS   86/13   PARTS   88/19   PARTS   89/03
    PARTS   89/18   PARTS   91/06   PARTS   94/18   CLAY   102/23
    PNFUL 116/19   IVY D 127/10   MOTHR 137/34   GRACE 153/02
COUNTER-ORDERS (1) .... DEAD   197/26
COUNTERPARTS (1) .... PARTS   86/ T
COUNTING (2) .... ARABY   35/01
    RACE   48/30
COUNTRIES (1) .... EVELN   39/10
COUNTRY (22) .... EVELN   37/31
    EVELN   38/09   EVELN   39/16   RACE   45/09   HOUSE   68/01
    LITTL   75/16   LITTL   78/30   IVY D 125/18   IVY D 125/20
    IVY D 131/19   IVY D 131/27   IVY D 131/29   IVY D 131/32
    GRACE 160/24   GRACE 160/30   GRACE 161/09   DEAD 187/05
    DEAD 189/29   DEAD 189/31   DEAD 202/33   DEAD 207/07
    DEAD 221/04
COUNTY (1) .... PNFUL 116/12
COUPLES (4) .... GALNT   58/33
    DEAD 182/03   DEAD 186/08   DEAD 190/33
COURAGE (4) .... SISTR   12/26
    SISTR   13/15   PNFUL 110/12   DEAD 192/19
COURSE (44) .... SISTR   17/27
    SISTR   18/15   ENCTR   25/16   EVELN   37/21   EVELN   39/16
    RACE   44/34   RACE   48/21   HOUSE   63/08   HOUSE   64/11
    HOUSE   66/08   HOUSE   66/22   LITTL   72/26   LITTL   76/22
    LITTL   77/19   LITTL   82/15   PARTS   91/16   PARTS   92/23
    PARTS   93/32   CLAY   101/20   CLAY   103/27   PNFUL 116/02
    IVY D 121/28   IVY D 129/34   IVY D 130/14   MOTHR 140/04
    MOTHR 140/25   MOTHR 140/33   MOTHR 141/05   MOTHR 148/14
    GRACE 164/08   GRACE 164/18   GRACE 165/14   GRACE 166/08
    GRACE 168/06   GPACE 168/12   GRACE 168/20   GRACE 168/24
    DEAD 176/24   DEAD 181/15   DEAD 188/26   DEAD 190/04
    DEAD 190/26   DEAD 191/07   DEAD 199/02
COURSE (1) .... GRACE 165/28
COURSES (4) .... RACE   43/24
    RACE   45/12   PARTS   87/21   MOTHR 144/04
COURSING (1) .... DEAD   213/31
COURTED (1) .... LITTL   72/15
COURTEOUS (1) .... DEAD   203/09
COURTING (1) .... EVELN   39/06
COURTS (2) .... GRACE 157/21
    DEAD 213/02
COURTSHIP (1) .... GRACE 156/02
COUSINS (3) .... RACE   43/08

```
        RACE    44/04    IVY D 121/33
COVER (7) ...................................................  SISTR   17/21
        RACE    48/29    PNFUL 108/02    PNFUL 108/19    DEAD   190/05
        DEAD   193/12    DEAD   215/13
COVERED (8) .................................................  HOUSE   6./01
        LITTL   71/06    LITTL   73/15    PNFUL 107/14    IVY D  118/03
        MOTHR 142/34    GRACE 153/28    DEAD   198/16
COVERING (1) ................................................  GRACE 173/15
COVERINGS (1) ...............................................  GALNT   54/11
COVERS (1) ..................................................  DEAD   188/11
COVERTLY (1) ................................................  RACE    43/28
COW (1) .....................................................  IVY D 130/13
COWARD (2) ..................................................  IVY D 134/11
        IVY D 134/27
COWLEY (2) ..................................................  IVY D 127/11
        IVY D 127/14
CRABBED-LOOKING (1) .........................................  GRACE 170/19
CRACK (1) ...................................................  CLAY   104/16
CRACKERS (1) ................................................  SISTR   15/05
CRAMMED (3) .................................................  SISTR   11/16
        PARTS   89/12    GRACE 162/20
CRANES (1) ..................................................  ENCTR   23/02
CRANING (1) .................................................  DEAD   181/28
CRANNY (1) ..................................................  GRACE 174/02
CRAPE (2) ...................................................  SISTR   12/03
        SISTR   12/05
CRAWLED (1) .................................................  LITTL   71/30
CRAZINESS (1) ...............................................  EVELN   40/13
CREAM (1) ...................................................  SISTR   15/05
CREASED (1) .................................................  DEAD   196/18
CREASES (1) .................................................  DEAD   179/30
CREATED (1) .................................................  GRACE 171/30
CREATURE (1) ................................................  ARABY   35/32
CREATURES (1) ...............................................  PNFUL 117/18
CREDIT (1) ..................................................  HOUSE   62/08
CREDO (2) ...................................................  GRACE 169/34
        GRACE 170/02
CREED (1) ...................................................  PNFUL 109/08
CREPT (2) ...................................................  ARABY   34/17
        PNFUL 116/07
CREST (3) ...................................................  RACE    42/02
        RACE    42/13    PNFUL 117/09
CRETONNE (2) ................................................  EVELN   36/03
        EVELN   39/34
CREVICES (1) ................................................  DEAD   177/20
CRICKET (1) .................................................  ENCTR   22/29
CRIED (21) ..................................................  RACE    47/29
        GALNT   60/17    HOUSE   66/29    LITTL   84/32    LITTL   85/07
        PARTS   86/18    PARTS   98/12    PARTS   98/22    CLAY   104/03
        CLAY   104/24    IVY D 135/31    GRACE 169/22    DEAD   178/29
        DEAD   191/16    DEAD   195/32    DEAD   196/03    DEAD   196/12
        DEAD   196/15    DEAD   209/21    DEAD   210/34    DEAD   211/04
CRIES (2) ...................................................  ARABY   33/09
        PNFUL 114/02
CRIMSON (1) .................................................  DEAD   202/30
CRIPPLE (1) .................................................  EVELN   36/13
CRITICAL (2) ................................................  GALNT   58/22
        DEAD   192/17
CRITICISMS (1) ..............................................  PNFUL 111/12
CRITICS (1) .................................................  LITTL   74/03
CROFTON (17) ................................................  IVY D 129/33
        IVY D 129/33    IVY D 130/10    IVY D 130/17    IVY D 130/32
```

IVY D 131/12	IVY D 132/11	IVY D 132/12	IVY D 132/31
IVY D 132/33	IVY D 133/03	IVY D 133/25	IVY D 135/31
IVY D 135/33	GRACE 165/18	GRACE 165/25	GRACE 165/27

CROFTON'S (1) .... IVY D 132/32
CROLY (1) .... PNFUL 114/10
CROOKED (1) .... DEAD 223/33
CROPPED (1) .... LITTL 75/04
CROSBIE (3) .... PARTS 87/16
    PARTS 87/26   PARTS 88/10
CROSS (10) .... ENCTR 21/15
    CLAY 104/15   CLAY 105/18   PNFUL 113/25   PNFUL 114/04
    GRACE 167/19   GRACE 167/19   DEAD 188/23   DEAD 188/26
    DEAD 214/27
CROSS-DIRECTIONS (1) .... DEAD 209/07
CROSSED (7) .... SISTR 17/18
    ENCTR 23/17   GALNT 54/19   GALNT 55/21   LITTL 73/12
    DEAD 185/05   DEAD 216/12
CROSSES (1) .... DEAD 223/33
CROSS-EXAMINATION (1) .... DEAD 189/23
CROSSING (5) .... PNFUL 114/24
    PNFUL 114/27   MOTHR 138/01   DEAD 190/18   DEAD 190/21
CROSSINGS (1) .... PNFUL 114/26
CROUCHING (1) .... IVY D 118/05
CROW (2) .... DEAD 187/25
    DEAD 211/12
CROWD (18) .... ENCTR 22/22
    ENCTR 23/29   ARABY 34/19   EVELN 40/22   RACE 47/09
    GALNT 49/04   GALNT 52/05   GALNT 54/20   GALNT 56/26
    GALNT 58/22   GALNT 58/31   LITTL 74/02   LITTL 75/24
    PARTS 93/10   MOTHR 137/31   GRACE 151/12   GRACE 152/24
    GRACE 152/32
CROWDED (2) .... PARTS 93/07
    DEAD 213/21
CROWDS (3) .... EVELN 38/21
    CLAY 102/12   GRACE 166/01
CROWE (1) .... GRACE 154/07
CROWN (3) .... ENCTR 24/24
    LITTL 75/10   PARTS 93/03
CROWNED (1) .... GRACE 173/12
CRUMBS (2) .... ENCTR 24/15
    DEAD 196/20
CRUMPLED (1) .... LITTL 82/23
CRUNCHING (1) .... EVELN 36/06
CRUSADE (1) .... GRACE 160/22
CRUSH (1) .... DEAD 217/17
CRUST (1) .... DEAD 196/20
CRUSTS (1) .... HOUSE 64/05
CRUX (2) .... GRACE 167/18
    GRACE 167/19
CRY (10) .... EVELN 37/30
    EVELN 41/11   HOUSE 66/32   LITTL 84/07   LITTL 84/09
    LITTL 85/04   LITTL 85/12   PARTS 88/09   DEAD 217/17
    DEAD 218/23
CRYING (5) .... HOUSE 67/31
    HOUSE 68/19   DEAD 183/30   DEAD 183/32   DEAD 222/32
CUFFS (3) .... GRACE 173/04
    DEAD 179/06   DEAD 206/20
CULTIVATED (1) .... DEAD 203/06
CULTURE (3) .... ENCTR 20/02
    GRACE 166/27   DEAD 179/14
CUNNING (1) .... GALNT 49/19
CUNNINGHAM (57) .... GRACE 157/04

GRACE 157/06	GRACE 157/12	GRACE 157/18	GRACE 157/27
GRACE 158/02	GRACE 158/09	GRACE 158/15	GRACE 158/30
GRACE 159/04	GRACE 159/05	GRACE 159/11	GRACE 159/16
GRACE 159/17	GRACE 160/17	GRACE 160/33	GRACE 161/07
GRACE 161/23	GRACE 162/01	GRACE 162/12	GRACE 162/16
GRACE 162/22	GRACE 162/27	GRACE 162/30	GRACE 163/01
GRACE 163/10	GRACE 163/27	GRACE 163/33	GRACE 164/04
GRACE 164/12	GRACE 164/18	GRACE 164/23	GRACE 164/26
GRACE 164/31	GRACE 165/07	GRACE 165/12	GRACE 165/20
GRACE 166/08	GRACE 167/05	GRACE 167/10	GRACE 167/17
GRACE 167/21	GRACE 167/24	GRACE 168/04	GRACE 168/08
GRACE 168/18	GRACE 168/23	GRACE 168/32	GRACE 169/07
GRACE 169/10	GRACE 169/25	GRACE 170/02	GRACE 171/09
GRACE 171/16	GRACE 171/22	GRACE 172/15	GRACE 172/24

CUNNINGHAM'S (1) .... GRACE 170/06
CUNNINGLY (1) .... HOUSE 62/07
CUP (3) .... SISTR 16/27
   IVY D 135/19   MOTHR 143/30
CURATE (6) .... PARTS 89/01
   PARTS 89/03   PARTS 96/20   GRACE 151/27   GRACE 153/02
   DEAD 186/33
CURATES (3) .... GALNT 57/11
   GRACE 150/09   GRACE 150/13
CURBSTONE (2) .... GALNT 54/24
   DEAD 215/07
CURIOUS (6) .... RACE 45/23
   HOUSE 67/02   GRACE 157/31   GRACE 163/33   DEAD 198/28
   DEAD 222/10
CURIOUSLY (2) .... RACE 43/26
   LITTL 74/22
CURLED (3) .... ARABY 29/12
   GRACE 150/02   DEAD 178/21
CURLING (1) .... PARTS 93/13
CURLS (1) .... ENCTR 23 08
CURRANT (1) .... ENCTR 23/05
CURS (1) .... IVY D 133/05
CURSE (1) .... GALNT 59/22
CURSED (3) .... PARTS 95/24
   PARTS 95/24   PARTS 97/01
CURSES (1) .... ARABY 31/05
CURTAIN (3) .... ARABY 34/34
   EVELN 39/33   DEAD 213/19
CURTAINS (3) .... SISTR 13/32
   EVELN 36/02   HOUSE 63/28
CURTLY (3) .... ARABY 32/30
   IVY D 122/28   MOTHR 146/11
CURVE (2) .... ARABY 32/07
   DEAD 178/21
CURVED (2) .... ARABY 33/14
   DEAD 215/23
CUSTARD (1) ....?. DEAD 196/27
CUSTOMERS (2) .... HOUSE 61/09
   GRACE 153/02
CUSTOMS (1) .... SISTR 13/34
CUT (7) .... GALNT 57/05
   PARTS 98/19   CLAY 99/07   CLAY 99/09   CLAY 102/27
   DEAD 196/32   DEAD 216/03
CUTE (1) .... DEAD 187/05
CYCLING (1) .... DEAD 189/10
CYCLING-SUIT (3) .... GRACE 151/22
   GRACE 151/33   GRACE 152/23
CYLINDER (2) .... PARTS 93/05

IVY D 118/14

```
DAILY (2) ........................................ DEAD   187/34
     DEAD   188/07
DAIRY (1) ........................................ ENCTR   24/03
DAIRYMAN (1) ..................................... GALNT   51/03
DALKEY (1) ....................................... DEAD   176/12
DALY (8) ......................................... DEAD   182/15
     DEAD   182/17   DEAD   182/22   DEAD   183/25   DEAD   184/05
     DEAD   184/06   DEAD   191/01   DEAD   197/15
DAME (3) ......................................... RACE    45/13
     GALNT   50/30   GALNT   58/16
DAMN (14) ........................................ GALNT   52/34
     GALNT   53/27   GALNT   54/30   LITTL   73/05   LITTL   75/14
     PARTS   90/33   IVY D  124/29   IVY D  125/11   IVY D  129/34
     IVY D  132/07   IVY D  132/18   GRACE  159/12   GRACE  171/23
     GRACE  171/26
DAMNED (2) ....................................... EVELN   40/10
     GRACE  165/28
DAMP (3) ......................................... ARABY   29/12
     PARTS   89/28   IVY. D  125/30
DAN (3) .......................................... PNFUL  108/32
     GRACE  172/30   DEAD   214/33
DANCE (4) ........................................ ENCTR   19/09
     RACE    47/26   DEAD   175/14   DEAD   190/06
DANCED (2) ....................................... CLAY   104/13
     DEAD   215/09
DANCERS (1) ...................................... DEAD   194/28
DANCES (1) ....................................... DEAD   184/07
DANCING (4) ...................................... DEAD   191/06
     DEAD   192/01   DEAD   195/19   DEAD   222/23
DANGER (4) ....................................... EVELN   38/01
     RACE    46/26   IVY D  130/04   DEAD   209/10
DANGLED (2) ...................................... RACE    46/32
     DEAD   222/19
D'ARCY (25) ...................................... DEAD   184/09
     DEAD   191/10   DEAD   198/18   DEAD   198/25   DEAD   198/27
     DEAD   199/18   DEAD   199/21   DEAD   199/30   DEAD   200/01
     DEAD   201/25   DEAD   206/30   DEAD   210/27   DEAD   211/02
     DEAD   211/04   DEAD   211/10   DEAD   211/13   DEAD   211/17
     DEAD   211/28   DEAD   211/30   DEAD   212/08   DEAD   212/10
     DEAD   212/16   DEAD   212/26   DEAD   213/04   DEAD   214/30
D'ARCY'S (1) ..................................... DEAD   215/01
DARED (1) ........................................ MOTHR  148/10
DARK (45) ........................................ SISTR   11/20
     SISTR   12/12   SISTR   18/07   ARABY   30/07   ARABY   30/10
     ARABY   30/11   ARABY   31/21   ARABY   33/11   ARABY   35/18
     ARABY   35/31   EVELN   40/05   RACE    48/28   GALNT   57/01
     GALNT   57/30   LITTL   83/15   PARTS   86/10   PARTS   88/30
     PARTS   88/32   PARTS   88/32   PARTS   89/28   PARTS   95/18
     PARTS   96/08   PNFUL  109/31   PNFUL  111/19   PNFUL  111/20
     IVY D  119/20   IVY D  119/23   IVY D  120/22   IVY D  120/24
     IVY D  126/16   MOTHR  145/19   GRACE  151/03   GRACE  172/09
     DEAD   176/04   DEAD   177/09   DEAD   177/13   DEAD   185/09
     DEAD   196/33   DEAD   209/25   DEAD   210/08   DEAD   212/31
     DEAD   219/10   DEAD   223/25   DEAD   223/28   DEAD   223/30
DARK-COMPLEXIONED (2) ............................ ENCTR   22/28
     DEAD   198/18
DARKENED (2) ..................................... SISTR    9/06
     RACE    47/15
DARKER (2) ....................................... PARTS   96/08
```

```
DEAD    179/25
DARKEST (1) ....................................... LITTL   72/16
DARKNESS (12) ..................................... ARABY   34/30
      ARABY   35/32     PARTS   89/06     PARTS   97/20     PARTS   97/31
      PNFUL  117/04     PNFUL  117/23     PNFUL  117/31     IVY D  118/04
      GRACE  167/14     DEAD   210/08     DEAD   223/15
DART (1) .......................................... PARTS   92/32
DAUGHER (1) ....................................... DEAD   190/19
DAUGHTER (29) ..................................... HOUSE   61/01
      HOUSE   62/26     HOUSE   63/01     HOUSE   63/04     HOUSE   63/05
      HOUSE   63/19     LITTL   79/15     PNFUL  109/27     PNFUL  110/22
      PNFUL  115/11     MOTHR  137/19     MOTHR  138/08     MOTHR  139/06
      MOTHR  139/10     MOTHR  139/31     MOTHR  141/04     MOTHR  141/29
      MOTHR  144/01     MOTHR  144/09     MOTHR  144/12     MOTHR  148/12
      MOTHR  148/23     MOTHR  148/27     MOTHR  149/03     MOTHR  149/13
      MOTHR  149/24     DEAD   175/01     DEAD   176/17     DEAD   190/23
DAUGHTERS (2) ..................................... HOUSE   65/22
      MOTHR  137/17
DAUGHTER'S (6) .................................... HOUSE   65/05
      PNFUL  110/05     PNFUL  110/19     MOTHR  137/26     MOTHR  141/32
      MOTHR  149/20
DAVY (1) .......................................... PARTS   93/20
DAWNED (1) ........................................ ENCTR   20/18
DAWNING (1) ....................................... IVY D  135/16
DAWSON (2) ........................................ IVY D  129/32
      IVY D  131/16
DAY (47) .......................................... SISTR   12/29
      SISTR   17/04     SISTR   17/09     ENCTR   20/13     ENCTR   20/17
      ENCTR   20/17     ENCTR   20/18     ENCTR   21/10     ENCTR   23/33
      ARABY   32/16     EVELN   39/20     EVELN   39/27     EVELN   39/29
      RACE    44/17     GALNT   58/20     HOUSE   61/18     HOUSE   63/03
      LITTL   72/13     LITTL   79/03     LITTL   81/10     LITTL   82/28
      PARTS   88/03     PARTS   89/21     PARTS   92/18     CLAY    99/15
      PNFUL  107/15     IVY D  118/ T     IVY D  119/18     IVY D  119/20
      IVY D  124/28     IVY D  128/01     IVY D  135/16     IVY D  135/17
      IVY D  135/18     MOTHR  138/07     MOTHR  138/24     GRACE  154/33
      GRACE  156/19     GRACE  156/31     DEAD   176/07     DEAD   188/12
      DEAD   191/26     DEAD   194/15     DEAD   194/16     DEAD   203/26
      DEAD   207/25     DEAD   221/29
DAYBREAK (1) ...................................... RACE    48/33
DAYS (15) ......................................... SISTR   12/01
      ENCTR   25/04     ARABY   30/01     ARABY   32/15     HOUSE   61/08
      LITTL   71/18     LITTL   75/15     PNFUL  112/11     GRACE  156/02
      GRACE  160/12     DEAD   178/06     DEAD   199/07     DEAD   203/28
      DEAD   203/29     DEAD   212/03
DAY'S (2) ......................................... ENCTR   21/11
      IVY D  129/29
DAYS' (2) ......................................... RACE    45/08
      HOUSE   65/25
DE (1) ............................................ DEAD   199/05
DEAD (26) ......................................... SISTR    9/05
      SISTR   10/15     SISTR   12/10     SISTR   12/12     EVELN   37/03
      EVELN   37/03     EVELN   38/06     EVELN   38/07     HOUSE   61/05
      CLAY   104/24     PNFUL  114/11     PNFUL  116/24     IVY D  132/03
      IVY D  132/30     IVY D  134/07     IVY D  134/07     IVY D  134/09
      DEAD   175/ T     DEAD   179/33     DEAD   203/32     DEAD   219/25
      DEAD   219/30     DEAD   221/30     DEAD   223/18     DEAD   223/21
      DEAD   224/04
DEADLY (1) ........................................ SISTR    9/15
DEAD-ROOM (1) ..................................... SISTR   14/13
DEAL (14) ......................................... SISTR   10/22
      SISTR   13/02     GALNT   56/29     CLAY   100/32     CLAY   101/08
```

CLAY 104/10	CLAY 105/15	IVY D 127/18	MOTHR 137/01
MOTHR 142/02	MOTHR 148/08	GRACE 165/34	DEAD 197/25
DEAD 208/33			

DEALS (1) .... HOUSE 63/24
DEALT (1) .... HOUSE 63/24
DEAR (8) .... HOUSE 69/05

			CLAY 99/13
LITTL 74/33	LITTL 75/18	CLAY 99/12	
MOTHR 139/33	MOTHR 142/14	DEAD 218/07	

DEATH (18) .... SISTR 12/32

SISTR 15/17	SISTR 18/12	PNFUL 113/19	PNFUL 113/28
PNFUL 114/19	PNFUL 114/20	PNFUL 115/19	PNFUL 115/23
PNFUL 117/07	PNFUL 117/17	IVY D 134/03	IVY D 135/07
GRACE 157/31	DEAD 176/02	DEAD 206/05	DEAD 221/23
DEAD 222/16			

DEBATED (2) .... MOTHR 147/32
    GRACE 152/11
DEBONAIR (1) .... GRACE 154/23
DEBT (1) .... HOUSE 61/06
DEBTS (1) .... GRACE 154/22
DECANTER (4) .... SISTR 15/01

MOTHR 138/12	MOTHR 138/26	DEAD 183/07	

DECANTERS (1) .... DEAD 196/32
DECEASED (6) .... PNFUL 113/25

PNFUL 114/11	PNFUL 114/16	PNFUL 114/27	PNFUL 114/32
PNFUL 114/32			

DECEIVED (1) .... PNFUL 115/32
DECENCY (2) .... MOTHR 149/01
    GRACE 154/02
DECENT (12) .... ARABY 29/05

GALNT 54/04	CLAY 104/11	IVY D 119/31	IVY D 124/25
IVY D 124/26	IVY D 129/34	IVY D 132/07	GRACE 160/09
GRACE 160/14	GRACE 165/28	DEAD 217/02	

DECEPTION (1) .... PNFUL 116/27
DECIDED (5) .... RACE 46/04

LITTL 82/17	CLAY 102/19	IVY D 118/17	MOTHR 140/07

DECIDEDLY (1) .... RACE 44/05
DECIPHER (1) .... ENCTR 23/24
DECISIVE (1) .... HOUSE 65/20
DECISIVELY (1) .... LITTL 81/06
DECK (2) .... EVELN 39/10
    RACE 48/18
DECLARE (1) .... IVY D 128/05
DECLARED (1) .... GRACE 169/31
DECLINE (3) .... GRACE 154/18
    GRACE 154/19   DEAD 220/32
DECLINED (2) .... SISTR 15/06
    GRACE 161/34
DECORATING (1) .... EVELN 38/08
DECOROUS (1) .... GRACE 172/22
DECREPIT (1) .... LITTL 71/08
DEED (1) .... DEAD 202/20
DEEP (9) .... SISTR 17/24

RACE 44/06	GALNT 54/16	GALNT 57/31	PNFUL 114/23
IVY D 127/10	IVY D 132/34	GRACE 170/07	DEAD 187/12

DEEP-DRAWN (1) .... DEAD 222/06
DEEPENED (1) .... EVELN 39/22
DEFEATED (2) .... PARTS 96/09
    PARTS 97/06
DEFENCE (1) .... DEAD 194/27
DEFEND (1) .... DEAD 213/14
DEFERRED (1) .... LITTL 79/33
DEFIANCE (1) .... PNFUL 110/03

```
DEFIANT (1) ...................................... PNFUL 109/31
DEFIANTLY (1) .................................... DEAD   199/20
DEFIED (1) ....................................... LITTL   83/13
DEFINED (1) ...................................... ARABY   30/21
DEFINITE (1) ..................................... PARTS   94/23
DEFINITELY (1) ................................... PNFUL  110/03
DEFT (1) ......................................... RACE    44/10
DEFTLY (2) ....................................... LITTL   71/32
     LITTL   82/19
DEGRADED (2) ..................................... PNFUL  115/24
     PNFUL  115/24
DEGREE (1) ....................................... DEAD   187/01
DELACOUR (7) ..................................... PARTS   89/11
     PARTS   89/23     PARTS   89/31     PARTS   90/01     PARTS   90/10
     PARTS   91/05     PARTS   91/27
DELAY (2) ........................................ ARABY   34/16
     DEAD   195/18
DELAYED (1) ...................................... ENCTR   27/33
DELIBERATE (1) ................................... PNFUL  109/32
DELIBERATED (1) .................................. GRACE  165/05
DELICATE (5) ..................................... LITTL   80/18
     MOTHR  138/17     DEAD   178/19     DEAD   219/06     DEAD   219/08
DELIGHT (3) ...................................... GALNT   59/24
     MOTHR  137/01     DEAD   217/27
DELIGHTED (3) .................................... LITTL   79/22
     LITTL   83/06     CLAY   104/33
DELIRIUM (2) ..................................... HOUSE   67/21
     HOUSE   67/22
DELIVERED (1) .................................... MOTHR  147/18
DELIVERING (1) ................................... GALNT   51/32
DELUSION (1) ..................................... GRACE  151/18
DEMEANOUR (1) .................................... HOUSE   63/32
DEMURE (1) ....................................... CLAY   103/07
DENIAL (1) ....................................... LITTL   75/10
DENIED (3) ....................................... HOUSE   66/09
     LITTL   72/30     PNFUL  117/16
DENUDED (1) ...................................... IVY D  120/33
DENY (2) ......................................... DEAD   205/20
     DEAD   205/31
DEOC (1) ......................................... LITTL   80/11
DEPARTURE (1) .................................... DEAD   196/08
DEPEND (1) ....................................... DEAD   181/23
DEPLORABLE (1) ................................... GRACE  152/16
DEPLORING (1) .................................... RACE    46/16
DEPOSED (1) ...................................... PNFUL  114/10
DEPOSIT (1) ...................................... PNFUL  113/02
DEPOSITING (1) ................................... IVY D  128/17
DEPOT (1) ........................................ GRACE  161/09
DEPRECATION (1) .................................. DEAD   178/32
DEPRESS (1) ...................................... GALNT   55/26
DEPUTY (2) ....................................... PNFUL  113/21
     PNFUL  115/10
DEREVAUN (2) ..................................... EVELN   40/16
     EVELN   40/16
DERIDED (1) ...................................... ARABY   35/33
DESCENDANT (1) ................................... IVY D  125/16
DESCENDANTS (1) .................................. DEAD   203/11
DESCENDED (2) .................................... GALNT   49/01
     CLAY   105/12
DESCENDING (2) ................................... PARTS   91/12
     DEAD   212/32
DESCENT (1) ...................................... DEAD   224/03
```

DESCRIBE (1) .... LITTL 84/04
DESCRIBED (2) .... ENCTR 27/26
   LITTL 78/21
DESERTED (2) .... ARABY 34/16
   PNFUL 109/20
DESERVED (1) .... LITTL 70/06
DESERVEDLY (1) .... MOTHR 147/19
DESIGNED (1) .... GRACE 174/06
DESIRE (8) .... ARABY 31/26
   ARABY 32/26   RACE 46/03   MOTHR 139/26   DEAD 215/25
   DEAD 217/21   DEAD 218/01   DEAD 219/32
DESIRED (1) .... SISTR 11/24
DESIRES (1) .... MOTHR 136/18
DESIST (1) .... HOUSE 65/25
DESISTED (1) .... GRACE 172/21
DESISTING (1) .... ENCTR 27/02
DESK (16) .... LITTL 71/01
   LITTL 71/25   LITTL 82/30   PARTS 86/06   PARTS 88/12
   PARTS 88/19   PARTS 89/26   PARTS 90/04   PARTS 90/09
   PARTS 90/14   PARTS 91/08   PNFUL 107/11   PNFUL 108/04
   PNFUL 108/04   PNFUL 108/10   PNFUL 112/17
DESPAIR (2) .... PNFUL 117/14
   DEAD 196/11
DESPERATELY (1) .... MOTHR 146/13
DESPISE (1) .... HOUSE 66/21
DESPISED (1) .... ENCTR 28/12
DESSERT (1) .... PNFUL 112/27
DESTINY (1) .... IVY D 134/18
DETACHED (1) .... ARABY 29/04
DETACHMENT (1) .... GRACE 159/20
DETAIL (1) .... HOUSE 65/30
DETAILS (5) .... HOUSE 65/12
   LITTL 78/22   PNFUL 115/23   MOTHR 138/13   GRACE 160/02
DETECTIVE (1) .... ENCTR 20/09
DETERMINED (3) .... HOUSE 61/02
   PARTS 96/05   MOTHR 137/26
DEUCED (1) .... LITTL 75/15
DEVELOPED (1) .... GRACE 173/26
DEVELOPMENT (1) .... GRACE 157/06
DEVICE (1) .... DEAD 187/23
DEVIL (6) .... GALNT 54/01
   GALNT 57/34   HOUSE 61/05   IVY D 130/11   GRACE 169/30
   GRACE 171/10
DEVILS (2) .... RACE 48/14
   GRACE 161/16
DEVINES (1) .... EVELN 36/12
DEVIOUS (1) .... MOTHR 144/04
DEVISING (1) .... RACE 47/26
DEVLIN (1) .... MOTHR 136/09
DEVOTIONS (1) .... GRACE 158/06
DEVOUT (1) .... ARABY 29/12
DEW (1) .... DEAD 210/25
DEXTERITY (1) .... RACE 46/12
D'HONNEUR (1) .... LITTL 80/03
DIAL (1) .... ARABY 34/23
DIALOGUES (1) .... GALNT 52/02
DIAMOND-BONE (1) .... DEAD 176/19
DIAMONDS (1) .... RACE 48/08
DICKY (2) .... IVY D 122/08
   IVY D 123/16
DICKY'S (1) .... IVY D 123/28
DID (123)

DIDN'T (31) .... ARABY 35/10
    ARABY 35/11   GALNT 53/15   LITTL 79/04   LITTL 79/25
    LITTL 85/13   PARTS 92/32   CLAY 100/30   CLAY 101/11
    CLAY 104/04   CLAY 104/11   CLAY 104/17   CLAY 104/21
    IVY D 119/03   IVY D 127/12   IVY D 128/05   IVY D 132/02
    IVY D 133/20   MOTHR 140/13   MOTHR 144/11   MOTHR 144/15
    MOTHR 148/13   GRACE 165/15   GRACE 167/29   DEAD 188/04
    DEAD 191/07   DEAD 195/22   DEAD 206/16   DEAD 208/03
    DEAD 212/25   DEAD 217/04
DIE (6) .... LITTL 79/08
    PNFUL 117/30   GRACE 173/24   DEAD 203/33   DEAD 219/26
    DEAD 220/16
DIED (14) .... SISTR 11/29
    ARABY 29/07   ARABY 31/21   LITTL 84/29   PNFUL 109/11
    PNFUL 112/23   PNFUL 116/32   MOTHR 147/07   DEAD 187/11
    DEAD 219/25   DEAD 220/18   DEAD 221/28   DEAD 222/07
    DEAD 223/01
DIFFERED (1) .... DEAD 179/14
DIFFERENCE (3) .... IVY D 121/18
    GRACE 166/03   GRACE 167/19
DIFFERENCES (1) .... ENCTR 20/02
DIFFERENT (7) .... SISTR 13/05
    SISTR 13/06   ENCTR 25/13   EVELN 39/13   LITTL 73/28
    CLAY 100/15   GRACE 165/31
DIFFERENTLY (1) .... DEAD 209/03
DIFFICULT (3) .... SISTR 13/07
    GRACE 173/27   DEAD 186/02
DIFFICULTIES (1) .... GRACE 156/13
DIFFICULTY (6) .... ARABY 35/03
    RACE 44/27   PNFUL 113/05   PNFUL 116/01   MOTHR 141/09
    DEAD 209/05
DIFFIDENCE (1) .... DEAD 216/29
DIFFIDENT (1) .... DEAD 218/03
DIFFUSED (1) .... ENCTR 20/01
DIG (1) .... MOTHR 143/21
DIGNITY (3) .... GRACE 154/01
    GRACE 163/20   DEAD 186/32
DIGNITY' (1) .... PNFUL 109/12
DILIGENCE (1) .... HOUSE 66/07
DILIGENTLY (1) .... ENCTR 21/31
DILLON (12) .... ENCTR 19/01
    ENCTR 19/10   ENCTR 20/14   ENCTR 20/16   ENCTR 20/20
    ENCTR 20/29   ENCTR 20/33   ENCTR 21/10   ENCTR 21/13
    ENCTR 21/17   ENCTR 22/14   ENCTR 22/31
DILLON'S (1) .... ENCTR 19/08
DILUTED (1) .... LITTL 75/20
DIMINUTIVE (1) .... CLAY 101/32
DIMMED (1) .... HOUSE 67/32
DIN (1) .... DEAD 209/12
DINE (1) .... RACE 45/18
DINED (2) .... PNFUL 108/34
    PNFUL 112/26
DINGED (1) .... GRACE 151/08
DINNER (15) .... ARABY 33/03
    ARABY 33/31   EVELN 38/18   RACE 45/26   RACE 46/03
    RACE 46/04   GALNT 58/04   HOUSE 62/12   HOUSE 67/13
    PARTS 97/27   PARTS 98/03   PNFUL 113/04   IVY D 128/09
    GRACE 161/13   DEAD 191/27
DINNERS (1) .... ARABY 30/02
DINORAH (1) .... DEAD 199/15
DIPPED (2) .... HOUSE 68/21
    PARTS 88/14

DIRECT (1) .... EVELN 40/30
DIRECTED (5) .... RACE   46/13
    PARTS 87/25   GRACE 172/04   DEAD 180/33   DEAD 209/02
DIRECTION (5) .... ENCTR 26/20
    GALNT 60/08   PARTS 95/11   IVY D 124/14   MOTHR 143/28
DIRECTIONS (2) .... PNFUL 108/05
    GRACE 153/12
DIRECTORY (1) .... SISTR 13/17
DIRTY (5) .... LITTL 75/18
    PARTS 86/12   PARTS 94/05   PARTS 94/31   MOTHR 136/03
DISAPPOINTED (5) .... SISTR 15/07
    SISTR 17/19   PARTS 95/24   CLAY 101/13   PNFUL 108/23
DISAPPOINTMENT (3) .... RACE   45/23
    CLAY 104/01   IVY D 125/32
DISAPPOINTMENTS (1) .... MOTHR 139/21
DISAPPROVAL (1) .... GRACE 159/32
DISARRAY (1) .... DEAD 185/23
DISBELIEVE (1) .... GALNT 53/12
DISBELIEVED (1) .... GALNT 52/31
DISC (1) .... GALNT 53/05
DISCHARGED (1) .... ENCTR 23/10
DISCHARGING (1) .... ENCTR 23/21
DISCIPLE (1) .... GALNT 60/29
DISCLOSED (3) .... RACE   44/20
    GRACE 157/05   GRACE 157/25
DISCOLOURED (1) .... SISTR 13/26
DISCOMFITURE (1) .... HOUSE 68/04
DISCOMPOSED (1) .... DEAD 179/04
DISCONTENTED (1) .... PARTS 96/33
DISCONTINUED (1) .... PNFUL 111/02
DISCOURSE (1) .... GRACE 165/18
DISCOURSES (1) .... PNFUL 111/30
DISCOURTEOUSLY (1) .... DEAD 203/15
DISCOURTESY (1) .... GALNT 50/25
DISCOVER (2) .... RACE   46/15
    PARTS 89/32
DISCOVERED (2) .... ENCTR 20/14
    ENCTR 24/11
DISCOVERING (1) .... SISTR 12/30
DISCOVERY (2) .... DEAD 193/31
    DEAD 194/01
DISCREET (3) .... PNFUL 111/20
    IVY D 126/06   MOTHR 144/08
DISCREETLY (2) .... ARABY 33/13
    LITTL 70/16
DISCREPANCIES (1) .... GRACE 174/27
DISCUSSED (2) .... HOUSE 62/14
    GRACE 163/22
DISCUSSING (1) .... PNFUL 116/12
DISCUSSION (3) .... DEAD 195/11
    DEAD 209/06   DEAD 209/11
DISCUSSIONS (1) .... PNFUL 111/03
DISFIGURED (1) .... IVY D 118/13
DISH (8) .... SISTR 11/09
    GALNT 57/06   DEAD 196/23   DEAD 196/24   DEAD 196/26
    DEAD 196/27   DEAD 196/34   DEAD 197/17
DISHES (1) .... DEAD 182/32
DISILLUSIONED (2) .... LITTL 77/01
    PNFUL 111/34
DISLIKED (1) .... ENCTR 25/33
DISMAL (1) .... IVY D 119/21
DISMALLY (1) .... DEAD 223/08

DISMISSED (1)			PNFUL	110/19
DISORDER (4)			ENCTR	21/02
PNFUL 108/15	GRACE 157/01	DEAD 184/30		
DISORDERED (1)			GALNT	55/30
DISPEL (1)			DEAD	179/06
DISPLAYED (2)			ARABY	34/25
LITTL 75/03				
DISPLAYING (1)			IVY D	122/13
DISPOSING (1)			MOTHR	138/18
DISPUTE (1)			DEAD	209/32
DISREPUTABLE (2)			HOUSE	63/02
HOUSE 66/15				
DISSIPATIONS (1)			PNFUL	109/06
DISSOLVING (1)			DEAD	223/22
DISSUADED (1)			MOTHR	138/14
DISTANCE (8)			ENCTR	20/34
GALNT 55/20	GALNT 59/34	PNFUL 108/24	GRACE	158/20
GRACE 172/25	DEAD 202/09	DEAD 210/21		
DISTANT (7)			ARABY	31/24
EVELN 37/31	EVELN 39/10	GRACE 172/12	DEAD	210/05
DEAD 210/09	DEAD 214/08			
DISTANTLY (1)			MOTHR	144/19
DISTASTE (1)			PNFUL	110/16
DISTENDED (1)			GRACE	151/02
DISTILLERS (1)			GRACE	166/22
DISTILLERY (3)			SISTR	10/06
PNFUL 107/06	PNFUL 115/17			
DISTRACTED (1)			SISTR	14/21
DISTRESS (2)			EVELN	40/29
EVELN 41/02				
DISTRESSING (1)			PNFUL	109/18
DISTRIBUTED (1)			IVY D	129/25
DISTRIBUTION (2)			CLAY	101/07
GRACE 162/09				
DISTRICT (1)			GRACE	166/25
DISTURB (3)			IVY D	126/07
IVY D 135/09	GRACE 170/10			
DISTURBED (1)			SISTR	12/11
DISUSED (1)			PNFUL	107/05
DITTO (1)			GALNT	53/01
DIVED (1)			PARTS	88/29
DIVERGED (1)			ARABY	30/30
DIVERTED (2)			PNFUL	110/06
MOTHR 138/23				
DIVIDE (1)			CLAY	103/18
DIVIDED (4)			EVELN	37/10
RACE 43/25	PNFUL 111/01	GRACE 152/24		
DIVINE (2)			GRACE	159/32
GRACE 174/02				
DIVINED (1)			HOUSE	64/17
DIVING (1)			DEAD	180/29
DO (100)				
DOCILE (1)			ENCTR	21/32
DOCKS (1)			DEAD	179/34
DOCTOR (2)			PNFUL	108/15
DEAD 183/15				
DOCTOR'S (2)			DEAD	183/10
DEAD 200/23				
DOCTRINE (1)			GRACE	168/27
DOCUMENTS (1)			PARTS	87/04
DODDER (1)			ENCTR	24/08
DODGE (1)			GALNT	51/08

DOES (12) .... RACE   44/14
    RACE   44/15   LITTL   75/16   PNFUL 113/17   IVY D 123/01
    IVY D 123/34   IVY D 124/16   IVY D 126/33   GRACE 155/07
    DEAD   194/24   DEAD   202/33   DEAD   218/23
DOESN'T (7) .... GALNT   51/11
    IVY D 124/32   IVY D 131/23   MOTHR 140/33   GRACE 158/16
    GRACE 171/06   DEAD   211/28
DOG (2) .... IVY D 130/01
    GRACE 169/30
DOGMA (1) .... GRACE 169/31
DOGS (2) .... LITTL   75/31
    IVY D 133/05
DOING (7) .... ENCTR   21/19
    ENCTR   26/24   GALNT   53/10   LITTL   75/30   IVY D 120/22
    IVY D 120/24   MOTHR 140/05
DOLL (1) .... DEAD   177/28
DOLLAR (1) .... LITTL   81/21
DOLLING (1) .... GRACE 169/16
DOME (2) .... IVY D 118/02
    IVY D 118/03
DOMESTIC (2) .... GRACE 155/04
    GRACE 157/13
DOMINANT (1) .... LITTL   73/31
DONATION (1) .... DEAD   200/33
DONE (28) .... SISTR   16/01
    SISTR   16/10   SISTR   16/18   EVELN   41/01   HOUSE   65/33
    HOUSE   66/10   HOUSE   66/22   HOUSE   66/22   HOUSE   66/24
    LITTL   79/05   LITTL   80/26   LITTL   85/07   PARTS   87/31
    PARTS   97/02   PNFUL 116/01   PNFUL 116/22   PNFUL 116/28
    IVY D 119/29   IVY D 120/03   IVY D 120/13   MOTHR 139/04
    MOTHR 139/04   MOTHR 147/33   MOTHR 149/11   MOTHR 149/26
    MOTHR 149/27   GRACE 163/30   DEAD   178/03
DONNA (1) .... DEAD   199/13
DONNELLY (11) .... CLAY   103/19
    CLAY   103/30   CLAY   104/12   CLAY   104/19   CLAY   104/26
    CLAY   105/04   CLAY   105/17   CLAY   105/22   CLAY   105/24
    CLAY   105/31   CLAY   105/33
DONNYBROOK (2) .... GALNT   51/02
    GALNT   56/15
DON'T (45) .... SISTR   16/10
    EVELN   37/28   GALNT   54/30   LITTL   75/21   LITTL   77/10
    LITTL   77/32   LITTL   81/28   LITTL   81/32   LITTL   82/03
    LITTL   82/20   PARTS   91/23   PARTS   93/18   PARTS   98/22
    PARTS   98/24   IVY D 120/12   IVY D 122/02   IVY D 122/27
    IVY D 122/27   IVY D 125/01   IVY D 125/11   IVY D 126/07
    IVY D 126/15   IVY D 129/02   IVY D 132/29   MOTHR 138/30
    MOTHR 138/30   MOTHR 144/20   MOTHR 145/17   GRACE 153/10
    GRACE 159/12   GRACE 166/06   GRACE 171/01   GRACE 171/19
    DEAD   180/04   DEAD   180/15   DEAD   181/02   DEAD   181/24
    DEAD   182/07   DEAD   183/20   DEAD   184/08   DEAD   194/34
    DEAD   195/33   DEAD   212/16   DEAD   216/04   DEAD   216/26
DOOR (54) .... SISTR   14/13
    ARABY   30/21   ARABY   30/26   ARABY   32/07   ARABY   35/05
    RACE   48/31   GALNT   60/06   HOUSE   66/26   HOUSE   67/05
    HOUSE   67/27   HOUSE   68/09   LITTL   72/07   LITTL   74/17
    LITTL   74/17   LITTL   82/28   LITTL   84/30   PARTS   86/16
    PARTS   88/08   PARTS   88/28   PARTS   89/09   PARTS   94/17
    PARTS   98/08   CLAY   103/17   IVY D 120/18   IVY D 122/21
    IVY D 124/09   IVY D 124/14   IVY D 125/21   IVY D 126/14
    IVY D 128/13   IVY D 129/21   MOTHR 139/11   MOTHR 149/12
    GRACE 151/11   GRACE 151/13   GRACE 155/21   GRACE 156/04
    GRACE 161/06   GRACE 165/21   GRACE 166/11   DEAD   177/01

```
        DEAD    178/28    DEAD    179/02    DEAD    182/03    DEAD    192/29
        DEAD    202/06    DEAD    205/33    DEAD    206/05    DEAD    206/15
        DEAD    209/24    DEAD    212/19    DEAD    215/15    DEAD    215/32
        DEAD    216/11
DOOR-KNOCKER (1) ................................... SISTR    12/03
DOORS (8) .......................................... ENCTR    20/08
        ARABY    30/09    ARABY    34/19    EVELN    40/26    LITTL    71/30
        IVY D 119/21      GRACE 152/33      GRACE 162/20
DOORSTEP (4) ....................................... ARABY    30/16
        ARABY    30/28    DEAD    206/18    DEAD    209/07
DOORWAY (9) ........................................ LITTL    74/18
        PARTS    88/29    PARTS    92/03    IVY D 125/24      IVY D 126/13
        IVY D 133/07      MOTHR 149/25      DEAD    186/07    DEAD    187/16
DORAN (4) .......................................... HOUSE    64/22
        HOUSE    65/23    HOUSE    66/05    HOUSE    69/05
DORAN'S (1) ........................................ HOUSE    65/07
DORSET (1) ......................................... GALNT    50/17
DORUIS (1) ......................................... LITTL    80/11
DOSED (1) .......................................... ENCTR    23/14
DOUBLE (5) ......................................... RACE     42/12
        GALNT    52/07    PNFUL 107/11      IVY D 130/09      GRACE 167/27
DOUBLED (2) ........................................ PNFUL 112/33
        DEAD    180/31
DOUBLY (1) ......................................... RACE     46/25
DOUBT (7) .......................................... SISTR    10/03
        LITTL    73/10    LITTL    79/18    PNFUL 117/28      GRACE 166/10
        GRACE 166/34      DEAD    199/24
DOUBTED (1) ........................................ DEAD    186/04
DOUBTFUL (2) ....................................... PNFUL 108/25
        MOTHR 138/23
DOWLING (3) ........................................ GRACE 169/17
        GRACE 169/18      GRACE 170/04
DOWN (136)
DOWNES'S (3) ....................................... CLAY    102/12
        CLAY    102/20    CLAY    103/24
DOWNRIGHT (1) ...................................... DEAD    211/04
DOWNSTAIRS (9) ..................................... SISTR     9/17
        SISTR    14/33    ARABY    33/16    HOUSE    68/02    PARTS    88/06
        IVY D 126/14      GRACE 154/26      GRACE 161/34      DEAD    221/18
DOWNWARD (1) ....................................... DEAD    221/32
DOWNWARDS (1) ...................................... GRACE 150/06
DOWRY (1) .......................................... MOTHR 137/18
DOYLE (1) .......................................... RACE     43/03
DOZE (1) ........................................... SISTR    12/16
DOZEN (4) .......................................... CLAY    102/14
        IVY D 127/05      IVY D 127/09      MOTHR 139/01
DOZING (1) ......................................... DEAD    215/18
DR (1) ............................................. PNFUL 114/15
DRAG (1) ........................................... IVY D 121/33
DRAGGING (2) ....................................... PNFUL 116/14
        DEAD    214/22
DRANK (21) ......................................... RACE     47/30
        RACE     47/31    RACE     48/07    HOUSE    61/06    LITTL    72/27
        LITTL    75/28    LITTL    77/24    PARTS    89/02    PARTS    95/06
        PNFUL 112/33      PNFUL 116/13      IVY D 129/03      IVY D 129/18
        IVY D 129/26      IVY D 135/24      MOTHR 142/29      GRACE 162/11
        GRACE 164/21      GRACE 168/03      GRACE 168/09      GRACE 169/26
DRAPED (1) ......................................... GRACE 173/08
DRAPER'S (1) ....................................... GRACE 156/15
DRAPERY (2) ........................................ SISTR    11/33
        SISTR    11/33
DRAUGHT (3) ........................................ DEAD    197/30
```

```
          DEAD  198/13     DEAD  208/27
DRAW (2) .........................................  EVELN   41/01
     GRACE 171/23
DRAWERS (1) ......................................  DEAD   216/15
DRAWING (3) ......................................  EVELN   41/07
     PARTS  94/05     DEAD  218/05
DRAWING-ROOM (12) ................................  ARABY   29/08
     ARABY   31/20     HOUSE  62/24     MOTHR 138/11     DEAD   179/02
     DEAD   182/02     DEAD  185/14     DEAD  186/03     DEAD   191/34
     DEAD   195/12     DEAD  202/06     DEAD  222/29
DRAWN (7) ........................................  HOUSE   65/30
     LITTL   72/07     MOTHR 138/14     GRACE 154/11     DEAD   179/24
     DEAD   197/02     DEAD  222/31
DREADFUL (2) .....................................  DEAD   180/07
     DEAD   211/08
DREADFULLY (1) ...................................  DEAD   176/26
DREAM (3) ........................................  SISTR   13/32
     SISTR   14/02     IVY D 134/23
DREAMED (2) ......................................  EVELN   37/10
     IVY D 134/23
DREAMS (1) .......................................  IVY D  134/13
DREAMT (3) .......................................  CLAY   106/02
     CLAY  106/04     CLAY  106/10
DRESS (19) .......................................  SISTR   15/34
     ARABY   30/23     ARABY  32/09     ARABY  33/15     RACE    45/20
     RACE    45/31     GALNT  54/23     HOUSE  67/03     CLAY   101/30
     MOTHR 138/33     MOTHR 139/10     MOTHR 140/21     MOTHR 143/18
     MOTHR 143/29     MOTHR 144/25     DEAD  177/04     DEAD   180/23
     DEAD   185/23     DEAD  185/27
DRESS-BOOTS (1) ..................................  CLAY   101/28
DRESSED (12) .....................................  ENCTR   24/22
     RACE    45/30     HOUSE  67/29     LITTL  72/08     MOTHR 143/32
     GRACE 156/08     GRACE 172/06     DEAD  179/22     DEAD   183/29
     DEAD   186/30     DEAD  206/19     DEAD  222/30
DRESSES (3) ......................................  LITTL   72/09
     LITTL   72/10     CLAY  103/16
DRESSING-ROOM (10) ...............................  MOTHR  139/14
     MOTHR 139/21     MOTHR 142/15     MOTHR 143/24     MOTHR 144/23
     MOTHR 145/30     MOTHR 147/22     DEAD  175/08     DEAD   177/15
     DEAD   179/22
DREW (10) ........................................  SISTR   11/22
     ARABY   34/22     RACE   45/15     IVY D 129/28     MOTHR 137/02
     GRACE 151/18     GRACE 154/14     GRACE 172/24     DEAD   182/04
     DEAD   214/34
DRIBBLED (1) .....................................  SISTR   12/20
DRIED (2) ........................................  HOUSE   68/20
     DEAD   218/24
DRIFTED (1) ......................................  DEAD   223/33
DRILL (1) ........................................  GRACE  161/10
DRINK (19) .......................................  ENCTR   20/27
     RACE    48/19     LITTL  72/05     LITTL  75/22     LITTL   75/23
     LITTL   76/18     LITTL  76/21     LITTL  81/34     PARTS   93/23
     PARTS   94/21     CLAY  100/15     CLAY  101/17     IVY D  127/06
     IVY D 128/24     IVY D 129/11     IVY D 130/14     IVY D  130/27
     GRACE 153/14     DEAD  205/09
DRINKING (7) .....................................  LITTL   81/04
     PARTS   87/29     PARTS  89/29     IVY D 131/26     GRACE 154/34
     GRACE 160/05     DEAD  183/02
DRINKS (5) .......................................  GALNT   58/28
     LITTL   78/06     LITTL  80/13     LITTL  80/33     IVY D  120/16
DRIPPING (2) .....................................  ARABY   30/10
     DEAD   223/16
```

```
DRIVE (6) ...................................... SISTR    17/04
      SISTR   17/10    DEAD   207/07    DEAD   207/24    DEAD   207/26
      DEAD   209/16
DRIVEN (2) ..................................... ARABY    35/33
      GRACE  158/21
DRIVER (4) ..................................... RACE     42/11
      RACE    44/20    PNFUL  113/29    DEAD   215/02
DRIVERS (1) .................................... ENCTR    23/03
DRIVING (2) .................................... GALNT    53/08
      IVY D  127/28
DRIZZLING (1) .................................. PARTS    94/13
DRONE (1) ...................................... PNFUL   117/25
DROP (3) ....................................... CLAY    103/13
      DEAD   209/05    DEAD   211/17
DROPS (3) ...................................... GALNT    60/08
      PARTS   94/06    IVY D  120/27
DROVE (8) ...................................... RACE     45/13
      RACE    47/01    RACE    47/09    GRACE  153/16    GRACE  155/25
      DEAD   207/32    DEAD   208/06    DEAD   214/25
DROWN (1) ...................................... EVELN    41/07
DROWSED (1) .................................... LITTL    71/08
DRUM (1) ....................................... LITTL    84/15
DRUMCONDRA (2) ................................. CLAY    100/05
      CLAY   102/29
DRUNK (7) ...................................... RACE     46/28
      LITTL   81/05    PARTS   97/01    PARTS   97/03    PARTS    97/18
      CLAY   100/15    IVY D  129/27
DRUNKARD (3) ................................... HOUSE    61/16
      GRACE  157/16    GRACE  168/26
DRUNKEN (2) .................................... ARABY    31/04
      IVY D  120/13
DRY (3) ........................................ GALNT    56/30
      PNFUL  108/18    IVY D  127/07
DRYING (2) ..................................... GRACE   170/09
      DEAD   212/03
DUBIOUSLY (3) .................................. GALNT    52/13
      IVY D  125/01    GRACE  169/23
DUBLIN (38) .................................... RACE     42/01
      RACE    43/17    RACE    43/21    RACE    43/23    HOUSE    66/02
      LITTL   71/34    LITTL   73/11    LITTL   75/18    LITTL    77/28
      LITTL   78/26    CLAY   100/23    PNFUL  107/03    PNFUL   107/06
      PNFUL  108/17    PNFUL  110/11    PNFUL  111/08    PNFUL   111/15
      PNFUL  113/21    PNFUL  114/15    PNFUL  114/33    PNFUL   117/10
      PNFUL  117/21    IVY D  121/34    IVY D  128/08    IVY D   131/30
      MOTHR  136/02    MOTHR  141/15    MOTHR  147/27    MOTHR   148/13
      GRACE  154/17    DEAD   183/23    DEAD   184/10    DEAD    190/20
      DEAD   199/05    DEAD   199/08    DEAD   204/16    DEAD    206/23
      DEAD   221/11
DUBLIN'S (2) ................................... ENCTR    23/07
      PNFUL  109/02
DUCHESS (1) .................................... LITTL    78/23
DUCKIE (1) ..................................... GRACE   162/04
DUE (1) ........................................ PNFUL   114/20
DUFFY (8) ...................................... PNFUL   107/01
      PNFUL  108/14    PNFUL  110/15    PNFUL  110/23    PNFUL   111/33
      PNFUL  112/12    PNFUL  115/15    PNFUL  116/16
DUGGAN (3) ..................................... MOTHR   142/17
      MOTHR  143/03    MOTHR  143/06
DUKE (1) ....................................... PARTS    94/11
DUKE'S (1) ..................................... GALNT    56/19
DULL (9) ....................................... ARABY    34/08
      LITTL   73/09    LITTL   78/27    LITTL   83/22    DEAD    212/31
```

DEAD 214/01	DEAD 214/06	DEAD 218/33	DEAD 219/01
DULY (1)			GRACE 159/23
DUMB-BELLS (1)			DEAD 180/17
DUMMY (3)			CLAY 100/01
CLAY 101/05	CLAY 101/23		
DUNN (1)			EVELN 37/03
DUNNE (1)			PNFUL 114/03
DUNNS (1)			EVELN 36/13
DURING (13)			ENCTR 20/31
ENCTR 23/20	EVELN 37/10	CLAY 101/09	PNFUL 107/15
PNFUL 111/30	GRACE 155/04	GRACE 156/31	GRACE 158/11
GRACE 160/33	DEAD 187/06	DEAD 201/19 ·	DEAD 206/12
DUSK (2)			ARABY 30/01
PARTS 89/07			
DUSKY (1)			SISTR 14/17
DUST (4)			EVELN 37/08
LITTL 71/07	LITTL 73/15	LITTL 83/34	
DUSTED (1)			EVELN 37/07
DUSTY (3)			EVELN 36/03
EVELN 39/34	DEAD 212/01		
DUTIES (6)			SISTR 13/12
SISTR 17/16	HOUSE 66/12	PNFUL 109/12	DEAD 204/08
DEAD 215/16			
DUTIFULLY (1)			GRACE 156/22
DUTY (2)			ARABY 35/17
EVELN 40/30			
DWARF'S (1)			PARTS 91/29
DWELL (1)			DEAD 223/17
DWELLINGS (1)			GRACE 173/25
DWELT (2)			CLAY 106/02
CLAY 106/04			
DWINDLING (1)			DEAD 223/22
DWYER (1)			GRACE 170/18
EACH (29)			SISTR 13/25
ENCTR 21/11	ENCTR 24/05	ENCTR 26/30	EVELN 37/19
EVELN 39/01	RACE 42/12	RACE 42/13	RACE 46/25
GALNT 54/10	GALNT 54/15	GALNT 56/23	GALNT 59/20
HOUSE 67/18	PARTS 96/04	PNFUL 111/01	IVY D 129/27
MOTHR 137/18	GRACE 157/17	GRACE 160/04	GRACE 164/12
GRACE 173/19	GRACE 174/15	DEAD 175/10	GRACE 197/33
DEAD 197/33	DEAD 197/34	DEAD 204/19	DEAD 209/03
EAGERLY (3)			GALNT 60/11
GRACE 167/13	DEAD 189/07		
EAGERNESS (1)			RACE 45/28
EAGLE (2)			IVY D 126/09
IVY D 128/16			
EAR (12)			ENCTR 27/14
HOUSE 68/23	LITTL 84/15	PNFUL 117/05	PNFUL 117/31
MOTHR 145/34	MOTHR 149/20	DEAD 182/05	DEAD 190/11
DEAD 190/33	DEAD 209/31	DEAD 213/13	
EARL (1)			GALNT 53/08
EARLIER (1)			LITTL 79/25
EARLSFORT (1)			PNFUL 110/05
EARLY (4)			ARABY 33/04
RACE 43/16	HOUSE 63/26	MOTHR 141/16	
EARNESTLY (6)			RACE 43/24
GALNT 51/30	GALNT 52/08	GALNT 57/07	MOTHR 146/08
GRACE 162/19			
EARS (8)			SISTR 9/11
PNFUL 111/21	PNFUL 117/25	PNFUL 117/28	IVY D 122/21

	DEAD 178/21	DEAD 179/24	DEAD 184/27		
EARSHOT (1)				DEAD	182/28
EARTH (6)				ARABY	31/23
	EVELN 37/08	LITTL 72/11	MOTHR 140/28	GRACE	169/29
	DEAD 196/12				
EASE (6)				ARABY	32/10
	GALNT 57/01	LITTL 82/29	PNFUL 116/25	DEAD	188/28
	DEAD 197/07				
EASIER (2)				IVY D	126/27
	DEAD 182/14				
EASILY (1)				DEAD	218/05
EAST (2)				GRACE	153/17
	DEAD 180/06				
EASTERN (2)				ARABY	32/19
	ARABY 35/17				
EASY (5)				GALNT	55/12
	LITTL 74/08	PARTS 88/04	CLAY 103/12	PNFUL	115/30
EAT (10)				ENCTR	23/06
	GALNT 54/31	LITTL 72/05	LITTL 77/13	CLAY	103/28
	GRACE 156/23	DEAD 180/17	DEAD 197/21	DEAD	198/01
	DEAD 213/20				
EATEN (5)				ARABY	30/02
	GALNT 57/11	GALNT 57/28	GALNT 58/08	CLAY	103/27
EATING (6)				SISTR	10/18
	SISTR 15/07	ENCTR 23/05	HOUSE 67/13	MOTHR	137/01
	DEAD 176/19				
EATING-HOUSE (1)				PNFUL	108/34
EBULLIENT (1)				MOTHR	143/01
E.C. (1)				GRACE	154/09
ECHO (1)				DEAD	183/12
ECHOED (3)				ARABY	30/06
	HOUSE 67/22	LITTL 84/25			
ECLOGUES (1)				PARTS	93/28
ECOD (1)				GALNT	53/24
ECSTASY (1)				DEAD	214/02
EDDIE (1)				IVY D	124/06
EDGE (6)				EVELN	37/26
	GALNT 59/34	IVY D 130/28	MOTHR 140/23	MOTHR	143/11
	DEAD 197/06				
EDGES (1)				PNFUL	111/22
EDITIONS (1)				PARTS	93/09
EDMUND (1)				GRACE	170/17
EDUCATED (5)				ENCTR	20/28
	RACE 43/22	MOTHR 136/10	GRACE 163/24	DEAD	203/24
EDUCATION (4)				SISTR	11/05
	LITTL 80/25	GRACE 167/33	DEAD 179/17		
EDWARD (2)				IVY D	122/03
	IVY D 132/27				
EDWARD'S (1)				IVY D	132/14
E'EN (1)				LITTL	83/32
'EET (1)				GRACE	153/07
EFFACED (1)				MOTHR	142/12
EFFECT (3)				SISTR	11/15
	MOTHR 146/27	GRACE 171/30			
EFFECTIVELY (1)				GRACE	166/08
EFFORT (2)				GRACE	168/17
	DEAD 220/23				
EGAN'S (2)				GALNT	58/25
	GALNT 58/28				
EGG (1)				PARTS	87/05
EGGS (1)				HOUSE	64/02
EGG-SHAPED (1)				PARTS	91/20

```
EH (8) ..........................................  GALNT  52/11
    GALNT  53/28    LITTL  75/01    PARTS  88/03   IVY D 121/19
    IVY D 127/30    IVY D 132/11    DEAD  178/07
EIDER-DOWN (1) ..................................  MOTHR 137/15
EIGHT (13) ......................................  ARABY  33/22
    LITTL  70/01    LITTL  71/02    LITTL  72/23   LITTL  80/19
    CLAY  100/07    MOTHR 138/15    MOTHR 139/13   MOTHR 139/25
    MOTHR 144/12    MOTHR 146/12    MOTHR 148/27   DEAD  216/01
EIGHT-O'CLOCK (1) ...............................  ENCTR  19/09
EIRE (1) ........................................  MOTHR 136/01
EITHER (5) ......................................  ARABY  35/18
    CLAY  101/12    PNFUL 109/03    DEAD  201/24   DEAD  201/25
ELABORATE (2) ...................................  ENCTR  27/28
    GRACE 173/20
ELASTICALLY (1) .................................  GRACE 151/02
ELATED (1) ......................................  EVELN  39/03
ELATES (1) ......................................  RACE   44/14
ELBOW (3) .......................................  PARTS  95/15
    DEAD  186/13    DEAD  222/04
ELBOWED (1) .....................................  EVELN  38/20
ELBOWS (5) ......................................  RACE   48/29
    GALNT  57/22    LITTL  72/32    PARTS  96/03   PNFUL 113/01
ELDER (3) .......................................  MOTHR 137/19
    GRACE 157/13    DEAD  179/33
ELDERLY (2) .....................................  CLAY  102/31
    MOTHR 145/22
ELDEST (2) ......................................  CLAY  103/18
    GRACE 156/14
ELECTED (1) .....................................  GRACE 172/28
ELECTION (2) ....................................  IVY D 119/13
    IVY D 121/01
ELECTIONS (1) ...................................  IVY D 119/10
ELECTRIC (2) ....................................  RACE   46/08
    PARTS  91/31
ELECTRICIAN (1) .................................  RACE   43/01
ELECTRIC-LIGHT (1) ..............................  DEAD  216/02
ELEGANCE (1) ....................................  MOTHR 147/12
ELEGANTLY (1) ...................................  RACE   46/10
ELEMENTS (1) ....................................  GALNT  56/25
ELEVEN (1) ......................................  HOUSE  64/21
ELEVENPENCE (2) .................................  LITTL  82/26
    LITTL  83/04
ELIZA (13) ......................................  SISTR  14/33
    SISTR  15/11    SISTR  15/13    SISTR  15/16   SISTR  15/34
    SISTR  16/06    SISTR  16/16    SISTR  16/22   SISTR  16/26
    SISTR  17/13    SISTR  17/23    SISTR  17/31   SISTR  18/13
ELLEN (1) .......................................  DEAD  179/33
ELOQUENCE (1) ...................................  GALNT  50/19
ELSE (13) .......................................  LITTL  81/15
    PARTS  92/14    CLAY  102/16    PNFUL 110/21   PNFUL 116/26
    IVY D 121/20    IVY D 123/15    MOTHR 148/15   GRACE 159/14
    GRACE 160/32    GRACE 161/01    GRACE 161/24   DEAD  193/14
ELSE'S (1) ......................................  HOUSE  66/03
ELSEWHERE (1) ...................................  GRACE 173/29
ELUCIDATING (1) .................................  SISTR  13/19
ELY (1) .........................................  GALNT  60/21
'EM (2) .........................................  IVY D 123/18
    IVY D 131/24
EMBELLISH (1) ...................................  DEAD  193/03
EMBITTERED (1) ..................................  GALNT  58/07
EMBRACED (1) ....................................  GRACE 159/29
EMBRASURE (1) ...................................  DEAD  191/32
```

```
EMERGED (1) ......................................... LITTL  71/25
EMERGING (1) ........................................ LITTL  78/08
EMILY (1) ........................................... PNFUL 113/23
EMOTION (3) ......................................... IVY D 135/30
     DEAD  216/13      DEAD  221/31
EMOTIONAL (1) ....................................... PARTS  91/03
EMOTIONALISED (1) ................................... PNFUL 111/22
EMOTIONS (1) ........................................ DEAD  222/21
EMPHASIS (2) ........................................ MOTHR 145/34
     DEAD  205/24
EMPHASISED (1) ...................................... LITTL  81/16
EMPHATICALLY (3) .................................... GALNT  51/14
     PNFUL 113/12      DEAD  194/08
EMPLOYED (2) ........................................ HOUSE  65/13
     GRACE 154/16
EMPLOYER (2) ........................................ HOUSE  66/01
     HOUSE  68/03
EMPLOYMENT (1) ...................................... PNFUL 113/30
EMPTIED (2) ......................................... SISTR  12/17
     GRACE 155/31
EMPTY (7) ........................................... SISTR  15/09
     SISTR  17/15      ARABY  33/07      LITTL  82/29   PARTS  97/13
     PNFUL 109/23      PNFUL 115/17
ENABLE (1) .......................................... GRACE 160/23
ENCHANTMENT (1) ..................................... ARABY  32/19
ENCLOSED (2) ........................................ ARABY  29/08
     LITTL  82/22
ENCORES (1) ......................................... DEAD  199/10
ENCOUNTER (1) ....................................... ENCTR  19/ T
ENCOURAGED (2) ...................................... PNFUL 110/18
     GRACE 163/04
ENCOURAGEMENT (3) ................................... MOTHR 136/18
     MOTHR 146/01      DEAD  202/01
ENCOURAGING (1) ..................................... ARABY  35/15
ENCOURAGINGLY (2) ................................... SISTR  14/12
     MOTHR 139/31
ENCUMBERED (1) ...................................... PNFUL 112/14
END (45) ............................................ SISTR  14/02
     SISTR  14/16      ENCTR  21/21      ENCTR  21/28   ENCTR  24/18
     ENCTR  25/10      ENCTR  26/21      ENCTR  27/03   ARABY  29/04
     ARABY  35/29      EVELN  38/17      RACE   43/20   RACE   48/19
     HOUSE  65/31      HOUSE  66/31      HOUSE  68/21   LITTL  72/27
     LITTL  72/32      PARTS  93/04      CLAY  102/02   CLAY  106/17
     PNFUL 108/01      PNFUL 108/03      PNFUL 111/29   PNFUL 115/18
     PNFUL 115/28      IVY D 124/17      IVY D 129/24   MOTHR 136/07
     MOTHR 139/20      MOTHR 140/15      GRACE 152/12   GRACE 156/25
     GRACE 168/18      DEAD  177/34      DEAD  182/30   DEAD  182/30
     DEAD  187/08      DEAD  187/10      DEAD  196/17   DEAD  196/18
     DEAD  201/17      DEAD  221/19      DEAD  221/25   DEAD  224/04
ENDEAVOUR (1) ....................................... DEAD  202/21
ENDEAVOURS (1) ...................................... DEAD  204/09
ENDED (10) .......................................... ENCTR  19/08
     GALNT  50/08      LITTL  78/22      CLAY  106/13   MOTHR 147/20
     MOTHR 147/27      MOTHR 148/20      DEAD  182/02   DEAD  187/11
     DEAD  188/13
ENDLESS (1) ......................................... SISTR  10/06
ENDS (6) ............................................ GALNT  55/29
     GRACE 152/06      GRACE 159/07      GRACE 160/07   GRACE 169/29
     DEAD  196/22
ENDURE (1) .......................................... ARABY  33/19
ENERGETIC (1) ....................................... GALNT  57/31
ENERGETICALLY (1) ................................... ARABY  34/03
```

ENERGY (2) .... GRACE 163/03
    DEAD   190/06
ENFORCE (1) .... GALNT 50./11
ENGAGE (1) .... DEAD   177/03
ENGAGED (3) .... IVY D 119/15
    IVY D 131/06   DEAD 185/26
ENGAGEMENTS (1) .... GRACE 160/23
ENGINE (5) .... PNFUL 113/26
    PNFUL 113/29   PNFUL 114/06   PNFUL 117/25   PNFUL 117/28
ENGINES (1) .... ENCTR 23/02
ENGLAND (4) .... EVELN 37/04
    RACE   43/22   RACE   47/31   IVY D 132/02
ENGLISH (5) .... ARABY 35/06
    RACE   46/16   LITTL 74/03   LITTL 78/23   DEAD 200/06
ENGLISHMAN (2) .... RACE   46/06
    RACE   46/16
ENGLISHMAN'S (1) .... RACE   46/11
ENJOY (5) .... LITTL 77/11
    CLAY 103/06   MOTHR 140/21   DEAD 180/32   DEAD 195/22
ENJOYING (2) .... LITTL 77/10
    PNFUL 110/23
ENJOYMENT (1) .... GALNT 49/19
ENLIST (1) .... HOUSE 61/15
ENLIVENED (1) .... GRACE 167/03
ENMITY (1) .... GRACE 163/22
ENOUGH (24) .... ARABY 34/05
    RACE   43/19   RACE   43/20   GALNT 52/30   GALNT 53/21
    GALNT 58/05   HOUSE 66/13   LITTL 74/25   PARTS 90/29
    PARTS 92/07   PARTS 95/07   CLAY 102/21   MOTHR 145/04
    MOTHR 145/05   GRACE 169/03   GRACE 171/24   DEAD 175/16
    DEAD 180/04   DEAD 197/20   DEAD 198/02   DEAD 200/15
    DEAD 200/17   DEAD 214/07   DEAD 216/04
ENRAGED (2) .... PARTS 90/26
    PARTS 90/31
ENSURED (1) .... MOTHR 137/17
ENTANGLED (2) .... PNFUL 110/26
    PNFUL 111/17
ENTER (4) .... SISTR 14/14
    LITTL 72/08   CLAY 105/25   GRACE 161/05
ENTERED (13) .... GALNT 60/10
    HOUSE 66/26   LITTL 74/17   PARTS 87/02   PARTS 89/05
    PNFUL 117/01   IVY D 130/03   MOTHR 138/13   GRACE 151/11
    GRACE 154/32   GRACE 161/30   GRACE 172/03   DEAD 222/13
ENTERPRISE (1) .... MOTHR 138/13
ENTERTAINED (1) .... MOTHR 139/26
ENTERTAINING (4) .... RACE   44/01
    IVY D 128/03   IVY D 128/03   MOTHR 145/27
ENTHUSIASM (6) .... MOTHR 142/07
    MOTHR 142/12   GRACE 163/27   DEAD 199/12   DEAD 200/07
    DEAD 203/20
ENTHUSIAST (1) .... DEAD 190/27
ENTHUSIASTIC (1) .... DEAD 203/20
ENTIRE (2) .... EVELN 38/11
    PNFUL 108/16
ENTRANCE (2) .... ARABY 34/26
    ARABY 35/18
ENTRUSTED (2) .... PNFUL 111/13
    GRACE 157/06
ENTRY (1) .... GALNT 57/20
ENUNCIATED (1) .... GRACE 168/03
ENUNCIATION (1) .... GRACE 166/26
ENVELOPE (1) .... DEAD 213/17

ENVIOUSLY (1) .... LITTL 77/08
EPILEPTIC (1) .... GRACE 158/11
EQUAL (1) .... GRACE 166/30
EQUALLY (1) .... GRACE 160/18
EQUATION (1) .... RACE 45/31
EQUIPOISE (1) .... LITTL 80/22
ERECT (3) .... GALNT 51/21
   DEAD 179/26   DEAD 213/11
ERIN (4) .... IVY D 134/08
   IVY D 134/19   IVY D 135/14   IVY D 135/18
ERIN'S (3) .... IVY D 134/13
   IVY D 134/13   IVY D 135/08
ERNEST (4) .... EVELN 36/14
   EVELN 38/04   EVELN 38/07   EVELN 39/24
ERRAND (1) .... LITTL 74/23
ERRORS (1) .... RACE 44/25
'ERY (2) .... GRACE 152/28
   GRACE 153/07
ESCALADED (1) .... ENCTR 27/02
ESCAPE (6) .... ENCTR 20/08
   ENCTR 21/01   EVELN 40/17   EVELN 40/18   LITTL 83/23
   PARTS 98/15
ESCAPED (9) .... ENCTR 24/06
   ENCTR 26/33   ENCTR 27/01   PNFUL 108/10   DEAD 177/20
   DEAD 187/14   DEAD 213/30   DEAD 215/15   DEAD 215/16
ESCORTED (2) .... LITTL 72/08
   DEAD 192/31
ESCORTING (2) .... PNFUL 109/10
   DEAD 192/29
ESPECIALLY (2) .... EVELN 37/26
   LITTL 83/06
ESTABLISHING (1) .... LITTL 80/14
ESTABLISHMENT (2) .... RACE 43/05
   RACE 43/07
ESTABLISHMENTS (1) .... PARTS 92/22
ESTATE (1) .... PNFUL 116/12
ESTEEMED (1) .... GRACE 154/21
ETERNAL (1) .... SISTR 16/20
ETHICAL (1) .... GRACE 159/30
EUCHARIST (1) .... SISTR 13/13
EUCLID (1) .... SISTR 9/12
EUROPE (1) .... GRACE 167/09
EUSTACE (1) .... PARTS 89/07
EVA (1) .... DEAD 180/17
EVASIVE (1) .... GRACE 162/30
EVE (4) .... ENCTR 21/23
   CLAY 103/04   CLAY 104/32   DEAD 185/13
EVELINE (3) .... EVELN 36/ T
   EVELN 37/32   EVELN 41/12
EVEN (34) .... SISTR 12/19
   SISTR 12/30   ENCTR 23/12   ENCTR 23/27   ARABY 31/01
   EVELN 37/34   RACE 43/34   RACE 45/32   RACE 46/26
   HOUSE 67/24   LITTL 72/13   LITTL 72/32   LITTL 76/09
   PARTS 96/33   PARTS 97/03   CLAY 99/08   CLAY 103/13
   PNFUL 112/12   IVY D 132/30   IVY D 135/23   GRACE 156/26
   GRACE 172/22   GRACE 172/22   DEAD 175/17   DEAD 178/16
   DEAD 180/27   DEAD 190/30   DEAD 193/04   DEAD 200/01
   DEAD 203/04   DEAD 203/20   DEAD 205/22   DEAD 208/01
   DEAD 222/14
EVENING (45) .... SISTR 14/03
   SISTR 17/10   ENCTR 19/03   ENCTR 21/03   ARABY 31/20
   ARABY 31/21   ARABY 32/14   ARABY 32/29   EVELN 36/01

EVELN	36/08	EVELN	39/02	EVELN	39/22	RACE	45/18
RACE	45/25	GALNT	49/01	GALNT	49/07	LITTL	71/19
LITTL	79/21	LITTL	80/01	LITTL	82/11	LITTL	83/31
PARTS	87/15	PARTS	88/10	PARTS	88/16	PARTS	93/09
CLAY	99/02	CLAY	100/13	CLAY	102/07	PNFUL	109/17
PNFUL	110/14	PNFUL	112/25	PNFUL	112/26	PNFUL	112/28
PNFUL	112/30	PNFUL	113/24	PNFUL	115/16	MOTHR	139/10
MOTHR	140/26	MOTHR	141/17	MOTHR	141/19	MOTHR	141/31
GRACE	174/10	DEAD	202/15	DEAD	211/07	DEAD	212/21

EVENINGS (3) .... ARABY   31/02

PNFUL	109/03	PNFUL	111/16

EVENLY (3) .... SISTR   9/05

RACE	42/02	PNFUL	109/16

EVER (35) .... SISTR   13/15

ENCTR	21/29	ENCTR	27/20	ENCTR	27/25	ARABY	31/16
GALNT	51/14	GALNT	52/34	HOUSE	67/29	LITTL	70/08
LITTL	80/26	LITTL	80/26	LITTL	81/09	LITTL	81/21
PARTS	92/18	PARTS	93/22	CLAY	100/18	CLAY	104/25
PNFUL	108/22	PNFUL	115/20	PNFUL	116/01	IVY D	120/13
IVY D	130/24	IVY D	133/24	MOTHR	137/13	MOTHR	147/26
GRACE	165/08	GRACE	165/09	GRACE	168/27	DEAD	176/01
DEAD	195/24	DEAD	198/24	DEAD	199/29	DEAD	199/34
DEAD	212/23	DEAD	213/33				

EVER-CHANGING (1) .... ARABY   30/04
EVERLASTING (2) .... IVY D   135/01

GRACE	173/25

EVERY (57) .... SISTR   9/09

SISTR	11/03	ENCTR	19/03	ENCTR	19/09	ENCTR	23/30
ENCTR	25/09	ENCTR	25/30	ARABY	30/25	EVELN	36/08
EVELN	39/22	RACE	47/18	GALNT	49/19	GALNT	51/04
GALNT	56/13	HOUSE	63/03	HOUSE	65/26	HOUSE	65/30
HOUSE	66/11	LITTL	73/24	LITTL	77/19	LITTL	79/07
PARTS	95/11	CLAY	101/07	PNFUL	107/08	PNFUL	108/31
PNFUL	111/31	PNFUL	112/07	PNFUL	112/24	PNFUL	112/25
PNFUL	114/24	PNFUL	114/26	MOTHR	137/10	MOTHR	137/17
MOTHR	137/21	MOTHR	137/34	MOTHR	138/24	MOTHR	139/22
MOTHR	142/31	GRACE	163/34	GRACE	172/03	GRACE	174/02
GRACE	174/15	GRACE	174/24	DEAD	176/10	DEAD	176/32
DEAD	180/08	DEAD	187/10	DEAD	188/07	DEAD	188/12
DEAD	189/10	DEAD	191/24	DEAD	199/11	DEAD	202/32
DEAD	205/07	DEAD	209/10	DEAD	223/28	DEAD	223/31

EVERYBODY (6) .... ENCTR   26/12

CLAY	103/14	CLAY	103/29	DEAD	175/14	DEAD	211/20
DEAD	211/20						

EVERYBODY'S (1) .... DEAD   209/13
EVERYDAY (2) .... DEAD   195/02

DEAD	204/13

EVERYONE (27) .... ENCTR   19/17

ENCTR	20/21	HOUSE	66/02	HOUSE	66/02	HOUSE	68/13
LITTL	71/10	LITTL	81/15	PARTS	91/26	PARTS	92/13
PARTS	94/01	CLAY	100/02	MOTHR	140/16	MOTHR	146/28
MOTHR	149/11	GRACE	150/12	GRACE	157/18	GRACE	161/05
GRACE	161/18	GRACE	171/32	DEAD	181/06	DEAD	193/14
DEAD	196/13	DEAD	197/29	DEAD	198/05	DEAD	202/28
DEAD	208/01	DEAD	211/32				

EVERYONE'S (1) .... ENCTR   20/20
EVERYTHING (13) .... SISTR   15/19

EVELN	37/04	LITTL	77/09	PARTS	97/02	CLAY	100/33
CLAY	104/33	IVY D	121/31	MOTHR	136/08	MOTHR	138/31
MOTHR	139/03	GRACE	161/24	DEAD	176/19	DEAD	208/06

EVERYWHERE (1) .... DEAD   206/08
EVES (1) .... CLAY   101/11

```
EVE'S (1) ...................................... DEAD   176/15
EVIDENCE (3) ................................... PNFUL  113/24
     PNFUL  114/32     PNFUL  115/09
EVIDENT (1) .................................... HOUSE   64/32
EVIDENTLY (6) .................................. HOUSE   6C/22
     PARTS   89/11     CLAY  102/23     PNFUL  115/28     MOTHR 142/14
     MOTHR 145/32
EVILS (1) ...................................... IVY D  131/05
EVOCATION (1) .................................. DEAD   219/30
EVOKED (1) ..................................... GRACE  154/05
EVOKING (1) .................................... PNFUL  116/22
EVVY (1) ....................................... EVELN   41/12
EX (3) ......................................... GRACE  168/27
     GRACE 168/30     GRACE 169/31
EXACTIONS (1) .................................. GRACE  159/31
EXACTITUDE (1) ................................. PNFUL  111/06
EXACTLY (5) .................................... SISTR    9/19
     RACE    48/10     IVY D 126/26     GRACE 165/03     GRACE 168/21
EXAGGERATION (1) ............................... DEAD   203/29
EXALTED (2) .................................... PNFUL  111/22
     IVY D 135/03
EXAMINED (4) ................................... ENCTR   23/25
     ARABY   35/04     GALNT   57/23     PARTS   95/34
EXAMINING (2) .................................. SISTR   10/26
     LITTL   82/33
EXAMPLE (5) .................................... LITTL   84/05
     GRACE 164/21     GRACE 167/30     GRACE 173/11     DEAD  199/22
EXCELLENT (2) .................................. RACE    44/05
     RACE    46/04
EXCEPT (8) ..................................... ARABY   29/02
     ARABY   30/32     GALNT   57/10     PNFUL  114/25     IVY D 121/01
     MOTHR 147/09     GRACE 169/13     DEAD  200/18
EXCESS (1) ..................................... RACE    43/28
EXCHANGE (4) ................................... HOUSE   67/19
     PARTS   94/18     IVY D 119/11     IVY D 119/14
EXCHANGED (2) .................................. GRACE  162/01
     DEAD  197/15
EXCHANGING (1) ................................. MOTHR  140/24
EXCITED (7) .................................... ENCTR   21/23
     RACE    43/12     RACE    47/07     RACE    48/21     HOUSE  66/04
     LITTL   80/16     MOTHR 146/10
EXCITEDLY (3) .................................. LITTL   72/15
     DEAD  183/30     DEAD  191/15
EXCITEMENT (7) ................................. EVELN   39/08
     RACE    44/16     RACE    48/20     LITTL   76/24     PNFUL  111/31
     MOTHR 147/22     DEAD  193/06
EXCLAIM (1) .................................... ENCTR   26/23
EXCLAIMED (5) .................................. ENCTR   26/25
     GRACE 168/07     GRACE 170/23     DEAD  181/02     DEAD  210/27
EXCLAIMING (1) ................................. GRACE  154/32
EXCLUDED (1) ................................... HOUSE   62/12
EXCURSION (1) .................................. DEAD   188/32
EXCUSE (4) ..................................... ENCTR   21/13
     HOUSE   64/29     HOUSE   64/29     PARTS   87/14
EXCUSED (1) .................................... MOTHR  144/05
EXECRATE (1) ................................... PARTS   90/25
EXECUTE (1) .................................... GALNT   51/17
EXECUTED (1) ................................... GALNT   55/16
EXEMPLARS (1) .................................. GRACE  174/07
EXERCISE (2) ................................... SISTR   11/03
     RACE    45/23
EXERTIONS (1) .................................. DEAD   208/23
```

```
EXHIBITION (1) ...................................... MOTHR 147/26
EXHILARATING (1) ................................... PARTS  94/01
EXIST (2) .......................................... PNFUL 116/24
   PNFUL 116/32
EXISTENCE (4) ...................................... HOUSE  66/09
   DEAD 198/13      DEAD  214/01      DEAD  223/19
EXONERATED (1) ..................................... PNFUL 115/09
EXOTIC (1) ......................................... PNFUL 111/18
EXPECT (4) ......................................... CLAY  104/16
   IVY D 123/34     IVY D 124/01      DEAD  217/04
EXPECTANTLY (1) .................................... DEAD  205/08
EXPECTED (2) ....................................... GALNT  59/07
   MOTHR 142/04
EXPENSE (4) ........................................ PARTS  94/33
   MOTHR 138/34     MOTHR 140/12      MOTHR 148/07
EXPERIENCE (3) ..................................... GALNT  58/07
   LITTL  78/19     DEAD  203/01
EXPERT (1) ......................................... DEAD  197/07
EXPIRED (1) ........................................ MOTHR 140/16
EXPLAIN (2) ........................................ RACE   46/18
   GRACE 155/01
EXPLAINED (9) ...................................... SISTR  10/19
   SISTR  13/05     ENCTR  22/09      MOTHR 142/03   MOTHR 145/12
   GRACE 168/31     DEAD  198/28      DEAD  201/09   DEAD  207/17
EXPLANATION (1) .................................... DEAD  201/12
EXPLODED (1) ....................................... DEAD  185/29
EXPLORE (1) ........................................ EVELN  38/27
EXPOSED (1) ........................................ GALNT  57/05
EXPRESS (10) ....................................... LITTL  73/18
   LITTL  73/21     LITTL  73/29      LITTL  84/03   IVY D 125/32
   IVY D 125/33     MOTHR 139/26      DEAD  187/34   DEAD  188/08
   DEAD  202/21
EXPRESSED (6) ...................................... ENCTR  25/05
   RACE   46/01     GALNT  50/04      PNFUL 114/23   PNFUL 115/10
   GRACE 153/13
EXPRESSING (2) ..................................... LITTL  77/01
   DEAD  210/22
EXPRESSION (15) .................................... GALNT  49/16
   GALNT  50/06     HOUSE  65/20      LITTL  73/33   PARTS  95/19
   PARTS  96/27     IVY D 130/06      MOTHR 142/07   GRACE 171/05
   GRACE 171/15     DEAD  190/07      DEAD  196/05   DEAD  218/20
   DEAD  219/10     DEAD  219/11
EXPRESSIONS (1) .................................... PNFUL 115/21
EXPRESSIVELY (2) ................................... GALNT  52/12
   LITTL  81/04
EXQUISITE (1) ...................................... RACE   46/04
EXTENDED (4) ....................................... GALNT  60/28
   LITTL  79/06     MOTHR 146/26      DEAD  193/28
EXTENSIVE (1) ...................................... IVY D 131/20
EXTENT (2) ......................................... GRACE 174/05
   DEAD  204/15
EXTINGUISHED (1) ................................... MOTHR 144/33
EXTRACT (1) ........................................ SISTR  11/19
EXTRAORDINARY (1) .................................. DEAD  208/16
EXTRAVAGANT (2) .................................... GRACE 158/04
   GRACE 174/11
EXTREMELY (2) ...................................... MOTHR 142/33
   MOTHR 142/34
EYE (10) ........................................... ARABY  30/29
   GALNT  52/12     LITTL  76/26      LITTL  77/31   LITTL  81/04
   IVY D 127/14     GRACE 170/24      GRACE 170/25   DEAD  184/34
   DEAD  185/33
```

```
EYEBROW  (1) ......................................... MOTHR  137/13
EYEBROWS  (5) ........................................ HOUSE   61/17
     PARTS   86/11    PNFUL  108/22    GRACE  166/18    GRACE  170/20
EYED  (2) ............................................ GALNT   57/07
     DEAD   183/09
EYEGLASSES  (1) ...................................... DEAD   218/21
EYES  (96) ........................................... SISTR   10/26
     SISTR   16/16    SISTR   17/13    ENCTR   23/15    ENCTR   23/20
     ENCTR   23/26    ENCTR   23/27    ENCTR   23/28    ENCTR   24/27
     ENCTR   25/13    ENCTR   26/25    ENCTR   27/17    ENCTR   27/18
     ARABY   31/13    ARABY   35/33    EVELN   41/15    RACE    43/14
     GALNT   49/17    GALNT   49/18    GALNT   53/04    GALNT   53/29
     GALNT   54/12    GALNT   55/22    GALNT   55/31    GALNT   55/33
     GALNT   56/25    GALNT   59/16    GALNT   59/20    HOUSE   61/17
     HOUSE   62/32    HOUSE   67/20    HOUSE   68/06    HOUSE   68/20
     HOUSE   68/22    LITTL   75/05    LITTL   81/11    LITTL   83/09
     LITTL   83/13    LITTL   83/15    LITTL   83/17    LITTL   84/10
     LITTL   85/10    LITTL   85/22    PARTS   86/11    PARTS   94/05
     PARTS   94/31    PARTS   95/11    PARTS   95/19    CLAY   101/12
     CLAY   106/15    PNFUL  108/21    PNFUL  109/30    PNFUL  111/24
     PNFUL  112/29    PNFUL  115/15    PNFUL  117/20    IVY D  118/07
     IVY D  123/19    IVY D  125/33    IVY D  130/06    MOTHR  143/18
     MOTHR  144/03    GRACE  150/06    GRACE  151/07    GRACE  151/29
     GRACE  155/29    GRACE  166/19    DEAD   178/20    DEAD   179/26
     DEAD   180/16    DEAD   180/22    DEAD   180/33    DEAD   184/30
     DEAD   186/14    DEAD   187/21    DEAD   187/29    DEAD   188/02
     DEAD   188/21    DEAD   190/06    DEAD   190/31    DEAD   192/18
     DEAD   202/04    DEAD   205/06    DEAD   212/06    DEAD   213/07
     DEAD   217/12    DEAD   218/24    DEAD   219/09    DEAD   219/10
     DEAD   219/20    DEAD   221/24    DEAD   222/10    DEAD   222/17
     DEAD   223/10    DEAD   223/12    DEAD   223/14

FACE  (108)
FACES  (9) ........................................... ARABY   29/06
     HOUSE   68/03    LITTL   72/10    GRACE  151/30    GRACE  164/24
     GRACE  173/02    GRACE  173/21    DEAD   202/04    DEAD   204/04
FACING  (1) .......................................... CLAY   102/02
FACT  (11) ........................................... ENCTR   26/11
     RACE    42/17    PNFUL  110/29    IVY D  123/24    IVY D  125/10
     MOTHR  138/26    GRACE  154/19    GRACE  160/24    GRACE  164/04
     DEAD   184/23    DEAD   189/08
FACTORIES  (2) ....................................... IVY D  131/30
     IVY D  131/33
FADE  (1) ............................................ DEAD   223/08
FADED  (4) ........................................... SISTR   12/23
     MOTHR  143/18    MOTHR  143/29    DEAD   180/32
FADING  (1) .......................................... DEAD   223/20
FAIL  (3) ............................................ GALNT   59/29
     DEAD   179/17    DEAD   192/18
FAILED  (4) .......................................... PNFUL  116/03
     GRACE  166/20    DEAD   179/18    DEAD   193/19
FAILING  (4) ......................................... ENCTR   23/24
     PNFUL  113/16    DEAD   203/04    DEAD   203/05
FAILINGS  (2) .......................................: GRACE  174/19
     GRACE  174/22
FAILURE  (6) ......................................... ENCTR   22/30
     CLAY   104/01    PNFUL  109/19    PNFUL  114/21    DEAD   179/20
     DEAD   219/29
FAINT  (4) ........................................... RACE    46/30
     GALNT   52/07    HOUSE   67/11    PNFUL  108/10
FAINTED  (1) ......................................... GRACE  151/01
```

```
FAINTLY (4) .......................................... SISTR    9/04
     DEAD   210/21     DEAD   224/02     DEAD   224/03
FAINTS (1) ........................................... SISTR   10/05
FAIR (10) ............................................ LITTL   70/15
     PARTS   86/11     PARTS   91/23     PARTS   93/18   PARTS   96/12
     PARTS   96/13     IVY D  132/19     GRACE  152/11   GRACE  166/18
     GRACE  166/18
FAIR-HAIRED (1) ...................................... MOTHR  142/31
FAIRLY (3) ........................................... ENCTR   24/24
     EVELN   38/16     DEAD   192/34
FAITH (7) ............................................ LITTL   73/32
     IVY D  127/34     GRACE  157/08     GRACE  158/06   GRACE  165/29
     GRACE  166/09     GRACE  170/02
FAITHFUL (1) ......................................... PARTS   91/10
FALL (10) ............................................ SISTR   16/05
     ARABY   35/02     ARABY   35/28     PNFUL  111/19   PNFUL  114/08
     PNFUL  114/18     IVY D  135/05     MOTHR  145/08   DEAD   199/11
     DEAD   222/01
FALLEN (12) .......................................... SISTR   12/25
     SISTR   16/33     SISTR   17/24     EVELN   39/15   GALNT   54/12
     MOTHR  142/23     GRACE  150/03     GRACE  174/19   DEAD   175/17
     DEAD   202/15     DEAD   218/02     DEAD   222/20
FALLING (16) ......................................... ARABY   32/08
     PARTS   88/16     CLAY   102/09     PNFUL  117/07   IVY D  130/05
     GRACE  169/05     DEAD   204/01     DEAD   215/20   DEAD   215/29
     DEAD   223/25     DEAD   223/28     DEAD   223/29   DEAD   223/30
     DEAD   223/31     DEAD   224/02     DEAD   224/03
FALLS (1) ............................................ DEAD   210/24
FALSE (2) ............................................ GRACE  168/27
     DEAD   217/03
FALSETTO (1) ......................................... IVY D  119/02
FAME (2) ............................................. HOUSE   66/16
     DEAD   203/33
FAMED (1) ............................................ IVY D  134/19
FAMILIAR (3) ......................................... EVELN   37/06
     EVELN   37/09     GRACE  173/01
FAMILIARITY (1) ...................................... PARTS   96/22
FAMILIARLY (3) ....................................... MOTHR  144/26
     DEAD   198/31     DEAD   214/32
FAMILIES (2) ......................................... ENCTR   24/02
     DEAD   176/12
FAMILY (9) ........................................... GALNT   51/08
     HOUSE   66/14     IVY D  127/33     MOTHR  137/30   GRACE  155/09
     DEAD   175/15     DEAD   175/15     DEAD   186/26   DEAD   186/32
FAMOUS (1) ........................................... DEAD   183/19
FAN (2) .............................................. IVY D  118/04
     IVY D  119/26
FANCY (2) ............................................ SISTR   14/24
     LITTL   82/03
FANLIGHT (1) ......................................... DEAD   212/01
FANNING (5) .......................................... IVY D  123/21
     IVY D  126/08     IVY D  126/28     IVY D  129/05   GRACE  172/25
FAR (21) ............................................. SISTR   13/34
     ENCTR   23/08     ENCTR   24/18     ENCTR   27/03   EVELN   39/34
     GALNT   49/14     GALNT   54/07     GALNT   56/07   GALNT   58/34
     GALNT   59/20     HOUSE   63/08     LITTL   74/27   PNFUL  107/02
     IVY D  127/27     GRACE  152/12     GRACE  154/07   GRACE  174/04
     DEAD   181/18     DEAD   192/31     DEAD   200/04   DEAD   203/01
FARCICAL (1) ......................................... GRACE  171/27
FARE (3) ............................................. CLAY   100/13
     PNFUL  109/03     DEAD   215/02
FAREWELL (3) ......................................... ARABY   34/10
```

```
        EVELN   41/16    GALNT   55/10
FARLEY  (7) .................................................. RACE    47/04
        RACE    47/05    RACE    47/25    RACE    47/25    RACE    47/28
        RACE    48/01    RACE    48/26
FARRINGTON  (19) ............................................. PARTS   86/04
        PARTS   87/07    PARTS   88/04    PARTS   93/21    PARTS   93/22
        PARTS   93/29    PARTS   94/03    PARTS   94/04    PARTS   94/14
        PARTS   94/21    PARTS   94/22    PARTS   94/26    PARTS   94/30
        PARTS   95/04    PARTS   95/15    PARTS   95/32    PARTS   95/33
        PARTS   96/05    PARTS   96/24
FARRINGTON'S  (8) ........................................... PARTS   93/29
        PARTS   94/02    PARTS   94/31    PARTS   95/05    PARTS   95/10
        PARTS   96/07    PARTS   96/15    PARTS   96/28
FARTHER  (5) ................................................ LITTL   73/24
        GRACE  172/31    GRACE  173/14    DEAD   199/04    DEAD   223/30
FARTHING  (2) ............................................... MOTHR  148/13
        DEAD   200/32
FASCINATED  (1) ............................................. PARTS   95/19
FASHION  (4) ................................................ SISTR   13/33
        GALNT   50/03    HOUSE   64/13    DEAD   185/03
FASHIONABLE  (1) ............................................ LITTL   78/21
FAST  (3) ................................................... RACE    45/28
        DEAD   207/07    DEAD   222/03
FASTER  (1) ................................................. LITTL   84/10
FAT  (12) ................................................... ENCTR   19/05
        RACE    46/33    RACE    46/34    RACE    47/01    GALNT   55/33
        LITTL   81/23    IVY D  121/32    IVY D  130/04    IVY D  130/10
        GRACE  159/28    DEAD   196/17    DEAD   200/31
FATHER  (50) ................................................ SISTR   10/14
        SISTR   15/20    SISTR   16/09    SISTR   17/07    SISTR   18/04
        ENCTR   20/13    ENCTR   20/21    ENCTR   21/17    ENCTR   21/19
        ENCTR   22/12    EVELN   36/15    EVELN   36/17    EVELN   36/18
        EVELN   37/15    EVELN   37/16    EVELN   38/13    EVELN   39/17
        EVELN   39/24    EVELN   39/25    EVELN   39/30    EVELN   40/08
        RACE    43/15    RACE    43/28    RACE    43/34    RACE    45/05
        RACE    45/31    RACE    45/33    RACE    46/23    HOUSE   66/15
        PNFUL  112/23    IVY D  120/09    IVY D  123/06    IVY D  123/23
        IVY D  123/28    IVY D  124/26    IVY D  126/01    IVY D  126/03
        IVY D  126/06    IVY D  126/12    IVY D  127/24    IVY D  127/32
        MOTHR  137/16    GRACE  164/27    GRACE  164/30    GRACE  164/30
        GRACE  165/06    GRACE  165/07    GRACE  166/01    GRACE  173/26
        DEAD   195/03
FATHER-IN-LAW  (1) .......................................... HOUSE   61/04
FATHERS  (2) ................................................ SISTR   13/16
        IVY D  127/22
FATHER'S  (5) ............................................... EVELN   38/02
        RACE    45/03    GALNT   51/19    HOUSE   61/03    GRACE  154/29
FATTY'D  (1) ................................................ ENCTR   22/15
FATUOUS  (1) ................................................ DEAD   220/04
FAULT  (4) .................................................. SISTR   17/28
        RACE    48/12    HOUSE   67/01    MOTHR  146/17
FAULTS  (1) ................................................. DEAD   192/22
FAVOUR  (3) ................................................. RACE    45/01
        IVY D  119/13    IVY D  131/19
FAVOURED  (1) ............................................... CLAY   103/07
FAVOURITE  (2) .............................................. EVELN   39/24
        DEAD   179/32
FAVOURITES  (2) ............................................. HOUSE   62/15
        MOTHR  138/24
FAWNING  (1) ................................................ IVY D  134/30
FEAR  (11) .................................................. SISTR    9/14
        SISTR   11/16    ENCTR   20/04    ENCTR   28/02    GALNT   59/02
```

```
        HOUSE   66/33      HOUSE   67/30      LITTL   72/16      LITTL   81/07
        IVY D 121/08       DEAD   203/23
FEARED (3) ...............................................      ENCTR   26/01
        GRACE 151/17       DEAD   179/09
FEARING (3) ..............................................      ARABY   34/26
        PNFUL 112/09       DEAD   216/29
FEARLESS (1) .............................................      LITTL   70/04
FEAST (2) ................................................      PNFUL 117/15
        PNFUL 117/20
FEATHER (1) ..............................................      PARTS   90/06
FEATS (1) ................................................      PARTS   95/30
FEATURES (7) .............................................      GALNT   56/01
        GALNT   60/23      LITTL   75/07      PNFUL 109/30      MOTHR 142/13
        GRACE 151/15       DEAD   184/28
FEBRUARY (1) .............................................      PARTS   89/07
FEEBLE (3) ...............................................      ARABY   30/05
        DEAD   176/15      DEAD   190/15
FEEBLY (2) ...............................................      SISTR   11/30
        HOUSE   66/32
FEED (1) .................................................      GRACE 160/31
FEEL (23) ................................................      SISTR   13/28
        GALNT   57/33      HOUSE   63/07      LITTL   75/17      LITTL   76/34
        PARTS   95/04      PARTS   96/33      PARTS   97/04      PNFUL 116/25
        PNFUL 117/05       PNFUL 117/30      GRACE 158/29      GRACE 173/02
        DEAD   182/14      DEAD   183/21      DEAD   188/11      DEAD   190/08
        DEAD   193/06      DEAD   195/15      DEAD   202/32      DEAD   207/03
        DEAD   216/26      DEAD   219/20
FEELING (9) ..............................................      ARABY   31/27
        RACE    45/23      HOUSE   67/13      LITTL   77/12      LITTL   78/31
        MOTHR 142/25       GRACE 164/09      DEAD   220/13      DEAD   223/13
FEELINGS (1) .............................................      DEAD   202/22
FEELS (1) ................................................      DEAD   192/12
FEES (1) .................................................      MOTHR 137/21
FEET (18) ................................................      ENCTR   24/25
        EVELN   39/15      RACE    47/16      RACE    47/18      RACE    48/22
        GALNT   56/21      HOUSE   69/01      LITTL   74/27      MOTHR 137/15
        MOTHR 146/02       GRACE 151/31      GRACE 152/01      DEAD   175/01
        DEAD   177/14      DEAD   177/32      DEAD   179/04      DEAD   186/30
        DEAD   215/20
FEIS (1) .................................................      MOTHR 142/32
FELICITOUS (1) ...........................................      PARTS   91/22
FELL (22) ................................................      SISTR   11/18
        ENCTR   23/30      ARABY   30/01      ARABY   32/09      GALNT   50/05
        GALNT   60/09      HOUSE   68/27      LITTL   82/22      PARTS   98/15
        PNFUL 110/01       PNFUL 114/06      IVY D 118/08      IVY D 120/18
        IVY D 122/11       IVY D 134/09      IVY D 135/05      MOTHR 143/30
        MOTHR 145/09       GRACE 152/27      GRACE 164/02      GRACE 172/07
        DEAD   208/08
FELLOW (31) ..............................................      EVELN   37/24
        EVELN   39/09      GALNT   51/06      HOUSE   68/16      LITTL   74/32
        LITTL   75/16      LITTL   79/28      PARTS   88/34      PARTS   94/19
        CLAY   100/19      IVY D 121/21      IVY D 121/26      IVY D 124/29
        IVY D 124/30       IVY D 125/17      IVY D 132/07      MOTHR 149/07
        GRACE 160/09       GRACE 160/14      GRACE 164/32      GRACE 170/19
        GRACE 171/08       DEAD   182/06      DEAD   185/12      DEAD   216/33
        DEAD   217/02      DEAD   217/06      DEAD   220/04      DEAD   221/02
        DEAD   221/19      DEAD   222/20
FELLOW-CATHOLICS (1) .....................................      GRACE 159/30
FELLOW-CLERKS (1) ........................................      LITTL   71/25
FELLOW-MEN (1) ...........................................      GRACE 174/12
FELLOWS (14) .............................................      RACE    48/02
        RACE    48/14      GALNT   53/09      LITTL   70/04      LITTL   72/26
```

GRACE 159/10	GRACE 161/09	DEAD 189/11	DEAD 205/17
DEAD 205/18	DEAD 205/19	DEAD 205/28	DEAD 205/29
DEAD 205/30			

FELLOW-SUFFERER (1) .... MOTHR 143/07
FELLOW-TRAVELLERS (1) .... GRACE 159/24
FELT (59) .... SISTR 10/25

SISTR 11/24	SISTR 11/29	SISTR 12/30	SISTR 13/33
ENCTR 24/06	ENCTR 26/01	EVELN 38/01	EVELN 39/03
EVELN 39/07	EVELN 40/28	EVELN 41/04	RACE 45/32
RACE 46/23	RACE 48/08	GALNT 56/34	GALNT 58/08
GALNT 58/09	HOUSE 65/08	HOUSE 66/03	HOUSE 66/33
LITTL 71/14	LITTL 73/08	LITTL 73/29	LITTL 74/21
LITTL 75/09	LITTL 80/15	LITTL 80/23	LITTL 84/01
LITTL 85/19	PARTS 87/29	PARTS 88/18	PARTS 90/29
PARTS 92/07	PARTS 92/12	PARTS 92/24	PARTS 96/33
CLAY 100/17	CLAY 105/13	PNFUL 109/01	PNFUL 110/33
PNFUL 111/05	PNFUL 117/07	PNFUL 117/15	PNFUL 117/33
IVY D 125/29	MOTHR 149/30	GRACE 171/14	DEAD 178/12
DEAD 188/28	DEAD 197/07	DEAD 210/07	DEAD 214/02
DEAD 215/09	DEAD 215/15	DEAD 217/33	DEAD 219/29
DEAD 220/24	DEAD 223/12		

FENDER (1) .... PNFUL 107/10
FENIANS (1) .... IVY D 125/05
FERNS (1) .... CLAY 100/28
FERRETED (1) .... CLAY 102/11
FERRYBOAT (2) .... ENCTR 21/16
    ENCTR 23/17
FERVENT (2) .... EVELN 41/03
    PNFUL 111/26
FEUDAL (1) .... LITTL 71/26
FEVER (1) .... DEAD 217/21
FEW (65) .... ENCTR 26/19

ENCTR 26/23	ENCTR 27/33	ARABY 29/11	ARABY 29/15
ARABY 30/32	ARABY 32/22	ARABY 34/21	ARABY 34/33
EVELN 36/04	EVELN 38/32	RACE 47/11	GALNT 51/17
GALNT 55/19	GALNT 59/32	GALNT 60/05	HOUSE 61/08
LITTL 70/04	LITTL 74/19	LITTL 75/15	LITTL 80/14
LITTL 81/19	LITTL 84/04	PARTS 87/27	PARTS 88/16
PARTS 90/19	CLAY 101/01	CLAY 105/15	PNFUL 110/04
PNFUL 112/10	PNFUL 113/05	IVY D 123/31	IVY D 124/13
IVY D 126/22	IVY D 126/32	IVY D 131/08	IVY D 131/13
MOTHR 136/12	MOTHR 137/23	MOTHR 139/08	MOTHR 139/22
MOTHR 139/25	MOTHR 140/10	MOTHR 145/20	MOTHR 146/32
MOTHR 147/07	GRACE 150/04	GRACE 151/29	GRACE 157/29
DEAD 178/17	DEAD 186/09	DEAD 198/14	DEAD 201/32
DEAD 202/21	DEAD 203/02	DEAD 209/33	DEAD 209/33
DEAD 211/02	DEAD 212/03	DEAD 214/20	DEAD 215/09
DEAD 216/17	DEAD 218/22	DEAD 222/04	DEAD 223/23

FEWER (3) .... LITTL 70/05
    MOTHR 140/11   MOTHR 140/11
FIB (2) .... ARABY 35/13
    DEAD 211/10
FIELD (15) .... ENCTR 24/06

ENCTR 24/07	ENCTR 24/16	ENCTR 24/18	ENCTR 26/22
ENCTR 26/34	ENCTR 27/03	ENCTR 28/05	ENCTR 28/10
EVELN 36/07	EVELN 36/09	EVELN 36/12	EVELN 36/16
GALNT 51/02	DEAD 202/12		

FIERCE (1) .... ENCTR 20/10
FIERCELY (4) .... ENCTR 19/12
    PARTS 96/25   IVY D 133/03   DEAD 194/19
FIERY (1) .... PNFUL 117/23
FIFTEEN (4) .... HOUSE 62/11

```
              PNFUL 113/30    DEAD  188/08    DEAD  202/12
FIFTY (1) ...........................................  ENCTR   24/28
FIGHTING (3) ........................................  ARABY   32/05
    HOUSE  61/08    GRACE 169/29
FIGS (2) ............................................  DEAD  196/27
    DEAD  201/22
FIGURE (17) .........................................  ARABY   30/21
    ARABY  30/29    ARABY  33/13    GALNT  50/04    GALNT   60/04
    LITTL  71/04    LITTL  71/27    PNFUL 110/33    IVY D  130/05
    GRACE 152/16    GRACE 156/03    GRACE 173/01    GRACE  173/07
    GRACE 173/11    DEAD  184/13    DEAD  219/30    DEAD   220/02
FIGURES (5) .........................................  RACE    47/27
    GALNT  58/21    LITTL  71/09    LITTL  72/18    PNFUL  117/13
FILL (1) ............................................  DEAD   185/19
FILLED (15) .........................................  SISTR    9/14
    ARABY  30/14    EVELN  37/25    CLAY  101/05    CLAY   106/15
    PNFUL 115/28    PNFUL 117/14    MOTHR 140/19    MOTHR  143/12
    GRACE 158/12    DEAD  183/07    DEAD  185/24    DEAD   201/27
    DEAD  201/28    DEAD  223/12
FILLING (1) .........................................  PARTS   88/30
FILTH (1) ...........................................  GRACE  150/05
FILTHY (1) ..........................................  GRACE  153/33
FINAL (6) ...........................................  EVELN   40/13
    GALNT  51/32    MOTHR 139/01    MOTHR 139/30    DEAD   182/01
    DEAD  187/12
FINALLY (7) .........................................  SISTR   10/28
    LITTL  74/17    LITTL  82/32    PARTS  92/05    PARTS   96/01
    CLAY  102/26    MOTHR 138/14
FINANCES (1) ........................................  MOTHR  145/26
FINANCIAL (1) .......................................  GRACE  166/21
FINANCIER (1) .......................................  GRACE  159/26
FIND (27) ...........................................  SISTR   12/11
    SISTR  12/13    SISTR  16/33    SISTR  18/01    ENCTR   20/25
    ENCTR  24/03    ARABY  34/26    EVELN  38/26    LITTL   77/19
    LITTL  78/27    LITTL  81/15    CLAY  103/26    CLAY   104/14
    CLAY  106/16    IVY D 124/01    IVY D 124/23    MOTHR  141/34
    GRACE 156/11    GRACE 172/18    GRACE 174/26    GRACE  174/29
    DEAD  197/08    DEAD  198/30    DEAD  204/07    DEAD   208/25
    DEAD  211/15    DEAD  223/02
FINDING (3) .........................................  LITTL   75/13
    LITTL  80/19    PNFUL 110/16
FINE (24) ...........................................  SISTR   11/05
    SISTR  17/04    ARABY  31/23    RACE   47/14    GALNT   50/31
    GALNT  51/03    GALNT  51/06    GALNT  54/04    PNFUL  111/14
    IVY D 131/16    IVY D 132/06    IVY D 132/20    IVY D  135/32
    IVY D 135/33    MOTHR 145/25    MOTHR 146/24    GRACE  160/12
    GRACE 163/32    GRACE 164/32    DEAD  178/06    DEAD   199/02
    DEAD  207/07    DEAD  207/25    DEAD  217/30
FINERY (1) ..........................................  GALNT   55/24
FINEST (1) ..........................................  DEAD   198/23
FINGER (5) ..........................................  SISTR   17/01
    RACE   45/10    PARTS  88/23    PARTS  90/11    CLAY   105/04
FINGERED (2) ........................................  SISTR   15/14
    DEAD  205/07
FINGERING (1) .......................................  PARTS   92/30
FINGERS (11) ........................................  SISTR   12/21
    ARABY  31/18    GALNT  56/22    HOUSE  67/03    LITTL   75/09
    PARTS  93/06    CLAY  105/13    GRACE 169/10    DEAD   192/02
    DEAD  202/02    DEAD  217/29
FINISH (7) ..........................................  RACE    48/16
    PARTS  89/09    PARTS  90/20    PARTS  90/24    DEAD   179/03
    DEAD  182/27    DEAD  195/11
```

```
FINISHED (9) ......................................... RACE    42/10
     LITTL  76/18    LITTL  76/25    LITTL  81/34    CLAY   101/22
     IVY D 135/21    GRACE 169/03    DEAD  197/28    DEAD   200/08
FINISHING (1) ........................................ PARTS   89/27
FINLAY (1) ........................................... PNFUL  114/22
FIRE (42) ............................................ SISTR    9/16
     SISTR  12/13    ARABY  33/17    EVELN  39/28    GALNT   58/04
     PARTS  97/13    PARTS  98/05    PARTS  98/06    PARTS   98/06
     PARTS  98/10    PARTS  98/16    CLAY   99/04    CLAY   104/05
     CLAY  104/22    IVY D 118/04    IVY D 118/07    IVY D  119/18
     IVY D 119/26    IVY D 120/18    IVY D 120/25    IVY D  120/32
     IVY D 120/34    IVY D 121/13    IVY D 122/22    IVY D  123/08
     IVY D 123/32    IVY D 124/11    IVY D 124/15    IVY D  124/18
     IVY D 124/20    IVY D 126/21    IVY D 130/26    IVY D  130/27
     IVY D 131/10    IVY D 132/33    IVY D 133/11    IVY D  133/26
     MOTHR 149/30    GRACE 156/29    DEAD  212/03    DEAD   213/27
     DEAD  214/04
FIREPLACE (2) ........................................ SISTR   15/09
     MOTHR 144/25
FIRES (2) ............................................ DEAD   213/32
     DEAD  219/01
FIRM (3) ............................................. RACE    46/10
     GRACE 154/09    GRACE 158/24
FIRMLY (7) ........................................... HOUSE   62/08
     PNFUL 108/29    GRACE 158/30    GRACE 173/05    DEAD   190/08
     DEAD  197/06    DEAD  201/06
FIRST (63) ........................................... SISTR   10/04
     SISTR  14/11    ENCTR  21/20    ENCTR  21/30    ARABY   31/30
     ARABY  34/01    EVELN  38/31    EVELN  39/08    RACE    45/05
     GALNT  52/02    GALNT  52/25    GALNT  60/27    HOUSE   63/01
     HOUSE  66/15    HOUSE  67/03    LITTL  73/07    LITTL   73/09
     LITTL  73/16    LITTL  81/08    LITTL  83/05    LITTL   83/30
     PARTS  91/17    PARTS  92/17    PNFUL 108/09    PNFUL  110/13
     PNFUL 116/04    PNFUL 117/01    IVY D 123/30    IVY D  128/24
     IVY D 130/14    IVY D 131/01    MOTHR 137/07    MOTHR  137/10
     MOTHR 138/21    MOTHR 139/12    MOTHR 140/07    MOTHR  143/31
     MOTHR 145/31    MOTHR 146/02    MOTHR 146/24    MOTHR  147/05
     MOTHR 147/09    MOTHR 147/15    MOTHR 147/17    MOTHR  148/20
     MOTHR 149/19    GRACE 169/03    DEAD  179/19    DEAD   184/13
     DEAD  185/22    DEAD  188/19    DEAD  191/04    DEAD   192/04
     DEAD  197/03    DEAD  197/28    DEAD  201/25    DEAD   202/23
     DEAD  202/25    DEAD  209/26    DEAD  215/12    DEAD   217/12
     DEAD  220/27    DEAD  222/12
FIRSTCOMER (1) ....................................... ENCTR   21/26
FIRST-RATE (1) ....................................... MOTHR  142/21
FISH (2) ............................................. DEAD   191/26
     DEAD  191/26
FISHER (1) ........................................... DEAD   191/26
FISHERMEN (1) ........................................ ENCTR   24/03
FISHING (2) .......................................... ENCTR   23/09
     DEAD  191/25
FIST (8) ............................................. ENCTR   19/14
     PARTS  90/25    PARTS  91/12    PARTS  91/30    PARTS   94/02
     PARTS  98/01    DEAD  184/33    DEAD  185/32
FISTS (1) ............................................ ARABY   33/24
FIT (3) .............................................. IVY D  132/26
     GRACE 158/12    DEAD  185/33
FITZPATRICK (15) ..................................... MOTHR  139/15
     MOTHR 139/27    MOTHR 140/21    MOTHR 141/02    MOTHR  141/03
     MOTHR 141/07    MOTHR 141/34    MOTHR 144/10    MOTHR  144/11
     MOTHR 144/18    MOTHR 144/20    MOTHR 146/30    MOTHR  146/32
     MOTHR 147/23    MOTHR 148/20
```

FITZPATRICK'S (1) .... MOTHR 140/13
FIVE (18) .... ENCTR 22/05
   · RACE   46/13   RACE   46/29   LITTL 77/15   LITTL 84/23
   PARTS 89/21   PARTS 89/28   PARTS 90/23   PARTS 93/34
   PARTS 97/18   CLAY 100/10   CLAY 100/12 PNFUL 116/11
   IVY D 130/19   GRACE 154/12   GRACE 167/01 GRACE 169/18
   DEAD 199/10
FIX (2) .... ENCTR 27/34
   PNFUL 109/26
FIXED (6) .... GALNT 52/07
   GALNT 59/06   HOUSE 68/33   PNFUL 112/29 MOTHR 141/24
   DEAD 187/23
FIXEDLY (3) .... PARTS 87/25
   PARTS 87/32   IVY D 130/32
FLACCID (1) .... DEAD 179/25
FLAG (1) .... IVY D 134/20
FLAKES (1) .... DEAD 223/25
FLAME (2) .⁴ .... IVY D 119/23
   DEAD 212/02
FLAMES (2) .... SISTR 14/18
   IVY D 135/15
FLANKED (1) .... ENCTR 23/01
FLANNEL (1) .... HOUSE 67/08
FLARING (1) .... ARABY 31/04
FLASHED (1) .... DEAD 202/11
FLASHING (1) .... RACE 48/09
FLAT (4) .... PARTS 97/33
   MOTHR 139/18   MOTHR 139/30   DEAD 175/18
FLATTERED (1) .... GRACE 166/23
FLATTERY (1) .... GALNT 52/20
FLAVOUR (2) .... LITTL 74/31
   LITTL 76/21
FLEET (3) .... ENCTR 23/09
   HOUSE 62/17   PARTS 92/31
FLEMING (2) .... CLAY 101/09
   CLAY 101/10
FLESH (1) .... CLAY 104/28
FLESHY (1) .... DEAD 184/26
FLEW (4) .... IVY D 131/09
   IVY D 132/32   IVY D 135/26   DEAD 219/15 PARTS 90/12
FLICKED (3) .... LITTL 71/09
   DEAD 178/13   DEAD 178/23
FLICKERED (2) .... DEAD 223/19
   GRACE 171/15
FLICKERING (1) .... GRACE 163/30
FLIES (1) .... HOUSE 68/04
FLIGHT (5) .... DEAD 209/26
   LITTL 72/29   DEAD 181/32   DEAD 193/07 LITTL 81/18
FLINCH (1) .... ENCTR 22/24
FLING (2) .... RACE 48/06
   LITTL 81/08
FLINGING (1) .... HOUSE 63/08
FLIRTED (1) .... MOTHR 144/34
FLOATED (1) .... HOUSE 62/04
FLOATING (1) .... DEAD 196/16
FLOCK (1) .... ARABY 31/14
FLOOD (2) .... SISTR 12/19
   DEAD 213/31
FLOOR (18) .... CLAY 102/03
   SISTR 16/33   ARABY 30/25   LITTL 85/05 GRACE 150/10
   PNFUL 116/14   IVY D 128/17   GRACE 150/06 GRACE 150/10
   GRACE 151/04   GRACE 151/17   GRACE 153/03 DEAD 175/03

```
            DEAD   176/06    DEAD   177/32    DEAD   186/14    DEAD   213/19
            DEAD   222/19
FLORENTINES (1) ..................................  GALNT    52/03
FLORID (1) ........................................  HOUSE    65/20
FLORIN (1) ........................................  ARABY    34/12
FLOURISH (1) ......................................  DEAD    182/01
FLOURY (1) ........................................  DEAD    197/17
FLOWERED (1) ......................................  ARABY    35/04
FLOWERS (4) .......................................  SISTR    14/31
            SISTR   16/11    GALNT   55/30    LITTL   83/34
FLUNG (5) .........................................  RACE    44/07
            GALNT   59/22    LITTL   85/05    DEAD   215/24    DEAD   221/32
FLUSH (2) .........................................  LITTL    73/01
            LITTL   76/02
FLUSHED (3) .......................................  PARTS    91/28
            PARTS   96/08    IVY D  135/27
FLUTTER (1) .......................................  MOTHR   141/10
FLY (1) ...........................................  HOUSE    67/34
FLYING (1) ........................................  GALNT    57/04
FLYNN (6) .........................................  SISTR    10/14
            SISTR   12/07    SISTR   15/31    PARTS   91/02    PARTS    93/20
            PARTS   94/11
FOES (1) ..........................................  ARABY    31/11
FOG (2) ...........................................  PARTS    89/06
            PARTS   92/25
FOGARTY (15) ......................................  GRACE   166/15
            GRACE  166/19    GRACE  166/28    GRACE  166/33    GRACE   167/03
            GRACE  167/13    GRACE  167/25    GRACE  168/02    GRACE   168/15
            GRACE  168/31    GRACE  169/01    GRACE  169/23    GRACE   170/01
            GRACE  171/12    GRACE  172/17
FOGARTY'S (1) .....................................  GRACE   155/13
FOLD (1) ..........................................  EVELN    40/21
FOLDING (1) .......................................  DEAD    177/34
FOLDS (1) .........................................  DEAD    177/20
FOLLIES (1) .......................................  ARABY    32/13
FOLLOW (4) ........................................  EVELN    41/13
            DEAD   177/13    DEAD   186/10    DEAD   193/05
FOLLOWED (23) .....................................  SISTR    11/23
            ENCTR   24/26    ARABY   30/29    RACE    47/05    GALNT    49/18
            GALNT   56/10    GALNT   57/20    GALNT   59/30    PARTS    98/13
            MOTHR  140/10    MOTHR  143/18    MOTHR  144/03    MOTHR   146/30
            MOTHR  149/24    MOTHR  149/28    GRACE  151/12    GRACE   169/26
            GRACE  173/11    DEAD   201/29    DEAD   205/32    DEAD    208/18
            DEAD   215/20    DEAD   218/17
FOLLOWING (6) .....................................  GALNT    54/18
            MOTHR  141/18    MOTHR  148/23    GRACE  164/21    GRACE   167/29
            DEAD   178/29
FOLLY (1) .........................................  RACE    48/29
FOL-THE-DIDDLE-I-DO (1) ...........................  MOTHR   149/07
FOND (9) ..........................................  EVELN    39/05
            GALNT   51/31    HOUSE   62/18    CLAY   100/02    CLAY    100/09
            IVY D  132/17    GRACE  157/10    DEAD   182/26    DEAD    221/02
FOOD (5) ..........................................  EVELN    37/20
            GALNT   57/07    GALNT   57/26    HOUSE   61/14    PNFUL   112/32
FOOL (5) ..........................................  SISTR    10/04
            EVELN   37/24    PARTS   91/18    PARTS   91/19    PARTS    92/15
FOOLED (1) ........................................  MOTHR   148/12
FOOLISH (5) .......................................  SISTR    13/20
            ARABY   30/33    EVELN   40/14    DEAD   213/13    DEAD    222/23
FOOT (11) .........................................  SISTR    14/19
            ENCTR   26/17    HOUSE   68/08    HOUSE   68/24    PARTS    90/08
            CLAY   101/28    PNFUL  107/14    MOTHR  148/28    GRACE   150/03
```

GRACE 170/11   DEAD 177/06
FOOTING (1) .... GRACE 153/01
FOOTPATH (3) .... RACE   45/17
    GALNT 59/31   GRACE 155/22
FOOTPATHS (1) .... PARTS 93/07
FOOTSTEPS (2) .... EVELN 36/05
    LITTL 72/18
FOR (509)
FORBID (1) .... GRACE 158/15
FORBIDDEN (1) .... EVELN 39/17
FORCE (1) .... HOUSE 68/02
FORCED (4) .... ENCTR 28/07
    PNFUL 110/17   GRACE 151/28   GRACE 174/04
FORCES (1) .... DEAD 220/21
FORCING (1) .... DEAD 180/17
FOREFATHERS (2) .... DEAD 203/10
    DEAD 208/05
FOREFINGER (1) .... DEAD 185/16
FOREHEAD (7) .... ENCTR 27/18
    ARABY 33/10   GALNT 49/14   PARTS 96/16   DEAD 178/16
    DEAD 189/26   DEAD 220/07
FOREIGN (4) .... ENCTR 23/25
    RACE   45/29   RACE   46/01   IVY D 122/04
FOREMAN (1) .... HOUSE 61/03
FORFEIT (1) .... ENCTR 22/17
FORGET (11) .... SISTR 16/20
    ARABY 31/32   IVY D 123/14   GRACE 160/21   GRACE 165/17
    GRACE 165/21   GRACE 170/13   GRACE 171/19   DEAD 177/03
    DEAD 198/13   DEAD 214/01
FORGETS (1) .... IVY D 123/22
FORGETTING (2) .... LITTL 82/31
    GRACE 171/10
FORGIVE (1) .... IVY D 127/04
FORGOT (2) .... IVY D 133/10
    MOTHR 139/03
FORGOTTEN (6) .... ENCTR 27/19
    ARABY 33/33   ARABY 34/06   LITTL 82/13   PNFUL 108/13
    IVY D 127/17
FORK (3) .... GALNT 57/26
    DEAD 197/06   DEAD 206/02
FORKS (3) .... DEAD 182/33
    DEAD 197/27   DEAD 200/09
FORM (3) .... IVY D 129/21
    GRACE 172/20   DEAD 223/15
FORM' (1) .... RACE   47/30
FORMALLY (1) .... GRACE 172/12
FORMED (3) .... PARTS 94/17
    GRACE 151/03   GRACE 159/20
FORMER (4) .... SISTR   9/18
    ARABY 29/07   LITTL 74/15   LITTL 76/34
FORMERLY (1) .... SISTR 12/07
FORMING (2) .... GALNT 50/19
    DEAD 192/06
FORMLESS (1) .... DEAD 178/17
FORMS (1) .... DEAD 223/16
FORSAKE (1) .... GALNT 56/18
FORTH (3) .... GALNT 49/16
    PARTS 94/05   GRACE 154/14
FORTUNATE (1) .... RACE   43/19
FORTUNE (1) .... LITTL 71/14
FORTUNES (1) .... ENCTR 24/20
FORTY (1) .... DEAD 184/25

```
FORTY-THREE (1) .................................... PNFUL 113/23
FORWARD (9) ....................................... SISTR  14/12
     EVELN  38/34     RACE   44/08     LITTL  72/17     PARTS  86/11
     CLAY   99/02     GRACE 166/17     DEAD  183/22     DEAD  198/10
FORWARDS (2) ...................................... DEAD  184/34
     DEAD  185/32
FOUGHT (2) ........................................ ENCTR  19/06
     ENCTR  19/07
FOUND (37) ........................................ SISTR   9/04
     SISTR  11/26     SISTR  12/29     SISTR  13/15     SISTR  14/33
     ENCTR  27/20     ARABY  29/11     ARABY  29/16     ARABY  33/16
     ARABY  34/28     EVELN  37/11     EVELN  37/23     EVELN  39/17
     RACE   43/31     GALNT  55/22     GALNT  56/27     GALNT  57/26
     LITTL  72/13     LITTL  83/11     LITTL  83/19     PARTS  91/22
     PARTS  95/29     PARTS  97/13     CLAY  101/33     PNFUL 107/03
     PNFUL 109/17     PNFUL 110/12     PNFUL 114/11     MOTHR 137/22
     MOTHR 145/22     GRACE 156/10     GRACE 172/05     DEAD  187/19
     DEAD  187/33     DEAD  188/30     DEAD  195/12     DEAD  197/31
FOUR (29) ......................................... ENCTR  20/13
     ENCTR  24/10     RACE   42/15     RACE   42/17     LITTL  77/15
     LITTL  84/23     PARTS  87/10     CLAY   99/05     CLAY  101/08
     PNFUL 107/10     PNFUL 108/34     PNFUL 112/12     PNFUL 117/03
     MOTHR 138/09     MOTHR 138/16     MOTHR 140/03     MOTHR 140/03
     MOTHR 140/34     MOTHR 141/04     MOTHR 141/07     MOTHR 146/33
     MOTHR 147/03     MOTHR 148/22     MOTHR 148/27     GRACE 154/11
     GRACE 163/16     DEAD  186/06     DEAD  187/15     DEAD  213/02
FOUR-HANDED (1) ................................... GRACE 163/15
FOURPENCE (2) ..................................... CLAY  104/02
     IVY D 125/18
FOURTEEN (1) ...................................... PARTS  90/24
FOURTH (2) ........................................ RACE   43/11
     MOTHR 142/32
FOWNES'S (1) ...................................... PARTS  93/27
FOXES' (1) ........................................ DEAD  186/23
FRACTURED (1) ..................................... PNFUL 114/16
FRAGILE (1) ....................................... LITTL  70/13
FRAGILITY (1) ..................................... PARTS  87/26
FRAGRANCE (4) ..................................... PNFUL 108/10
     PNFUL 108/11     MOTHR 145/06     MOTHR 145/09
FRAGRANT (2) ...................................... DEAD  177/19
     DEAD  213/24
FRAIL (3) ......................................... ENCTR  21/31
     DEAD  213/14     DEAD  215/22
FRAILER (1) ....................................... IVY D 130/08
FRAME (3) ......................................... GALNT  51/20
     LITTL  70/13     LITTL  82/23
FRAMEWORK (1) ..................................... RACE   46/11
FRANCE (4) ........................................ RACE   43/33
     RACE   47/32     DEAD  189/13     DEAD  189/15
FRANCOIS (1) ...................................... LITTL  78/04
FRANK (11) ........................................ EVELN  38/27
     EVELN  38/27     EVELN  39/20     EVELN  40/18     EVELN  40/20
     EVELN  40/32     GALNT  55/32     HOUSE  64/10     HOUSE  64/10
     GRACE 174/28     DEAD  205/21
FRANKLY (3) ....................................... DEAD  179/32
     DEAD  188/03     DEAD  196/02
FRANK-MANNERED (1) ................................ DEAD  187/20
FREAK (1) ......................................... RACE   44/30
FRECKLED (1) ...................................... DEAD  187/21
FREDDY (34) ....................................... DEAD  176/27
     DEAD  176/30     DEAD  176/33     DEAD  181/34     DEAD  182/11
     DEAD  184/22     DEAD  184/24     DEAD  185/01     DEAD  185/02
```

	DEAD	185/18	DEAD	185/21	DEAD	185/23	DEAD	185/24
	DEAD	185/28	DEAD	190/14	DEAD	190/17	DEAD	191/30
	DEAD	193/12	DEAD	193/32	DEAD	198/03	DEAD	198/22
	DEAD	198/28	DEAD	198/32	DEAD	200/20	DEAD	201/09
	DEAD	205/22	DEAD	206/01	DEAD	208/20	DEAD	208/21
	DEAD	208/30	DEAD	208/32	DEAD	209/03	DEAD	209/08
	DEAD	210/13						

FREE (8) .... ARABY 29/03
    HOUSE 66/23   HOUSE 68/11   PARTS 98/11   PNFUL 107/07
    PNFUL 108/34   DEAD 191/31   DEAD 220/22
FREED (1) .... SISTR 12/32
FREEDOM (1) .... SISTR 12/31
FREEDOM'S (1) .... IVY D 135/17
FREELY (2) .... ENCTR 22/12
    LITTL 72/27
FREEMAN (4) .... MOTHR 144/27
    MOTHR 144/27   MOTHR 144/31   MOTHR 145/27
FREEMAN'S (3) .... SISTR 16/12
    GRACE 158/23   GRACE 172/32
FREEMASON (1) .... ARABY 32/21
FREEMASONS' (1) .... IVY D 120/20
FREE-THINKING (1) .... HOUSE 66/08
FRENCH (8) .... RACE 42/08
    RACE 42/09   RACE 43/09   RACE 44/18   RACE 46/19
    LITTL 72/06   MOTHR 136/11   MOTHR 137/20
FRENCHMEN (2) .... RACE 44/07
    RACE 46/10
FRENZY (1) .... EVELN 41/11
FREQUENT (1) .... GRACE 156/21
FREQUENTLY (1) .... RACE 48/12
FRESH (3) .... HOUSE 63/27
    DEAD 193/25   DEAD 193/25
FRIDAY (5) .... MOTHR 137/10
    MOTHR 139/05   MOTHR 140/26   MOTHR 141/16   GRACE 154/34
FRIEND (34) .... SISTR 10/12
    ENCTR 27/05   EVELN 37/14   RACE 44/05   RACE 45/16
    RACE 45/19   GALNT 51/17   GALNT 51/28   GALNT 52/04
    GALNT 54/27   GALNT 60/18   GALNT 60/24   LITTL 70/01
    LITTL 70/07   LITTL 71/02   LITTL 72/25   LITTL 77/03
    LITTL 77/08   LITTL 78/15   LITTL 79/09   LITTL 79/10
    LITTL 79/17   LITTL 80/26   LITTL 80/34   LITTL 81/12
    IVY D 124/15   IVY D 124/28   MOTHR 137/22   MOTHR 148/18
    GRACE 152/21   GRACE 153/19   GRACE 155/07   GRACE 172/33
    DEAD 188/28
FRIENDLINESS (2) .... LITTL 80/31
    MOTHR 143/01
FRIENDLY (7) .... RACE 45/34
    IVY D 132/11   MOTHR 138/25   GRACE 165/04   DEAD 178/01
    DEAD 188/25   DEAD 222/13
FRIENDS (49) .... SISTR 10/21
    SISTR 16/17   SISTR 16/17   SISTR 16/18   RACE 42/08
    RACE 44/17   GALNT 50/19   GALNT 58/05   GALNT 58/06
    GALNT 58/17   GALNT 58/18   GALNT 58/20   GALNT 58/29
    HOUSE 62/19   HOUSE 66/18   LITTL 78/05   LITTL 78/18
    PARTS 89/30   PARTS 95/28   CLAY 102/10   PNFUL 109/08
    IVY D 134/30   MOTHR 136/05   MOTHR 136/12   MOTHR 137/02
    MOTHR 137/28   MOTHR 137/29   MOTHR 137/32   MOTHR 137/33
    MOTHR 137/33   MOTHR 139/02   MOTHR 140/25   MOTHR 143/16
    GRACE 151/10   GRACE 154/20   GRACE 154/22   GRACE 155/09
    GRACE 156/27   GRACE 157/04   GRACE 157/23   GRACE 160/03
    GRACE 160/04   GRACE 163/22   GRACE 173/24   DEAD 175/15
    DEAD 188/18   DEAD 190/23   DEAD 204/13   DEAD 215/16

```
FRIEND'S (6) ......................................... GALNT  53/33
     GALNT  59/11    LITTL  76/33    LITTL  80/24    LITTL  81/18
     GRACE 154/18
FRIENDS' (1) ......................................... GRACE 162/25
FRIENDSHIP (2) ....................................... RACE   45/02
     PNFUL 112/20
FRIEZE (1) ........................................... DEAD  177/19
FRIGHT (3) ........................................... LITTL  84/20
     LITTL  84/29    PARTS  98/21
FRIGHTENED (1) ....................................... LITTL  85/16
FRILL (1) ............................................ DEAD  196/20
FRINGE (2) ........................................... PNFUL 113/08
     DEAD  177/16
FRINGED (1) .......................................... HOUSE  65/26
FRO (5) .............................................. GALNT  53/13
     GALNT  53/30    LITTL  84/09    GRACE 171/31    DEAD  185/17
FROCK-COAT (2) ....................................... IVY D 125/27
     GRACE 156/08
FROM (239)
FRONT (18) ........................................... SISTR  12/21
     ARABY  30/25    ARABY  32/32    ARABY  33/08    ARABY  34/24
     RACE   44/04    GALNT  56/03    GALNT  60/01    GALNT  60/03
     HOUSE  62/24    LITTL  79/20    MOTHR 138/33    MOTHR 145/03
     GRACE 172/31    DEAD  187/23    DEAD  194/12    DEAD  208/28
     DEAD  209/32
FRONTAL (1) .......................................... MOTHR 146/27
FROWNED (2) .......................................... SISTR  17/01
     DEAD  180/08
FROWNING (4) ......................................... ENCTR  20/22
     LITTL  74/23    DEAD  185/16    DEAD  211/18
FRUIT-STAND (1) ...................................... DEAD  196/31
FUGITIVE (1) ......................................... LITTL  72/19
FULFIL (1) ........................................... GRACE 160/23
FULHAM (1) ........................................... DEAD  176/05
FULL (29) ............................................ ARABY  31/13
     EVELN  40/25    GALNT  54/16    HOUSE  62/32    LITTL  72/02
     LITTL  74/21    LITTL  81/12    LITTL  83/16    PARTS  93/12
     PARTS  94/15    PARTS  96/32    CLAY  102/01    CLAY  102/13
     CLAY  103/04    CLAY  105/27    PNFUL 110/31    IVY D 128/20
     MOTHR 136/03    GRACE 154/12    GRACE 172/03    DEAD  185/24
     DEAD  186/02    DEAD  191/11    DEAD  196/23    DEAD  196/28
     DEAD  218/19    DEAD  219/31    DEAD  219/32    DEAD  223/07
FULLY (2) ............................................ GALNT  50/09
     DEAD  211/30
FULNESS (1) .......................................... PNFUL 110/03
FUMES (1) ............................................ PARTS  93/14
FUN (2) .............................................. EVELN  39/08
     MOTHR 147/15
FUNDS (1) ............................................ PARTS  95/06
FUNK (2) ............................................. ENCTR  22/15
     ENCTR  22/32
FUNNY (1) ............................................ DEAD  181/12
FUR (3) .............................................. SISTR  14/30
     LITTL  76/07    DEAD  206/20
FUREY (5) ............................................ DEAD  219/05
     DEAD  220/10    DEAD  221/06    DEAD  222/16    DEAD  223/32
FURIOUS (1) .......................................... PARTS  86/02
FURIOUSLY (2) ........................................ PARTS  86/01
     PARTS  98/05
FURLONG (5) .......................................... DEAD  182/22
     DEAD  183/25    DEAD  184/01    DEAD  197/10    DEAD  198/21
FURNACE (3) .......................................... DEAD  213/24
```

```
                    DEAD  213/26    DEAD  213/28
FURNITURE (5) ......................................... ARABY   29/18
       LITTL  83/20    LITTL  83/25    PNFUL 107/08    GRACE  157/17
FURRY (1) ............................................. HOUSE   67/09
FURTHER (4) ........................................... ENCTR   26/30
       PNFUL 109/12    IVY D 129/17    MOTHR 146/24
FURTIVE (1) ........................................... PNFUL  117/13
FURTIVELY (2) ......................................... PARTS   88/28
       PARTS  89/04
FURY (2) .............................................. PARTS   97/07
       PARTS  97/09
FUSSING (2) ........................................... ARABY   32/29
       DEAD  175/10
FUSSY (2) ............................................. DEAD   176/22
       DEAD  176/24
FUTURE (4) ............................................ ARABY   31/15
       HOUSE  68/31    LITTL  72/24    PNFUL 115/13

G. (1) ................................................ DEAD   187/29
GAB (1) ............................................... PARTS   96/25
GABRIEL (141)
GABRIEL'S (16) ........................................ DEAD   177/10
       DEAD  180/24    DEAD  184/25    DEAD  185/09    DEAD   186/14
       DEAD  188/06    DEAD  192/02    DEAD  200/09    DEAD   203/14
       DEAD  208/01    DEAD  208/18    DEAD  213/07    DEAD   216/22
       DEAD  218/33    DEAD  219/15    DEAD  223/12
GAIETY (3) ............................................ GALNT   56/17
       LITTL  76/23    DEAD  198/23
GAILY (5) ............................................. RACE    46/31
       GALNT  49/04    GRACE 155/26    DEAD  178/05    DEAD   214/33
GAINED (3) ............................................ ARABY   33/06
       PNFUL 117/09    DEAD  178/33
GAINING (1) ........................................... PARTS   89/06
GAIT (1) .............................................. GALNT   51/20
GAITERS (1) ........................................... GRACE  154/03
GALLAHER (49) ......................................... LITTL   70/02
       LITTL  70/09    LITTL  70/10    LITTL  72/21    LITTL   72/25
       LITTL  72/31    LITTL  73/05    LITTL  73/19    LITTL   74/13
       LITTL  74/26    LITTL  75/03    LITTL  75/11    LITTL   75/22
       LITTL  75/26    LITTL  75/29    LITTL  76/04    LITTL   76/11
       LITTL  76/18    LITTL  76/20    LITTL  76/28    LITTL   77/07
       LITTL  77/09    LITTL  77/18    LITTL  77/24    LITTL   77/29
       LITTL  78/05    LITTL  78/08    LITTL  78/13    LITTL   78/25
       LITTL  78/29    LITTL  79/04    LITTL  79/12    LITTL   79/17
       LITTL  79/24    LITTL  79/31    LITTL  80/02    LITTL   80/06
       LITTL  80/10    LITTL  80/18    LITTL  80/19    LITTL   80/24
       LITTL  80/31    LITTL  81/03    LITTL  81/04    LITTL   81/11
       LITTL  81/19    LITTL  81/26    LITTL  83/14    LITTL   83/24
GALLAHER'S (8) ........................................ LITTL   70/05
       LITTL  70/09    LITTL  73/02    LITTL  77/01    LITTL   80/17
       LITTL  80/20    LITTL  80/21    LITTL  80/30
GALLANTLY (3) ......................................... RACE    45/11
       DEAD  192/29    DEAD  205/07
GALLANTRIES (1) ....................................... GALNT   57/31
GALLANTS (1) .......................................... GALNT   49/ T
GALLERY (6) ........................................... ARABY   34/29
       ARABY  35/29    PNFUL 110/20    MOTHR 142/26    DEAD   199/08
       DEAD  199/11
GALLICISM (1) ......................................... RACE    42/17
GALLOPED (1) .......................................... DEAD   214/21
GALLOPING (2) ......................................... DEAD   214/23
```

```
      DEAD   214/24
GALWAY (6) ......................................  DEAD   191/16
      DEAD   218/31    DEAD   219/14    DEAD   219/16    DEAD   220/31
      DEAD   221/08
GAME (13) ........................................  RACE    48/06
      RACE    48/06    RACE    48/16    RACE    48/18    RACE    48/19
      GALNT   52/13    GALNT   52/33    GALNT   52/33    HOUSE   68/16
      PARTS   89/21    IVY D  127/21    MOTHR  136/04    GRACE  160/25
GAMES (3) ........................................  ENCTR   25/13
      CLAY   103/17    CLAY   104/32
GANG (2) .........................................  LITTL   75/29
      IVY D  134/09
GANTLET (1) ......................................  ARABY   30/08
GAPING (1) .......................................  LITTL   71/30
GAPS (1) .........................................  ENCTR   25/20
GARCON (1) .......................................  LITTL   74/31
GARDEN (7) .......................................  ENCTR   19/04
      ENCTR   19/13    ENCTR   21/28    ARABY   29/14    CLAY   105/17
      DEAD   221/19    DEAD   221/19
GARDENS (3) ......................................  ARABY   30/10
      HOUSE   61/04    LITTL   71/11
GARDINER (2) .....................................  ENCTR   19/10
      GRACE  172/02
GARMENTS (1) .....................................  SISTR   12/22
GARRET (2) .......................................  PNFUL  110/34
      PNFUL  111/02
GARRULOUS (1) ....................................  ARABY   33/17
GAS (7) ..........................................  ENCTR   22/11
      ARABY   34/14    PARTS   88/17    PARTS   89/30    DEAD   177/25
      DEAD   206/11    DEAD   212/02
GASPING (1) ......................................  MOTHR  147/11
GASWORKS (2) .....................................  DEAD   219/28
      DEAD   219/30
GATE (3) .........................................  EVELN   38/33
      PNFUL  117/01    DEAD   224/01
GATES (2) ........................................  PNFUL  114/26
      DEAD   209/16
GATHER (3) .......................................  SISTR   14/20
      RACE    48/25    DEAD   219/01
GATHERED (8) .....................................  ARABY   34/33
      RACE    42/03    GALNT   53/31    HOUSE   65/27    MOTHR  147/04
      DEAD   202/24    DEAD   204/12    DEAD   223/14
GATHERING (1) ....................................  DEAD   220/21
GATHERINGS (2) ...................................  DEAD   203/30
      DEAD   204/02
GAUDY (1) ........................................  LITTL   77/06
GAUGING (1) ......................................  PARTS   87/26
GAUNT (3) ........................................  LITTL   71/33
      PNFUL  117/02    DEAD   176/04
GAVAN (1) ........................................  EVELN   37/25
GAVE (31) ........................................  SISTR   12/22
      SISTR   14/19    ENCTR   26/07    EVELN   38/11    EVELN   41/16
      RACE    48/15    LITTL   70/12    LITTL   71/31    LITTL   82/15
      CLAY   100/29    CLAY   103/18    PNFUL  108/20    PNFUL  108/22
      PNFUL  108/28    PNFUL  109/18    PNFUL  110/29    PNFUL  114/32
      MOTHR  136/17    MOTHR  141/07    MOTHR  142/13    GRACE  152/02
      GRACE  156/29    GRACE  161/23    DEAD   176/10    DEAD   176/16
      DEAD   179/27    DEAD   191/15    DEAD   192/19    DEAD   211/32
      DEAD   215/02    DEAD   217/03
GAY (10) .........................................  ENCTR   21/34
      GALNT   52/17    LITTL   77/09    PNFUL  112/16    DEAD   205/17
      DEAD   205/18    DEAD   205/19    DEAD   205/28    DEAD   205/29
```

```
DEAD    205/30                                              ENCTR    26/16
GAZE (15) ...........................................      GALNT    52/06
    ENCTR   26/20    ENCTR   27/17    GALNT   51/26         LITTL    71/05
    GALNT   59/06    GALNT   60/29    HOUSE   68/32         PNFUL   109/31
    LITTL   81/18    LITTL   85/09    PARTS   95/18
    MOTHR  143/29    DEAD   181/27                          SISTR     9/09
GAZED (11) ..........................................      GALNT    53/04
    SISTR   15/09    SISTR   17/14    ARABY   29/06         GRACE   172/12
    PARTS   95/16    PNFUL  115/15    PNFUL  116/16
    DEAD   194/12    DEAD   196/05                          RACE     45/22
GAZERS (1) ..........................................      ARABY    35/32
GAZING (6) ..........................................      DEAD    209/25
    PARTS   87/32    IVY D  120/18    DEAD   202/08
    DEAD   210/02                                           DEAD    196/16
GEESE (1) ...........................................      SISTR    16/12
GENERAL (10) ........................................      GRACE   162/10
    GALNT   50/20    MOTHR  141/23    GRACE  157/22         DEAD    211/24
    GRACE  163/27    GRACE  173/11    DEAD   198/04
    DEAD   223/27                                           PARTS    93/11
GENERALLY (2) .......................................
    GRACE  158/05                                           GRACE   173/22
GENERATION (6) ......................................      DEAD    203/18
    DEAD   192/21    DEAD   192/24    DEAD   203/18
    DEAD   203/23                                           RACE     46/23
GENEROUS (3) ........................................
    DEAD   217/26    DEAD   223/12                          MOTHR   147/17
GENEROUSLY (1) ......................................      CLAY    100/32
GENTEEL (1) .........................................      GALNT    57/19
GENTILITY (1) .......................................      LITTL    71/13
GENTLE (2) ..........................................
    DEAD   221/03                                           CLAY    102/31
GENTLEMAN (18) ......................................      CLAY    103/13
    CLAY   102/32    CLAY   103/01    CLAY   103/03         CLAY    103/13
    CLAY   103/32    IVY D  133/01    GRACE  150/14         GRACE   152/27
    GRACE  153/01    GRACE  159/28    DEAD   175/02         DEAD    207/18
    DEAD   207/21    DEAD   207/25    DEAD   207/30         DEAD    208/13
    DEAD   208/14
GENTLEMAN'S (2) .....................................      PNFUL   116/12
    DEAD   207/23
GENTLEMEN (32) ......................................      ARABY    35/06
    RACE    48/33    MOTHR  139/28    MOTHR  145/20         MOTHR   145/21
    GRACE  150/01    GRACE  150/09    GRACE  150/16         GRACE   151/08
    GRACE  152/11    GRACE  157/33    GRACE  158/09         GRACE   161/32
    GRACE  162/11    GRACE  164/21    GRACE  169/26         GRACE   172/03
    GRACE  172/06    GRACE  172/10    DEAD   183/33         DEAD    184/04
    DEAD   192/21    DEAD   197/24    DEAD   198/13         DEAD    200/18
    DEAD   201/32    DEAD   202/14    DEAD   202/23         DEAD    203/17
    DEAD   204/25    DEAD   205/02    DEAD   207/03
GENTLY (3) ..........................................      HOUSE    63/29
    DEAD   201/32    DEAD   222/01
GENUINE (3) .........................................      RACE     45/10
    DEAD   193/09    DEAD   203/09
GENUINELY (2) .......................................      RACE     43/12
    GRACE  165/30
GEOGRAPHY (1) .......................................      ENCTR    23/13
GEORGE'S (6) ........................................      GALNT    58/16
    GALNT   58/29    HOUSE   63/30    HOUSE   64/20         PNFUL   109/01
    PNFUL  112/26
GEORGINA (1) ........................................      DEAD    199/03
GERMAN (7) ..........................................      RACE     42/11
    LITTL   72/06    IVY D  121/34    GRACE  169/16         GRACE   169/18
    GRACE  169/20    GRACE  170/05
```

GERMANS (1) .... LITTL 81/30
GERMANY (1) .... DEAD 189/14
GESTICULATING (2) .... RACE   48/23
    MOTHR 149/13
GESTURE (4) .... GALNT 53/16
    GALNT 60/28   LITTL 77/18   GRACE 173/20
GESTURES (2) .... ARABY 31/18
    GRACE 161/12
GET (61) .... SISTR 17/06

ENCTR 20/30	ENCTR 22/32	ENCTR 27/05	ENCTR 27/15
EVELN 38/13	GALNT 51/07	GALNT 52/15	GALNT 54/29
GALNT 58/02	HOUSE 65/22	HOUSE 66/16	LITTL 73/19
LITTL 74/07	LITTL 74/30	LITTL 75/16	LITTL 82/07
LITTL 83/26	LITTL 84/05	PARTS 87/20	PARTS 87/30
PARTS 89/22	PARTS 89/26	PARTS 92/27	PARTS 94/28
CLAY 100/04	CLAY 101/09	CLAY 102/14	CLAY 105/07
CLAY 105/32	IVY D 119/07	IVY D 120/07	IVY D 120/14
IVY D 121/27	IVY D 124/32	IVY D 130/18	IVY D 130/19
IVY D 131/14	MOTHR 146/12	MOTHR 147/01	MOTHR 148/27
MOTHR 149/04	MOTHR 149/22	GRACE 152/10	GRACE 152/25
GRACE 161/09	GRACE 161/24	GRACE 161/25	GRACE 161/26
GRACE 171/12	DEAD 178/11	DEAD 184/02	DEAD 184/10
DEAD 191/10	DEAD 195/26	DEAD 199/16	DEAD 206/05
DEAD 208/24	DEAD 210/28	DEAD 221/13	DEAD 221/23

GETS (2) .... IVY D 120/15
    IVY D 121/30
GETTING (11) .... SISTR 16/07

RACE 48/14	LITTL 75/01	PARTS 92/29	CLAY 103/09
CLAY 104/15	IVY D 124/24	IVY D 130/23	DEAD 197/33
DEAD 206/27	DEAD 215/06		

GHOST (2) .... EVELN 39/28
    GRACE 158/08
GHOSTLY (1) .... DEAD 216/10
GIFT (4) .... LITTL 74/08
    GRACE 166/28   GRACE 166/29   GRACE 166/31
GIFTED (1) .... DEAD 204/32
GILDED (1) .... PNFUL 109/02
GILT (2) .... HOUSE 64/18
    DEAD 178/19
GILT-RIMMED (1) .... DEAD 218/21
GINGER (7) .... GALNT 57/05

GALNT 57/05	GALNT 57/17	GALNT 57/26	GALNT 57/28
CLAY 99/18	CLAY 101/14		

GIRDLED (1) .... ARABY 34/29
GIRL (34) .... ENCTR 26/06

ENCTR 27/21	ENCTR 27/23	EVELN 38/05	EVELN 39/03
GALNT 57/14	GALNT 57/16	GALNT 57/24	GALNT 58/12
GALNT 58/13	HOUSE 62/28	HOUSE 62/31	HOUSE 65/01
LITTL 81/15	LITTL 82/30	CLAY 101/31	CLAY 105/05
PNFUL 109/27	PNFUL 113/03	MOTHR 138/05	MOTHR 148/08
DEAD 176/07	DEAD 177/24	DEAD 177/33	DEAD 178/08
DEAD 178/29	DEAD 178/33	DEAD 179/18	DEAD 181/23
DEAD 181/25	DEAD 186/19	DEAD 190/26	DEAD 196/01
DEAD 219/17			

GIRLISH (1) .... DEAD 222/12
GIRLS (22) .... ENCTR 20/10

ENCTR 22/22	ENCTR 24/19	ENCTR 26/03	ENCTR 26/04
ENCTR 27/21	ENCTR 27/23	GALNT 52/06	GALNT 52/25
GALNT 52/26	GALNT 58/05	GALNT 58/06	GALNT 58/31
PARTS 94/29	CLAY 103/17	CLAY 104/14	CLAY 104/32
CLAY 105/01	CLAY 105/04	CLAY 105/18	GRACE 154/28
DEAD 186/20			

GIRL'S (1)						DEAD	179/04
GIRT (1)						DEAD	215/23
GIUGLINI (1)						DEAD	199/06
GIVE (28)						SISTR	11/16
ENCTR	25/04	ENCTR	27/24	ARABY	33/32	ARABY	34/04
EVELN	38/15	EVELN	38/17	EVELN	40/18	RACE	45/01
GALNT	51/29	HOUSE	61/14	HOUSE	62/08	HOUSE	63/06
LITTL	73/33	PARTS	87/31	PARTS	88/34	PARTS	90/33
PARTS	92/14	PARTS	93/33	PARTS	98/11	PNFUL	111/29
IVY D	133/22	IVY D	133/24	MOTHR	138/10	GRACE	151/01
GRACE	174/06	DEAD	199/26	DEAD	200/33		
GIVEN (9)						SISTR	12/15
EVELN	38/02	EVELN	40/08	GALNT	59/15	HOUSE	67/04
CLAY	99/01	IVY D	131/05	DEAD	177/23	DEAD	199/01
GIVING (11)						SISTR	10/10
RACE	45/31	HOUSE	68/30	LITTL	85/14	PNFUL	110/22
MOTHR	144/30	GRACE	153/12	GRACE	157/10	GRACE	164/27
DEAD	194/30	DEAD	197/34				
GLAD (10)						EVELN	37/25
RACE	48/28	RACE	48/28	GALNT	58/18	LITTL	75/15
LITTL	81/31	CLAY	101/22	CLAY	102/01	MOTHR	141/26
DEAD	214/18						
GLANCE (1)						MOTHR	139/11
GLANCED (24)						ENCTR	24/26
ENCTR	27/16	ARABY	35/23	GALNT	49/19	GALNT	54/27
HOUSE	64/18	HOUSE	68/08	LITTL	74/22	LITTL	83/18
PARTS	88/24	PARTS	89/17	PARTS	91/20	PARTS	95/20
MOTHR	139/23	MOTHR	143/15	MOTHR	146/28	DEAD	177/24
DEAD	177/33	DEAD	178/08	DEAD	179/08	DEAD	180/21
DEAD	189/24	DEAD	205/04	DEAD	207/01		
GLANCES (2)						GALNT	56/28
MOTHR	145/10						
GLANCING (5)						GALNT	54/09
GALNT	57/08	GALNT	60/09	HOUSE	62/33	PARTS	91/17
GLARE (2)						PARTS	89/30
PARTS	90/21						
GLARED (2)						MOTHR	149/25
GRACE	170/22						
GLARING (2)						ARABY	34/14
LITTL	85/07						
GLASGOW (3)						GRACE	156/15
DEAD	190/19	DEAD	190/23				
GLASNEVIN (2)						GRACE	154/24
GRACE	166/23						
GLASS (32)						SISTR	15/03
SISTR	15/30	ARABY	33/11	RACE	46/27	GALNT	57/04
LITTL	76/33	LITTL	77/15	LITTL	79/19	LITTL	80/34
LITTL	81/05	LITTL	81/06	LITTL	81/34	PARTS	89/01
PARTS	95/06	CLAY	105/23	PNFUL	112/33	IVY D	132/17
MOTHR	140/30	GRACE	151/13	GRACE	151/28	GRACE	168/09
DEAD	185/19	DEAD	185/24	DEAD	185/25	DEAD	185/28
DEAD	185/31	DEAD	196/29	DEAD	196/33	DEAD	201/27
DEAD	205/06	DEAD	205/08	DEAD	205/14		
GLASSES (17)						SISTR	15/04
HOUSE	65/27	HOUSE	67/32	LITTL	75/28	LITTL	76/29
LITTL	76/33	LITTL	81/01	PARTS	87/03	PARTS	89/30
PARTS	94/16	GRACE	162/11	GRACE	162/11	GRACE	167/01
GRACE	169/05	DEAD	178/19	DEAD	182/32	DEAD	201/28
GLASS-STOPPERS (1)						DEAD	197/27
GLEAMED (1)						ARABY	31/25
GLEAMING (2)						PNFUL	117/21
DEAD	202/11						

GLIMMERING (1) .... DEAD 218/21
GLIMPSE (3) .... EVELN 40/27
    LITTL 70/17   DEAD 220/05
GLITTERED (1) .... DEAD 186/14
GLOBES (1) .... RACE 45/24
GLOBULAR (1) .... GALNT 51/22
GLOOM (4) .... LITTL 83/31
    PARTS 89/04   DEAD 179/05   DEAD 210/01
GLOOMY (3) .... ARABY 33/07
    PNFUL 117/01   DEAD 204/11
GLORIOUSLY (1) .... IVY D 134/20
GLORY (4) .... ENCTR 20/32
    IVY D 134/12   IVY D 135/12   DEAD 223/07
GLOSSY (2) .... IVY D 119/23
    DEAD 178/20
GLOVE (2) .... GRACE 151/18
    DEAD 213/22
GLOVED (2) .... HOUSE 63/33
    MOTHR 142/27
GLOVES (1) .... PARTS 95/15
GLOW (2) .... LITTL 71/06
    DEAD 219/02
GLOWED (3) .... ARABY 30/06
    GALNT 55/32   HOUSE 67/09
GLUE (1) .... DEAD 207/21
GLUE-BOILER (1) .... DEAD 207/18
GLYNN (3) .... MOTHR 143/20
    MOTHR 143/26   MOTHR 143/26
GLYNN'S (1) .... MOTHR 147/10
GNAWED (1) .... PNFUL 117/14
GNOMON (1) .... SISTR 9/11
GO (96) .... SISTR 12/26
    SISTR 17/04   SISTR 17/34   ENCTR 20/17   ENCTR 21/14
    ENCTR 26/31   ENCTR 28/01   ARABY 30/19   ARABY 31/03
    ARABY 31/34   ARABY 32/03   ARABY 32/12   ARABY 32/20
    ARABY 32/29   ARABY 32/32   ARABY 33/21   ARABY 33/32
    ARABY 34/04   EVELN 37/05   EVELN 37/18   EVELN 38/04
    EVELN 38/28   EVELN 40/07   EVELN 41/14   RACE   45/20
    GALNT 51/03   GALNT 52/25   GALNT 55/01   GALNT 59/29
    HOUSE 61/05   HOUSE 64/34   HOUSE 67/18   LITTL 73/11
    LITTL 76/12   LITTL 77/11   LITTL 77/20   LITTL 77/26
    LITTL 79/22   LITTL 79/29   LITTL 81/32   LITTL 82/18
    LITTL 83/25   PARTS 88/06   PARTS 90/12   PARTS 93/01
    PARTS 94/29   PARTS 94/30   PARTS 96/03   CLAY   99/01
    CLAY   100/16   IVY D 123/12   IVY D 123/26   IVY D 124/02
    IVY D 124/23   IVY D 125/18   IVY D 127/13   IVY D 132/09
    IVY D 133/26   MOTHR 138/20   MOTHR 138/20   MOTHR 140/08
    MOTHR 142/15   MOTHR 145/16   MOTHR 146/12   MOTHR 146/18
    GRACE 160/01   GRACE 163/30   GRACE 169/03   DEAD   176/15
    DEAD   177/12   DEAD   178/01   DEAD   189/08   DEAD   189/09
    DEAD   189/10   DEAD   189/13   DEAD   189/15   DEAD   190/02
    DEAD   191/13   DEAD   191/16   DEAD   191/17   DEAD   191/25
    DEAD   194/07   DEAD   195/10   DEAD   195/30   DEAD   195/32
    DEAD   199/04   DEAD   200/30   DEAD   204/07   DEAD   208/15
    DEAD   209/17   DEAD   219/13   DEAD   219/16   DEAD   221/03
    DEAD   221/21   DEAD   221/22   DEAD   221/26
GOD (33) .... SISTR 10/24
    SISTR 15/18   SISTR 16/01   SISTR 17/29   EVELN 40/30
    GALNT 53/15   HOUSE 66/09   HOUSE 67/31   LITTL 74/33
    PARTS 98/06   CLAY   104/24   PNFUL 115/28   IVY D 121/05
    IVY D 122/09   IVY D 122/18   IVY D 123/09   IVY D 123/25
    IVY D 126/31   IVY D 127/04   IVY D 127/24   IVY D 128/05

IVY D 132/22	IVY D 133/20	IVY D 133/20	GRACE 158/15
GRACE 165/24	GRACE 166/07	GRACE 170/23	GRACE 170/33
GRACE 174/24	DEAD 183/10	DEAD 194/17	DEAD 194/20

GOD-FEARING (1) .... GRACE 170/30

GOD'S (2) .... GRACE 165/30

GRACE 174/30

GODSPEED (1) .... LITTL 70/02
                                                     DEAD 207/08

GOER (1) .... ENCTR 25/13

GOES (8) .... IVY D 122/06

IVY D 119/30	IVY D 120/29	IVY D 121/26	
IVY D 127/27	DEAD 203/01	DEAD 210/29	

GOING (46) .... ENCTR 24/12

ENCTR 27/06	ARABY 31/32	ARABY 34/08	EVELN 37/05
EVELN 38/14	EVELN 39/11	GALNT 50/30	GALNT 54/31
HOUSE 63/13	HOUSE 67/32	LITTL 81/07	PARTS 88/03
PARTS 93/02	PARTS 95/07	PARTS 98/04	CLAY 102/04
CLAY 103/11	CLAY 103/17	PNFUL 114/02	PNFUL 115/05
IVY D 121/33	IVY D 123/03	IVY D 123/14	IVY D 128/12
IVY D 132/10	MOTHR 138/10	MOTHR 140/27	MOTHR 144/09
MOTHR 149/04	GRACE 162/34	GRACE 163/02	GRACE 163/10
GRACE 170/29	GRACE 170/32	DEAD 178/05	DEAD 179/28
DEAD 180/01	DEAD 181/31	DEAD 181/31	DEAD 185/19
DEAD 188/33	DEAD 200/24	DEAD 220/29	DEAD 221/05
DEAD 221/10			

GOLD (5) .... SISTR 14/05

GALNT 60/30	LITTL 80/06	MOTHR 146/25	DEAD 196/29

GOLDBERG (1) .... GRACE 159/28

GOLDEN (3) .... SISTR 14/17

LITTL 71/07	LITTL 71/27

GOLD-RIMMED (1) .... PARTS 87/03

GOLOSHES (9) .... DEAD 177/05

DEAD 177/17	DEAD 178/13	DEAD 180/26	DEAD 180/27
DEAD 181/01	DEAD 181/02	DEAD 181/03	DEAD 208/11

GONE (40) .... SISTR 10/12

SISTR 12/12	SISTR 15/12	SISTR 16/20	SISTR 16/24
SISTR 18/16	ENCTR 24/27	ENCTR 26/22	ARABY 33/23
EVELN 37/04	EVELN 38/03	EVELN 39/29	RACE 48/17
GALNT 52/16	GALNT 59/21	HOUSE 66/06	LITTL 75/31
LITTL 80/16	LITTL 82/11	CLAY 100/10	PNFUL 116/30
PNFUL 117/19	IVY D 132/30	IVY D 134/17	GRACE 151/10
DEAD 175/18	DEAD 181/32	DEAD 184/15	DEAD 185/18
DEAD 186/08	DEAD 186/20	DEAD 187/16	DEAD 196/09
DEAD 203/15	DEAD 203/29	DEAD 203/32	DEAD 206/29
DEAD 206/31	DEAD 209/24	DEAD 214/10	

GONGS (1) .... RACE 45/14

GOOD (101)

GOOD-BYE (2) .... PNFUL 112/10

MOTHR 138/10

GOOD-DAY (2) .... ENCTR 24/32

ENCTR 28/01

GOOD-EVENING (2) .... DEAD 185/01

DEAD 185/02

GOOD-FELLOWSHIP (1) .... DEAD 204/14

GOOD-HUMOUREDLY (1) .... DEAD 206/13

GOODLY (1) .... DEAD 183/08

GOODNESS (3) .... DEAD 181/02

DEAD 195/32	DEAD 206/16

GOOD-NIGHT (22) .... GALNT 50/32

GALNT 58/33	GRACE 155/27	DEAD 177/02	DEAD 212/19
DEAD 212/20	DEAD 212/22	DEAD 212/22	DEAD 212/23
DEAD 212/23	DEAD 212/25	DEAD 212/26	DEAD 212/26
DEAD 212/27	DEAD 212/28	DEAD 212/29	DEAD 212/30

DEAD	212/30	DEAD	214/33	DEAD	215/08	DEAD	216/08
DEAD	222/24						

GOOD-NIGHTS (1) .... HOUSE 67/19
GOODS (1) .... PNFUL 117/22
GOOSE (7) .... DEAD 191/01

DEAD	196/14	DEAD	196/17	DEAD	197/07	DEAD	197/15
DEAD	197/19	DEAD	197/20				

GOSSIP (2) .... ARABY 33/19

MOTHR 137/34

GOSSIPING (1) .... DEAD 175/09
GOSTER (1) .... IVY D 127/11
GOT (39) .... SISTR 18/03

ENCTR	27/25	EVELN	38/24	RACE	44/27	RACE	47/07
RACE	47/20	RACE	47/28	GALNT	52/34	HOUSE	61/12
LITTL	70/02	LITTL	72/28	LITTL	80/28	PARTS	89/31
PARTS	91/07	PARTS	97/03	CLAY	100/22	CLAY	101/07
CLAY	101/34	CLAY	102/11	CLAY	105/02	CLAY	105/03
CLAY	105/04	CLAY	105/21	CLAY	105/26	IVY D	123/19
IVY D	129/32	IVY D	131/13	IVY D	131/15	IVY D	131/15
IVY D	131/16	IVY D	132/33	IVY D	133/23	MOTHR	148/12
GRACE	155/25	DEAD	176/21	DEAD	180/05	DEAD	197/22
DEAD	201/03	DEAD	208/34				

GOVERNED (1) .... HOUSE 62/07
G.P. (2) .... PARTS 88/34

PARTS 92/29

GRACE (9) .... PARTS 95/17

GRACE	150/ T	GRACE	154/03	GRACE	166/25	GRACE	174/30
DEAD	193/05	DEAD	210/03	DEAD	213/07	DEAD	215/10

GRACEFUL (3) .... ENCTR 23/21

RACE 46/11   LITTL 74/08

GRACEFULLY (1) .... GRACE 156/09
GRACES (3) .... DEAD 192/10

DEAD 204/16   DEAD 204/21

GRADE (1) .... DEAD 179/14
GRADUALLY (5) .... ENCTR 23/14

HOUSE	68/30	GRACE	173/01	DEAD	192/34	DEAD	201/27

GRAFTON (5) .... RACE   45/21

RACE 46/33   GALNT 56/25   GALNT 58/31   GRACE 153/04

GRAINS (1) .... SISTR 12/25
GRAMMAR (1) .... HOUSE 66/20
GRAND (7) .... MOTHR 138/09

MOTHR 138/16   MOTHR 141/28 . MOTHR 142/22   DEAD 198/29
DEAD 199/15   DEAD 207/32

GRANDEST (1) .... GRACE 163/26
GRANDFATHER (1) .... DEAD 207/16
GRANDIOSE (1) .... DEAD 188/20
GRANDMOTHER (1) .... DEAD 218/32
GRANDMOTHER'S (2) .... DEAD 220/29

DEAD 221/15

GRANITE (1) .... ENCTR 22/02
GRANTED (1) .... DEAD 203/04
GRASP (2) .... DEAD 188/25

DEAD 193/27

GRASS (4) .... ENCTR 19/07

ENCTR 21/28   ENCTR 24/31   LITTL 71/06

GRATE (3) .... SISTR 10/28

SISTR 17/15   GRACE 154/15

GRATED (2) .... DEAD 196/27

DEAD 213/23

GRATEFULLY (1) .... RACE   42/07
GRATITUDE (2) .... GRACE 153/13

DEAD 195/03

GRATTAN (2)						LITTL	73/12
LITTL	84/05						
GRAVE (2)						SISTR	13/14
GALNT	60/28						
GRAVEL (2)						LITTL	71/10
DEAD	221/16						
GRAVELY (6)						GALNT	52/32
GRACE	160/17	GRACE	160/18	GRACE	168/03	DEAD	187/27
DEAD	193/15						
GRAVITY (1)						GRACE	171/27
GRAY (1)						GRACE	170/18
GRAYS (1)						GRACE	170/26
GRAY'S (1)						GRACE	170/17
GREASE (1)						PNFUL	113/03
GREAT (66)						SISTR	10/21
SISTR	10/22	SISTR	10/22	SISTR	11/32	SISTR	13/01
SISTR	14/06	SISTR	15/31	SISTR	16/22	ENCTR	24/34
ENCTR	25/20	ARABY	35/17	RACE	43/31	RACE	44/23
RACE	44/25	RACE	45/29	RACE	47/34	RACE	48/16
GALNT	55/25	GALNT	56/29	GALNT	57/06	HOUSE	65/14
HOUSE	65/20	LITTL	70/10	LITTL	77/12	PARTS	86/10
PARTS	90/06	PARTS	92/24	PARTS	93/34	PARTS	95/14
PARTS	97/11	CLAY	101/08	CLAY	104/27	CLAY	105/15
CLAY	106/08	PNFUL	109/34	PNFUL	115/11	IVY D	119/17
MOTHR	137/01	MOTHR	137/06	MOTHR	142/02	MOTHR	142/25
MOTHR	148/18	MOTHR	149/07	GRACE	154/05	GRACE	157/14
GRACE	167/06	GRACE	167/22	GRACE	168/12	GRACE	168/14
GRACE	169/20	DEAD	175/13	DEAD	178/09	DEAD	187/13
DEAD	190/06	DEAD	193/03	DEAD	196/19	DEAD	197/25
DEAD	199/06	DEAD	199/13	DEAD	203/26	DEAD	203/32
DEAD	209/10	DEAD	211/10	DEAD	211/32	DEAD	215/18
DEAD	220/12						
GREAT-COAT (1)						SISTR	12/14
GREATER (3)						ARABY	34/30
RACE	44/32	DEAD	209/02				
GREATEST (2)						LITTL	70/14
GRACE	169/08						
GREAT-GREAT-GRANDFATHER (1)						PNFUL	110/09
GREATLY (5)						ENCTR	25/02
IVY D	124/28	MOTHR	146/04	GRACE	157/31	DEAD	194/04
GREATNESS (1)						LITTL	72/24
GREEDILY (1)						GALNT	57/26
GREEK (1)						GRACE	167/07
GREEN (18)						SISTR	12/23
ENCTR	22/01	ENCTR	23/26	ENCTR	23/28	ENCTR	24/19
RACE	46/30	GALNT	54/19	GALNT	56/24	GALNT	59/02
GALNT	60/07	HOUSE	62/33	LITTL	74/20	IVY D	134/20
GRACE	172/09	DEAD	180/16	DEAD	196/24	DEAD	197/04
DEAD	206/19						
GREENISH-BLACK (1)						ENCTR	24/23
GREET (1)						PNFUL	108/22
GREETED (1)						DEAD	187/13
GRESHAM (1)						DEAD	181/17
GRETTA (24)						DEAD	180/01
DEAD	180/05	DEAD	180/07	DEAD	180/12	DEAD	181/04
DEAD	181/11	DEAD	181/15	DEAD	181/19	DEAD	187/05
DEAD	187/05	DEAD	187/06	DEAD	189/03	DEAD	206/26
DEAD	210/34	DEAD	212/22	DEAD	212/25	DEAD	214/13
DEAD	216/19	DEAD	216/31	DEAD	218/07	DEAD	218/10
DEAD	218/27	DEAD	220/10	DEAD	220/16		
GREW (15)						SISTR	10/06
ENCTR	27/30	EVELN	39/23	RACE	46/25	RACE	46/25

```
            GALNT  54/24     LITTL  84/09     LITTL  85/21     CLAY  105/29
            PNFUL 108/18     MOTHR 140/11     MOTHR 146/09     GRACE 154/31
            DEAD  202/01     DEAD  209/02
GREY (20) .....................................................  SISTR  11/21
            SISTR  11/23     SISTR  14/29     ENCTR  22/06     ENCTR  23/27
            RACE   43/14     RACE   48/32     GALNT  49/01     GALNT  49/07
            GALNT  50/05     GALNT  52/08     HOUSE  62/32     LITTL  75/02
            PNFUL 117/20     IVY D 132/05     GRACE 151/05     DEAD  176/14
            DEAD  179/24     DEAD  179/24     DEAD  223/20
GREY-GREEN (1) ...............................................  CLAY  101/12
GREY-HAIRED (2) ..............................................  IVY D 118/12
            MOTHR 144/32
GREYISH (2) ..................................................  CLAY  102/33
            CLAY  103/32
GREYSTONES (1) ...............................................  MOTHR 137/24
GRIEF (4) ....................................................  IVY D 134/08
            IVY D 135/20     DEAD  210/23     DEAD  222/01
GRIMES (3) ...................................................  IVY D 122/33
            GRACE 172/29     DEAD  183/20
GRIMLY (1) ...................................................  GALNT  60/27
GRIMY (1) ....................................................  LITTL  71/29
GRIN (1) .....................................................  GALNT  54/28
GRINNED (1) ..................................................  DEAD  201/13
GRINNING (2) .................................................  DEAD  185/04
            DEAD  194/32
GRIPPED (2) ..................................................  EVELN  41/07
            PARTS  87/27
GRIZZLED (2) .................................................  IVY D 130/07
            DEAD  182/18
GROANING (1) .................................................  ENCTR  23/03
GROCER (1) ...................................................  GRACE 166/20
GROCERIES (1) ................................................  GRACE 166/32
GROCER'S (1) .................................................  GALNT  57/25
GROCERS' (1) .................................................  ENCTR  23/34
GROG (1) .....................................................  IVY D 132/17
GROOMED (1) ..................................................  RACE   43/03
GROOVE (2) ...................................................  RACE   42/02
            DEAD  178/22
GROPE (1) ....................................................  PARTS  89/03
GROPED (1) ...................................................  SISTR  14/34
GROTESQUE (1) ................................................  GRACE 161/12
GROUND (9) ...................................................  ENCTR  24/30
            ARABY  29/04     RACE   46/22     PNFUL 113/08     PNFUL 113/12
            PNFUL 114/07     DEAD  175/03     DEAD  176/06     DEAD  211/27
GROUP (3) ....................................................  GALNT  54/15
            GALNT  56/23     MOTHR 148/17
GROUPS (3) ...................................................  GALNT  58/33
            HOUSE  63/31     DEAD  192/02
GROVE (1) ....................................................  LITTL  83/32
GROW (1) .....................................................  HOUSE  63/21
GROWING (4) ..................................................  EVELN  38/03
            DEAD  177/24     DEAD  192/24     DEAD  203/18
GROWN (10) ...................................................  ENCTR  23/33
            ARABY  30/03     EVELN  36/15     EVELN  37/02     GALNT  51/24
            LITTL  71/28     IVY D 119/20     GRACE 156/24     DEAD  175/16
            DEAD  201/18
GRUDGING (1) .................................................  GALNT  57/11
GRUDGINGLY (1) ...............................................  IVY D 129/13
GRUFF (1) ....................................................  GRACE 163/07
GRUNTING (1) .................................................  GRACE 150/07
GUARD (2) ....................................................  ARABY  31/06
            DEAD  202/34
```

GUARDIAN (1) .... IVY D 131/23
GUARDS (1) .... ARABY 35/18
GUARD'S (1) .... PNFUL 113/31
GUESS (2) .... RACE   44/10
    DEAD 180/19
GUESSING (1) .... ENCTR 22/32
GUEST (3) .... DEAD 175/06
    DEAD 197/16   DEAD 197/17
GUESTS (6) .... GRACE 157/01
    DEAD 200/28   DEAD 201/24   DEAD 204/15   DEAD 205/14
    DEAD 205/33
GUIDANCE (1) .... GRACE 173/31
GUINEAS (4) .... MOTHR 138/15
    MOTHR 144/12   MOTHR 146/12   MOTHR 148/22
GUISE (1) .... LITTL 71/03
GULP (1) .... PARTS 89/02
GULPED (1) .... PARTS 89/25
GUM (1) .... PNFUL 108/11
GUMS (1) .... GRACE 153/28
GUST (1) .... HOUSE 67/06
GUTTAPERCHA (1) .... DEAD 181/05
GUTTERING (1) .... DEAD 215/28

H. (2) .... PNFUL 114/22
    IVY D 127/16
HA (1) .... GRACE 169/15
HABIT (8) .... SISTR 13/27
    GALNT 52/20   HOUSE 62/33   LITTL 72/12   PNFUL 108/25
    PNFUL 114/27   PNFUL 115/05   GRACE 157/29
HABITS (2) .... PNFUL 115/03
    PNFUL 115/30
HABITUAL (1) .... DEAD 185/03
HACKS (1) .... IVY D 125/11
HAD (810)
HADDINGTON (1) .... DEAD 176/09
HADN'T (4) .... CLAY 101/17
    GRACE 165/24   DEAD 180/04   DEAD 194/07
HAD'VE (1) .... HOUSE 66/19
HAGGARD (2) .... MOTHR 149/12
    DEAD 222/27
HAIL (3) .... PARTS 98/23
    PARTS 98/23   PARTS 98/24
HAIR (23) .... ENCTR 26/03
    ENCTR 26/07   ARABY 30/24   ARABY 32/08   EVELN 38/34
    GALNT 50/05   HOUSE 62/31   LITTL 70/15   LITTL 75/09
    PNFUL 108/18   GRACE 159/13   DEAD 177/25   DEAD 178/20
    DEAD 179/23   DEAD 179/30   DEAD 180/23   DEAD 184/30
    DEAD 190/15   DEAD 210/07   DEAD 212/02   DEAD 217/28
    DEAD 222/05   DEAD 222/11
HAIRLESS (2) .... PARTS 87/05
    DEAD 178/17
HAIRPIN (1) .... HOUSE 68/23
HAIRY (2) .... GALNT 51/11
    IVY D 118/07
HALF (15) .... SISTR 12/18
    ARABY 34/29   GALNT 50/09   GALNT 55/07   GALNT 55/16
    LITTL 73/03   PARTS 87/20   PARTS 87/21   PARTS 89/28
    PARTS 97/34   IVY D 125/08   MOTHR 147/01   GRACE 154/12
    DEAD 192/33   DEAD 194/01
HALF-A-DOZEN (1) .... LITTL 77/29
HALF-AN-HOUR (1) .... GALNT 59/17

HALF-CROWNS (1) .... CLAY 100/11
HALF-DISCLOSED (1) .... PNFUL 110/01
HALF-HOUR (1) .... HOUSE 65/19
HALF-MOONS (1) .... LITTL 70/16
HALF-ONE (2) .... LITTL 75/24
    PARTS 93/22
HALF-OPEN (1) .... DEAD 222/05
HALF-OPENED (1) .... ARABY 30/21
HALF-PAST (2) .... MOTHR 139/25
    GRACE 153/17
HALFPENCE (2) .... GALNT 57/16
    IVY D 121/31
HALFPENNY (3) .... ENCTR 19/03
    ENCTR 20/15   GALNT 58/13
HALF-PINT (1) .... GRACE 166/28
HALF-SEVEN (2) .... GRACE 162/21
    GRACE 162/23
HALFWAY (1) .... DEAD 181/32
HALL (34) .... SISTR 14/06
    ENCTR 19/11   ARABY 30/28   ARABY 32/32   ARABY 34/29
    ARABY 34/30   ARABY 35/30   EVELN 40/06   RACE 45/31
    GALNT 58/15   LITTL 71/19   LITTL 82/08   IVY D 124/02
    MOTHR 139/11   MOTHR 139/26   MOTHR 140/11   MOTHR 142/01
    MOTHR 142/19   MOTHR 142/20   MOTHR 143/31   MOTHR 146/01
    MOTHR 146/09   MOTHR 146/13   MOTHR 146/31   MOTHR 147/06
    MOTHR 147/14   DEAD 206/03   DEAD 206/25   DEAD 208/11
    DEAD 209/25   DEAD 210/01   DEAD 210/12   DEAD 215/18
    DEAD 222/24
HALLDOOR (1) .... ARABY 33/28
HALL-DOOR (7) .... GALNT 60/02
    DEAD 175/04   DEAD 196/07   DEAD 206/17   DEAD 208/20
    DEAD 210/11   DEAD 210/16
HALLO (4) .... GALNT 60/13
    GALNT 60/17   LITTL 74/28   GRACE 152/14
HALLOOED (1) .... ENCTR 28/09
HALLOW (3) .... CLAY 101/10
    CLAY 103/03   CLAY 104/32
HALLS (2) .... HOUSE 62/06
    CLAY 106/04
HALLSTAND (3) .... ARABY 32/29
    ARABY 33/29   CLAY 103/25
HALLWAY (1) .... DEAD 175/05
HALO (1) .... GALNT 52/07
HALPIN (1) .... PNFUL 114/15
HALTED (10) .... GALNT 56/08
    GALNT 60/27   LITTL 74/16   PARTS 86/17   PNFUL 117/09
    PNFUL 117/29   GRACE 154/24   DEAD 215/27   DEAD 215/28
    DEAD 218/21
HALTING (1) .... SISTR 13/20
HALVES (1) .... LITTL 74/31
HAM (4) .... GALNT 57/05
    DEAD 191/01   DEAD 196/19   DEAD 197/16
HAND (67) .... SISTR 12/20
    SISTR 14/15   ENCTR 21/08   ENCTR 24/21   ENCTR 24/21
    ENCTR 27/14   ARABY 32/08   ARABY 33/14   ARABY 34/12
    EVELN 38/20   EVELN 40/23   EVELN 41/04   GALNT 54/13
    GALNT 54/14   GALNT 54/24   GALNT 56/05   GALNT 56/19
    GALNT 60/16   GALNT 60/28   HOUSE 65/24   HOUSE 67/21
    LITTL 79/06   LITTL 83/29   PARTS 96/04   PARTS 96/07
    PARTS 96/19   CLAY 101/26   CLAY 105/11   CLAY 105/12
    PNFUL 110/19   PNFUL 111/32   PNFUL 112/29   PNFUL 116/04
    PNFUL 117/05   IVY D 120/07   IVY D 121/21   MOTHR 139/16

MOTHR 139/19	MOTHR 142/27	MOTHR 143/07	MOTHR 144/34
MOTHR 146/33	MOTHR 147/01	MOTHR 148/28	GRACE 151/09
GRACE 159/09	GRACE 162/05	GRACE 173/04	GRACE 173/06
DEAD 178/32	DEAD 185/25	DEAD 185/26	DEAD 188/24
DEAD 189/07	DEAD 190/08	DEAD 193/18	DEAD 193/27
DEAD 193/28	DEAD 203/11	DEAD 205/14	DEAD 210/18
DEAD 213/18	DEAD 214/32	DEAD 218/25	DEAD 220/23
DEAD 220/25	DEAD 221/33		

HANDBILLS (1) .... MOTHR 141/16

HANDED (7) .... ENCTR 20/20

CLAY 99/08	CLAY 104/14	IVY D 129/13	IVY D 133/12
DEAD 185/24	DEAD 203/10		

HANDING (2) .... ARABY 34/28

IVY D 129/09

HANDIWORK (1) .... IVY D 118/15

HANDKERCHIEF (4) .... SISTR 12/23

SISTR 17/13	LITTL 70/16	DEAD 205/21

HANDKERCHIEFS (1) .... GRACE 173/10

HANDLE (3) .... PARTS 90/05

IVY D 121/22	DEAD 196/25

HAND-ME-DOWN (1) .... IVY D 123/23

HAND-MIRROR (1) .... PNFUL 107/14

HANDS (50) .... SISTR 12/17

SISTR 14/08	SISTR 14/28	ENCTR 21/24	ENCTR 22/03
ENCTR 26/04	ENCTR 26/07	ARABY 31/28	EVELN 41/08
EVELN 41/10	RACE 47/34	RACE 48/30	GALNT 51/20
GALNT 54/13	HOUSE 63/33	HOUSE 65/22	HOUSE 67/10
LITTL 70/13	PARTS 96/03	PARTS 96/17	PARTS 98/20
CLAY 101/02	IVY D 122/22	IVY D 123/07	IVY D 128/31
IVY D 134/27	MOTHR 136/03	MOTHR 138/01	MOTHR 138/02
MOTHR 148/33	MOTHR 149/11	GRACE 153/11	GRACE 153/25
GRACE 157/27	GRACE 170/09	GRACE 171/17	GRACE 173/15
DEAD 178/26	DEAD 182/01	DEAD 183/30	DEAD 186/10
DEAD 191/15	DEAD 193/18	DEAD 196/11	DEAD 213/06
DEAD 215/26	DEAD 217/24	DEAD 217/28	DEAD 218/04
DEAD 220/15			

HAND'S (1) .... IVY D 129/28

HANDSOME (3) .... RACE 46/34

PNFUL 109/29	DEAD 216/06

HANDY (1) .... HOUSE 62/22

HANG (1) .... SISTR 12/01

HANGING (3) .... PARTS 86/10

DEAD 184/27	DEAD 192/30

HAPPEN (5) .... ENCTR 21/05

ENCTR 21/06	GRACE 160/15	GRACE 174/27	DEAD 223/03

SISTR 13/31

HAPPENED (7) .... LITTL 71/12

ARABY 30/31	HOUSE 64/34	HOUSE 67/01
GRACE 153/20	GRACE 160/16	

HAPPIEST (1) .... ENCTR 25/03

HAPPILY (2) .... GALNT 58/11

PNFUL 115/01

HAPPINESS (7) .... EVELN 40/20 ... DEAD 213/08

LITTL 81/03	PNFUL 117/16	DEAD 205/10
DEAD 213/20	DEAD 217/31	

HAPPY (8) .... ENCTR 22/04 ... GRACE 157/14

EVELN 36/18	RACE 43/12	HOUSE 67/17
DEAD 180/22	DEAD 215/10	DEAD 215/10

HARBOUR (1) .... RACE 47/15

HARD (18) .... SISTR 10/09

EVELN 37/21	EVELN 38/22	EVELN 38/25	EVELN 38/25
GALNT 51/29	HOUSE 62/17	CLAY 102/18	CLAY 102/32
PNFUL 109/23	IVY D 119/27	IVY D 124/18	IVY D 124/29

```
        IVY D 125/29    IVY D 127/19      GRACE 164/28       GRACE 174/18
        DEAD  176/30
HARD-EARNED (1) ................................. EVELN   38/15
HARDER (2) ...................................... RACE    46/25
        HOUSE  65/11
HARD-FEATURED (1) ...............................
HARDLY (10) ..................................... PNFUL 111/05
        ENCTR  20/17    ENCTR   26/32     ARABY   32/25     ENCTR   20/17
        DEAD  175/02    DEAD   184/15     DEAD   185/11     PARTS   91/12
        DEAD  222/07                                        DEAD   191/28
HARDWICKE (1) ................................... HOUSE   62/03
HARD-WORKING (1) ................................ DEAD   205/01
HARFORD (4) ..................................... GRACE  159/15
        GRACE 159/20    GRACE  160/04     GRACE  172/24
HARFORD'S (1) ................................... GRACE  160/05
HARM (4) ........................................ HOUSE   65/33
        HOUSE  68/15    LITTL   78/01     GRACE  158/04
HARMONIUM (1) ................................... EVELN   37/12
HARNESS (1) ..................................... ARABY   30/12
HARNESSED (1) ................................... DEAD   207/30
HARP (2) ........................................ ARABY   31/18
        GALNT  54/11
HARPIST (2) ..................................... GALNT   54/07
        GALNT  56/20
HARRY (5) ....................................... EVELN   38/04
        EVELN  38/08    EVELN   38/12     EVELN   39/23     EVELN   39/25
HARSH (1) ....................................... PNFUL  108/20
HARSHER (1) ..................................... PNFUL  116/01
HARSHNESS (1) ................................... PNFUL  108/20
HAS (30) ........................................ SISTR   10/16
        SISTR  11/15    ENCTR   25/30     GALNT   52/24     HOUSE   65/01
        LITTL  74/08    LITTL   75/32     PARTS   89/15     CLAY   103/13
        PNFUL 115/31    IVY D  121/04     IVY D  121/14     IVY D  127/17
        IVY D 129/05    IVY D  131/20     IVY D  135/07     MOTHR  148/27
        GRACE 155/08    GRACE  155/17     GRACE  161/13     GRACE  163/14
        GRACE 171/04    DEAD   181/24     DEAD   194/03     DEAD   198/29
        DEAD  202/15    DEAD   202/33     DEAD   204/31     DEAD   206/11
        DEAD  211/20
HASN'T (4) ...................................... LITTL   75/32
        IVY D 121/19    IVY D  123/19     IVY D  130/01
HASTE (1) .......................................
HASTENED (1) .................................... MOTHR  146/20
HASTILY (4) ..................................... DEAD   205/06
        PARTS  89/25    DEAD   194/33     DEAD   211/14     LITTL   84/22
HAT (38) ........................................ ENCTR   24/24
        GALNT  51/23    GALNT   54/23     GALNT   56/06     LITTL   75/03
        LITTL  75/11    PARTS   90/06     PARTS   95/14     PARTS   97/08
        CLAY  102/32    CLAY   103/10     PNFUL  116/06     IVY D  120/27
        IVY D 121/21    IVY D  122/12     IVY D  125/29     IVY D  130/09
        IVY D 130/28    IVY D  133/34     MOTHR  139/17     GRACE  150/04
        GRACE 151/09    GRACE  152/03     GRACE  154/02     GRACE  155/25
        GRACE 156/09    GRACE  173/02     GRACE  173/05     GRACE  173/18
        DEAD  178/22    DEAD   195/14     DEAD   207/31     DEAD   208/21
        DEAD  209/10    DEAD   210/07     DEAD   216/11     DEAD   216/15
        DEAD  222/30
HAT-BRUSH (1) ................................... ARABY   32/30
HATED (1) ....................................... PARTS   95/27
HATES (1) ....................................... DEAD   180/18
HAT-RACK (1) .................................... PARTS   88/24
HATRED (1) ...................................... LITTL   85/10
HATS (2) ........................................ PARTS   95/08
        GRACE 172/11
```

```
HAUGHTY (1) ....................................... MOTHR 149/05
HAUPTMANN'S (1) ................................... PNFUL 108/04
HAVE (167)
HAVEN'T (10) ...................................... LITTL  76/05
     PARTS  87/08    IVY D 126/31    IVY D 128/03   MOTHR 148/26
     GRACE 163/23    GRACE 164/18    DEAD  189/19   DEAD  189/27
     DEAD  211/22
HAVING (20) ....................................... ENCTR  27/21
     ARABY  29/08    RACE   45/32    GALNT  58/08   HOUSE  65/01
     LITTL  78/31    PARTS  96/09    PARTS  97/06   PARTS  97/30
     CLAY  103/15    PNFUL 112/25    IVY D 127/10   IVY D 129/27
     GRACE 161/34    GRACE 171/29    GRACE 172/10   DEAD  185/22
     DEAD  186/23    DEAD  197/05    DEAD  200/08
HAWK (1) .......................................... GRACE 170/25
HAY-COLOURED (1) .................................. DEAD  177/25
HAZE (1) .......................................... RACE   45/25
HAZEL (2) ......................................... PNFUL 108/29
     PNFUL 113/08
HE (1645)
HEAD (90) ......................................... SISTR   9/07
     SISTR  11/19    SISTR  11/22    SISTR  13/21   SISTR  13/24
     SISTR  14/10    SISTR  14/26    SISTR  15/13   SISTR  16/04
     SISTR  16/16    ENCTR  19/14    ENCTR  22/04   ARABY  32/06
     EVELN  36/02    EVELN  38/14    EVELN  38/34   EVELN  39/33
     RACE   48/30    GALNT  51/21    GALNT  51/22   GALNT  53/13
     GALNT  53/30    GALNT  55/12    GALNT  55/18   GALNT  56/12
     GALNT  57/21    GALNT  59/12    GALNT  60/14   LITTL  72/12
     LITTL  75/04    LITTL  75/09    LITTL  75/10   LITTL  76/07
     LITTL  77/24    LITTL  80/16    LITTL  81/09   LITTL  81/14
     LITTL  81/25    PARTS  87/04    PARTS  87/05   PARTS  87/24
     PARTS  87/32    PARTS  88/02    PARTS  88/27   PARTS  90/20
     PARTS  91/12    PARTS  91/21    PARTS  93/12   PARTS  96/21
     CLAY  103/12    CLAY  104/29    PNFUL 108/18   PNFUL 113/27
     PNFUL 114/18    PNFUL 117/23    IVY D 120/17   IVY D 120/30
     IVY D 123/12    IVY D 128/14    IVY D 132/12   MOTHR 139/18
     MOTHR 140/24    MOTHR 146/25    MOTHR 149/05   GRACE 151/04
     GRACE 151/16    GRACE 152/03    GRACE 155/11   GRACE 159/05
     GRACE 167/27    GRACE 170/21    GRACE 170/24   GRACE 171/27
     GRACE 171/31    DEAD  175/10    DEAD  180/08   DEAD  181/08
     DEAD  187/27    DEAD  192/30    DEAD  193/13   DEAD  193/15
     DEAD  197/05    DEAD  197/08    DEAD  206/20   DEAD  208/21
     DEAD  209/04    DEAD  209/09    DEAD  215/22   DEAD  218/04
     DEAD  218/24
HEADINGS (2) ...................................... DEAD  179/08
     DEAD  192/09
HEADLINE (1) ...................................... PNFUL 108/08
HEADLONG (1) ...................................... HOUSE  61/06
HEADS (3) ......................................... DEAD  179/10
     DEAD  186/23    DEAD  194/23
HEADSTONES (1) .................................... DEAD  223/33
HEALED (1) ........................................ GRACE 156/22
HEALTH (5) ........................................ RACE   48/07
     GALNT  55/32    CLAY  101/15    DEAD  205/10   DEAD  221/05
HEALTHIER (1) ..................................... DEAD  179/29
HEALY (12) ........................................ MOTHR 143/16
     MOTHR 143/22    MOTHR 143/23    MOTHR 144/26   MOTHR 145/03
     MOTHR 146/03    MOTHR 146/21    MOTHR 148/04   MOTHR 148/17
     MOTHR 148/17    MOTHR 149/15    DEAD  195/04
HEAPED (1) ........................................ IVY D 121/02
HEAR (30) ......................................... SISTR  10/12
     SISTR  16/23    EVELN  40/01    RACE   47/33   RACE   47/33
     HOUSE  66/02    HOUSE  68/01    PARTS  87/16   PARTS  87/18
```

PARTS 88/10	PNFUL 117/32	IVY D 123/25	IVY D 133/24
GRACE 165/08	GRACE 165/09	DEAD 182/10	DEAD 193/13
DEAD 195/32	DEAD 198/29	DEAD 199/26	DEAD 201/03
DEAD 202/06	DEAD 203/34	DEAD 203/34	DEAD 206/16
DEAD 209/31	DEAD 213/28	DEAD 214/14	DEAD 215/29
DEAD 217/22			

HEARD (55) .... SISTR 17/30

ENCTR 26/23	ARABY 31/23	ARABY 33/28	ARABY 33/29
ARABY 33/29	ARABY 35/12	ARABY 35/29	EVELN 36/05
EVELN 40/06	EVELN 40/14	GALNT 51/14	GALNT 57/31
GALNT 58/32	HOUSE 66/04	HOUSE 69/01	LITTL 72/05
LITTL 77/13	LITTL 77/23	LITTL 78/10	LITTL 83/03
PARTS 88/09	PARTS 93/21	PARTS 93/22	CLAY 99/17
PNFUL 111/27	PNFUL 116/20	PNFUL 117/25	IVY D 131/08
IVY D 135/28	MOTHR 138/03	MOTHR 140/29	MOTHR 143/22
MOTHR 147/08	GRACE 161/06	GRACE 165/10	GRACE 165/17
GRACE 167/08	DEAD 191/28	DEAD 193/21	DEAD 193/22
DEAD 193/24	DEAD 194/01	DEAD 198/24	DEAD 198/25
DEAD 199/08	DEAD 199/29	DEAD 199/32	DEAD 200/01
DEAD 201/19	DEAD 210/17	DEAD 211/01	DEAD 221/16
DEAD 221/29	DEAD 224/02		

HEARERS (6) .... GRACE 170/07

GRACE 173/30	GRACE 174/10	GRACE 174/15	GRACE 174/23
DEAD 179/10			

HEARING (5) .... ENCTR 20/13

LITTL 85/01	PNFUL 113/31	PNFUL 116/17	DEAD 200/04

HEART (33) .... SISTR 13/23

ENCTR 20/20	ENCTR 25/32	ENCTR 26/08	ENCTR 28/02
ENCTR 28/09	ENCTR 28/11	ARABY 30/28	ARABY 31/14
ARABY 33/02	EVELN 41/04	EVELN 41/06	RACE 44/26
GALNT 58/07	HOUSE 66/03	LITTL 70/06	LITTL 85/10
PARTS 97/07	IVY D 134/16	MOTHR 138/13	GRACE 158/05
DEAD 187/11	DEAD 203/08	DEAD 204/07	DEAD 204/30
DEAD 204/31	DEAD 206/18	DEAD 212/07	DEAD 213/30
DEAD 215/30	DEAD 217/06	DEAD 217/30	DEAD 223/09

HEARTH (1) .... IVY D 120/30

HEARTILY (5) .... GRACE 171/32

DEAD 180/24	DEAD 180/31	DEAD 184/31	DEAD 193/32

HEARTS (4) .... RACE 48/08

DEAD 203/32	DEAD 205/13	DEAD 215/17	

HEART'S (2) .... PNFUL 114/21

IVY D 125/17

HEARTY (1) .... DEAD 203/13

HEAT (1) .... HOUSE 63/27

HEATED (2) .... GALNT 57/21

DEAD 189/33

HEAVEN (1) .... MOTHR 140/28

HEAVIEST (1) .... RACE 48/26

HEAVILY (4) .... GALNT 55/22

PARTS 86/15	PARTS 88/08	PARTS 97/32	

HEAVY (10) .... SISTR 11/21

SISTR 14/31	LITTL 75/04	PARTS 86/14	PARTS 94/05
PARTS 94/31	PNFUL 116/15	DEAD 186/15	DEAD 210/24
DEAD 213/03			

HEAVY-LIDDED (1) .... DEAD 184/30

HECKLING (1) .... DEAD 190/31

HE'D (9) .... SISTR 15/27

SISTR 17/04	HOUSE 68/17	LITTL 77/31	IVY D 119/01
IVY D 119/28	IVY D 122/10	IVY D 128/04	DEAD 207/26

HEED (1) .... LITTL 85/14

HEEDLESS (1) .... GALNT 54/11

HEEDLESSLY (1) .... GALNT 54/09

```
HEELS (6) ................................................  SISTR  14/23
    GALNT  55/16     DEAD  179/13     DEAD  183/32     DEAD  197/33
    DEAD  214/22
HEIGHT (1) ..............................................  ARABY  34/29
HEIGHTENED (1) .........................................  LITTL  81/17
HELD (27) ...............................................  ENCTR  19/05
    ENCTR  24/21     ARABY  32/06     ARABY  34/12     EVELN  40/23
    GALNT  55/24     LITTL  71/21     LITTL  74/18     PARTS  93/03
    PNFUL 108/06     PNFUL 113/22     PNFUL 115/20     MOTHR 139/18
    MOTHR 143/07     MOTHR 144/33     MOTHR 146/32     GRACE 151/08
    GRACE 169/10     GRACE 169/12     GRACE 173/05     DEAD  186/28
    DEAD  193/18     DEAD  200/11     DEAD  210/18     DEAD  215/24
    DEAD  215/26     DEAD  221/33
HELIOTROPE (1) .........................................  DEAD  213/16
HELL (4) ................................................  PARTS  92/15
    PARTS  93/01     PARTS  96/24     IVY D 123/22
HE'LL (6) ...............................................  IVY D 121/05
    IVY D 121/08     IVY D 121/09     IVY D 123/03     GRACE 154/33
    DEAD  180/29
HELLO (2) ...............................................  IVY D 120/20
    IVY D 130/10
HELMET (1) ..............................................  GRACE 152/19
HELP (10) ...............................................  HOUSE  64/05
    LITTL  78/31     LITTL  82/11     CLAY  102/07     IVY D 124/01
    MOTHR 138/28     GRACE 151/25     GRACE 161/32     DEAD  177/22
    DEAD  183/10
HELPED (8) ..............................................  IVY D 128/19
    MOTHR 138/19     GRACE 152/01     GRACE 154/25     GRACE 169/01
    DEAD  175/03     DEAD  208/28     DEAD  209/06
HELPING (2) .............................................  MOTHR 138/29
    DEAD  208/31
HELPINGS (1) ...........................................  DEAD  197/28
HELPLESS (3) ...........................................  EVELN  41/15
    HOUSE  67/29     GRACE 150/02
HELPLESSLY (1) .........................................  HOUSE  66/25
HELPLESSNESS (1) .......................................  GRACE 154/29
HEMS (1) ................................................  CLAY  103/08
HENCHY (53) ............................................  IVY D 122/25
    IVY D 122/27     IVY D 123/07     IVY D 123/12     IVY D 123/13
    IVY D 123/18     IVY D 123/20     IVY D 123/25     IVY D 124/01
    IVY D 124/08     IVY D 124/13     IVY D 124/19     IVY D 124/26
    IVY D 125/06     IVY D 125/10     IVY D 125/22     IVY D 126/01
    IVY D 126/09     IVY D 126/13     IVY D 126/20     IVY D 126/27
    IVY D 127/03     IVY D 127/08     IVY D 127/21     IVY D 127/28
    IVY D 127/34     IVY D 128/07     IVY D 128/24     IVY D 128/27
    IVY D 128/28     IVY D 128/31     IVY D 129/02     IVY D 129/05
    IVY D 129/10     IVY D 129/18     IVY D 129/24     IVY D 129/29
    IVY D 130/10     IVY D 130/18     IVY D 130/23     IVY D 130/31
    IVY D 131/12     IVY D 131/27     IVY D 132/03     IVY D 132/15
    IVY D 132/22     IVY D 133/03     IVY D 133/09     IVY D 133/16
    IVY D 133/19     IVY D 133/24     IVY D 133/32     IVY D 135/31
HENDRICK (3) ...........................................  MOTHR 145/14
    MOTHR 145/17     GRACE 172/31
HENRIETTA (1) ..........................................  LITTL  71/27
HENRY (2) ...............................................  CLAY  102/22
    DEAD  217/20
HER (794)
HERALD (1) .............................................  PNFUL 116/20
HERE (53) ..............................................  SISTR  10/16
    EVELN  40/10     RACE  46/22     GALNT  53/01     GALNT  54/19
    HOUSE  66/05     LITTL  74/28     LITTL  74/31     LITTL  75/18
    LITTL  78/25     LITTL  78/30     LITTL  79/27     LITTL  79/32
```

```
          LITTL   82/20    PARTS   86/04    PARTS   86/17    PARTS   88/34
          PARTS   93/08    PARTS   94/03    CLAY   102/22    CLAY   105/12
          PNFUL  112/08    IVY D  122/03    IVY D  122/25    IVY D  123/32
          IVY D  124/16    IVY D  124/34    IVY D  127/29    IVY D  128/27
          IVY D  130/03    IVY D  131/28    IVY D  132/01    IVY D  132/11
          IVY D  133/10    IVY D  133/10    GRACE  155/20    GRACE  161/20
          GRACE  163/02    GRACE  170/18    GRACE  170/29    GRACE  172/08
          DEAD   177/04    DEAD   177/12    DEAD   182/14    DEAD   182/15
          DEAD   194/02    DEAD   196/15    DEAD   204/04    DEAD   204/11
          DEAD   204/11    DEAD   204/13    DEAD   206/11    DEAD   220/30
HERE'S (11) ...........................................  LITTL   75/26
          CLAY   103/14    IVY D  129/18    IVY D  132/03    IVY D  132/04
          GRACE  166/13    DEAD   177/08    DEAD   178/27    DEAD   181/34
          DEAD   182/21    DEAD   183/34
HERO (1) ..............................................  LITTL   74/28
HEROES (1) ............................................  IVY D  135/08
HERS (5) ..............................................  GALNT   60/04
          HOUSE   67/06    PNFUL  110/26    DEAD   188/28    DEAD   214/03
HERSELF (26) ..........................................  EVELN   38/01
          GALNT   53/15    HOUSE   61/02    HOUSE   65/19    HOUSE   66/31
          HOUSE   68/22    LITTL   82/18    LITTL   83/21    CLAY    99/09
          CLAY   100/17    CLAY   102/14    CLAY   102/22    PNFUL  115/24
          MOTHR  140/12    MOTHR  144/05    DEAD   177/04    DEAD   180/31
          DEAD   186/10    DEAD   192/32    DEAD   194/26    DEAD   200/15
          DEAD   204/30    DEAD   206/13    DEAD   217/24    DEAD   220/25
          DEAD   221/32
HE'S (50) .............................................  SISTR   15/12
          SISTR   16/20    SISTR   16/24    ENCTR   26/24    ENCTR   26/27
          LITTL   75/31    LITTL   75/33    IVY D  123/18    IVY D  124/18
          IVY D  124/22    IVY D  124/22    IVY D  125/03    IVY D  125/12
          IVY D  126/09    IVY D  126/30    IVY D  126/32    IVY D  127/03
          IVY D  128/33    IVY D  128/33    IVY D  129/05    IVY D  129/34
          IVY D  129/34    IVY D  131/18    IVY D  131/18    IVY D  131/19
          IVY D  131/22    IVY D  132/05    IVY D  132/06    IVY D  132/16
          IVY D  132/17    IVY D  132/17    IVY D  132/18    IVY D  132/30
          GRACE  151/01    GRACE  154/34    GRACE  155/19    GRACE  164/32
          GRACE  165/27    DEAD   180/15    DEAD   182/06    DEAD   182/07
          DEAD   182/07    DEAD   182/14    DEAD   185/08    DEAD   191/11
          DEAD   198/33    DEAD   200/04    DEAD   210/13    DEAD   217/02
          DEAD   217/05
HESITATED (4) .........................................  SISTR   14/14
          IVY D  133/33    GRACE  166/05    DEAD   195/28
HICKEY'S (1) ..........................................  DEAD   188/14
HID (4) ...............................................  ENCTR   21/27
          ARABY   30/15    GALNT   60/04    DEAD   218/16
HIDE (2) ..............................................  LITTL   82/32
          IVY D  135/30
HIGGINS (6) ...........................................  PARTS   92/19
          PARTS   92/21    PARTS   92/21    PARTS   93/32    PARTS   94/11
          DEAD   197/13
HIGH (20) .............................................  SISTR   12/15
          SISTR   18/01    ENCTR   23/01    ENCTR   23/12    ENCTR   24/24
          ARABY   33/07    RACE    44/12    RACE    48/10    LITTL   78/22
          CLAY   106/09    IVY D  128/10    IVY D  130/08    IVY D  135/11
          MOTHR  147/15    GRACE  164/23    GRACE  172/13    DEAD   178/15
          DEAD   184/31    DEAD   199/11    DEAD   206/02
HIGH-CLASS (1) ........................................  MOTHR  136/10
HIGHER (2) ............................................  RACE    44/31
          LITTL   80/27
HIGHEST (1) ...........................................  GRACE  154/20
HIGHLY (2) ............................................  DEAD   198/20
          DEAD   208/14
```

HIGH-PITCHED (1)					DEAD	185/30
HILARIOUS (2)					RACE	42/18
RACE 44/03						
HILL (10)					ENCTR	21/33
ENCTR 22/06	EVELN 37/28		EVELN 37/29		EVELN	39/30
RACE 42/03	RACE 42/13		GALNT 49/09		PNFUL	117/09
DEAD 223/32						
HILLS (1)					DEAD	223/29
HILLSIDERS (1)					IVY D	125/05
HIM (493)						
HIMSELF (76)					SISTR	13/07
SISTR 13/15	SISTR 17/33		SISTR 17/34		SISTR	18/07
SISTR 18/08	SISTR 18/14		ARABY 33/29		GALNT	50/21
GALNT 51/21	GALNT 51/34		GALNT 52/20		HOUSE	61/15
HOUSE 67/23	LITTL 71/23		LITTL 72/14		LITTL	73/08
LITTL 77/02	LITTL 80/19		LITTL 80/29		LITTL	81/17
LITTL 83/18	PARTS 89/20		PARTS 92/13		PARTS	92/15
PARTS 92/22	PARTS 93/01		PARTS 97/02		PARTS	97/34
PNFUL 107/08	PNFUL 108/27		PNFUL 109/01		PNFUL	109/14
PNFUL 109/17	PNFUL 109/28		PNFUL 110/33		PNFUL	111/12
PNFUL 111/23	PNFUL 115/32		PNFUL 116/26		IVY D	118/04
IVY D 124/03	IVY D 126/28		IVY D 132/02		IVY D	132/08
MOTHR 137/11	MOTHR 138/29		MOTHR 140/21		MOTHR	142/21
MOTHR 149/29	GRACE 150/15		GRACE 154/33		GRACE	155/22
GRACE 166/22	GRACE 166/24		GRACE 166/25		GRACE	169/30
DEAD 179/15	DEAD 183/08		DEAD 185/28		DEAD	187/01
DEAD 187/19	DEAD 192/11		DEAD 193/32		DEAD	196/07
DEAD 197/08	DEAD 197/29		DEAD 203/16		DEAD	210/04
DEAD 217/15	DEAD 218/19		DEAD 220/01		DEAD	220/22
DEAD 222/14	DEAD 223/04		DEAD 223/13			
HIP (1)					ENCTR	24/21
HIPS (2)					GALNT	51/27
DEAD 215/24						
HIRE (1)					LITTL	83/21
HIS (1160)						
HISSING (1)					IVY D	124/20
HISTORIAN'S (1)					LITTL	78/14
HISTORY (5)					ENCTR	20/14
ENCTR 20/24	GRACE 164/04		GRACE 169/08		DEAD	211/31
HIT (1)					GRACE	153/18
HITCHED (1)					GRACE	172/10
HIVE (1)					MOTHR	147/22
HM (3)					LITTL	83/08
IVY D 126/25	GRACE 159/16					
HO (2)					RACE	47/19
RACE 47/19						
HOARSE (1)					DEAD	211/12
HOARSENESS (1)					DEAD	210/21
HOB (3)					IVY D	130/26
IVY D 130/33	IVY D 133/13					
HOBBLED (1)					MOTHR	146/19
HOBBLING (1)					PNFUL	115/26
HOGAN (3)					LITTL	75/32
LITTL 77/30	LITTL 78/33					
HOGAN'S (1)					GRACE	172/30
HOHE (1)					RACE	47/19
HOISTED (2)					GRACE	153/11
DEAD 208/29						
HOLD (6)					HOUSE	67/24
GRACE 161/11	DEAD 183/07		DEAD 205/11		DEAD	205/12
DEAD 205/13						
HOLDING (7)					EVELN	38/19

```
      GALNT  50/21      GALNT  51/21      LITTL  82/08      MOTHR 143/27
      DEAD  213/06      DEAD  218/04
HOLIDAY (2) ...................................... EVELN  39/16
      LITTL  75/17
HOLIDAYS (1) ..................................... ENCTR  21/08
HOLLAND (1) ...................................... PNFUL 110/11
HOLOHAN (38) ..................................... GALNT  58/27
      MOTHR 136/01      MOTHR 136/05      MOTHR 138/08      MOTHR 138/17
      MOTHR 138/24      MOTHR 138/28      MOTHR 139/21      MOTHR 139/34
      MOTHR 140/01      MOTHR 140/06      MOTHR 140/29      MOTHR 141/01
      MOTHR 141/34      MOTHR 143/23      MOTHR 143/25      MOTHR 144/04
      MOTHR 144/06      MOTHR 144/10      MOTHR 144/13      MOTHR 144/18
      MOTHR 145/13      MOTHR 145/14      MOTHR 145/27      MOTHR 146/06
      MOTHR 146/07      MOTHR 146/09      MOTHR 146/13      MOTHR 146/19
      MOTHR 146/30      MOTHR 147/23      MOTHR 148/21      MOTHR 148/29
      MOTHR 149/01      MOTHR 149/08      MOTHR 149/27      MOTHR 149/28
      MOTHR 149/32
HOLOHAN'S (1) .................................... MOTHR 149/25
HOLY (3) ......................................... GRACE 154/34
      GRACE 158/08      GRACE 170/30
HOMAGE (1) ....................................... RACE   45/17
HOME (54) ........................................ ENCTR  21/06
      ENCTR  23/15      ENCTR  24/10      ENCTR  24/13      ENCTR  25/15
      ARABY  33/03      ARABY  33/04      EVELN  36/05      EVELN  37/05
      EVELN  37/06      EVELN  37/18      EVELN  37/19      EVELN  37/31
      EVELN  38/21      EVELN  38/30      EVELN  39/02      EVELN  40/03
      RACE   43/29      RACE   45/20      GALNT  58/02      GALNT  59/15
      GALNT  59/21      HOUSE  62/19      HOUSE  63/05      LITTL  71/18
      LITTL  82/12      LITTL  82/13      LITTL  82/14      LITTL  82/25
      LITTL  83/01      PARTS  96/32      PARTS  97/12      CLAY  100/22
      CLAY  103/15      PNFUL 112/25      PNFUL 115/07      IVY D 124/02
      MOTHR 140/16      GRACE 152/18      GRACE 155/16      GRACE 155/17
      GRACE 155/23      GRACE 156/17      GRACE 173/02      DEAD  180/12
      DEAD  195/26      DEAD  195/29      DEAD  207/04      DEAD  207/09
      DEAD  212/29      DEAD  215/16      DEAD  221/22      DEAD  221/26
      DEAD  221/27
HOMELY (2) ....................................... MOTHR 138/26
      GRACE 163/03
HOMEWARD (1) ..................................... RACE   42/04
HONEST (5) ....................................... GALNT  53/15
      IVY D 121/18      IVY D 121/25      GRACE 167/33      DEAD  194/02
HONESTY (1) ...................................... PNFUL 109/03
HONEYMOON (1) .................................... DEAD  214/24
HONOUR (11) ...................................... RACE   44/21
      HOUSE  64/26      HOUSE  65/05      HOUSE  67/24      PARTS  95/32
      IVY D 121/34      DEAD  193/24      DEAD  194/17      DEAD  194/20
      DEAD  202/33      DEAD  205/12
HONOURABLE (2) ................................... GRACE 160/29
      DEAD  194/21
HONOURED (1) ..................................... GRACE 164/13
HOODED (1) ....................................... DEAD  215/18
HOOKED (1) ....................................... SISTR  14/22
HOP-BITTERS (1) .................................. DEAD  183/02
HOPE (14) ........................................ SISTR   9/01
      GALNT  58/08      LITTL  73/23      LITTL  79/03      LITTL  79/21
      PARTS  95/23      CLAY  106/07      IVY D 121/05      IVY D 121/09
      MOTHR 149/14      GRACE 153/07      DEAD  200/16      DEAD  203/30
      DEAD  206/16
HOPED (8) ........................................ ARABY  32/21
      ARABY  32/23      PARTS  89/32      CLAY  100/14      CLAY  102/06
      MOTHR 142/10      DEAD  197/21      DEAD  220/20
HOPELESS (1) ..................................... PARTS  89/27
```

```
HOPELESSLY (1) ....................................... DEAD   195/23
HOPES (3) ............................................ HOUSE   68/30
     HOUSE   68/31      IVY D 134/13
HOPING (1) ........................................... DEAD   221/11
HOP-O'-MY-THUMB (1) .................................. IVY D  127/16
HOPPY (1) ............................................ MOTHR  136/05
HORDE (1) ............................................ LITTL   71/28
HORIZON (1) .......................................... LITTL   73/25
HORN (1) ............................................. LITTL   82/23
HORNET'S (1) ......................................... PARTS   92/09
HORNS (1) ............................................ RACE    45/14
HORSE (10) ........................................... ARABY   30/12
     HOUSE   62/21     DEAD  207/09     DEAD  207/22     DEAD   208/08
     DEAD   208/17     DEAD  209/22     DEAD  214/21     DEAD   214/28
     DEAD   222/27
HORSEPLAY (1) ........................................ GRACE  154/30
HORSES (2) ........................................... ENCTR   21/32
     DEAD   199/12
HOSPITABLE (3) ....................................... DEAD   200/27
     DEAD   202/24     DEAD  202/24
HOSPITABLY (1) ....................................... PNFUL  117/11
HOSPITAL (3) ......................................... PNFUL  113/21
     PNFUL  114/16     GRACE 152/02
HOSPITALITY (8) ...................................... HOUSE   64/27
     PARTS   94/27     DEAD  192/09     DEAD  192/23     DEAD   202/27
     DEAD   202/34     DEAD  203/10     DEAD  203/25
HOST (3) ............................................. RACE    46/02
     RACE    46/13     RACE   46/26
HOSTESS (2) .......................................... DEAD   204/30
     DEAD   205/01
HOSTESSES (1) ........................................ DEAD   205/27
HOSTILE (1) .......................................... ARABY   31/01
HOSTS (1) ............................................ DEAD   223/18
HOT (17) ............................................. ENCTR   25/01
     RACE    46/25     GALNT  57/25     LITTL  76/30     PARTS   90/22
     PARTS   93/25     PARTS  93/34     PARTS  94/25     PARTS   95/03
     PARTS   97/05     CLAY  101/05     PNFUL 116/09     DEAD   183/04
     DEAD   183/22     DEAD  197/17     DEAD  197/31     DEAD   213/27
HOTEL (8) ............................................ RACE    45/19
     GALNT   56/07     DEAD  191/27     DEAD  199/14     DEAD   200/31
     DEAD   214/11     DEAD  214/34     DEAD  215/15
HOTELS (1) ........................................... RACE    43/33
HOTLY (1) ............................................ MOTHR  147/32
HOUNDED (1) .......................................... PARTS   92/11
HOUNDS (1) ........................................... IVY D  134/11
HOUR (18) ............................................ ENCTR   22/13
     ARABY   29/02     ARABY  33/12     ARABY  33/20     GALNT   58/23
     LITTL   71/24     LITTL  82/10     LITTL  82/11     PARTS   87/20
     PARTS   87/21     PNFUL 115/07     MOTHR 136/06     MOTHR  139/13
     MOTHR  141/30     DEAD  207/05     DEAD  215/34     DEAD   220/20
     DEAD   222/21
HOURS (8) ............................................ ENCTR   20/31
     GALNT   56/31     HOUSE  62/19     LITTL  84/05     PNFUL  112/06
     GRACE  160/34     DEAD  177/04     DEAD  215/09
HOUR'S (1) ........................................... PARTS   92/14
HOUSE (77) ........................................... SISTR    9/02
     SISTR   10/17     SISTR  11/32     SISTR  14/03     SISTR   16/23
     SISTR   17/05     SISTR  18/10     ENCTR  19/11     ENCTR   21/16
     ENCTR   21/19     ENCTR  24/10     ARABY  29/03     ARABY   29/07
     ARABY   29/15     ARABY  29/19     ARABY  31/22     ARABY   32/33
     ARABY   33/07     ARABY  33/11     EVELN  36/04     EVELN   37/22
     EVELN   38/22     EVELN  38/32     RACE   45/26     GALNT   50/33
```

GALNT	59/33	GALNT	60/10	HOUSE	61/ T	HOUSE	61/11
HOUSE	62/03	HOUSE	62/04	HOUSE	62/07	HOUSE	63/20
HOUSE	63/28	HOUSE	63/34	HOUSE	65/12	HOUSE	66/16
HOUSE	67/14	LITTL	83/20	LITTL	83/24	PARTS	94/15
PARTS	95/01	CLAY	103/15	CLAY	104/20	PNFUL	107/05
PNFUL	109/18	PNFUL	109/20	PNFUL	109/22	PNFUL	110/18
PNFUL	113/14	PNFUL	114/15	PNFUL	115/18	IVY D	127/28
IVY D	128/11	IVY D	131/20	IVY D	133/01	MOTHR	137/12
MOTHR	137/27	MOTHR	140/19	MOTHR	140/28	MOTHR	142/10
MOTHR	143/11	MOTHR	144/30	MOTHR	147/16	MOTHR	148/19
GRACE	154/24	GRACE	154/25	GRACE	155/12	GRACE	155/30
GRACE	156/14	GRACE	157/16	GRACE	166/20	DEAD	176/02
DEAD	176/04	DEAD	187/07	DEAD	190/23	DEAD	221/16

HOUSE-BOOTS (1) .... CLAY 101/27
HOUSED (1) .... ARABY 30/15
HOUSEHOLD (2) .... DEAD 176/08
    DEAD 214/04
HOUSEMAID'S (1) .... DEAD 176/17
HOUSE-ROOM (1) .... HOUSE 61/14
HOUSES (15) .... SISTR 14/05

ARABY	29/05	ARABY	30/03	ARABY	30/08	ARABY	34/18
EVELN	36/07	EVELN	36/10	EVELN	36/10	EVELN	36/11
LITTL	73/13	LITTL	78/20	PARTS	89/08	IVY D	123/26
MOTHR	136/13	DEAD	212/32				

HOUSEWIVES (1) .... GRACE 166/24
HOUSEWORK (1) .... HOUSE 63/05
HOW (76) .... SISTR 10/31

SISTR	13/10	SISTR	13/14	SISTR	14/22	SISTR	14/23
ENCTR	22/32	ENCTR	25/23	ENCTR	25/26	ENCTR	26/03
ENCTR	26/04	ENCTR	27/27	ENCTR	28/09	ARABY	31/17
EVELN	38/30	RACE	44/31	RACE	45/08	RACE	48/21
GALNT	50/25	GALNT	53/24	GALNT	56/31	GALNT	57/15
GALNT	58/03	LITTL	71/14	LITTL	74/32	LITTL	74/33
LITTL	78/21	LITTL	82/27	LITTL	83/16	LITTL	84/02
PARTS	87/21	PARTS	89/27	PARTS	90/16	CLAY	101/30
CLAY	102/04	CLAY	103/01	CLAY	103/12	CLAY	103/32
CLAY	104/10	CLAY	104/16	PNFUL	116/29	PNFUL	116/30
IVY D	120/29	IVY D	123/01	IVY D	123/15	IVY D	123/33
IVY D	124/23	IVY D	126/33	IVY D	128/02	IVY D	130/21
MOTHR	140/14	MOTHR	148/07	GRACE	152/25	GRACE	153/20
GRACE	156/05	GRACE	160/15	GRACE	161/01	GRACE	169/09
DEAD	188/16	DEAD	188/30	DEAD	192/03	DEAD	192/03
DEAD	192/07	DEAD	195/26	DEAD	199/08	DEAD	199/09
DEAD	199/11	DEAD	200/26	DEAD	200/26	DEAD	200/27
DEAD	209/11	DEAD	217/08	DEAD	219/22	DEAD	220/13
DEAD	222/08	DEAD	222/32	DEAD	223/08		

HOW-DO-YOU-DO (1) .... IVY D 123/33.
HOWEVER (14) .... ENCTR 19/07

ENCTR	25/19	EVELN	36/14	RACE	42/07	RACE	43/12
RACE	47/31	LITTL	72/15	PNFUL	110/15	MOTHR	137/01
MOTHR	140/14	MOTHR	147/16	MOTHR	147/30	GRACE	158/02
DEAD	202/19						

HOW'S (2) .... IVY D 122/01
    IVY D 128/09
HOWTH (2) .... EVELN 39/30
    MOTHR 137/24
HUBBY (1) .... GRACE 162/08
HUCKSTER'S (1) .... ENCTR 24/04
HUDDLED (2) .... LITTL 73/14
    GRACE 153/19
HUE (2) .... GALNT 49/07
    PARTS 91/29

```
HUGE (7) ........................................... SISTR   13/25
        RACE    43/02    CLAY   101/04    CLAY   101/06    PNFUL  116/13
        DEAD   196/34    DEAD   200/08
HUM (1) ............................................ RACE    44/06
HUMAN (7) .......................................... RACE    45/11
        LITTL   78/32    PNFUL  117/13    PNFUL  117/15    IVY D  135/10
        GRACE  157/20    GRACE  174/02
HUMANITY (3) ....................................... RACE    46/27
        DEAD   192/23    DEAD   203/25
HUMBLE (2) ......................................... MOTHR  142/20
        DEAD   220/09
HUMBLY (1) ......................................... ARABY   35/17
HUME (2) ........................................... GALNT   54/22
        GALNT   55/21
HUMILIATED (2) ..................................... PARTS   96/33
        DEAD   219/29
HUMILIATION (1) .................................... PARTS   96/09
HUMMING (2) ........................................ RACE    44/12
        MOTHR  146/26
HUMOUR (12) ........................................ ARABY   32/33
        RACE    43/03    RACE    43/06    RACE    43/08    RACE    43/09
        GALNT   50/12    LITTL   82/15    MOTHR  143/01    DEAD   189/25
        DEAD   192/23    DEAD   196/08    DEAD   203/25
HUMPED (1) ......................................... DEAD   208/22
HUNDRED (1) ........................................ MOTHR  137/18
HUNDREDS (1) ....................................... LITTL   81/29
HUNG (6) ........................................... ARABY   29/09
        EVELN   37/12    RACE    45/24    PNFUL  107/15    IVY D  120/27
        DEAD   186/17
HUNGARIAN (5) ...................................... RACE    43/02
        RACE    44/04    RACE    46/02    RACE    46/19    RACE    48/31
HUNGARY (1) ........................................ RACE    47/32
HUNGER (1) ......................................... ENCTR   21/01
HUNGRY (4) ......................................... GALNT   57/10
        DEAD   195/06    DEAD   195/06    DEAD   195/16
HUNKER-SLIDING (1) ................................. IVY D  121/25
HUNT (1) ........................................... EVELN   36/15
HURRIED (5) ........................................ ENCTR   21/29
        GALNT   60/08    LITTL   72/14    GRACE  156/04    DEAD   193/17
HURRIEDLY (1) ...................................... DEAD   182/04
HURRY (4) .......................................... LITTL   75/12
        LITTL   82/03    PARTS   90/17    MOTHR  141/01
HURRYING (1) ....................................... GALNT   59/02
HURT (1) ........................................... GRACE  153/21
HUSBAND (22) ....................................... PARTS   97/17
        CLAY   104/27    PNFUL  110/07    PNFUL  110/10    PNFUL  110/22
        PNFUL  114/31    MOTHR  141/20    MOTHR  141/23    MOTHR  141/29
        MOTHR  141/33    MOTHR  143/13    MOTHR  145/28    MOTHR  148/04
        MOTHR  149/13    MOTHR  149/21    GRACE  156/01    GRACE  156/14
        GRACE  162/02    GRACE  162/07    DEAD   180/22    DEAD   191/20
        DEAD   222/08
HUSBANDS (1) ....................................... GRACE  156/23
HUSBAND'S (3) ...................................... PNFUL  110/09
        GRACE  155/31    GRACE  157/30
HUSH (2) ........................................... LITTL   84/08
        MOTHR  146/07
HUSHED (3) ......................................... LITTL   83/31
        LITTL   84/08    DEAD   186/03
HUSKY (1) .......................................... IVY D  119/02
HYNES (23) ......................................... IVY D  120/23
        IVY D  120/24    IVY D  121/03    IVY D  121/07    IVY D  121/11
        IVY D  121/15    IVY D  121/22    IVY D  121/30    IVY D  122/07
```

IVY D 122/12	IVY D 122/28	IVY D 123/16	IVY D 124/03
IVY D 124/27	IVY D 125/02	IVY D 125/11	IVY D 133/07
IVY D 133/08	IVY D 133/17	IVY D 133/27	IVY D 133/33
IVY D 135/21	IVY D 135/26		

HYNES' (1) .... IVY D 135/26
HYPEREDUCATED (2) .... DEAD 192/24
   DEAD 203/24
HYPOCRITES (1) .... IVY D 134/10

I (670)
I' (2) .... GRACE 152/28
   GRACE 153/07
ICE (1) .... LITTL 79/33
ICING (1) .... CLAY 102/21
I'D (13) .... SISTR 16/32
   SISTR 16/33   LITTL 79/04   PARTS 87/22   IVY D 120/01
   IVY D 120/02 IVY D 130/18 GRACE 155/10 DEAD 191/16
   DEAD 195/03   DEAD 198/28   DEAD 199/26   DEAD 207/06
IDEA (12) .... SISTR 10/33
   GALNT 59/14   LITTL 70/12   LITTL 73/19   LITTL 73/21
   GRACE 157/05 GRACE 163/16 GRACE 167/06 DEAD 192/19
   DEAD 197/18   DEAD 201/14   DEAD 216/08
IDEALISING (1) .... DEAD 220/04
IDEALS (1) .... IVY D 132/24
IDEAS (4) .... PNFUL 110/27
   MOTHR 137/09 DEAD 203/19 DEAD 203/20
IDENTITY (1) .... DEAD 223/20
IDIOT (1) .... GRACE 159/33
IDLE (5) .... SISTR 9/08
   SISTR 18/12   ARABY 32/24   IVY D 131/31 MOTHR 139/09
IDLENESS (1) .... MOTHR 139/12
IDLER (1) .... ENCTR 19/05
IDLY (1) .... GALNT 56/22
IDOL (1) .... IVY D 134/25
IF (138)
IGNATIUS (38) .... LITTL 72/21
   LITTL 72/25   LITTL 72/31   LITTL 73/02   LITTL 73/05
   LITTL 74/25   LITTL 75/03   LITTL 75/10   LITTL 75/21
   LITTL 75/26   LITTL 75/29   LITTL 76/04   LITTL 76/11
   LITTL 76/18   LITTL 76/20   LITTL 76/28   LITTL 77/09
   LITTL 77/18   LITTL 77/24   LITTL 77/29   LITTL 78/05
   LITTL 78/08   LITTL 78/13   LITTL 78/25   LITTL 78/29
   LITTL 79/04   LITTL 79/12   LITTL 79/17   LITTL 79/24
   LITTL 79/31   LITTL 80/02   LITTL 80/06   LITTL 80/10
   LITTL 81/03   LITTL 81/04   LITTL 81/11   LITTL 81/19
   LITTL 81/26
IGNOMINY (1) .... PNFUL 117/17
IGNORANCE (1) .... HOUSE 64/29
IGNORANT (3) .... GRACE 160/32
   GRACE 164/10 DEAD 192/27
IGNORED (1) .... DEAD 183/27
ILL (6) .... PNFUL 116/25
   MOTHR 141/31 MOTHR 142/23 DEAD 196/08 DEAD 216/26
   DEAD 220/30
I'LL (34) .... SISTR 10/02
   ENCTR 26/29   GALNT 53/32   GALNT 55/01   GALNT 55/01
   LITTL 78/08   PARTS 87/15   PARTS 91/32   PARTS 98/06
   PARTS 98/10   PARTS 98/22   PARTS 98/22   PARTS 98/23
   PARTS 98/24   IVY D 119/07 IVY D 127/32 IVY D 132/09
   IVY D 133/11 IVY D 133/20 MOTHR 145/13 GRACE 152/18
   GRACE 155/13 GRACE 155/19 GRACE 163/31 GRACE 170/12

```
        GRACE  171/07     GRACE  171/24     GRACE  171/24     DEAD   177/03
        DEAD   177/12     DEAD   184/10     DEAD   191/01     DEAD   195/29
        DEAD   210/28
ILL-FEELING (1) .....................................  DEAD   192/15
ILLITERATE (1) ......................................  GRACE  159/32
ILLNESS (2) .........................................  EVELN   40/05
        DEAD   187/07
ILLUMINATED (1) .....................................  DEAD   210/22
ILLUMINED (3) .......................................  EVELN   40/28
        GALNT   49/04     DEAD   213/33
ILLUSIONS (1) .......................................  GRACE  157/29
ILLUSTRATED (1) .....................................  GRACE  161/11
ILMA (1) ............................................  DEAD   199/05
I'M (54) ............................................  SISTR   11/02
        SISTR   16/19     ENCTR   20/27     ARABY   33/26     GALNT   51/12
        GALNT   53/25     GALNT   54/31     HOUSE   62/28     LITTL   74/29
        LITTL   74/30     LITTL   75/15     LITTL   79/24     LITTL   79/27
        LITTL   79/27     LITTL   81/07     LITTL   82/03     PARTS   92/02
        PARTS   98/04     IVY D  120/01     IVY D  123/03     IVY D  124/07
        IVY D  124/28     IVY D  125/13     IVY D  126/07     IVY D  127/07
        IVY D  127/24     MOTHR 143/22     MOTHR 148/29     MOTHR 148/34
        MOTHR 149/06     MOTHR 149/26     MOTHR 149/27     GRACE  155/12
        GRACE  158/14     GRACE  159/08     GRACE  164/18     GRACE  171/07
        DEAD   178/03     DEAD   181/24     DEAD   182/07     DEAD   182/08
        DEAD   182/24     DEAD   183/15     DEAD   183/19     DEAD   185/19
        DEAD   188/03     DEAD   189/30     DEAD   191/10     DEAD   194/34
        DEAD   195/33     DEAD   200/16     DEAD   200/17     DEAD   211/12
        DEAD   212/14
IMAGE (6) ...........................................  ARABY   31/01
        ARABY   32/16     RACE    46/11     MOTHR 149/19     GRACE  170/06
        DEAD   223/10
IMAGES (1) ..........................................  PNFUL  116/23
IMAGINARY (1) .......................................  GRACE  160/23
IMAGINATION (5) .....................................  ARABY   33/13
        RACE    46/09     GALNT   57/29     HOUSE   66/04     PARTS   91/04
IMAGINE (1) .........................................  HOUSE   66/17
IMAGINED (4) ........................................  SISTR   11/21
        ENCTR   23/13     ARABY   31/10     DEAD   223/15
IMBECILE (1) ........................................  SISTR   11/17
IMITATED (2) ........................................  LITTL   82/05
        PARTS   94/03
IMITATION (1) .......................................  DEAD   208/18
IMMEDIATELY (1) .....................................  GRACE  172/27
IMMENSE (3) .........................................  RACE    46/15
        PARTS   95/13     GRACE  151/11
IMMENSELY (1) .......................................  DEAD   188/31
IMMERSIONS (1) ......................................  GRACE  157/22
IMMINENT (1) ........................................  IVY D  120/27
IMMOBILE (1) ........................................  GRACE  151/15
IMMOBILITY (1) ......................................  ENCTR   23/03
IMMORAL (3) .........................................  LITTL   77/16
        LITTL   77/19     LITTL   77/27
IMMORALITY (2) ......................................  LITTL   78/10
        LITTL   78/12
IMPALPABLE (2) ......................................  DEAD   220/20
        DEAD   223/20
IMPATIENT (1) .......................................  RACE    45/15
IMPATIENTLY (1) .....................................  DEAD   185/22
IMPERFECTIONS (1) ...................................  SISTR   13/10
IMPERSONAL (1) ......................................  PNFUL  111/27
IMPERTINENCE (2) ....................................  PARTS   92/01
        PARTS   92/09
```

ENCTR 19/13   ENCTR 22/21
INDIANS (1) .... ENCTR 20/05
INDICATE (1) .... PARTS 88/23
INDICATED (1) .... IVY D 125/31
INDIFFERENT (2) .... IVY D 131/24
    DEAD 220/09
INDIGNANT (3) .... GRACE 160/27
    GRACE 161/19   DEAD 208/15
INDIGNANTLY (1) .... ENCTR 27/06
INDIGNITIES (1) .... PARTS 90/31
INDISTINCT (3) .... ARABY 33/10
    EVELN 39/23   DEAD 201/20
INDITE (1) .... GRACE 151/20
INDUCED (1) .... PNFUL 115/06
INDULGENT (1) .... IVY D 126/06
INDUSTRIES (1) .... IVY D 131/32
INDUSTRY (2) .... RACE   42/06
    HOUSE 66/06
INEFFICACIOUS (1) .... SISTR 12/25
INEFFICIENT (1) .... PNFUL 110/34
INELEGANCE (1) .... LITTL 73/09
INEXPERIENCE (1) .... HOUSE 64/31
INEXPLICABLE (1) .... GRACE 154/22
INFALLIBILITY (3) .... GRACE 168/33
    GRACE 169/07   GRACE 169/31
INFALLIBLE (1) .... GRACE 168/31
INFANT (1) .... LITTL 73/23
INFERENCE (1) .... GRACE 167/21
INFERIOR (1) .... LITTL 80/24
INFLAMED (1) .... PARTS 88/31
INFLECTION (1) .... DEAD 204/02
INFLUENCE (7) .... ENCTR 20/02
    ENCTR 20/34   PNFUL 112/02   IVY D 119/13   GRACE 163/31
    GRACE 167/02   DEAD 176/29
INFLUENCES (2) .... ENCTR 23/16
    RACE   46/23
INFLUENTIAL (1) .... GRACE 157/19
INFLUX (1) .... IVY D 131/29
INFORMAL (1) .... MOTHR 140/21
INFORMATION (1) .... GRACE 159/18
INFORMED (1) .... GRACE 157/23
INGENUOUSLY (1) .... RACE . 46/17
INGRATIATE (1) .... GRACE 166/24
INHALING (1) .... EVELN 39/33
INHERITED (1) .... GALNT 51/19
INHERITOR (1) .... RACE   44/26
INIQUITY (1) .... GRACE 173/24
INITIALS (1) .... DEAD 193/12
INJURED (7) .... PNFUL 114/18
    GRACE 151/10   GRACE 151/23   GRACE 151/25   GRACE 151/34
    GRACE 152/28   GRACE 153/05
INJURIES (2) .... PNFUL 113/27
    PNFUL 114/18
INK (2) .... PARTS 88/14
    PNFUL 108/06
INNER (3) .... ENCTR 22/09
    GALNT 51/31   PARTS 88/28
INNOCENCE (1) .... HOUSE 64/16
INNOCENT (2) .... ENCTR 20/21
    DEAD 187/33
INNOCENT-LOOKING (1) .... RACE   43/14
INNS (2) .... LITTL 71/01

```
          LITTL   71/26
INNUMERABLE (1) ................................... ARABY   32/13
INORDINATE (1) .................................... PNFUL  111/05
INQUEST (1) ....................................... PNFUL  113/22
INQUIRED (1) ...................................... GRACE  156/29
INQUIRINGLY (1) ................................... PARTS   88/21
INQUIRY (1) ....................................... GRACE  158/24
INSCRIBED (1) ..................................... PNFUL  108/07
INSCRIPTION (1) ................................... PARTS   86/16
INSCRIPTIONS (1) .................................. GALNT   57/05
INSECT (1) ........................................ GALNT   53/31
INSENSITIVE (1) ................................... GALNT   50/24
INSERT (1) ........................................ LITTL   74/11
INSIDE (2) ........................................ GALNT   54/29
          DEAD   213/21
INSISTED (2) ...................................... CLAY   104/21
          CLAY   105/05
INSISTENCE (2) .................................... EVELN   40/15
          LITTL   77/28
INSISTENT (1) ..................................... GALNT   53/31
INSISTING (1) ..................................... PNFUL  111/28
INSPECT (1) ....................................... GRACE  152/34
INSPECTOR (1) ..................................... GALNT   51/19
INSTANCE (1) ...................................... LITTL   77/20
INSTANT (5) ....................................... LITTL   84/20
          PNFUL  109/33     MOTHR  149/18     GRACE  151/07    DEAD   217/23
INSTANTER (1) ..................................... PARTS   92/01
INSTEAD (5) ....................................... ENCTR   20/24
          ENCTR   22/18     PARTS   90/27     IVY D  123/20    DEAD   189/16
INSTEP (1) ........................................ HOUSE   67/08
INSTINCT (5) ...................................... HOUSE   66/22
          HOUSE   67/23     PNFUL  108/23     MOTHR  145/22    DEAD   183/24
INSTINCTIVELY (2) ................................. HOUSE   64/18
          DEAD   220/05
INSTINCTS (1) ..................................... RACE    44/26
INSTITUTION (2) ................................... IVY D  127/01
          DEAD   201/01
INSTITUTIONS (2) .................................. SISTR   13/11
          ARABY   29/18
INSTRUMENT (1) .................................... GALNT   59/29
INSTRUMENTS (1) ................................... RACE    46/17
INSULT (1) ........................................ IVY D  132/10
INSUPERABLE (1) ................................... GRACE  156/12
INSURANCE (1) ..................................... SISTR   16/14
INTELLECTUAL (2) .................................. PNFUL  110/27
          GRACE  167/08
INTELLIGENCE (1) .................................. RACE    44/31
INTELLIGENT (2) ................................... PNFUL  109/29
          GRACE  157/19
INTEMPERANCE (1) .................................. GRACE  156/21
INTEMPERATE (1) ................................... PNFUL  115/02
INTEND (1) ........................................ MOTHR  144/21
INTENDED (3) ...................................... IVY D  122/23
          MOTHR  145/01     DEAD   218/26
INTENTION (6) ..................................... ENCTR   20/11
          EVELN   38/18     HOUSE   63/06     HOUSE   64/17    GRACE  159/19
          GRACE  167/27
INTENTLY (1) ...................................... PARTS   90/14
INTERCOURSE (3) ................................... PNFUL  112/06
          PNFUL  112/20     PNFUL  112/22
INTEREST (4) ...................................... ARABY   35/26
          PNFUL  110/21     PNFUL  111/04     GRACE  159/27
```

```
INTERESTED (4) ..........................................  SISTR   10/19
    GRACE 158/27     GRACE 167/04     DEAD  219/08
INTERESTING (1) ...................................  SISTR   10/05
INTERLUDE (1) .....................................  GRACE  169/05
INTERPRET (2) .....................................  ARABY   33/30
    GRACE 173/28
INTERPRETATION (2) ................................  GALNT   52/21
    PNFUL 111/33
INTERPRETED (1) ...................................  PNFUL  115/33
INTERROGATION (1) .................................  DEAD   220/08
INTERROGATIVELY (1) ...............................  SISTR   14/09
INTERRUPTED (2) ...................................  GRACE  169/01
    DEAD  208/19
INTERRUPTION (1) ..................................  DEAD   191/22
INTERSECTED (1) ...................................  GRACE  154/18
INTERVAL (5) ......................................  ENCTR   27/04
    MOTHR 147/01     MOTHR 147/21     MOTHR 147/33    GRACE  173/16
INTERVALS (3) .....................................  PNFUL  116/13
    MOTHR 137/06     MOTHR 146/11
INTERVENE (1) .....................................  HOUSE   63/21
INTERVENED (3) ....................................  HOUSE   63/23
    GRACE 171/09     DEAD  194/29
INTERVENING (2) ...................................  ARABY   32/15
    GRACE 163/23
INTERVIEW (3) .....................................  HOUSE   64/08
    PNFUL 112/02     PNFUL 112/18
INTIMACY (1) ......................................  GRACE  156/01
INTIMATE (2) ......................................  PARTS   89/18
    PNFUL 110/06
INTIMATION (1) ....................................  GALNT   59/27
INTO (146)
INTOLERABLE (1) ...................................  ARABY   34/16
INTONATION (1) ....................................  MOTHR  147/12
INTRICATE (2) .....................................  SISTR   13/19
    HOUSE  68/31
INTRIGUES (1) .....................................  GALNT   58/01
INTRODUCE (1) .....................................  PARTS   94/28
INTRODUCED (3) ....................................  ENCTR   19/01
    PARTS  94/19     MOTHR 139/14
INTRODUCING (2) ...................................  DEAD   193/29
    DEAD  199/11
INTRODUCTION (1) ..................................  GALNT   54/30
INTRUDE (1) .......................................  DEAD   204/11
INTRUDING (1) .....................................  DEAD   222/01
INUNDATED (1) .....................................  MOTHR  148/32
INVADE (2) ........................................  EVELN   36/01
    DEAD  189/26
INVALID (5) .......................................  GRACE  158/14
    GRACE 159/08     GRACE 163/13     GRACE 164/30    GRACE  165/09
INVARIABLE (1) ....................................  EVELN   38/09
INVARIABLY (1) ....................................  MOTHR  138/25
INVENT (2) ........................................  GALNT   56/29
    LITTL  74/06
INVENTED (1) ......................................  HOUSE   65/13
INVENTION (1) .....................................  GRACE  168/05
INVESTMENT (2) ....................................  RACE    44/34
    RACE   45/05
INVIDIOUS (1) .....................................  DEAD   204/28
INVISIBLE (1) .....................................  DEAD   193/09
INVITATION (4) ....................................  LITTL   70/09
    LITTL  80/31     PNFUL 109/24     IVY D 135/28
INVITED (7) .......................................  SISTR   15/03
```

GALNT 56/28	MOTHR 148/19	DEAD 183/03	DEAD 198/09
DEAD 201/24	DEAD 208/33		

INVOLUNTARILY (1) .... ENCTR 27/16
I.O.U.'S (1) .... RACE 48/13
IRELAND (8) .... RACE 47/31

LITTL 77/13	LITTL 80/32	PARTS 86/02	PARTS 92/19
DEAD 191/13	DEAD 211/24	DEAD 223/28	

IRIS (1) .... PNFUL 109/33
IRISH (25) .... SISTR 13/02

RACE 45/02	LITTL 77/12	PARTS 94/22	PARTS 94/27
PNFUL 110/33	IVY D 132/09	IVY D 132/18	IVY D 134/16
MOTHR 137/25	MOTHR 137/27	MOTHR 137/28	MOTHR 137/29
MOTHR 138/02	MOTHR 147/17	GRACE 154/17	GRACE 158/22
GRACE 159/32	GRACE 164/13	DEAD 187/23	DEAD 189/20
DEAD 189/21	DEAD 192/09	DEAD 203/10	DEAD 210/19

IRISH-LOOKING (1) .... LITTL 74/10
IRISHTOWN (1) .... SISTR 17/05
IRKSOME (1) .... GRACE 156/10
IRON (6) .... ENCTR 22/29

EVELN 41/08	EVELN 41/11	HOUSE 68/27	PNFUL 107/09
PNFUL 107/09			

IRONICAL (1) .... PNFUL 108/08
IRONICALLY (2) .... DEAD 219/03

DEAD 219/27

IRONING (1) .... GRACE 161/34
IRONS (2) .... CLAY 100/02

PNFUL 107/11

IRONY (1) .... DEAD 219/29
IRREGULAR (1) .... DEAD 192/31
IRREGULARLY (1) .... PNFUL 113/12
IRRESOLUTELY (1) .... DEAD 221/33
IRRITABLE (1) .... GRACE 156/31
IRRITATE (1) .... ARABY 33/05
IRRITATED (3) .... LITTL 83/13

MOTHR 140/14	DEAD 186/14

IS (177)
ISLAND (2) .... DEAD 176/04

DEAD 221/16

ISLE (3) .... HOUSE 62/05

LITTL 76/10	LITTL 76/12

ISLES (1) .... DEAD 188/33
ISN'T (19) .... LITTL 78/31

LITTL 80/01	IVY D 121/14	IVY D 121/22	IVY D 131/17
IVY D 131/21	IVY D 132/11	IVY D 135/32	MOTHR 144/15
GRACE 165/27	GRACE 168/10	GRACE 168/28	DEAD 178/27
DEAD 181/04	DEAD 185/12	DEAD 189/04	DEAD 194/17
DEAD 210/13	DEAD 219/26		

ISOLATION (1) .... PNFUL 111/20
ISSUE (1) .... MOTHR 141/08
ISSUING (1) .... PNFUL 113/12
IT (581)
ITALIAN (3) .... GRACE 169/24

DEAD 199/04	DEAD 199/10

ITALIANS (1) .... EVELN 40/10
ITALY (1) .... EVELN 40/07
ITEM (3) .... MOTHR 145/31

MOTHR 147/05	MOTHR 147/10

ITEMS (3) .... MOTHR 138/18

MOTHR 138/23	MOTHR 140/09

IT'LL (2) .... IVY D 123/06

IVY D 124/06

ITS (42) .... SISTR 9/15

ENCTR	20/02	ENCTR	27/10	ARABY	29/04	ARABY	29/14
ARABY	33/05	ARABY	34/29	EVELN	37/06	EVELN	40/11
RACE	42/05	RACE	44/03	RACE	45/24	GALNT	52/09
HOUSE	62/06	LITTL	82/22	LITTL	84/09	LITTL	84/23
LITTL	85/01	PARTS	87/26	CLAY	101/33	PNFUL	111/02
PNFUL	111/02	PNFUL	111/13	PNFUL	111/14	IVY D	120/34
GRACE	154/01	GRACE	157/06	GRACE	159/23	GRACE	166/17
GRACE	173/12	GRACE	173/17	GRACE	173/18	DEAD	179/31
DEAD	192/22	DEAD	196/19	DEAD	196/20	DEAD	202/34
DEAD	203/20	DEAD	214/18	DEAD	220/22	DEAD	222/20
DEAD	222/20						

IT'S (63) .... SISTR 10/09

SISTR	10/32	SISTR	11/11	SISTR	11/13	SISTR	16/25
SISTR	16/25	ARABY	32/11	RACE	47/04	GALNT	52/33
GALNT	53/27	LITTL	76/21	LITTL	76/22	LITTL	77/29
LITTL	78/10	LITTL	78/29	LITTL	78/30	LITTL	79/03
LITTL	79/33	LITTL	85/03	LITTL	85/03	LITTL	85/12
PARTS	88/22	PNFUL	109/22	IVY D	119/27	IVY D	120/15
IVY D	121/31	IVY D	123/12	IVY D	129/04	IVY D	131/33
MOTHR	144/16	MOTHR	144/17	MOTHR	149/06	GRACE	152/18
GRACE	155/23	GRACE	158/28	GRACE	161/24	GRACE	161/28
GRACE	162/27	GRACE	162/27	GRACE	162/30	GRACE	163/33
GRACE	164/10	GRACE	164/26	GRACE	164/27	GRACE	165/03
GRACE	165/03	DEAD	178/26	DEAD	180/27	DEAD	181/11
DEAD	182/13	DEAD	183/10	DEAD	184/22	DEAD	189/17
DEAD	194/21	DEAD	194/25	DEAD	194/25	DEAD	195/27
DEAD	210/27	DEAD	211/04	DEAD	211/19	DEAD	212/10
DEAD	212/14	DEAD	217/04				

ITSELF (13) .... ENCTR 20/01

ARABY	31/14	LITTL	80/14	LITTL	83/11	PARTS	87/05
CLAY	101/19	PNFUL	109/34	IVY D	127/06	IVY D	131/01
GRACE	151/03	DEAD	178/17	DEAD	195/19	DEAD	223/21

I'VE (14) .... LITTL 76/10

LITTL	76/15	LITTL	76/28	LITTL	76/29	LITTL	77/23
LITTL	78/10	LITTL	78/11	LITTL	79/32	LITTL	81/27
IVY D	120/08	IVY D	123/21	GRACE	155/12	DEAD	181/16
DEAD	184/09						

IVORS (26) .... DEAD 187/20

DEAD	187/29	DEAD	188/03	DEAD	188/24	DEAD	189/06
DEAD	189/09	DEAD	189/12	DEAD	189/16	DEAD	189/20
DEAD	189/28	DEAD	189/32	DEAD	190/01	DEAD	190/03
DEAD	190/26	DEAD	191/08	DEAD	192/13	DEAD	192/26
DEAD	195/13	DEAD	195/14	DEAD	195/21	DEAD	195/24
DEAD	195/29	DEAD	195/31	DEAD	196/03	DEAD	203/14
DEAD	219/17						

IVORY (1) .... MOTHR 136/14
IVY (4) .... IVY D 118/ T

IVY D	119/24	IVY D	122/14	DEAD	213/18

IX. (1) .... GRACE 167/18

J. (2) .... IVY D 119/12

DEAD	179/34

JACK (20) .... SISTR 10/34

ENCTR	19/02	ARABY	34/08	HOUSE	62/16	HOUSE	68/04
HOUSE	68/09	HOUSE	68/15	IVY D	118/01	IVY D	119/19
IVY D	121/11	IVY D	122/27	IVY D	123/09	IVY D	127/29
IVY D	129/02	IVY D	130/20	IVY D	133/09	GRACE	160/19
GRACE	162/14	GRACE	163/01	GRACE	166/34		

JACKET (2) .... GALNT 55/28

PNFUL	110/02

JACKET-COAT (1) .... IVY D 120/28

```
JACK'S (1) ......................................... HOUSE    68/13
JADED (1) .......................................... ENCTR    24/14
JAM (2) ............................................ DEAD    196/24
     DEAD   200/13
JAMES (8) .......................................... SISTR    12/07
     SISTR   16/01     SISTR   16/22     SISTR   16/28     SISTR    17/11
     SISTR   17/29     PNFUL  107/01     PNFUL  113/29
JAMES'S (1) ........................................ SISTR    16/14
JANE (49) .......................................... DEAD    176/03
     DEAD    176/07    DEAD    183/33    DEAD    183/34    DEAD    184/03
     DEAD    184/05    DEAD    184/14    DEAD    186/01    DEAD    186/06
     DEAD    186/10    DEAD    187/08    DEAD    187/13    DEAD    192/32
     DEAD    194/18    DEAD    194/20    DEAD    194/25    DEAD    194/28
     DEAD    195/05    DEAD    195/10    DEAD    195/13    DEAD    195/19
     DEAD    195/22    DEAD    196/05    DEAD    197/21    DEAD    197/31
     DEAD    198/34    DEAD    199/26    DEAD    200/12    DEAD    200/34
     DEAD    201/16    DEAD    202/30    DEAD    204/22    DEAD    206/07
     DEAD    206/09    DEAD    206/15    DEAD    206/30    DEAD    207/01
     DEAD    207/11    DEAD    208/20    DEAD    209/06    DEAD    210/12
     DEAD    210/13    DEAD    210/27    DEAD    210/30    DEAD    210/31
     DEAD    211/04    DEAD    211/22    DEAD    212/14    DEAD    212/16
JANE'S (4) ......................................... DEAD    175/17
     DEAD    176/28    DEAD    183/25    DEAD    197/18
JARS (1) ........................................... ARABY    35/17
JAUNTILY (2) ....................................... GALNT    50/04
     PARTS    90/08
JAWS (1) ........................................... HOUSE    65/26
JEALOUS (1) ........................................ MOTHR   142/34
JEALOUSLY (1) ...................................... DEAD    202/34
JEALOUSY (1) ....................................... MOTHR   143/01
JELLY (2) .......................................... DEAD    196/23
     DEAD   200/13
JERKS (1) .......................................... DEAD    183/13
JERRY (1) .......................................... ENCTR    24/24
JEST (2) ........................................... ENCTR    20/04
     DEAD   183/04
JESUIT (4) ......................................... GRACE   163/30
     GRACE  163/34     GRACE  164/01     GRACE  172/02
JESUITS (5) ........................................ GRACE   163/22
     GRACE  163/23     GRACE  163/27     GRACE  163/32     GRACE   164/07
JESUS (3) .......................................... GRACE   173/30
     GRACE  174/01     GRACE  174/18
JETS (1) ........................................... GALNT    49/17
JEW (2) ............................................ ENCTR    23/18
     GRACE  159/32
JEWESSES (1) ....................................... LITTL    83/15
JEWISH (2) ......................................... PARTS    90/02
     GRACE  159/29
JEWS (1) ........................................... LITTL    81/30
JIMMY (24) ......................................... RACE     43/23
     RACE    43/31     RACE    44/04     RACE    44/08     RACE     44/25
     RACE    45/03     RACE    45/07     RACE    45/16     RACE     45/19
     RACE    45/29     RACE    46/04     RACE    46/06     RACE     46/09
     RACE    46/18     RACE    46/22     RACE    47/11     RACE     47/13
     RACE    47/27     RACE    47/32     RACE    48/08     RACE     48/10
     RACE    48/19     RACE    48/20     RACE    48/26
JIMMY'S (2) ........................................ RACE     44/16
     RACE    45/26
JOB (11) ........................................... GALNT    51/10
     GALNT   51/28     GALNT   53/27     GALNT   58/02     HOUSE    62/01
     IVY D  120/14     IVY D  120/15     IVY D  121/27     IVY D   127/25
     GRACE  171/24     GRACE  172/30
```

JOBS (1) .... IVY D 121/**32**
JOE (34) .... ENCTR 19/**01**
    ENCTR 19/08   CLAY 100/09   CLAY 100/14   CLAY 100/19
    CLAY 100/20   CLAY 102/08   CLAY 103/15   CLAY 104/04
    CLAY 104/07   CLAY 104/10   CLAY 104/15   CLAY 104/18
    CLAY 104/21   CLAY 104/24   CLAY 104/28   CLAY 104/30
    CLAY 104/34   CLAY 105/23   CLAY 105/26   CLAY 105/29
    CLAY 106/13   IVY D 122/09   IVY D 124/12   IVY D 124/17
    IVY D 124/25   IVY D 125/02   IVY D 133/06   IVY D 133/14
    IVY D 133/20   IVY D 133/22   IVY D 133/26   IVY D 133/32
    IVY D 135/29
JOE'S (2) .... CLAY 100/17
    CLAY 103/14
JOG-ALONG (1) .... LITTL 78/25
JOHN (10) .... IVY D 126/23
    IVY D 127/31   IVY D 129/31   IVY D 132/01   GRACE 169/21
    GRACE 169/22   GRACE 169/25   GRACE 169/32   GRACE 170/12
    GRACE 170/17
JOHNNY (11) .... SISTR 17/09
    DEAD 207/11   DEAD 207/14   DEAD 207/22   DEAD 207/22
    DEAD 207/25   DEAD 207/31   DEAD 208/06   DEAD 208/07
    DEAD 208/15   DEAD 208/16
JOIN (5) .... PARTS 93/32
    PNFUL 115/06   MOTHR 148/17   GRACE 163/15   DEAD 211/34
JOKE (4) .... GRACE 167/28
    DEAD 180/25   DEAD 180/32   DEAD 190/30
JOKERS (1) .... IVY D 125/07
JOKING (3) .... CLAY 101/08
    CLAY 105/10   DEAD 188/26
JOLLY (9) .... IVY D 132/06
    GRACE 164/32   DEAD 180/07   DEAD 205/17   DEAD 205/18
    DEAD 205/19   DEAD 205/28   DEAD 205/29   DEAD 205/30
JOSSER (1) .... ENCTR 26/27
JOSTLED (1) .... ARABY 31/04
JOURNAL (2) .... GRACE 158/23
    GRACE 172/32
JOURNALISM (1) .... LITTL 80/27
JOURNEY (5) .... ARABY 34/15
    RACE 45/10   PARTS 88/23   DEAD 207/04   DEAD 223/26
JOVIAL (2) .... RACE 48/02
    GRACE 156/07
JOVIALITY (1) .... GRACE 170/28
JOY (7) .... LITTL 72/02
    LITTL 73/33   LITTL 79/07   IVY D 135/19   DEAD 212/07
    DEAD 213/30   DEAD 219/32
JOYFUL (1) .... DEAD 213/09
JOYFULLY (1) .... PARTS 93/05
JOYS (1) .... LITTL 78/33
JUDGE (4) .... HOUSE 63/09
    GRACE 154/15   GRACE 164/20   GRACE 164/24
JUDGED (2) .... HOUSE 63/23
    PNFUL 109/28
JUDGMENTS (1) .... GALNT 51/32
JUDICIOUSLY (1) .... IVY D 118/02
JULIA (49) .... DEAD 175/07
    DEAD 175/09   DEAD 176/01   DEAD 176/13   DEAD 177/01
    DEAD 177/09   DEAD 179/23   DEAD 181/02   DEAD 181/07
    DEAD 181/30   DEAD 181/31   DEAD 181/31   DEAD 181/32
    DEAD 182/15   DEAD 182/21   DEAD 182/22   DEAD 182/30
    DEAD 184/15   DEAD 184/17   DEAD 184/19   DEAD 185/01
    DEAD 186/18   DEAD 186/26   DEAD 192/20   DEAD 192/29
    DEAD 192/33   DEAD 193/18   DEAD 193/26   DEAD 193/31

```
DEAD   194/05    DEAD   194/08    DEAD   194/12    DEAD   197/23
DEAD   197/32    DEAD   200/19    DEAD   201/24    DEAD   202/29
DEAD   204/19    DEAD   204/21    DEAD   204/23    DEAD   205/22
DEAD   207/10    DEAD   209/06    DEAD   210/11    DEAD   211/19
DEAD   211/25    DEAD   212/24    DEAD   222/25    DEAD   222/32
JULIA'S (7) ...................................... DEAD   175/15
DEAD   180/32    DEAD   193/01    DEAD   193/10     DEAD   195/03
DEAD   200/14    DEAD   205/05
JULIET (1) ....................................... DEAD   186/17
JULY (2) ......................................... SISTR   12/06
MOTHR 137/22
JUMP (1) ......................................... DEAD   191/15
JUMPED (5) ....................................... ENCTR   22/14
LITTL   84/21    PARTS   98/05    IVY D 131/09    DEAD   214/34
JUMPING (1) ...................................... IVY D 126/01
JUNE (1) ......................................... ENCTR   21/30
JUNIOR (1) ....................................... PNFUL 112/23
JUROR (1) ........................................ PNFUL 114/08
JURY (1) ......................................... PNFUL 115/08
JUST (47) ........................................ SISTR   10/16
SISTR   15/26    SISTR   17/04    ARABY   32/10    EVELN  .39/16
RACE    46/12    RACE    48/18    GALNT   49/10    LITTL   73/27
LITTL   80/04    LITTL   80/32    LITTL   81/33    PARTS   93/16
PARTS   93/31    PARTS   94/33    PARTS   95/04    PARTS   96/28
PNFUL 115/28    IVY D 118/13    IVY D 124/09     IVY D 124/23
IVY D 126/07    IVY D 126/11    IVY D 127/14    IVY D 131/12
IVY D 132/08    IVY D 132/16    IVY D 133/14    GRACE 162/30
GRACE 163/14    GRACE 164/26    GRACE 165/03    GRACE 171/07
DEAD   178/27    DEAD   179/17    DEAD   179/21    DEAD   184/02
DEAD   185/07    DEAD   185/20    DEAD   190/10    DEAD   193/21
DEAD   194/25    DEAD   197/12    DEAD   200/22    DEAD   213/29
DEAD   217/31    DEAD   220/26
JUSTIFIABLE (1) .................................. MOTHR 138/34
JUTTING (1) ...................................... MOTHR 140/24


KATE (73) ........................................ DEAD   175/07
DEAD   175/09    DEAD   176/01    DEAD   176/15    DEAD   177/01
DEAD   177/08    DEAD   177/09    DEAD   177/12    DEAD   179/28
DEAD   180/02    DEAD   180/05    DEAD   180/08    DEAD   180/15
DEAD   180/31    DEAD   181/14    DEAD   181/18    DEAD   181/22
DEAD   182/04    DEAD   182/13    DEAD   182/21    DEAD   182/27
DEAD   183/32    DEAD   184/03    DEAD   184/12    DEAD   184/17
DEAD   184/22    DEAD   185/08    DEAD   186/12    DEAD   186/25
DEAD   190/34    DEAD   192/20    DEAD   194/08    DEAD   194/14
DEAD   194/17    DEAD   194/19    DEAD   194/30    DEAD   194/32
DEAD   195/05    DEAD   196/10    DEAD   196/15    DEAD   197/19
DEAD   197/23    DEAD   197/32    DEAD   198/03    DEAD   199/27
DEAD   199/32    DEAD   200/07    DEAD   201/06    DEAD   201/08
DEAD   202/29    DEAD   205/21    DEAD   206/04    DEAD   206/07
DEAD   206/08    DEAD   206/11    DEAD   206/27    DEAD   206/30
DEAD   207/13    DEAD   207/19    DEAD   207/28    DEAD   208/02
DEAD   208/26    DEAD   209/06    DEAD   210/11    DEAD   210/30
DEAD   211/10    DEAD   211/16    DEAD   211/20    DEAD   211/29
DEAD   212/16    DEAD   212/20    DEAD   212/23    DEAD   222/31
KATE'S (2) ....................................... DEAD   175/16
DEAD   205/06
KATHLEEN (13) .................................... MOTHR 137/19
MOTHR 137/27    MOTHR 138/03    MOTHR 138/15    MOTHR 143/14
MOTHR 143/21    MOTHR 146/15    MOTHR 146/16    MOTHR 147/04
MOTHR 147/16    MOTHR 147/26    MOTHR 149/28    DEAD   189/02
KATHLEEN'S (3) ................................... MOTHR 138/33
```

```
         MOTHR 145/34      MOTHR 148/18
KAVANAGH'S (1) ....................................  IVY D 126/29
KEARNEY (51) ......................................  MOTHR 136/08
         MOTHR 136/09      MOTHR 137/04      MOTHR 137/07      MOTHR 137/22
         MOTHR 137/25      MOTHR 137/30      MOTHR 138/03      MOTHR 138/06
         MOTHR 138/19      MOTHR 138/31      MOTHR 139/06      MOTHR 139/30
         MOTHR 140/04      MOTHR 140/09      MOTHR 140/19      MOTHR 140/22
         MOTHR 140/26      MOTHR 141/02      MOTHR 141/19      MOTHR 141/28
         MOTHR 141/32      MOTHR 142/03      MOTHR 142/06      MOTHR 142/15
         MOTHR 143/10      MOTHR 144/01      MOTHR 144/09      MOTHR 144/11
         MOTHR 144/15      MOTHR 144/21      MOTHR 145/28      MOTHR 145/32
         MOTHR 145/34      MOTHR 146/08      MOTHR 146/11      MOTHR 146/15
         MOTHR 146/15      MOTHR 146/17      MOTHR 146/28      MOTHR 147/02
         MOTHR 147/31      MOTHR 148/03      MOTHR 148/05      MOTHR 148/21
         MOTHR 148/26      MOTHR 148/29      MOTHR 148/31      MOTHR 149/16
         MOTHR 149/23      DEAD  189/03
KEARNEYS (2) .....................................  MOTHR 137/33
         MOTHR 148/19
KEARNEY'S (5) ....................................  MOTHR 141/10
         MOTHR 146/33      MOTHR 147/26      MOTHR 147/28      MOTHR 149/10
KEEGAN (1) .......................................  IVY D 128/01
KEEN (3) .........................................  MOTHR 143/18
         GRACE 153/17      DEAD  215/13
KEENER (1) .......................................  LITTL  84/10
KEENLY (3) .......................................  GALNT  57/33
         GALNT  60/18      GRACE 160/27
KEEP (22) ........................................  EVELN  36/17
         EVELN  38/22      EVELN  40/03      GALNT  56/33      HOUSE  61/02
         PARTS  92/16      PARTS  92/22      PARTS  95/07      IVY D 120/14
         IVY D 127/34      IVY D 128/29      IVY D 131/21      IVY D 133/04
         MOTHR 138/22      MOTHR 141/11      GRACE 155/08      DEAD  189/17
         DEAD  189/19      DEAD  189/25      DEAD  208/26      DEAD  217/05
         DEAD  220/08
KEEPING (3) ......................................  GALNT  59/24
         IVY D 132/05      DEAD  176/31
KEEPS (2) ........................................  GRACE 158/32
         GRACE 159/01
KELLY'S (2) ......................................  PARTS  92/31
         PARTS  93/02
KEOGH (2) ........................................  EVELN  36/13
         EVELN  36/16
KEON (5) .........................................  IVY D 126/01
         IVY D 126/03      IVY D 126/06      IVY D 126/12      IVY D 127/32
KEPT (20) ........................................  SISTR  17/03
         ENCTR  25/06      ARABY  30/29      ARABY  34/05      EVELN  41/02
         RACE   44/06      RACE   44/28      GALNT  56/14      GALNT  59/06
         GALNT  59/26      GALNT  60/23      HOUSE  63/15      HOUSE  68/14
         HOUSE  68/15      LITTL  72/33      LITTL  82/09      PNFUL 112/22
         IVY D 123/23      GRACE 156/13      DEAD  190/23
KERNAN (66) ......................................  GRACE 153/08
         GRACE 153/11      GRACE 153/18      GRACE 153/26      GRACE 153/32
         GRACE 153/34      GRACE 154/13      GRACE 154/25      GRACE 154/32
         GRACE 155/03      GRACE 155/18      GRACE 155/28      GRACE 156/03
         GRACE 156/19      GRACE 157/05      GRACE 157/07      GRACE 157/25
         GRACE 158/28      GRACE 158/31      GRACE 160/01      GRACE 160/08
         GRACE 160/13      GRACE 160/18      GRACE 160/26      GRACE 160/27
         GRACE 161/18      GRACE 161/26      GRACE 161/30      GRACE 162/05
         GRACE 162/24      GRACE 162/29      GRACE 162/32      GRACE 163/17
         GRACE 164/09      GRACE 164/17      GRACE 164/22      GRACE 165/05
         GRACE 165/17      GRACE 165/28      GRACE 165/31      GRACE 166/10
         GRACE 166/11      GRACE 166/29      GRACE 166/31      GRACE 167/23
         GRACE 167/32      GRACE 168/07      GRACE 168/16      GRACE 168/29
```

```
        GRACE  169/22    GRACE  170/09    GRACE  170/12    GRACE  170/16
        GRACE  170/21    GRACE  170/27    GRACE  170/29    GRACE  171/01
        GRACE  171/02    GRACE  171/21    GRACE  171/23    GRACE  171/29
        GRACE  172/01    GRACE  172/16    GRACE  173/02    GRACE  173/11
        GRACE  173/17
KERNAN'S (9) .......................................... GRACE  153/24
        GRACE  154/19    GRACE  155/29    GRACE  156/29    GRACE  158/01
        GRACE  158/27    GRACE  171/05    GRACE  172/24    GRACE  172/33
KERRIGAN (2) .......................................... DEAD   183/34
        DEAD   184/01
KEY (2) ............................................... HOUSE   64/07
        DEAD   184/31
KEY-BOARD (1) ......................................... DEAD   186/11
KEYS (1) .............................................. SISTR   18/04
KICKED (1) ............................................ DEAD   178/13
KICKS (1) ............................................. IVY D  121/30
KID (1) ............................................... GALNT   53/14
KILDARE (2) ........................................... GALNT   54/06
        PNFUL  116/12
KILKELLY (1) .......................................... DEAD   189/02
KILLARNEY (1) ......................................... MOTHR  147/10
KILLED (1) ............................................ PNFUL  113/23
KIND (13) ............................................. SISTR   15/33
        ENCTR   19/13    ENCTR   27/11    EVELN   38/28    GALNT   52/18
        HOUSE   64/15    IVY D  126/32    IVY D  128/12    GRACE  155/23
        GRACE  161/21    GRACE  165/04    DEAD   183/16    DEAD   186/20
KINDER (1) ............................................ DEAD   218/25
KINDLING (2) .......................................... RACE    46/09
        DEAD   215/11
KINDLY (5) ............................................ LITTL   71/07
        PARTS   87/12    MOTHR  149/15    DEAD   198/13    DEAD   203/25
KINDNESS (1) .......................................... SISTR   16/21
KINDRED (1) ........................................... LITTL   74/03
KINDS (1) ............................................. GALNT   50/25
KING (9) .............................................. IVY D  122/04
        IVY D  124/06    IVY D  131/25    IVY D  132/02    IVY D  132/13
        IVY D  134/07    MOTHR  142/24    DEAD   208/07    DEAD   208/08
KING'S (3) ............................................ LITTL   71/01
        LITTL   71/26    IVY D  131/28
KINGSBRIDGE (1) ....................................... PNFUL  117/22
KINGSTOWN (4) ......................................... RACE    43/17
        RACE    47/12    PNFUL  113/27    DEAD   176/12
KINK (1) .............................................. DEAD   185/30
KIRWAN (1) ............................................ PARTS   87/09
KISS (3) .............................................. HOUSE   67/20
        IVY D  134/28    DEAD   217/27
KISSED (5) ............................................ LITTL   83/02
        LITTL   83/07    DEAD   177/10    DEAD   179/32    DEAD   217/25
KITCHEN (9) ........................................... ARABY   29/10
        ARABY   30/13    ARABY   34/10    PARTS   97/13    PARTS   97/13
        CLAY    99/03    GRACE  154/26    GRACE  154/32    GRACE  158/07
KNACK (1) ............................................. PARTS   96/23
KNEE (2) .............................................. PARTS   90/08
        GRACE  173/18
KNEES (9) ............................................. SISTR   15/34
        GALNT   54/12    PARTS   98/15    IVY D  125/19    GRACE  172/11
        GRACE  173/04    DEAD   186/29    DEAD   209/01    DEAD   222/30
KNELT (5) ............................................. SISTR   14/19
        GRACE  151/23    GRACE  151/24    GRACE  173/10    GRACE  173/14
KNEW (57) ............................................. SISTR    9/06
        SISTR    9/09    SISTR   10/04    SISTR   10/18    SISTR   13/29
        SISTR   15/22    SISTR   18/10    ENCTR   22/15    ENCTR   26/05
```

ENCTR	26/12	ARABY	35/25	EVELN	38/02	EVELN	39/05
EVELN	40/01	EVELN	40/23	RACE	44/26	RACE	47/06
RACE	48/11	RACE	48/27	GALNT	50/25	GALNT	51/31
GALNT	56/28	GALNT	58/06	GALNT	58/06	GALNT	59/29
GALNT	59/29	HOUSE	62/08	HOUSE	63/10	HOUSE	63/16
HOUSE	65/12	HOUSE	65/16	HOUSE	65/21	HOUSE	67/13
LITTL	72/03	LITTL	72/04	LITTL	78/23	PARTS	91/01
PARTS	91/09	PARTS	92/09	CLAY	101/20	CLAY	104/10
PNFUL	117/18	MOTHR	138/19	MOTHR	138/21	MOTHR	141/13
MOTHR	141/25	GRACE	150/13	GRACE	150/18	GRACE	151/14
GRACE	156/25	GRACE	160/05	DEAD	175/14	DEAD	187/08
DEAD	213/32	DEAD	220/33	DEAD	222/15	DEAD	223/13

KNIT (1) .... DEAD 187/31
KNITTED (2) .... GRACE 170/21
    DEAD 181/09
KNIVES (3) .... DEAD 182/33
    DEAD 191/34   DEAD 197/27
KNOB (1) .... PARTS 91/31
KNOCK (6) .... SISTR 12/27
    LITTL 76/08   IVY D 125/21   IVY D 126/33   IVY D 128/13
    DEAD 208/19
KNOCKABOUT (2) .... PARTS 94/20
    IVY D 132/16
KNOCKED (3) .... LITTL 76/15
    PARTS 86/18   PNFUL 113/26
KNOCKER (1) .... GRACE 168/22
KNOCKING (1) .... GALNT 57/34
KNOT (2) .... RACE 45/16
    RACE 45/22
KNOTTED (1) .... PARTS 95/14
KNOW (113)
KNOWING (2) .... RACE 43/34
    IVY D 125/09
KNOWLEDGE (2) .... RACE 44/27
    GRACE 157/20
KNOWN (12) .... EVELN 37/21
    HOUSE 65/03   HOUSE 66/19   LITTL 71/03   LITTL 78/11
    LITTL 78/26   GRACE 154/20   GRACE 157/15   GRACE 158/10
    GRACE 159/18   DEAD 177/26   DEAD 207/17
KNOWS (6) .... SISTR 16/01
    HOUSE 66/02   LITTL 79/31   LITTL 81/01   MOTHR 142/14
    GRACE 170/33
KNUCKLES (2) .... DEAD 184/33
    DEAD 185/32
KOWTOWING (1) .... IVY D 122/04
KRAMER (1) .... PNFUL 108/05

LABELS (1) .... DEAD 197/03
LABORIOUS (1) .... PNFUL 117/25
LABORIOUSLY (1) .... PNFUL 117/24
LABOUR (4) .... RACE 44/29
    PARTS 86/17   IVY D 121/26   IVY D 121/31
LABOURERS (3) .... ENCTR 23/04
    ENCTR 23/18   ARABY 31/05
LACE (2) .... SISTR 14/16
    HOUSE 63/28
LACK (3) .... RACE 48/09
    DEAD 192/25   DEAD 203/24
LACKING (1) .... ENCTR 20/05
LAD (3) .... SISTR 10/33
    IVY D 130/31   GRACE 170/25

LADEN (1) .... CLAY 102/15
LADIES (27) .... EVELN 37/28

RACE 46/34	LITTL 72/08	CLAY 99/17	PNFUL 109/17
MOTHR 139/28	MOTHR 143/24	DEAD 175/06	DEAD 182/24
DEAD 182/28	DEAD 183/12	DEAD 183/24	DEAD 183/33
DEAD 184/03	DEAD 184/04	DEAD 184/07	DEAD 192/20
DEAD 197/25	DEAD 198/13	DEAD 202/14	DEAD 202/23
DEAD 202/27	DEAD 203/07	DEAD 203/17	DEAD 204/25
DEAD 205/02	DEAD 205/15		

LADIES' (5) .... LITTL 82/30

DEAD 175/08	DEAD 177/15	DEAD 179/21

DEAD 183/04
LADLING (1) .... SISTR 9/17
LADS (1) .... SISTR 10/34
LADY (21) .... ARABY 35/05

ARABY 35/14	ARABY 35/21	ARABY 35/23	RACE 47/26
PARTS 91/18	CLAY 102/23	CLAY 102/26	CLAY 102/26
PNFUL 109/19	PNFUL 113/19	PNFUL 113/25	PNFUL 114/08
MOTHR 140/31	MOTHR 147/10	MOTHR 147/19	MOTHR 148/04
MOTHR 149/08	MOTHR 149/31	MOTHR 149/31	DEAD 187/21

LADYLIKE (1) .... MOTHR 141/13
LADY-LIKE (1) .... LITTL 83/12
LADY'S (2) .... PARTS 91/20
PNFUL 110/24
LAGER (1) .... PNFUL 108/33
LAID (14) .... SISTR 11/09

SISTR 17/01	ARABY 32/13	EVELN 39/27	EVELN 40/11
RACE 45/10	CLAY 101/27	IVY D 118/10	IVY D 133/34
IVY D 134/10	IVY D 135/13	GRACE 150/10	GRACE 172/11
DEAD 206/11			

LAIN (2) .... ENCTR 24/17
GRACE 150/06
LAKES (1) .... DEAD 191/25
LAMB (1) .... LITTL 85/18
LAMBABAUN (1) .... LITTL 85/17
LAME (1) .... DEAD 223/02
LAMELY (1) .... DEAD 188/21
LAMENTED (1) .... DEAD 207/16
LAMP (12) .... SISTR 13/13

ARABY 31/24	ARABY 32/07	GALNT 59/04	GALNT 60/27
LITTL 82/21	PARTS 97/30	PARTS 97/33	PARTS 98/01
PNFUL 107/16	PNFUL 111/20	DEAD 216/10	

LAMPLIGHT (4) .... ARABY 33/14

LITTL 85/20	CLAY 100/23	DEAD 223/25

LAMP-POST (2) .... GALNT 59/06
GALNT 59/24
LAMPS (6) .... ARABY 30/04

ARABY 35/01	GALNT 49/05	PARTS 89/07

DEAD 213/01   GRACE 172/07
LANCERS (2) .... DEAD 187/19
DEAD 190/13
LAND (6) .... SISTR 13/34

ARABY 31/09	LITTL 75/33	DEAD 189/16

DEAD 200/31   DEAD 189/27
LANDED (2) .... ENCTR 23/21
LITTL 75/17
LANDING (6) .... SISTR 14/11

HOUSE 67/19	PARTS 86/15	PARTS 88/25

DEAD 195/12   DEAD 184/24
LANDLADY'S (1) .... PNFUL 109/04
LANDSCAPE (1) .... PNFUL 115/16
LANE (4) .... ENCTR 24/05

IVY D 123/23	DEAD 207/33	DEAD 208/03

```
LANES (1) ........................................ ARABY  30/08
LANEWAY (2) ...................................... GRACE 151/12
   GRACE  152/33
LANGUAGE (4) ..................................... MOTHR 138/06
   DEAD  189/19    DEAD  189/22    DEAD  217/16
LANGUAGES (1) .................................... DEAD  189/18
LANTERNS (1) ..................................... ARABY  30/05
LAP (1) .......................................... EVELN  39/23
LAPEL (2) ........................................ IVY D 119/24
   IVY D 122/14
LAPSED (1) ....................................... IVY D 118/03
LARGE (21) ....................................... SISTR  11/06
   SISTR  12/19    SISTR  14/28    ARABY  34/25    GALNT  51/22
   GALNT  51/23    GALNT  52/07    LITTL  75/03    LITTL  80/06
   PARTS  87/05    PARTS  95/18    PNFUL 108/18    MOTHR 141/24
   MOTHR 145/23    GRACE 173/20    DEAD  179/25    DEAD  182/31
   DEAD  187/22    DEAD  196/24    DEAD  205/04    DEAD  216/16
LARRY (1) ........................................ IVY D 124/27
LASS (5) ......................................... EVELN  39/06
   DEAD  212/10    DEAD  212/12    DEAD  218/14    DEAD  219/05
LAST (45) ........................................ ENCTR  21/03
   ENCTR  21/23    ENCTR  22/14    ARABY  29/14    ARABY  31/30
   EVELN  36/04    EVELN  40/04    RACE   45/31    RACE   46/24
   RACE   48/22    GALNT  57/02    GALNT  59/10    GALNT  59/18
   HOUSE  63/22    HOUSE  68/04    HOUSE  69/01    LITTL  74/33
   LITTL  79/02    LITTL  80/08    PARTS  88/15    PARTS  89/32
   PARTS  90/16    PARTS  92/28    CLAY  102/15    CLAY  105/17
   CLAY  105/29    PNFUL 112/02    PNFUL 112/18    IVY D 135/06
   MOTHR 148/13    GRACE 169/30    DEAD  179/19    DEAD  180/04
   DEAD  184/07    DEAD  185/33    DEAD  187/06    DEAD  193/16
   DEAD  198/03    DEAD  201/17    DEAD  201/28    DEAD  204/34
   DEAD  208/32    DEAD  209/11    DEAD  212/05    DEAD  224/03
LATCHKEY (1) ..................................... ARABY  33/28
LATE (22) ........................................ SISTR  11/18
   ENCTR  24/09    ARABY  29/16    ARABY  33/23    ARABY  34/05
   EVELN  38/21    RACE   48/15    HOUSE  67/04    HOUSE  67/12
   LITTL  71/06    LITTL  72/14    LITTL  79/03    LITTL  82/13
   LITTL  83/24    PARTS  92/29    PNFUL 114/28    PNFUL 115/04
   MOTHR 146/05    GRACE 162/19    GRACE 165/22    DEAD  176/31
   DEAD  207/16
LATELY (2) ....................................... EVELN  39/25
   DEAD  181/24
LATENT (1) ....................................... RACE   44/29
LATER (7) ........................................ PARTS  94/34
   PNFUL 112/11    IVY D 124/07    GRACE 156/10    GRACE 159/27
   DEAD  184/10    DEAD  207/17
LATEST (3) ....................................... GALNT  58/19
   DEAD  180/26    DEAD  193/31
LATIN (4) ........................................ SISTR  13/03
   GRACE 167/07    GRACE 167/24    GRACE 168/06
LATTER (2) ....................................... ENCTR  20/04
   DEAD  184/24
LATTERLY (2) ..................................... SISTR  16/32
   EVELN  38/05
LAUGH (6) ........................................ EVELN  39/31
   PARTS  89/20    CLAY  101/11    MOTHR 140/24    DEAD  182/11
   DEAD  196/03
LAUGHED (31) ..................................... ENCTR  23/20
   RACE   48/02    GALNT  50/09    GALNT  51/13    GALNT  53/23
   GALNT  55/18    LITTL  76/04    LITTL  76/11    LITTL  82/01
   CLAY  101/12    CLAY  101/18    CLAY  104/08    CLAY  105/08
   CLAY  105/08    IVY D 121/07    IVY D 124/03    IVY D 127/26
```

MOTHR 143/07	GRACE 160/33	GRACE 161/05	GRACE 161/18
GRACE 171/32	DEAD 180/14	DEAD 180/24	DEAD 180/30
DEAD 183/12	DEAD 202/29	DEAD 206/09	DEAD 206/13
DEAD 207/13	DEAD 208/01		

LAUGHING (20) .... ENCTR 21/24

ARABY 35/06	HOUSE 66/18	PARTS 94/01	CLAY 101/08
CLAY 105/10	IVY D 130/15	MOTHR 138/01	MOTHR 145/04
GRACE 169/19	GRACE 171/12	DEAD 175/09	DEAD 177/15
DEAD 184/31	DEAD 193/32	DEAD 196/09	DEAD 206/18
DEAD 207/11	DEAD 207/19	DEAD 210/12	

LAUGHING-LIKE (2) .... SISTR 18/08
SISTR 18/14
LAUGHTER (18) .... RACE 44/07

RACE 47/08	GALNT 49/17	LITTL 72/19	MOTHR 145/09
DEAD 180/21	DEAD 185/30	DEAD 185/34	DEAD 197/26
DEAD 198/04	DEAD 204/18	DEAD 208/12	DEAD 208/18
DEAD 209/08	DEAD 209/09	DEAD 209/13	DEAD 209/23
DEAD 209/32			

LAUNCHED (1) .... GRACE 156/15
LAUNDRY (2) .... CLAY 100/19
CLAY 100/23
LAVATORY (1) .... GRACE 150/01
LAVENDER (1) .... GRACE 156/08
LAW (3) .... SISTR 13/18
RACE 43/23   IVY D 131/23
LAWN (1) .... GALNT 56/19
LAY (33) .... SISTR 14/25

SISTR 14/27	ENCTR 23/34	ARABY 30/25	RACE 47/15
RACE 48/20	GALNT 56/02	GALNT 57/06	HOUSE 64/01
LITTL 83/28	PARTS 87/15	PARTS 89/34	PNFUL 107/11
PNFUL 108/04	PNFUL 112/17	PNFUL 115/16	GRACE 150/02
DEAD 177/16	DEAD 186/30	DEAD 196/17	DEAD 196/19
DEAD 196/25	DEAD 196/26	DEAD 196/34	DEAD 202/09
DEAD 212/34	DEAD 214/31	DEAD 216/10	DEAD 222/20
DEAD 223/05	DEAD 223/09	DEAD 223/32	DEAD 223/33

LAY-BROTHER (1) .... GRACE 172/04
LAYING (2) .... SISTR 16/08
DEAD 189/06
LAYMAN'S (1) .... IVY D 125/26
LAZILY (1) .... ENCTR 24/18
LEAD (7) .... SISTR 14/19
IVY D 132/26   GRACE 151/19   GRACE 169/26   GRACE 173/32
GRACE 173/33   DEAD 220/14
LEADEN (1) .... GRACE 154/10
LEADER (2) .... PNFUL 111/02
DEAD 205/16
LEADING (3) .... CLAY 105/06
DEAD 176/14   DEAD 198/20
LEADS (1) .... PNFUL 113/10
LEAF (5) .... LITTL 72/20
IVY D 119/32   IVY D 122/14   IVY D 122/15   GRACE 155/19
LEAF-SHAPED (1) .... DEAD 196/24
LEAGUE (1) .... PNFUL 115/07
LEANED (14) .... SISTR 16/04

EVELN 36/02	RACE 48/29	GALNT 59/05	IVY D 121/03
GRACE 153/23	GRACE 170/11	DEAD 183/22	DEAD 192/30
DEAD 196/06	DEAD 202/02	DEAD 215/06	DEAD 215/08
DEAD 216/14			

LEANING (8) .... ARABY 33/10

EVELN 39/33	LITTL 74/26	IVY D 127/10	MOTHR 145/02
GRACE 156/07	DEAD 209/29	DEAD 222/04	

LEAP (1) .... HOUSE 66/03

LEAPED (1) .... ARABY   30/28
LEAPING (1) .... DEAD   212/07
LEARN (3) .... SISTR   11/01
    SISTR   13/23   GRACE 167/29
LEARNED (5) .... ENCTR   26/08
    PNFUL 109/27   MOTHR 136/10   MOTHR 137/20   MOTHR 140/26
LEAST (13) .... ENCTR   20/08
    ENCTR   21/10   ENCTR   22/31   RACE   45/29   RACE   47/28
    LITTL   72/29   GRACE 158/03   GRACE 174/08   DEAD   184/08
    DEAD   195/16   DEAD   203/06   DEAD   203/30   DEAD   204/34
LEATHER (2) .... EVELN   38/20
    GALNT   55/25
LEATHER-BOUND (1) .... DEAD   193/11
LEAVE (22) .... ENCTR   26/19
    ARABY   32/20   EVELN   37/05   EVELN   37/18   EVELN   38/26
    GALNT   53/32   GALNT   59/10   LITTL   71/24   LITTL   79/25
    PARTS   95/22   CLAY   99/01   IVY D 121/05   IVY D 124/05
    IVY D 128/29   MOTHR 137/14   MOTHR 144/30   MOTHR 145/11
    GRACE 157/27   GRACE 162/02   DEAD   200/34   DEAD   220/29
    DEAD   221/08
LEAVES (2) .... ENCTR   22/01
    ARABY   29/14
LEAVING (7) .... EVELN   37/30
    GALNT   52/20   PARTS   87/28   PARTS   89/03   PARTS   95/21
    PARTS   97/27   DEAD   185/15
LECTURE (2) .... LITTL   76/06
    MOTHR 144/29
LED (12) .... ENCTR   27/29
    CLAY 105/01   CLAY 105/10   PNFUL 108/26   PNFUL 113/28
    DEAD   177/06   DEAD   182/28   DEAD   183/03   DEAD   184/14
    DEAD   194/14   DEAD   198/34   DEAD   215/32
LEECH (1) .... GALNT   50/18
LEER (2) .... GALNT   56/02
    GALNT   57/32
LEERED (1) .... PARTS   94/31
LEFT (42) .... ENCTR   24/14
    ARABY   29/18   ARABY   30/19   ARABY   32/33   ARABY   33/05
    ARABY   34/10   EVELN   38/24   GALNT   56/33   GALNT   58/08
    GALNT   58/29   GALNT   58/30   GALNT   60/22   HOUSE   67/31
    LITTL   74/23   LITTL   82/33   LITTL   83/29   PARTS   90/08
    PARTS   94/10   PARTS   94/12   CLAY 103/31   PNFUL 108/12
    PNFUL 112/10   PNFUL 116/34   IVY D 120/14   IVY D 120/30
    IVY D 123/10   GRACE 151/16   GRACE 152/32   GRACE 157/29
    GRACE 159/21   GRACE 170/05   DEAD   176/02   DEAD   178/22
    DEAD   184/33   DEAD   184/34   DEAD   185/25   DEAD   185/32
    DEAD   185/33   DEAD   189/24   DEAD   191/31   DEAD   200/20
    DEAD   221/15
LEG (4) .... SISTR   11/06
    GALNT   55/04   GALNT   55/07   MOTHR 136/04
LEGEND (2) .... ENCTR   23/24
    GRACE 154/06
LEGHORN (1) .... PNFUL 110/09
LEGITIMATE (1) .... DEAD   199/01
LEGS (2) .... IVY D 130/29
    DEAD   185/06
LEISURE (1) .... PNFUL 111/07
LEMONADE (5) .... ENCTR   24/04
    MOTHR 140/31   DEAD   183/06   DEAD   185/20   DEAD   185/24
LEND (3) .... IVY D 128/28
    DEAD   202/20   DEAD   217/13
LENDING (1) .... GRACE 159/26
LENEHAN (29) .... GALNT   50/17

GALNT	51/09	GALNT	51/13	GALNT	52/04	GALNT 52/13
GALNT	52/17	GALNT	52/24	GALNT	52/32	GALNT 53/01
GALNT	53/10	GALNT	53/12	GALNT	53/16	GALNT 53/18
GALNT	53/23	GALNT	53/26	GALNT	53/33	GALNT 54/24
GALNT	54/30	GALNT	55/03	GALNT	55/05	GALNT 55/10
GALNT	55/19	GALNT	56/03	GALNT	56/07	GALNT 58/24
GALNT	58/27	GALNT	60/08	GALNT	60/15	GALNT 60/23

LENEHAN'S (2) .... GALNT 52/06
    GALNT 55/31
LENGTH (4) .... GALNT 52/09
    GRACE 163/24   DEAD 218/19   DEAD 219/25
LENNON (2) .... PNFUL 113/29
    PNFUL 115/09
LENSES (1) .... DEAD 178/18
LENT (3) .... PNFUL 110/26
    MOTHR 147/12   DEAD 217/04
LEO (11) .... ENCTR 19/05
    ENCTR 20/14   ENCTR 20/20   ENCTR 20/33   ENCTR 21/10
    ENCTR 21/13   ENCTR 21/16   ENCTR 22/14   ENCTR 22/31
    GRACE 167/05   GRACE 167/22
LEONARD (7) .... HOUSE 66/04
    PARTS 91/01   PARTS 93/24   PARTS 94/19   PARTS 94/29
    PARTS 95/29   PARTS 96/03
LEO'S (1) .... GRACE 168/05
LEOVILLE (1) .... PNFUL 114/31
LESS (9) .... GALNT 58/09
    GALNT 58/09   HOUSE 63/33   LITTL 85/21   LITTL 85/21
    PARTS 91/26   PNFUL 111/17   PNFUL 113/12   DEAD 203/28
LESSER (1) .... IVY D 131/05
LESSONS (2) .... PNFUL 110/23
    DEAD 176/16
LEST (5) .... ENCTR 24/11
    ENCTR 27/33   LITTL 83/29   PNFUL 112/22   DEAD 220/06
LET (42) .... SISTR 10/33
    SISTR 11/01   SISTR 13/27   ENCTR 20/24   ENCTR 26/28
    ARABY 34/04   GALNT 53/22   HOUSE 62/09   LITTL 77/22
    LITTL 80/10   PARTS 87/14   PARTS 97/10   PARTS 98/06
    PARTS 98/10   PARTS 98/16   CLAY 104/22   PNFUL 110/31
    IVY D 119/17   IVY D 124/33   IVY D 126/07   IVY D 128/24
    IVY D 129/02   IVY D 132/15   IVY D 132/29   MOTHR 138/32
    MOTHR 140/07   DEAD 175/05   DEAD 180/13   DEAD 182/07
    DEAD 195/25   DEAD 196/13   DEAD 198/08   DEAD 199/10
    DEAD 203/30   DEAD 203/33   DEAD 204/10   DEAD 205/09
    DEAD 205/09   DEAD 208/20   DEAD 220/31   DEAD 221/10
    DEAD 222/01
LET'S (1) .... GALNT 54/26
LETTER (7) .... GALNT 52/02
    PARTS 90/17   GRACE 156/19   GRACE 161/19   DEAD 214/05
    DEAD 220/27   DEAD 221/10
LETTERS (6) .... EVELN 39/23
    GALNT 57/04   PARTS 89/33   PARTS 90/18   PARTS 91/09
    PARTS 91/14
LEVEL (5) .... SISTR 14/11
    ENCTR 24/32   RACE 42/17   GALNT 60/18   PNFUL 114/26
LEVERETT (1) .... PNFUL 113/22
LIBERAL (2) .... ENCTR 25/31
    PARTS 93/28
LIBERALISM (1) .... ENCTR 27/20
LIBERATED (1) .... ARABY 33/07
LIBERTY (1) .... IVY D 134/24
LIBH (1) .... DEAD 196/03
LIBRARY (1) .... ENCTR 19/02

LICENSED (1) .... GRACE 166/20
LICK (1) .... IVY D 118/17
LICKED (1) .... GRACE 151/19
LID (1) .... PNFUL 108/10
LIE (5) .... SISTR 13/27
   ARABY 32/33   IVY D 133/05   DEAD 205/25   DEAD 205/26
                                                                   ENCTR 27/24
LIES (4) ....
   IVY D 134/09   IVY D 134/11   DEAD 210/26
LIFE (79) .... SISTR 11/04
   SISTR 17/17   ENCTR 25/03   ARABY 31/10   ARABY 32/25
   EVELN 37/21   EVELN 38/25   EVELN 38/26   EVELN 38/27
   EVELN 40/11   EVELN 40/12   EVELN 40/18   RACE   43/15
   RACE   43/27   RACE   45/11   RACE   46/24   RACE   47/28
   GALNT 58/09   HOUSE 66/13   LITTL 71/12   LITTL 71/13
   LITTL 71/33   LITTL 73/08   LITTL 73/22   LITTL 73/25
   LITTL 75/12   LITTL 76/22   LITTL 77/10   LITTL 79/08
   LITTL 80/22   LITTL 80/23   LITTL 81/03   LITTL 81/08
   LITTL 83/23   LITTL 84/16   PARTS 90/31   PARTS 92/15
   CLAY 100/19   CLAY 102/10   PNFUL 109/07   PNFUL 109/09
   PNFUL 109/13   PNFUL 109/15   PNFUL 110/27   PNFUL 110/30
   PNFUL 111/23   PNFUL 112/13   PNFUL 116/22   PNFUL 116/30
   PNFUL 116/31   PNFUL 117/06   PNFUL 117/14   PNFUL 117/16
   IVY D 122/19   IVY D 132/14   MOTHR 136/16   MOTHR 137/07
   GRACE 156/10   GRACE 157/13   GRACE 157/28   GRACE 158/19
   GRACE 159/25   GRACE 167/07   GRACE 173/32   GRACE 173/33
   GRACE 174/04   GRACE 174/07   GRACE 174/16   GRACE 174/20
   DEAD 176/18   DEAD 186/32   DEAD 192/14   DEAD 204/05
   DEAD 205/10   DEAD 213/16   DEAD 213/32   DEAD 219/31
   DEAD 222/07   DEAD 222/09
LIFE'S (2) .... PNFUL 117/15
   PNFUL 117/20
LIFFEY (2) .... ENCTR 23/17
   GRACE 159/28
LIFT (1) .... GRACE 150/02
LIFTED (7) .... ARABY 30/05
   RACE   46/27   LITTL 81/01   PARTS 86/12   CLAY 101/14
   MOTHR 137/13   DEAD 186/11
LIFTING (2) .... PARTS 88/19
   PNFUL 108/10
LIFTS (1) .... IVY D 135/19
LIGHT (52) .... SISTR 14/17
   SISTR 18/05   ENCTR 22/01   ARABY 30/13   ARABY 30/21
   ARABY 32/06   ARABY 35/30   RACE   43/13   RACE   44/07
   RACE   45/24   RACE   47/29   RACE   48/32   GALNT 50/02
   GALNT 51/17   GALNT 55/27   GALNT 57/07   GALNT 60/09
   GALNT 60/29   HOUSE 62/31   LITTL 73/25   LITTL 74/18
   LITTL 82/22   PARTS 97/30   PNFUL 113/16   PNFUL 115/17
   PNFUL 116/03   IVY D 118/06   IVY D 120/25   IVY D 120/26
   IVY D 123/30   IVY D 126/14   GRACE 152/07   GRACE 166/17
   GRACE 167/11   GRACE 167/12   GRACE 167/14   GRACE 169/04
   GRACE 172/06   GRACE 172/13   GRACE 173/15   GRACE 173/23
   DEAD 177/16   DEAD 210/09   DEAD 212/31   DEAD 216/04
   DEAD 216/04   DEAD 216/10   DEAD 216/15   DEAD 216/21
   DEAD 219/23   DEAD 220/06   DEAD 223/23
LIGHTED (6) .... SISTR 9/03
   SISTR 9/04   ARABY 31/25   ARABY 34/23   GRACE 171/17
   DEAD 202/08
LIGHT-HEARTEDLY (1) .... LITTL 73/03
LIGHTING (4) .... PARTS 88/17
   PNFUL 111/20   IVY D 119/22   IVY D 126/23
LIGHTLY (11) .... ENCTR 24/22
   ENCTR 25/22   GALNT 56/10   HOUSE 66/26   LITTL 76/33

	MOTHR 139/21	GRACE 173/05	DEAD 213/11	DEAD 215/08
	DEAD 215/08	DEAD 217/24		
LIGHTS (4)				GALNT 54/20
	LITTL 80/20	PNFUL 117/10	GRACE 167/06	
LIKE (131)				
LIKED (9)				ENCTR 20/08
	ENCTR 26/05	ARABY 29/13	EVELN 39/24	CLAY 100/23
	CLAY 100/27	DEAD 186/03	DEAD 188/30	DEAD 197/08
LIKELY (3)				HOUSE 62/21
	HOUSE 62/21	PNFUL 111/08		
LIKING (1)				PNFUL 109/05
LILY (14)				DEAD 175/01
	DEAD 175/11	DEAD 176/17	DEAD 176/20	DEAD 176/33
	DEAD 176/34	DEAD 177/06	DEAD 177/21	DEAD 177/29
	DEAD 178/01	DEAD 178/26	DEAD 181/24	DEAD 197/18
	DEAD 198/10			
LILY'S (1)				DEAD 198/16
LIMERICKS (1)				GALNT 50/24
LIMIT (1)				MOTHR 137/02
LIMITS (1)				RACE 44/28
LIMP (1)				DEAD 222/20
LIMPED (1)				MOTHR 143/23
LIMPING (2)				MOTHR 140/30
	MOTHR 144/04			
LINE (6)				EVELN 39/11
	RACE 44/20	PNFUL 113/26	GRACE 158/19	GRACE 171/23
	DEAD 176/13			
LINEAL (1)				IVY D 125/16
LINED (2)				ENCTR 21/34
	DEAD 186/23			
LINES (7)				ARABY 34/11
	LITTL 71/23	PNFUL 114/04	PNFUL 114/25	PNFUL 114/27
	DEAD 179/09	DEAD 196/22		
LINGER (1)				DEAD 204/10
LINGERED (1)				ARABY 35/25
LINKED (1)				RACE 47/17
LINKS (1)				MOTHR 146/25
LION (1)				GRACE 169/34
LIP (5)				SISTR 13/27
	GALNT 50/29	GALNT 53/03	LITTL 79/20	PARTS 94/07
LIPS (14)				SISTR 11/28
	ARABY 31/11	EVELN 41/03	LITTL 75/07	LITTL 81/06
	LITTL 82/24	PNFUL 113/17	IVY D 126/03	IVY D 131/26
	MOTHR 138/04	DEAD 179/27	DEAD 182/25	DEAD 184/29
	DEAD 216/22			
LIQUEURS (1)				LITTL 72/05
LIQUID (1)				GRACE 154/12
LIQUOR (2)				LITTL 77/32
	PARTS 94/06			
LIST (1)				IVY D 135/14
LISTEN (12)				SISTR 18/09
	LITTL 74/01	CLAY 105/33	PNFUL 117/06	IVY D 131/27
	IVY D 133/25	GRACE 171/04	GRACE 171/28	DEAD 186/01
	DEAD 189/23	DEAD 196/06	DEAD 209/31	
LISTENED (14)				SISTR 18/09
	ARABY 35/02	ARABY 35/07	GALNT 49/15	LITTL 85/20
	PARTS 90/19	PNFUL 110/28	PNFUL 117/33	MOTHR 141/21
	GRACE 151/15	GRACE 163/21	DEAD 177/32	DEAD 182/09
	DEAD 193/13			
LISTENERS (2)				GALNT 54/08
	DEAD 186/05			
LISTENING (15)				ENCTR 26/17

EVELN	37/27	GALNT	49/13	GALNT	51/32	LITTL 80/20
PNFUL	111/23	PNFUL	117/32	DEAD	179/03	DEAD 192/12
DEAD	202/08	DEAD	203/26	DEAD	209/30	DEAD 210/05
DEAD	211/05	DEAD	222/05			

LISTLESSLY (1) .... GALNT 56/24
LIT (15) .... ARABY 32/08

ARABY	32/08	RACE	46/08	GALNT	59/05	GALNT 59/18
HOUSE	67/10	LITTL	78/06	PARTS	89/08	PARTS 97/33
PARTS	98/01	PNFUL	110/34	IVY D	119/22	IVY D 119/23
DEAD	212/02	DEAD	215/19			

LITANIES (1) .... ARABY 31/05
LITERALLY (2) .... PARTS 93/04
   DEAD 175/01
LITERARY (2) .... ENCTR 20/12
   DEAD 188/07
LITERATURE (2) .... ENCTR 20/06
   DEAD 188/17
LITHIA (1) .... LITTL 74/30
LITTERED (1) .... ARABY 29/10
LITTLE (210)
LIVE (22) .... ENCTR 24/03

EVELN	38/29	EVELN	40/19	GALNT	58/11	HOUSE 64/26
LITTL	83/24	CLAY	100/16	CLAY	100/26	PNFUL 107/02
PNFUL	115/29	IVY D	128/04	GRACE	152/05	GRACE 152/09
GRACE	158/21	GRACE	160/28	GRACE	170/13	GRACE 174/04
DEAD	176/03	DEAD	200/31	DEAD	208/03	DEAD 221/24
DEAD	223/11					

LIVED (15) .... ENCTR 21/27

ARABY	33/12	HOUSE	61/12	HOUSE	66/13	LITTL 70/10
LITTL	77/07	PNFUL	107/01	PNFUL	107/04	PNFUL 108/23
PNFUL	109/09	PNFUL	115/01	PNFUL	116/28	DEAD 190/19
DEAD	222/10	DEAD	223/21			

LIVELY (6) .... EVELN 37/29

RACE	46/10	GALNT	54/25	HOUSE	63/06	LITTL 77/21
MOTHR	144/24					

LIVERPOOL (1) .... HOUSE 62/06
LIVES (3) .... ARABY 29/05
   DEAD 194/22   DEAD 215/16
LIVING (12) .... GALNT 49/06

GALNT	50/26	LITTL	77/04	PNFUL	116/22	IVY D 128/10
DEAD	203/22	DEAD	203/28	DEAD	204/08	DEAD 204/08
DEAD	204/08	DEAD	218/31	DEAD	224/04	

LIZZIE (1) .... CLAY 101/09
LOAD (1) .... EVELN 38/22
LOAN (2) .... IVY D 129/06
   GRACE 159/28
LOANS (1) .... GRACE 155/05
LOATHED (1) .... PARTS 97/12
LOBES (1) .... DEAD 184/27
LOCK (2) .... HOUSE 64/07
   DEAD 216/09
LOCKED (1) .... DEAD 223/09
LOCKS (1) .... DEAD 210/24
LODGERS (1) .... HOUSE 65/12
LODGING (1) .... EVELN 38/31
LODGINGS (2) .... HOUSE 62/12
   DEAD 220/30
LOFT (1) .... ENCTR 19/05
LOFTY (2) .... PNFUL 107/07
   GRACE 173/29
LONDON (16) .... LITTL 70/10

LITTL	71/04	LITTL	72/22	LITTL	73/19	LITTL 73/24

```
LITTL   76/01      LITTL   76/12      LITTL   77/04      LITTL   77/28
LITTL   77/29      LITTL   77/31      LITTL   83/25      PARTS   95/22
MOTHR  143/26      GRACE  154/09      DEAD   199/21
LONDONER (1) ................................................ HOUSE   68/11
LONELINESS (1) ............................................... PNFUL  111/28
LONELY (5) ................................................... PNFUL  113/10
PNFUL  116/21      PNFUL  116/30      PNFUL  116/32      DEAD   223/32
LONG (61) .................................................... SISTR    9/08
SISTR   13/32      SISTR   17/25      ENCTR   21/27      ENCTR   22/34
ENCTR   25/02      ENCTR   26/18      ARABY   29/08      EVELN   37/02
EVELN   39/26      EVELN   40/04      EVELN   40/31      RACE    47/33
GALNT   49/10      GALNT   58/05      GALNT   59/27      HOUSE   61/18
HOUSE   63/11      HOUSE   66/06      HOUSE   68/25      LITTL   75/08
LITTL   81/02      LITTL   82/12      PARTS   90/03      PARTS   96/18
CLAY    99/07      CLAY    99/11      CLAY    99/11      CLAY   102/13
CLAY   102/22      CLAY   104/11      CLAY   106/14      PNFUL  108/17
PNFUL  116/18      IVY D  125/32      IVY D  129/28      IVY D  134/02
GRACE  152/12      GRACE  155/08      GRACE  155/33      GRACE  157/21
GRACE  163/21      GRACE  170/13      DEAD   176/01      DEAD   176/25
DEAD   178/21      DEAD   187/06      DEAD   190/07      DEAD   194/02
DEAD   197/30      DEAD   203/06      DEAD   203/07      DEAD   203/08
DEAD   205/10      DEAD   205/11      DEAD   206/19      DEAD   208/30
DEAD   216/10      DEAD   218/28      DEAD   218/30      DEAD   222/11
LONGED (11) .................................................. SISTR    9/14
HOUSE   67/34      PARTS   89/29      PARTS   90/25      PARTS   97/04
DEAD   213/12      DEAD   213/14      DEAD   213/34      DEAD   214/09
DEAD   217/12      DEAD   217/17
LONGER (10) .................................................. ARABY   33/22
HOUSE   68/28      HOUSE   68/32      IVY D  133/33      MOTHR  145/11
DEAD   192/33      DEAD   213/06      DEAD   221/33      DEAD   222/14
DEAD   222/15
LONGING (1) .................................................. LITTL   83/16
LOOK (39) .................................................... SISTR    9/15
SISTR   11/31      SISTR   12/23      SISTR   12/26      SISTR   18/06
ENCTR   26/24      EVELN   37/29      GALNT   50/07      GALNT   54/31
GALNT   54/33      GALNT   57/01      HOUSE   62/34      HOUSE   66/14
LITTL   72/12      LITTL   74/25      PARTS   89/22      PARTS   95/23
CLAY   103/24      PNFUL  107/05      IVY D  121/09      IVY D  131/30
IVY D  131/31      IVY D  132/01      IVY D  132/04      IVY D  132/20
MOTHR  139/08      MOTHR  140/13      GRACE  151/13      GRACE  164/05
GRACE  164/05      DEAD   177/26      DEAD   181/21      DEAD   184/31
DEAD   188/06      DEAD   207/03      DEAD   211/25      DEAD   214/16
DEAD   216/24      DEAD   222/27
LOOKED (63) .................................................. SISTR   10/25
SISTR   14/05      SISTR   14/18      SISTR   15/26      SISTR   15/26
SISTR   18/01      ENCTR   19/12      ENCTR   24/12      ARABY   33/11
ARABY   35/17      EVELN   37/06      RACE    45/30      GALNT   51/23
GALNT   56/17      GALNT   58/21      GALNT   60/18      HOUSE   68/22
LITTL   73/12      LITTL   74/19      LITTL   77/08      LITTL   79/19
LITTL   80/06      LITTL   82/01      LITTL   82/24      LITTL   83/09
LITTL   84/26      PARTS   88/20      PARTS   88/31      PARTS   93/16
PARTS   93/16      PARTS   93/17      PARTS   94/04      PARTS   96/05
PARTS   98/14      CLAY    99/02      CLAY   101/31      CLAY   103/28
PNFUL  109/20      PNFUL  117/10      PNFUL  117/11      IVY D  130/32
MOTHR  142/06      MOTHR  142/11      MOTHR  145/33      MOTHR  146/16
MOTHR  147/13      MOTHR  148/33      GRACE  151/29      GRACE  151/30
GRACE  157/02      GRACE  159/04      GRACE  174/29      DEAD   177/31
DEAD   190/09      DEAD   191/18      DEAD   197/06      DEAD   201/30
DEAD   204/23      DEAD   216/13      DEAD   216/21      DEAD   219/18
DEAD   219/23      DEAD   222/04
LOOKING (28) ................................................. SISTR   10/27
SISTR   16/06      ENCTR   23/12      ENCTR   24/30      ENCTR   26/06
```

ENCTR 28/04	ARABY 30/23	ARABY 32/30	LITTL 75/13
PARTS 93/10	CLAY 100/27	CLAY 106/16	PNFUL 108/21
IVY D 121/32	IVY D 126/08	IVY D 130/17	MOTHR 141/33
GRACE 170/19	GRACE 171/13	DEAD 178/13	DEAD 184/16
DEAD 192/17	DEAD 193/05	DEAD 206/25	DEAD 213/22
DEAD 214/19	DEAD 216/28	DEAD 217/23	

LOOKING-GLASS (1) .... HOUSE 68/20
LOOKS (3) .... SISTR 15/24
    RACE 44/23   IVY D 130/02
LOOPED (1) .... GRACE 166/19
LOOPHOLE (1) .... HOUSE 65/32
LOOSE (4) .... RACE 45/28
    HOUSE 67/07   LITTL 77/22   DEAD 218/15
LOOSELY (1) .... SISTR 14/28
LOOSEN (1) .... MOTHR 137/02
LOOSENED (1) .... RACE 46/14
LORD (10) .... SISTR 17/12
    ENCTR 25/08   ENCTR 25/14   ENCTR 25/16   ARABY 33/27
    IVY D 127/23   IVY D 127/23   IVY D 128/08   IVY D 134/28
    DEAD 207/28
LORDLY (1) .... RACE 45/08
LOSE (3) .... RACE 48/21
    PARTS 87/06   CLAY 104/30
LOSERS (1) .... RACE 48/26
LOSING (2) .... RACE 48/11
    LITTL 84/23
LOSS (3) .... RACE 46/17
    HOUSE 65/05   HOUSE 65/15
LOST (5) .... RACE 46/02
    PARTS 95/27   PARTS 97/05   IVY D 120/34   DEAD 179/31
LOT (3) .... IVY D 123/21
    GRACE 173/32   DEAD 202/15
LOTHARIO (2) .... GALNT 52/17
    GALNT 52/18
LOTS (3) .... ENCTR 25/29
    HOUSE 64/21   GRACE 168/24
LOUD (4) .... RACE 45/14
    PARTS 94/15   PNFUL 114/02   DEAD 193/08
LOUDER (2) .... MOTHR 146/09
    DEAD 202/01
LOUDLY (8) .... ENCTR 28/04
    RACE 46/31   RACE 48/02   LITTL 82/01   DEAD 193/07
    DEAD 197/29   DEAD 203/34   DEAD 205/08
LOUD-VOICED (1) .... HOUSE 65/09
LOUTISH (1) .... PARTS 96/22
LOVE (19) .... ENCTR 27/28
    ARABY 31/29   ARABY 31/29   ARABY 31/34   EVELN 40/19
    EVELN 41/16   LITTL 83/34   LITTL 85/17   LITTL 85/17
    PNFUL 112/19   PNFUL 117/16   IVY D 123/09   DEAD 191/16
    DEAD 208/08   DEAD 211/25   DEAD 219/03   DEAD 219/12
    DEAD 220/10   DEAD 223/14
LOVED (4) .... HOUSE 66/20
    CLAY 106/11   IVY D 134/26   DEAD 188/11
LOVELY (5) .... CLAY 100/28
    MOTHR 138/32   DEAD 182/17   DEAD 184/12   DEAD 184/12
LOVER (1) .... EVELN 39/21
LOVERS (1) .... GALNT 57/30
LOVER'S (2) .... HOUSE 68/06
    DEAD 223/10
LOVES (2) .... EVELN 39/06
    PNFUL 117/13
LOW (10) .... SISTR 18/01

LITTL 72/19	PARTS 95/06	PNFUL 115/31	IVY D 134/10	
IVY D 135/13	GRACE 158/19	GRACE 160/25	DEAD 179/24	
DEAD 183/23				

LOW-CUT (1) .... DEAD 187/22
LOWER (10) .... SISTR 13/27

LITTL 73/13	LITTL 79/20	PARTS 88/12	PARTS 90/13
PARTS 94/07	PNFUL 112/15	PNFUL 114/16	MOTHR 145/29
GRACE 153/28			

LOWERED (1) .... ENCTR 26/12
LOWERING (2) .... GRACE 170/21
    DEAD 206/08
LOWEST (2) .... PNFUL 108/01
    DEAD 177/27
LUCAN (1) .... PNFUL 115/18
LUCK (2) .... RACE 48/19
    MOTHR 141/31
LUCREZIA (1) .... DEAD 199/15
LUDICROUS (1) .... DEAD 220/02
LUGUBRIOUS (2) .... GRACE 172/09
    DEAD 201/18
LUMPS (1) .... IVY D 123/31
LUNCH (2) .... PARTS 87/21
    PNFUL 108/32
LUNCHEON (1) .... RACE 43/10
LUNCHES (1) .... ENCTR 23/05
LUNCH-TIME (1) .... LITTL 70/08
LURCH (1) .... IVY D 121/06
LUST (2) .... DEAD 215/13
    DEAD 219/02
LUSTRE (1) .... DEAD 178/23
LUSTS (1) .... DEAD 220/04
LUTES (1) .... RACE 46/20
LUX (5) .... GRACE 167/11

GRACE 167/11	GRACE 167/14	GRACE 167/17

LUXURIATED (1) .... GRACE 167/18
LYING (7) .... ARABY 32/19

SISTR 18/11	EVELN 40/27	PNFUL 114/11
DEAD 192/05	DEAD 213/17	

LYONS (12) ....

IVY D 130/14	IVY D 130/16	IVY D 130/27
IVY D 131/14	IVY D 131/25	IVY D 132/13
IVY D 132/24	IVY D 133/17	IVY D 135/23

LYONS' (1) .... IVY D 131/09
LYTTON (1) .... ENCTR 25/09
LYTTON'S (2) .... ENCTR 25/14
    ENCTR 25/16

MA'AM (2) .... SISTR 15/16
    SISTR 16/27
MAC (4) .... GALNT 58/23

GALNT 58/24	GALNT 58/25	GALNT 58/26

MACHALE (3) .... GRACE 169/21

GRACE 169/32	GRACE 170/12

MACHINE (3) .... PARTS 86/05

PARTS 90/19	PARTS 91/31

MACHINERY (1) .... RACE 45/11
MADAM (6) .... HOUSE 62/10

HOUSE 68/03	MOTHR 143/20	MOTHR 143/26
MOTHR 147/10		

MADAM'S (2) .... HOUSE 62/16
    HOUSE 62/26

MADE (90) .... SISTR 13/23

SISTR 13/28	SISTR 18/15	ENCTR 19/02	ENCTR 21/08
ENCTR 22/10	ENCTR 24/07	EVELN 37/13	EVELN 39/28
RACE 43/16	RACE 43/18	RACE 45/06	RACE 46/32
RACE 47/20	RACE 47/32	GALNT 49/15	GALNT 51/17
GALNT 53/16	GALNT 55/22	GALNT 57/27	GALNT 57/32
GALNT 58/22	GALNT 60/12	HOUSE 62/04	HOUSE 62/06
HOUSE 62/34	HOUSE 63/25	HOUSE 64/04	HOUSE 64/12
HOUSE 64/14	HOUSE 64/15	HOUSE 64/33	HOUSE 65/24
HOUSE 66/27	HOUSE 67/25	HOUSE 68/11	LITTL 72/20
LITTL 77/18	LITTL 80/15	LITTL 82/05	PARTS 87/09
PARTS 91/10	PARTS 92/15	PARTS 93/26	PARTS 94/32
CLAY 102/25	CLAY 102/31	CLAY 103/20	CLAY 103/33
CLAY 104/04	CLAY 104/07	CLAY 104/08	CLAY 105/23
PNFUL 107/12	IVY D 124/04	IVY D 127/23	MOTHR 136/07
MOTHR 136/12	MOTHR 137/15	MOTHR 138/11	MOTHR 140/02
MOTHR 145/32	MOTHR 147/14	GRACE 151/19	GRACE 152/07
GRACE 156/20	GRACE 156/30	GRACE 156/33	GRACE 158/26
GRACE 159/17	GRACE 159/33	GRACE 160/22	GRACE 160/27
GRACE 168/16	GRACE 169/05	DEAD 176/21	DEAD 177/26
DEAD 178/12	DEAD 179/08	DEAD 182/17	DEAD 184/30
DEAD 185/13	DEAD 199/03	DEAD 202/28	DEAD 209/28
DEAD 210/20	DEAD 211/16	DEAD 217/30	DEAD 219/20
DEAD 223/23			

MADNESS (1) .... GRACE 168/14

MADONNA (1) .... HOUSE 63/01

MADRIGAL (1) .... RACE 46/16

MAGAZINE (1) .... PNFUL 117/09

MAGELLAN (1) .... EVELN 39/14

MAGICAL (2) .... ARABY 34/25
RACE 45/10

MAGIC-LANTERN (1) .... GRACE 171/31

MAGNETISED (2) .... ENCTR 26/09
ENCTR 27/09

MAGNIFICENT (1) .... GRACE 165/23

MAGNIFIED (1) .... HOUSE 65/31

MAGNILOQUENT (1) .... MOTHR 145/24

MAHONY (21) .... ENCTR 21/10

ENCTR 21/18	ENCTR 21/24	ENCTR 22/11	ENCTR 22/14
ENCTR 22/17	ENCTR 22/21	ENCTR 22/27	ENCTR 23/11
ENCTR 24/05	ENCTR 24/11	ENCTR 25/12	ENCTR 25/17
ENCTR 25/19	ENCTR 25/22	ENCTR 25/26	ENCTR 26/23
ENCTR 26/25	ENCTR 26/32	ENCTR 27/01	ENCTR 28/09

MAHONY'S (2) .... ENCTR 21/12
ENCTR 22/06

MAIL (2) .... PNFUL 113/09
DEAD 177/12

MAIN (3) .... EVELN 38/32
DEAD 176/08 | DEAD 203/21

MAINLY (2) .... SISTR 11/34
GALNT 51/33

MAJOR (1) .... IVY D 125/16

MAJORITY (1) .... GRACE 174/04

MAKE (41) .... SISTR 13/20

SISTR 15/06	SISTR 15/27	ARABY 35/26	EVELN 39/31
RACE 44/10	HOUSE 64/10	HOUSE 64/32	HOUSE 65/05
HOUSE 66/21	LITTL 74/23	LITTL 77/32	LITTL 83/06
PARTS 91/32	PARTS 92/12	PARTS 94/25	PNFUL 110/08
PNFUL 110/13	IVY D 119/30	IVY D 123/18	IVY D 127/23
IVY D 127/31	IVY D 127/32	MOTHR 148/13	GRACE 155/18
GRACE 155/27	GRACE 156/23	GRACE 162/34	GRACE 170/29
GRACE 170/32	GRACE 172/20	GRACE 173/23	DEAD 179/14

DEAD	183/21	DEAD	188/09	DEAD	190/30	DEAD	193/34
DEAD	201/11	DEAD	209/20	DEAD	213/34	DEAD	218/23

MAKER (1) .... GRACE 172/26
MAKES (5) .... SISTR 17/07
    ARABY 34/07   GRACE 161/10   DEAD 180/19   DEAD 207/03
MAKING (10) .... ENCTR 21/22
    HOUSE 61/07   PARTS 93/05   CLAY 99/14   DEAD 180/17
    DEAD 189/25   DEAD 190/32   DEAD 200/14   DEAD 205/21
    DEAD 213/23
MALE (2) .... PARTS 89/19
    MOTHR 141/26
MALEFICENT (1) .... SISTR 9/13
MALINS (35) .... DEAD 176/27
    DEAD 176/30   DEAD 184/24   DEAD 185/02   DEAD 185/18
    DEAD 185/21   DEAD 185/29   DEAD 191/18   DEAD 191/20
    DEAD 191/22   DEAD 191/30   DEAD 193/12   DEAD 193/33
    DEAD 198/03   DEAD 198/22   DEAD 198/28   DEAD 198/33
    DEAD 200/20   DEAD 200/23   DEAD 201/09   DEAD 201/19
    DEAD 205/22   DEAD 206/01   DEAD 206/05   DEAD 208/01
    DEAD 208/20   DEAD 208/21   DEAD 208/26   DEAD 208/28
    DEAD 208/30   DEAD 208/32   DEAD 209/03   DEAD 209/08
    DEAD 216/33   DEAD 217/16
MALINS' (4) .... DEAD 182/11
    DEAD 185/23   DEAD 185/25   DEAD 190/14
MALL (1) .... ENCTR 21/34
MALODOROUS (1) .... PNFUL 115/25
MALONE (2) .... LITTL 74/12
    LITTL 74/12
MALT (2) .... LITTL 74/32
    PARTS 93/25
MAMMA (4) .... HOUSE 69/04
    CLAY 100/21   CLAY 100/21   CLAY 103/23
MAMMA'S (1) .... LITTL 85/18
MAMMON (2) .... GRACE 173/24
    GRACE 174/08
MAN (221)
MANAGE (1) .... DEAD 176/30
MANAGED (2) .... RACE 45/01
    GALNT 59/09
MANAGER (11) .... RACE 43/07
    CLAY 104/07   CLAY 104/09   GRACE 150/12   GRACE 150/15
    GRACE 151/04   GRACE 151/09   GRACE 151/14   GRACE 151/16
    GRACE 152/01   GRACE 152/33
MANGAN'S (2) .... ARABY 30/16
    ARABY 30/20
MANHOOD (2) .... LITTL 80/30
    IVY D 124/31
MANIFEST (1) .... GRACE 159/33
MANIKIN (1) .... PARTS 91/13
MANLY (2) .... EVELN 38/28
    GRACE 174/24
MANNER (13) .... RACE 45/34
    RACE 46/11   GALNT 50/20   GALNT 52/03   GALNT 52/19
    HOUSE 63/21   LITTL 77/06   PARTS 93/28   MOTHR 136/12
    GRACE 173/33   DEAD 187/28   DEAD 193/29   DEAD 208/01
MANNERISMS (1) .... MOTHR 147/11
MANNERS (6) .... LITTL 70/14
    MOTHR 136/14   MOTHR 144/33   GRACE 154/30   GRACE 160/05
    GRACE 166/24
MANNIE (1) .... LITTL 85/16
MANOEUVRES (1) .... DEAD 208/29
MAN-O'-WAR (1) .... DEAD 186/30

MAN'S (11) .... PARTS 88/01
 PARTS 91/30 IVY D 118/06 GRACE 151/03 GRACE 151/05
 GRACE 151/26 GRACE 151/28 GRACE 152/03 GRACE 170/24
 DEAD 199/34 DEAD 209/33
MANSION (5) .... IVY D 127/28
 IVY D 128/11 MOTHR 144/30 DEAD 207/33 DEAD 208/05
MANSIONS (1) .... LITTL 71/34
MANTELPIECE (7) .... HOUSE 64/19
 PNFUL 107/16 IVY D 121/03 IVY D 124/04 IVY D 129/27
 MOTHR 145/03 GRACE 154/09
MANUSCRIPT (1) .... PNFUL 108/04
MANY (42) .... ENCTR 22/32
 ENCTR 25/23 ENCTR 25/26 ARABY 31/29 EVELN 37/07
 EVELN 37/30 RACE 43/18   RACE 44/16   GALNT 56/25
 GALNT 58/32 LITTL 71/18 LITTL 72/09 LITTL 72/24
 LITTL 73/28 LITTL 74/20 LITTL 78/16 LITTL 78/20
 LITTL 84/04 PARTS 87/21 CLAY 101/10 PNFUL 108/30
 PNFUL 110/13 PNFUL 110/23 PNFUL 111/18 IVY D 118/13
 IVY D 120/03 IVY D 124/27 IVY D 126/31 MOTHR 136/13
 MOTHR 138/02 MOTHR 140/03 GRACE 155/04 GRACE 167/31
 DEAD 176/11 DEAD 188/18 DEAD 203/08 DEAD 203/08
 DEAD 204/05 DEAD 205/33 DEAD 208/29 DEAD 215/11
 DEAD 223/09
MANY'S (1) .... IVY D 129/03
MARBLE (2) .... CLAY 106/04
 GRACE 172/09
MARGARET (1) .... EVELN 37/14
MARGARET'S (1) .... LITTL 83/33
MARIA (40) .... CLAY 99/02
 CLAY 99/08   CLAY 99/10   CLAY 99/16   CLAY 100/02
 CLAY 100/02 CLAY 100/21 CLAY 101/06 CLAY 101/09
 CLAY 101/11 CLAY 101/17 CLAY 101/22 CLAY 102/25
 CLAY 102/33 CLAY 103/07 CLAY 103/14 CLAY 103/17
 CLAY 103/21 CLAY 103/22 CLAY 103/31 CLAY 103/31
 CLAY 104/07 CLAY 104/16 CLAY 104/17 CLAY 104/20
 CLAY 104/22 CLAY 104/23 CLAY 104/25 CLAY 104/33
 CLAY 105/06 CLAY 105/08 CLAY 105/19 CLAY 105/23
 CLAY 105/24 CLAY 105/26 CLAY 105/30 CLAY 105/31
 CLAY 105/32 CLAY 105/34 CLAY 105/34
MARIA'S (2) .... CLAY 101/15
 CLAY 105/33
MARITANA (1) .... MOTHR 142/24
MARKED (1) .... PNFUL 109/30
MARKETING (2) .... ARABY 31/02
 EVELN 38/19
MARKETS (1) .... GALNT 58/30
MARLBOROUGH (1) .... HOUSE 64/23
MARRED (1) .... MOTHR 142/26
MARRIAGE (4) .... HOUSE 65/05
 MOTHR 136/13 GRACE 157/08 DEAD 187/03
MARRIED (12) .... EVELN 37/32
 HOUSE 61/03 HOUSE 66/23 LITTL 79/02 LITTL 83/17
 PARTS 94/30 PNFUL 115/01 MOTHR 137/07 GRACE 157/15
 GRACE 157/28 DEAD 179/33 DEAD 190/19
MARRY (4) .... GALNT 51/09
 HOUSE 65/33 HOUSE 66/23 LITTL 81/22
MARRYING (1) .... MOTHR 137/03
MARTIN (6) .... GRACE 155/19
 GRACE 157/18 GRACE 161/21 GRACE 165/02 GRACE 168/19
 GRACE 169/09
MARVEL (2) .... ENCTR 19/03
 ENCTR 20/15

```
MARY (63) ...................................................  EVELN   37/14
        HOUSE   64/04   HOUSE   64/04   HOUSE   65/06   HOUSE   67/26
        PARTS   98/23   PARTS   98/23   PARTS   98/24   PNFUL  115/04
        DEAD   175/17   DEAD   176/03   DEAD   176/07   DEAD   176/28
        DEAD   183/20   DEAD   183/25   DEAD   183/33   DEAD   183/34
        DEAD   184/03   DEAD   184/05   DEAD   184/14   DEAD   186/01
        DEAD   186/06   DEAD   186/10   DEAD   187/08   DEAD   187/13
        DEAD   192/32   DEAD   194/18   DEAD   194/20   DEAD   194/25
        DEAD   194/28   DEAD   195/05   DEAD  ·195/10   DEAD   195/13
        DEAD   195/19   DEAD   195/22   DEAD   196/05   DEAD   197/18
        DEAD   197/21   DEAD   197/31   DEAD   198/34   DEAD   199/26
        DEAD   200/12   DEAD   200/34   DEAD   201/16   DEAD   202/29
        DEAD   204/21   DEAD   206/07   DEAD   206/09   DEAD   206/15
        DEAD   206/30   DEAD   207/01   DEAD   207/11   DEAD   208/20
        DEAD   209/06   DEAD   210/12   DEAD   210/13   DEAD   210/27
        DEAD   210/30   DEAD   210/31   DEAD   211/04   DEAD   211/22
        DEAD   212/14   DEAD   212/16
MARY'S (1) ................................................  IVY D  123/23
MASK (1) ..................................................  RACE    46/29
MASS (8) ..................................................  SISTR   13/06
        SISTR   13/23   SISTR   16/09   ENCTR   19/09   EVELN   40/27
        CLAY   101/25   CLAY   101/30   MOTHR  137/31
MASSEY'S (1) ..............................................  DEAD   188/15
MASSIVE (2) ...............................................  SISTR   14/29
        GRACE 173/13
MASTER (2) ................................................  IVY D  128/02
        DEAD   217/12
MASTERFULLY (1) ...........................................  PARTS   93/11
MASTER'S (2) ..............................................  ARABY   32/22
        GALNT   54/13
MASTS (1) .................................................  ENCTR   23/13
MAT (4) ...................................................  IVY D  120/29
        IVY D  121/22   IVY D  123/16   DEAD   177/05
MATCH (5) .................................................  GALNT   58/27
        IVY D  119/07   GRACE 153/24   GRACE 153/27   GRACE 153/30
MATCH-SELLERS (1) .........................................  PARTS   94/17
MATERIALS (1) .............................................  PNFUL  108/03
MATERNAL (1) ..............................................  PNFUL  110/30
MATES (1) .................................................  ENCTR   21/25
MATRON (3) ................................................  CLAY    99/01
        CLAY   99/15   CLAY   100/31
MATRONLY (1) ..............................................  DEAD   186/27
MATTER (15) ...............................................  GALNT   52/01
        HOUSE   64/22   HOUSE   66/20   PARTS   87/15   PARTS   87/18
        PARTS   88/11   CLAY   104/04   CLAY   104/26   IVY D  126/11
        IVY D  127/15   MOTHR  141/09   GRACE 162/28   GRACE 162/31
        DEAD   184/17   DEAD   218/10
MATTERS (3) ...............................................  RACE    45/04
        MOTHR  138/17   GRACE 174/09
MATURITY (1) ..............................................  LITTL   73/27
M'AULEY'S (2) .............................................  GRACE 162/17
        GRACE 162/23
MAY (26) ..................................................  SISTR   12/21
        ARABY   33/12   ARABY   33/26   RACE    45/32   GALNT   50/13
        LITTL   77/25   LITTL   79/02   LITTL   79/08   LITTL   79/32
        LITTL   81/02   LITTL   81/21   PARTS   87/08   IVY D  123/14
        IVY D  135/01   IVY D  135/14   IVY D  135/18   GRACE 163/05
        GRACE 173/25   DEAD   182/20   DEAD   184/01   DEAD   192/22
        DEAD   199/24   DEAD   202/19   DEAD   203/08   DEAD   203/22
        DEAD   205/10
MAYBE (2) .................................................  GALNT   51/09
        DEAD   199/24
```

```
MAYNOOTH ( 1 ) .....................................  PNFUL 108/01
MAYOR ( 4 ) ........................................  IVY D 127/23
     IVY D 127/23     IVY D 128/08     GRACE 172/26
MAZE ( 1 ) ........................................  EVELN  40/29
MCCLOUD'S ( 1 ) ...................................  CLAY  105/22
M'COY ( 32 ) ......................................  GRACE 157/04
     GRACE 158/16     GRACE 158/17     GRACE 158/34     GRACE 159/03
     GRACE 160/19     GRACE 160/21     GRACE 160/23     GRACE 161/05
     GRACE 161/28     GRACE 162/17     GRACE 162/21     GRACE 163/01
     GRACE 163/09     GRACE 163/29     GRACE 164/03     GRACE 164/07
     GRACE 164/16     GRACE 165/05     GRACE 165/13     GRACE 165/16
     GRACE 166/03     GRACE 167/16     GRACE 167/26     GRACE 168/10
     GRACE 169/02     GRACE 169/06     GRACE 169/15     GRACE 170/04
     GRACE 171/19     GRACE 172/16     GRACE 172/18
M'COY'S ( 1 ) .....................................  GRACE 167/30
ME ( 180 )
MEADE ( 1 ) .......................................  HOUSE  65/10
MEADE'S ( 1 ) .....................................  MOTHR 138/22
MEAGRE ( 1 ) ......................................  MOTHR 143/19
MEAL ( 2 ) ........................................  ARABY  33/19
     CLAY  101/09
MEALS ( 1 ) .......................................  EVELN  38/24
MEAN ( 22 ) .......................................  SISTR  10/31
     SISTR  10/32     SISTR  17/28     HOUSE  65/15     LITTL  77/28
     LITTL  81/22     LITTL  81/33     LITTL  83/11     LITTL  83/19
     PARTS  97/30     PNFUL 107/04     IVY D 123/15     IVY D 123/22
     IVY D 131/29     IVY D 132/24     MOTHR 144/17     GRACE 163/25
     GRACE 167/09     DEAD  199/28     DEAD  200/29     DEAD  208/15
     DEAD  211/04
MEANING ( 5 ) .....................................  SISTR  11/20
     SISTR  13/05     RACE   44/11     PARTS  87/07     GRACE 163/18
MEANS ( 4 ) .......................................  PNFUL 107/12
     IVY D 121/09     IVY D 129/06     IVY D 132/06
MEANT ( 6 ) .......................................  GALNT  56/27
     HOUSE  63/11     HOUSE  68/15     CLAY  101/20     MOTHR 140/01
     MOTHR 140/02
MEANWHILE ( 1 ) ...................................  RACE   45/19
MEASURE ( 2 ) .....................................  GRACE 169/04
     DEAD  183/08
MEASURES ( 2 ) ....................................  PNFUL 115/12
     GRACE 167/02
MEAT ( 3 ) ........................................  HOUSE  61/09
     HOUSE  63/24     PARTS  88/32
MEATH ( 1 ) .......................................  SISTR  12/08
MECHANIC ( 2 ) ....................................  GALNT  57/13
     GALNT  57/22
MECHANICAL ( 1 ) ..................................  DEAD  185/26
MECHANICALLY ( 2 ) ................................  IVY D 118/09
     DEAD  185/25
MECHANICIANS ( 1 ) ................................  RACE   46/19
MEDAL ( 2 ) .......................................  MOTHR 142/33
     GRACE 151/03
MEDIAEVAL ( 1 ) ...................................  PNFUL 108/15
MEDICAL ( 2 ) .....................................  PNFUL 115/08
     GRACE 160/09
MEDIOCRE ( 1 ) ....................................  MOTHR 140/09
MEDITATE ( 1 ) ....................................  GALNT  53/05
MEDITATIVELY ( 2 ) ................................  IVY D 118/09
     IVY D 118/16
MEEK ( 1 ) ........................................  DEAD  194/05
MEEKLY ( 1 ) ......................................  MOTHR 149/28
MEET ( 16 ) .......................................  ENCTR  21/12
```

ENCTR 21/17	EVELN 39/02	EVELN 39/21	GALNT 55/06
LITTL 75/24	LITTL 79/22	LITTL 79/25	PARTS 91/01
PARTS 94/34	PNFUL 110/17	PNFUL 112/01	PNFUL 112/23
GRACE 162/17	GRACE 162/21	DEAD 188/16	

MEETING (6) .... LITTL 70/09
LITTL 80/18	PNFUL 110/12	IVY D 120/20	MOTHR 148/22
DEAD 202/04			

MEETINGS (2) .... PNFUL 110/14
PNFUL 110/32

MELANCHOLY (8) .... EVELN 40/06
LITTL 71/13	LITTL 73/30	LITTL 73/32	LITTL 74/05
LITTL 84/02	LITTL 84/03	MOTHR 142/11	

MELBOURNE (1) .... EVELN 37/17
MELLERAY (2) .... DEAD 200/25
DEAD 200/26

MELLOW (2) .... PARTS 95/04
DEAD 200/06

MELODIES (1) .... DEAD 179/12
MELODIOUS (1) .... DEAD 205/24
MELODY (6) .... RACE 44/06
GALNT 54/14	GALNT 56/21	DEAD 186/04	DEAD 186/05
DEAD 187/09			

MEMBER (3) .... RACE 43/11
MOTHR 142/01 DEAD 205/07

MEMBERS (3) .... GRACE 159/23
DEAD 175/14 DEAD 175/15

MEMOIRS (1) .... ARABY 29/13
MEMORANDA (1) .... IVY D 122/32
MEMORIES (6) .... HOUSE 68/26
HOUSE 68/30	DEAD 192/10	DEAD 204/06	DEAD 215/12
DEAD 219/31			

MEMORY (17) .... GALNT 49/02
GALNT 59/12	HOUSE 67/02	LITTL 72/01	PNFUL 109/26
PNFUL 116/03	PNFUL 116/25	PNFUL 116/32	PNFUL 117/29
IVY D 135/02	IVY D 135/20	GRACE 154/05	DEAD 187/04
DEAD 190/25	DEAD 203/32	DEAD 213/16	DEAD 213/33

MEN (69) .... ARABY 31/04
ARABY 35/01	ARABY 35/22	RACE 42/16	RACE 42/18
RACE 43/07	RACE 45/21	RACE 46/07	RACE 46/14
RACE 46/30	RACE 47/07	RACE 47/26	RACE 47/30
RACE 48/06	RACE 48/13	RACE 48/22	GALNT 49/09
GALNT 52/05	GALNT 54/17	GALNT 58/31	HOUSE 62/09
HOUSE 62/11	HOUSE 63/07	HOUSE 63/07	HOUSE 63/09
HOUSE 63/10	HOUSE 63/14	LITTL 71/08	LITTL 74/01
PARTS 93/07	PARTS 93/33	PARTS 94/15	PARTS 94/16
PARTS 96/02	CLAY 102/30	CLAY 103/02	IVY D 122/11
IVY D 123/26	IVY D 129/26	IVY D 130/03	MOTHR 136/17
MOTHR 139/08	MOTHR 143/10	MOTHR 144/24	MOTHR 145/18
MOTHR 147/20	MOTHR 147/30	GRACE 150/11	GRACE 152/32
GRACE 161/21	GRACE 163/32	GRACE 164/12	GRACE 164/27
GRACE 167/08	GRACE 169/12	GRACE 174/01	GRACE 174/03
GRACE 174/08	GRACE 174/12	DEAD 178/10	DEAD 183/01
DEAD 183/06	DEAD 183/08	DEAD 183/28	DEAD 186/06
DEAD 187/15	DEAD 199/23	DEAD 201/21	DEAD 201/21

MENACE (1) .... GALNT 60/25
MENACINGLY (1) .... DEAD 213/03
MEN'S (2) .... RACE 48/24
DEAD 179/13

MENTAL (2) .... PNFUL 108/15
PNFUL 111/23

MENTALLY (1) .... GALNT 57/27
MENTION (1) .... GRACE 153/10

```
MENTIONED (5) ..................................... ENCTR  25/09
    ENCTR  25/22   CLAY  104/26   IVY D 123/06   DEAD  199/23
MERCANTILE (1) .................................... PNFUL 110/10
MERCER (2) ........................................ ARABY  33/16
    ARABY  33/21
MERCHANT (1) ...................................... RACE   43/21
MERCIFUL (1) ...................................... SISTR  17/29
MERCY (3) ......................................... SISTR  10/24
    SISTR  17/12   DEAD  207/28
MERE (2) .......................................... LITTL  80/27
    PARTS  97/06
MERELY (3) ........................................ RACE   44/30
    HOUSE  64/14   PNFUL 115/24
MEREST (1) ........................................ GRACE 155/02
MERRILY (1) ....................................... RACE   44/03
MERRIMENT (2) ..................................... RACE   47/27
    GRACE 162/10
MERRION (4) ....................................... GALNT  55/09
    GALNT  56/11   GALNT  59/03   DEAD  180/06
MERRY (4) ......................................... RACE   47/10
    CLAY  104/33   CLAY  104/34   CLAY  105/24
MERRY-MAKING (1) .................................. DEAD  222/23
MESS (1) .......................................... GRACE 152/25
MET (23) .......................................... ENCTR  19/04
    ENCTR  23/20   ENCTR  27/17   ARABY  30/02   RACE   43/30
    GALNT  51/01   GALNT  56/31   GALNT  58/17   HOUSE  62/19
    LITTL  75/29   LITTL  76/01   LITTL  85/10   CLAY  101/14
    CLAY  101/18   CLAY  105/09   PNFUL 110/04   PNFUL 110/14
    PNFUL 112/03   PNFUL 116/06   MOTHR 136/17   DEAD  190/07
    DEAD  204/13   DEAD  214/17
METAL (1) ......................................... ENCTR  23/06
METAPHOR (2) ...................................... GRACE 163/03
    GRACE 174/14
METHODS (1) ....................................... GRACE 154/06
MICE (1) .......................................... LITTL  71/31
MICHAEL (7) ....................................... PNFUL 108/05
    GRACE 172/29   DEAD  219/05   DEAD  220/10   DEAD  221/06
    DEAD  222/15   DEAD  223/32
MICHING (1) ....................................... ENCTR  21/11
MIDDAY (1) ........................................ PNFUL 108/32
MIDDLE (7) ........................................ ARABY  35/27
    PARTS  87/30   PNFUL 111/13   IVY D 121/01   GRACE 155/32
    DEAD  178/20   DEAD  182/29
MIDDLE-AGED (1) ................................... PARTS  90/01
MIDLAND (1) ....................................... GRACE 158/22
MIDST (1) ......................................... DEAD  203/18
MIDWAY (2) ........................................ ARABY  33/31
    DEAD  200/11
MIGHT (37) ........................................ SISTR  11/06
    SISTR  11/16   SISTR  17/18   ENCTR  21/17   GALNT  58/10
    HOUSE  65/16   LITTL  73/19   LITTL  73/27   LITTL  74/02
    LITTL  83/27   PARTS  87/19   PARTS  87/31   PARTS  92/20
    CLAY  104/24   CLAY  106/15   PNFUL 108/12   MOTHR 147/31
    MOTHR 149/01   MOTHR 149/03   GRACE 158/03   GRACE 160/11
    GRACE 163/15   GRACE 173/28   GRACE 174/13   GRACE 174/20
    GRACE 174/21   GRACE 174/27   DEAD  176/27   DEAD  184/04
    DEAD  193/34   DEAD  197/21   DEAD  203/28   DEAD  213/29
    DEAD  216/05   DEAD  216/13   DEAD  220/06   DEAD  223/02
MIGHTY (1) ........................................ IVY D 135/05
MIGNON (1) ........................................ DEAD  199/02
MILAN (1) ......................................... DEAD  199/21
MILD (2) .......................................... ENCTR  21/29
```

GALNT 49/02

MILDLY (1)				RACE 46/15
MILES (1)				RACE 44/06
MILITARY (1)				DEAD 207/26
MILK (2)				CLAY 101/06
MOTHR 142/30				
MILL (5)				DEAD 207/20
DEAD 207/23	DEAD 207/24	DEAD 208/04		DEAD 208/09
MILLS (1)				IVY D 131/32
MIMIC (2)				ENCTR 21/03
PARTS 97/33				
MIMICKING (1)				PARTS 92/18
MIMICRY (2)				GRACE 154/06
DEAD 183/18				
MIND (42)				SISTR 10/04
SISTR 10/22	SISTR 16/31	SISTR 17/11	SISTR 17/32	
ENCTR 21/09	ENCTR 26/10	ENCTR 27/09	GALNT 52/21	
GALNT 59/08	HOUSE 63/25	HOUSE 66/21	HOUSE 68/26	
LITTL 72/01	LITTL 73/26	LITTL 77/12	LITTL 80/17	
PARTS 87/22	PARTS 90/21	CLAY 102/04	PNFUL 108/26	
PNFUL 112/13	IVY D 119/08	IVY D 123/29	IVY D 134/01	
MOTHR 145/17	GRACE 163/18	GRACE 164/23	GRACE 168/16	
GRACE 171/01	DEAD 180/15	DEAD 182/14	DEAD 184/08	
DEAD 190/25	DEAD 192/19	DEAD 195/33	DEAD 203/05	
DEAD 203/14	DEAD 219/01	DEAD 219/15	DEAD 219/33	
DEAD 223/01				
MINDS (6)				SISTR 11/13
LITTL 74/03	GRACE 168/12	GRACE 168/14	GRACE 170/07	
DEAD 204/03				
MINE (2)				SISTR 10/29
LITTL 75/22				
MINERAL (1)				LITTL 74/30
MINERALS (2)				DEAD 197/02
DEAD 197/25				
MINGLED (1)				RACE 45/27
MINSTERS (1)				DEAD 196/22
MINSTRELS (1)				DEAD 181/12
MINUTE (10)				ENCTR 26/19
GALNT 50/09	LITTL 71/33	CLAY 101/19	IVY D 126/10	
IVY D 128/29	MOTHR 142/05	GRACE 153/29	GRACE 155/13	
DEAD 207/06				
MINUTES (25)				ENCTR 22/05
ENCTR 26/20	ENCTR 26/23	ARABY 34/22	ARABY 34/24	
GALNT 55/19	GALNT 60/01	HOUSE 64/21	HOUSE 65/26	
PARTS 88/16	PARTS 90/19	CLAY 100/05	CLAY 100/06	
CLAY 100/06	CLAY 101/01	PNFUL 117/32	IVY D 130/19	
IVY D 131/08	MOTHR 139/13	MOTHR 139/22	GRACE 150/11	
DEAD 176/32	DEAD 186/09	DEAD 195/17	DEAD 198/14	
MIRE (1)				IVY D 134/12
MIRROR (7)				RACE 47/16
CLAY 101/29	MOTHR 139/24	DEAD 216/16	DEAD 216/20	
DEAD 218/21	DEAD 220/05			
MIRTH (1)				DEAD 185/28
MIRTHLESS (1)				DEAD 180/33
MISDIRECTED (1)				DEAD 203/21
MISERABLE (1)				PNFUL 115/25
MISGAVE (1)				ARABY 33/02
MISS (99)				SISTR 15/31
SISTR 16/25	EVELN 37/25	EVELN 37/28	EVELN 37/29	
EVELN 39/26	PARTS 86/01	PARTS 86/05	PARTS 89/11	
PARTS 90/01	PARTS 90/10	PARTS 90/17	PARTS 91/05	
PARTS 91/27	PARTS 92/19	CLAY 105/22	PNFUL 115/04	

MOTHR 136/09	MOTHR 138/03	MOTHR 142/03	MOTHR 142/04
MOTHR 143/16	MOTHR 143/22	MOTHR 143/23	MOTHR 144/26
MOTHR 145/03	MOTHR 146/02	MOTHR 146/21	MOTHR 147/23
MOTHR 147/26	MOTHR 148/01	MOTHR 148/04	MOTHR 148/17
MOTHR 148/17	MOTHR 149/15	DEAD 175/07	DEAD 175/07
DEAD 175/09	DEAD 175/09	DEAD 177/01	DEAD 177/01
DEAD 177/08	DEAD 182/15	DEAD 182/15	DEAD 182/16
DEAD 182/20	DEAD 182/22	DEAD 182/22	DEAD 182/23
DEAD 182/26	DEAD 183/24	DEAD 183/25	DEAD 184/01
DEAD 184/01	DEAD 184/05	DEAD 184/06	DEAD 184/08
DEAD 187/20	DEAD 187/29	DEAD 188/03	DEAD 188/24
DEAD 189/06	DEAD 189/09	DEAD 189/12	DEAD 189/15
DEAD 189/20	DEAD 189/27	DEAD 189/32	DEAD 190/01
DEAD 190/03	DEAD 190/26	DEAD 191/01	DEAD 192/13
DEAD 192/26	DEAD 193/04	DEAD 193/31	DEAD 195/13
DEAD 195/14	DEAD 195/21	DEAD 195/24	DEAD 195/29
DEAD 195/31	DEAD 196/03	DEAD 197/10	DEAD 197/13
DEAD 197/15	DEAD 198/20	DEAD 199/30	DEAD 200/03
DEAD 200/16	DEAD 203/14	DEAD 204/04	DEAD 206/31
DEAD 211/03	DEAD 211/07	DEAD 211/26	DEAD 212/26
DEAD 212/27	DEAD 214/25		

MISSED (2) .... GRACE 153/01
   GRACE 160/04
MISSES (3) .... DEAD 175/13
   DEAD 185/02   DEAD 201/30
MISSING (2) .... PARTS 89/33
   PARTS 91/09
MISSUS (1) .... HOUSE 67/27
MIST (2) .... EVELN 40/31
   HOUSE 65/27
MISTAKE (9) .... CLAY 103/27
   CLAY 106/12   MOTHR 140/03   MOTHR 148/10   GRACE 160/03
   GRACE 163/29   DEAD 176/21   DEAD 178/12   DEAD 179/19
MISTAKEN (1) .... MOTHR 139/13
MISTOOK (1) .... RACE 48/12
MISTRESSES (1) .... DEAD 176/22
MISUNDERSTOOD (1) .... HOUSE 63/17
MITE (1) .... RACE 45/02
MITIGATED (1) .... GRACE 154/19
MITS (1) .... HOUSE 62/22
MIX (1) .... LITTL 72/26
MIXED (3) .... LITTL 72/28
   CLAY 101/05   CLAY 102/15
MMMNO (1) .... GRACE 165/03
'MMMYES (1) .... IVY D 126/30
MOANING (1) .... HOUSE 67/31
MOCK (1) .... DEAD 206/19
MOCKERY (1) .... GALNT 52/19
MODEL (1) .... MOTHR 137/16
MODERATELY (1) .... PNFUL 112/26
MODERN (5) .... PNFUL 107/04
   IVY D 134/10   GRACE 154/06   GRACE 167/34   DEAD 203/02
MODEST (3) .... LITTL 71/26
   GRACE 166/20   DEAD 176/18
MODESTLY (1) .... LITTL 75/23
MODIFIED (1) .... RACE 43/16
MOIST (7) .... SISTR 11/28
   PARTS 89/10   PARTS 89/34   IVY D 118/07   IVY D 118/08
   MOTHR 139/20   DEAD 220/25
MOISTENED (1) .... GALNT 53/03
MOISTURE (1) .... HOUSE 67/33
MOLLY (3) .... DEAD 191/08

DEAD 195/17	DEAD 196/01			

MOLTEN (1) .... DEAD 215/30

MOMENT (39) .... RACE 46/25

GALNT 49/19	GALNT 56/13	HOUSE 63/23	HOUSE 65/01
LITTL 73/22	LITTL 85/09	PARTS 87/06	PARTS 88/01
PARTS 91/22	PARTS 95/11	PNFUL 108/08	MOTHR 143/24
MOTHR 144/06	MOTHR 145/01	MOTHR 145/05	MOTHR 145/09
MOTHR 146/07	GRACE 166/05	GRACE 169/32	GRACE 170/03
GRACE 172/03	DEAD 177/33	DEAD 182/01	DEAD 190/09
DEAD 191/18	DEAD 195/28	DEAD 196/10	DEAD 204/12
DEAD 206/17	DEAD 209/10	DEAD 215/06	DEAD 216/23
DEAD 218/17	DEAD 219/09	DEAD 221/01	DEAD 221/13
DEAD 221/33	DEAD 222/28		

MOMENTARY (1) .... DEAD 186/12

MOMENTS (18) .... ENCTR 27/34

ARABY 31/11	GALNT 59/32	LITTL 74/19	LITTL 80/14
LITTL 81/19	PARTS 87/27	PNFUL 110/05	PNFUL 117/04
IVY D 124/13	IVY D 126/22	DEAD 202/21	DEAD 213/15
DEAD 213/32	DEAD 213/34	DEAD 214/02	DEAD 216/17
DEAD 222/04			

MOMENT'S (1) .... IVY D 118/16

MONARCH (1) .... IVY D 121/34

MONARCH'S (1) .... IVY D 134/14

MONASTERY (1) .... DEAD 200/33

MONEY (50) .... ARABY 29/18

ARABY 33/32	ARABY 34/04	ARABY 35/02	EVELN 38/10
EVELN 38/13	EVELN 38/14	EVELN 38/15	EVELN 38/17
RACE 43/16	RACE 43/18	RACE 43/25	RACE 44/15
RACE 44/23	RACE 44/30	RACE 45/02	RACE 45/05
RACE 45/06	GALNT 52/29	HOUSE 61/14	HOUSE 62/02
HOUSE 65/03	HOUSE 66/13	LITTL 72/27	LITTL 72/28
LITTL 72/32	LITTL 79/08	LITTL 81/22	LITTL 81/30
LITTL 82/09	PARTS 90/03	PARTS 92/21	PARTS 92/28
PARTS 92/29	PARTS 94/09	PARTS 95/24	PARTS 97/03
CLAY 102/06	IVY D 122/24	IVY D 123/21	IVY D 127/22
IVY D 127/27	IVY D 131/29	IVY D 131/31	MOTHR 146/18
MOTHR 147/30	GRACE 155/08	GRACE 155/16	GRACE 156/17
GRACE 159/26			

MONEYLENDER (1) .... GRACE 172/25

MONICA (2) .... LITTL 82/10

| LITTL 82/11 | | | |

MONKS (4) .... DEAD 200/27

| DEAD 201/03 | DEAD 201/10 | DEAD 201/21 | |

MONKSTOWN (2) .... DEAD 180/02

| DEAD 187/07 | | | |

MONOLOGUE (4) .... ENCTR 26/18

| ENCTR 27/19 | ENCTR 27/32 | GALNT 49/10 | |

MONOSYLLABLE (1) .... GRACE 159/19

MONOTONOUS (2) .... ENCTR 26/16

| ARABY 32/27 | | | |

MONOTONOUSLY (1) .... ENCTR 27/29

MONTH (5) .... EVELN 39/11

| PARTS 87/30 | MOTHR 136/02 | MOTHR 137/21 | DEAD 189/01 |

MONTHS (2) .... LITTL 79/02

| PNFUL 112/18 | | | |

MONUMENT (2) .... DEAD 192/07

| DEAD 202/11 | | | |

MOOD (5) .... SISTR 12/30

| GALNT 57/02 | LITTL 84/06 | DEAD 217/12 | DEAD 218/02 |

MOODILY (2) .... IVY D 124/10

| DEAD 191/12 | | | |

MOODS (1) .... LITTL 73/28

MOODY (1) .... DEAD   196/05
MOON (2) .... GALNT 52/07
   GALNT 53/05
MOONEY (16) .... HOUSE 61/01
   HOUSE 61/05   HOUSE 62/01   HOUSE 62/16   HOUSE 62/26
   HOUSE 63/01   HOUSE 63/09   HOUSE 63/12   HOUSE 63/20
   HOUSE 63/23   HOUSE 64/03   HOUSE 64/18   HOUSE 68/04
   CLAY   99/18   CLAY 101/14   CLAY 101/20
MOONEY'S (2) .... HOUSE 62/11
   HOUSE 62/24
MOONING (1) .... LITTL 81/22
MOORE (2) .... ENCTR 25/08
   GRACE 165/29
MOPE (1) .... SISTR 17/33
MORAL (4) .... HOUSE 63/24
   PNFUL 117/07   MOTHR 145/24   GRACE 159/19
MORALISING (1) .... DEAD   204/11
MORALITY (2) .... PNFUL 111/13
   GRACE 173/29
MORE (53) .... SISTR 15/30
   SISTR 16/23   SISTR 16/27   ENCTR 19/12   ENCTR 20/25
   ENCTR 22/13   ENCTR 27/01   ARABY 35/26   EVELN 38/16
   RACE   43/30   RACE   44/31   GALNT 53/33   GALNT 54/33
   GALNT 55/16   GALNT 56/34   HOUSE 67/29   LITTL 74/10
   LITTL 80/05   LITTL 84/25   PARTS 92/27   PARTS 95/18
   PARTS 96/29   CLAY 103/01   CLAY 104/31   PNFUL 110/03
   PNFUL 111/26   PNFUL 111/26   IVY D 122/11   IVY D 130/18
   MOTHR 143/31   GRACE 156/31   GRACE 159/29   GRACE 160/24
   GRACE 166/31   GRACE 169/02   GRACE 173/02   DEAD 178/04
   DEAD 178/24   DEAD 179/28   DEAD 183/28   DEAD 185/27
   DEAD 188/10   DEAD 188/28   DEAD 192/07   DEAD 193/17
   DEAD 198/07   DEAD 202/31   DEAD 202/32   DEAD 205/27
   DEAD 210/17   DEAD 213/30   DEAD 220/06   DEAD 223/14
MOREOVER (5) .... RACE   42/09
   RACE   45/06   LITTL 82/13   MOTHR 138/05   GRACE 157/10
MORKAN (13) .... DEAD   182/20
   DEAD 182/26   DEAD 184/08   DEAD 185/02   DEAD 186/26
   DEAD 193/31   DEAD 199/30   DEAD 200/03   DEAD 200/16
   DEAD 201/30   DEAD 207/16   DEAD 212/27   DEAD 222/26
MORKAN'S (1) .... DEAD   175/13
MORNING (32) .... SISTR 11/04
   SISTR 11/31   ENCTR 19/10   ENCTR 21/04   ENCTR 21/12
   ENCTR 21/26   ENCTR 21/30   ARABY 30/25   ARABY 30/31
   ARABY 30/32   ARABY 32/28   RACE   48/27   HOUSE 63/26
   HOUSE 65/23   HOUSE 66/28   LITTL 82/10   CLAY 101/25
   CLAY 101/25   CLAY 101/31   PNFUL 108/31   PNFUL 112/24
   PNFUL 114/34   IVY D 123/24   MOTHR 141/16   DEAD 194/16
   DEAD 201/04   DEAD 206/03   DEAD 211/23   DEAD 212/31
   DEAD 214/22   DEAD 215/34   DEAD 220/27
MORNINGS (1) .... LITTL 76/07
MOROSELY (1) .... GALNT 56/26
MORSEL (2) .... PNFUL 112/28
   PNFUL 112/31
MORSELS (1) .... HOUSE 64/02
MORTAL (2) .... SISTR 13/09
   DEAD 177/04
MOST (18) .... ENCTR 25/22
   ARABY 31/01   GALNT 50/17   CLAY 106/10   PNFUL 110/15
   PNFUL 115/10   MOTHR 147/25   GRACE 158/05   GRACE 162/18
   GRACE 164/19   GRACE 167/08   GRACE 167/10   GRACE 168/26
   GRACE 173/27   DEAD 187/14   DEAD 190/22   DEAD 200/33
   DEAD 208/16

MOTHER (29) .... EVELN 37/01
    EVELN   37/03   EVELN   37/34   EVELN   39/29   EVELN   40/03
    HOUSE   63/18   HOUSE   64/25   HOUSE   66/28   HOUSE   66/28
    HOUSE   69/01   PARTS   97/25   CLAY 100/21   PNFUL 115/04
    PNFUL 115/06   IVY D 120/03   IVY D 132/05   MOTHR 136/ T
    MOTHR 149/28   GRACE 156/12   GRACE 156/12   GRACE 166/07
    DEAD 185/13   DEAD 186/21   DEAD 186/24   DEAD 190/14
    DEAD 191/31   DEAD 193/15   DEAD 193/21   DEAD 209/11
MOTHER-OF-PEARL (1) .... GALNT 55/28
    HOUSE 65/21   HOUSE 65/02
MOTHERS (2) .... HOUSE 65/02
    HOUSE 65/21
MOTHER'S (11) .... EVELN 38/06
    EVELN   39/31   EVELN   40/05   EVELN   40/11   EVELN   40/14
    HOUSE   63/17   HOUSE   64/17   HOUSE   66/16   LITTL   74/11
    LITTL   85/01   GRACE 154/29
MOTION (2) .... RACE 44/14
    PNFUL 113/31
MOTOR (3) .... RACE 43/05
    RACE   45/06   RACE   45/17
MOTORING (1) .... RACE 43/26
MOTORISTS (1) .... RACE 45/14
MOTTLED (1) .... GRACE 172/09
MOTTO (2) .... GRACE 167/11
    GRACE 167/18
MOULDING (1) .... PNFUL 110/02
MOULIN (1) .... LITTL 76/28
MOUNT (2) .... DEAD 200/25
    DEAD 200/26
MOUNTED (2) .... ARABY 33/06
    DEAD 215/21
MOURN (1) .... IVY D 134/08
MOURNFUL (2) .... EVELN 40/31
    GALNT 54/18
MOURNING (2) .... SISTR 12/30
    SISTR 14/04
MOUSTACHE (17) .... ENCTR 24/25
    RACE   43/14   HOUSE   61/16   LITTL   70/15   PARTS   86/11
    PARTS   94/06   CLAY 102/33   CLAY 103/32   PNFUL 108/18
    IVY D 120/26   IVY D 130/07   MOTHR 142/18   GRACE 152/07
    GRACE 166/18   DEAD 182/18   DEAD 182/25   DEAD 198/19
MOUTH (25) .... SISTR 11/16
    SISTR   16/34   ENCTR   25/20   ENCTR   25/34   GALNT   49/17
    GALNT   56/02   GALNT   57/32   HOUSE   62/32   LITTL   81/34
    LITTL   82/05   PARTS   91/29   PNFUL 108/19   PNFUL 112/29
    IVY D 118/08   IVY D 119/04   IVY D 125/32   IVY D 129/20
    GRACE 150/08   GRACE 151/26   GRACE 153/18   GRACE 153/24
    GRACE 153/26   GRACE 153/28   GRACE 153/32   DEAD 222/05
                                                      GRACE 154/13
MOUTHFUL (1) .... PNFUL 113/05
MOUTHFULS (1) .... GALNT 51/27
MOVE (3) .... ARABY 30/23
    MOTHR 140/28   DEAD 183/07
MOVED (10) .... CLAY 105/11
    ARABY   34/17   ARABY   34/20   PARTS   95/16   DEAD 205/22
    CLAY 106/13   GRACE 151/16   GRACE 165/30
    DEAD 222/17
MOVEMENT (3) .... LITTL 76/23
    MOTHR 138/06   GRACE 153/27
MOVEMENTS (1) .... GALNT 56/20
MOVING (4) .... EVELN 41/02
    LITTL   71/09   PNFUL 113/17   MOTHR 146/16
MOYA (1) .... IVY D 123/27
MOYLE (1) .... GALNT 54/14

```
MOZART'S (1) ...................................... PNFUL 109/05
MR (577)
MRS (117)
MUCH (47) ........................................ SISTR  10/29
       SISTR  12/18     SISTR  15/06     SISTR  17/17     ENCTR  20/31
       ENCTR  22/17     ENCTR  26/06     EVELN  38/16     RACE   43/30
       RACE   43/32     RACE   44/31     RACE   47/08     RACE   48/21
       GALNT  57/15     HOUSE  65/11     LITTL  75/20     PARTS  95/05
       PARTS  95/17     PARTS  95/31     CLAY  102/05     CLAY  103/01
       CLAY  104/08     CLAY  105/05     CLAY  106/01     CLAY  106/13
       CLAY  106/16     PNFUL 111/33     IVY D 128/03     IVY D 130/07
       MOTHR 136/14     MOTHR 137/05     MOTHR 140/14     MOTHR 145/14
       GRACE 154/16     GRACE 158/28     GRACE 159/08     GRACE 165/11
       GRACE 166/03     GRACE 170/24     DEAD  176/16     DEAD  192/07
       DEAD  193/20     DEAD  195/24     DEAD  201/14     DEAD  202/33
       DEAD  212/23     DEAD  221/09
MUCUS (1) ........................................ GRACE 158/34
MUD (1) ..... .' ................................. IVY D 121/34
MUDDY (1) ........................................ ARABY  30/08
MUFFLED (1) ...................................... DEAD  207/03
MUFFLER (1) ...................................... DEAD  178/14
MUG (1) .......................................... CLAY  101/15
MUGS (2) ......................................... CLAY  101/04
       CLAY  101/16
MUG'S (1) ........................................ GALNT  52/33
MULBERRY (1) ..................................... DEAD  186/24
MULLIGAN'S (2) ................................... PARTS  94/34
       PARTS  95/01
MUMBLED (1) ...................................... DEAD  216/08
MUNCHING (1) ..................................... IVY D 118/08
MUNICIPAL (1) .................................... IVY D 119/10
MURDERED (1) ..................................... DEAD  186/18
MURKY (2) ........................................ DEAD  213/02
       DEAD  214/21
MURMUR (5) ....................................... RACE   44/19
       GALNT  49/08     PARTS  96/19     DEAD  192/28     DEAD  203/13
MURMURED (5) ..................................... SISTR  11/23
       ARABY  35/18     DEAD  181/07     DEAD  188/21     DEAD  193/26
MURMURING (3) .................................... SISTR  11/27
       ARABY  31/28     LITTL  85/15
MURPHY (2) ....................................... ENCTR  26/28
       ENCTR  28/06
MURZKA (1) ....................................... DEAD  199/05
MUSCLE (2) ....................................... PARTS  95/31
       PARTS  95/34
MUSCULAR (1) ..................................... GALNT  55/32
MUSED (1) ........................................ EVELN  40/11
MUSHA (1) ........................................ IVY D 122/18
MUSIC (31) ....................................... ARABY  30/12
       EVELN  39/05     RACE   47/10     RACE   47/21     GALNT  54/18
       HOUSE  62/06     LITTL  79/23     CLAY  106/14     PNFUL 109/05
       PNFUL 110/23     PNFUL 111/21     PNFUL 112/11     PNFUL 112/14
       MOTHR 136/11     MOTHR 137/20     MOTHR 138/05     MOTHR 139/25
       MOTHR 141/32     MOTHR 142/25     MOTHR 143/27     MOTHR 145/31
       GRACE 169/04     DEAD  176/16     DEAD  186/03     DEAD  186/10
       DEAD  187/14     DEAD  192/13     DEAD  202/09     DEAD  210/05
       DEAD  210/09     DEAD  214/08
MUSICAL (7) ...................................... RACE   43/26
       MOTHR 137/33     MOTHR 147/27     DEAD  183/12     DEAD  186/25
       DEAD  204/17     DEAD  215/12
MUSIC-HALL (3) ................................... HOUSE  62/24
       HOUSE  68/10     HOUSE  68/14
```

MUSIC-LOVING (1) .... MOTHR 141/17
MUSIC-STAND (2) .... PNFUL 112/14
    DEAD   193/11
MUSKETRY (1) .... DEAD   192/31
MUSLIN (1) .... PARTS 95/13
MUST (46) .... SISTR   9/07

SISTR	15/31	SISTR	15/33	ENCTR	21/07	ENCTR	22/30
ENCTR	25/25	EVELN	40/18	RACE	48/01	RACE	48/17
GALNT	59/21	HOUSE	64/33	HOUSE	67/25	LITTL	77/11
LITTL	78/27	LITTL	79/25	LITTL	80/01	LITTL	82/07
PARTS	87/10	PARTS	87/29	PARTS	88/18	PARTS	92/27
CLAY	104/09	PNFUL	109/29	PNFUL	112/20	PNFUL	112/21
PNFUL	116/30	IVY D	120/14	IVY D	123/10	IVY D	123/21
IVY D	127/22	MOTHR	146/12	MOTHR	149/06	GRACE	153/01
GRACE	164/31	GRACE	171/21	DEAD	177/10	DEAD	180/27
DEAD	187/08	DEAD	192/03	DEAD	195/25	DEAD	203/11
DEAD	203/27	DEAD	204/33	DEAD	217/11	DEAD	222/12
DEAD	223/14						

MUSTER (1) .... GRACE 154/04
MUSTN'T (1) .... GRACE 162/19
MUSTY (2) .... ENCTR 23/34
    ARABY   29/08
MUTINOUS (1) .... DEAD   223/30
MUTTERED (2) .... PARTS 86/08
    DEAD   216/03
MUTTERING (2) .... PARTS 93/01
    IVY D 129/21
MUTTERINGS (1) .... SISTR 14/21
MUTTON (1) .... SISTR 11/07
MUTUALLY (1) .... GRACE 160/29
MY (181)
MYSELF (14) .... SISTR   9/10

SISTR	12/11	SISTR	12/31	ENCTR	21/05	ENCTR	25/11
ARABY	31/12	ARABY	34/28	ARABY	35/32	LITTL	82/04
IVY D	127/25	IVY D	129/33	IVY D	132/09	DEAD	188/01
DEAD	195/34						

MYSTERIOUS (1) .... SISTR 13/10
MYSTERIOUSLY (1) .... ENCTR 26/13
MYSTERY (5) .... ENCTR 27/28

| ENCTR | 27/30 | CLAY | 103/30 | IVY D | 126/34 | DEAD | 210/03 |

NAAS (1) .... RACE   42/02
NABS (1) .... PARTS 94/03
NA'E (1) .... GRACE 153/08
NAILS (2) .... LITTL 70/16
    DEAD   215/26
NAME (38) .... SISTR   9/13

SISTR	11/33	ENCTR	28/08	ARABY	30/33	ARABY	31/11
ARABY	34/25	EVELN	37/11	GALNT	50/26	GALNT	51/11
GALNT	52/03	LITTL	72/04	LITTL	74/10	LITTL	74/11
PARTS	91/04	CLAY	106/09	PNFUL	110/08	PNFUL	117/26
IVY D	121/22	IVY D	123/06	IVY D	132/22	IVY D	135/03
MOTHR	137/26	MOTHR	138/03	MOTHR	145/24	GRACE	151/21
GRACE	154/08	GRACE	159/12	GRACE	159/13	GRACE	160/20
GRACE	164/16	GRACE	169/16	GRACE	169/20	DEAD	183/26
DEAD	199/32	DEAD	207/22	DEAD	212/08	DEAD	212/13
DEAD	214/07						

NAMED (7) .... ENCTR 21/10

| RACE | 43/02 | RACE | 43/03 | RACE | 46/06 | PARTS | 94/19 |
| MOTHR | 142/03 | DEAD | 219/04 | | | | |

NAMES (7) .... ENCTR 26/28

EVELN 39/12	EVELN 39/13	RACE 45/28	PARTS 93/09
DEAD 186/31	DEAD 203/26		

NAMING (1) .... PARTS 93/31
NANNIE (6) .... SISTR 14/06

SISTR 14/19	SISTR 15/01	SISTR 16/04	SISTR 16/06
SISTR 17/06			

NAPE (2) .... HOUSE 68/26
   IVY D 130/28
NAPKIN (1) .... DEAD 197/18
NAPOLEON (2) .... SISTR 13/04
   GRACE 154/05
NARRATE (2) .... PARTS 93/15
   GRACE 151/14
NARRATIVE (4) .... GALNT 49/15

GALNT 50/08	PNFUL 115/19	GRACE 160/27

NARROW (3) .... SISTR 14/10

LITTL 84/12	PARTS 92/33

NARROWEST (1) .... LITTL 72/16
NASAL (1) .... ARABY 31/07
NASSAU (1) .... GALNT 54/06
NATIONAL (3) .... ENCTR 20/29

ENCTR 27/07	PARTS 95/32

NATIONALIST (6) .... RACE 43/15

IVY D 122/06	IVY D 131/06	IVY D 131/18	MOTHR 137/33
MOTHR 143/16		

NATIONS (2) .... IVY D 134/22
   DEAD 203/03
NATIVE (1) .... ARABY 31/09
NATURAL (3) .... GALNT 57/21

GRACE 157/20	GRACE 170/23

NATURALLY (1) .... MOTHR 136/11
NATURE (11) .... ENCTR 20/07

RACE 43/11	LITTL 78/32	LITTL 80/22	PARTS 91/03
PNFUL 110/01	PNFUL 110/31	PNFUL 111/26	PNFUL 117/07
GRACE 174/03	GRACE 174/19		

NAUGHTY (1) .... HOUSE 62/28
NAUSEA (1) .... EVELN 41/02
NEAR (26) .... ENCTR 21/08

ENCTR 21/28	ENCTR 22/34	ENCTR 26/21	ARABY 30/30
RACE 45/15	GALNT 57/06	HOUSE 61/04	LITTL 74/15
LITTL 82/16	PNFUL 112/03	PNFUL 117/04	PNFUL 117/30
IVY D 133/17	MOTHR 137/02	MOTHR 144/34	GRACE 151/03
GRACE 165/21	GRACE 168/14	GRACE 172/15	DEAD 187/08
DEAD 191/29	DEAD 193/29	DEAD 207/33	DEAD 209/26
DEAD 223/17			

NEARER (2) .... SISTR 9/14
   LITTL 73/24
NEAREST (1) .... ENCTR 21/27
NEARING (1) .... DEAD 185/21
NEARLY (23) .... SISTR 12/13

ARABY 34/29	EVELN 38/08	RACE 44/10	GALNT 53/05
HOUSE 65/19	HOUSE 66/10	PARTS 97/09	PARTS 97/14
CLAY 101/14	CLAY 101/18	CLAY 101/19	CLAY 104/03
CLAY 104/15	CLAY 104/29	CLAY 105/09	PNFUL 112/06
IVY D 124/20	MOTHR 136/02	MOTHR 139/25	DEAD 180/31
DEAD 188/12	DEAD 190/17		

NEAT (4) .... LITTL 71/26

LITTL 75/22	GRACE 166/26	DEAD 196/20

NEATLY (1) .... RACE 43/02
NECESSARY (3) .... GALNT 51/26

GALNT 54/02	DEAD 196/16

NECESSITOUS (1) .... LITTL 71/03

```
NECK (10) ..................................... ARABY   32/08
   ARABY   33/14   HOUSE   66/29   HOUSE   68/26   IVY D  125/28
   IVY D  130/29   GRACE  153/33   GRACE  163/20   DEAD   181/28
   DEAD   211/18
NECKTIE (1) ..................................... GRACE  151/06
NEEDLES (1) ..................................... ARABY   31/23
NEEDN'T (4) ..................................... HOUSE   62/29
   PARTS   88/06   GRACE  155/06   GRACE  161/21
NEGRO (1) ....................................... DEAD   198/22
NEICE (1) ....................................... DEAD   176/03
NEIGHBOUR (1) ................................... DEAD   201/20
NEIGHBOURS (5) .................................. ARABY   29/04
   PARTS   91/27   DEAD   189/23   DEAD   201/26   DEAD   204/19
NEIGHBOUR'S (1) ................................. HOUSE   61/11
NEITHER (13) .................................... SISTR   12/29
   ENCTR   26/25   HOUSE   61/14   LITTL   78/19   PARTS   90/09
   PARTS   94/09   PNFUL  109/08   PNFUL  110/24   PNFUL  110/25
   IVY D  124/08   MOTHR  141/34   MOTHR  148/06   DEAD   194/03
NEPHEW (3) ...................................... PARTS   92/12
   GRACE  172/30   DEAD   179/33
NEPHEWS (1) ..................................... IVY D  121/32
NEPHEW'S (1) .................................... DEAD   180/33
NERVES (3) ...................................... RACE    45/11
   PNFUL  116/05   MOTHR  146/03
NERVOUS (5) ..................................... SISTR   17/29
   MOTHR  142/33   MOTHR  142/34   DEAD   183/13   DEAD   220/02
NERVOUSLY (8) ................................... GALNT   59/19
   LITTL   83/18   MOTHR  139/23   GRACE  171/01   DEAD   180/30
   DEAD   187/14   DEAD   189/24   DEAD   202/03
NERVOUSNESS (1) ................................. LITTL   82/27
NEST (1) ........................................ PARTS   92/09
NETTLED (1) ..................................... GRACE  165/09
NEVER (70) ...................................... ENCTR   19/07
   ENCTR   25/15   ARABY   30/32   ARABY   35/08   EVELN   36/14
   EVELN   37/09   EVELN   37/10   EVELN   37/11   EVELN   38/03
   GALNT   52/14   GALNT   58/02   GALNT   58/02   HOUSE   66/33
   HOUSE   67/30   HOUSE   68/01   LITTL   72/03   LITTL   74/01
   LITTL   76/09   LITTL   79/08   PARTS   90/18   PARTS   92/14
   PARTS   92/17   PARTS   92/21   CLAY   105/26   PNFUL  108/28
   PNFUL  109/15   IVY D  119/08   IVY D  120/13   IVY D  121/08
   IVY D  123/25   IVY D  132/08   MOTHR  137/08   MOTHR  137/11
   MOTHR  142/29   MOTHR  143/22   MOTHR  148/30   GRACE  154/01
   GRACE  155/17   GRACE  156/24   GRACE  159/24   GRACE  159/29
   GRACE  161/06   GRACE  164/01   GRACE  164/02   GRACE  170/12
   GRACE  170/23   DEAD   175/17   DEAD   177/02   DEAD   180/19
   DEAD   183/05   DEAD   183/15   DEAD   192/15   DEAD   193/21
   DEAD   193/22   DEAD   193/22   DEAD   193/24   DEAD   193/25
   DEAD   194/01   DEAD   194/09   DEAD   197/21   DEAD   199/15
   DEAD   200/01   DEAD   200/19   DEAD   200/27   DEAD   201/03
   DEAD   211/26   DEAD   214/27   DEAD   220/33   DEAD   222/10
   DEAD   223/12
NEVERTHELESS (1) ................................ ENCTR   19/18
NEVER-TO-BE-FORGOTTEN (1) ....................... DEAD   207/11
NEW (22) ........................................ ENCTR   27/10
   EVELN   36/07   EVELN   37/31   LITTL   75/14   LITTL   77/06
   PNFUL  108/11   PNFUL  112/14   IVY D  128/02   MOTHR  146/17
   GRACE  155/19   GRACE  155/27   GRACE  158/26   GRACE  167/02
   DEAD   185/13   DEAD   192/23   DEAD   203/18   DEAD   203/19
   DEAD   203/19   DEAD   203/20   DEAD   203/23   DEAD   215/04
   DEAD   215/17
NEW-COMER (2) ................................... GALNT   54/10
   GRACE  152/16
```

NEW-FANGLED (1) .... SISTR 17/07
NEWLY (2) .... GRACE 172/28
    DEAD 188/11
NEWPORT (1) .... RACE   48/15
NEWS (2) .... SISTR 10/19
    HOUSE 64/13
NEWSPAPER (2) .... SISTR 13/18
    HOUSE 66/11
NEWSPAPERS (3) .... RACE   43/21
    DEAD 211/23   DEAD 223/27
NEXT (14) .... SISTR 11/31
    GALNT 51/01   LITTL 79/32   LITTL 79/34   LITTL 80/02
    LITTL 81/02   PARTS 98/16   CLAY 101/25   CLAY 103/17
    PNFUL 109/19   IVY D 122/03   GRACE 156/19   GRACE 163/28
    DEAD 180/28
NEXT-DOOR (5) .... CLAY 104/13
    CLAY 104/32   CLAY 105/01   CLAY 105/03   CLAY 105/18
NICE (29) .... ENCTR 26/03
    ENCTR 26/06   ENCTR 26/06   ENCTR 27/15   EVELN 39/26
    PARTS 94/29   CLAY 99/04   CLAY 100/13   CLAY 100/18
    CLAY 100/25   CLAY 100/26   CLAY 100/32   CLAY 101/33
    CLAY 102/06   CLAY 102/17   CLAY 103/08   CLAY 104/05
    CLAY 105/26   IVY D 123/33   MOTHR 138/05   MOTHR 149/31
    MOTHR 149/31   GRACE 155/09   GRACE 163/05   GRACE 171/33
    DEAD 184/09   DEAD 190/23   DEAD 191/20   DEAD 212/14
NIECE (1) .... DEAD 194/19
NIECES (1) .... DEAD 205/02
NIETZSCHE (1) .... PNFUL 112/15
NIGHT (72) .... SISTR   9/02
    SISTR   9/02   SISTR   9/03   SISTR   9/04   SISTR   9/09
    SISTR 13/01   SISTR 17/34   ENCTR 21/26   ARABY 32/15
    ARABY 32/20   ARABY 33/23   ARABY 33/26   EVELN 38/17
    EVELN 40/02   EVELN 40/04   RACE   46/29   RACE   47/14
    RACE   47/15   GALNT 50/30   GALNT 51/01   GALNT 51/04
    GALNT 51/05   GALNT 53/09   GALNT 58/24   HOUSE 61/10
    HOUSE 64/08   HOUSE 65/29   HOUSE 67/04   HOUSE 67/07
    HOUSE 67/14   HOUSE 67/15   HOUSE 68/10   LITTL 72/07
    LITTL 72/14   LITTL 73/17   LITTL 76/01   LITTL 79/25
    PARTS 89/28   PARTS 90/22   PARTS 93/02   CLAY 104/30
    CLAY 105/27   PNFUL 111/30   PNFUL 114/28   PNFUL 115/05
    PNFUL 115/33   PNFUL 116/31   PNFUL 116/31   PNFUL 116/34
    PNFUL 117/11   PNFUL 117/32   MOTHR 139/07   MOTHR 140/09
    MOTHR 140/18   MOTHR 140/29   MOTHR 141/22   MOTHR 141/28
    MOTHR 142/22   GRACE 162/14   DEAD 176/24   DEAD 177/29
    DEAD 180/16   DEAD 181/20   DEAD 192/16   DEAD 194/15
    DEAD 194/15   DEAD 199/09   DEAD 199/09   DEAD 199/09
    DEAD 210/28   DEAD 211/33   DEAD 221/15
NIGHT-BOAT (1) .... EVELN 38/29
NIGHTS (5) .... EVELN 38/10
    HOUSE 62/23   HOUSE 67/12   GRACE 155/20   GRACE 156/27
NIGHT'S (1) .... PARTS 87/29
NIMBLY (1) .... GALNT 50/22
NINE (4) .... ARABY 33/28
    LITTL 82/12   PNFUL 116/34   GRACE 153/17
NINETEEN (4) .... EVELN 38/01
    HOUSE 62/31   IVY D 120/11   IVY D 124/28
NINE-TENTHS (1) .... HOUSE 66/12
NIPPER (1) .... SISTR 11/03
NIX (1) .... EVELN 36/17
NO (169)
NOBILITY (1) .... LITTL 71/34
NOBLEMAN (1) .... IVY D 125/13

NOBLY (1)						IVY D	135/06
NOBODY (12)						**ENCTR**	**21/28**
ENCTR	24/16	EVELN	38/07	LITTL	72/29	LITTL	74/24
CLAY	104/14	CLAY	105/14	DEAD	196/13	DEAD	198/34
DEAD	205/20	DEAD	205/31	DEAD	206/29		
NOD (3)						SISTR	13/21
SISTR	13/24	GRACE	162/01				
NODDED (14)						SISTR	17/31
GALNT	52/32	PARTS	96/21	IVY D	122/28	IVY D	124/13
IVY D	125/15	IVY D	132/12	GRACE	159/05	GRACE	170/16
DEAD	180/08	DEAD	185/17	DEAD	187/27	DEAD	193/15
DEAD	214/32						
NODDING (3)						SISTR	14/09
PARTS	90/06	DEAD	181/07				
NODS (2)						RACE	42/14
CLAY	103/08						
NOISE (21)						SISTR	15/06
SISTR	17/07	RACE	44/13	GALNT	54/19	LITTL	74/18
LITTL	80/20	PARTS	94/16	IVY D	128/17	MOTHR	143/12
MOTHR	143/31	MOTHR	146/09	MOTHR	146/29	MOTHR	147/06
GRACE	150/07	DEAD	177/18	DEAD	197/26	DEAD	197/26
DEAD	201/29	DEAD	209/32	DEAD	213/28	DEAD	214/18
NOISELESSLY (3)						GALNT	50/09
GALNT	51/13	DEAD	213/12				
NOISES (2)						ARABY	31/09
PARTS	93/12						
NOISIEST (1)						RACE	47/07
NOISILY (1)						DEAD	182/12
NOISY (2)						ENCTR	23/01
LITTL	72/09						
NOMINATORS (1)						IVY D	123/05
NONE (7)						ENCTR	25/24
HOUSE	63/11	CLAY	102/30	MOTHR	139/09	GRACE	167/34
GRACE	170/26	DEAD	199/29				
NONSENSE (1)						IVY D	132/07
NOON (2)						ENCTR	23/04
GRACE	159/21						
NOR (15)						SISTR	12/29
SISTR	16/27	ENCTR	26/25	HOUSE	61/14	HOUSE	61/14
HOUSE	64/29	LITTL	78/19	PARTS	90/10	PNFUL	109/08
PNFUL	109/08	PNFUL	110/24	PNFUL	117/31	IVY D	124/09
MOTHR	148/07	DEAD	218/08				
NORMAL (1)						PNFUL	114/19
NORTH (6)						ENCTR	22/19
ARABY	29/01	EVELN	40/23	LITTL	70/01	PARTS	86/02
PARTS	92/19						
NORTHERN (1)						GALNT	59/01
NORTHWARD (1)						RACE	45/22
NORWEGIAN (1)						ENCTR	23/23
NOSE (15)						SISTR	12/20
SISTR	17/01	GALNT	49/17	PARTS	89/11	PARTS	93/13
CLAY	99/11	CLAY	99/12	CLAY	101/13	CLAY	101/18
CLAY	105/08	IVY D	122/21	MOTHR	142/27	DEAD	184/28
DEAD	184/28	DEAD	222/32				
NOSEY (3)						PARTS	91/02
PARTS	93/20	PARTS	94/11				
NOSTRIL (1)						SISTR	13/25
NOSTRILS (3)						SISTR	14/30
EVELN	36/03	GALNT	56/01				
NOT (287)							
NOTE (9)						GALNT	56/25
GALNT	57/27	GALNT	60/24	LITTL	73/31	LITTL	74/09

PNFUL 109/32	PNFUL 110/03	MOTHR 140/23	DEAD 218/25
NOTEBOOK (1)			PNFUL 108/02
NOTED (1)			GALNT 55/31
NOTES (10)			GALNT 54/15
GALNT 54/15	GALNT 56/23	MOTHR 136/07	MOTHR 142/20
MOTHR 146/27	MOTHR 147/15	MOTHR 149/19	DEAD 193/05
DEAD 209/33			
NOTHING (57)			SISTR 17/27
ENCTR 20/11	ENCTR 26/05	ENCTR 26/30	ENCTR 27/12
ENCTR 27/25	ARABY 38/12	EVELN 40/28	GALNT 52/22
GALNT 57/11	GALNT 60/19	HOUSE 64/34	HOUSE 66/06
LITTL 73/11	LITTL 75/31	LITTL 76/32	LITTL 78/26
LITTL 85/03	LITTL 85/03	LITTL 85/12	PARTS 91/10
PARTS 91/14	PARTS 91/16	PARTS 91/16	CLAY 104/03
PNFUL 109/12	PNFUL 117/32	IVY D 123/19	IVY D 129/04
IVY D 129/17	IVY D 131/01	IVY D 133/18	MOTHR 139/03
MOTHR 140/09	MOTHR 140/15	MOTHR 148/02	MOTHR 148/25
GRACE 151/34	GRACE 152/07	GRACE 152/15	GRACE 153/32
GRACE 155/11	GRACE 155/12	GRACE 160/32	GRACE 161/28
GRACE 162/04	GRACE 162/08	GRACE 162/27	GRACE 165/14
GRACE 171/14	DEAD 181/11	DEAD 188/22	DEAD 189/28
DEAD 197/08	DEAD 207/06	DEAD 210/15	DEAD 211/15
NOTICE (6)			SISTR 12/01
SISTR 12/02	SISTR 16/12	PARTS 90/10	CLAY 102/30
MOTHR 145/12			
NOTICEABLE (1)			DEAD 185/11
NOTICED (7)			SISTR 13/32
SISTR 14/22	SISTR 16/31	ENCTR 26/02	EVELN 39/25
HOUSE 63/13	MOTHR 139/17		
NOTICES (3)			SISTR 13/18
LITTL 74/07	PNFUL 114/25		
NOTION (2)			ENCTR 23/26
HOUSE 66/17			
NOTIONS (2)			PARTS 94/23
CLAY 101/21			
NOTORIETY (1)			RACE 44/14
NOVEL (1)			DEAD 216/08
NOVEMBER (2)			GALNT 58/01
PNFUL 113/07			
NOVICE (1)			MOTHR 138/17
NOW (131)			
NOWADAYS (1)			IVY D 127/22
NOWHERE (1)			CLAY 103/26
NUDGED (1)			DEAD 201/26
NUDGES (1)			RACE 44/22
NUMBER (2)			ENCTR 20/04
MOTHR 141/25			
NUMBERS (1)			ENCTR 19/02
NUNS' (1)			DEAD 221/16
NURSED (2)			CLAY 100/19
DEAD 187/06			
NURSES (1)			LITTL 71/08
NURSING (2)			HOUSE 68/05
DEAD 177/27			
NUT (1)			DEAD 179/31
NUTCRACKER (1)			CLAY 104/16
NUTCRACKERS (1)			CLAY 104/14
NUTMEG (1)			DEAD 196/28
NUTS (4)			CLAY 102/18
CLAY 104/14	CLAY 104/16	CLAY 104/17	

O -- OCCASIONAL

O (99)						SISTR	15/16
ARABY	31/29	ARABY	31/29	ARABY	35/08	ARABY	35/09
ARABY	35/10	ARABY	35/13	GALNT	51/06	GALNT	54/14
GALNT	54/33	HOUSE	66/30	HOUSE	67/31	LITTL	78/01
LITTL	79/30	LITTL	80/09	PARTS	95/22	PARTS	98/12
PARTS	98/22	CLAY	103/14	CLAY	105/05	IVY D	121/08
IVY D	122/27	IVY D	123/13	IVY D	123/18	IVY D	123/20
IVY D	125/10	IVY D	125/17	IVY D	126/01	IVY D	126/03
IVY D	126/15	IVY D	129/02	IVY D	130/14	IVY D	133/09
IVY D	133/22	IVY D	133/24	IVY D	133/30	IVY D	134/08
MOTHR	149/31	GRACE	154/33	GRACE	155/06	GRACE	155/18
GRACE	160/11	GRACE	161/26	GRACE	162/05	GRACE	162/27
GRACE	162/32	GRACE	164/14	GRACE	164/26	GRACE	164/31
GRACE	165/07	GRACE	165/14	GRACE	165/22	GRACE	166/16
GRACE	167/16	GRACE	168/12	GRACE	168/24	GRACE	168/33
GRACE	171/19	GRACE	171/22	DEAD	176/34	DEAD	178/03
DEAD	178/05	DEAD	178/26	DEAD	178/29	DEAD	180/19
DEAD	181/07	DEAD	181/16	DEAD	181/20	DEAD	183/15
DEAD	183/34	DEAD	184/02	DEAD	184/06	DEAD	185/11
DEAD	187/33	DEAD	188/32	DEAD	189/30	DEAD	191/16
DEAD	194/34	DEAD	195/27	DEAD	197/14	DEAD	199/18
DEAD	199/26	DEAD	200/33	DEAD	206/30	DEAD	207/19
DEAD	208/03	DEAD	208/25	DEAD	210/24	DEAD	210/27
DEAD	210/28	DEAD	210/30	DEAD	210/34	DEAD	211/04
DEAD	211/10	DEAD	212/25	DEAD	217/19	DEAD	218/14
DEAD	219/12	DEAD	221/29				

OATS (1)						HOUSE	66/08
OBDURATELY (1)						GRACE	172/01
OBEDIENTLY (1)						GRACE	153/26
OBEYED (1)						ARABY	30/22
OBJECTED (1)						ENCTR	22/25
OBJECTIVE (1)						PARTS	88/23
OBJECTS (2)						EVELN	37/07
EVELN	37/09						
OBLIGE (1)						HOUSE	62/25
OBLIGED (7)						ENCTR	28/01
GALNT	49/12	HOUSE	61/15	HOUSE	65/25	PARTS	92/08
GRACE	159/08	DEAD	195/30				
OBLIQUE (1)						PARTS	95/19
OBLIQUELY (2)						GALNT	55/21
DEAD	223/25						
OBSCENITIES (1)						HOUSE	62/18
OBSCURE (1)						GRACE	159/25
OBSCURELY (1)						RACE	48/08
OBSEQUIOUSLY (1)						PNFUL	116/10
OBSERVATION (1)						SISTR	10/18
OBSERVE (1)						MOTHR	146/27
OBSERVED (6)						ENCTR	23/22
GALNT	55/19	GALNT	60/11	LITTL	77/03	PNFUL	114/04
GRACE	173/08						
OBSERVER (1)						GRACE	173/29
OBSERVING (3)						ARABY	35/14
LITTL	74/22	PARTS	96/27				
OBSTINATELY (1)						PNFUL	117/24
OBTUSE (1)						PNFUL	111/12
O'CALLAGHAN (6)						DEAD	206/31
DEAD	211/03	DEAD	211/07	DEAD	211/26	DEAD	212/26
DEAD	214/25						
O'CARROLL (1)						GRACE	172/32
OCCASION (4)						RACE	45/26
MOTHR	137/22	DEAD	202/22	DEAD	204/27		
OCCASIONAL (1)						GRACE	156/30

```
OCCASIONALLY (2) ..................................  GALNT   52/05
     HOUSE   62/05
OCCASIONS (1) .....................................  MOTHR  138/34
OCCUPATIONS (1) ...................................  HOUSE   62/13
OCCUPIED (1) ......................................  DEAD   182/29
OCCURRED (1) ......................................  GRACE  163/14
OCCURS (1) ........................................  LITTL   81/21
O'CLOCK (11) ......................................  ENCTR   22/33
     ENCTR   24/11    ARABY   33/22    ARABY   33/28   PARTS   87/10
     CLAY   100/03    PNFUL  108/34    PNFUL  113/26   PNFUL  116/34
     DEAD   176/25    DEAD   194/16
O'CLOHISSEY'S (1) .................................  DEAD   188/15
O'CONNELL (3) .....................................  PARTS   96/30
     DEAD   214/25    DEAD   214/27
O'CONNOR (45) .....................................  IVY D  118/11
     IVY D 118/12    IVY D 119/04    IVY D 119/08   IVY D 119/15
     IVY D 119/22    IVY D 120/05    IVY D 120/10   IVY D 120/17
     IVY D 120/23    IVY D 120/29    IVY D 120/30   IVY D 121/05
     IVY D 121/10    IVY D 121/23    IVY D 121/24   IVY D 122/05
     IVY D 122/09    IVY D 122/17    IVY D 122/30   IVY D 122/31
     IVY D 123/24    IVY D 123/33    IVY D 124/10   IVY D 124/17
     IVY D 124/25    IVY D 125/01    IVY D 125/15   IVY D 126/23
     IVY D 126/33    IVY D 127/06    IVY D 127/12   IVY D 127/18
     IVY D 127/26    IVY D 128/07    IVY D 129/04   IVY D 130/15
     IVY D 130/20    IVY D 132/01    IVY D 132/28   IVY D 133/14
     IVY D 133/22    IVY D 133/26    IVY D 133/31   IVY D 135/29
OCTAVE (1) ........................................  DEAD   187/12
OCTAVES (1) .......................................  DEAD   187/12
OCTOBER (2) .......................................  IVY D  119/21
     IVY D 134/04
ODD (3) ...........................................  LITTL   75/24
     LITTL   82/31    PNFUL  108/25
O'DONOVAN (1) .....................................  ARABY   31/08
ODOROUS (1) .......................................  ARABY   30/11
ODOUR (6) .........................................  SISTR   14/31
     ENCTR   19/10    EVELN   36/03    EVELN   39/34   PARTS   89/10
     GRACE 156/29
ODOURS (1) ........................................  ARABY   30/10
OF (1865)
O'FARRELL'S (1) ...................................  IVY D  128/27
OFF (51) ..........................................  ARABY   33/26
     RACE    47/01    GALNT   52/11    GALNT   52/26   GALNT   53/02
     GALNT   53/27    GALNT   53/32    GALNT   56/03   GALNT   59/01
     GALNT   59/14    GALNT   60/20    HOUSE   65/22   HOUSE   65/27
     HOUSE   67/33    LITTL   70/01    LITTL   71/19   LITTL   75/03
     LITTL   77/24    LITTL   82/08    PARTS   93/30   PARTS   94/11
     PARTS   96/29    CLAY   101/26    CLAY   105/14   PNFUL  112/06
     IVY D 119/22    IVY D 122/12    IVY D 124/07   IVY D 131/09
     IVY D 133/34    MOTHR 137/23    GRACE 151/18   GRACE 153/16
     GRACE 153/30    GRACE 155/25    GRACE 158/11   GRACE 158/29
     GRACE 172/01    GRACE 172/25    DEAD   175/01   DEAD   175/03
     DEAD   175/18    DEAD   177/22    DEAD   178/13   DEAD   181/27
     DEAD   195/25    DEAD   209/22    DEAD   210/07   DEAD   210/08
     DEAD   211/05    DEAD   216/15
OFFER (6) .........................................  ENCTR   21/02
     LITTL   79/03    PARTS   92/08    MOTHR 136/16   GRACE 155/13
     DEAD   185/22
OFFERED (2) .......................................  GALNT   52/04
     PARTS   88/25
OFFERING (2) ......................................  IVY D  122/25
     GRACE 161/33
OFFHAND (1) .......................................  DEAD   185/03
```

OFFICE (36) .... SISTR 13/17
    HOUSE 63/02   HOUSE   63/03   HOUSE   65/14   LITTL   71/05
    PARTS 86/13   PARTS   88/12   PARTS   88/20   PARTS   89/09
    PARTS 89/13   PARTS   89/31   PARTS   90/03   PARTS   90/13
    PARTS 90/29   PARTS   92/01   PARTS   92/03   PARTS   92/09
    PARTS 92/11   PARTS   94/14   PARTS   97/02   CLAY   104/06
    MOTHR 141/24   MOTHR 142/19   MOTHR 144/31   GRACE 153/17
    GRACE 154/07   GRACE 154/10   GRACE 154/17   GRACE 156/19
    GRACE 158/25   GRACE 158/26   GRACE 160/34   GRACE 172/31
    DEAD 175/03   DEAD   206/24   DEAD   215/19
OFFICE-GIRLS (1) .... PARTS 93/12
OFFICER (1) .... DEAD 206/01
OFFICES (1) .... GRACE 155/03
OFFICIAL (1) .... GRACE 160/33
OFFICIALS (1) .... PNFUL 114/30
OFFICIATE (1) .... GRACE 161/33
OFFICIATED (1) .... GRACE 167/01
OFTEN (29) .... SISTR   9/07
    SISTR 13/19   ENCTR   23/02   ENCTR   27/06   ARABY   31/13
    EVELN 36/15   RACE   44/08   RACE   45/33   GALNT   51/29
    HOUSE 62/23   LITTL   71/04   PARTS   90/03   PARTS   95/17
    CLAY 100/16   CLAY   100/20   CLAY   101/32   PNFUL 108/23
    PNFUL 110/22   PNFUL 111/15   PNFUL 111/15   PNFUL 115/05
    PNFUL 116/14   IVY D 126/28   MOTHR 138/04   MOTHR 143/15
    MOTHR 148/19   GRACE 167/08   GRACE 170/15   DEAD   194/08
OFTENER (1) .... MOTHR 137/11
O'HALLORAN (8) .... PARTS 91/02
    PARTS 93/23   PARTS   93/25   PARTS   94/08   PARTS   94/25
    PARTS 94/29   PARTS   95/02   PARTS   96/27
O'HARA (2) .... LITTL 75/30
    LITTL 76/02
OIL-LAMP (1) .... PNFUL 111/01
OIL-RAG (1) .... IVY D 128/04
OILY (1) .... GALNT 51/22
OLD (144)
OLDER (3) .... GALNT 56/17
    MOTHR 137/05   DEAD   203/26
OLD-FASHIONED (3) .... MOTHR 147/11
    DEAD 179/31   DEAD   196/32
OLDISH (1) .... MOTHR 142/06
O'LIGED (2) .... GRACE 152/28
    GRACE 153/07
O'MADDEN (8) .... MOTHR 144/27
    MOTHR 145/12   MOTHR 145/21   MOTHR 146/06   MOTHR 147/24
    MOTHR 147/25   MOTHR 148/01   MOTHR 149/32
OMADHAUNS (1) .... GRACE 161/10·
ON (458)
ONCE (46) .... ENCTR 23/19
    ENCTR 24/07   ENCTR   25/34   ENCTR   27/01   ARABY   35/23
    EVELN 37/07   GALNT   50/01   GALNT   55/15   GALNT   55/17
    GALNT 59/14   GALNT   59/31   HOUSE   66/23   LITTL   70/03
    LITTL 84/13   PARTS   87/20   PARTS   88/29   PARTS   95/20
    CLAY 105/19   PNFUL 109/20   PNFUL 110/07   PNFUL 113/14
    IVY D 118/08   IVY D 133/27   IVY D 134/05   MOTHR 140/19
    MOTHR 142/27   MOTHR 149/23   GRACE 151/14   GRACE 158/10
    GRACE 160/08   GRACE 164/02   GRACE 165/17   GRACE 170/12·
    GRACE 173/04   DEAD   175/17   DEAD   177/09   DEAD   182/28
    DEAD 185/27   DEAD   187/04   DEAD   190/20   DEAD   201/31
    DEAD 202/01   DEAD   205/27   DEAD   214/14   DEAD   218/12
    DEAD 221/22
ONE (208)
O'NEILL'S (3) .... PARTS 88/30

```
PARTS   89/12      PARTS   92/26
ONES (10) ...................................................  GALNT   51/14
     CLAY  103/05    IVY D  135/05    GRACE 161/25    GRACE 161/25
     GRACE 161/26    DEAD  191/04    DEAD  203/32    DEAD  210/09
     DEAD  223/02
ONE'S (2) ....................................................  ENCTR   25/03
     ENCTR  25/04
'ONGUE (1) ...................................................  GRACE 153/21
ONLOOKERS (1) ................................................  GRACE 151/02
ONLY (69) ....................................................  SISTR   13/09
     SISTR  13/20    SISTR  16/09    SISTR  17/06    ENCTR   23/27
     ENCTR  25/20    ENCTR  26/05    EVELN  38/06    GALNT   53/02
     GALNT  58/11    HOUSE  63/10    HOUSE  65/04    LITTL   77/04
     LITTL  79/29    LITTL  79/33    LITTL  80/27    LITTL   80/31
     LITTL  81/27    LITTL  81/31    LITTL  83/26    PARTS   97/01
     CLAY  100/14    CLAY  103/05    PNFUL 109/06    PNFUL 114/34
     IVY D 120/01    IVY D 120/07    IVY D 121/27    IVY D 129/05
     IVY D 131/32    IVY D 133/04    MOTHR 148/08    GRACE 152/08
     GRACE 154/07    GRACE 160/10    GRACE 160/11    GRACE 160/33
     GRACE 162/27    GRACE 165/14    GRACE 166/06    GRACE 174/22
     DEAD  176/03    DEAD  176/23    DEAD  178/10    DEAD  179/14
     DEAD  184/22    DEAD  184/27    DEAD  186/09    DEAD  188/26
     DEAD  191/12    DEAD  192/26    DEAD  194/34    DEAD  195/17
     DEAD  195/27    DEAD  198/33    DEAD  199/28    DEAD  201/29
     DEAD  202/19    DEAD  208/03    DEAD  208/24    DEAD  212/33
     DEAD  214/02    DEAD  214/20    DEAD  215/25    DEAD  217/09
     DEAD  219/25    DEAD  221/05    DEAD  221/27    DEAD  223/02
ONWARD (2) ...................................................  ARABY   34/17
     LITTL  73/23
OOZE (1) .....................................................  GRACE 150/05
OPEN (27) ....................................................  SISTR   14/13
     SISTR  16/34    ENCTR  25/12    ARABY  34/34    RACE    46/28
     GALNT  52/20    GALNT  56/02    HOUSE  63/18    HOUSE   63/19
     HOUSE  63/28    HOUSE  67/07    LITTL  77/31    LITTL   83/27
     LITTL  84/30    CLAY  104/31    PNFUL 110/31    IVY D 118/08
     IVY D 123/27    IVY D 130/20    IVY D 133/09    MOTHR 139/11
     MOTHR 139/29    GRACE 166/34    GRACE 174/15    DEAD  186/28
     DEAD  193/28    DEAD  208/20
OPENED (27) ..................................................  SISTR   18/04
     ENCTR  20/08    RACE   48/31    GALNT  60/02    GALNT   60/29
     HOUSE  61/03    LITTL  74/17    LITTL  83/29    IVY D 120/18
     IVY D 125/31    IVY D 125/33    IVY D 129/09    IVY D 129/13
     IVY D 129/26    GRACE 151/06    GRACE 151/11    GRACE 151/29
     GRACE 153/26    GRACE 153/28    GRACE 166/23    DEAD  176/34
     DEAD  182/03    DEAD  183/05    DEAD  197/23    DEAD  206/17
     DEAD  215/32    DEAD  217/19
OPEN-HEARTED (1) .............................................  EVELN   38/28
OPENING (4) ..................................................  ARABY   34/11
     RACE   43/17    HOUSE  67/08    DEAD  187/09
OPENLY (1) ...................................................  PNFUL 116/28
OPERA (6) ....................................................  PNFUL 109/06
     MOTHR 142/22    MOTHR 142/24    GRACE 162/29    DEAD  198/17
     DEAD  199/01
OPERAS (1) ...................................................  DEAD  199/15
OPERATIC (1) .................................................  MOTHR 142/23
OPINION (12) .................................................  SISTR   10/02
     SISTR  10/03    HOUSE  64/24    LITTL  78/08    CLAY  100/24
     PNFUL 114/20    IVY D 124/21    IVY D 125/07    GRACE 161/29
     GRACE 163/23    GRACE 164/23    DEAD  198/29
OPINIONS (1) .................................................  GRACE 157/23
OPPONENT'S (2) ...............................................  PARTS   96/07
     PARTS  96/18
```

OPPORTUNE (1) .... GRACE 155/04
OPPORTUNITIES (1) .... PNFUL 110/23
OPPORTUNITY (2) .... RACE 46/27
    MOTHR 139/34
OPPOSITE (5) .... ENCTR 23/11
    ARABY 32/07   GALNT 57/13   PARTS 92/03   IVY D 118/05
OPPOSITION (1) .... DEAD 187/03
OPPRESSED (1) .... RACE 42/07
OPTIMIST (1) .... RACE 43/11
OPTION (1) .... GRACE 160/12
OPULENCE (1) .... MOTHR 143/33
OR (158)
ORANGE (3) .... LITTL 75/07
    LITTL 81/11   DEAD 200/12
ORANGEMAN (2) .... GRACE 165/27
    GRACE 165/28
ORANGES (2) .... DEAD 196/31
    DEAD 201/22
ORATING (1) .... DEAD 220/03
ORATOR (1) .... GRACE 165/08
ORATORY (1) .... GRACE 165/23
ORBIT (1) .... ENCTR 26/10
ORDEAL (2) .... MOTHR 143/02
    DEAD 189/25
ORDER (16) .... GALNT 57/19
    PARTS 87/31   PARTS 92/12   PARTS 98/11   IVY D 133/04
    MOTHR 149/29   GRACE 151/27   GRACE 156/26   GRACE 163/24
    GRACE 163/26   GRACE 163/34   GRACE 163/34   GRACE 164/01
    DEAD 201/06   DEAD 207/23   DEAD 216/13
ORDERED (6) .... EVELN 40/07
    LITTL 76/26   LITTL 80/13   PARTS 95/03   PNFUL 116/09
    DEAD 183/15
ORDERLINESS (1) .... PNFUL 112/13
ORDERLY (1) .... GRACE 172/06
ORDERS (5) .... RACE 43/04
    DEAD 176/21   DEAD 183/10   DEAD 197/26   DEAD 197/34
ORDINARY (3) .... SISTR 12/01
    IVY D 132/16   MOTHR 136/17
ORGAN (2) .... EVELN 40/01
    DEAD 176/09
ORGAN PLAYER (1) .... EVELN 40/07
ORIENTAL (1) .... LITTL 83/15
ORIGIN (1) .... GRACE 159/25
ORIGINAL (4) .... RACE 47/27
    LITTL 73/20   GRACE 166/09   GRACE 173/18
ORIGINALLY (1) .... MOTHR 141/06
ORMOND (1) .... MOTHR 137/04
ORNAMENT (1) .... PNFUL 107/16
O'ROURKE (4) .... SISTR 15/20
    SISTR 16/10   SISTR 17/08   SISTR 18/05
ORTHODOX (1) .... GRACE 165/15
OTHER (69) .... ENCTR 21/21
    ENCTR 23/22   ENCTR 24/21   ENCTR 26/30   ARABY 29/05
    ARABY 32/04   EVELN 36/08   EVELN 39/01   EVELN 39/23
    EVELN 40/06   RACE 48/05   RACE 48/13   GALNT 49/11
    GALNT 54/14   GALNT 55/07   GALNT 59/31   HOUSE 63/03
    LITTL 76/03   LITTL 77/30   LITTL 78/28   LITTL 80/34
    PARTS 91/14   PARTS 92/28   PARTS 94/09   PARTS 94/12
    PARTS 95/32   PARTS 96/13   PARTS 97/31   CLAY 101/15
    CLAY 105/03   CLAY 106/15   PNFUL 107/03   PNFUL 114/29
    IVY D 120/32   IVY D 121/14   IVY D 121/15   IVY D 121/27
    IVY D 124/22   IVY D 130/07   IVY D 130/33   MOTHR 137/29

```
        MOTHR 142/34    MOTHR 147/01    MOTHR 148/17    MOTHR 148/21
        GRACE 152/24    GRACE 153/23    GRACE 156/09    GRACE 156/16
        GRACE 156/18    GRACE 159/10    GRACE 159/34    GRACE 160/04
        GRACE 163/34    GRACE 164/01    GRACE 164/15    GRACE 169/21
        GRACE 169/26    GRACE 171/07    GRACE 173/06    DEAD  175/10
        DEAD  186/05    DEAD  194/31    DEAD  196/18    DEAD  196/33
        DEAD  197/34    DEAD  205/33    DEAD  223/07    DEAD  223/16
OTHERS (25) ...................................... ENCTR  26/14
        EVELN  37/05    GALNT  53/11    HOUSE  65/09    LITTL  78/18
        PARTS  93/32    PNFUL 108/23    PNFUL 109/09    MOTHR 145/30
        GRACE 155/07    GRACE 169/02    GRACE 169/04    GRACE 169/13
        GRACE 171/13    GRACE 172/19    DEAD  193/08    DEAD  194/11
        DEAD  208/12    DEAD  209/24    DEAD  210/31    DEAD  211/15
        DEAD  211/17    DEAD  214/10    DEAD  214/20    DEAD  215/07
OTHER'S (3) ...................................... PARTS  96/04
        DEAD  197/33    DEAD  197/34
OTHERWISE (1) .................................... MOTHR 139/02
'OU (1) ...+...................................... LITTL  85/16
OUGHT (3) ........................................ ENCTR  27/11
        DEAD  189/01    DEAD  190/28
OUGHTERARD (2) ................................... DEAD  220/32
        DEAD  221/28
OUR (59) ......................................... SISTR  13/28
        ENCTR  19/08    ENCTR  23/03    ENCTR  23/17    ENCTR  23/20
        ENCTR  24/09    ENCTR  24/11    ENCTR  24/14    ENCTR  24/15
        ENCTR  24/25    ENCTR  24/27    ENCTR  25/28    ENCTR  26/28
        ARABY  29/07    ARABY  30/02    ARABY  30/06    ARABY  30/06
        ARABY  30/07    ARABY  30/17    ARABY  30/19    ARABY  30/30
        ARABY  31/09    ARABY  32/07    ARABY  33/27    PARTS  89/23
        PNFUL 111/29    IVY D 122/05    IVY D 124/15    IVY D 124/28
        IVY D 132/24    IVY D 133/01    IVY D 134/07    MOTHR 142/14
        GRACE 165/32    GRACE 166/09    GRACE 168/20    GRACE 170/33
        GRACE 171/17    GRACE 171/17    GRACE 174/02    GRACE 174/18
        GRACE 174/19    GRACE 174/21    GRACE 174/22    DEAD  201/01
        DEAD  202/32    DEAD  203/10    DEAD  203/11    DEAD  203/18
        DEAD  203/32    DEAD  204/03    DEAD  204/05    DEAD  204/07
        DEAD  204/09    DEAD  204/13    DEAD  204/30    DEAD  205/01
        DEAD  205/13    DEAD  207/16
OURSELVES (9) .................................... SISTR  14/32
        ENCTR  20/03    ENCTR  22/31    ENCTR  23/07    ENCTR  24/16
        PNFUL 111/29    IVY D 129/33    GRACE 164/32    DEAD  191/05
OUT (231)
OUT-AND-OUT (1) .................................. GRACE 168/26
OUTBURST (2) ..................................... PNFUL 115/33
        DEAD  218/12
OUTCAST (2) ...................................... PNFUL 117/15
        PNFUL 117/20
OUTDOOR (1) ...................................... MOTHR 144/24
OUTER (1) ........................................ DEAD  196/19
OUTGENERALLED (1) ................................ GRACE 171/14
OUT-OF-DOORS (1) ................................. DEAD  177/19
OUTRAGED (1) ..................................... HOUSE  64/25
OUTRIGHT (1) ..................................... CLAY  104/03
OUTSIDE (12) ..................................... EVELN  39/02
        EVELN  40/06    PARTS  91/06    CLAY  101/34    PNFUL 111/15
        PNFUL 116/21    GRACE 151/13    DEAD  179/02    DEAD  192/03
        DEAD  195/12    DEAD  201/11    DEAD  202/07
OUTSIDER (1) ..................................... GRACE 153/05
OUTSIDERS (1) .................................... HOUSE  62/15
OUTSKIRTS (2) .................................... PNFUL 109/04
        GRACE 159/23
OVAL (3) ......................................... PNFUL 109/30
```

GRACE 166/17   DEAD   206/20
OVER (108)
OVERBEARING (1) .... CLAY   104/09
OVERCOAT (11) .... ARABY   33/30
   PNFUL 116/06   DEAD 175/04   DEAD 177/17   DEAD 177/18
   DEAD 177/23   DEAD 177/34   DEAD 206/19   DEAD 206/25
   DEAD 211/14   DEAD 216/11
OVER-COAT (1) .... PNFUL 113/10
OVERCOME (1) .... DEAD   221/31
OVERFLOWING (1) .... DEAD   185/31
OVERHEAR (1) .... ENCTR   26/14
OVERHEARD (1) .... PARTS   92/18
OVERLOOK (1) .... GRACE 159/25
OVERMASTER (2) .... LITTL   74/16
   DEAD 217/18
OVERNIGHT (1) .... ENCTR   21/32
OVER-RIPE (1) .... PNFUL 108/12
OVERSTAYED (1) .... DEAD   195/16
OWE (1) .... IVY D 127/22
OWED (1) .... GRACE 163/20
OWING (2) .... GALNT   49/12
   IVY D 127/27
OWN (48) .... SISTR   10/08
   SISTR 10/34   ENCTR 21/22   ENCTR 26/09   RACE   43/33
   RACE   48/12   GALNT 57/33   GALNT 58/03   GALNT 59/12
   HOUSE 63/15   LITTL 73/25   LITTL 80/23   PARTS 92/12
   CLAY 102/05   CLAY 104/28   PNFUL 108/24   PNFUL 110/30
   PNFUL 111/02   PNFUL 111/02   PNFUL 111/24   PNFUL 111/28
   PNFUL 111/29   IVY D 124/33   IVY D 127/03   IVY D 129/06
   IVY D 131/21   MOTHR 137/09   GRACE 157/13   GRACE 163/04
   GRACE 163/07   GRACE 163/08   GRACE 163/09   GRACE 164/13
   DEAD 189/16   DEAD 189/19   DEAD 189/27   DEAD 189/28
   DEAD 189/29   DEAD 189/31   DEAD 192/14   DEAD 198/09
   DEAD 215/30   DEAD 217/10   DEAD 217/32   DEAD 220/01
   DEAD 220/04   DEAD 222/23   DEAD 223/19
OWNER (2) .... RACE   43/01
   GRACE 172/29
OX'S (1) .... IVY D 130/06
OXTER (1) .... GRACE 167/32
OYSTERS (1) .... LITTL   72/05

P. (1) .... PNFUL 114/03
PA (8) .... PARTS   97/22
   PARTS 97/24   PARTS 97/29   PARTS 98/04   PARTS 98/12
   PARTS 98/22   PARTS 98/22   PARTS 98/24
PACE (6) .... ARABY   30/31
   GALNT 55/12   GALNT 56/12   LITTL 73/07   PNFUL 113/11
   MOTHR 149/29
PACED (1) .... DEAD   208/11
PACES (2) .... ENCTR   24/28
   DEAD 218/22
PACIFICALLY (1) .... DEAD   194/29
PACK (1) .... IVY D 119/05
PACKED (1) .... DEAD   199/09
PACKET (2) .... SISTR   12/15
   SISTR 12/17
PACKING (2) .... MOTHR 137/23
   DEAD 221/16
PADDED (1) .... GALNT   56/21
PADDY (3) .... PARTS   93/24
   PARTS 95/29   PARTS 96/03

PAGE (6) .... ENCTR   20/16
      ENCTR   20/16   ENCTR   20/16   ARABY   32/17   LITTL   84/08
      DEAD   186/13
PAGES (5) .... ENCTR   20/13
      ENCTR   20/22   ARABY   29/11   PARTS   90/24   DEAD   188/11
PAID (14) .... RACE   43/28
      GALNT   58/13   HOUSE   62/11   LITTL   83/26   PNFUL 113/06
      IVY D 121/04   MOTHR 137/21   MOTHR 144/09   MOTHR 144/13
      MOTHR 147/29   MOTHR 148/22   MOTHR 149/04   DEAD   188/08
      DEAD   215/01
PAIN (7) .... HOUSE   65/29
      PARTS   98/19   IVY D 135/10   GRACE 153/09   GRACE 156/30
      GRACE 158/16   GRACE 158/28
PAINED (2) .... ENCTR   25/18
      DEAD   222/07
PAINFUL (4) .... PNFUL 107/ T
      PNFUL 113/20   PNFUL 115/10   MOTHR 146/21
PAINT (1) .... DEAD   210/06
PAINTER (2) .... DEAD   210/06
      DEAD   210/10
PAINTERS (1) .... RACE   46/21
PAIR (8) .... ENCTR   27/17
      GALNT   56/14   GALNT   57/30   HOUSE   63/14   HOUSE   68/07
      GRACE 154/02   GRACE 156/05   DEAD   181/06
PALACE (2) .... IVY D 134/15
      DEAD   213/02
PALATE (1) .... GRACE 154/14
PALAVER (1) .... DEAD   178/10
PALE (12) .... SISTR   14/18
      EVELN   40/29   RACE   45/24   GALNT   53/04   LITTL   75/04
      LITTL   82/25   MOTHR 136/11   MOTHR 143/17   GRACE 157/09
      GRACE 166/17   DEAD   177/25   DEAD   178/17
PALED (1) .... ENCTR   20/31
PALER (2) .... HOUSE   68/14
      DEAD   177/26
PALLID (1) .... DEAD   184/26
PALLOR (3) .... LITTL   75/06
      PARTS   96/16   GRACE 151/05
PALM (3) .... GALNT   60/30
      LITTL   78/17   DEAD   213/22
PALMS (2) .... ARABY   31/28
      DEAD   215/26
PALPITATED (1) .... ENCTR   20/20
PALPITATIONS (1) .... EVELN   38/03
PALTRY (2) .... ENCTR   28/08
      DEAD   188/10
PANE (2) .... DEAD   192/03
      DEAD   223/23
PANELS (3) .... GRACE 151/13
      DEAD   209/28   DEAD   210/08
PANES (1) .... ARABY   31/22
PANG (1) .... DEAD   215/13
PANGS (1) .... GALNT   59/11
PANORAMA (1) .... LITTL   73/16
PANSY (1) .... DEAD   183/29
PANT (1) .... GALNT   60/12
PANTING (2) .... LITTL   84/30
      MOTHR 146/31
PANTOMIME (1) .... DEAD   198/23
PANTRY (10) .... HOUSE   68/05
      DEAD   175/02   DEAD   177/22   DEAD   177/26   DEAD   177/31
      DEAD   179/18   DEAD   182/10   DEAD   206/24   DEAD   211/14

         DEAD   211/30
PAPA (1) .... CLAY   103/22
PAPAL (1) .... GRACE 169/07
PAPER (15) .... ENCTR   20/20
   RACE   48/10   GALNT   59/21   LITTL   73/20   PNFUL 112/27
   PNFUL 112/30   PNFUL 113/01   PNFUL 113/15   PNFUL 115/15
   IVY D 118/17   MOTHR 136/03   MOTHR 140/19   DEAD   179/07
   DEAD   196/18   DEAD   196/20
PAPER-COVERED (1) .... ARABY   29/11
PAPERS (13) .... SISTR   16/13
   ARABY   29/10   PARTS   87/06   PARTS   87/24   PARTS   87/33
   PARTS   87/34   PNFUL 108/06   PNFUL 112/17   IVY D 121/02
   IVY D 135/30   MOTHR 141/17   GRACE 161/19   DEAD   196/29
PARADE (4) .... GALNT   51/25
   PNFUL 113/19   PNFUL 113/24   PNFUL 114/31
PARAGRAPH (5) .... PNFUL 112/30
   PNFUL 112/32   PNFUL 113/02   PNFUL 113/15   PNFUL 113/18
PARALLEL (2) .... DEAD   188/19
   DEAD   196/22
PARALYSIS (2) .... SISTR   9/10
   SISTR   11/29
PARALYTIC (1) .... SISTR   11/22
PARAPETS (1) .... DEAD   212/34
PARCEL (4) .... LITTL   82/14
   LITTL   82/33   PNFUL 112/11   DEAD   213/05
PARCELLED (1) .... CLAY   102/27
PARCELS (2) .... ARABY   31/03
   LITTL   85/05
PARDON (2) .... PARTS   95/22
   PARTS   97/09
PARENTS (1) .... ENCTR   19/09
PARENTS' (1) .... RACE   45/27
PARIS (13) .... RACE   43/05
   LITTL   76/12   LITTL   76/12   LITTL   76/14   LITTL   76/22
   LITTL   76/23   LITTL   77/09   LITTL   77/11   LITTL   77/16
   LITTL   77/20   DEAD   192/10   DEAD   199/21   DEAD   204/26
PARISIENNE (1) .... LITTL   77/26
PARK (7) .... PNFUL 112/05
   PNFUL 112/08   PNFUL 117/01   PNFUL 117/12   DEAD   192/05
   DEAD   202/09   DEAD   207/27
PARKER (4) .... PARTS   86/01
   PARTS   86/05   PARTS   90/17   PARTS   92/20
PARKES (1) .... IVY D 131/15
PARKGATE (2) .... PNFUL 112/04
   PNFUL 113/10
PARKINSON (2) .... DEAD   199/32
   DEAD   200/04
PARLOUR (5) .... ARABY   30/25
   ARABY   32/32   HOUSE   67/28   PARTS   95/02   GRACE 157/05
PARNELL (6) .... IVY D 132/02
   IVY D 132/03   IVY D 132/21   IVY D 132/26   IVY D 134/03
   IVY D 135/20
PARNELL'S (1) .... IVY D 132/28
PAROLE (1) .... LITTL   80/03
PAROXYSM (2) .... LITTL   85/01
   LITTL   85/20
PARSLEY (1) .... DEAD   196/19
PART (34) .... ARABY   33/06
   ARABY   34/30   ARABY   35/30   EVELN   39/04   RACE   44/32
   RACE   47/27   GALNT   59/06   PNFUL 112/10   IVY D 119/16
   IVY D 119/17   MOTHR 137/16   MOTHR 141/20   MOTHR 142/23
   MOTHR 144/08   MOTHR 147/09   MOTHR 147/18   MOTHR 148/20
```
```

MOTHR	148/24	MOTHR	149/14	GRACE	156/12	GRACE	156/21
GRACE	163/21	GRACE	173/07	DEAD	176/05	DEAD	190/05
DEAD	192/22	DEAD	198/15	DEAD	198/23	DEAD	204/26
DEAD	207/25	DEAD	209/25	DEAD	222/08	DEAD	223/28
DEAD	223/31						

PARTED (2) .... DEAD 178/20
DEAD 179/26
PARTIAL (1) .... DEAD 223/15
PARTICULARISED (1) .... GRACE 157/20
PARTICULARLY (1) .... PARTS 95/25
PARTICULARS (1) .... GRACE 164/25
PARTLY (3) .... GRACE 153/09
DEAD 189/17   DEAD 189/18
PARTNER (5) .... PNFUL 112/23
GRACE 159/27   DEAD 182/19   DEAD 184/02   DEAD 184/09
PARTNERED (1) .... DEAD 187/19
PARTS (1) .... MOTHR 147/14
PARTY (16) .... RACE   42/15

RACE	43/11	RACE	45/18	RACE	46/05	RACE	46/21
RACE	47/02	GALNT	50/21	PARTS	94/10	PARTS	94/17
PARTS	95/20	PNFUL	110/33	PNFUL	111/01	IVY D	127/33
IVY D	131/23	MOTHR	137/12	GRACE	172/19		

PASS (11) .... ARABY 32/23

EVELN	37/16	RACE	48/10	GALNT	55/02	GALNT	56/31
HOUSE	62/09	MOTHR	149/18	GRACE	154/04	DEAD	199/02
DEAD	216/22	DEAD	223/06				

PASSAGE (2) .... EVELN 40/24
EVELN 40/33
PASSAGES (2) .... MOTHR 145/18
DEAD 186/02
PASSED (39) .... SISTR   9/02

SISTR	15/04	ENCTR	24/25	ARABY	30/31	ARABY	34/23
ARABY	34/27	EVELN	36/04	EVELN	36/04	GALNT	50/06
GALNT	53/18	GALNT	56/03	GALNT	56/26	GALNT	60/01
HOUSE	66/10	HOUSE	68/04	LITTL	71/11	LITTL	72/12
LITTL	73/08	LITTL	74/14	PARTS	87/27	PARTS	87/30
PARTS	88/19	PARTS	89/31	PARTS	92/04	PARTS	93/10
PNFUL	112/12	PNFUL	117/24	MOTHR	139/10	MOTHR	142/29
MOTHR	143/10	MOTHR	149/24	GRACE	153/16	GRACE	156/06
DEAD	180/06	DEAD	187/02	DEAD	200/10	DEAD	201/23
DEAD	218/18	DEAD	218/33				

PASSES (1) .... HOUSE 67/22
PASSING (8) .... SISTR 10/16

GALNT	52/06	GALNT	52/08	GALNT	56/33	HOUSE	63/10
PARTS	86/13	PARTS	88/20	DEAD	182/19		

PASSION (5) .... LITTL 83/14
LITTL 83/16   PARTS 91/30   DEAD 194/26   DEAD 223/07
PASSIONATELY (1) .... PNFUL 111/32
PASSIVE (1) .... EVELN 41/15
PAST (14) .... SISTR 16/29

HOUSE	64/21	LITTL	72/01	LITTL	72/23	PARTS	89/28
PARTS	94/16	PNFUL	108/28	IVY D	135/08	DEAD	202/15
DEAD	203/27	DEAD	204/03	DEAD	204/10	DEAD	210/31
DEAD	214/09						

PASTEBOARD (2) .... IVY D 119/05
IVY D 126/24
PASTED (1) .... PNFUL 108/09
PAT (6) .... ENCTR 22/03
PARTS 88/34   PARTS 92/26   IVY D 128/02   MOTHR 146/22
DEAD 176/02
PATAGONIANS (1) .... EVELN 39/14
PATCH (1) .... HOUSE 65/02

PATCHES (3) .... DEAD 178/17
    DEAD 212/33   DEAD 214/31
PATENT (1) .... PNFUL 114/26
PATENT-LEATHER (1) .... DEAD 178/14
PATH (6) .... EVELN 36/06
    GALNT 49/11   GALNT 51/18   GALNT 59/34   PARTS 88/29
    DEAD 204/05
PATHS (1) .... LITTL 71/10
PATIENCE (1) .... ARABY 32/25
PATIENT (1) .... HOUSE 67/02
PATIENTLY (1) .... HOUSE 68/29
PATRICK (2) .... DEAD 207/16
    DEAD 222/26
PATRIOT (2) .... IVY D 125/13
    IVY D 125/17
PATRIOTIC (2) .... MOTHR 147/18
    MOTHR 148/05
PATRONISING (2) .... LITTL 80/31
    LITTL 80/32
PATTED (2) .... DEAD 180/30
    DEAD 201/32
PATTERED (1) .... SISTR 13/23
PATTERSON (1) .... PNFUL 114/22
PATTING (1) .... DEAD 202/01
PAUSE (14) .... SISTR 17/25
    RACE   47/34   GALNT 57/20   PARTS 91/25   PARTS 94/08
    CLAY 105/15   IVY D 129/30   IVY D 134/02   MOTHR 147/07
    GRACE 170/27   DEAD 180/34   DEAD 201/29   DEAD 211/19
    DEAD 217/14
PAUSED (10) .... ENCTR 26/18
    ENCTR 27/32   GALNT 57/02   LITTL 84/01   GRACE 154/15
    GRACE 162/12   DEAD 202/28   DEAD 216/17   DEAD 221/01
    DEAD 221/13
PAUSES (1) .... DEAD 186/11
PAUSING (2) .... LITTL 76/20
    LITTL 82/24
PAVEMENT (1) .... EVELN 36/06
PAWNBROKER'S (2) .... ARABY 33/17
    GRACE 172/29
PAWNED (2) .... PARTS 97/02
    GRACE 157/17
PAWN-OFFICE (2) .... PARTS 92/31
    PARTS 93/05
PAY (9) .... RACE 45/17
    GALNT 52/27   IVY D 121/08   IVY D 123/20   IVY D 125/08
    MOTHR 148/01   MOTHR 148/13   MOTHR 148/25   GRACE 160/31
PAYING (6) .... ENCTR 23/17
    GALNT 51/04   LITTL 82/30   CLAY 100/13   MOTHR 137/16
    DEAD 200/32
PEACE (2) .... CLAY 99/14
    MOTHR 147/30
PEACEFUL (2) .... SISTR 15/26
    ENCTR 19/10
PEACEFULLY (2) .... SISTR 15/15
    SISTR 15/16
PEACE-MAKER (1) .... CLAY 99/16
PEACOCK-BLUE (1) .... PARTS 95/13
PEAKE (1) .... PARTS 92/11
PEAKED (1) .... EVELN 38/33
PEAKS (1) .... IVY D 135/12
PEAL (1) .... DEAD 180/21
PEALS (2) .... HOUSE 63/30

```
            DEAD   208/18
PEARLS (1) ........................................ GALNT  49/05
PEAS (4) .......................................... GALNT  57/15
    GALNT  57/17    GALNT  57/25    GALNT  57/28
PECULIAR (1) ...................................... SISTR  10/09
PEELED (1) ........................................ DEAD   196/26
PEEPING (1) ....................................... PNFUL  113/09
PEER (1) .......................................... ARABY  30/17
PEERED (3) ........................................ GALNT  53/19
    GRACE  153/23    GRACE  153/25
PEERING (3) ....................................... ENCTR  27/17
    PARTS  97/20    DEAD  175/11
PEGS (1) .......................................... GRACE  161/15
PELLETS (1) ....................................... RACE   42/02
PELOOTHERED (1) ................................... GRACE  160/16
PEN (2) ........................................... PARTS  88/13
    IVY D  125/03
PENCIL (1) ........................................ GRACE  151/19
PENCILLED (1) ..................................... HOUSE  61/17
PENCILS (1) ....................................... PNFUL  108/11
PENDING (1) ....................................... PNFUL  114/12
PENITENT (1) ...................................... ENCTR  28/11
PENNIES (1) ....................................... ARABY  35/28
PENNY (5) ......................................... LITTL  82/31
    PARTS  89/03    PARTS  92/28    CLAY  102/15    MOTHR  138/33
PENNY-A-WEEK (2) .................................. GRACE  167/30
    GRACE  167/31
PENNYBOY (1) ...................................... DEAD   220/02
PENNY-PIECE (1) ................................... DEAD   200/28
PENSIVELY (2) ..................................... SISTR  13/24
    GALNT  56/05
PEONY (1) ......................................... PARTS  96/17
PEOPLE (45) ....................................... ENCTR  21/06
    ENCTR  21/33    ARABY  34/01    ARABY  34/19    ARABY  34/33
    EVELN  36/04    EVELN  37/27    EVELN  37/33    EVELN  39/05
    RACE   42/06    RACE   45/16    RACE   46/32    GALNT  50/17
    HOUSE  63/19    LITTL  72/04    LITTL  72/25    LITTL  73/08
    LITTL  74/21    LITTL  74/22    CLAY  100/25    CLAY  100/26
    CLAY  102/03    CLAY  102/13    CLAY  106/15    PNFUL  109/23
    PNFUL  114/24   IVY D  128/12   IVY D  130/02   MOTHR  137/31
    MOTHR  138/04   MOTHR  139/25   MOTHR  140/10   MOTHR  143/02
    GRACE  157/14   GRACE  159/17   GRACE  161/21   DEAD   189/05
    DEAD   189/28   DEAD   190/29   DEAD   190/30   DEAD   198/07
    DEAD   200/33   DEAD   202/06   DEAD   220/31   DEAD   221/29
PEOPLED (1) ....................................... PNFUL  109/18
PEOPLE'S (2) ...................................... EVELN  36/09
    MOTHR  138/04
PEPPER (1) ........................................ GALNT  57/25
PEPPERED (1) ...................................... DEAD   196/19
PERCEIVED (2) ..................................... MOTHR  137/07
    MOTHR  146/07
PERCHED (1) ....................................... DEAD   193/13
PERENNIAL (1) ..................................... DEAD   204/32
PERFECT (1) ....................................... LITTL  70/17
PERFECTLY (2) ..................................... PNFUL  117/33
    PNFUL  117/33
PERFORM (1) ....................................... DEAD   202/16
PERFORMED (1) ..................................... PNFUL  109/11
PERFORMING (1) .................................... PARTS  94/20
PERFUME (3) ....................................... HOUSE  67/11
    LITTL  70/15    PARTS  89/34
PERFUMED (2) ...................................... HOUSE  67/10
```

DEAD   215/13
PERFUMES (2) .... PARTS   89/10
    PARTS   90/05
PERHAPS (32) .... SISTR   12/14
    ENCTR   24/28   EVELN   37/08   EVELN   37/24   EVELN   40/19
    RACE   44/24   GALNT   59/14   HOUSE   65/15   HOUSE   67/17
    LITTL   73/19   LITTL   74/01   LITTL   74/04   LITTL   74/10
    LITTL   77/04   LITTL   79/26   IVY D 122/09   IVY D 132/18
    MOTHR 141/21   GRACE 164/17   DEAD   189/13   DEAD   190/28
    DEAD   192/18   DEAD   202/07   DEAD   202/26   DEAD   203/03
    DEAD   214/14   DEAD   217/32   DEAD   217/33   DEAD   219/16
    DEAD   219/22   DEAD   222/17   DEAD   222/29
PERIODS (1) .... GRACE 158/20
PERISH (1) .... IVY D 134/14
PERISHED (1) .... DEAD   177/10
PERMANENTLY (1) .... PNFUL 109/26
PERPLEXED (1) .... DEAD   188/23
PERPLEXITY (1) .... DEAD   188/06
PERSIA (1) .... SISTR   14/01
PERSISTENT (1) .... HOUSE   63/17
PERSON (21) .... RACE   43/33
    GALNT   51/34   GALNT   51/34   LITTL   76/06   LITTL   80/18
    PARTS   91/28   CLAY   99/10   CLAY   100/32   CLAY   104/09
    PNFUL 108/28   PNFUL 114/19   IVY D 125/23   MOTHR 137/08
    GRACE 151/17   GRACE 159/31   GRACE 159/33   DEAD   217/26
    DEAD   218/28   DEAD   218/30   DEAD   218/31   DEAD   220/01
PERSONAL (4) .... RACE   46/26
    LITTL   77/05   LITTL   78/19   GRACE 156/29
PERSONALLY (1) .... IVY D 132/16
PERSONS (2) .... DEAD   182/10
    DEAD   186/09
PERSUADE (1) .... DEAD   195/13
PERSUADED (1) .... SISTR   12/10
PERSUASION (1) .... DEAD   194/31
PERSUASIVELY (1) .... GRACE 164/28
PERTLY (1) .... ENCTR   25/26
PERTURBATION (1) .... HOUSE   68/28
PERTURBED (1) .... HOUSE   63/22
PERVADES (2) .... ARABY   34/31
    LITTL   74/09
PERVERSE (1) .... HOUSE   62/34
PETTICOAT (2) .... ARABY   32/10
    DEAD   222/19
PETTICOATS (1) .... CLAY   101/02
PHILOSOPHICALLY (1) .... GALNT   53/11
PHILOSOPHY (1) .... GRACE 157/22
PHLEGM (1) .... GRACE 158/32
PHOENIX (1) .... IVY D 135/15
PHOTOGRAPH (10) .... EVELN   37/12
    EVELN   37/15   LITTL   82/22   LITTL   82/23   LITTL   83/09
    LITTL   83/17   GRACE 168/05   GRACE 168/07   GRACE 168/10
    DEAD   186/28
PHRASE (8) .... RACE   44/09
    HOUSE   67/22   PARTS   90/14   DEAD   185/33   DEAD   188/20
    DEAD   192/11   DEAD   203/22   DEAD   217/28
PHRASEMONGERS (1) .... PNFUL 111/11
PHRASES (4) .... ENCTR   26/15
    LITTL   74/07   PNFUL 115/21   DEAD   187/03
PHYSICAL (1) .... PNFUL 108/14
PIANIST (2) .... RACE   44/02
    DEAD   182/02
PIANO (23) .... RACE   47/24

RACE 48/05	RACE 48/17	CLAY 104/12	CLAY 105/32
PNFUL 109/04	MOTHR 147/08	GRACE 158/19	DEAD 176/16
DEAD 177/33	DEAD 182/34	DEAD 184/13	DEAD 186/08
DEAD 186/16	DEAD 187/17	DEAD 192/32	DEAD 196/34
DEAD 197/24	DEAD 202/05	DEAD 206/32	DEAD 209/33
DEAD 210/17	DEAD 210/32		

PIANO-STOOL (1) .... DEAD 194/18
PICK (3) .... SISTR 11/06
   GALNT 50/28   DEAD 195/19
PICKED (1) .... LITTL 71/32
PICKING (1) .... DEAD 199/27
PICNIC (1) .... EVELN 39/29
PICTURE (5) .... MOTHR 137/28
   MOTHR 137/29   DEAD 186/16   DEAD 186/17   DEAD 210/09
PICTURES (2) .... LITTL 78/15
   PNFUL 107/08
PIECE (15) .... ARABY 34/11
   IVY D 118/01   IVY D 118/10   IVY D 119/25   IVY D 133/27
   IVY D 134/01   IVY D 135/33   MOTHR 148/05   GRACE 153/29
   GRACE 158/11   DEAD 186/02   DEAD 186/03   DEAD 187/08
   DEAD 187/11   DEAD 187/17
PIECES (4) .... HOUSE 64/05
   PNFUL 112/14   PNFUL 117/08   MOTHR 136/03
PIERCED (2) .... GALNT 60/25
   LITTL 84/15
PIERCING (2) .... PARTS 86/02
   DEAD 206/03
PIERGLASS (1) .... DEAD 186/28
PIER-GLASS (1) .... HOUSE 65/20
PIGEON (3) .... ENCTR 21/16
   ENCTR 21/19   ENCTR 24/10
PIGS' (2) .... ARABY 31/06
   IVY D 123/19
PILE (3) .... PARTS 87/04
   PARTS 87/24   PARTS 87/33
PILED (1) .... LITTL 82/30
PILLAR (3) .... CLAY 100/05
   CLAY 100/05   CLAY 102/11
PILLARS (1) .... GRACE 172/09
PILLOWS (3) .... HOUSE 68/24
   HOUSE 68/32   GRACE 156/32
PILOTING (1) .... DEAD 184/23
PIMPLES (1) .... IVY D 118/13
PIM'S (1) .... GALNT 51/11
PIN (1) .... PNFUL 108/07
PINCHES (1) .... SISTR 13/25
PINK (1) .... PARTS 87/05
PINK-VEINED (1) .... HOUSE 61/18
PINNED (2) .... SISTR 12/05
   GALNT 55/30
PINT (1) .... PNFUL 116/13
PIOUS (5) .... ARABY 33/18
   LITTL 76/30   MOTHR 137/10   GRACE 170/30   DEAD 201/21
PIOUSLY (1) .... SISTR 10/24
PIPE (3) .... SISTR 10/03
   SISTR 10/10   SISTR 10/27
PIPECLAYED (1) .... ENCTR 21/32
PIPING (1) .... ENCTR 23/06
PIT (1) .... GRACE 165/19
PITCH (1) .... DEAD 192/33
PITCHED (1) .... ENCTR 19/06
PITEOUSLY (1) .... LITTL 84/23

PITIABLE (1) .... DEAD 220/04
PITIED (1) .... LITTL 73/13
PITIFUL (1) .... EVELN 40/11
PITILESSLY (1) .... ARABY 33/01
PITY (8) .... LITTL 74/09
    CLAY 102/08   PNFUL 109/22   GRACE 171/04   DEAD 210/34
    DEAD 211/32   DEAD 217/04   DEAD 222/13
PIUS (1) .... GRACE 167/18
PIVOT (1) .... GALNT 56/14
PLACE (12) .... EVELN 37/24
    GALNT 60/21   HOUSE 68/30   LITTL 70/06   LITTL 77/19
    PARTS 97/30   MOTHR 137/06   GRACE 161/08   GRACE 162/10
    GRACE 162/18   GRACE 172/18   DEAD 195/03
PLACED (8) .... RACE 42/10
    IVY D 123/32   IVY D 129/27   IVY D 133/12   MOTHR 141/32
    GRACE 152/03   GRACE 166/29   DEAD 182/30
PLACES (6) .... ARABY 31/01
    LITTL 78/28   IVY D 131/21   DEAD 187/24   DEAD 191/23
    DEAD 203/02
PLACIDLY (1) .... DEAD 190/20
PLACING (3) .... PNFUL 114/25
    GRACE 161/30   DEAD 213/21
PLAID (1) .... PARTS 88/26
PLAIN (8) .... GALNT 51/30
    PARTS 89/01   CLAY 103/30   PNFUL 109/03   IVY D 121/25
    GRACE 167/33   DEAD 197/19   DEAD 223/29
PLAINLY (3) .... LITTL 75/06
    DEAD 179/22   DEAD 219/09
PLAINTIVE (1) .... DEAD 210/21
PLANKS (1) .... ENCTR 23/30
PLANNED (1) .... ENCTR 21/11
PLANS (1) .... MOTHR 141/27
PLANTED (2) .... GALNT 57/22
    LITTL 74/27
PLANTS (1) .... CLAY 100/27
PLATE (9) .... SISTR 10/27
    GALNT 57/06   GALNT 57/15   GALNT 57/17   GALNT 57/25
    PARTS 86/16   PNFUL 112/32   PNFUL 112/33   PNFUL 113/03
PLATES (9) .... HOUSE 64/01
    GRACE 161/11   GRACE 161/17   DEAD 182/32   DEAD 191/34
    DEAD 197/15   DEAD 197/16   DEAD 198/16   DEAD 200/11
PLATFORM (8) .... ARABY 34/22
    PNFUL 114/11   PNFUL 114/28   PNFUL 114/28   MOTHR 140/10
    MOTHR 148/28   MOTHR 149/18   DEAD 213/21
PLAUSIBLE (1) .... MOTHR 144/32
PLAY (23) .... SISTR 10/33
    ENCTR 22/21   ARABY 30/07   ARABY 32/27   ARABY 32/27
    ARABY 34/07   EVELN 36/08   EVELN 36/12   RACE 45/28
    RACE 48/09   RACE 48/22   GALNT 52/28   LITTL 81/32
    PARTS 96/12   PARTS 98/11   CLAY 105/19   IVY D 132/19
    MOTHR 148/24   MOTHR 149/16   GRACE 158/19   DEAD 186/06
    DEAD 199/15   DEAD 204/26
PLAYED (18) .... ENCTR 19/11
    ARABY 30/06   EVELN 36/14   RACE 47/24   RACE 48/05
    RACE 48/06   GALNT 54/13   GALNT 56/20   GALNT 56/21
    HOUSE 62/25   CLAY 104/12   CLAY 105/22   CLAY 105/34
    MOTHR 137/34   MOTHR 147/16   DEAD 183/26   DEAD 204/27
    DEAD 222/08
PLAYING (14) .... ARABY 31/24
    ARABY 33/09   EVELN 40/01   GALNT 54/08   PARTS 96/13
    MOTHR 136/14   GRACE 160/25   DEAD 184/06   DEAD 186/01
    DEAD 186/04   DEAD 187/09   DEAD 194/13   DEAD 202/05

```
DEAD   206/28
PLEAD (1) ........................................ ENCTR  27/31
PLEADED (2) ...................................... HOUSE  64/28
   GRACE 169/03
PLEASANT (9) ..................................... SISTR  11/25
   RACE   44/09    RACE   44/21    GALNT  58/03    CLAY  105/27
   MOTHR 143/12    DEAD  192/03    DEAD  192/07    DEAD  212/20
PLEASANTLY (3) ................................... EVELN  39/07
   MOTHR 145/07    GRACE 166/19
PLEASANTRY (1) ...................................'.............. DEAD  183/12
PLEASE (10) ...................................... EVELN  37/29
   HOUSE  66/05    LITTL  77/02    PARTS  94/04    PARTS  98/01
   CLAY  102/28    CLAY  105/31    IVY D 121/34    IVY D 129/12
   DEAD  199/28
PLEASED (4) ...................................... ENCTR  23/07
   CLAY  106/10    MOTHR 140/08    GRACE 171/15
PLEASING (1) ..................................... DEAD  202/16
PLEASURE (9) ..................................... RACE   43/31
   HOUSE  65/01    LITTL  79/33    LITTL  81/02    IVY D 125/34
   GRACE 156/05    DEAD  184/05    DEAD  202/30    DEAD  222/24
PLEASURES (1) .................................... PNFUL 110/20
PLEDGE (3) ....................................... HOUSE  61/07
   IVY D 135/19    DEAD  185/13
PLENTY (1) ....................................... CLAY  102/18
P.L.G. (1) ....................................... IVY D 119/12
PLOT (3) ......................................... ENCTR  21/20
   GRACE 157/03    GRACE 157/25
PLOTS (1) ........................................ LITTL  71/06
PLUCK (2) ........................................ ENCTR  19/03
   DEAD  187/25
PLUCKED (1) ...................................... GALNT  54/08
PLUMCAKE (4) ..................................... CLAY  102/20
   CLAY  102/20    CLAY  102/27    CLAY  103/24
PLUMP (2) ........................................ PARTS  95/16
   DEAD  178/24
PLUMPED (1) ...................................... DEAD  198/04
PLUM-PUDDING (1) ................................. GALNT  57/07
PLUNDERED (1) .................................... HOUSE  61/06
PLUNGED (1) ...................................... DEAD  197/06
PLYING (1) ....................................... PNFUL 110/10
POCKET (12) ...................................... SISTR  17/14
   ENCTR  20/19    ENCTR  22/09    ARABY  35/29    PARTS  88/26
   PARTS  89/13    PARTS  97/01    CLAY  102/06    PNFUL 113/15
   GRACE 155/08    DEAD  178/25    DEAD  179/07
POCKET-HANDKERCHIEF (1) .......................... HOUSE  65/28
POCKETS (5) ...................................... CLAY  103/25
   IVY D 119/05    IVY D 122/31    MOTHR 136/03    GRACE 155/31
POEM (2) ......................................... LITTL  73/18
   LITTL  83/30
POEMS (6) ........................................ LITTL  74/01
   LITTL  74/05    LITTL  74/09    LITTL  83/28    GRACE 168/05
   DEAD  188/29
POET (2) ......................................... GRACE 167/22
   GRACE 168/14
POETIC (1) ....................................... LITTL  73/22
POETRY (4) ....................................... ENCTR  25/07
   LITTL  71/17    GRACE 167/24    DEAD  179/15
POET'S (1) ....................................... LITTL  73/30
POINT (18) ....................................... ENCTR  23/19
   ENCTR  25/31    ARABY  30/30    GALNT  53/28    GALNT  57/23
   GALNT  57/23    GALNT  59/28    LITTL  73/27    IVY D 128/13
   MOTHR 136/07    MOTHR 138/25    MOTHR 141/08    MOTHR 146/16
```

```
        GRACE 152/11    GRACE 154/20    GRACE 163/31    GRACE 174/24
        DEAD  181/27
POINT-BLANK (1) ................................... GRACE 162/33
POINTED (7) ....................................... SISTR  14/08
        PARTS  98/05    MOTHR 146/13    DEAD  206/21    DEAD  210/15
        DEAD  214/31    DEAD  216/02
POINTING (6) ...................................... ENCTR  25/12
        PARTS  88/22    IVY D 122/15    DEAD  186/29    DEAD  214/20
        DEAD  216/05
POINTS (3) ........................................ GRACE 158/20
        GRACE 159/34    GRACE 168/17
POISED (1) ........................................ MOTHR 149/33
POISONS (1) ....................................... PARTS  93/31
POK (3) ........................................... IVY D 131/08
        IVY D 132/32    IVY D 135/26
POLES (1) ......................................... GALNT  49/06
POLICE (4) ........................................ RACE   43/19
        GALNT  51/19    PNFUL 114/10    GRACE 157/21
POLICEMAN (2) ..................................... GRACE 151/05
        GRACE 160/14
POLICEMEN (2) ..................................... GALNT  51/30
        PNFUL 111/13
POLICY (1) ........................................ GALNT  50/20
POLISH (3) ........................................ HOUSE  65/28
        HOUSE  67/33    PARTS  93/30
POLISHED (2) ...................................... PARTS  87/25
        DEAD  178/18
POLITE (3) ........................................ CLAY  103/01
        MOTHR 144/03    GRACE 156/31
POLITELY (2) ...................................... GRACE 166/29
        DEAD  199/31
POLITENESS (2) .................................... MOTHR 145/05
        DEAD  195/02
POLITICAL (1) ..................................... DEAD  188/22
POLITICS (2) ...................................... RACE   46/22
        DEAD  188/17
POLKAS (1) ........................................ HOUSE  62/25
POLLY (15) ........................................ HOUSE  62/26
        HOUSE  62/31    HOUSE  63/05    HOUSE  63/08    HOUSE  63/12
        HOUSE  63/14    HOUSE  63/16    HOUSE  63/21    HOUSE  64/09
        HOUSE  64/10    HOUSE  64/14    HOUSE  68/12    HOUSE  68/19
        HOUSE  69/03    HOUSE  69/03
POLLY'S (1) ....................................... HOUSE  64/31
POMPOUS (1) ....................................... DEAD  208/14
POMPS (1) ......................................... GRACE 171/11
PONTIFICATES (1) .................................. GRACE 167/20
PONY (1) .......................................... PARTS  96/28
POOLBEG (1) ....................................... PARTS  94/34
POOR (40) ......................................... SISTR  12/04
        SISTR  16/01    SISTR  16/02    SISTR  16/06    SISTR  16/13
        SISTR  16/22    SISTR  16/28    SISTR  17/11    SISTR  17/29
        RACE   44/02    LITTL  73/13    LITTL  76/02    CLAY  106/14
        PNFUL 109/22    IVY D 124/17    IVY D 124/25    IVY D 124/27
        IVY D 125/23    IVY D 125/23    IVY D 131/23    MOTHR 147/10
        GRACE 157/18    GRACE 161/16    GRACE 162/08    GRACE 171/04
        GRACE 172/32    GRACE 174/19    DEAD  180/18    DEAD  185/12
        DEAD  199/03    DEAD  202/17    DEAD  204/29    DEAD  211/28
        DEAD  216/33    DEAD  217/02    DEAD  221/02    DEAD  221/06
        DEAD  221/19    DEAD  222/08    DEAD  222/25
POOR-LOOKING (1) .................................. GALNT  57/02
POPE (15) ......................................... GRACE 163/28
        GRACE 165/22    GRACE 165/22    GRACE 166/07    GRACE 167/05
```

GRACE 167/09	GRACE 167/11	GRACE 167/22	GRACE 168/05
GRACE 168/30	GRACE 168/33	GRACE 169/30	GRACE 170/03
DEAD 194/21	DEAD 194/24		

POPES (2) .... GRACE 168/19
GRACE 168/21
POPE'S (1) .... DEAD 194/34
POPPED (1) .... DEAD 209/05
POPPENS (1) .... EVELN 39/08
POPULAR (2) .... RACE 43/25
LITTL 74/01
POPULATED (1) .... LITTL 71/29
POPULATION (2) .... HOUSE 62/04
HOUSE 62/06
PORCELAIN (1) .... ARABY 35/04
PORCH (1) .... GALNT 54/07
PORT (5) .... CLAY 104/19
DEAD 179/34   DEAD 196/33   DEAD 201/24   DEAD 205/06
PORTER (11) .... PARTS 89/01
PARTS 89/25   CLAY 101/17   PNFUL 114/03   IVY D 128/02
MOTHR 142/19   DEAD 215/22   DEAD 215/27   DEAD 215/32
DEAD 216/02   DEAD 216/07
PORTERS (1) .... ARABY 34/20
PORTHOLES (1) .... EVELN 40/28
PORTMANTEAUS (1) .... GRACE 160/22
POSITION (7) .... ARABY 35/21
GALNT 56/06   PARTS 92/07   CLAY 100/22   GRACE 173/18
DEAD 205/11   DEAD 205/12
POSITIVELY (2) .... LITTL 80/09
GRACE 167/17
POSSESSION (4) .... SISTR 17/21
RACE 44/15   LITTL 71/13   MOTHR 144/25
POSSIBILITY (1) .... PNFUL 115/13
POSSIBLE (4) .... LITTL 72/22
PNFUL 107/02   PNFUL 115/32   GRACE 159/22
POST (3) .... SISTR 13/17
PARTS 90/18   MOTHR 141/23
POSTCARDS (2) .... MOTHR 137/28
MOTHR 137/29
POT (2) .... GRACE 163/02
GRACE 163/10
POTATOES (2) .... DEAD 197/17
DEAD 198/10
POTS (1) .... RACE 45/06
POUCH (1) .... IVY D 135/30
POUND (6) .... EVELN 39/11
LITTL 82/18   IVY D 128/09   IVY D 128/10   DEAD 217/13
DEAD 217/16
POUNDING (1) .... PNFUL 117/28
POUNDS (3) .... LITTL 82/18
MOTHR 137/18   MOTHR 148/27
POUR (1) .... ARABY 31/14
POURED (3) .... SISTR 15/04
GRACE 167/02   DEAD 185/28
POVERTY (2) .... RACE 42/05
GALNT 57/33
POWDERED (2) .... LITTL 72/10
IVY D 127/30
POWER (52) .... GRACE 152/20
GRACE 152/21   GRACE 152/26   GRACE 153/04   GRACE 153/12
GRACE 153/31   GRACE 154/16   GRACE 154/21   GRACE 154/26
GRACE 155/01   GRACE 155/06   GRACE 155/11   GRACE 155/15
GRACE 155/18   GRACE 155/24   GRACE 157/04   GRACE 157/13

```
GRACE  159/04      GRACE  159/06      GRACE  159/09      GRACE  160/06
GRACE  160/11      GRACE  160/20      GRACE  161/33      GRACE  162/13
GRACE  162/15      GRACE  162/19      GRACE  162/33      GRACE  163/07
GRACE  163/08      GRACE  163/16      GRACE  163/32      GRACE  164/05
GRACE  164/08      GRACE  164/14      GRACE  164/28      GRACE  165/27
GRACE  165/34      GRACE  167/01      GRACE  167/09      GRACE  167/29
GRACE  168/01      GRACE  168/12      GRACE  169/09      GRACE  169/19
GRACE  170/26      GRACE  170/27      GRACE  171/14      GRACE  172/17
DEAD   182/15      DEAD   182/23      DEAD   184/01
```
POWERFUL-LOOKING (1) .... GRACE 173/07
POWERS (2) .... DEAD   202/17
```
     DEAD   204/29
```
POWER'S (4) .... GRACE 155/03
```
     GRACE  156/02      GRACE  157/06      GRACE  162/02
```
PRACTICAL (1) .... GRACE 155/32
PRACTICES (1) .... LITTL   78/21
PRAISED (3) .... SISTR   15/18
```
     DEAD   192/13      DEAD   198/19
```
PRAISES (2) .... ARABY   31/12
```
     DEAD   200/14
```
PRAY (2) .... SISTR   14/20
```
     MOTHR  141/12
```
PRAYED (2) .... EVELN   40/30
```
     GRACE  173/15
```
PRAYER (1) .... EVELN   41/03
PRAYER-BOOK (3) .... CLAY   105/02
```
     CLAY   105/21      CLAY   105/26
```
PRAYERS (2) .... ARABY   31/12
```
     PNFUL  113/18
```
PREACH (1) .... GRACE 165/15
PREACHED (2) .... GRACE 168/27
```
     GRACE  173/30
```
PREACHER (3) .... GRACE 165/02
```
     GRACE  173/19      GRACE  173/19
```
PREACHING (1) .... GRACE 166/02
PRECAUTION (1) .... PNFUL 114/24
PRECEDED (1) .... DEAD   177/22
PRECONSIDERED (1) .... PARTS   93/14
PREDECESSOR (1) .... GRACE 168/20
PREDECESSOR'S (1) .... GRACE 167/18
PREDICATE (1) .... PNFUL 108/28
PREFER (1) .... CLAY   104/20
PRELUDE (3) .... CLAY   105/34
```
     DEAD   184/13      DEAD   193/01
```
PREPARATORY (1) .... DEAD   198/12
PREPARED (2) .... SISTR   15/21
```
     GRACE  162/02
```
PRESENCE (4) .... HOUSE   61/08
```
     PARTS   88/01      PARTS   89/18      PARTS   89/24
```
PRESENT (11) .... SISTR   12/15
```
     RACE    42/16      RACE    48/27      GALNT   51/27      LITTL   72/02
     LITTL   82/26      CLAY   100/08      IVY D  122/02      IVY D  124/07
     GRACE  168/20      DEAD   186/22
```
PRESENTED (3) .... RACE   44/18
```
     GRACE  156/12      GRACE  173/18
```
PRESENTLY (1) .... PARTS   95/07
PRESS (4) .... LITTL   71/04
```
     LITTL   72/22      LITTL   75/12      LITTL   77/05
```
PRESSED (6) .... SISTR   15/05
```
     ARABY   31/27      ARABY   34/19      PNFUL  111/32      DEAD   190/08
     DEAD   215/14
```
PRESUME (2) .... DEAD   195/01

```
                  DEAD   199/18
PRETENDED (3) ..........................................  SISTR   14/20
     ENCTR   25/09     GRACE  161/06
PRETENDING (1) .........................................  ENCTR   27/34
PRETENTIOUS (1) ........................................  PNFUL  107/04
PRETTY (7) .............................................  LITTL   83/02
     LITTL   83/10     LITTL   83/11     LITTL   83/20    LITTL   83/22
     MOTHR  138/33     DEAD   183/26
PREVAIL (1) ............................................  RACE    46/20
PREVALENT (1) ..........................................  ENCTR   19/11
PREVENT (2) ............................................  PNFUL  114/24
     PNFUL  115/13
PREVENTED (2) ..........................................  GALNT   50/19
     PARTS   89/18
PREVIOUSLY (1) .........................................  RACE    44/27
PREY (1) ...............................................  PNFUL  115/30
PRICE (1) ..............................................  LITTL   83/03
PRICKED (1) ............................................  GALNT   59/28
PRIDE (7) ..............................................  RACE    45/27
     LITTL   73/01     CLAY   106/07     IVY D  135/04    GRACE  157/02
     DEAD   194/06     DEAD   203/31
PRIEST (15) ............................................  SISTR   13/06
     SISTR   13/12     SISTR   14/24     SISTR   18/05    SISTR   18/10
     ARABY   29/07     ARABY   29/17     ARABY   31/21    EVELN   37/11
     HOUSE   61/12     HOUSE   65/30     PNFUL  113/17    IVY D  126/29
     MOTHR  144/29     GRACE  171/04
PRIESTESS (1) .........................................· DEAD   186/12
PRIESTHOOD (3) .........................................  SISTR   17/17
     ENCTR   19/18     GRACE  164/13
PRIESTHOODS (1) ........................................  GRACE  164/15
PRIESTLY (1) ...........................................  SISTR   12/22
PRIESTS (2) ............................................  IVY D  134/30
     GRACE  164/10
PRIEST'S (1) ...........................................  GRACE  173/11
PRIM (1) ...............................................  LITTL   83/22
PRIMA (1) ..............................................  DEAD   199/13
PRIME (1) ..............................................  DEAD   199/33
PRINCE (1) .............................................  RACE    43/21
PRINCELY (1) ...........................................  DEAD   203/05
PRINCES (1) ............................................  DEAD   186/18
PRINCIPAL (1) ..........................................  MOTHR  141/15
PRINCIPLE (1) ..........................................  SISTR   11/01
PRINCIPLES (1) .........................................  DEAD   203/19
PRINT (1) ..............................................  EVELN   37/13
PRINTED (5) ............................................  SISTR   13/18
     GALNT   57/03     HOUSE   67/08     IVY D  119/09    DEAD   188/12
PRINTERS (1) ...........................................  LITTL   75/15
PRISONER (2) ...........................................  LITTL   84/16
     GRACE  165/24
PRIVATE (6) ............................................  PNFUL  108/30
     IVY D  124/21     IVY D  125/06     IVY D  127/31    IVY D  127/32
     GRACE  158/24
PRIVATELY (2) ..........................................  PARTS   90/32
     MOTHR  143/13
PRIZE (1) ..............................................  DEAD   205/03
PRIZES (1) .............................................  MOTHR  142/32
PROBABLY (3) ...........................................  RACE    46/02
     PNFUL  114/20     DEAD   186/19
PROBLEM (2) ............................................  GALNT   56/31
     MOTHR  145/25
PROBLEMS (1) ...........................................  HOUSE   63/24
PROCATHEDRAL (1) .......................................  MOTHR  137/30
```

```
PROCEEDED  (6) ...................................... SISTR  14/09
     ENCTR  26/01      RACE   47/16     LITTL  78/14   GRACE 163/04
     DEAD  222/22
PRODIGY  (1) ........................................ DEAD  193/30
PRODUCE  (1) ........................................ IVY D 122/23
PRODUCED  (3) ....................................... LITTL  78/05
     GRACE 151/18     GRACE 173/10
PRODUCES  (1) ....................................... IVY D 121/31
PRODUCT  (1) ........................................ PNFUL 111/06
PRODUCTION  (1) ..................................... DEAD  198/21
PROFANE  (1) ........................................ RACE   44/22
PROFESSION  (1) ..................................... DEAD  205/12
PROFESSIONAL  (1) ................................... GRACE 174/01
PROFESSIONALLY  (1) ................................. GRACE 158/26
PROFILE  (1) ........................................ HOUSE  68/23
PROGRAMME  (2) ...................................... MOTHR 138/18
     MOTHR 139/19
PROGRESSING  (1) .................................... DEAD  209/11
PROJECT  (1) ........................................ ENCTR  24/09
PROJECTING  (1) ..................................... GALNT  56/02
PROLONGED  (3) ...................................... ARABY  33/19
     MOTHR 142/20     DEAD  206/22
PROMINENT  (2) ...................................... IVY D 131/22
     DEAD  187/21
PROMISE  (3) ........................................ EVELN  40/02
     EVELN  40/03     IVY D 123/02
PROMISED  (2) ....................................... PARTS  94/27
     PARTS  94/33
PROMISES  (1) ....................................... EVELN  37/13
PROMISING  (1) ...................................... HOUSE  63/26
PROMPTLY  (5) ....................................... GRACE 151/23
     GRACE 162/16     GRACE 171/09     DEAD  183/27   DEAD  188/24
PRONOUNCE  (1) ...................................... SISTR  13/03
PRONOUNCED  (1) ..................................... RACE   45/26
PRONUNCIATION  (1) .................................. MOTHR 147/12
PROOFS  (1) ......................................... LITTL  75/15
PROP  (1) ........................................... DEAD  176/08
PROPAGANDISM  (1) ................................... DEAD  192/14
PROPER  (4) ......................................... GALNT  52/18
     PARTS  92/15     CLAY  100/21     MOTHR 149/32
PROPERLY  (9) ....................................... SISTR  13/03
     ENCTR  27/34     LITTL  77/11     LITTL  81/32    PNFUL 113/04
     IVY D 123/14     GRACE 170/25     GRACE 173/28    DEAD  212/11
PROPERTY  (1) ....................................... IVY D 131/20
PROPHECY  (1) ....................................... PNFUL 109/19
PROPOSAL  (1) ....................................... GRACE 163/17
PROPOSED  (4) ....................................... ENCTR  22/24
     RACE   48/16     CLAY  101/15     MOTHR 138/08
PROPPED  (2) ........................................ PNFUL 112/31
     GRACE 156/32
PROPRIETOR  (2) ..................................... PNFUL 116/10
     PNFUL 116/19
PROSPERITY  (1) ..................................... DEAD  205/10
PROSPEROUS  (1) ..................................... DEAD  215/04
PROSTRATE  (1) ...................................... PNFUL 117/18
PROTECT  (1) ........................................ EVELN  38/07
PROTEST  (3) ........................................ IVY D 124/20
     GRACE 169/04     DEAD  215/01
PROTESTANT  (2) ..................................... GRACE 157/07
     GRACE 168/17
PROTESTANTS  (3) .................................... ENCTR  22/27
     CLAY  100/24     GRACE 166/01
```

```
PROTESTED (1) .....................................  DEAD   197/29
PROTESTING (1) ....................................  PARTS   94/27
PROTRUDED (1) .....................................  DEAD   184/29
PROUD (7) .........................................  RACE    43/28
   PARTS   93/11    DEAD  186/27    DEAD  205/11    DEAD   213/09
   DEAD  215/09    DEAD  215/10
PROUDLY (1) .......................................  GRACE  157/02
PROVED (1) ........................................  DEAD   193/20
PROVIDED (1) ......................................  PNFUL  110/27
PROVINCIAL (2) ....................................  GRACE  151/20
   GRACE  161/02
PROVISIONS (2) ....................................  ENCTR   24/15
   EVELN   38/22
PROXY (1) .........................................  GRACE  159/31
PRUDENCE (1) ......................................  PNFUL  110/02
PUBLIC (3) ........................................  ENCTR   22/22
   PARTS   89/24    MOTHR 141/18
PUBLICAN (1) ......................................  IVY D  121/18
PUBLIC-HOUSE (6) ..................................  GALNT   50/17
   PARTS   90/22    PARTS  92/25    PARTS  97/05    PNFUL  116/08
   GRACE  159/22
PUBLIC-HOUSES (1) .................................  HOUSE   66/09
PUBLICITY (2) .....................................  HOUSE   65/11
   HOUSE   65/15
PUBLISHED (1) .....................................  LITTL   83/26
PUCKERS (1) .......................................  DEAD   179/29
PUDDING (7) .......................................  DEAD   191/02
   DEAD  196/34    DEAD  200/08    DEAD  200/10    DEAD   200/13
   DEAD  200/18    DEAD  200/21
PUDDING-FORK (1) ..................................  DEAD   205/23
PUFF (2) ..........................................  SISTR   10/03
   SISTR   10/10
PUFFED (2) ........................................  LITTL   78/06
   LITTL   78/13
PUFFING (2) .......................................  PARTS   86/17
   DEAD  208/22
PUFFS (1) .........................................  MOTHR  141/17
PUFFY (2) .........................................  ENCTR   20/32
   GRACE  156/33
PULL (5) ..........................................  GALNT   52/11
   GALNT   53/32    GALNT  59/13    CLAY  100/34    DEAD   199/13
PULLED (6) ........................................  ARABY   30/26
   PARTS   88/26    PARTS  92/17    PARTS  95/33    GRACE  173/04
   DEAD  178/24
PULLING (5) .......................................  ENCTR   21/33
   GALNT   57/34    LITTL  74/33    CLAY  101/02    GRACE  153/32
PULLS (1) .........................................  LITTL   75/12
PULP (1) ..........................................  MOTHR  139/20
PULPIT (4) ........................................  GRACE  172/15
   GRACE  172/27    GRACE 173/09    GRACE 173/12
PULSE (1) .........................................  RACE    45/11
PUNCH (7) .........................................  HOUSE   67/16
   LITTL   77/32    PARTS  93/14    PNFUL 116/09    PNFUL  116/18
   MOTHR 137/15    DEAD  183/04
PUNCHES (1) .......................................  PARTS   90/22
PUNCTILIOUSLY (1) .................................  LITTL   71/25
PUNCTUATED (1) ....................................  MOTHR  146/32
PUNGENT (2) .......................................  PARTS   89/10
   PARTS   89/34
PUPIL (2) .........................................  PNFUL  109/33
   PNFUL  109/34
PUPILS (7) ........................................  DEAD   175/16
```

DEAD 175/17	DEAD 176/11	DEAD 176/28	DEAD 183/25
DEAD 197/22	DEAD 199/01		

PUPILS' (1) .... DEAD 176/10
PURDON (5) .... GRACE 164/27
    GRACE 164/30   GRACE 164/30   GRACE 173/14   GRACE 173/26
PURE (2) .... DEAD 200/06
    DEAD 202/09
PUREST (1) .... DEAD 199/33
PURPLE (3) .... PNFUL 108/06
    DEAD 186/22   DEAD 196/25
PURPOSE (6) .... ARABY 33/18
    ARABY 34/15   HOUSE 63/32   PNFUL 115/29   GRACE 159/21
    GRACE 174/11
PURPOSED (1) .... DEAD 220/14
PURSE (5) .... EVELN 38/20
    GALNT 57/33   CLAY 100/07   CLAY 100/09   CLAY 100/11
PURSING (2) .... IVY D 126/03
    DEAD 182/24
PURSUED (2) .... ENCTR 26/34
    LITTL 74/14
PUSHED (13) .... EVELN 38/33
    RACE 45/21   GALNT 57/21   HOUSE 68/02   LITTL 80/33
    PARTS 86/08   PARTS 94/16   PNFUL 112/33   IVY D 122/21
    IVY D 130/28   MOTHR 138/26   DEAD 178/16   DEAD 201/33
PUSHING (1) .... SISTR 13/25
PUT (52) .... SISTR 13/22
    SISTR 17/14   ARABY 33/26   GALNT 50/34   HOUSE 62/01
    HOUSE 65/18   HOUSE 66/31   HOUSE 67/28   HOUSE 68/17
    LITTL 74/06   LITTL 75/11   LITTL 81/08   LITTL 81/14
    LITTL 82/19   PARTS 88/26   PARTS 89/02   PARTS 90/08
    PARTS 91/23   PARTS 93/18   PARTS 96/11   PARTS 96/25
    CLAY 104/23   CLAY 105/01   CLAY 105/11   PNFUL 112/28
    PNFUL 116/05   IVY D 119/04   IVY D 120/12   IVY D 124/20
    IVY D 126/20   IVY D 128/13   IVY D 128/21   IVY D 129/19
    IVY D 130/26   IVY D 133/11   MOTHR 137/09   MOTHR 137/14
    MOTHR 140/12   MOTHR 148/28   GRACE 154/25   GRACE 158/07
    GRACE 160/29   GRACE 165/33   DEAD 180/27   DEAD 180/28
    DEAD 194/23   DEAD 195/14   DEAD 199/34   DEAD 200/30
    DEAD 207/31   DEAD 211/14   DEAD 217/28
PUTTING (4) .... SISTR 13/07
    EVELN 39/30   RACE 46/33   CLAY 105/07
PUZZLED (4) .... SISTR 11/19
    GRACE 155/29   DEAD 196/05   DEAD 218/20
PYRAMID (1) .... DEAD 196/31
PYRE (1) .... IVY D 134/14

QUADRILLES (2) .... DEAD 183/31
    DEAD 183/31
QUAINT (1) .... CLAY 101/32
QUAINTNESS (1) .... DEAD 217/28
QUALIFIED (2) .... GRACE 159/23
    GRACE 161/23
QUALITIES (3) .... RACE 45/33
    DEAD 192/23   DEAD 203/24
QUALITY (1) .... DEAD 207/26
QUARRELLED (2) .... EVELN 39/20
    CLAY 99/13
QUARRELS (1) .... GRACE 155/04
QUARRELSOME (2) .... DEAD 195/06
    DEAD 195/08
QUARTER (6) .... ENCTR 22/13

```
GALNT   58/29     LITTL   82/12     LITTL   82/18     IVY D 127/18
GRACE  157/28
QUARTERS (3) ........................................ GALNT  55/17
  PNFUL 110/15     DEAD   200/14
QUAVERING (1) ....................................... CLAY  106/01
QUAY (12) ........................................... ENCTR  23/11
  ENCTR  23/22     ENCTR   23/29     EVELN   40/27     MOTHR 137/04
  DEAD  188/15     DEAD   195/27     DEAD   202/07     DEAD  206/21
  DEAD  208/25     DEAD   209/23     DEAD   212/34
QUAYS (4) ........................................... ENCTR  23/04
  LITTL  73/13     IVY D  131/31     DEAD   188/13
QUEEN (2) ........................................... RACE   48/07
  RACE   48/08
QUEEN'S (1) ......................................... MOTHR 142/24
QUEER (3) ........................................... SISTR  10/01
  SISTR  16/31     ENCTR   26/27
QUENCHED (2) ........................................ DEAD  214/03
  DEAD  214/04
QUESTION (15) ....................................... ENCTR  25/18
  EVELN  37/19     RACE    44/30     HOUSE   64/32     LITTL  83/18
  PARTS  91/23     PARTS   93/18     PNFUL  110/19     PNFUL 111/04
  GRACE 160/26     DEAD   184/20     DEAD   188/28     DEAD  194/34
  DEAD  198/34     DEAD   220/24
QUESTIONS (6) ....................................... SISTR  13/07
  SISTR  13/10     SISTR   13/19     ARABY   32/22     HOUSE  64/10
  DEAD  181/26
QUICK (5) ........................................... EVELN  40/12
  RACE   44/09     GALNT   59/26     MOTHR  139/11     MOTHR 139/31
QUICKENED (2) ....................................... ARABY  30/31
  LITTL  73/07
QUICKLY (27) ........................................ ENCTR  24/26
  ENCTR  28/02     ARABY   34/27     EVELN   38/19     GALNT  54/09
  GALNT  55/16     GALNT   57/09     GALNT   59/25     LITTL  72/09
  LITTL  74/22     PARTS   88/27     PARTS   92/33     CLAY  102/12
  PNFUL 110/01     PNFUL  112/10     PNFUL  113/07     PNFUL 116/06
  IVY D 122/22     IVY D  126/03     IVY D  130/24     MOTHR 140/17
  MOTHR 140/30     MOTHR  141/08     DEAD   184/14     DEAD  185/09
  DEAD  206/14     DEAD   216/33
QUIET (9) ........................................... ARABY  29/01
  GALNT  57/01     HOUSE   68/13     LITTL   70/14     CLAY  100/25
  CLAY  105/33     PNFUL  110/15     PNFUL  115/17     PNFUL 116/19
QUIETLY (9) ......................................... SISTR  15/08
  SISTR  17/23     RACE    48/04     GALNT   53/23     GRACE 166/08
  DEAD  186/08     DEAD   192/01     DEAD   197/31     DEAD  222/02
QUILT (2) ........................................... MOTHR 137/15
  DEAD  221/33
QUINCUNX (1) ........................................ GRACE 172/20
QUIT (2) ............................................ PARTS  92/01
  PARTS  92/02
QUITE (23) .......................................... SISTR  12/25
  SISTR  15/16     SISTR   15/23     SISTR   15/24     GALNT  50/08
  HOUSE  61/02     CLAY   105/24     PNFUL  108/19     MOTHR 140/22
  GRACE 150/02     GRACE  157/03     GRACE  160/05     GRACE 165/15
  GRACE 168/01     DEAD   176/14     DEAD   180/03     DEAD  180/10
  DEAD  180/10     DEAD   195/33     DEAD   197/07     DEAD  199/22
  DEAD  200/15     DEAD   213/25
QUIVERING (1) ....................................... LITTL  84/26
QUIZZICALLY (1) ..................................... DEAD  190/09
QUIZZING (1) ........................................ DEAD  192/17
QUOTATION (3) ....................................... DEAD  179/10
  DEAD  191/30     DEAD   192/10
QUOTING (1) ......................................... DEAD  179/15
```

RABBIT'S (1) .... DEAD 190/31
RABBLE-ROUT (1) .... IVY D 134/29
RACE (1) .... RACE 4?/ T
RACING (2) .... GALNT 50/27
    DEAD 186/10
RADIANT (1) .... DEAD 215/17
RAG (2) .... DEAD 177/28
    DEAD 188/04
RAGE (3) .... PARTS 87/27
    MOTHR 149/12   DEAD 217/21
RAGGED (5) .... ENCTR 22/22
    ENCTR 22/23   ENCTR 22/26   GALNT 55/28   PARTS 93/08
RAIL (1) .... GRACE 170/11
RAILING (2) .... ARABY 32/09
    EVELN 41/08
RAILINGS (7) .... ARABY 30/23
    ARABY 32/05   ARABY 33/15   GALNT 53/18   GALNT 56/18
    GALNT 56/22   DEAD 213/01
RAILLERY (1) .... GALNT 52/21
RAILWAY (6) .... PNFUL 113/30
    PNFUL 114/03   PNFUL 114/22   PNFUL 114/29   PNFUL 115/12
    GRACE 158/22
RAIN (10) .... ARABY 31/23
    GALNT 60/09   PARTS 94/13   CLAY 101/34   CLAY 103/12
    IVY D 120/27   IVY D 130/17   MOTHR 142/11   DEAD 210/24
    DEAD 221/23
RAINCLOAK (2) .... CLAY 102/01
    CLAY 103/25
RAINDROPS (1) .... IVY D 125/30
RAINY (3) .... ARABY 31/21
    CLAY 103/04   MOTHR 141/31
RAISED (14) .... SISTR 12/19
    ENCTR 26/31   RACE 42/06   HOUSE 63/29   CLAY 103/10
    PNFUL 115/15   IVY D 134/12   IVY D 134/21   MOTHR 142/21
    GRACE 155/25   DEAD 185/09   DEAD 202/04   DEAD 205/06
    DEAD 218/24
RAISING (2) .... GALNT 56/05
    DEAD 217/23
RAISINS (2) .... DEAD 196/25
    DEAD 201/22
RAKE (2) .... IVY D 122/11
    IVY D 132/17
RAKED (1) .... IVY D 118/01
RAKISH (2) .... HOUSE 65/09
    LITTL 72/26
RAMBLED (1) .... DEAD 190/24
RAN (26) .... ENCTR 28/10
    ARABY 30/08   ARABY 30/28   RACE 44/03   RACE 45/09
    RACE 48/09   GALNT 50/29   GALNT 60/11   GALNT 60/15
    HOUSE 61/06   HOUSE 69/02   LITTL 71/10   LITTL 71/29
    LITTL 84/30   PARTS 88/27   PARTS 93/08   PARTS 98/12
    PNFUL 114/05   DEAD 192/09   DEAD 196/03   DEAD 196/22
    DEAD 203/13   DEAD 208/20   DEAD 210/31   DEAD 218/15
    DEAD 221/18
RANDOM (1) .... MOTHR 146/27
RANG (1) .... PARTS 86/01
RANK (1) .... LITTL 78/19
RANKLED (1) .... DEAD 187/04
RAPID (1) .... RACE 44/14
RAPIDLY (6) .... GALNT 55/20

MOTHR 143/12	GRACE 159/06	DEAD 178/25	DEAD 178/28
DEAD 193/04			
RAPTURE (1)			LITTL 83/14
RAPTURES (1)			DEAD 211/05
RASPBERRY (2)			ENCTR 24/04
DEAD 200/12			
RASPING (1)			HOUSE 66/05
RATE (1)			SISTR 15/31
RATEPAYER (1)			IVY D 131/19
RATES (2)			IVY D 131/22
GRACE 160/31			
RATHER (14)			SISTR 10/05
ENCTR 24/06	EVELN 36/18	RACE 43/14	HOUSE 68/11
CLAY 104/20	PNFUL 108/18	PNFUL 115/02	IVY D 134/01
GRACE 164/34	GRACE 165/09	DEAD 185/05	DEAD 198/21
DEAD 203/03			
RATTLE (1)			PARTS 90/21
RATTLED (1)			DEAD 209/22
RATTLING (4)			DEAD 180/05
DEAD 207/07	DEAD 214/18	DEAD 214/22	
RAUCOUS (1)			GRACE 170/07
RAVAGED (1)			GALNT 50/07
RAVELLI (1)			DEAD 199/06
RAVING (1)			DEAD 184/10
RAW (2)			ARABY 33/01
HOUSE 61/18			
REACH (3)			PNFUL 111/07
PNFUL 114/05	IVY D 129/28		
REACHED (14)			ENCTR 23/04
ENCTR 24/07	ENCTR 28/03	ARABY 33/10	GALNT 54/18
GALNT 59/03	GALNT 60/21	HOUSE 68/08	PARTS 89/08
PARTS 94/14	PNFUL 113/14	DEAD 185/29	DEAD 190/33
DEAD 210/32			
REACHING (1)			PARTS 95/15
READ (22)			SISTR 12/05
ENCTR 20/24	ENCTR 25/07	ENCTR 25/09	ENCTR 25/17
ENCTR 25/17	ARABY 32/17	EVELN 39/27	GALNT 59/24
LITTL 71/20	LITTL 83/30	LITTL 84/10	LITTL 84/14
CLAY 100/08	PNFUL 112/19	PNFUL 112/26	PNFUL 112/32
PNFUL 113/01	PNFUL 113/15	PNFUL 113/16	IVY D 119/09
DEAD 211/23			
READER (1)			GRACE 164/24
READILY (1)			DEAD 211/20
READING (7)			SISTR 12/04
SISTR 12/10	SISTR 12/28	ENCTR 20/28	ENCTR 25/15
PNFUL 116/19	GRACE 168/04		
READJUSTED (1)			HOUSE 68/23
READJUSTMENT (1)			DEAD 185/26
READS (1)			PNFUL 113/17
READY (13)			GALNT 51/29
GALNT 58/12	HOUSE 67/16	LITTL 77/13	PARTS 87/10
CLAY 99/08	CLAY 100/33	IVY D 124/04	MOTHR 139/33
MOTHR 145/31	GRACE 151/20	DEAD 196/16	DEAD 212/18
REAL (5)			ENCTR 21/05
ENCTR 21/05	ARABY 35/26	RACE 46/01	GALNT 51/06
REALISED (2)			PARTS 89/27
PNFUL 116/24			
REALISTS (1)			PNFUL 111/05
REALITY (1)			PNFUL 117/28
REALLY (20)			RACE 44/23
HOUSE 66/20	LITTL 76/16	LITTL 77/34	CLAY 102/17
MOTHR 140/05	DEAD 178/29	DEAD 180/15	DEAD 184/06

DEAD	192/14	DEAD	195/05	DEAD	195/21	DEAD	195/24
DEAD	195/30	DEAD	198/30	DEAD	206/10	DEAD	208/03
DEAD	210/13	DEAD	211/27	DEAD	217/04		

REAPPEARED (1) .... GALNT 60/05
REARED (2) .... PNFUL 115/31
    DEAD 223/21
REARRANGED (1) .... GALNT 50/01
REASON (10) .... HOUSE 62/13
    LITTL 74/05   PNFUL 115/06   IVY D 131/01   IVY D 131/02
    MOTHR 145/04   DEAD 176/24   DEAD 182/26   DEAD 185/03
    DEAD 220/23
REASONABLE (2) .... ENCTR 25/33
    RACE   44/28
REASONS (2) .... RACE   44/15
    IVY D 130/33
REASSERTED (1) .... PNFUL 109/34
REASSURANCE (1) .... GALNT 53/30
REASSURED (2) .... ENCTR 21/20
    MOTHR 141/19
REASSURINGLY (1) .... DEAD 180/30
REBUKE (1) .... ENCTR 20/31
RECALL (3) .... GRACE 168/17
    DEAD 203/30   DEAD 213/34
RECALLED (2) .... ARABY 34/14
    GRACE 156/05
RECEDE (1) .... ENCTR 23/15
RECEDING (2) .... SISTR 11/25
    DEAD 184/29
RECEIVE (4) .... HOUSE 64/12
    MOTHR 138/15   MOTHR 141/06   GRACE 173/25
RECEIVED (9) .... SISTR 14/06
    ARABY 33/30   RACE   42/12   RACE   43/04   PNFUL 112/11
    GRACE 172/21   DEAD 183/24   DEAD 188/09   DEAD 200/14
RECENT (1) .... ENCTR 27/20
RECENTLY (2) .... GRACE 158/25
    GRACE 160/22
RECHERCHE (1) .... GALNT 50/14
RECIPIENTS (1) .... DEAD 202/26
RECIPROCATED (1) .... LITTL 76/34
RECITATION (2) .... IVY D 135/22
    MOTHR 147/18
RECITE (2) .... ARABY 34/11
    IVY D 134/05
RECITED (1) .... MOTHR 148/05
RECKLESSNESS (1) .... RACE   44/28
RECLINES (1) .... LITTL 84/12
RECOGNISE (2) .... LITTL 74/04
    DEAD 179/11
RECOGNISED (6) .... ARABY 34/31
    PARTS 87/28   PNFUL 111/27   GRACE 173/01   DEAD 182/11
    DEAD 192/34
RECOGNITION (1) .... EVELN 41/16
RECOLLECTION (2) .... GALNT 53/04
    HOUSE 65/28
RECONSTRUCT (1) .... HOUSE 64/08
RE-COVERED (1) .... SISTR 12/02
RECRUITS (1) .... DEAD 184/14
RECTANGLE (1) .... DEAD 196/27
RECTIFY (1) .... GRACE 174/30
RECTITUDE (1) .... PNFUL 117/14
RECUR (1) .... DEAD 204/03
RECURRENCES (1) .... LITTL 73/32

```
RECURRING (1) ....................................... DEAD   202/32
RED (19) ............................................ SISTR   12/23
     EVELN   36/07    GALNT  55/30     GALNT  55/33   LITTL   74/20
     PARTS   96/21    CLAY  101/03     CLAY  102/32   MOTHR  146/10
     GRACE  164/34    GRACE 172/13     GRACE 173/13   GRACE  173/14
     DEAD   178/17    DEAD  179/30     DEAD  186/19   DEAD   196/23
     DEAD   196/24    DEAD  197/03
REDDISH (1) ......................................... HOUSE   65/25
REDEEMER (1) ........................................ GRACE  166/06
REDEEMING (1) ....................................... PNFUL  108/23
RED-FACED (1) ....................................... DEAD   183/29
REDLY (2) ........................................... PNFUL  117/11
     DEAD   213/01
RED-NOSED (1) ....................................... SISTR   11/17
REEFER (1) .......................................... PNFUL  113/09
REEKING (1) ......................................... PARTS   97/05
REEL (2) ............................................ CLAY   105/22
     GRACE  163/15
RE-EMERGED (1) ...................................... IVY D  118/06
RE-ENTERED (1) ...................................... PARTS   89/13
REFINED (2) ......................................... RACE    46/05
     LITTL   70/14
REFLECTED (4) ....................................... SISTR   14/05
     ENCTR   21/05    CLAY  103/01     IVY D 125/27
REFLECTING (1) ...................................... IVY D  133/28
REFLECTION (1) ...................................... SISTR    9/05
REFORMED (2) ........................................ GRACE  164/01
     GRACE  164/02
REFRACTORY (1) ...................................... DEAD   194/12
REFRAINING (1) ...................................... PNFUL  111/19
REFRESHED (2) ....................................... ENCTR   24/05
     HOUSE   68/21
REFRESHMENT (3) ..................................... GALNT   57/03
     DEAD   182/16    DEAD  182/20
REFRESHMENT-ROOM (2) ................................ DEAD   186/07
     DEAD   187/16
REFUGE (1) .......................................... LITTL   78/10
REFUSAL (2) ......................................... SISTR   15/07
     LITTL   80/30
REFUSED (1) ......................................... DEAD   201/25
REGAINED (1) ........................................ ENCTR   24/13
REGARDED (2) ........................................ SISTR   13/12
     HOUSE   68/24
REGARDING (3) ....................................... ENCTR   25/12
     HOUSE   68/09    PNFUL 108/24
REGION (2) .......................................... SISTR   11/25
     DEAD   223/17
REGISTERED (1) ...................................... SISTR   11/33
REGISTRATION (1) .................................... GRACE  172/26
REGRET (3) .......................................... RACE    48/27
     PNFUL  114/23    MOTHR 140/11
REGRETFULLY (4) ..................................... ENCTR   24/12
     GALNT   53/06    PARTS  94/10     MOTHR 145/11
REGRETTED (1) ....................................... GRACE  153/13
REGULAR (3) ......................................... HOUSE   66/13
     LITTL   83/04    IVY D 131/17
REGULARLY (4) ....................................... EVELN   38/24
     EVELN   38/25    PNFUL 113/08     GRACE 156/17
REGULATE (1) ........................................ PNFUL  109/13
REHABILITATED (1) ................................... GRACE  173/03
REHEARSAL (1) ....................................... MOTHR  140/21
REHEARSING (1) ...................................... IVY D  134/01
```

REIGN (2) .... PNFUL 110/01
   IVY D 135/17
REITERATING (1) .... PNFUL 117/25
RELATED (1) .... ENCTR 20/06
RELATIVES (1) .... PNFUL 109/10
RELAXATION (1) .... LITTL 78/29
RELEASED (2) .... GALNT 54/20
   DEAD 193/27
RELENTING (1) .... GRACE 164/17
RELIEF (2) .... PARTS 95/05
   DEAD 182/13
RELIEVED (3) .... GALNT 52/19
   LITTL 75/05   GRACE 172/08
RELIGHT (1) .... HOUSE 67/05
RELIGION (7) .... MOTHR 137/11
   GRACE 157/29   GRACE 158/02   GRACE 158/03   GRACE 166/09
   GRACE 166/09   DEAD 194/33
RELIGIOUS (6) .... HOUSE 66/12
   LITTL 78/20   GRACE 172/23   GRACE 174/03   GRACE 174/07
   GRACE 174/09
RELISH (1) .... GRACE 160/20
RELUCTANT (2) .... ENCTR 20/05
   HOUSE 67/19
REMAIN (5) .... ENCTR 21/06
   ARABY 30/19   HOUSE 66/23   LITTL 70/05   GRACE 160/02
REMAINED (13) .... ENCTR 26/22
   ENCTR 27/07   ARABY 30/19   ARABY 34/21   GALNT 59/34
   HOUSE 62/02   LITTL 71/22   PARTS 88/13   PNFUL 109/29
   IVY D 135/27   MOTHR 145/02   GRACE 156/19   DEAD 191/34
REMARK (5) .... SISTR 9/18
   GALNT 58/22   PARTS 88/25   PNFUL 109/24   GRACE 159/17
REMARKED (1) .... ARABY 35/06
REMARKS (1) .... GRACE 172/21
REMEMBER (19) .... SISTR 13/31
   SISTR 14/01   LITTL 72/24   PARTS 92/10   IVY D 125/04
   IVY D 133/23   IVY D 133/27   GRACE 160/13   GRACE 160/13
   GRACE 165/22   GRACE 165/25   GRACE 165/30   GRACE 168/04
   GRACE 168/33   DEAD 176/01   DEAD 180/04   DEAD 200/03
   DEAD 212/11   DEAD 214/01
REMEMBERED (18) .... SISTR 11/28
   SISTR 13/30   SISTR 13/32   EVELN 38/30   EVELN 39/30
   EVELN 40/04   EVELN 40/08   HOUSE 67/01   HOUSE 67/20
   HOUSE 68/10   HOUSE 68/33   HOUSE 69/06   LITTL 71/17
   LITTL 72/33   PNFUL 115/33   PNFUL 116/33   GRACE 159/34
   DEAD 187/02
REMEMBERING (4) .... ARABY 35/03
   CLAY 101/24   CLAY 103/31   GRACE 155/03
REMEMBRANCE (1) .... LITTL 73/01
REMIND (3) .... EVELN 40/02
   IVY D 127/12   DEAD 201/16
REMINDED (3) .... ARABY 32/28
   LITTL 83/21   DEAD 179/13
REMINDING (1) .... MOTHR 141/17
REMINDS (1) .... DEAD 181/12
REMINISCENCE (1) .... DEAD 194/13
REMINISCENCES (1) .... CLAY 105/27
REMONSTRATIVE (1) .... RACE 43/28
REMORSE (1) .... LITTL 85/22
REMOTE (3) .... ENCTR 20/07
   PNFUL 111/17   DEAD 190/13
REMOVAL (1) .... DEAD 198/16
REMOVE (2) .... HOUSE 64/04

```
      DEAD   216/06
REMOVED (1) ......................................... LITTL  76/29
REMOVING (1) ........................................ GRACE 153/02
RENEGE (1) .......................................... IVY D 133/20
RENEW (1) ........................................... GRACE 171/17
RENEWED (2) ......................................... GRACE 155/33
      DEAD   205/33
RENOUNCE (1) ........................................ GRACE 171/10
RENTED (1) .......................................... DEAD  176/05
REPAID (1) .......................................... MOTHR 148/07
REPARATION (5) ...................................... HOUSE  64/32
      HOUSE  64/33    HOUSE  65/04    HOUSE  65/32    HOUSE  67/25
REPEAT (1) .......................................... DEAD  185/06
REPEATED (15) ....................................... ENCTR  26/14
      LITTL  71/23    LITTL  81/14    PARTS  93/24    MOTHR 144/20
      MOTHR 146/17    GRACE 151/27    GRACE 152/09    GRACE 166/18
      GRACE 169/25    GRACE 172/01    DEAD  190/01    DEAD  192/11
      DEAD  201/08    DEAD  212/12
REPEATEDLY (2) ...................................... SISTR  14/15
      GRACE 151/09
REPEATING (3) ....................................... ENCTR  26/08
      CLAY  104/06    DEAD  185/33
REPELLED (1) ........................................ LITTL  83/13
REPENTANT (1) ....................................... DEAD  211/31
REPLACE (1) ......................................... DEAD  193/11
REPLACED (2) ........................................ PNFUL 112/31
      IVY D 119/32
REPLENISHED (1) ..................................... DEAD  200/12
REPLIED (2) ......................................... GALNT  58/19
      DEAD  181/16
REPLY (1) ........................................... ENCTR  27/06
REPORT (2) .......................................... MOTHR 144/29
      MOTHR 144/31
REPORTED (5) ........................................ ENCTR  19/17
      RACE   42/11    GALNT  52/02    GRACE 156/04    DEAD  183/20
REPORTER (2) ........................................ PNFUL 115/22
      GRACE 172/32
REPORTS (1) ......................................... MOTHR 139/22
REPOSE (1) .......................................... GALNT  49/03
REPOSING (1) ........................................ PARTS  87/06
REPRESENT (1) ....................................... IVY D 121/26
REPRESENTED (1) ..................................... IVY D 121/28
REPUTATION (4) ...................................... GALNT  50/18
      HOUSE  62/17    PARTS  97/05    GRACE 158/17
REPUTED (1) ......................................... RACE   43/32
REQUIRED (1) ........................................ PARTS  89/26
RESEMBLE (1) ........................................ GRACE 156/33
RESEMBLED (1) ....................................... IVY D 130/05
RESEMBLING (1) ...................................... IVY D 125/23
RESENTED (4) ........................................ PNFUL 111/06
      GRACE 160/24    GRACE 160/25    GRACE 160/29
RESENTMENT (2) ...................................... LITTL  83/22
      DEAD  187/11
RESERVE (2) ......................................... RACE   46/09
      MOTHR 140/08
RESERVED (2) ........................................ GALNT  59/05
      DEAD  198/10
RESIDENT (2) ........................................ HOUSE  62/06
      HOUSE  62/09
RESIGNATION (1) ..................................... LITTL  73/32
RESIGNED (3) ........................................ SISTR  15/23
      SISTR  15/24    SISTR  15/27
```

RESIGNEDLY (1) .... ARABY 30/20
RESOLVE (1) .... MOTHR 141/09
RESONANT (2) .... RACE 46/19
    GRACE 173/26
RESOUNDING (2) .... MOTHR 142/20
    DEAD 208/19
RESPECT (6) .... EVELN 37/33
    RACE 45/03   RACE 46/01   RACE 46/15   IVY D 132/29
    GRACE 157/18
RESPECTABLE (2) .... IVY D 124/26
    IVY D 131/18
RESPECTED (4) .... IVY D 131/22
    MOTHR 141/22   MOTHR 141/23   MOTHR 145/26
RESPECTFULLY (4) .... SISTR 17/24
    PARTS 90/09   IVY D 119/12   DEAD 183/09
RESPECTS (2) .... IVY D 129/18
    IVY D 133/01
RESPOND (2) .... GRACE 172/23
    DEAD 220/25
RESPONSE (1) .... PNFUL 114/01
RESPONSES (1) .... SISTR 13/22
RESPONSIBLE (1) .... GRACE 155/02
REST (6) .... RACE 48/28
    GALNT 58/18   PARTS 92/14   PNFUL 114/01   IVY D 124/18
    MOTHR 145/23
RESTED (7) .... ARABY 32/08
    RACE 48/30   HOUSE 68/06   HOUSE 68/26   PARTS 96/02
    GRACE 173/03   DEAD 222/11
RESTING (1) .... DEAD 217/24
RESTLESS (1) .... DEAD 178/20
RESTLESSLY (1) .... DEAD 178/18
RESTORED (1) .... GRACE 173/17
RESTRAIN (2) .... PARTS 91/12
    DEAD 217/15
RESTRAINING (1) .... ENCTR 20/34
RESTS (1) .... IVY D 135/10
RESULT (3) .... GALNT 59/25
    GALNT 59/28   LITTL 77/04
RESUMED (2) .... SISTR 18/13
    GRACE 169/27
RESUMING (2) .... GALNT 57/23
    GRACE 170/23
RESURRECTED (1) .... MOTHR 147/13
RETAINING (1) .... SISTR 14/28
RETCH (1) .... GRACE 158/29
RETIRED (2) .... PNFUL 112/23
    DEAD 191/32
RETORT (5) .... PARTS 93/26
    PARTS 93/27   PARTS 93/29   DEAD 179/05   DEAD 189/33
RETORTED (1) .... DEAD 189/30
RETRACE (1) .... ENCTR 24/28
RETREAT (5) .... ARABY 32/03
    GRACE 162/34   GRACE 164/26   GRACE 170/32   GRACE 171/24
RETREATED (2) .... PARTS 89/04
    IVY D 126/13
RETURN (5) .... RACE 44/22
    GALNT 59/02   GALNT 59/07   LITTL 83/33   PNFUL 110/29
RETURNED (17) .... SISTR 10/27
    SISTR 17/22   ARABY 30/13   RACE 48/04   GALNT 56/04
    LITTL 76/32   PARTS 86/05   PARTS 88/12   PARTS 90/13
    PNFUL 112/12   PNFUL 115/08   IVY D 120/31   IVY D 121/13
    IVY D 123/31   IVY D 126/20   IVY D 132/33   GRACE 153/02

RETURNING (4) .... SISTR   9/18
    EVELN 38/21   PARTS 93/08   PARTS 97/12
RETURN-ROOM (1) .... HOUSE   68/09
REUNION (2) .... HOUSE   62/23
    HOUSE 68/12
REV. (1) .... SISTR   12/07
REVEALED (1) .... LITTL   78/19
REVEALING (2) .... HOUSE   63/32
    PNFUL 109/33
REVEL (1) .... PARTS   90/31
REVELATION (1) .... DEAD   204/34
REVENGED (1) .... ENCTR   22/31
REVENGEFUL (1) .... PARTS   92/13
REVENGEFULLY (1) .... MOTHR 143/30
REVENGEFULNESS (1) .... PARTS   96/32
REVERY (4) .... SISTR   17/24
    HOUSE 64/20   HOUSE 68/27   LITTL 74/14
REVIEW (6) .... DEAD   188/10
    DEAD 188/29   DEAD 188/30   DEAD 192/11   DEAD   192/13
    DEAD 207/27
REVIEWED (1) .... LITTL   72/23
REVIEWING (1) .... EVELN   37/06
REVIEWS (1) .... DEAD   188/22
REVIVAL (1) .... MOTHR 137/25
REVOLTED (3) .... LITTL   73/09
    PNFUL 115/19   PNFUL 115/19
REVOLUTION (1) .... PNFUL 111/07
REVOLVING (2) .... GALNT   56/14
    GALNT 59/12
REWARD (1) .... SISTR   16/20
REWARDED (1) .... MOTHR 139/30
REX (1) .... IVY D 122/03
REYNOLDS'S (1) .... HOUSE   66/11
RHEUMATIC (1) .... SISTR   17/08
RHYTHM (3) .... LITTL   84/01
    PNFUL 117/27   PNFUL 117/30
RIBBON (1) .... SISTR   12/04
RIBS (2) .... PNFUL 114/16
    DEAD 215/31
RICH (4) .... RACE   43/20
    LITTL 81/30   LITTL 83/15   DEAD 212/02
RICHARD (1) .... IVY D 119/12
RICHES (1) .... CLAY   106/08
RICHLY (1) .... LITTL   72/08
RICHMOND (1) .... ARABY   29/01
RICKETY (1) .... PARTS   88/27
RIDDLES (1) .... GALNT   50/24
RIDE (1) .... MOTHR 148/09
RIDGE (1) .... ENCTR   24/08
RIDICULE (1) .... RACE   46/20
RIDICULOUS (3) .... HOUSE   65/30
    DEAD 179/15   DEAD 190/30
RIFE (1) .... LITTL   78/15
RIGHT (74) .... SISTR   10/34
    SISTR 17/27   ENCTR 22/20   ENCTR   23/11   ENCTR   23/31
    ENCTR 23/31   EVELN 40/20   GALNT   52/11   GALNT   52/15
    GALNT 52/30   GALNT 53/06   GALNT   53/21   GALNT   53/27
    GALNT 55/03   GALNT 55/10   GALNT   56/09   GALNT   59/14
    HOUSE 63/23   HOUSE 66/33   HOUSE   67/30   LITTL   70/06
    LITTL 72/21   LITTL 74/23   LITTL   77/10   LITTL   77/18
    LITTL 78/03   PARTS 88/22   PARTS   90/08   PARTS   90/12
    PARTS 97/27   CLAY 103/05   PNFUL 113/28   PNFUL 114/17

PNFUL 114/18	IVY D 121/19	IVY D 121/20	IVY D 121/24
IVY D 122/09	IVY D 123/03	IVY D 123/06	IVY D 124/06
IVY D 126/18	IVY D 126/19	IVY D 127/16	IVY D 132/11
IVY D 133/03	GRACE 151/16	GRACE 151/32	GRACE 152/18
GRACE 152/20	GRACE 155/08	GRACE 164/17	GRACE 164/18
GRACE 168/01	GRACE 171/24	GRACE 172/28	GRACE 174/31
DEAD 177/12	DEAD 180/10	DEAD 180/10	DEAD 181/16
DEAD 182/07	DEAD 184/23	DEAD 185/25	DEAD 189/24
DEAD 190/18	DEAD 190/29	DEAD 191/03	DEAD 194/25
DEAD 194/34	DEAD 200/03	DEAD 209/21	DEAD 212/01
DEAD 223/27			

RIGHTLY (2) .... DEAD 204/09
  DEAD 220/33
RIGHTO (2) .... GRACE 162/16
  GRACE 162/22
RIGHTS (2) .... MOTHR 148/12
  MOTHR 148/34
RIM (1) .... LITTL 81/05
RIMS (1) .... DEAD 178/19
RING (8) .... GALNT 54/08
  CLAY 101/10 CLAY 101/11 CLAY 105/04 MOTHR 148/13
  GRACE 150/11 GRACE 151/02 GRACE 151/23
RINGING (1) .... HOUSE 64/20
RINGSEND (2) .... ENCTR 23/09
  ENCTR 23/33
RINSED (1) .... GRACE 167/01
RIOT (2) .... PARTS 91/03
  DEAD 222/21
RIOTING (1) .... DEAD 213/09
R.I.P. (1) .... SISTR 12/09
RIPE (1) .... DEAD 179/31
RISE (4) .... IVY D 135/15
  MOTHR 145/08 GRACE 151/31 GRACE 154/18
RISEN (3) .... LITTL 80/14
  MOTHR 146/29 DEAD 205/05
RISK (1) .... DEAD 188/20
RIVAL (2) .... LITTL 75/07
  DEAD 196/22
RIVER (14) .... ENCTR 22/34
  ENCTR 23/07 ARABY 34/18 LITTL 73/12 PNFUL 107/06
  PNFUL 115/16 PNFUL 117/10 PNFUL 117/21 PNFUL 117/22
  GRACE 153/18 DEAD 192/04 DEAD 212/32 DEAD 213/02
  DEAD 222/25
RIVER-BANKS (1) .... LITTL 73/15
RIVIERE (6) .... RACE 43/01
  RACE 43/06 RACE 46/17 RACE 47/06 RACE 47/25
  RACE 47/25
ROAD (22) .... ENCTR 21/15
  ENCTR 22/19 ENCTR 22/21 ARABY 34/23 EVELN 38/32
  RACE 42/02 RACE 44/07 GALNT 49/12 GALNT 53/19
  GALNT 54/19 GALNT 55/11 GALNT 55/21 GALNT 57/30
  GALNT 59/22 GALNT 60/11 PARTS 97/10 PNFUL 113/10
  PNFUL 115/18 PNFUL 116/21 GRACE 154/24 GRACE 166/23
  DEAD 176/09
ROADS (2) .... RACE 45/10
  PNFUL 112/05
ROADWAY (3) .... GALNT 51/18
  GALNT 54/08 LITTL 71/30
ROAMING (1) .... PNFUL 109/04
ROARED (1) .... PARTS 94/01
ROARING (1) .... DEAD 213/24
ROAST (1) .... DEAD 197/20

ROB (1) .... PNFUL 109/14
ROBERT (1) .... DEAD 179/09
ROBUSTNESS (1) .... ENCTR 20/06
ROCK (1) .... LITTL 84/09
ROCKED (1) .... LITTL 84/10
ROCKING (1) .... ARABY 33/29
ROISTERED (1) .... LITTL 71/34
ROLL (2) .... IVY D 118/16
    MOTHR 143/27
ROLLED (3) .... PNFUL 109/15
    MOTHR 139/24   GRACE 150/04
ROLLING (2) .... PARTS 98/10
    DEAD 187/13
ROMAN (3) .... ENCTR 20/13
    ENCTR 20/24   GRACE 170/30
ROMANCE (2) .... ARABY 31/02
    DEAD 222/06
ROMANTIC (4) .... RACE 46/21
    MOTHR 136/18   MOTHR 137/08   MOTHR 137/09
ROME (1) .... SISTR 13/02
ROMEO (1) .... DEAD 186/16
ROOF (4) .... HOUSE 64/26
    HOUSE 67/34   DEAD 202/24   DEAD 203/07
ROOFS (2) .... EVELN 36/11
    DEAD 212/34
ROOM (88) .... SISTR 11/21
    SISTR   12/12   SISTR   14/16   SISTR   14/31   SISTR   14/32
    SISTR   17/21   ARABY   29/09   ARABY   33/05   ARABY   33/08
    ARABY   33/08   ARABY   33/24   EVELN   37/06   EVELN   40/05
    RACE   46/07   RACE   46/24   HOUSE   62/01   HOUSE   65/07
    LITTL   71/19   LITTL   82/08   LITTL   83/19   LITTL   84/02
    LITTL   84/22   LITTL   84/24   LITTL   85/15   PARTS   87/02
    PARTS   88/09   PARTS   90/01   PARTS   92/12   PARTS   95/21
    PARTS   95/23   CLAY   100/34   CLAY   102/31   PNFUL 107/07
    PNFUL 107/09   PNFUL 111/20   PNFUL 112/13   PNFUL 112/15
    PNFUL 116/31   IVY D 118/ T   IVY D 119/18   IVY D 120/19
    IVY D 120/31   IVY D 120/33   IVY D 120/34   IVY D 121/02
    IVY D 122/20   IVY D 123/11   IVY D 124/08   IVY D 130/03
    MOTHR 139/27   MOTHR 143/17   MOTHR 143/27   MOTHR 144/24
    MOTHR 145/19   MOTHR 145/22   MOTHR 146/06   MOTHR 146/20
    MOTHR 146/30   MOTHR 148/03   MOTHR 149/29   GRACE 157/01
    GRACE 161/16   GRACE 161/30   GRACE 162/02   GRACE 170/09
    DEAD   176/11   DEAD   176/17   DEAD   181/15   DEAD   181/16
    DEAD   182/29   DEAD   182/29   DEAD   183/30   DEAD   184/14
    DEAD   184/16   DEAD   185/05   DEAD   185/15   DEAD   187/14
    DEAD   190/14   DEAD   191/21   DEAD   191/31   DEAD   191/32
    DEAD   191/33   DEAD   192/28   DEAD   192/34   DEAD   193/17
    DEAD   214/11   DEAD   216/12   DEAD   223/04
ROOMS (6) .... ARABY 29/09
    ARABY   33/07   MOTHR 138/11   MOTHR 139/07   MOTHR 141/30
    DEAD   176/11
ROPE (1) .... ARABY 30/24
ROSE (6) .... SISTR 14/26
    RACE   48/22   PARTS 91/29   MOTHR 145/08   GRACE 173/16
    GRACE 173/17
ROSICRUCIAN (1) .... SISTR 11/02
ROSSA (1) .... ARABY 31/08
ROSY (1) .... IVY D 125/31
ROTTEN (1) .... LITTL 81/30
ROTTERDAM (1) .... PNFUL 114/34
ROTUNDA (1) .... PNFUL 109/18
ROTUNDITY (1) .... GALNT 50/05

ROUGE (1)						LITTL	76/28
ROUGH (4)						ENCTR	27/05
ENCTR 27/12	ARABY 30/09		PNFUL 111/22				
ROUGHLY (2)						GALNT	57/19
DEAD 211/13							
ROUGHSHOD (1)						MOTHR	148/09
ROUND (54)						ENCTR	19/13
ENCTR 26/10	ENCTR 26/10	ENCTR 27/10		ENCTR 27/10			
ENCTR 28/04	ARABY 32/02	ARABY 32/02		EVELN 37/06			
RACE 42/12	GALNT 50/23	GALNT 50/32		GALNT 50/34			
GALNT 51/23	GALNT 56/24	HOUSE 66/29		LITTL 83/19			
PARTS 90/07	PARTS 91/07	PARTS 93/25		PARTS 94/08			
PARTS 94/21	PARTS 94/26	PARTS 94/26		PARTS 95/01			
PARTS 95/03	PARTS 95/04	PARTS 95/14		PARTS 98/12			
CLAY 99/08	CLAY 104/14	PNFUL 109/20		IVY D 124/23			
IVY D 125/29	IVY D 126/09	MOTHR 149/23		GRACE 155/13			
GRACE 169/03	GRACE 170/31	DEAD 184/26		DEAD 186/23			
DEAD 194/18	DEAD 196/20	DEAD 196/21		DEAD 197/28			
DEAD 197/33	DEAD 203/13	DEAD 206/25		DEAD 207/23			
DEAD 207/23	DEAD 208/10	DEAD 208/11		DEAD 208/13			
DEAD 208/13							
ROUNDLY (1)						GRACE	156/20
ROUNDS (1)						PARTS	95/25
ROUSED (1)						SISTR	12/16
ROUSSEL (1)						RACE	47/17
ROUTE (1)						DEAD	209/06
ROUTH (4)						RACE	46/06
RACE 46/24	RACE 48/20	RACE 48/23					
ROUTINE (2)						ENCTR	21/04
DEAD 204/13							
ROW (7)						ARABY	34/18
RACE 47/11	LITTL 70/18	PARTS 88/24		CLAY 104/29			
GRACE 161/11	DEAD 202/04						
ROWBOAT (1)						RACE	47/20
ROYAL (6)						IVY D	119/11
IVY D 119/14	GRACE 154/17	DEAD 187/01		DEAD 198/18			
DEAD 199/09							
RUB (4)						CLAY	104/11
IVY D 123/07	IVY D 128/31	DEAD 185/32					
RUBBER (1)						GALNT	50/03
RUBBING (2)						IVY D	122/22
DEAD 184/33							
RUBBISH (1)						ENCTR	20/23
RUDDY (1)						GALNT	49/14
RUDE (2)						GALNT	55/32
DEAD 211/15							
RUDELY (2)						SISTR	10/28
DEAD 213/29							
RUDENESS (1)						GALNT	49/12
RUFFIAN (3)						PARTS	91/32
PARTS 91/32	GRACE 168/26						
RUFFLE (1)						GALNT	53/33
RUG (2)						PNFUL	107/14
DEAD 209/01							
RUINED (2)						HOUSE	61/09
PNFUL 112/03							
RUINOUS (1)						ARABY	34/17
RUINS (1)						IVY D	120/05
RULE (3)						LITTL	75/23
DEAD 201/06	DEAD 201/08						
RUM (3)						LITTL	78/10
MOTHR 137/15	GRACE 150/14						

RUN (13)						SISTR	10/33
	ENCTR	23/11	EVELN	37/23	GALNT 56/19	GALNT	60/12
	HOUSE	63/06	HOUSE	65/34	PARTS 89/24	IVY D	128/27
	DEAD	175/01	DEAD	195/25	DEAD 213/12	DEAD	215/16
RUNNING (12)						ENCTR	28/10
	ARABY	31/19	EVELN	39/32	RACE 42/01	GALNT	53/03
	GALNT	54/03	GALNT	60/03	GALNT 60/05	PARTS	95/06
	PARTS	97/18	GRACE	151/28	DEAD 217/33		
RUNS (3)						DEAD	186/02
	DEAD	187/09	DEAD	193/03			
RUSH (3)						EVELN	38/19
	PARTS	90/30	DEAD	204/13			
RUSHED (1)						EVELN	41/13
RUSH'S (1)						SISTR	17/09
RUSTY (1)						ARABY	29/17
RUTLAND (2)						GALNT	49/09
	GALNT	56/34					
RYAN (1)						ENCTR	22/33

'S (3)						GRACE	151/34
	GRACE	152/15	GRACE	153/32			
S. (1)						SISTR	12/07
SACK (2)						LITTL	81/09
	LITTL	81/14					
SACRAMENTS (1)						GRACE	158/06
SACRED (3)						PNFUL	115/21
	GRACE	158/05	GRACE	169/11			
SACRIFICES (1)						EVELN	40/13
SAD (4)						LITTL	71/13
	DEAD	192/09	DEAD	204/05	DEAD 220/13		
SADDER (1)						DEAD	204/02
SADLY (3)						DEAD	207/10
	DEAD	211/25	DEAD	220/15			
SADNESS (1)						LITTL	74/08
SAFE (5)						SISTR	11/09
	HOUSE	64/07	PARTS	88/30	PNFUL 109/01	DEAD	212/29
SAFELY (2)						ARABY	30/15
	ARABY	31/10					
SAID (754)							
SAILED (1)						EVELN	39/13
SAILING-VESSEL (1)						ENCTR	23/10
SAILOR (4)						ENCTR	23/28
	EVELN	39/07	EVELN	39/19	GALNT 54/23		
SAILORS (1)						ENCTR	23/25
SAILORS' (1)						ENCTR	23/27
SAKE (7)						EVELN	38/06
	RACE	47/30	PNFUL	109/12	MOTHR 142/30	MOTHR	148/14
	DEAD	195/32	DEAD	222/07			
SALLY (1)						DEAD	204/18
SALMONPINK (1)						DEAD	209/28
SALUTATION (1)						IVY D	129/21
SALUTE (1)						GALNT	56/04
SALUTED (5)						RACE	47/12
	HOUSE	68/06	PARTS	89/11	PARTS 95/09	DEAD	215/02
SALUTING (1)						GALNT	55/15
SALVER (1)						ARABY	35/02
SAME (25)						SISTR	9/04
	ENCTR	21/21	ENCTR	26/10	ARABY 35/23	GALNT	60/08
	LITTL	74/30	LITTL	76/06	LITTL 76/26	LITTL	78/02
	LITTL	78/04	PARTS	90/17	CLAY 106/11	IVY D	125/33
	MOTHR	141/23	GRACE	157/01	GRACE 159/04	GRACE	165/32

DEAD	179/31	DEAD	182/01	DEAD	184/33	DEAD	204/24
DEAD	206/12	DEAD	212/04	DEAD	215/05	DEAD	222/29

SANDY (1) .... GRACE 159/13
SANDYMOUNT (2) .... PARTS 96/31
    GRACE 156/06
SANG (14) .... ARABY 31/07

EVELN	39/05	EVELN	39/06	HOUSE	62/22	HOUSE	62/27
CLAY	104/13	CLAY	106/02	CLAY	106/03	MOTHR	142/24
MOTHR	147/10	DEAD	193/04	DEAD	205/15	DEAD	205/24
DEAD	205/27						

SASH (1) .... ARABY 30/27
SASHES (2) .... HOUSE 63/29
    DEAD 197/04
SAT (51) .... SISTR 15/08

ENCTR	21/30	ENCTR	23/06	ENCTR	24/33	ENCTR	26/32
ENCTR	26/32	ARABY	33/04	EVELN	36/01	EVELN	39/04
RACE	44/04	RACE	44/05	RACE	45/08	RACE	47/30
RACE	48/01	GALNT	57/12	GALNT	57/28	HOUSE	61/18
HOUSE	64/03	HOUSE	68/19	HOUSE	68/24	LITTL	71/01
LITTL	71/19	LITTL	82/08	PARTS	89/26	PARTS	90/13
PARTS	95/09	PARTS	97/32	CLAY	104/22	PNFUL	109/19
PNFUL	116/16	PNFUL	116/18	PNFUL	116/22	IVY D	122/28
IVY D	126/21	IVY D	130/26	IVY D	130/27	IVY D	130/32
IVY D	133/17	IVY D	135/21	MOTHR	136/14	GRACE	154/26
GRACE	156/31	GRACE	166/30	GRACE	172/10	GRACE	172/12
GRACE	172/15	GRACE	172/16	GRACE	172/17	GRACE	172/25
GRACE	172/28	GRACE	172/31				

SATAN (1) .... GRACE 171/12
SATIN (1) .... DEAD 186/23
SATIRICALLY (1) .... IVY D 121/11
SATISFACTION (3) .... PARTS 93/11
    IVY D 129/28   GRACE 171/02
SATISFACTORY (1) .... RACE 43/10
SATISFIED (3) .... RACE 45/32
    HOUSE 65/21   GRACE 161/27
SATISFY (1) .... SISTR 10/26
SATURATED (1) .... GRACE 154/14
SATURDAY (10) .... ARABY 31/02

ARABY	32/20	ARABY	32/28	EVELN	38/10	EVELN	38/16
LITTL	82/26	MOTHR	139/06	MOTHR	140/08	MOTHR	140/28
MOTHR	141/22						

SATURNINE (1) .... PNFUL 108/16
SAUCE (2) .... DEAD 197/19
    DEAD 197/20
SAUCERS (2) .... CLAY 105/01
    CLAY 105/13
SAUNTERED (1) .... GALNT 55/11
SAVAGE (1) .... PARTS 92/12
SAVE (6) .... EVELN 40/18

EVELN	40/21	GALNT	52/20	LITTL	82/09	IVY D	125/30
DEAD	209/32						

SAVED (2) .... ENCTR 21/11
    DEAD 214/18
SAW (49) .... SISTR 10/11

SISTR	11/21	SISTR	14/27	SISTR	18/15	ENCTR	22/05
ENCTR	23/13	ENCTR	24/17	ENCTR	24/27	ENCTR	25/20
ENCTR	26/21	ENCTR	28/09	ARABY	33/09	ARABY	34/23
ARABY	35/32	EVELN	36/17	RACE	48/31	GALNT	53/08
GALNT	56/08	GALNT	57/31	GALNT	59/23	HOUSE	68/09
HOUSE	68/32	LITTL	74/02	LITTL	74/24	LITTL	74/33
LITTL	80/30	CLAY	101/07	PNFUL	114/08	PNFUL	115/25
PNFUL	117/13	PNFUL	117/22	IVY D	123/30	IVY D	127/19

MOTHR	140/19	MOTHR	143/03	MOTHR	145/08	GRACE	155/21
GRACE	159/32	GRACE	170/12	GRACE	170/24	DEAD	188/21
DEAD	190/32	DEAD	191/30	DEAD	197/22	DEAD	211/01
DEAD	212/05	DEAD	218/20	DEAD	220/01	DEAD	223/15

SAWDUST (1) .... PNFUL 116/15
SAY (73) .... SISTR 9/19

SISTR	10/09	SISTR	10/22	SISTR	10/30	SISTR	15/33
SISTR	17/18	SISTR	17/27	SISTR	17/28	ENCTR	21/14
ENCTR	26/24	ENCTR	26/27	ARABY	35/11	EVELN	37/22
EVELN	37/24	EVELN	38/05	EVELN	39/18	HOUSE	62/21
HOUSE	63/04	HOUSE	65/07	LITTL	72/25	LITTL	73/03
LITTL	75/15	LITTL	75/18	LITTL	76/16	LITTL	77/17
LITTL	77/25	LITTL	77/32	LITTL	78/31	LITTL	81/27
PARTS	87/12	PARTS	90/12	PARTS	92/06	PARTS	98/23
PARTS	98/23	PARTS	98/24	CLAY	100/20	CLAY	101/11
CLAY	103/20	CLAY	105/05	CLAY	106/15	IVY D	119/01
IVY D	119/03	IVY D	121/17	IVY D	125/11	IVY D	125/25
IVY D	128/29	IVY D	131/02	IVY D	133/20	MOTHR	137/22
MOTHR	144/28	MOTHR	147/29	GRACE	161/08	GRACE	161/28
GRACE	163/06	GRACE	165/11	GRACE	165/15	GRACE	170/24
GRACE	174/25	GRACE	174/28	DEAD	188/04	DEAD	188/17
DEAD	191/09	DEAD	192/20	DEAD	194/01	DEAD	200/29
DEAD	202/26	DEAD	203/03	DEAD	211/16	DEAD	211/22
DEAD	213/13	DEAD	214/27	DEAD	216/05	DEAD	222/14

SAYING (38) .... SISTR 11/02

SISTR	12/01	SISTR	17/03	ENCTR	22/31	ENCTR	25/01
ENCTR	26/03	ENCTR	26/19	ENCTR	27/34	ARABY	34/07
ARABY	34/20	EVELN	40/09	EVELN	40/14	EVELN	40/24
RACE	47/33	HOUSE	66/29	HOUSE	68/15	LITTL	78/11
LITTL	81/29	PARTS	86/05	PARTS	88/02	PARTS	90/17
PARTS	91/08	PARTS	93/22	PARTS	94/03	PARTS	97/34
CLAY	99/18	IVY D	121/13	IVY D	128/32	MOTHR	138/27
GRACE	152/17	GRACE	161/34	GRACE	165/25	GRACE	167/27
GRACE	169/06	DEAD	181/15	DEAD	201/20	DEAD	221/10
DEAD	222/24						

SAYINGS (1) .... LITTL 73/02
SAYS (15) .... PARTS 87/13

PARTS	93/19	IVY D	120/14	IVY D	128/02	IVY D	128/03
IVY D	128/04	IVY D	128/10	IVY D	128/10	IVY D	128/11
IVY D	128/11	IVY D	132/08	GRACE	168/14	DEAD	181/06
DEAD	181/12	DEAD	204/21				

SCALE (1) .... GALNT 56/22
SCALES (1) .... DEAD 187/10
SCAMPER (1) .... DEAD 175/05
SCANDAL (1) .... DEAD 194/30
SCANDALOUS (1) .... MOTHR 147/25
SCANDALOUSLY (1) .... MOTHR 148/06
SCANT (1) .... GALNT 50/05
SCANTILY (1) .... ENCTR 23/13
SCANTY (2) .... SISTR 14/30
    DEAD 184/30
SCARCELY (3) .... SISTR 14/11
    HOUSE 67/13   DEAD 217/29
SCARF (1) .... PARTS 95/13
SCARLET (1) .... PNFUL 107/14
SCATTER (1) .... LITTL 83/34
SCATTERED (2) .... MOTHR 142/18
    DEAD 178/16
SCENE (5) .... LITTL 71/11
    GRACE 152/34   GRACE 155/02   GRACE 169/08   DEAD 186/16
SCENERY (1) .... DEAD 191/24
SCENES (1) .... PARTS 94/28

SCENTED (1) . . . . GALNT   55/22
SCEPTICAL (1) . . . . DEAD   203/22
SCHEME (1) . . . . GRACE 158/03
SCHOLAR (1) . . . . GRACE 167/22
SCHOOL (26) . . . . ENCTR   19/03
     ENCTR   20/12   ENCTR   20/29   ENCTR   20/31   ENCTR   20/34
     ENCTR   21/04   ENCTR   23/14   ENCTR   23/15   ENCTR   25/06
     ENCTR   27/06   ENCTR   27/07   ARABY   29/02   ARABY   32/15
     ARABY   33/01   EVELN   37/14   EVELN   38/24   LITTL   74/04
     IVY D 120/14   MOTHR 136/12   GRACE 153/34   GRACE 154/27
     GRACE 156/18   GRACE 167/30   GRACE 167/32   DEAD   178/02
     DEAD   186/20
SCHOOLBOY (1) . . . . ENCTR   25/04
SCHOOLING (1) . . . . DEAD   178/03
SCHOOL-LIFE (1) . . . . ENCTR   21/09
SCIENCE (1) . . . . PNFUL 112/16
SCINTILLATED (1) . . . . DEAD   178/18
SCOLDED (1) . . . . GRACE 156/20
SCORE (1) . . . . PNFUL 110/34
SCORN (1) . . . . PNFUL 111/10
SCORNFULLY (1) . . . . IVY D 121/16
SCOTCH (2) . . . . PARTS   94/15
     PARTS   95/01
SCOTLAND (1) . . . . DEAD   191/23
SCOTT (2) . . . . ENCTR   25/08
     ARABY   29/12
SCOTT'S (1) . . . . ENCTR   25/14
SCOUNDRELS (1) . . . . GRACE 163/06
SCRAPING (2) . . . . DEAD   177/05
     DEAD   177/14
SCREAM (1) . . . . LITTL   84/21
SCREAMING (2) . . . . ENCTR   22/26
     LITTL   71/10
SCREEN (3) . . . . MOTHR 140/23
     MOTHR 141/03   MOTHR 143/11
SCREENED (1) . . . . DEAD   178/19
SCREW (1) . . . . HOUSE   65/17
SCREWED (4) . . . . MOTHR 142/07
     DEAD   176/27   DEAD   182/07   DEAD   182/08
SCRIBBLER (1) . . . . ENCTR   20/26
SCRIPTURES (1) . . . . GRACE 173/27
SCRUPULOUS (1) . . . . SISTR   17/16
SCRUTINY (1) . . . . GALNT   55/23
SCUDDING (1) . . . . RACE   42/01
SCUFFLING (1) . . . . CLAY   105/16
SCURRY (1) . . . . LITTL   75/13
SEA (3) . . . . ENCTR   23/12
     EVELN   40/32   GRACE 156/06
SEARCH (3) . . . . IVY D 119/05
     IVY D 122/31   GRACE 160/22
SEARCHED (2) . . . . GALNT   53/29
     GALNT   59/16
SEARCHING (1) . . . . PARTS   87/34
SEARCHINGLY (1) . . . . MOTHR 142/06
SEAS (2) . . . . EVELN   41/06
     EVELN   41/11
SEASONED (1) . . . . GALNT   57/25
SEASONS (1) . . . . ENCTR   25/02
SEAT (5) . . . . ARABY   34/15
     RACE   44/04   IVY D 121/13   DEAD   197/05   DEAD   208/31
SEATED (3) . . . . SISTR   14/33
     DEAD   192/32   DEAD   205/15

SEATING (1) .... GRACE 172/05
SEATS (1) .... MOTHR 143/11
SECLUDED (1) .... MOTHR 145/19
SECOND (15) .... ARABY 34/09
     RACE   42/10   HOUSE 68/07   LITTL 84/11   PARTS 86/15
     CLAY 106/03   PNFUL 114/01   IVY D 131/02   MOTHR 142/16
     MOTHR 142/31   MOTHR 148/15   MOTHR 148/24   MOTHR 149/14
     DEAD 197/28   DEAD 198/23
SECOND-CLASS (1) .... GRACE 166/22
SECOND-HAND (1) .... DEAD 188/13
SECONDS (9) .... RACE   47/11
     GALNT 56/04   GALNT 60/05   LITTL 84/23   PARTS 96/06
     CLAY 105/15   PNFUL 111/12   MOTHR 147/07   GRACE 151/29
SECRECY (1) .... SISTR 13/13
SECRET (7) .... ENCTR 26/13
     HOUSE 68/26   MOTHR 137/01   GRACE 159/18   DEAD 188/30
     DEAD 213/15   DEAD 219/31
SECRETARIES (3) .... MOTHR 142/04
     MOTHR 147/32   MOTHR 149/15
SECRETARY (5) .... IVY D 127/31
     MOTHR 136/01   MOTHR 139/15   MOTHR 149/06   GRACE 158/25
SECRETLY (2) .... ENCTR 20/12
     EVELN 39/21
SECRETO (1) .... PNFUL 113/18
SECRETS (1) .... LITTL 78/20
SECTIONS (1) .... PNFUL 111/01
SECULAR (1) .... GRACE 164/10
SECURE (4) .... RACE   43/19
     MOTHR 140/28   MOTHR 141/24   DEAD 193/07
SECURED (1) .... RACE   45/32
SECURELY (1) .... LITTL 83/01
SECURITY (1) .... GRACE 172/12
SEDULOUSLY (1) .... ENCTR 24/01
SEE (82) .... SISTR   9/05
     SISTR 11/14   SISTR 16/02   SISTR 17/04   SISTR 17/20
     SISTR 18/02   ENCTR 21/16   ENCTR 23/25   ENCTR 24/08
     ENCTR 25/11   ARABY 30/18   ARABY 31/26   EVELN 37/09
     EVELN 37/28   EVELN 38/23   EVELN 39/02   EVELN 39/03
     RACE   43/27   GALNT 59/07   GALNT 60/11   GALNT 60/14
     GALNT 60/19   HOUSE 67/27   LITTL 73/30   LITTL 75/01
     LITTL 76/05   LITTL 79/27   LITTL 81/08   LITTL 81/31
     LITTL 82/33   PARTS 88/05   PARTS 88/06   PARTS 91/33
     PARTS 92/03   CLAY   99/04   CLAY   99/07   CLAY 104/33
     CLAY 105/06   IVY D 122/07   IVY D 123/14   IVY D 124/07
     IVY D 126/17   IVY D 130/24   IVY D 132/08   IVY D 132/09
     MOTHR 138/24   MOTHR 140/15   MOTHR 142/04   MOTHR 144/17
     MOTHR 144/21   MOTHR 144/31   MOTHR 145/13   MOTHR 145/15
     MOTHR 148/11   GRACE 152/18   GRACE 153/24   GRACE 156/27
     GRACE 157/31   GRACE 158/12   GRACE 162/24   GRACE 163/05
     GRACE 168/12   GRACE 174/16   DEAD 176/28   DEAD 182/06
     DEAD 183/19   DEAD 191/07   DEAD 191/16   DEAD 192/18
     DEAD 195/29   DEAD 209/27   DEAD 209/27   DEAD 211/12
     DEAD 212/25   DEAD 214/29   DEAD 217/11   DEAD 219/09
     DEAD 219/22   DEAD 220/06   DEAD 221/10   DEAD 221/17
     DEAD 221/24
SEED (1) .... PARTS 89/02
SEEING (17) .... SISTR 14/14
     ARABY 33/12   RACE   47/28   PARTS 88/24   PARTS 98/14
     PNFUL 116/16   GRACE 152/13   GRACE 156/05   GRACE 169/02
     DEAD 178/33   DEAD 182/27   DEAD 183/27   DEAD 185/04
     DEAD 194/28   DEAD 205/04   DEAD 212/18   DEAD 214/27
SEEM (12) .... ENCTR 20/05

```
ARABY  35/26      GALNT  59/27      HOUSE  64/13      IVY D 126/28
IVY D 133/27      IVY D 135/28      GRACE 157/33      GRACE 173/28
DEAD  196/08      DEAD  214/06      DEAD  217/07
SEEMED (69) .................................................  SISTR  12/30
SISTR  13/14      SISTR  15/07      SISTR  16/05      SISTR  17/23
ENCTR  21/02      ENCTR  23/05      ENCTR  23/15      ENCTR  23/16
ENCTR  24/24      ENCTR  26/05      ENCTR  27/09      ENCTR  27/19
ENCTR  27/31      ARABY  31/14      ARABY  31/26      ARABY  32/26
ARABY  35/16      EVELN  36/18      EVELN  38/32      RACE   42/16
RACE   47/11      GALNT  50/11      GALNT  53/05      GALNT  54/12
GALNT  55/26      GALNT  56/18      LITTL  73/14      LITTL  74/21
LITTL  76/01      LITTL  78/16      LITTL  80/24      PARTS  87/05
PARTS  91/30      PARTS  94/09      CLAY   99/06      CLAY  102/30
PNFUL 109/25      PNFUL 109/32      PNFUL 116/29      PNFUL 117/04
PNFUL 117/04      PNFUL 117/16      IVY D 130/04      IVY D 134/01
MOTHR 139/20      MOTHR 140/21      MOTHR 141/01      MOTHR 141/08
GRACE 153/29      GRACE 156/03      GRACE 160/15      GRACE 163/12
GRACE 164/22      GRACE 168/16      GRACE 173/31      DEAD  185/03
DEAD  186/09      DEAD  186/27      DEAD  192/01      DEAD  201/09
DEAD  203/27      DEAD  205/22      DEAD  210/19      DEAD  210/19
DEAD  212/04      DEAD  212/32      DEAD  213/14      DEAD  214/19
SEEMS (4) ....................................................  LITTL  75/30
GRACE 155/17      DEAD  192/25      DEAD  204/32
SEEN (33) ....................................................  SISTR  18/11
ARABY  30/14      ARABY  30/15      ARABY  30/27      EVELN  38/31
RACE   43/32      RACE   44/16      RACE   46/06      GALNT  51/30
GALNT  56/15      GALNT  58/19      GALNT  58/23      GALNT  58/25
GALNT  59/15      GALNT  59/17      HOUSE  64/30      HOUSE  66/19
LITTL  70/01      LITTL  72/07      LITTL  76/14      LITTL  77/07
LITTL  78/28      CLAY  105/26      PNFUL 115/27      MOTHR 146/22
MOTHR 146/23      MOTHR 148/26      GRACE 154/02      GRACE 164/19
DEAD  181/15      DEAD  184/23      DEAD  190/06      DEAD  212/03
SEES (1) .....................................................  IVY D 120/08
SEGMENT (1) ..................................................  GALNT  57/06
SEGOUIN (12) .................................................  RACE   42/18
RACE   43/03      RACE   43/30      RACE   44/18      RACE   44/24
RACE   44/34      RACE   45/06      RACE   45/15      RACE   46/04
RACE   46/07      RACE   46/21      RACE   48/20
SEGOUIN'S (2) ................................................  RACE   45/18
RACE   46/25
SEIZE (3) ....................................................  ENCTR  28/03
EVELN  41/04      DEAD  215/25
SEIZED (5) ...................................................  ARABY  30/28
PARTS  98/04      PNFUL 110/05      DEAD  193/18      DEAD  220/19
SEIZING (1) ..................................................  IVY D 126/13
SELDOM (2) ...................................................  PNFUL 112/17
DEAD  176/21
SELECTED (1) .................................................  IVY D 119/09
SELECTION (1) ................................................  MOTHR 147/16
SELF-CONTAINED (1) ...........................................  HOUSE  63/32
SELF-WON (1) .................................................  DEAD  205/11
SELL (2) .....................................................  IVY D 125/18
IVY D 125/20
SEND (5) .....................................................  HOUSE  66/05
PARTS  86/04      IVY D 127/09      GRACE 155/13      DEAD  197/10
SENDING (5) ..................................................  SISTR  16/27
HOUSE  63/12      HOUSE  65/06      IVY D 128/09      DEAD  191/04
SENIOR (1) ...................................................  DEAD  186/33
SENSATION (5) ................................................  SISTR  12/31
ARABY  31/09      LITTL  84/04      PARTS  87/28      PARTS  87/29
SENSATIONS (1) ...............................................  ENCTR  21/01
SENSE (5) ....................................................  ARABY  35/16
```

HOUSE   67/24   PNFUL 116/01   MOTHR 149/01   DEAD 194/11
SENSES (2) .... ARABY 31/26
   MOTHR 145/07
SENSIBILITY (1) .... PNFUL 109/34
SENSIBLE (3) .... GRACE 157/19
   GRACE 172/22   DEAD 186/32
SENSIBLY (2) .... ENCTR 21/18
   GRACE 171/23
SENSITIVE (1) .... LITTL 80/22
SENT (21) .... EVELN 38/12
   EVELN 41/11   RACE   43/21   RACE   43/23   RACE   43/27
   GALNT 49/07   GALNT 54/01   HOUSE 63/01   HOUSE 63/30
   CLAY   99/13   IVY D 119/29   MOTHR 136/13   MOTHR 137/19
   MOTHR 137/28   MOTHR 137/29   MOTHR 139/01   MOTHR 141/15
   GRACE 151/05   GRACE 156/17   GRACE 156/19   DEAD 215/13
SENTENCE (4) .... PNFUL 108/07
   PNFUL 108/27   GRACE 174/05   DEAD 182/27
SENTENCED (2) .... PNFUL 117/07
   PNFUL 117/17
SENTENCES (3) ....: SISTR 11/20
   LITTL 74/06   PNFUL 112/18
SENTENTIOUSLY (1) .... GRACE 167/32
SENTIMENT (1) .... ENCTR 27/15
SENTIMENTALIST (1) .... DEAD 220/03
SENTIMENTS (1) .... ENCTR 25/05
SENTRIES (1) .... DEAD 196/30
SEPARATION (1) .... HOUSE 61/13
SERAUN (2) .... EVELN 40/16
   EVELN 40/16
SERENE (1) .... RACE   47/15
SERFS (1) .... CLAY 106/05
SERGE (2) .... GALNT 55/24
   IVY D 130/04
SERGEANT (2) .... PNFUL 114/10
   GRACE 161/10
SERIES (2) .... MOTHR 136/04
   MOTHR 138/09
SERIOUS (15) .... ENCTR 23/19
   ARABY 32/25   RACE   44/33   GALNT 50/15   HOUSE 65/08
   LITTL 74/24   LITTL 76/06   PARTS 96/05   CLAY 100/25
   MOTHR 137/06   DEAD 186/27   DEAD 192/24   DEAD 193/34
   DEAD 203/19   DEAD 216/21
SERIOUSLY (2) .... CLAY 102/26
   IVY D 127/24
SERMON (1) .... GRACE 165/03
SERVANT (2) .... HOUSE 64/03
   LITTL 82/09
SERVE (1) .... IVY D 122/30
SERVED (6) .... LITTL 78/07
   PNFUL 116/10   GRACE 150/14   DEAD 182/34   DEAD 198/05
   DEAD 200/10
SERVICE (2) .... ARABY 34/32
   HOUSE 66/06
SERVICES (2) .... EVELN 39/13
   MOTHR 138/16
SERVILITY (1) .... GALNT 52/19
SERVING (1) .... DEAD 197/29
SET (24) .... SISTR   9/07
   SISTR 15/02   SISTR 17/11   ARABY 29/02   EVELN 41/14
   RACE   45/07   GALNT 51/23   GALNT 59/01   HOUSE 62/03
   HOUSE 63/05   LITTL 72/26   LITTL 81/06   PARTS 90/20
   PARTS 91/03   PNFUL 108/34   PNFUL 113/31   IVY D 118/04

GRACE 153/02	GRACE 157/16	GRACE 162/11	GRACE 174/31
DEAD 198/15	DEAD 215/33	DEAD 223/26	
SETTING (2)			GRACE 174/06
DEAD 185/31			
SETTLE (4)			GALNT 52/01
GALNT 58/10	HOUSE 66/13	DEAD 215/28	
SETTLED (6)			CLAY 101/04
GRACE 172/19	GRACE 173/17	DEAD 197/31	DEAD 208/32
DEAD 209/01			
SETTLING (2)			GALNT 60/15
DEAD 208/31			
SEVEN (5)			EVELN 38/11
LITTL 84/27	CLAY 100/04	CLAY 101/26	GRACE 160/12
SEVENTEEN (3)			HOUSE 64/21
IVY D 129/16	DEAD 219/26		
SEVENTH (1)			IVY D 132/27
SEVENTY (2)			GRACE 158/11
GRACE 158/14			
SEVERE (1)			PNFUL 114/17
SEVERELY (2)			PARTS 89/16
DEAD 180/08			
SEWN (1)			PNFUL 108/02
SEXUAL (2)			PNFUL 112/20
PNFUL 112/22			
SH (2)			PARTS 96/27
PARTS 96/27			
'SH (2)			IVY D 133/32
IVY D 133/32			
SHA (3)			GRACE 151/34
GRACE 152/15	GRACE 153/32		
SHABBILY (1)			ENCTR 24/22
SHABBY (3)			HOUSE 61/15
LITTL 71/03	IVY D 125/27		
SHADE (5)			GALNT 52/19
HOUSE 62/32	LITTL 82/21	DEAD 222/26	DEAD 222/26
SHADES (2)			DEAD 180/16
DEAD 223/06			
SHADOW (13)			ARABY 30/15
ARABY 30/17	ARABY 30/19	GALNT 59/04	LITTL 71/33
PARTS 97/11	PNFUL 117/12	IVY D 118/05	MOTHR 143/29
DEAD 187/02	DEAD 209/26	DEAD 209/28	DEAD 210/05
SHADOWS (1)			DEAD 179/25
SHADY (1)			LITTL 72/28
SHAFT (4)			RACE 48/32
DEAD 216/10	DEAD 216/21	DEAD 219/23	
SHAFTS (1)			DEAD 207/08
SHAKE (3)			LITTL 73/17
MOTHR 143/09	GRACE 171/30		
SHAKEN (1)			IVY D 128/17
SHAKESPEARE (1)			DEAD 179/11
SHAKESPEARE'S (1)			GRACE 157/24
SHAKING (5)			IVY D 123/12
MOTHR 147/05	DEAD 177/31	DEAD 185/16	DEAD 193/19
SHAKY (1)			DEAD 185/06
SHALL (5)			PARTS 88/15
PARTS 90/15	DEAD 197/10	DEAD 203/31	DEAD 204/16
SHALLOW (2)			PNFUL 107/06
DEAD 196/23			
SHAM (1)			HOUSE 62/29
SHAME (7)			LITTL 85/19
CLAY 103/33	CLAY 104/27	PNFUL 117/17	IVY D 134/27
IVY D 135/01	DEAD 220/06		

SHAMEFUL (1) .... DEAD 219/33
SHANNON (1) .... DEAD 223/31
SHAPE (1) .... GALNT 49/06
SHAPELESS (1) .... LITTL 75/08
SHAPELY (1) .... IVY D 118/14
SHARE (2) .... DEAD 176/13
    DEAD 193/06
SHARED (2) .... HOUSE 62/13
    PNFUL 110/27
SHARING (1) .... LITTL 80/21
SHARP (5) .... RACE 46/03
    GALNT 59/28   LITTL 71/28   PARTS 87/28   PARTS 89/22
SHARP-FACED (1) .... PARTS 97/16
SHARPLY (1) .... DEAD 198/33
SHAVE (1) .... HOUSE 65/24
SHE (697)
SHEAF (2) .... PNFUL 108/06
    PNFUL 112/17
SHE'D (4) .... GALNT 51/04
    GALNT 51/07   DEAD 180/12 - DEAD 189/03
SHEDS (1) .... EVELN 40/26
SHEEP (1) .... IVY D 126/31
SHEET (2) .... PARTS 90/28
    PNFUL 108/10
SHEETS (3) .... PARTS 88/13
    PNFUL 108/07   DEAD 223/05
SHELBOURNE (2) .... GALNT 56/07
    PARTS 97/10
SHELF (3) .... PNFUL 108/01
    PNFUL 108/03   DEAD 177/34
SHELL (1) .... GRACE 153/25
SHE'LL (2) .... GALNT 53/21
    LITTL 81/23
SHELLEY (4) .... PARTS 87/11
    PARTS 87/12   PARTS 87/13   PARTS 88/22
SHELTER (2) .... EVELN 37/20
    MOTHR 143/29
SHELTERING (1) .... GRACE 153/25
SHELTERS (1) .... DEAD 203/07
SHELVES (5) .... LITTL 71/17
    LITTL 71/22   PNFUL 107/12   PNFUL 107/17   PNFUL 112/15
SHEPHERDED (2) .... RACE 46/21
    DEAD 212/18
SHEPHERDS (1) .... PARTS 93/28
SHEPHERD'S (1) .... PARTS 88/26
SHERIDAN (2) .... HOUSE 62/25
    HOUSE 65/09
SHERIFF'S (2) .... HOUSE 61/15
    HOUSE 63/02
SHERRY (5) .... SISTR 15/02
    SISTR 15/04   SISTR 17/22   DEAD 196/33   DEAD 201/25
SHE'S (12) .... SISTR 16/06
    GALNT 51/08   GALNT 52/15   GALNT 52/16   GALNT 53/08
    GALNT 54/04   PARTS 97/26   MOTHR 149/31   DEAD 181/25
    DEAD 189/04   DEAD 191/04   DEAD 206/27
SHIFTS (1) .... GALNT 58/01
SHILLING (2) .... ARABY 34/28
    DEAD 215/02
SHILLINGS (7) .... EVELN 38/11
    HOUSE 62/11   PARTS 93/03   PARTS 93/04   CLAY 100/12
    MOTHR 147/03   DEAD 188/08
SHIMMERING (1) .... DEAD 213/19

```
SHIN (1) ........................................... DEAD   196/21
SHINING (6) ........................................ EVELN   36/11
      RACE    44/21    LITTL  74/20    CLAY  101/34    IVY D 125/29
      DEAD   212/06
SHIP (1) ........................................... EVELN   39/11
SHIPBUILDING (1) ................................... IVY D 131/33
SHIPS (3) .......................................... ENCTR   21/15
      ENCTR  23/12    EVELN  39/12
SHIRKING (1) ....................................... PARTS   87/14
SHIRT (2) .......................................... HOUSE   66/25
      HOUSE  66/33
SHIRT-FRONT (1) .................................... DEAD   218/19
SHIRT-SLEEVES (1) .................................. IVY D 127/10
SHIVER (1) ......................................... DEAD   207/02
SHIVERED (1) ....................................... ENCTR   25/34
SHIVERING (1) ...................................... DEAD   221/20
SHOCK (3) .......................................... PNFUL 114/20
      PNFUL 116/04    GRACE 153/09
SHOE (2) ........................................... ENCTR   27/34
      MOTHR 146/17
SHOEBOY (3) ........................................ IVY D 123/13
      IVY D 123/22    IVY D 127/08
SHOES (6) .......................................... ENCTR   21/31
      GALNT  50/03    GALNT  56/10    DEAD  178/14    DEAD  178/23
      DEAD   213/05
SHONE (4) .......................................... GALNT   49/05
      GALNT  60/30    HOUSE  67/08    LITTL  75/06
SHONEENS (1) ....................................... IVY D 121/21
SHOOK (24) ......................................... SISTR   14/08
      SISTR  16/16    ENCTR  21/24    ARABY  30/12    RACE   48/23
      GALNT  53/12    LITTL  75/10    LITTL  77/24    LITTL  81/25
      PARTS  91/30    PARTS  94/02    PARTS  98/20    CLAY  101/19
      CLAY  105/04    IVY D 120/17    IVY D 120/30    IVY D 122/12
      MOTHR 137/34    MOTHR 139/16    GRACE 153/11    GRACE 155/11
      GRACE 167/26    GRACE 171/27    DEAD  220/22
SHOOT (1) .......................................... LITTL   79/09
SHOP (24) .......................................... SISTR   11/32
      SISTR  12/13    ENCTR  24/04    GALNT  57/03    GALNT  57/09
      GALNT  57/27    GALNT  58/14    HOUSE  61/04    LITTL  82/17
      LITTL  82/28    LITTL  82/28    LITTL  82/33    PARTS  88/30
      PARTS  94/10    CLAY  102/13    CLAY  102/15    CLAY  102/21
      PNFUL 116/11    PNFUL 116/18    PNFUL 116/34    IVY D 123/23
      GRACE 156/15    GRACE 166/23    DEAD  217/20
SHOP-BOYS (1) ...................................... ARABY   31/06
SHOPS (3) .......................................... ENCTR   23/34
      RACE   43/17    GRACE 172/29
SHOP-WINDOWS (1) ................................... SISTR   12/28
SHORT (21) ......................................... ENCTR   23/20
      ARABY  30/01    RACE   46/33    RACE   47/01    GALNT  55/28
      GALNT  55/32    GALNT  59/26    HOUSE  64/23    HOUSE  68/07
      LITTL  82/15    PARTS  91/33    PNFUL 108/27    IVY D 119/20
      IVY D 125/25    MOTHR 147/03    GRACE 158/20    GRACE 159/28
      GRACE 162/24    DEAD  176/07    DEAD  184/07    DEAD  216/03
SHORTENED (1) ...................................... GRACE 158/01
SHORTEST (1) ....................................... GRACE 158/20
SHORTLY (4) ........................................ LITTL   76/03
      MOTHR 140/16    GRACE 159/21    DEAD  189/05
SHOT (4) ........................................... PARTS   87/04
      PARTS  88/01    DEAD  203/13    DEAD  216/09
SHOULD (26) ........................................ SISTR   13/08
      ENCTR  22/24    ENCTR  24/11    ENCTR  27/31    ENCTR  27/33
      EVELN  40/02    EVELN  40/19    GALNT  59/02    LITTL  76/15
```

LITTL	82/07	LITTL	83/29	PARTS	93/31	CLAY	103/06
PNFUL	112/22	IVY D	121/28	IVY D	132/01	MOTHR	138/09
MOTHR	138/20	MOTHR	138/20	MOTHR	141/06	MOTHR	147/33
DEAD	176/28	DEAD	179/03	DEAD	188/01	DEAD	202/34
DEAD	205/03						

SHOULDER (4) .... ARABY 35/24

| GALNT | 50/02 | PNFUL | 114/17 | DEAD | 178/08 |

SHOULDERS (14) .... RACE 44/08

RACE	46/32	GALNT	60/16	IVY D	124/04	DEAD	177/16
DEAD	183/13	DEAD	184/26	DEAD	194/05	DEAD	208/22
DEAD	213/12	DEAD	215/22	DEAD	217/24	DEAD	219/21
DEAD	223/04						

SHOUT (1) .... RACE 44/11
SHOUTED (8) .... SISTR 14/07

| ENCTR | 23/02 | EVELN | 41/14 | LITTL | 84/18 | PARTS | 98/02 |
| PNFUL | 114/05 | GRACE | 169/33 | DEAD | 209/12 | | |

SHOUTING (1) .... HOUSE 68/15
SHOUTS (1) .... ARABY 30/06
SHOVED (1) .... GALNT 49/14
SHOVEL (1) .... GRACE 161/15
SHOVING (1) .... IVY D 124/03
SHOW (9) .... EVELN 40/30

| CLAY | 106/12 | IVY D | 133/10 | MOTHR | 148/10 | GRACE | 153/22 |
| GRACE | 163/20 | GRACE | 167/19 | DEAD | 210/07 | DEAD | 210/08 |

SHOWED (9) .... SISTR 13/10

| EVELN | 37/15 | LITTL | 77/30 | PARTS | 94/01 | PARTS | 95/33 |
| PNFUL | 113/25 | MOTHR | 139/11 | GRACE | 153/17 | GRACE | 170/02 |

SHOWER (1) .... LITTL 71/07
SHOWERS (1) .... SISTR 12/22
SHOWING (2) .... ENCTR 21/22

| PARTS | 95/30 |

SHOWMAN (1) .... DEAD 193/29
SHOWN (2) .... PNFUL 111/31

| DEAD | 188/29 |

SHREWD (1) .... HOUSE 63/09
SHREWDLY (2) .... SISTR 16/30

| GRACE | 156/14 |

SHREWDNESS (1) .... RACE 45/04
SHRILL (3) .... ARABY 31/05

| PARTS | 86/18 | DEAD | 206/22 |

SHRIVELLED (1) .... DEAD 179/30
SHRUGGED (2) .... DEAD 194/05

| DEAD | 219/20 |

SHUFFLING (3) .... DEAD 177/32

| DEAD | 179/04 | DEAD | 179/13 |

SHUTTERED (1) .... GALNT 49/03
SHUTTERS (1) .... SISTR 12/02
SHY (1) .... DEAD 222/01
SHYNESS (2) .... LITTL 71/21

| CLAY | 101/13 |

SICK (4) .... ENCTR 21/14

| GRACE | 156/22 | DEAD | 189/31 | DEAD | 189/31 |

SICKENING (2) .... GRACE 158/28

| GRACE | 159/01 |

SICKROOM (1) .... EVELN 40/09
SIDE (31) .... SISTR 12/27

SISTR	14/24	ARABY	30/24	ARABY	30/24	ARABY	32/09
ARABY	35/18	EVELN	37/19	EVELN	40/06	GALNT	51/21
GALNT	51/21	GALNT	51/31	GALNT	55/12	GALNT	55/12
GALNT	56/11	GALNT	59/01	GALNT	60/22	HOUSE	64/25
HOUSE	66/25	HOUSE	67/26	HOUSE	68/19	PARTS	88/28
CLAY	106/05	PNFUL	112/33	PNFUL	113/28	PNFUL	114/18

IVY D 124/33	IVY D 133/01	IVY D 133/17	MOTHR 139/18
DEAD 215/14	DEAD 222/21		
SIDEBOARD (5)			SISTR 15/01
DEAD 182/32	DEAD 182/34	DEAD 183/01	DEAD 185/05
SIDE-DISHES (1)			DEAD 196/22
SIDE-DOOR (2)			PARTS 97/13
GRACE 172/04			
SIDE-GLANCES (1)			PNFUL 108/25
SIDE-POCKET (1)			PNFUL 113/09
SIDES (3)			GALNT 51/20
LITTL 72/27	GRACE 164/19		
SIDE-TABLES (1)			CLAY 99/05
SIDE-THRUSTS (1)			GRACE 157/10
SIDEWAYS (5)			GALNT 51/23
GALNT 54/27	IVY D 128/16	IVY D 129/21	DEAD 193/13
SIDLING (1)			DEAD 183/18
SIEGE (2)			ENCTR 19/08
ENCTR 22/30			
SIFTED (1)			GRACE 152/32
SIGH (1)			MOTHR 142/13
SIGHED (5)			SISTR 15/11
SISTR 15/13	IVY D 118/10	GRACE 151/07	DEAD 221/01
SIGHING (1)			PNFUL 113/13
SIGHT (17)			SISTR 18/02
ENCTR 22/22	ENCTR 23/32	ENCTR 26/33	ARABY 34/13
RACE 47/01	HOUSE 68/25	LITTL 74/19	LITTL 74/24
PARTS 93/34	PNFUL 117/24	IVY D 133/06	GRACE 154/33
GRACE 155/30	DEAD 180/18	DEAD 208/07	DEAD 218/18
SIGHTSEERS (1)			RACE 42/03
SIGN (6)			ENCTR 22/14
EVELN 41/16	GALNT 59/16	PNFUL 111/31	MOTHR 145/32
DEAD 176/26			
SIGNAL (1)			DEAD 201/32
SIGNALLED (2)			ENCTR 23/08
DEAD 185/15			
SIGNED (2)			MOTHR 141/04
MOTHR 144/12			
SIGNIFICANT (1)			RACE 44/23
SIGNIFICANTLY (1)			RACE 46/28
SIGNS (4)			ARABY 33/31
LITTL 72/24	LITTL 75/01	DEAD 211/16	
SILENCE (27)			SISTR 17/21
SISTR 17/25	ENCTR 26/22	ARABY 32/18	ARABY 34/31
GALNT 54/20	HOUSE 63/17	LITTL 72/17	LITTL 78/06
PNFUL 112/08	IVY D 126/21	IVY D 133/33	IVY D 135/22
IVY D 135/25	MOTHR 146/20	GRACE 162/24	GRACE 162/33
GRACE 168/23	GRACE 170/10	DEAD 183/24	DEAD 201/18
DEAD 201/32	DEAD 201/33	DEAD 215/14	DEAD 215/20
DEAD 215/29	DEAD 219/24		
SILENCED (1)			MOTHR 137/03
SILENT (25)			ENCTR 25/06
ENCTR 25/25	ENCTR 26/22	ENCTR 27/08	ARABY 30/06
EVELN 41/03	GALNT 50/15	GALNT 53/07	GALNT 54/14
LITTL 72/18	PNFUL 109/18	PNFUL 117/33	PNFUL 117/33
IVY D 120/18	IVY D 122/11	IVY D 122/20	IVY D 130/33
MOTHR 141/14	MOTHR 146/20	GRACE 159/17	GRACE 160/05
GRACE 163/17	DEAD 200/23	DEAD 210/18	DEAD 219/07
SILK (6)			MOTHR 145/24
GRACE 151/08	GRACE 152/03	GRACE 154/02	GRACE 156/09
DEAD 222/30			
SILKEN (1)			LITTL 70/15
SILVER (8)			ENCTR 22/28

ARABY 32/02	GALNT 55/25	CLAY 100/08	MOTHR 138/12
GRACE 155/33	DEAD 196/29	DEAD 223/25	

SIMILAR (2) .... PNFUL 115/13
GRACE 158/10
SIMONIAC (1) .... SISTR 11/30
SIMONY (1) .... SISTR 9/12
SIMPLE (1) .... LITTL 73/33
SIMPLE-MINDED (1) .... GALNT 58/12
SIMPLEST (1) .... SISTR 13/12
SIMPLY (7) .... ENCTR 26/11

HOUSE 64/27	HOUSE 64/30	CLAY 103/02	DEAD 180/18
DEAD 184/20	DEAD 194/09		

SIMULTANEOUSLY (3) .... PARTS 87/02
IVY D 129/26   GRACE 173/09
SIN (4) .... SISTR 11/30

HOUSE 65/31	HOUSE 67/24	HOUSE 67/25	

SINCE (14) .... ENCTR 25/02

GALNT 57/12	GALNT 59/17	HOUSE 64/29	LITTL 70/08
LITTL 74/33	LITTL 75/17	PARTS 92/18	IVY D 119/20
IVY D 120/13	GRACE 154/34	GRACE 156/24	GRACE 166/31
DEAD 176/01			

SINCERE (3) .... LITTL 79/09
DEAD 192/13   DEAD 203/21
SINCERELY (1) .... PNFUL 110/20
SINFUL (1) .... SISTR 9/13
SING (15) .... HOUSE 62/27

CLAY 105/30	CLAY 106/01	PNFUL 109/23	DEAD 184/10
DEAD 191/11	DEAD 193/22	DEAD 194/01	DEAD 199/16
DEAD 199/26	DEAD 210/28	DEAD 210/28	DEAD 211/09
DEAD 218/28	DEAD 219/05		

SINGER (2) .... MOTHR 147/05
DEAD 210/19
SINGERS (3) .... DEAD 199/19
DEAD 203/27   DEAD 205/23
SINGER'S (2) .... DEAD 193/06
DEAD 210/21
SINGING (14) .... ARABY 33/08

RACE 47/17	CLAY 100/14	MOTHR 147/13	DEAD 198/22
DEAD 199/07	DEAD 204/33	DEAD 209/34	DEAD 210/02
DEAD 210/27	DEAD 210/32	DEAD 212/09	DEAD 221/05
DEAD 222/28			

SINGLE (1) .... ARABY 31/09
SINGLE-HANDED (1) .... PARTS 90/29
SINGLY (1) .... HOUSE 63/31
SINICO (8) .... PNFUL 110/08

PNFUL 110/18	PNFUL 111/31	PNFUL 112/19	PNFUL 113/23
PNFUL 114/31	PNFUL 115/04	PNFUL 115/11	

SINNERS (1) .... DEAD 201/11
SINS (3) .... SISTR 13/09
GRACE 170/33   DEAD 201/11
SINUS (1) .... MOTHR 146/27
SIP (2) .... DEAD 183/09
DEAD 183/17
SIPPED (3) .... SISTR 15/30
GALNT 57/28   LITTL 76/18
SIPPING (1) .... SISTR 15/14
SIPS (1) .... LITTL 77/15
SIR (27) .... ENCTR 25/08

ENCTR 25/14	RACE 47/14	GALNT 57/16	PARTS 87/11
PARTS 87/12	PARTS 87/13	PARTS 87/17	PARTS 87/23
PARTS 91/23	IVY D 129/12	IVY D 129/18	GRACE 150/16
GRACE 152/28	GRACE 153/07	GRACE 170/17	DEAD 178/03

```
DEAD    178/29     DEAD    178/29     DEAD    179/01     DEAD    208/15
DEAD    208/15     DEAD    209/15     DEAD    209/19     DEAD    209/21
DEAD    213/27     DEAD    215/04
SIRLOINS (1) ......................................... DEAD    176/20
SIRR (1) ............................................. IVY D  123/16
SISTER (14) .......................................... SISTR   15/09
     ENCTR   21/13     ARABY   29/19     ARABY   30/16     HOUSE   68/17
     LITTL   82/10     MOTHR  137/27     DEAD   179/33     DEAD   181/02
     DEAD   181/27     DEAD   184/20     DEAD   186/27     DEAD   194/27
     DEAD   204/32
SISTERS (3) .......................................... SISTR    9/ T
     EVELN   36/14     EVELN   37/02
SISTER'S (2) ......................................... SISTR   15/03
     DEAD   179/29
SIT (14) ............................................. EVELN   39/32
     GALNT   58/04     GALNT   58/04     HOUSE   65/15     LITTL   75/32
     CLAY   102/02     CLAY   104/04     IVY D  122/25     IVY D  126/05
     IVY D  126/10     IVY D  133/14     MOTHR  138/12     DEAD   177/27
     DEAD   198/01
SITS (1) ............................................. DEAD   208/08
SITTING (19) ......................................... SISTR    9/16
     SISTR   12/13     SISTR   18/07     ENCTR   22/05     ARABY   33/16
     HOUSE   66/25     HOUSE   67/26     PARTS   90/04     PARTS   93/20
     PNFUL  109/17     PNFUL  116/30     IVY D  119/18     IVY D  119/19
     IVY D  135/27     GRACE  167/03     GRACE  172/27     DEAD   190/14
     DEAD   222/29     DEAD   222/31
SITUATION (1) ........................................ GALNT   59/11
SIX (8) .............................................. LITTL   77/29
     PARTS   93/03     PARTS   93/04     CLAY   100/03     CLAY   101/26
     PNFUL  116/11     GRACE  157/16   · DEAD   194/16
SIXPENCE (6) ......................................... ENCTR   21/11
     ENCTR   21/21     ENCTR   21/22     ENCTR   22/16     ARABY   35/28
     EVELN   40/08
SIXPENNY (1) ......................................... ARABY   34/26
SIXTH (1) ............................................ IVY D  119/20
SIXTY (1) ............................................ PNFUL  111/11
SIXTY-FIVE (1) ....................................... SISTR   12/08
SIZE (1) ............................................. DEAD   184/20
SKERRIES (2) ......................................... MOTHR  137/23
     MOTHR  137/24
SKETCH (1) ........................................... LITTL   78/14
SKIN (6) ............................................. HOUSE   67/10
     IVY D  124/25     MOTHR  149/30     DEAD   182/19     DEAD   196/19
     DEAD   210/25
SKIP (1) ............................................. LITTL   79/32
SKIPPED (1) .......................................... GALNT   53/19
SKIPS (1) ............................................ GALNT   51/17
SKIRT (9) ............................................ SISTR   14/22
     GALNT   55/24     CLAY   101/27     CLAY   101/27     MOTHR  147/04
     DEAD   209/28     DEAD   210/08     DEAD   213/06     DEAD   215/23
SKIRTS (2) ........................................... DEAD   179/03
     DEAD   202/06
SKIT (1) ............................................. ENCTR   23/11
SKULL (1) ............................................ PARTS   87/25
SKY (5) .............................................. ARABY   30/03
     GALNT   54/11     DEAD   212/32     DEAD   213/03     DEAD   214/22
SLACKENED (1) ........................................ PNFUL  113/11
SLAIN (1) ............................................ IVY D  134/11
SLAKE (1) ............................................ PARTS   88/18
SLANG (1) ............................................ ENCTR   22/12
SLANTED (1) .......................................... ENCTR   22/01
SLAP (1) ............................................. ENCTR   27/13
```

SLAPPED (1) .... LITTL 79/17
SLATE-BLUE (1) .... LITTL 81/11
SLATE-COLOUR (1) .... LITTL 75/05
SLATTERNLY (2) .... GALNT 57/14
   GALNT 58/13
SLAVED (1) .... DEAD 194/22
SLAVEY (2) .... GALNT 50/33
   GALNT 52/22
SLAVING (1) .... DEAD 194/15
SLEEP (3) .... ARABY 34/01
   HOUSE 61/11   IVY D 135/09
SLEEPILY (1) .... DEAD 223/24
SLEEPING (3) .... ARABY 32/13
   HOUSE 67/14   LITTL 82/19
SLEEPY (2) .... CLAY 105/29
   DEAD 184/31
SLEEVE (4) .... PARTS 95/33
   PARTS 98/11   IVY D 129/20   GRACE 173/20
SLEEVES (3) .... LITTL 83/06
   CLAY 101/03   PNFUL 116/07
SLENDER (2) .... IVY D 120/26
   MOTHR 142/17
SLEPT (3) .... ENCTR 21/26
   DEAD 201/04   DEAD 222/09
SLICE (3) .... CLAY 102/27
   DEAD 197/11   DEAD 197/12
SLICES (3) .... CLAY 99/08
   CLAY 101/08   DEAD 197/22
SLIGHT (1) .... LITTL 73/01
SLIGHTING (1) .... DEAD 187/03
SLIGHTLY (10) .... LITTL 70/11
   LITTL 74/23   LITTL 81/16   PARTS 86/12   MOTHR 137/13
   MOTHR 144/24   GRACE 172/11   DEAD 178/22   DEAD 181/09
   DEAD 190/16
SLIM (2) .... HOUSE 62/31
   DEAD 177/24
SLIP (4) .... ARABY 31/27
   RACE 47/20   GALNT 59/15   DEAD 182/06
SLIPPED (3) .... MOTHR 138/23
   DEAD 177/18   DEAD 221/18
SLIPPERS (1) .... HOUSE 67/09
SLIPPING (1) .... DEAD 218/04
SLIPS (1) .... CLAY 100/29
SLOPE (5) .... ENCTR 24/33
   ENCTR 26/17   ENCTR 28/02   ENCTR 28/04   PNFUL 117/12
SLOPING (2) .... ENCTR 24/07
   IVY D 130/05
SLOW (2) .... PNFUL 113/26
   DEAD 179/26
SLOWLY (37) .... SISTR 12/27
   SISTR 16/16   SISTR 17/25   ENCTR 23/32   ENCTR 24/20
   ENCTR 24/29   ENCTR 24/30   ENCTR 24/34   ENCTR 26/10
   ENCTR 26/19   ENCTR 26/21   ENCTR 27/10   ARABY 33/01
   ARABY 34/17   ARABY 35/27   RACE 45/21   GALNT 56/11
   GALNT 59/12   GALNT 60/02   GALNT 60/29   PARTS 96/07
   PARTS 96/19   PNFUL 114/02   PNFUL 117/24   IVY D 118/06
   IVY D 119/26   IVY D 124/08   IVY D 133/08   MOTHR 145/08
   GRACE 151/16   GRACE 173/21   DEAD 181/08   DEAD 184/15
   DEAD 193/16   DEAD 216/07   DEAD 216/20   DEAD 224/02
SLUNG (2) .... GALNT 50/02
   GALNT 50/04
SLUSH (1) .... DEAD 213/06

SLUSHY (1) .... DEAD 212/33
SMACKED (1) .... LITTL 81/06
SMACKING (1) .... IVY D 131/26
SMAHAN (1) .... PARTS 96/29
SMALL (31) .... ENCTR 22/25
   GALNT 53/29   GALNT 60/30   HOUSE 62/19   HOUSE 62/32
   HOUSE 66/02   LITTL 70/13   LITTL 80/12   LITTL 80/16
   PARTS 93/34   PARTS 94/22   PARTS 95/03   CLAY 99/10
   PNFUL 108/33   IVY D 121/02   MOTHR 137/16   MOTHR 138/21
   MOTHR 141/25   GRACE 150/14   GRACE 151/18   GRACE 154/24
   GRACE 155/04   GRACE 156/26   GRACE 159/26   GRACE 166/23
   GRACE 166/32   GRACE 167/02   GRACE 167/04   DEAD 179/22
   DEAD 196/28   DEAD 197/12
SMALLER (1) .... DEAD 183/01
SMALLEST (2) .... DEAD 193/05
   DEAD 197/04
SMART (4) .... PARTS 93/22
   CLAY 104/06   IVY D 121/09 · DEAD 198/19
SMARTED (1) .... GRACE 159/30
SMARTLY (1) .... GRACE 156/08
SMEAR (1) .... IVY D 135/03
SMEARED (1) .... GRACE 150/05
SMELL (1) .... IVY D 128/04
SMILE (15) .... SISTR 13/21
   SISTR 13/24   ARABY 34/03   GALNT 52/06   PARTS 91/28
   CLAY 102/25   MOTHR 140/14   MOTHR 143/23   DEAD 180/32
   DEAD 183/11   DEAD 188/02   DEAD 188/21   DEAD 194/13
   DEAD 205/04   DEAD 218/33
SMILED (16) .... SISTR 11/27
   SISTR 13/26   ENCTR 25/20   ENCTR 25/28   GALNT 53/13
   LITTL 70/17   LITTL 79/01   LITTL 79/19   CLAY 103/10
   MOTHR 139/15   MOTHR 139/27   DEAD 177/23   DEAD 190/10
   DEAD 193/26   DEAD 202/03   DEAD 202/29
SMILES (1) .... RACE 42/14
SMILING (19) .... SISTR 11/29
   SISTR 14/24   SISTR 14/27   ENCTR 22/06   GALNT 60/29
   HOUSE 68/14   PARTS 94/05   MOTHR 146/26   GRACE 171/01
   DEAD 182/25   DEAD 183/10   DEAD 187/28   DEAD 192/30
   DEAD 192/33   DEAD 194/18   DEAD 198/05   DEAD 204/23
   DEAD 211/29   DEAD 218/30
SMITH (1) .... ENCTR 26/29
SMOKE (8) .... SISTR 12/20
   ENCTR 23/09   RACE 46/31   GALNT 51/07   GALNT 59/19
   LITTL 78/04   LITTL 78/09   MOTHR 144/34
SMOKED (2) .... PNFUL 116/14
   IVY D 119/26
SMOKING (1) .... SISTR 9/16
SMOOTH (1) .... GALNT 54/03
SMOOTHED (2) .... SISTR 15/34
   ARABY 30/11
SMOOTHING (4) .... ENCTR 22/29
   PARTS 90/05   DEAD 182/31   DEAD 217/29
SMOOTHLY (2) .... RACE 45/08
   MOTHR 138/31
SMOTE (1) .... IVY D 134/28
SMOTHERED (1) .... SISTR 12/14
SMOULDERING (1) .... PARTS 96/32
SMYRNA (1) .... DEAD 196/27
SNATCHED (1) .... LITTL 85/05
SNIFFED (1) .... PARTS 93/13
SNORTING (1) .... RACE 45/17
SNOW (18) .... DEAD 177/05

```
        DEAD   177/16      DEAD   180/13      DEAD   192/05      DEAD   202/07
        DEAD   202/10      DEAD   202/11      DEAD   211/22      DEAD   211/24
        DEAD   211/25      DEAD   211/27      DEAD   211/28      DEAD   212/34
        DEAD   214/32      DEAD   222/25      DEAD   223/24      DEAD   223/27
        DEAD   224/02
SNOW-COVERED (1)  ...............................  DEAD   206/21
SNOWING (1)  ....................................  DEAD   177/21
SNOW-STIFFENED (1)  .............................  DEAD   177/19
SNUFF (4)  ......................................  SISTR  12/19
        SISTR  12/22      SISTR  13/25      SISTR  16/28
SNUFF-BOX (1)  ..................................  SISTR  12/17
SNUFFLE (1)  ....................................  IVY D  123/07
SNUFFLED (1)  ...................................  IVY D  124/19
SNUFFLING (1)  ..................................  IVY D  122/21
SNUFF-STAINS (1)  ...............................  SISTR  12/24
SNUG (4)  .......................................  RACE   46/07
        GALNT  58/10      PARTS  88/30      PARTS  89/04
SO (173)
SOB (1)  ........................................  LITTL  84/23
SOBBED (1)  .....................................  LITTL  84/25
SOBBING (3)  ....................................  LITTL  85/02
        LITTL  85/21      DEAD   221/32
SOBER (5)  ......................................  ENCTR  20/31
        LITTL  73/25      PARTS  97/17      PNFUL  110/34      MOTHR  137/09
SOBERED (1)  ....................................  GRACE  153/09
SOBS (2)  .......................................  LITTL  84/27
        DEAD   221/31
SOCIAL (4)  .....................................  HOUSE  64/24
        PNFUL  109/11     PNFUL  111/07     GRACE  154/18
SOCIALIST (1)  ..................................  PNFUL  110/33
SOCIETY (9)  ....................................  RACE   43/31
        LITTL  78/22      PNFUL  109/02     PNFUL  110/24      MOTHR  136/01
        MOTHR  137/17     MOTHR  138/10     MOTHR  139/15      MOTHR  141/07
SOD (1)  ........................................  GRACE  167/32
SODA (1)  .......................................  LITTL  74/30
SODDEN (1)  .....................................  ARABY  31/24
SOFA (1)  .......................................  SISTR  15/08
SOFA-PILLOW (1)  ................................  SISTR  16/04
SOFT (11)  ......................................  ENCTR  26/03
        ENCTR  26/03      ENCTR  26/07      ARABY  30/24      RACE   43/13
        RACE   47/09      HOUSE  62/31      CLAY   105/13     MOTHR  139/17
        DEAD   188/25     DEAD   215/20
SOFTER (1)  .....................................  DEAD   204/01
SOFTLY (10)  ....................................  SISTR  9/10
        SISTR  18/08      GALNT  56/21      HOUSE  67/31      MOTHR  142/29
        DEAD   214/12     DEAD   218/06     DEAD   218/09     DEAD   223/29
        DEAD   223/30
SOIL (1)  .......................................  PNFUL  111/18
SOLDIER (1)  ....................................  DEAD   199/10
SOLDIERS (1)  ...................................  EVELN  40/25
SOLDIERS' (1)  ..................................  HOUSE  62/18
SOLE (1)  .......................................  PNFUL  107/16
SOLEMN (4)  .....................................  SISTR  14/27
        SISTR  18/11      GRACE  170/10     DEAD   187/28
SOLEMNITY (1)  ..................................  ENCTR  23/19
SOLES (1)  ......................................  DEAD   179/13
SOLICITOUS (1)  .................................  GRACE  174/08
SOLICITS (1)  ...................................  IVY D  119/12
SOLICITUDE (2)  .................................  PNFUL  110/30
        DEAD   180/24
SOLID (4)  ......................................  RACE   44/26
        GALNT  55/13      DEAD   196/26     DEAD   223/20
```

SOLIDLY (1) .... RACE   42/10
SOLITARY (2) .... GALNT   50/13
   MOTHR 143/17
SOLUTION (1) .... CLAY 103/30
SOMBRE (3) .... ARABY 30/03
   GALNT 57/01   PNFUL 107/04
SOME (135)
SOMEBODY (2) .... CLAY 105/16
   DEAD 206/05
SOMEONE (10) .... ENCTR 21/17
   RACE   48/15   RACE   48/16   GALNT   51/26   IVY D 120/18
   MOTHR 143/19   MOTHR 148/33   DEAD 201/31   DEAD 206/32
   DEAD 219/03
SOMETHING (61) .... SISTR 10/01
   SISTR   10/01   SISTR   11/24   SISTR   12/32   SISTR   16/31
   SISTR   17/30   SISTR   18/16   ENCTR 24/31   ENCTR 26/01
   ENCTR 26/08   ENCTR 26/13   ARABY 32/12   EVELN 40/24
   GALNT   52/29   GALNT   55/13   HOUSE 63/13   HOUSE 64/30
   HOUSE 65/12   LITTL 70/07   LITTL 71/21   LITTL 72/30
   LITTL 73/20   LITTL 75/14   LITTL 77/02   LITTL 78/32
   LITTL 80/26   LITTL 80/27   LITTL 83/11   LITTL 83/19
   PARTS 87/34   PARTS 90/26   PARTS 90/30   PARTS 91/07
   PARTS 95/12   CLAY 102/17   CLAY 103/22   CLAY 103/23
   CLAY 105/16   CLAY 105/17   IVY D 120/12   MOTHR 140/13
   MOTHR 141/24   MOTHR 145/15   MOTHR 145/32   GRACE 152/01
   GRACE 158/32   GRACE 164/22   DEAD 184/16   DEAD 186/06
   DEAD 186/29   DEAD 191/10   DEAD 193/26   DEAD 199/07
   DEAD 201/26   DEAD 209/30   DEAD 210/04   DEAD 213/13
   DEAD 213/15   DEAD 214/15   DEAD 217/09   DEAD 220/33
SOMETIMES (20) .... SISTR 13/07
   SISTR   13/22   ENCTR 20/12   EVELN 38/01   EVELN 39/26
   GALNT   58/22   HOUSE 66/19   LITTL 72/15   LITTL 75/13
   PNFUL 109/05   PNFUL 110/29   PNFUL 111/23   PNFUL 116/14
   MOTHR 137/10   GRACE 156/17   GRACE 159/20   GRACE 165/14
   DEAD 176/30   DEAD 199/12   DEAD 203/23
SOMEWAY (1) .... IVY D 119/31
SOMEWHAT (9) .... SISTR 15/07
   GALNT   59/13   HOUSE 64/11   LITTL 77/01   PARTS 94/10
   MOTHR 141/19   MOTHR 146/21   GRACE 156/31   GRACE 161/18
SOMEWHERE (4) .... EVELN 38/09
   GALNT   52/27   PARTS 92/28   DEAD 207/33
SON (10) .... RACE   43/22
   RACE   45/33   GALNT   51/19   HOUSE 62/16   LITTL 79/15
   MOTHR 142/18   GRACE 159/34   DEAD 179/33   DEAD 200/24
   DEAD 208/28
SONG (13) .... CLAY 105/30
   CLAY 105/33   CLAY 106/13   MOTHR 149/19   DEAD 193/01
   DEAD 193/08   DEAD 210/18   DEAD 210/28   DEAD 212/08
   DEAD 218/14   DEAD 218/23   DEAD 218/29   DEAD 219/05
SONG-BOOK (1) .... DEAD 193/11
SONGS (2) .... HOUSE 62/22
   CLAY 105/31
SON-IN-LAW (2) .... DEAD 191/24
   DEAD 191/25
SONOROUSLY (1) .... LITTL 79/17
SONS (5) .... IVY D 120/09
   IVY D 121/32   GRACE 156/14   GRACE 156/17   DEAD 186/31
SON'S (2) .... PARTS 97/33
   DEAD 190/16
SOON (21) .... SISTR 10/06
   ENCTR 22/21   GALNT   54/03   GALNT   59/02   HOUSE 61/04
   HOUSE 64/19   PARTS 88/25   PARTS 92/29   CLAY   99/01

CLAY 104/32	CLAY 105/23	MOTHR 138/03	MOTHR 144/04
MOTHR 148/20	GRACE 159/22	DEAD 180/32	DEAD 191/04
DEAD 197/28	DEAD 222/26	DEAD 222/29	DEAD 223/03

SOONER (1) .... PARTS 92/32
SOOT (1) .... LITTL 73/15
SOOTHE (1) .... LITTL 84/25
SOOTHINGLY (1) ....,.... CLAY 99/12
SOPRANO (3) .... MOTHR 143/20
   GRACE 158/18   DEAD 176/14
   DEAD 194/27
SORE (2) .... LITTL 76/07
SORROW (1) .... PNFUL 112/07
SORRY (11) .... SISTR 10/12

ARABY 33/21	ARABY 34/06	LITTL 79/25	LITTL 79/27
CLAY 101/17	CLAY 104/26	MOTHR 148/14	GRACE 155/12
DEAD 192/18	DEAD 212/14		

SORT (4) .... HOUSE 68/16
   CLAY 104/11   IVY D 129/05   DEAD 217/02
SOTTISH (1) .... DEAD 217/16
SOUGHT (2) .... ENCTR 21/07
   MOTHR 140/29
SOUL (17) .... SISTR 10/24

SISTR 11/25	SISTR 17/12	ARABY 32/19	LITTL 73/09
LITTL 73/30	LITTL 73/30	LITTL 84/03	IVY D 123/19
IVY D 130/18	MOTHR 138/13	DEAD 207/28	DEAD 214/03
DEAD 217/17	DEAD 222/13	DEAD 223/17	DEAD 224/01

SOUL'S (2) .... PNFUL 111/28
   PNFUL 115/26
SOULS' (1) .... DEAD 214/04
SOUND (12) .... SISTR 18/10

ENCTR 27/13	ARABY 31/22	GALNT 55/13	LITTL 72/19
LITTL 84/25	PNFUL 111/24	PNFUL 113/13	IVY D 135/09
DEAD 186/08	DEAD 193/25	DEAD 206/22	

SOUNDED (3) .... SISTR 9/11
   SISTR 9/13   DEAD 193/09
SOUNDS (1) .... MOTHR 146/01
SOUP (1) .... SISTR 16/32
SOUR (1) .... DEAD 190/07
SOURCES (1) .... GRACE 159/18
SOUTH (1) .... GALNT 52/26
SOVEREIGN (1) .... DEAD 217/03
SOWN (1) .... HOUSE 66/07
SPACE (3) .... ARABY 30/03
   RACE 44/14   LITTL 80/21
SPACIOUS (2) .... DEAD 203/28
   DEAD 203/29
SPAKE (1) .... PNFUL 112/16
SPAN (1) .... CLAY 99/03
SPANKING (1) .... DEAD 207/08
SPARED (3) .... LITTL 78/19
   MOTHR 148/06   GRACE 154/07
SPARK (2) .... IVY D 122/23
   IVY D 124/31
SPARKLED (1) .... CLAY 101/13
SPASM (2) .... LITTL 84/20
   PARTS 87/26
SPAT (3) .... SISTR 10/28
   IVY D 124/19   GRACE 154/14
SPEAK (18) .... ENCTR 26/02

ENCTR 27/08	ARABY 31/16	GALNT 56/29	HOUSE 65/07
HOUSE 66/28	HOUSE 69/05	LITTL 74/13	CLAY 104/27
IVY D 123/21	MOTHR 141/02	MOTHR 144/06	MOTHR 144/18

	MOTHR 149/06	GRACE 174/12	GRACE 174/13	DEAD	198/08
	DEAD 203/31				
SPEAKER (2)	....			GRACE	159/18
	DEAD 202/17				
SPEAKING (12)	....			SISTR	17/15
	ENCTR 24/17	EVELN 40/23	GALNT 54/17	GALNT	59/27
	CLAY 102/08	IVY D 126/06	IVY D 127/15	MOTHR	145/28
	MOTHR 146/09	GRACE 170/18	GRACE 174/12		
SPEAKS (2)	....			IVY D	120/09
	GRACE 168/30				
SPEARS (1)	....			DEAD	224/01
SPECIAL (5)	....			ARABY	34/20
	CLAY 103/22	MOTHR 137/29	MOTHR 141/13	GRACE	166/28
SPECIALLY (2)	....			GRACE	167/04
	GRACE 173/31				
SPECIALS (1)	....			PARTS	95/03
SPECK (2)	....			GRACE	172/13
	GRACE 173/14				
SPECTACLE (3)	....			ENCTR	23/07
	PARTS 93/10	GRACE 152/13			
SPECTATORS (2)	....			RACE	44/22
	PARTS 96/20				
SPECTRAL (1)	....			LITTL	71/34
SPED (1)	....			RACE	42/05
SPEECH (14)	....			ENCTR	26/09
	ENCTR 27/09	RACE 47/33	RACE 47/33	RACE	48/01
	GALNT 51/33	DEAD 179/08	DEAD 179/19	DEAD	183/24
	DEAD 191/29	DEAD 192/09	DEAD 192/19	DEAD	211/15
	DEAD 222/23				
SPEECHLESS (1)	....			DEAD	209/09
SPEED (1)	....			IVY D	123/08
SPELL (2)	....			EVELN	40/12
	PARTS 91/03				
SPEND (3)	....			GALNT	52/29
	LITTL 79/21	PARTS 89/29			
SPENT (9)	....			ENCTR	22/34
	GALNT 58/20	PARTS 92/28	PARTS 97/03	PNFUL	109/03
	PNFUL 111/16	IVY D 119/17	IVY D 123/21	DEAD	208/30
SPICED (2)	....			DEAD	196/21
	DEAD 197/16				
SPICK (1)	....			CLAY	99/03
SPICY (1)	....			LITTL	77/20
SPIKES (1)	....			ARABY	32/06
SPILLING (1)	....			SISTR	12/18
SPIRIT (8)	....			ENCTR	20/01
	GALNT 57/33	GALNT 58/10	IVY D 135/14	MOTHR	145/05
	DEAD 193/03	DEAD 204/14	DEAD 204/15		
SPIRITS (4)	....			RACE	42/16
	RACE 44/06	CLAY 104/34	PNFUL 115/05		
SPIRITUAL (5)	....			PNFUL	109/09
	GRACE 162/31	GRACE 163/18	GRACE 174/14	GRACE	174/16
SPITE (8)	....			RACE	44/25
	RACE 46/26	GALNT 50/18	LITTL 72/31	CLAY	101/33
	PNFUL 112/04	MOTHR 136/09	DEAD 215/01		
SPITS (1)	....			PNFUL	116/15
SPITTING (1)	....			PNFUL	116/14
SPITTLE (1)	....			SISTR	11/28
SPLENDID (7)	....			ARABY	31/33
	IVY D 133/25	GRACE 165/16	DEAD 175/18	DEAD	189/01
	DEAD 189/03	DEAD 191/25			
SPOILS (1)	....			LITTL	74/31
SPOKE (33)	....			SISTR	15/09

ENCTR	22/12	ENCTR	26/11	ENCTR	26/13	ENCTR	27/04
ARABY	31/16	ARABY	31/30	ARABY	32/02	GALNT	51/32
GALNT	55/17	GALNT	57/19	HOUSE	62/09	HOUSE	62/34
LITTL	72/06	CLAY	104/25	CLAY	105/14	PNFUL	111/17
MOTHR	142/28	MOTHR	143/13	MOTHR	145/34	MOTHR	146/08
MOTHR	146/10	GRACE	152/08	GRACE	159/31	GRACE	166/26
GRACE	170/03	DEAD	188/27	DEAD	190/22	DEAD	192/17
DEAD	200/25	DEAD	201/03	DEAD	214/20	DEAD	220/09

SPOKEN (5) .... ARABY 30/32
    ARABY 35/16   PNFUL 115/20   IVY D 118/15   DEAD 187/04
SPONDULICS (1) .... IVY D 122/10
SPONGE (1) .... PARTS 95/27
SPONGING (1) .... IVY D 124/30
SPOON (2) .... GRACE 161/14
    GRACE 161/15
SPOONFULS (1) .... DEAD 200/10
SPOONING (1) .... LITTL 81/22
SPOONS (2) .... DEAD 182/33
    DEAD 200/09
SPORTING (1) .... GALNT 50/23
SPORTSMAN (1) .... IVY D 132/18
SPOTS (2) .... IVY D 125/31
    IVY D 130/14
SPOTTED (1) .... GALNT 50/31
SPRANG (2) .... ENCTR 26/33
    ARABY 31/11
SPRAWLED (1) .... PNFUL 116/19
SPREAD (2) .... LITTL 72/17
    IVY D 118/02
SPRIGS (1) .... DEAD 196/18
SPRING (4) .... HOUSE 61/04
    PNFUL 114/26   DEAD 201/15   DEAD 220/27
SPURIOUS (1) .... RACE 46/20
SPURNED (1) .... IVY D 135/04
SPURS (1) .... IVY D 135/11
SPY (1) .... IVY D 124/22
SPYING (1) .... IVY D 124/34
SQUABBLE (1) .... EVELN 38/10
SQUAD (1) .... DEAD 197/04
SQUADS (1) .... DEAD 197/01
SQUALID (2) .... ENCTR 24/02
    PNFUL 115/25
SQUANDER (1) .... EVELN 38/14
SQUARE (13) .... SISTR 9/03
    ARABY 29/04   RACE 47/26   GALNT 49/09   GALNT 56/11
    GALNT 56/34   GALNT 59/20   CLAY 102/32   PNFUL 107/11
    DEAD 176/16   DEAD 182/30   DEAD 182/34   DEAD 196/34
SQUARED (1) .... GRACE 160/19
SQUAT (2) .... GALNT 49/13
    DEAD 196/32
SQUATTED (1) .... LITTL 71/31
SQUEAKING (1) .... DEAD 177/18
SQUEAL (1) .... PARTS 98/19
SQUEEZED (1) .... GALNT 50/34
SQUEEZING (1) .... RACE 47/08
SQUINT (1) .... GALNT 54/26
STABLE (1) .... ENCTR 19/05
STABLES (1) .... ARABY 30/11
STAGE (4) .... ENCTR 21/20
    PNFUL 108/05   MOTHR 139/14   DEAD 196/13
STAGE-WARDROBE (1) .... MOTHR 147/14
STAIRCASE (8) .... SISTR 14/10

```
      ARABY   33/06     HOUSE   68/08     MOTHR 145/19     DEAD   196/04
      DEAD   196/09     DEAD   209/25     DEAD   210/31
STAIRS (26) ............................................. GALNT   56/15
      HOUSE   67/32     HOUSE   68/04     PARTS   88/27     PARTS   89/10
      PARTS   97/19     IVY D  126/16     GRACE  150/03     GRACE  150/10
      GRACE  152/27     GRACE  152/34     DEAD   175/10     DEAD   177/06
      DEAD   177/09     DEAD   178/32     DEAD   178/33     DEAD   181/28
      DEAD   182/09     DEAD   182/11     DEAD   184/32     DEAD   210/05
      DEAD   210/15     DEAD   215/19     DEAD   215/21     DEAD   215/21
      DEAD   215/27
STAKE (1) .............................................. RACE   44/32
STALE (1) .............................................. LITTL   82/07
STALK (1) .............................................. DEAD   200/21
STALKS (1) ............................................. DEAD   196/30
STALK-SHAPED (1) ....................................... DEAD   196/25
STALL (3) .............................................. ARABY   35/05
      ARABY   35/18     ARABY   35/25
STALLS (3) ............................................. ARABY   34/30
      ARABY   34/33     ARABY   35/04
STAMMER (1) ............................................ LITTL   85/11
STAMPING (6) ........................................... RACE   47/17
      MOTHR 146/02     MOTHR 146/14     MOTHR 146/31     GRACE 155/21
      DEAD   177/32
STAMPS (1) ............................................. ARABY   33/18
STAND (14) ............................................. GALNT   59/04
      PARTS   86/09     PARTS   88/03     CLAY   102/29     CLAY   105/32
      IVY D  120/02     IVY D  123/01     MOTHR 143/27     MOTHR 149/17
      GRACE  151/34     GRACE  161/10     GRACE  171/16     DEAD   176/23
      DEAD   186/07
STANDING (28) .......................................... EVELN   38/33
      RACE    48/32     GALNT   54/22     GALNT   59/34     LITTL   82/29
      PARTS   89/17     PARTS   91/06     PARTS   95/04     PARTS   96/20
      PARTS   98/09     IVY D  127/29     DEAD   180/24     DEAD   183/02
      DEAD   186/12     DEAD   188/18     DEAD   202/07     DEAD   206/04
      DEAD   208/26     DEAD   209/26     DEAD   210/04     DEAD   210/16
      DEAD   212/01     DEAD   213/20     DEAD   213/22     DEAD   215/07
      DEAD   216/16     DEAD   221/24     DEAD   223/16
STANDS (3) ............................................. SISTR   11/05
      IVY D  130/01     GRACE  163/28
STANZA (1) ............................................. LITTL   84/11
STAR (1) ............................................... GRACE 156/06
STARCH (2) ............................................. DEAD   207/20
      DEAD   207/21
STARE (2) .............................................. PARTS   88/14
      MOTHR 139/31
STARED (7) ............................................. GALNT   51/24
      GALNT   60/27     HOUSE   68/03     PARTS   87/25     PARTS   90/14
      CLAY   103/02     DEAD   196/09
STARING (7) ............................................ SISTR   10/11
      ARABY   33/04     PARTS   93/11     PARTS   95/19     IVY D  124/10
      IVY D  130/06     DEAD   190/31
STARS (2) .............................................. DEAD   213/16
      DEAD   213/32
START (4) .............................................. RACE   43/05
      PNFUL 114/04     DEAD   190/10     DEAD   212/18
STARTED (4) ............................................ EVELN   39/10
      GALNT   59/23     HOUSE   69/01     LITTL   85/22
STARTLED (1) ........................................... MOTHR 143/29
STATE (2) .............................................. SISTR   14/33
      MOTHR 142/21
STATED (4) ............................................. PNFUL 113/29
      PNFUL 114/03     PNFUL 114/16     PNFUL 114/32
```

```
STATES (1) ......................................... RACE    47/32
STATESMEN (1) ...................................... IVY D  134/21
STATION (9) ........................................ ARABY   34/13
    ARABY   34/17    ARABY   34/18    EVELN   40/22   EVELN   40/25
    RACE    47/12    PNFUL  113/24    PNFUL  114/26   PNFUL  117/22
STATUE (4) ......................................... GRACE  170/17
    DEAD   208/07    DEAD   208/10    DEAD   214/31
STATURE (2) ........................................ LITTL   70/12
    PNFUL  111/25
STAY (6) ........................................... ARABY   35/25
    MOTHR  145/01    MOTHR  145/10    DEAD   188/33   DEAD   195/13
    DEAD   195/15
STAYED (1) ......................................... PARTS   90/03
STAYING (1) ........................................ RACE    45/19
STEADIED (1) ....................................... HOUSE   67/11
STEADILY (1) ....................................... GRACE  158/05
STEADY (1) ......................................... PNFUL  109/31
STEALING (1) ....................................... CLAY   103/29
STEALTHILY (1) ..................................... PNFUL  110/17
STEAMING (4) ....................................... EVELN   40/32
    CLAY   101/02    CLAY   101/03    DEAD   208/22
STEED (1) .......................................... ARABY   34/10
STEERED (2) ........................................ RACE    45/20
    PARTS   97/10
STEM (1) ........................................... SISTR   15/14
STEMS (2) .......................................... ENCTR   24/19
    GALNT   55/31
STEP (7) ........................................... GALNT   49/12
    HOUSE   68/02    HOUSE   68/02    LITTL   73/24   PARTS   86/14
    PARTS   98/08    DEAD   177/27
STEPHEN'S (4) ...................................... RACE    46/30
    GALNT   54/18    GALNT   56/24    GALNT   60/07
STEPPED (1) ........................................ LITTL   73/23
STEPPING (1) ....................................... GALNT   56/10
STEPS (13) ......................................... ENCTR   24/29
    ARABY   30/20    GALNT   59/26    GALNT   59/33   GALNT   60/01
    GALNT   60/03    GALNT   60/06    LITTL   71/30   DEAD   195/27
    DEAD   208/28    DEAD   209/32    DEAD   211/02   DEAD   215/28
STERN (4) .......................................... ENCTR   23/24
    GALNT   50/26    GALNT   60/23    HOUSE   62/08
STERNNESS (1) ...................................... ARABY   32/23
STEWARD (1) ........................................ MOTHR  142/02
STEWARDS (4) ....................................... MOTHR  142/01
    MOTHR  145/20    MOTHR  147/24    MOTHR  147/32
STEWARDS' (1) ...................................... MOTHR  139/12
STICK (8) .......................................... ENCTR   24/21
    ENCTR   24/30    EVELN   36/16    PARTS   98/17   PARTS   98/19
    PNFUL  113/08    PNFUL  113/11    IVY D  120/02
STIFF (2) .......................................... GRACE  163/20
    DEAD   182/18
STIFFLY (1) ........................................ MOTHR  143/27
STILL (63) ......................................... SISTR   11/23
    SISTR   16/23    SISTR   17/03    SISTR   17/28   SISTR   18/02
    SISTR   18/11    ENCTR   22/13    ENCTR   26/30   ARABY   33/04
    ARABY   33/20    ARABY   34/33    EVELN   36/17   EVELN   41/01
    EVELN   41/14    GALNT   60/21    HOUSE   63/16   HOUSE   63/20
    HOUSE   66/11    LITTL   70/05    LITTL   72/23   LITTL   74/12
    LITTL   77/06    LITTL   83/25    LITTL   83/31   PARTS   87/32
    PARTS   90/24    PARTS   95/18    PARTS   96/08   CLAY   100/26
    CLAY   106/11    PNFUL  111/21    PNFUL  112/13   PNFUL  112/24
    PNFUL  117/06    PNFUL  117/25    MOTHR  149/18   GRACE  154/21
    GRACE  156/03    GRACE  156/18    GRACE  158/18   GRACE  161/19
```

GRACE 172/03	DEAD 176/14	DEAD 177/26	DEAD 178/01
DEAD 179/04	DEAD 187/04	DEAD 188/23	DEAD 191/34
DEAD 193/14	DEAD 197/32	DEAD 199/04	DEAD 201/09
DEAD 203/12	DEAD 203/31	DEAD 203/31	DEAD 210/01
DEAD 210/12	DEAD 212/31	DEAD 213/01	DEAD 213/07
DEAD 215/24	DEAD 219/27		

STILLNESS (1) .... DEAD 209/31
STIMULUS (1) .... GRACE 172/23
STINGING (1) .... GRACE 156/30
STIPULATED (1) .... MOTHR 141/06
STIR (3) .... IVY D 122/27
    IVY D 122/27   IVY D 132/29
STIRABOUT (3) .... SISTR 9/17
    SISTR 11/16   DEAD 180/18
STIRRING (1) .... MOTHR 147/18
STOCK (3) .... GALNT 50/24
    GRACE 157/07   DEAD 207/32
STOCK-STILL (1) .... DEAD 218/16
STOMACH (2) .... PNFUL 115/23
    PNFUL 116/05
STONE (4) .... ENCTR 22/02
    ENCTR 23/01   CLAY 104/24   MOTHR 149/19
STONES (2) .... ENCTR 22/24
    ENCTR 27/02
STONEY (1) .... DEAD 176/03
STOOD (80) .... ENCTR 26/18

ENCTR 27/32	ARABY 29/03	ARABY 30/22	ARABY 31/06
ARABY 32/10	ARABY 32/26	ARABY 33/12	ARABY 33/21
ARABY 35/17	EVELN 40/17	EVELN 40/22	RACE 45/30
GALNT 54/07	GALNT 54/23	GALNT 58/28	HOUSE 65/19
HOUSE 67/28	LITTL 71/24	LITTL 71/29	LITTL 80/28
LITTL 82/21	LITTL 85/20	PARTS 86/09	PARTS 87/32
PARTS 88/18	PARTS 92/03	PARTS 93/21	PARTS 93/23
PARTS 93/25	PARTS 94/21	PARTS 94/25	PARTS 94/26
PARTS 95/25	PARTS 95/26	PARTS 96/15	PARTS 96/30
CLAY 101/29	PNFUL 107/16	PNFUL 107/18	PNFUL 108/02
PNFUL 112/15	PNFUL 117/05	IVY D 133/34	MOTHR 136/06
MOTHR 137/13	MOTHR 139/09	MOTHR 140/23	MOTHR 143/15
MOTHR 145/03	MOTHR 145/31	MOTHR 146/03	MOTHR 149/12
MOTHR 149/18	GRACE 154/11	GRACE 155/15	GRACE 161/33
GRACE 169/30	GRACE 169/33	GRACE 173/12	DEAD 177/05
DEAD 178/23	DEAD 179/26	DEAD 186/28	DEAD 190/11
DEAD 193/17	DEAD 196/29	DEAD 196/30	DEAD 198/03
DEAD 201/34	DEAD 205/14	DEAD 210/01	DEAD 211/17
DEAD 213/03	DEAD 215/15	DEAD 216/28	DEAD 217/22
DEAD 218/04	DEAD 218/16	DEAD 222/19	

STOOL (3) .... CLAY 102/02
    PNFUL 116/16   DEAD 192/32
STOOPED (1) .... HOUSE 61/16
STOP (3) .... RACE 47/29
    RACE 48/14   LITTL 84/19
STOPPED (17) .... SISTR 14/12
    SISTR 16/29   SISTR 18/09   ENCTR 24/32   RACE 48/17
    RACE 48/18   GALNT 58/17   GALNT 59/20   GALNT 59/31
    GALNT 59/32   HOUSE 64/20   LITTL 84/20   PNFUL 112/29
    MOTHR 149/25   DEAD 187/18   DEAD 210/32   DEAD 221/31
STORE (1) .... MOTHR 141/18
STORES (3) .... EVELN 37/23
    EVELN 37/30   EVELN 39/02
STOREYS (1) .... ARABY 29/03
STORIES (8) .... SISTR 10/06
    SISTR 13/03   ENCTR 20/09   ENCTR 20/11   EVELN 39/14

```
        GALNT  50/24    LITTL  80/21    PARTS  94/18
STORM (1) ...........................................  ENCTR  19/06
STORY (13) .........................................  EVELN  39/28
        LITTL  78/22    LITTL  78/23    PARTS  93/21    PARTS  93/24
        PARTS  93/26    GRACE 161/07    GRACE 161/12    DEAD  184/32
        DEAD  185/06    DEAD  185/21    DEAD  185/30    DEAD  222/17
STOUT (21) .........................................  GALNT  55/32
        HOUSE  62/12    PARTS  91/27    CLAY  102/31    CLAY  104/19
        CLAY  104/31    PNFUL 108/29    PNFUL 113/08    IVY D 127/05
        IVY D 127/09    IVY D 130/20    IVY D 133/09    MOTHR 143/33
        GRACE 162/10    DEAD  176/20    DEAD  178/15    DEAD  179/26
        DEAD  190/15    DEAD  197/01    DEAD  197/24    DEAD  197/30
STOUTLY (3) ........................................  LITTL  81/15
        GRACE 164/32    DEAD  207/06
STRAGGLING (2) .....................................  ARABY  29/15
        GALNT  56/01
STRAIGHT (6) .......................................  GALNT  51/25
        CLAY  103/02    IVY D 125/03    MOTHR 145/33    GRACE 174/23
        DEAD  195/04
STRAIGHTENING (1) ..................................  DEAD  182/31
STRAIGHT-LACED (1) .................................  GRACE 160/21
STRAIN (2) .........................................  RACE   44/08
        MOTHR 146/20
STRAINED (3) .......................................  GALNT  59/19
        MOTHR 145/30    DEAD  209/31
STRAITS (1) ........................................  EVELN  39/14
STRAND (1) .........................................  ENCTR  22/19
STRANGE (13) .......................................  SISTR  12/29
        SISTR  14/01    ARABY  31/12    EVELN  40/01    HOUSE  63/21
        PARTS  90/16    PNFUL 111/27    MOTHR 137/12    DEAD  186/24
        DEAD  200/01    DEAD  215/12    DEAD  217/12    DEAD  222/13
STRANGELY (3) ......................................  SISTR   9/11
        ENCTR  25/31    DEAD  217/23
STRANGERS (1) ......................................  GALNT  54/13
STRATAGEM (1) ......................................  ENCTR  28/08
STRAW (1) ..........................................  HOUSE  64/03
STRAY (1) ..........................................  PARTS  94/06
STREAKS (2) ........................................  HOUSE  64/02
        DEAD  212/33
STREAM (1) .........................................  GRACE 150/08
STREET (86) ........................................  SISTR  11/32
        SISTR  12/08    SISTR  12/28    ENCTR  19/10    ARABY  29/01
        ARABY  29/01    ARABY  29/05    ARABY  30/02    ARABY  30/05
        ARABY  30/07    ARABY  30/13    ARABY  30/18    ARABY  33/09
        ARABY  34/13    EVELN  40/01    RACE   45/13    RACE   45/13
        RACE   45/21    RACE   46/33    GALNT  50/17    GALNT  50/30
        GALNT  50/34    GALNT  51/26    GALNT  53/08    GALNT  54/06
        GALNT  54/07    GALNT  54/17    GALNT  54/22    GALNT  55/09
        GALNT  55/21    GALNT  56/25    GALNT  57/01    GALNT  57/09
        GALNT  58/15    GALNT  58/16    GALNT  58/16    GALNT  58/23
        GALNT  58/26    GALNT  58/30    GALNT  58/31    GALNT  58/32
        GALNT  59/03    GALNT  59/16    GALNT  59/30    GALNT  60/22
        HOUSE  62/03    HOUSE  62/17    HOUSE  63/29    HOUSE  64/23
        LITTL  71/27    LITTL  71/29    LITTL  72/13    LITTL  72/21
        LITTL  73/10    LITTL  74/14    PARTS  88/28    PARTS  89/07
        PARTS  92/31    PARTS  93/07    PARTS  93/27    PARTS  94/11
        PARTS  94/34    CLAY  102/22    PNFUL 108/31    PNFUL 109/01
        PNFUL 112/26    IVY D 119/19    IVY D 122/30    IVY D 127/20
        IVY D 129/32    IVY D 131/16    MOTHR 136/06    MOTHR 137/32
        MOTHR 142/12    GRACE 153/04    GRACE 153/16    GRACE 154/08
        GRACE 156/25    GRACE 165/29    GRACE 172/02    DEAD  214/17
        DEAD  214/21    DEAD  216/05    DEAD  216/10    DEAD  216/13
```

```
                                                           DEAD   217/20
STREETS (14) ............................................  ENCTR   23/01
       ENCTR   24/02    ARABY   31/04    ARABY   34/13     EVELN   38/15
       GALNT   49/03    GALNT   49/03    GALNT   58/05     LITTL   72/16
       PARTS   94/13    CLAY   101/34    PNFUL  108/17     MOTHR  141/15
       DEAD   199/14
STREET-SINGERS (1) ......................................  ARABY   31/07
STRENGTH (3) ............................................  PARTS   95/30
       PARTS   96/02    PNFUL  115/29
STRENUOUS (1) ...........................................  DEAD   204/09
STRESS (2) ..............................................  PARTS   96/18
       DEAD   215/26
STRETCHED (2) ...........................................  MOTHR  143/19
       DEAD   223/04
STREWN (2) ..............................................  DEAD   196/18
       DEAD   204/05
STRIDE (2) ..............................................  GALNT   51/16
       GALNT   59/27
STRIFE (1) ..............................................  IVY D  135/09
STRIKE (4) ..............................................  CLAY   104/24
       PNFUL  111/08    GRACE  163/12    DEAD   214/15
STRIKING (3) ............................................  PARTS   95/12
       PARTS   98/17    PNFUL  113/08
STRING (1) ..............................................  DEAD   222/19
STRIP (1) ...............................................  IVY D  119/22
STRIPLING (1) ...........................................  PARTS   96/09
STRIPPED (1) ............................................  DEAD   196/19
STRIVING (1) ............................................  LITTL   82/32
STRODE (1) ..............................................  ARABY   34/12
STROKE (4) ..............................................  SISTR    9/02
       GALNT   59/01    IVY D  125/12    MOTHR  146/15
STROKING (1) ............................................  MOTHR  145/33
STROLLED (1) ............................................  RACE    46/30
STRONG (9) ..............................................  LITTL   80/17
       PARTS   90/29    PARTS   97/06    PNFUL  115/12     MOTHR  137/15
       GRACE  167/23    DEAD   183/04    DEAD   183/05     DEAD   193/02
STRONGER (1) ............................................  MOTHR  142/30
STRONGLY (4) ............................................  ENCTR   20/29
       PNFUL  109/30    DEAD   199/25    DEAD   202/32
STROVE (6) ..............................................  ARABY   32/17
       RACE    45/11    IVY D  134/24    MOTHR  144/03     GRACE  151/31
       DEAD   217/15
STRUCK (10) .............................................  ENCTR   25/31
       GALNT   59/14    LITTL   71/24    PARTS   90/23     PNFUL  110/03
       PNFUL  113/11    MOTHR  149/19    GRACE  153/24     GRACE  165/32
       DEAD   209/33
STRUGGLE (3) ............................................  LITTL   71/14
       PARTS   96/18    MOTHR  146/19
STRUGGLED (2) ...........................................  PARTS   90/22
       DEAD   193/10
STRUGGLING (3) ..........................................  GRACE  151/13
       GRACE  173/08    DEAD   206/25
STRUMMING (1) ...........................................  DEAD   206/32
STRUTTING (1) ...........................................  EVELN   40/08
STUCK (1) ...............................................  IVY D  133/21
STUDENTS' (1) ...........................................  LITTL   77/20
STUDIED (3) .............................................  SISTR    9/03
       SISTR   13/02    ENCTR   20/18
STUDIOUS (1) ............................................  ENCTR   20/05
STUDY (3) ...............................................  RACE    43/23
       RACE    43/24    DEAD   221/05
STUDYING (1) ............................................  ENCTR   20/24
```

```
STUFF (7) .......................................... ENCTR   20/25
      ENCTR   20/28    GALNT   55/27    HOUSE  65/18    LITTL   74/29
      LITTL   75/14    LITTL   76/30
STUFFING (1) ....................................... DEAD   198/08
STUMBLING (1) ...................................... IVY D  120/31
STUMP (1) .......................................... IVY D  123/34
STUNG (1) .......................................... ARABY   30/05
STUNTED (1) ........................................ LITTL   73/13
STUPEFIED (2) ...................................... SISTR   12/16
      LITTL   73/16
STUPID (2) ......................................... ENCTR   25/19
      DEAD   195/01
STUPIDLY (2) ....................................... PARTS   88/14
      PARTS   91/14
STUPOR (1) ......................................... RACE    48/28
STUTTERED (1) ...................................... DEAD   190/16
STYLE (7) .......................................... RACE    45/09
      LITTL   77/26    IVY D  128/01    GRACE 165/23    DEAD   175/18
      DEAD   198/21    DEAD   207/32
STYLISH (2) ........................................ LITTL   83/02
      CLAY   102/23
SUAVE (1) .......................................... MOTHR  145/22
SUBDUED (2) ........................................ GALNT   57/24
      MOTHR  145/34
SUBJECT (9) ........................................ ENCTR   27/08
      ARABY   35/23    PNFUL  108/27    GRACE 160/08    GRACE  165/18
      DEAD   194/27    DEAD   198/17    DEAD   201/18    DEAD   211/17
SUBJECTS (1) ....................................... PNFUL  111/17
SUB-MATRON (1) ..................................... CLAY    99/17
SUBMISSION (1) ..................................... GRACE  170/08
SUBMIT (2) ......................................... PNFUL  111/12
      GRACE  170/05
SUBMITTED (1) ...................................... GRACE  170/03
SUB-SHERIFF (1) .................................... GRACE  158/25
SUBSTANCE (3) ...................................... ENCTR   23/14
      RACE    44/32    CLAY   105/13
SUBTLE (1) ......................................... GALNT   52/21
SUBTLETY (1) ....................................... RACE    46/02
SUBURBS (2) ........................................ RACE.   43/17
      PNFUL  107/03
SUCCEED (1) ........................................ LITTL   73/11
SUCCEEDED (3) ...................................... LITTL   76/26
      CLAY    99/14    GRACE  150/03
SUCCESS (3) ........................................ RACE    43/09
      LITTL   70/05    GRACE  154/20
SUCCESSFUL (2) ..................................... RACE    42/17
      MOTHR  147/09
SUCCESSFULLY (1) ................................... GALNT   59/09
SUCH (50) .......................................... SISTR   13/09
      SISTR   13/09    SISTR   15/27    ENCTR   20/28    ENCTR   27/24
      ENCTR   27/27    ARABY   35/08    RACE    43/33    GALNT   51/34
      GALNT   51/34    GALNT   56/30    HOUSE   64/33    HOUSE   65/03
      HOUSE   66/02    HOUSE   67/25    LITTL   70/05    LITTL   78/26
      PARTS   96/09    CLAY   100/24    CLAY   100/31    CLAY   102/10
      CLAY   103/19    CLAY   104/34    PNFUL  109/22    PNFUL  110/07
      PNFUL  110/24    IVY D  129/06    MOTHR  137/07    MOTHR  138/17
      MOTHR  140/12    GRACE  154/33    GRACE  157/12    GRACE  160/25
      GRACE  162/09    GRACE  163/23    GRACE  170/24    GRACE  171/07
      DEAD   176/24    DEAD   182/13    DEAD   195/01    DEAD   195/02
      DEAD   203/30    DEAD   204/02    DEAD   204/05    DEAD   216/08
      DEAD   217/21    DEAD   219/09    DEAD   219/10    DEAD   221/03
      DEAD   223/13
```

SUDDEN (7) .... ENCTR 26/01
    EVELN   40/17   PNFUL 114/21   DEAD   179/05   DEAD   196/15
    DEAD   212/06   DEAD   217/27
SUDDENLY (16) .... SISTR 18/09
    GALNT   59/23   HOUSE   68/10   LITTL   84/17   PARTS   87/33
    PARTS   92/30   IVY D 124/11   IVY D 125/32   IVY D 133/22
    GRACE 163/12   DEAD   181/27   DEAD   188/31   DEAD   189/30
    DEAD   193/17   DEAD   213/25   DEAD   217/23
SUFFER (1) .... GRACE 158/01
SUFFERED (2) .... GALNT   59/10
    LITTL   82/28
SUFFICIENT (2) .... PNFUL 114/19
    IVY D 131/01
SUFFOLK (1) .... IVY D 127/20
SUFFUSED (3) .... SISTR 14/17
    LITTL   85/19   MOTHR 144/24
SUGAR (3) .... HOUSE 64/07
    LITTL   82/19   CLAY   101/06
SUGGEST (1) .... ENCTR 24/12
SUGGESTED (5) .... SISTR 18/03
    RACE   45/05   PARTS   94/14   MOTHR 141/26   DEAD   197/18
SUIT (6) .... ENCTR 22/06
    ENCTR   24/23   LITTL   70/04   PARTS   95/08   DEAD   180/29
    DEAD   186/30
SUITABLE (1) .... RACE   44/11
SUITED (1) .... GALNT 57/01
SUITING (1) .... CLAY 102/22
SUITOR (1) .... MOTHR 136/16
SULLEN (1) .... DEAD 187/02
SULLEN-FACED (1) .... PARTS 96/30
SULTRY (1) .... ENCTR 23/33
SUM (5) .... RACE   44/24
    RACE   44/25   HOUSE   65/03   MOTHR 137/16   MOTHR 141/06
SUMMARILY (1) .... DEAD 182/21
SUMMARISED (1) .... LITTL 78/16
SUMMER (11) .... SISTR 11/04
    SISTR   17/03   ENCTR   21/08   ENCTR   25/01   RACE   45/25
    RACE   47/15   GALNT   49/02   HOUSE   63/26   LITTL 82/25
    DEAD   188/33   DEAD   221/11
SUMMITS (1) .... GALNT 49/05
SUMMONS (1) .... ARABY 30/33
SUMS (1) .... GRACE 159/26
SUN (2) .... SISTR 13/30
    ENCTR   24/13
SUNDAY (12) .... SISTR 17/10
    GALNT   49/04   GALNT   51/01   GALNT   55/24   HOUSE 62/23
    HOUSE   63/26   HOUSE   65/23   LITTL   76/07   CLAY 101/30
    CLAY   103/16   IVY D 123/26   GRACE 159/21
SUNDAYS (1) .... MOTHR 137/30
SUNDAY'S (1) .... EVELN 38/18
SUNDERED (1) .... IVY D 134/26
SUNG (2) .... MOTHR 142/19
    DEAD   199/10
SUNK (1) .... PNFUL 115/31
SUNLIGHT (1) .... ENCTR 22/01
SUNNY (3) .... SISTR 12/27
    ENCTR   21/30   DEAD   213/19
SUNSET (4) .... SISTR 14/04
    LITTL   71/06   LITTL   71/28   LITTL   73/16
SUNSHADE (2) .... GALNT 54/24
    GALNT   55/16
SUP (2) .... CLAY 101/17

```
          IVY D 120/08
SUPERFLUITIES (1)  ...............................  GRACE 168/02
SUPERINTENDED (1)  ...............................  CLAY  101/06
SUPERIOR (2)  ....................................  LITTL  73/08
          DEAD  179/17
SUPPED (1)  ......................................  RACE   46/07
SUPPER (11)  .....................................  SISTR   9/17
     RACE   47/21   RACE   47/29   DEAD  191/28   DEAD  195/10
     DEAD  195/14   DEAD  197/32   DEAD  198/09   DEAD  198/15
     DEAD  200/24   DEAD  222/22
SUPPER-ROOM (2)  .................................  DEAD  196/10
          DEAD  205/33
SUPPERS (2)  .....................................  DEAD  195/33
          DEAD  198/01
SUPPER-TABLE (3)  ................................  DEAD  192/08
          DEAD  192/16   DEAD  193/09
SUPPORT (1)  .....................................  IVY D 131/05
SUPPOSE (14)  ....................................  ENCTR  20/26
     GALNT  52/10   GALNT  53/10   LITTL  76/02   LITTL  77/22
     LITTL  78/02   IVY D 123/22   MOTHR 139/28   GRACE 160/19
     DEAD  178/05   DEAD  194/24   DEAD  199/22   DEAD  199/28
     DEAD  220/10
SUPPOSED (2)  ....................................  CLAY  103/04
          GRACE 161/08
SURE (37)  .......................................  SISTR  16/19
     ENCTR  25/24   GALNT  50/08   GALNT  53/26   GALNT  59/13
     HOUSE  61/07   HOUSE  62/20   HOUSE  64/23   HOUSE  65/08
     HOUSE  66/01   HOUSE  67/16   LITTL  73/21   LITTL  74/25
     LITTL  80/25   PARTS  92/21   CLAY  101/09   CLAY  102/07
     CLAY  102/18   CLAY  103/23   IVY D 120/06   IVY D 120/13
     IVY D 120/15   IVY D 123/15   IVY D 127/16   IVY D 129/32
     IVY D 133/30   MOTHR 143/22   GRACE 162/20   GRACE 169/18
     GRACE 169/23   DEAD  181/18   DEAD  181/22   DEAD  181/24
     DEAD  182/07   DEAD  182/08   DEAD  183/15   DEAD  203/06
SURELY (2)  ......................................  GALNT  59/17
          DEAD  188/09
SURGEON (1)  .....................................  PNFUL 114/15
SURGEONS (2)  ....................................  GALNT  58/34
          GALNT  59/18
SURNAME (2)  .....................................  LITTL  74/11
          DEAD  177/24
SURPLICE (2)  ....................................  GRACE 173/08
          GRACE 173/20
SURPRISE (4)  ....................................  CLAY  104/01
          IVY D 125/34   DEAD  204/33   DEAD  219/18
SURPRISED (15)  ..................................  SISTR  13/16
     ENCTR  20/27   ENCTR  27/15   ARABY  32/21   RACE   46/16
     CLAY  105/14   PNFUL 109/24   PNFUL 111/33   MOTHR 138/07
     MOTHR 148/29   GRACE 154/30   DEAD  184/21   DEAD  190/08
     DEAD  209/30   DEAD  216/08
SURROUNDED (2)  ..................................  LITTL  80/20
          GRACE 150/11
SURROUNDING (1)  .................................  ENCTR  26/15
SURVEYED (3)  ....................................  HOUSE  65/19
          GRACE 152/16   GRACE 173/21
SUSPECT (3)  .....................................  PNFUL 110/21
          IVY D 124/24   MOTHR 145/04
SUSPECTED (3)  ...................................  HOUSE  64/09
          HOUSE  65/17   GRACE 157/29
SUSPENDED (1)  ...................................  GRACE 172/13
SUSPICIONS (1)  ..................................  MOTHR 141/20
SUSPICIOUS (1)  ..................................  GRACE 151/20
```

SUSTAINED (2) .... LITTL 85/09
    PNFUL 114/17
SUSTAINING (1) .... PNFUL 113/27
SWADDLERS (2) .... ENCTR 22/26
    ENCTR 22/27
SWARMED (1) .... GALNT 49/04
SWARTHY (2) .... RACE 44/20
    DEAD 182/19
SWATHED (1) .... DEAD 211/30
SWATHING (1) .... DEAD 211/17
SWAY (1) .... LITTL 74/02
SWAYING (5) .... EVELN 40/22
    GALNT 51/21   GALNT 55/11   GRACE 153/26   DEAD 183/12
SWEATED (1) .... GALNT 51/22
SWEEPING (1) .... DEAD 202/06
SWEET (3) .... PARTS 90/02
    DEAD 183/04   DEAD 200/06
SWEETHEART (3) .... ENCTR 25/30
    ENCTR 27/21   ENCTR 27/23
SWEETHEARTS (3) .... ENCTR 25/22
    ENCTR 25/29   ENCTR 25/33
SWEETS (5) .... GALNT 52/29
    DEAD 183/01   DEAD 196/28   DEAD 200/19   DEAD 201/23
SWELLED (1) .... PARTS 97/07
SWEPT (3) .... GALNT 56/22
    GRACE 170/31   DEAD 179/03
SWERVED (1) .... GALNT 60/22
SWIFT (5) .... RACE 45/12
    GALNT 55/23   GALNT 60/12   MOTHR 146/19   DEAD 193/07
SWIFTLY (6) .... GALNT 50/29
    GALNT 60/07   LITTL 71/27   LITTL 72/06   LITTL 72/13
    DEAD 218/05
SWINDLE (1) .... LITTL 83/04
SWING (2) .... GALNT 51/16
    IVY D 130/29
SWINGING (4) .... SISTR 13/33
    GALNT 54/24   GRACE 155/22   DEAD 216/16
SWISHING (2) .... PARTS 93/13
    PNFUL 116/20
SWIVELLED (1) .... PARTS 90/07
SWOON (1) .... PNFUL 109/33
SWOONED (1) .... DEAD 224/02
SWUNG (3) .... ARABY 30/23
    GALNT 53/30   GALNT 55/15
SYDNEY (3) .... PNFUL 113/19
    PNFUL 113/24   PNFUL 114/31
SYLLABLE (1) .... MOTHR 139/30
SYLLABLES (3) .... ARABY 32/17
    PNFUL 117/26   DEAD 177/23
SYMBOL (2) .... DEAD 210/03
    DEAD 210/05
SYMPATHETIC (1) .... LITTL 75/09
SYMPATHY (5) .... RACE 42/07
    PNFUL 115/11   PNFUL 115/21   IVY D 120/17   GRACE 157/14
SYSTEM (2) .... LITTL 83/21
    GRACE 167/33

T. (2) .... LITTL 74/12
    DEAD 179/34
TABINET (1) .... DEAD 186/22
TABLE (62) .... SISTR 11/10

SISTR 15/02	SISTR 17/22	RACE 48/04	RACE 48/29
GALNT 57/13	GALNT 57/22	HOUSE 63/34	HOUSE 64/06
LITTL 82/21	LITTL 83/03	LITTL 83/28	PARTS 95/09
PARTS 96/02	PARTS 96/04	PARTS 96/07	PARTS 96/19
PARTS 96/21	PARTS 98/01	PARTS 98/13	CLAY 101/16
CLAY 105/01	CLAY 105/02	CLAY 105/06	CLAY 105/10
PNFUL 107/11	IVY D 120/33	IVY D 121/02	IVY D 126/21
IVY D 128/20	IVY D 129/19	IVY D 130/25	IVY D 130/28
IVY D 131/09	IVY D 131/11	IVY D 133/17	IVY D 133/34
IVY D 135/21	IVY D 135/27	GRACE 154/11	GRACE 161/14
GRACE 161/31	GRACE 162/12	GRACE 166/30	DEAD 191/05
DEAD 196/17	DEAD 196/30	DEAD 197/05	DEAD 197/09
DEAD 197/33	DEAD 198/16	DEAD 198/26	DEAD 198/31
DEAD 199/01	DEAD 200/09	DEAD 200/11	DEAD 200/25
DEAD 201/19	DEAD 201/23	DEAD 201/32	DEAD 203/13
DEAD 204/18			

TABLECLOTH (2) .... DEAD 201/31
DEAD 202/03

TABLE-NAPKINS (1) .... DEAD 184/19
TABLES (1) .... DEAD 182/30
TACT (3) .... GALNT 54/02
MOTHR 138/19   DEAD 181/14
TAIL (1) .... GALNT 57/34
TAILORS (1) .... PARTS 93/25
TAKE (45) .... SISTR 11/03

SISTR 11/06	SISTR 15/03	SISTR 15/05	SISTR 17/06
EVELN 40/20	GALNT 52/23	GALNT 52/26	GALNT 52/27
GALNT 53/24	HOUSE 61/07	HOUSE 65/27	HOUSE 67/33
LITTL 71/20	LITTL 79/32	LITTL 82/31	LITTL 83/05
PARTS 88/04	PARTS 91/18	PARTS 94/22	PARTS 96/31
PARTS 98/17	CLAY 104/11	CLAY 104/18	CLAY 104/21
CLAY 105/23	PNFUL 110/21	PNFUL 115/12	IVY D 120/02
MOTHR 137/14	MOTHR 137/26	GRACE 161/08	DEAD 178/30
DEAD 180/01	DEAD 182/15	DEAD 182/22	DEAD 183/20
DEAD 183/21	DEAD 184/01	DEAD 185/13	DEAD 195/19
DEAD 195/33	DEAD 201/25	DEAD 202/20	DEAD 217/10

TAKEN (20) .... HOUSE 62/02

HOUSE 63/04	HOUSE 64/31	LITTL 78/10	CLAY 103/13
PNFUL 114/12	PNFUL 114/24	PNFUL 116/02	IVY D 120/08
MOTHR 144/25	MOTHR 147/31	GRACE 162/25	DEAD 176/03
DEAD 179/18	DEAD 181/16	DEAD 187/01	DEAD 187/24
DEAD 205/32	DEAD 211/15	DEAD 216/15	

TAKES (7) .... GALNT 50/10

GALNT 50/13	GALNT 51/15	IVY D 120/07	GRACE 161/15
DEAD 177/04	DEAD 198/30		

TAKING (13) .... ENCTR 23/14

GALNT 59/26	GALNT 59/31	LITTL 74/29	PARTS 93/17
PNFUL 113/15	IVY D 119/25	IVY D 135/29	MOTHR 140/22
GRACE 152/21	DEAD 183/07	DEAD 190/05	DEAD 197/30

TALE (4) .... PNFUL 108/16
PNFUL 109/16   GRACE 171/04   GRACE 171/07
TALENT (3) .... LITTL 72/30
MOTHR 140/08   DEAD 186/25
TALENTED (1) .... DEAD 205/01
TALENTS (2) .... LITTL 70/04
MOTHR 141/25
TALES (1) .... EVELN 39/10
TALK (23) .... ENCTR 24/34

ENCTR 25/06	ARABY 35/22	RACE 47/05	RACE 47/06
GALNT 55/01	GALNT 57/20	HOUSE 63/20	LITTL 78/10
PARTS 94/25	CLAY 105/27	PNFUL 109/24	PNFUL 116/11
IVY D 122/16	IVY D 130/10	IVY D 131/24	GRACE 155/19

GRACE 155/20	GRACE 158/09	GRACE 165/04	DEAD	198/17
DEAD 208/34	DEAD 212/04			

TALKATIVE (1) .... DEAD 187/20
TALKED (10) .... RACE 46/08

RACE 46/31	GALNT 58/20	GALNT 59/32	HOUSE	66/01
CLAY 99/11	PNFUL 109/25	MOTHR 139/23	MOTHR	144/02
GRACE 161/19				

TALKING (22) .... SISTR 10/05

SISTR 17/33	ENCTR 27/21	ENCTR 27/23	ARABY	33/29
ARABY 35/05	RACE 48/23	GALNT 50/16	GALNT	51/30
HOUSE 66/18	PARTS 87/19	PARTS 87/19	PARTS	95/30
CLAY 104/22	IVY D 127/13	IVY D 128/01	IVY D	130/02
IVY D 133/14	MOTHR 139/19	MOTHR 145/03	DEAD	182/10
DEAD 193/14				

TALL (10) .... ENCTR 21/34

ENCTR 23/28	GALNT 49/05	PARTS 86/09	IVY D	120/26
GRACE 152/11	GRACE 164/34	DEAD 182/18	DEAD	196/30
DEAD 207/31				

TALLER (1) .... DEAD 179/23
TALLIED (2) .... GRACE 174/16

GRACE 174/24

TALLISH (1) .... DEAD 178/15
TALLY (1) .... IVY D 128/20
TANGLED (1) .... DEAD 222/05
TANNER (1) .... ENCTR 22/18
TAP (1) .... DEAD 216/02
TAPED (1) .... GRACE 170/25
TAPPED (5) .... ENCTR 24/22

HOUSE 66/26	HOUSE 67/05	PARTS 90/11	DEAD	192/02

TAPPING (1) .... ENCTR 24/29
TAPS (1) .... DEAD 223/23
TARDY (1) .... IVY D 132/32
TART (2) .... GALNT 50/31

GALNT 54/04

TARTLY (1) .... GRACE 162/06
TASK (8) .... RACE 46/25

GALNT 50/26	GALNT 56/30	HOUSE 65/10	PARTS	89/27
DEAD 202/16	DEAD 202/16	DEAD 204/28		

TASKMASTER (1) .... GRACE 174/18
TASTE (1) .... RACE 46/05
TASTED (4) .... SISTR 17/22

LITTL 78/33	GRACE 154/13	GRACE 167/26

TASTES (2) .... RACE 46/14

HOUSE 62/13

TASTING (1) .... LITTL 82/05
TAUGHT (5) .... SISTR 10/22

SISTR 13/01	SISTR 13/03	GRACE 158/18	DEAD	186/21

TAWDRY (1) .... LITTL 80/27
TAWNY (3) .... SISTR 14/05

PNFUL 108/18   PNFUL 108/21

TEA (12) .... ARABY 30/17

LITTL 82/13	LITTL 82/16	LITTL 82/18	CLAY	99/02
CLAY 99/08	CLAY 100/03	CLAY 101/05	CLAY	101/15
CLAY 101/23	GRACE 154/13	DEAD 176/20		

TEACH (3) .... ENCTR 27/22

PARTS 98/06   PARTS 98/10

TEACHER (1) .... MOTHR 137/27
TEACHERS (1) .... DEAD 188/19
TEACHING (1) .... DEAD 188/12
TEA-COSY (1) .... ENCTR 19/14
TEAM (1) .... RACE 42/09
TEA-MERCHANT (1) .... GRACE 156/16

TEARS (8) .... ARABY 31/13
    EVELN   37/30   LITTL   85/21   CLAY   106/16   DEAD   205/05
    DEAD   218/13   DEAD   223/12   DEAD   223/14
TEASED (1) .... ARABY 30/22
TEA-SETS (1) .... ARABY 35/05
TEA-TABLE (1) .... ARABY 33/19
TEA-THINGS (1) .... CLAY 101/24
TEDDY (3) .... DEAD 185/19
    DEAD   198/30   DEAD   206/23
TEDIOUS (1) .... ARABY 32/14
TEETH (9) .... SISTR 13/26
    ENCTR   25/21   RACE   44/11   RACE   44/21   GALNT   56/03
    HOUSE   68/17   LITTL   70/18   LITTL   79/20   GRACE 153/28
TELEGRAM (1) .... SISTR 12/04
TELL (54) .... SISTR 10/02
    SISTR   15/16   ENCTR   21/14   ENCTR   24/19   ENCTR   25/26
    ARABY   31/13   ARABY   31/17   GALNT   51/12   GALNT   52/10
    GALNT   53/15   GALNT   53/26   GALNT   55/01   GALNT   60/26
    HOUSE   62/20   LITTL   70/03   LITTL   75/16   LITTL   77/16
    LITTL   78/08   LITTL   78/32   LITTL   81/33   PARTS   87/14
    PARTS   91/17   CLAY   106/17   IVY D 123/02   IVY D 123/16
    IVY D 124/15   IVY D 124/21   IVY D 126/23   IVY D 128/29
    MOTHR 140/01   MOTHR 141/20   GRACE 153/20   GRACE 155/06
    GRACE 161/21   GRACE 162/34   GRACE 163/31   GRACE 165/02
    GRACE 165/30   GRACE 167/28   GRACE 168/19   GRACE 171/07
    DEAD   178/01   DEAD   181/14   DEAD   189/30   DEAD   191/22
    DEAD   195/03   DEAD   199/24   DEAD   204/19   DEAD   206/15
    DEAD   209/17   DEAD   211/11   DEAD   218/10   DEAD   220/24
    DEAD   221/21
TELLING (8) .... ENCTR 26/13
    HOUSE   66/32   LITTL   78/22   PARTS   92/02   IVY D 131/12
    DEAD   184/32   DEAD   193/21   DEAD   222/32
TELLS (3) .... DEAD 180/01
    DEAD   205/25   DEAD   205/26
TEMPER (2) .... GALNT 54/01
    CLAY   104/30
TEMPERAMENT (3) .... LITTL 73/26
    LITTL 73/31   PNFUL 109/33
TEMPERED (2) .... LITTL 73/32
    GRACE 157/22
TEMPLE (1) .... PARTS 92/33
TEMPLES (1) .... RACE   48/31
TEMPORARY (1) .... RACE   44/25
TEMPTATIONS (2) .... GRACE 174/20
    GRACE 174/21
TEMPTED (2) .... LITTL 71/20
    GRACE 157/31
TEN (15) .... ENCTR 21/12
    ENCTR   22/05   ARABY   34/24   ARABY   34/24   GALNT   55/07
    GALNT   56/04   GALNT   58/29   GALNT   59/01   LITTL   82/26
    LITTL   83/04   PNFUL 113/26   MOTHR 140/16   DEAD   176/25
    DEAD   195/17   DEAD   202/02
TENANT (1) .... ARABY 29/07
TENANT'S (1) .... ARABY 29/16
TENDER (5) .... DEAD 213/09
    DEAD   213/30   DEAD   213/31   DEAD   214/04   DEAD   214/07
TENDERNESS (1) .... DEAD 219/32
TENEBRAE (1) .... GRACE 167/16
TENEBRIS (1) .... GRACE 167/14
TENOR (16) .... MOTHR 138/21
    MOTHR 142/16   MOTHR 142/31   MOTHR 143/31   MOTHR 146/02
    MOTHR 146/25   MOTHR 147/15   MOTHR 148/15   GRACE 158/17

DEAD	184/10	DEAD	198/18	DEAD	198/24	DEAD	199/10
DEAD	199/28	DEAD	199/34	DEAD	200/06		

TENORS (1) .... MOTHR 142/34
TENSE (1) .... PNFUL 108/28
TERM (1) .... RACE   43/27
TERMS (6) .... PARTS 93/14
   MOTHR 141/05   MOTHR 144/02   GRACE 158/19   GRACE 160/29
   GRACE 166/30
TERRACE (2) .... CLAY 103/11
   PNFUL 110/05
TERRACOTTA (1) .... DEAD 209/27
TERRIBLE (6) .... EVELN 39/14
   RACE   48/18   DEAD 185/12   DEAD 210/13   DEAD 210/14
   DEAD 219/26
TERRIFIC (1) .... IVY D 123/08
TERRIFYING (1) .... GRACE 174/11
TERROR (2) .... EVELN 40/17
   DEAD 220/19
TERRY (2) .... PARTS 92/31
   PARTS 93/02
TESSELLATED (1) .... GRACE 151/04
TESTILY (1) .... DEAD 181/30
TEXT (4) .... GRACE 173/26
   GRACE 173/28   GRACE 173/31   GRACE 174/01
TEXTS (1) .... GRACE 173/27
TEXTURE (1) .... GALNT 49/06
TH' (1) .... IVY D 135/03
THAN (35) .... SISTR 16/23
   ENCTR 27/28   RACE   43/30   GALNT 58/08   HOUSE 63/33
   HOUSE 67/29   HOUSE 68/14   LITTL 74/29   LITTL 80/26
   LITTL 80/27   PARTS 91/27   PARTS 92/27   CLAY 103/02
   PNFUL 109/28   PNFUL 116/01   IVY D 121/20   IVY D 128/01
   IVY D 129/04   IVY D 130/19   MOTHR 137/05   MOTHR 137/09
   MOTHR 142/30   GRACE 159/29   GRACE 160/24   GRACE 173/23
   DEAD 175/04   DEAD 179/29   DEAD 188/10   DEAD 192/08
   DEAD 197/08   DEAD 199/23   DEAD 203/04   DEAD 207/07
   DEAD 218/25   DEAD 223/08
THANK (9) .... ARABY 35/20
   IVY D 125/19   IVY D 126/11   IVY D 126/12   IVY D 126/17
   IVY D 126/31   MOTHR 142/09   MOTHR 145/14   DEAD 179/01
THANKED (1) .... CLAY 103/09
THANKFUL (2) .... ARABY 31/25
   HOUSE 65/32
THANKS (11) .... LITTL 79/24
   CLAY 103/21   IVY D 120/06   IVY D 126/19   IVY D 126/19
   MOTHR 139/03   DEAD 182/16   DEAD 186/32   DEAD 186/33
   DEAD 212/20   DEAD 212/23
THAT (657)
THAT'D (3) .... LITTL 76/13
   LITTL 81/31   IVY D 125/18
THAT'LL (3) .... IVY D 127/16
   GRACE 162/17   DEAD 184/02
THAT'S (54) .... SISTR 11/01
   SISTR 11/02   SISTR 11/05   SISTR 15/25   SISTR 16/19
   ENCTR 22/17   GALNT 53/10   GALNT 54/04   LITTL 75/25
   LITTL 76/22   LITTL 77/21   LITTL 78/32   LITTL 79/09
   LITTL 80/01   LITTL 80/02   LITTL 80/11   PARTS 90/12
   PARTS 91/23   PARTS 93/18   PARTS 96/23   PARTS 97/27
   IVY D 118/11   IVY D 120/05   IVY D 122/17   IVY D 123/29
   IVY D 123/29   IVY D 123/33   IVY D 125/17   IVY D 126/34
   IVY D 129/23   IVY D 131/24   IVY D 132/20   IVY D 133/05
   IVY D 133/30   MOTHR 149/31   GRACE 153/31   GRACE 154/33

GRACE 158/30	GRACE 159/03	GRACE 161/29	GRACE 163/01
GRACE 164/04	GRACE 164/04	GRACE 164/09	GRACE 165/01
GRACE 167/28	GRACE 169/18	GRACE 172/01	DEAD 180/26
DEAD 193/23	DEAD 193/24	DEAD 194/02	DEAD 201/06
DEAD 216/27			

THE (4079)
THEATRE (5) . . . . EVELN 39/04

GALNT 52/28	LITTL 72/04	MOTHR 142/24	DEAD 198/18

THEATRICAL (2) . . . . SISTR 12/28

PARTS 94/25
THEATRICALS (1) . . . . MOTHR 147/19
THEIR (148)
THEIRS (2) . . . . GALNT 56/12

PARTS 94/25
THEM (171)
THEMSELVES (11) . . . . ARABY 31/26

RACE 47/08	RACE 48/06	LITTL 73/17	LITTL 77/22
CLAY 103/06	PNFUL 112/30	MOTHR 139/23	GRACE 159/23
GRACE 163/19	DEAD 199/14		

THEN (180)
THEOLOGIAN (1) . . . . GRACE 165/11
THEOLOGY (1) . . . . GRACE 168/17
THEORIES (1) . . . . PNFUL 110/29
THEORY (2) . . . . SISTR 10/08

SISTR 10/11
THERE (169)
THEREBY (1) . . . . PNFUL 113/27
THEREFORE (7) . . . . RACE 42/12

RACE 45/34	MOTHR 138/07	MOTHR 143/03	MOTHR 148/09
GRACE 160/26	DEAD 204/10		

THERE'LL (1) . . . . LITTL 81/21
THERE'S (24) . . . . SISTR 16/06

SISTR 16/17	ARABY 35/13	GALNT 52/22	LITTL 76/23
LITTL 77/25	IVY D 125/09	IVY D 125/12	IVY D 125/16
IVY D 127/18	IVY D 129/01	IVY D 130/21	IVY D 133/10
IVY D 133/19	GRACE 158/32	GRACE 163/29	GRACE 165/34
GRACE 166/03	GRACE 171/33	DEAD 181/23	DEAD 182/15
DEAD 191/20	DEAD 195/02	DEAD 196/13	

THESE (49) . . . . SISTR 12/21

SISTR 13/19	SISTR 15/02	ENCTR 20/04	ENCTR 20/11
ENCTR 20/27	ENCTR 25/05	ARABY 29/10	ARABY 31/09
ARABY 33/31	EVELN 37/28	EVELN 39/19	RACE 42/15
RACE 42/17	RACE 43/07	RACE 44/15	RACE 44/17
GALNT 52/02	LITTL 74/09	LITTL 75/07	CLAY 99/06
PNFUL 108/07	PNFUL 109/06	PNFUL 109/11	PNFUL 109/15
PNFUL 111/30	IVY D 125/05	IVY D 132/09	MOTHR 137/28
MOTHR 143/10	MOTHR 145/21	GRACE 150/09	GRACE 154/03
GRACE 154/13	GRACE 154/22	GRACE 155/20	GRACE 160/32
GRACE 161/09	GRACE 161/20	GRACE 169/14	GRACE 169/29
GRACE 172/21	DEAD 178/06	DEAD 182/30	DEAD 196/21
DEAD 203/20	DEAD 214/06	DEAD 214/08	DEAD 223/21

THEY (271)
THEY'LL (1) . . . . IVY D 127/23
THEY'RE (14) . . . . GALNT 53/27

LITTL 77/10	IVY D 124/23	IVY D 125/10	IVY D 126/28
IVY D 127/21	IVY D 132/09	GRACE 155/08	GRACE 160/32
GRACE 163/24	GRACE 163/26	GRACE 163/30	GRACE 164/12
DEAD 206/29			

THEY'VE (1) . . . . LITTL 77/12
THICK (11) . . . . SISTR 13/17

HOUSE 68/07	HOUSE 68/07	PARTS 89/06	CLAY 99/07
CLAY 102/27	IVY D 126/28	GRACE 151/15	GRACE 161/02

```
                GRACE 169/10    DEAD  184/27
THICKLY (4) ................................................... GRACE 152/08
     DEAD  215/21    DEAD  223/14    DEAD  223/33
THIGH (1) .................................................... PARTS  98/19
THIN (9) ..................................................... SISTR  14/18
     LITTL  75/02    LITTL  75/09    LITTL  82/24    LITTL  84/24
     IVY D 119/05    IVY D 129/24    IVY D 130/08    GRACE 150/07
THING (33) ................................................... ARABY  35/08
     RACE   44/33    GALNT  52/34    GALNT  59/18    HOUSE  62/21
     HOUSE  65/17    LITTL  76/23    LITTL  81/32    PARTS  93/22
     PARTS  95/26    CLAY  100/30    IVY D 125/04    IVY D 130/14
     IVY D 133/22    IVY D 133/25    IVY D 133/30    IVY D 134/26
     MOTHR 149/32    GRACE 159/02    GRACE 163/30    GRACE 163/33
     GRACE 168/25    GRACE 168/28    GRACE 171/07    GRACE 174/22
     DEAD  176/23    DEAD  180/28    DEAD  181/18    DEAD  195/01
     DEAD  195/02    DEAD  200/22    DEAD  203/06    DEAD  219/26
THINGS (22) .................................................. SISTR  11/14
     ENCTR  20/27    HOUSE  61/02    HOUSE  62/09    HOUSE  63/11
     HOUSE  64/04    HOUSE  64/09    LITTL  76/03    LITTL  78/17
     LITTL  78/26    LITTL  84/04    PARTS  88/04    CLAY  100/06
     CLAY  103/05    IVY D 129/32    MOTHR 139/08    MOTHR 140/13
     GRACE 168/13    DEAD  181/05    DEAD  190/27    DEAD  198/30
     DEAD  206/27
THINK (69) ................................................... SISTR  10/08
     SISTR  11/11    SISTR  11/22    SISTR  15/27    SISTR  18/06
     SISTR  18/15    ENCTR  25/19    RACE   44/24    GALNT  56/32
     HOUSE  63/12    HOUSE  65/11    LITTL  76/15    LITTL  77/10
     LITTL  81/13    LITTL  82/07    LITTL  83/07    PARTS  91/19
     PARTS  91/23    PARTS  92/32    PARTS  93/18    PARTS  97/27
     CLAY  102/19    PNFUL 109/14    PNFUL 114/29    PNFUL 115/20
     IVY D 119/28    IVY D 121/11    IVY D 121/24    IVY D 123/03
     IVY D 123/06    IVY D 124/22    IVY D 125/02    IVY D 125/12
     IVY D 126/30    IVY D 127/03    IVY D 127/21    IVY D 127/25
     IVY D 128/08    IVY D 132/25    IVY D 135/31    MOTHR 146/05
     MOTHR 147/28    GRACE 155/17    GRACE 158/31    GRACE 160/03
     GRACE 161/20    GRACE 164/34    GRACE 167/13    GRACE 167/14
     GRACE 168/11    DEAD  177/29    DEAD  179/16    DEAD  188/04
     DEAD  191/11    DEAD  191/29    DEAD  192/16    DEAD  192/22
     DEAD  194/03    DEAD  194/21    DEAD  198/29    DEAD  199/03
     DEAD  199/33    DEAD  207/33    DEAD  211/26    DEAD  212/12
     DEAD  218/10    DEAD  219/07    DEAD  220/18    DEAD  222/08
THINKING (9) ................................................. ENCTR  22/27
     GALNT  57/29    CLAY  102/08    PNFUL 110/18    PNFUL 111/11
     IVY D 127/24    DEAD  218/07    DEAD  218/14    DEAD  218/28
THINKS (3) ................................................... GALNT  51/09
     GALNT  51/12    DEAD  181/11
THINLY (2) ................................................... PNFUL 109/18
     IVY D 118/03
THINNED (1) .................................................. GALNT  58/32
THIRD (6) .................................................... SISTR   9/01
     RACE   42/10    HOUSE  67/19    PNFUL 108/27    PNFUL 110/12
     DEAD  197/04
THIRD-CLASS (1) .............................................. ARABY  34/15
THIRST (2) ................................................... PARTS  87/28
     PARTS  88/18
THIRSTY (3) .................................................. PARTS  92/13
     PARTS  97/04    DEAD  195/08
THIRTEEN (1) ................................................. HOUSE  65/14
THIRTY (4) ................................................... PARTS  96/06
     DEAD  176/06    DEAD  194/07    DEAD  211/23
THIRTY-FIVE (1) .............................................. HOUSE  64/28
THIRTY-FOUR (1) .............................................. HOUSE  64/27
```

THIRTY-ONE (1) .... GALNT 58/01
THIRTY-TWO (1) .... LITTL 73/26
THIS (124)
THIS'LL (1) .... IVY D 119/08
THITHER (1) .... DEAD 183/03
THOMAS (3) .... ENCTR 25/08
    LITTL 74/11   GRACE 156/25
THOMAS'S (1) .... MOTHR 138/32
THORAX (1) .... GRACE 159/03
THORNS (1) .... DEAD 224/01
THORNY (1) .... GRACE 168/17
THOROUGHLY (1) .... GRACE 157/19
THOSE (35) .... SISTR 10/09

ENCTR 21/02	ENCTR 23/12	ENCTR 24/19	EVELN 37/09
EVELN 37/10	EVELN 37/20	RACE 42/14	GALNT 58/06
GALNT 59/11	LITTL 71/02	LITTL 83/15	CLAY 106/06
PNFUL 117/13	IVY D 121/20	IVY D 123/19	IVY D 125/07
IVY D 135/02	MOTHR 139/02	GRACE 154/20	GRACE 155/07
GRACE 159/10	GRACE 160/30	GRACE 164/10	GRACE 173/32
GRACE 174/07	DEAD 186/11	DEAD 191/34	DEAD 193/28
DEAD 199/06	DEAD 203/24	DEAD 203/26	DEAD 203/28
DEAD 203/32	DEAD 213/34		

THOUGH (22) .... SISTR 11/18

ENCTR 20/10	ENCTR 20/11	ARABY 35/25	EVELN 37/34
GALNT 56/25	HOUSE 63/19	LITTL 70/11	LITTL 81/17
CLAY 100/17	CLAY 101/10	CLAY 101/20	MOTHR 141/24
GRACE 157/07	GRACE 159/29	DEAD 176/14	DEAD 176/18
DEAD 179/25	DEAD 186/05	DEAD 186/25	DEAD 193/04
DEAD 222/09			

THOUGHT (56) .... SISTR 9/05

SISTR 9/08	SISTR 13/19	SISTR 14/01	SISTR 15/06
ENCTR 24/30	ENCTR 25/32	ARABY 31/15	RACE 46/12
GALNT 58/03	HOUSE 64/16	HOUSE 65/21	LITTL 71/01
LITTL 71/12	LITTL 71/12	LITTL 71/32	LITTL 72/22
LITTL 73/21	LITTL 73/31	LITTL 83/14	LITTL 83/16
PARTS 90/15	PARTS 92/31	PARTS 97/07	CLAY 100/25
CLAY 101/30	CLAY 102/04	CLAY 102/16	CLAY 102/29
CLAY 102/33	CLAY 103/12	CLAY 104/01	CLAY 104/23
PNFUL 111/24	PNFUL 115/26	PNFUL 116/04	IVY D 118/17
IVY D 127/04	MOTHR 141/20	MOTHR 141/27	MOTHR 148/08
MOTHR 148/16	MOTHR 148/30	MOTHR 149/08	GRACE 163/12
GRACE 163/20	GRACE 169/24	GRACE 171/02	DEAD 175/07
DEAD 177/01	DEAD 198/21	DEAD 207/26	DEAD 208/09
DEAD 219/15	DEAD 222/11	DEAD 223/08	

THOUGHTFUL (1) .... GRACE 154/31
THOUGHTFULLY (3) .... LITTL 78/13
    LITTL 82/01   IVY D 127/19
THOUGHTFULNESS (1) .... HOUSE 67/15
THOUGHTLESSNESS (1) .... MOTHR 142/28
THOUGHTS (13) .... SISTR 14/21

ENCTR 24/14	ARABY 32/14	ARABY 32/24	GALNT 54/03
LITTL 70/08	PNFUL 110/26	PNFUL 111/09	PNFUL 111/17
DEAD 204/03	DEAD 204/03	DEAD 213/09	DEAD 217/33

THOUGHT-TORMENTED (2) .... DEAD 192/12
    DEAD 203/22
THOUSANDS (1) .... LITTL 81/30
THREADBARE (1) .... PNFUL 115/21
THREADING (1) .... DEAD 191/21
THREATEN (1) .... EVELN 38/05
THREE (45) .... SISTR 14/19

SISTR 17/10	ENCTR 22/31	ENCTR 22/33	ENCTR 25/23
RACE 44/15	GALNT 57/16	HOUSE 65/25	HOUSE 65/26

LITTL 79/20	LITTL 80/16	PARTS 90/16	PARTS 94/12
PARTS 94/16	PARTS 96/14	CLAY 105/03	PNFUL 111/01
PNFUL 112/06	IVY D 122/11	IVY D 127/08	IVY D 127/19
IVY D 129/09	IVY D 129/25	IVY D 131/21	MOTHR 140/07
GRACE 152/32	GRACE 156/10	GRACE 172/29	DEAD 176/22
DEAD 177/04	DEAD 177/14	DEAD 177/23	DEAD 182/28
DEAD 183/05	DEAD 183/11	DEAD 183/33	DEAD 184/03
DEAD 192/10	DEAD 197/01	DEAD 198/10	DEAD 201/30
DEAD 204/16	DEAD 204/21	DEAD 205/09	DEAD 205/15

THREE-MASTER (1) .... ENCTR 23/21
THREE-QUARTERS (1) .... MOTHR 141/30
THREES (1) .... CLAY 101/02
THREE-SHILLING (1) .... DEAD 176/20
THRESHOLD (1) .... PNFUL 116/07
THRESHOLDS (1) .... LITTL 71/31
THREW (4) .... RACE 46/28

HOUSE 66/29	LITTL 83/03	DEAD 216/11

THRICE (1) .... SISTR 13/22
THRIFTY (1) .... MOTHR 137/09
THRILLED (1) .... GRACE 170/08
THRILLS (1) .... GALNT 59/11
THROAT (11) .... GALNT 56/30

HOUSE 66/03	HOUSE 68/17	PARTS 87/27	PARTS 88/18
IVY D 134/05	GRACE 151/29	GRACE 158/32	GRACE 159/01
DEAD 199/34	DEAD 211/33		

THROBBED (1) .... GALNT 54/16
THRONE (1) .... IVY D 132/04
THRONG (1) .... ARABY 31/11
THRONGED (1) .... ARABY 34/14
THROUGH (55) .... SISTR 12/20

SISTR 13/22	SISTR 14/16	ENCTR 22/01	ENCTR 24/02
ENCTR 27/30	ARABY 30/07	ARABY 31/04	ARABY 31/11
ARABY 31/22	ARABY 32/18	ARABY 33/31	ARABY 34/27
EVELN 38/21	EVELN 39/13	EVELN 40/26	RACE 42/04
RACE 44/14	RACE 45/22	GALNT 52/05	GALNT 56/26
GALNT 60/25	HOUSE 62/33	HOUSE 64/19	HOUSE 67/34
LITTL 71/11	LITTL 71/32	LITTL 83/32	PARTS 92/33
PARTS 93/10	PARTS 97/20	CLAY 99/12	PNFUL 113/07
PNFUL 117/02	PNFUL 117/23	MOTHR 139/11	MOTHR 143/17
MOTHR 149/24	GRACE 151/13	GRACE 151/22	GRACE 152/32
GRACE 159/33	DEAD 176/09	DEAD 177/19	DEAD 190/32
DEAD 192/05	DEAD 199/14	DEAD 200/24	DEAD 203/14
DEAD 204/05	DEAD 209/04	DEAD 213/09	DEAD 213/23
DEAD 215/13	DEAD 224/02		

THROW (4) .... ENCTR 27/02

EVELN 38/15	CLAY 105/18	IVY D 130/01

THROWING (2) .... IVY D 124/17

DEAD 218/15

THROWN (7) .... GALNT 55/04

HOUSE 66/07	PARTS 90/07	CLAY 104/02
DEAD 221/16	DEAD 222/18	

THRUST (1) .... DEAD 194/09
THRUSTING (1) .... IVY D 120/32
THUDS (1) .... DEAD 178/26
THUMB (1) .... DEAD 215/20
THUMPING (1) .... PARTS 93/06
THUNDERING (1) .... DEAD 215/30
TH'UPPER (1) .... GRACE 161/09
THURSDAY (5) .... IVY D 120/07

MOTHR 140/18	GRACE 162/14	GRACE 162/15

THUS (2) .... MOTHR 139/05

IVY D 119/20	GRACE 162/28

PNFUL 112/16

TICKET (2) .... IVY D 122/06
    DEAD 213/21
TICKET-COLLECTOR (1) .... RACE   47/12
TICKETS (1) .... MOTHR 139/01
TICKING (1) .... ARABY 33/05
TICKLISH (1) .... GALNT 53/27
TIDE (1) .... DEAD 212/07
TIDY (1) .... CLAY 101/33
TIE (6) .... RACE   45/31
    LITTL 75/07   LITTL 81/11   GRACE 166/22   DEAD 179/07
    DEAD 180/30
TIED (2) .... SISTR 12/03
    LITTL 83/01
TIERNEY (5) .... IVY D 119/01
    IVY D 119/12   IVY D 122/08   IVY D 123/17   IVY D 131/07
TIERNEY'S (1) .... IVY D 119/15
TIETJENS (1) .... DEAD 199/05
TIGHT (3) .... LITTL 73/02
    LITTL 82/24   PNFUL 113/09
TIGHTLY (6) .... ARABY 34/12
    EVELN 38/20   LITTL 85/15   IVY D 125/24   DEAD 178/24
    DEAD 215/23
TILL (18) .... ENCTR 21/25
    ENCTR 22/19   ENCTR 27/32   ARABY 30/06   GALNT 56/31
    HOUSE 61/06   LITTL 79/08   PARTS 88/01   PARTS 91/30
    PARTS 91/33   CLAY 101/18   CLAY 101/19   CLAY 105/08
    IVY D 122/07   IVY D 127/14   IVY D 132/05   GRACE 155/29
    DEAD 209/11
TIM (1) .... PARTS 94/24
TIME (114)
TIMES (20) .... ENCTR 26/11
    ENCTR 26/12   ARABY 31/14   ARABY 31/29   RACE   43/18
    GALNT 49/11   LITTL 71/22   LITTL 72/19   LITTL 75/27
    PARTS 89/21   PARTS 94/05   CLAY 104/23   PNFUL 111/19
    IVY D 118/08   IVY D 122/18   IVY D 127/08   GRACE 154/06
    GRACE 157/16   GRACE 158/23   GRACE 159/34
TIMID (2) .... ENCTR 19/12
    LITTL 77/28
TIMIDITY (1) .... LITTL 80/29
TIMIDLY (2) .... ARABY 34/32
    HOUSE 67/05
TIMING (1) .... GALNT 56/11
TIMOROUS (1) .... PNFUL 111/04
TIN (2) .... ENCTR 19/14
    CLAY 101/06
TINCTURE (1) .... PARTS 94/33
TINKER (3) .... IVY D 121/14
    IVY D 121/15   IVY D 123/15
TINPOT (1) .... IVY D 129/06
TINT (1) .... PNFUL 108/17
TINY (3) .... CLAY 101/28
    CLAY 103/12   CLAY 106/01
TIP (7) .... GALNT 52/23
    CLAY 101/13   CLAY 101/14   CLAY 101/18   CLAY 101/18
    CLAY 105/08   CLAY 105/09
TIPTOE (5) .... SISTR 14/16
    HOUSE 67/18   GRACE 172/04   DEAD 190/11   DEAD 217/24
TIRADE (2) .... PARTS 91/08
    PARTS 91/11
TIRED (13) .... SISTR 10/06
    ENCTR 23/32   ENCTR 24/06   ENCTR 24/09   ENCTR 25/15
    EVELN 36/03   GALNT 50/16   GALNT 57/34   CLAY 105/29

	DEAD	192/01	DEAD	214/19	DEAD	216/24	DEAD	216/27
TIRESOME (3)							SISTR	10/04
	SISTR	11/17	LITTL	71/05				
TISSUES (1)							GALNT	50/27
TIVOLI (2)							PARTS	94/20
	PARTS	95/10						
TIZZIE (1)							EVELN	37/03
TO (1752)								
TOAST (7)							SISTR	12/15
	EVELN	39/28	RACE	46/27	RACE	48/15	LITTL	75/28
	LITTL	76/34	DEAD	205/09				
TOBACCO (3)							IVY D	118/14
	IVY D	118/16	IVY D	125/02				
TO-DAY (5)							LITTL	75/29
	PNFUL	113/21	IVY D	129/29	IVY D	131/13	DEAD	199/19
TODDLING (3)							DEAD	177/09
	DEAD	196/10	DEAD	197/32				
TOECAPS (1)							DEAD	177/17
TOES (2)							CLAY	102/03
	DEAD	177/17						
TOFF (1)							IVY D	131/17
TOGETHER (47)							SISTR	17/10
	ENCTR	20/03	ARABY	31/28	ARABY	32/24	EVELN	36/12
	EVELN	38/23	EVELN	40/03	RACE	44/27	RACE	45/18
	RACE	47/08	RACE	48/25	HOUSE	67/17	HOUSE	67/18
	LITTL	73/14	LITTL	80/01	LITTL	85/10	PARTS	92/17
	PARTS	98/20	CLAY	102/10	PNFUL	108/06	PNFUL	110/15
	IVY D	118/01	IVY D	122/12	IVY D	126/29	MOTHR	138/01
	MOTHR	143/32	MOTHR	146/03	MOTHR	147/06	GRACE	153/14
	GRACE	153/19	GRACE	163/10	GRACE	163/16	GRACE	170/32
	GRACE	171/10	DEAD	188/27	DEAD	190/02	DEAD	202/24
	DEAD	204/12	DEAD	205/09	DEAD	213/16	DEAD	213/32
	DEAD	214/01	DEAD	214/12	DEAD	215/17	DEAD	219/32
	DEAD	221/03	DEAD	222/10				
TOIL (1)							SISTR	14/09
TOILET-TABLE (1)							DEAD	215/33
TOKEN (1)							PARTS	94/32
TOLD (54)							SISTR	10/16
	SISTR	13/03	SISTR	13/16	SISTR	17/08	ENCTR	22/10
	ENCTR	27/24	ARABY	34/09	EVELN	39/12	EVELN	39/14
	GALNT	50/33	GALNT	51/03	GALNT	51/10	GALNT	51/17
	GALNT	54/01	HOUSE	66/27	HOUSE	67/25	LITTL	78/18
	LITTL	78/33	PARTS	87/10	PARTS	93/25	PARTS	93/30
	PARTS	94/24	PARTS	95/09	CLAY	100/33	CLAY	104/05
	CLAY	104/26	CLAY	105/11	CLAY	105/18	PNFUL	110/32
	PNFUL	111/07	PNFUL	117/29	IVY D	123/05	IVY D	128/05
	IVY D	128/08	IVY D	128/25	MOTHR	141/04	MOTHR	146/23
	MOTHR	148/21	GRACE	157/33	GRACE	170/15	GRACE	173/30
	GRACE	174/10	DEAD	182/02	DEAD	185/07	DEAD	190/17
	DEAD	194/08	DEAD	199/08	DEAD	200/21	DEAD	209/11
	DEAD	211/08	DEAD	211/31	DEAD	221/22	DEAD	222/17
	DEAD	223/10						
TOLERANCE (1)							HOUSE	64/17
TOLL (1)							ENCTR	23/17
TOM (17)							PARTS	97/24
	GRACE	152/14	GRACE	152/21	GRACE	160/16	GRACE	161/01
	GRACE	162/34	GRACE	163/14	GRACE	163/26	GRACE	164/28
	GRACE	164/31	GRACE	165/06	GRACE	165/07	GRACE	165/08
	GRACE	166/02	GRACE	167/29	GRACE	169/06	GRACE	171/19
TOMB (1)							LITTL	83/33
TOMMY (8)							LITTL	74/28
	LITTL	75/18	LITTL	76/05	LITTL	76/31	LITTL	77/32

LITTL 78/04	LITTL 79/07	LITTL 79/18	
TO-MORROW (5)			ENCTR 21/25
EVELN 40/32	LITTL 79/25	LITTL 81/27	IVY D 128/26
TOM'S (1)			DEAD 180/16
TON (1)			LITTL 75/17
TONALITY (1)			DEAD 210/19
TONE (17)			ARABY 35/15
GALNT 52/30	LITTL 74/05	LITTL 78/14	LITTL 81/16
LITTL 82/02	PNFUL 110/07	GRACE 161/02	GRACE 162/30
DEAD 178/01	DEAD 179/19	DEAD 188/25	DEAD 193/02
DEAD 206/09	DEAD 206/12	DEAD 211/31	DEAD 220/08
TONGUE (13)			SISTR 13/27
GALNT 50/16	GALNT 50/29	GALNT 53/03	LITTL 76/08
PARTS 91/22	PARTS 92/16	GRACE 153/29	GRACE 156/30
GRACE 158/01	GRACE 158/11	GRACE 158/12	DEAD 190/24
TONGUES (4)			RACE 46/14
PARTS 94/16	MOTHR 137/03	MOTHR 146/19	
TO-NIGHT (15)			LITTL 79/26
PNFUL 109/22	IVY D 121/06	GRACE 155/10	DEAD 180/02
DEAD 180/27	DEAD 184/07	DEAD 193/23	DEAD 202/19
DEAD 203/26	DEAD 204/04	DEAD 204/11	DEAD 204/26
DEAD 204/34	DEAD 212/15		
TONS (1)			LITTL 79/08
TOO (78)			SISTR 10/29
SISTR 11/01	SISTR 11/29	SISTR 12/18	SISTR 15/06
SISTR 17/16	SISTR 17/17	SISTR 18/09	ENCTR 19/11
ENCTR 22/25	ENCTR 24/09	ENCTR 24/09	EVELN 36/14
EVELN 37/03	EVELN 39/25	EVELN 40/19	RACE 43/12
RACE 44/13	RACE 45/29	RACE 48/21	GALNT 51/11
GALNT 52/18	GALNT 53/04	GALNT 54/11	GALNT 56/30
GALNT 58/06	GALNT 59/02	GALNT 59/32	HOUSE 64/13
HOUSE 66/22	HOUSE 67/10	LITTL 76/03	LITTL 79/03
LITTL 79/28	LITTL 81/31	LITTL 83/22	LITTL 83/24
LITTL 84/02	PARTS 92/29	PARTS 94/24	PARTS 94/27
CLAY 100/20	CLAY 101/29	CLAY 103/19	CLAY 104/19
CLAY 106/08	PNFUL 111/03	PNFUL 116/32	PNFUL 116/32
IVY D 125/03	IVY D 125/05	IVY D 127/07	IVY D 131/16
MOTHR 140/03	MOTHR 143/05	GRACE 163/25	GRACE 164/05
GRACE 164/28	GRACE 165/29	DEAD 175/17	DEAD 176/15
DEAD 180/11	DEAD 180/24	DEAD 182/20	DEAD 183/22
DEAD 189/03	DEAD 193/20	DEAD 198/32	DEAD 199/08
DEAD 200/04	DEAD 202/17	DEAD 204/31	DEAD 207/13
DEAD 211/08	DEAD 215/28	DEAD 217/09	DEAD 222/26
DEAD 223/31			
TOOK (63)			SISTR 14/03
SISTR 16/13	SISTR 17/13	SISTR 17/21	ARABY 34/15
EVELN 39/21	RACE 43/24	RACE 47/10	RACE 47/27
GALNT 56/03	GALNT 56/25	GALNT 59/03	GALNT 60/09
LITTL 70/14	LITTL 71/13	LITTL 71/24	LITTL 73/22
LITTL 75/03	LITTL 77/15	LITTL 79/06	LITTL 80/06
LITTL 80/34	PARTS 88/13	PARTS 90/10	PARTS 98/08
CLAY 100/07	CLAY 100/15	CLAY 101/26	CLAY 102/26
CLAY 105/14	PNFUL 108/32	PNFUL 109/24	PNFUL 111/04
IVY D 119/05	IVY D 122/12	IVY D 125/01	IVY D 129/17
IVY D 129/20	IVY D 130/25	IVY D 130/27	IVY D 131/10
IVY D 133/34	MOTHR 137/06	MOTHR 138/34	MOTHR 143/26
MOTHR 143/29	MOTHR 145/11	GRACE 152/23	GRACE 154/13
GRACE 162/10	GRACE 163/20	GRACE 169/01	DEAD 178/25
DEAD 179/07	DEAD 183/05	DEAD 183/09	DEAD 183/17
DEAD 188/24	DEAD 197/05	DEAD 198/12	DEAD 198/15
DEAD 200/20	DEAD 216/07		
TOP (8)			ENCTR 28/03

```
       LITTL  75/02    CLAY  102/21    PNFUL 108/03    DEAD   182/33
       DEAD  192/06    DEAD  199/08    DEAD  209/26
TOPPED (2) ................................................ RACE    42/13
       DEAD  196/27
TOPS (1) .................................................. DEAD   179/24
TORE (1) .................................................. IVY D  119/22
TOREADOR (1) .............................................. GALNT   50/03
TORPID (1) ................................................ RACE    46/24
TORRENT (1) ............................................... RACE    47/05
TORTUOUS (1) .............................................. MOTHR  145/18
TOSS (1) .................................................. GALNT   53/30
TOSSED (3) ................................................ ARABY   30/24
       LITTL  81/34    MOTHR 149/05
TOTTIES (1) ............................................... ENCTR   25/23
TOUCH (11) ................................................ GALNT   52/22
       HOUSE  67/21    PARTS  92/26    PARTS  92/26    PNFUL 117/05
       PNFUL 117/05    PNFUL 117/31    DEAD  189/17    DEAD   189/19
       DEAD  215/12    DEAD  220/26
TOUCHED (8) ............................................... ARABY   33/13
       LITTL  72/01    LITTL  72/11    LITTL  73/22    LITTL  76/33
       PNFUL 116/04    GRACE 152/19    DEAD  184/26
TOUCHING (2) .............................................. CLAY   102/03
       DEAD  217/29
TOUR (1) .................................................. DEAD   189/10
TOURISTS (1) .............................................. HOUSE   62/05
TOWARDS (59) .............................................. SISTR   13/12
       SISTR  13/13    SISTR  14/12    SISTR  14/34    ENCTR   24/29
       ENCTR  26/16    ENCTR  26/21    ARABY  30/04    ARABY   32/06
       ARABY  33/01    ARABY  34/13    EVELN  40/33    RACE    42/01
       RACE   47/16    GALNT  50/01    GALNT  56/09    GALNT   56/13
       GALNT  58/15    GALNT  59/23    GALNT  60/04    GALNT   60/07
       GALNT  60/10    GALNT  60/28    HOUSE  63/29    LITTL   72/21
       LITTL  73/13    LITTL  80/34    PARTS  88/08    PARTS   88/29
       PARTS  90/12    PARTS  94/12    PARTS  96/21    PNFUL  112/08
       PNFUL 114/05    PNFUL 117/10    PNFUL 117/21    IVY D  130/28
       MOTHR 138/26    MOTHR 146/13    GRACE 153/16    GRACE  162/12
       GRACE 170/14    GRACE 173/14    DEAD  178/28    DEAD   180/33
       DEAD  190/32    DEAD  193/28    DEAD  205/14    DEAD   205/23
       DEAD  205/27    DEAD  210/15    DEAD  211/02    DEAD   212/05
       DEAD  214/09    DEAD  216/12    DEAD  216/21    DEAD   218/05
       DEAD  219/23    DEAD  223/13
TOWEL (1) ................................................. HOUSE   68/21
TOWER (1) ................................................. DEAD   186/18
TOWN (3) .................................................. GALNT   51/28
       GRACE 158/23    GRACE 172/31
TRACE (1) ................................................. GRACE  158/13
TRACES (1) ................................................ GRACE  153/03
TRACT (1) ................................................. PNFUL  115/25
TRACTS (1) ................................................ CLAY   100/31
TRADITION (4) ............................................. GRACE  154/04
       DEAD  202/33    DEAD  203/01    DEAD  203/09
TRAFFIC (1) ............................................... RACE    45/14
TRAGIC (2) ................................................ GALNT   53/16
       DEAD  207/25
TRAILING (1) .............................................. GRACE  166/18
TRAIN (11) ................................................ ENCTR   24/13
       ARABY  34/16    ARABY  34/16    ARABY  34/20    ARABY   34/22
       RACE   47/10    PNFUL 113/27    PNFUL 113/31    PNFUL  114/02
       PNFUL 114/03    PNFUL 117/22
TRAM (16) ................................................. GALNT   51/05
       GALNT  52/27    GALNT  52/27    GALNT  56/15    GALNT   59/20
       PARTS  96/31    PARTS  97/10    CLAY  100/13    CLAY   102/01
```

```
        CLAY   102/11      CLAY   102/30      CLAY   103/31      PNFUL 108/32
        PNFUL 112/08      PNFUL 112/24      PNFUL 116/20
TRAM-DRIVERS (1) ....................................  RACE    45/15
TRAM-GOINGS (1) .....................................  PARTS   93/12
TRAMLOAD (1) ........................................  ENCTR   21/33
TRAMPS (1) ..........................................  LITTL   73/14
TRAMS (1) ...........................................  GALNT   54/19
TRANQUILLY (1) ......................................  MOTHR 146/03
TRANSACTION (1) .....................................  LITTL   72/28
TRANSEPT (1) ........................................  GRACE 172/02
TRANSFER (2) ........................................  IVY D 128/19
        IVY D 128/21
TRANSFERRED (1) .....................................  DEAD   200/08
TRANSLATE (1) .......................................  RACE    45/07
TRANSLATION (1) .....................................  PNFUL 108/04
TRANSPORTED (1) .....................................  ENCTR   23/18
TRANSVERSE (1) ......................................  DEAD   197/04
TRAP (1) ............................................  DEAD   207/09
TRAVELLED (1) .......................................  LITTL   70/03
TRAVELLER (2) .......................................  GRACE 153/34
        GRACE 158/23
TRAVELLERS (1) ......................................  GRACE 159/24
TRAVELLING (1) ......................................  IVY D 127/03
TRAVERSED (2) .......................................  ENCTR   20/09
        HOUSE   63/31
TRAY (2) ............................................  GRACE 161/30
        DEAD   215/30
TRAYFUL (1) .........................................  PNFUL 108/33
TREACHERY (1) .......................................  IVY D 134/25
TREAT (4) ...........................................  EVELN   37/33
        MOTHR 141/18      MOTHR 148/30      MOTHR 148/31
TREATED (5) .........................................  EVELN   37/34
        IVY D 133/05      MOTHR 148/06      MOTHR 148/11      MOTHR 148/16
TREBELLI (1) ........................................  DEAD   199/06
TREBLE (2) ..........................................  GALNT   54/15
        DEAD   187/12
TREE (3) ............................................  PNFUL 117/29
        DEAD   221/25      DEAD   223/16
TREELESS (1) ........................................  DEAD   223/29
TREES (4) ...........................................  ENCTR   21/34
        PNFUL 117/02      DEAD   192/06      DEAD   202/10
TREMBLE (3) .........................................  LITTL   72/20
        LITTL   73/25      PNFUL 112/09
TREMBLED (5) ........................................  SISTR   12/17
        ARABY   31/28      EVELN   40/13      LITTL   84/16      PARTS   96/17
TREMBLING (6) .......................................  SISTR   12/19
        DEAD   192/02      DEAD   202/02      DEAD   215/25      DEAD   217/07
        DEAD   217/27
TREPIDATION (1) .....................................  RACE    45/27
TRIAL (5) ...........................................  PARTS   96/01
        PARTS   96/06      PARTS   96/15      MOTHR 142/32      DEAD   183/09
TRIBES (1) ..........................................  ARABY   30/09
TRIBUTE (1) .........................................  MOTHR 145/10
TRICK (1) ...........................................  IVY D 130/24
TRICKLED (1) ........................................  GRACE 150/08
TRICKS (2) ..........................................  RACE    48/23
        GALNT   53/25
TRICKY (5) ..........................................  IVY D 122/08
        IVY D 123/16      IVY D 123/18      IVY D 123/27      IVY D 123/28
TRIED (31) ..........................................  SISTR   11/22
        SISTR   12/25      SISTR   13/31      ENCTR   19/06      ENCTR   23/24
        EVELN   37/19      GALNT   52/24      GALNT   59/24      HOUSE   68/13
```

HOUSE 68/16	LITTL 73/29	LITTL 83/05	LITTL 84/08
LITTL 84/25	PARTS 92/20	CLAY 103/24	CLAY 106/12
PNFUL 109/26	PNFUL 115/06	IVY D 119/30	IVY D 135/02
GRACE 150/01	GRACE 156/22	GRACE 172/18	GRACE 172/20
DEAD 179/06	DEAD 189/24	DEAD 190/05	DEAD 190/24
DEAD 190/30	DEAD 220/08		

TRIFLE (1) .... LITTL 80/15
TRILL (1) .... DEAD 187/12
TRIMLY (1) .... RACE 42/15
TRINITY (4) .... GALNT 53/18

DEAD 209/14	DEAD 209/16	DEAD 209/20

TRIP (3) .... LITTL 76/09

CLAY 100/11	DEAD 191/13

TRIUMPH (2) .... RACE 46/18

DEAD 220/20

TRIUMPHANT (1) .... LITTL 80/22
TRIVIAL (1) .... GALNT 56/27
TRODDEN (1) .... SISTR 14/23
TROLLEYS (1) .... PARTS 93/13
TROOP (1) .... ENCTR 22/26
TROTTING (1) .... DEAD 178/31
TROUBLE (9) .... SISTR 16/22

EVELN 38/12	HOUSE 68/01	LITTL 76/25	IVY D 126/15
IVY D 129/02	MOTHR 142/02	MOTHR 148/06	GRACE 152/14

TROUBLED (6) .... GALNT 56/32

LITTL 72/18	LITTL 72/19	PNFUL 112/02	MOTHR 137/14
GRACE 168/16			

TROUBLES (1) .... ARABY 31/08
TROUSERS (4) .... HOUSE 66/26

IVY D 123/27	GRACE 156/08	GRACE 172/11

TRUCULENT (2) .... SISTR 14/29

SISTR 18/11

TRUE (13) .... SISTR 9/09

SISTR 16/19	ENCTR 19/18	GALNT 58/26	LITTL 77/16
LITTL 78/23	IVY D 122/17	MOTHR 140/31	MOTHR 140/32
GRACE 160/18	DEAD 187/05	DEAD 188/06	DEAD 204/15

TRUMPERY (1) .... GRACE 167/34
TRUST (2) .... SISTR 16/18

DEAD 203/05

TRUSTED (1) .... MOTHR 139/02
TRUSTFULNESS (2) .... MOTHR 142/07

MOTHR 142/12

TRUTH (7) .... GRACE 162/34

GRACE 165/30	GRACE 174/28	DEAD 189/30	DEAD 193/23
DEAD 193/24	DEAD 194/02		

TRY (7) .... SISTR 18/03

GALNT 60/26	LITTL 83/24	PARTS 96/04	IVY D 124/23
GRACE 161/16	DEAD 220/14		

TRYING (12) .... GALNT 54/29

LITTL 82/29	PARTS 92/06	MOTHR 136/18	GRACE 151/34
GRACE 160/13	DEAD 188/02	DEAD 188/21	DEAD 191/10
DEAD 195/13	DEAD 201/10	DEAD 210/01	

TUAM (2) .... GRACE 169/22

GRACE 169/25

TUBE (1) .... PARTS 86/02
TUBS (1) .... CLAY 99/14
TUCKED (1) .... DEAD 213/05
TUESDAY (2) .... SISTR 15/20

MOTHR 148/23

TUESDAY'S (1) .... HOUSE 64/05
TULLE (1) .... GALNT 55/29
TUMBLED (2) .... EVELN 38/34

EVELN 41/06
TUMBLER (1) .... HOUSE 67/16
TUMBLERS (2) .... PNFUL 116/13
  IVY D 129/01
TUMID (1) .... DEAD 184/29
TUNE (2) .... IVY D 120/01
  DEAD 202/05
TURF (3) .... ENCTR 24/22
  GALNT 53/08   GRACE 167/32
TURKISH (1) .... MOTHR 137/01
TURN (19) .... LITTL 74/15
  PARTS 93/23   IVY D 119/28   IVY D 122/10   IVY D 124/27
  MOTHR 138/22 MOTHR 145/05   GRACE 155/18   DEAD 176/27
  DEAD 186/13   DEAD 188/11   DEAD 188/23   DEAD 194/21
  DEAD 203/11   DEAD 204/19   DEAD 204/29   DEAD 214/16
  DEAD 217/09   DEAD 223/23
TURNED (53) .... ENCTR 20/22
  ENCTR 22/20   ENCTR 24/28   ENCTR 27/18   ENCTR 28/04
  ARABY 32/02   ARABY 35/27   GALNT 52/05   GALNT 54/06
  GALNT 56/09   GALNT 56/12   GALNT 56/16   GALNT 56/33
  GALNT 58/16   GALNT 58/30   GALNT 59/30   GALNT 60/03
  GALNT 60/14   LITTL 71/04   LITTL 72/21   LITTL 74/25
  LITTL 81/11   LITTL 84/07   PARTS 91/07   PARTS 94/12
  PNFUL 117/20 PNFUL 117/27   IVY D 120/28   IVY D 122/13
  IVY D 125/28 GRACE 152/17   GRACE 162/12   GRACE 163/12
  GRACE 170/14 GRACE 170/27   GRACE 173/14   GRACE 173/19
  DEAD 183/27   DEAD 184/05   DEAD 184/20   ·DEAD 189/23
  DEAD 191/18   DEAD 192/33   DEAD 193/33   DEAD 194/11
  DEAD 194/19   DEAD 194/32   DEAD 202/30   DEAD 205/23
  DEAD 212/05   DEAD 216/14   DEAD 216/20   DEAD 220/06
TURNING (10) .... ARABY 30/14
  LITTL 72/12   PARTS 96/25   IVY D 132/31   GRACE 150/04
  GRACE 163/07 DEAD 180/03   DEAD 187/29   DEAD 205/14
  DEAD 205/27
TURNS (1) .... GALNT 55/16
TURNSTILE (1) .... ARABY 34/27
'TWAS (1) .... IVY D 134/23
TWEED (1) .... LITTL 70/03
TWEEDS (1) .... GRACE 172/08
TWELVE (2) .... HOUSE 64/23
  LITTL 79/02
TWENTY (6) .... GALNT 53/20
  CLAY 100/05   CLAY 100/06   CLAY 100/06   MOTHR 139/13
  GRACE 157/09
TWENTY-FIVE (1) .... GRACE 156/13
TWENTY-FOUR (1) .... MOTHR 137/19
TWENTY-SIX (1) .... RACE 43/13
TWENTY-TWO (1) .... PNFUL 115/01
TWICE (16) .... SISTR 13/21
  ENCTR 25/34   ARABY 35/23   GALNT 50/01   GALNT 55/17
  PARTS 91/05   PARTS 95/20   PARTS 97/06   PNFUL 109/20
  PNFUL 110/07 IVY D 118/08   IVY D 134/05   MOTHR 142/27
  GRACE 173/04 DEAD 184/13   DEAD 201/31
TWIG (1) .... IVY D 124/24
TWILIGHT (2) .... GALNT 52/08
  PNFUL 113/07
TWINED (1) .... RACE 46/10
TWINKLING (2) .... ARABY 34/18
  GALNT 49/19
TWIRL (1) .... GRACE 152/06
TWISTED '(1) .... MOTHR 142/13
TWISTING (1) .... DEAD 194/18

```
TWITCHED (1) ..................................... PARTS  91/29
TWITCHING (1) .................................... ENCTR  27/18
TWITTERING (1) ...................,............... DEAD  213/18
TWO (117)
TWO-AND-FOUR (1) ................................. CLAY  102/28
TWO'D (1) ........................................ IVY D 130/19
TWOPENCE (2) ..................................... GALNT  58/13
     PARTS  97/01
TWOS (1) ......................................... CLAY  101/01
TWO-SHILLING (1) ................................. MOTHR 139/01
TWO-THIRDS (1) ................................... GRACE 173/12
TYING (1) ........................................ LITTL  82/03
TYPE (1) ......................................... MOTHR 138/21
TYPED (1) ........................................ PARTS  90/18
TYPEWRITING (1) .................................. HOUSE  63/13
TYPIST (1) ....................................... HOUSE  63/02


'UCH (2) ......................................... GRACE 152/28
     GRACE 153/07
UGLY (2) ......................................... ARABY  32/27
     GRACE 153/31
ULSTER (1) ....................................... GRACE 152/12
UMBRELLA (4) ..................................... PARTS  90/05
     MOTHR 145/24    MOTHR 145/25    MOTHR 149/33
UMBRELLAS (2) .................................... SISTR  11/34
     SISTR  12/02
UNABASHED (1) .................................... GALNT  55/33
UNABLE (1) ....................................... MOTHR 141/08
UNACCUMSTOMED (1) ................................ EVELN  39/04
UNAMIABLE (1) .................................... PNFUL 108/19
UNANIMOUS (1) .................................... GRACE 169/14
UNASSUMING (2) ................................... SISTR  11/32
     MOTHR 142/28
UNAWARE (2) ...................................... PARTS  87/34
     DEAD  212/04
UNBEARABLE (1) ................................... GRACE 156/11
UNBENDING (1) .................................... MOTHR 136/11
UNBOSOMING (1) ................................... GALNT  52/25
UNCANNY (1) ...................................... SISTR  10/01
UNCARPETED (1) ................................... PNFUL 107/07
UNCEASING (1) .................................... GALNT  49/08
UNCEASINGLY (1) .................................. GALNT  49/07
UNCERTAIN (1) .................................... DEAD  210/20
UNCHANGING (1) ................................... GALNT  49/08
UNCLE (9) ........................................ SISTR  10/11
     SISTR  10/19    SISTR  11/01    SISTR  13/01   ARABY  30/14
     ARABY  32/28    ARABY  33/03    ARABY  33/20   ARABY  34/06
                                                    ARABY  33/28
UNCLE'S (1) ...................................... LITTL  83/12
UNCONSCIOUS (3) ..................................
     MOTHR 140/22    GRACE 157/03                   MOTHR 145/20
UNCORKING (1) .................................... SISTR  13/26
UNCOVER (1) ...................................... GALNT  57/12
UNCOVERED (3) ....................................
     IVY D 125/27    GRACE 173/16                   IVY D 134/07
UNCROWNED (1) .................................... CLAY   99/06
UNCUT (1) ........................................ IVY D 135/06
UNDAUNTED (1) .................................... DEAD  179/09
UNDECIDED (1) .................................... SISTR  10/18
UNDER (44) ....................................... ENCTR  23/14
     SISTR  11/33    SISTR  17/21    ENCTR  20/01   RACE   44/24
     ENCTR  27/18    ARABY  29/16    EVELN  38/21
```

RACE 46/22	GALNT 50/31	HOUSE 64/07	LITTL 70/11
LITTL 71/03	LITTL 71/26	LITTL 71/33	LITTL 77/06
PARTS 86/08	PARTS 95/14	PARTS 96/17	CLAY 103/12
PNFUL 108/21	PNFUL 110/01	PNFUL 111/02	PNFUL 117/02
PNFUL 117/29	GRACE 159/31	GRACE 167/32	GRACE 169/04
GRACE 170/20	GRACE 172/27	DEAD 176/29	DEAD 186/15
DEAD 189/25	DEAD 190/09	DEAD 200/23	DEAD 202/24
DEAD 212/01	DEAD 213/05	DEAD 214/21	DEAD 215/13
DEAD 221/13	DEAD 223/05	DEAD 223/16	

UNDERFOOT (2) .... DEAD 180/27
    DEAD 212/33
UNDERHAND (1) .... PNFUL 110/16
UNDERSTAND (13) .... ENCTR 20/28

ENCTR 27/31	ARABY 31/13	PARTS 87/20	CLAY 104/07
IVY D 124/29	IVY D 124/30	DEAD 179/16	DEAD 187/32
DEAD 201/09	DEAD 204/23	DEAD 208/16	DEAD 209/17

UNDERSTANDING (4) .... HOUSE 63/19
    GRACE 151/30   GRACE 163/18   GRACE 174/02
UNDERSTOOD (9) .... SISTR 11/24

RACE 48/19	PARTS 94/32	CLAY 105/19	PNFUL 116/30
GRACE 174/03	GRACE 174/18	GRACE 174/19	GRACE 174/20

UNDERTAKE (1) .... SISTR 13/15
UNDERTAKEN (1) .... MOTHR 142/23
UNDERTONE (2) .... DEAD 185/06
    DEAD 201/20
UNDERTOOK (1) .... RACE 46/18
UNDESIRABLE (1) .... EVELN 38/26
UNDID (1) .... IVY D 118/15
UNDONE (1) .... GRACE 151/06
UNDOUBTEDLY (1) .... ENCTR 25/03
UNDRESSING (2) .... HOUSE 67/04
    DEAD 214/14
UNEASILY (1) .... GALNT 60/24
UNEASY (1) .... SISTR 13/28
UNEXPECTEDLY (1) .... RACE 43/04
UNFASTENED (1) .... GRACE 151/06
UNFINISHED (1) .... SISTR 11/20
UNFIT (1) .... PNFUL 115/29
UNFOLDING (1) .... ENCTR 27/27
UNFORTUNATE (2) .... LITTL 80/28
    IVY D 126/32
UNFORTUNATELY (2) .... RACE 44/02
    MOTHR 142/26
UNFURLED (1) .... IVY D 134/20
UNGALLANT (1) .... GRACE 156/03
UNHAPPY (1) .... EVELN 40/20
UNHEALTHY (1) .... LITTL 75/06
UNHEEDED (1) .... DEAD 197/34
UNHOOKING (1) .... DEAD 216/16
UNIFORMS (1) .... DEAD 197/03
UNINHABITED (1) .... ARABY 29/03
UNION (3) .... ENCTR 19/02
    PNFUL 111/21   GRACE 167/06
UNIQUE (3) .... GALNT 50/13
    PNFUL 110/33   DEAD 203/01
UNISON (1)... DEAD 205/15
UNITED (3) .... RACE 47/32
    PNFUL 111/21   IVY D 135/07
UNIVERSE (1) .... DEAD 224/03
UNIVERSITY (4) .... RACE 43/23
    DEAD 187/01   DEAD 188/19   DEAD 188/27
UNJUST (1) .... LITTL 80/24

UNKEMPT (1) .... ENCTR 20/10
UNKNOWN (3) .... EVELN 37/31
   MOTHR 143/16   MOTHR 143/25
UNLESS (3) .... DEAD 205/25
   DEAD 205/26   DEAD 211/27
UNLOADED (1) .... ENCTR 22/23
UNMISTAKABLE (1) .... RACE 45/07
UNNERVED (1) .... DEAD 192/16
UNNOTICED (1) .... MOTHR 142/29
UNPLEASANT (2) .... GALNT 54/27
   DEAD 190/25
UNPRESENTABLE (1) .... GRACE 157/15
UNPURCHASABLE (1) .... RACE 45/33
UNRESENTFULLY (1) .... DEAD 222/05
UNROLLED (1) .... MOTHR 139/24
UNRULINESS (1) .... ENCTR 20/01
UNRULY (1) .... ENCTR 27/12
UNSEEMLY (1) .... SISTR 14/07
UNSETTLED (2) .... GRACE 166/32
   GRACE 173/09
UNSETTLINGS (1) .... DEAD 201/30
UNSPEAKABLY (1) .... EVELN 38/11
UNSPOILED (1) .... LITTL 70/05
UNSTABLE (1) .... DEAD 215/33
UNSTEADY (1) .... HOUSE 65/25
UNSUCCESSFULLY (2) .... GRACE 172/18
   GRACE 172/20
UNTASTED (1) .... DEAD 185/31
UNTIDY (1) .... LITTL 71/07
UNTIL (25) .... SISTR 15/11
   ENCTR   21/15   ARABY   30/15   ARABY   31/28   GALNT   50/22
   GALNT   56/14   LITTL   76/32   LITTL   78/06   LITTL   82/28
   PARTS   86/15   PARTS   89/08   PNFUL 115/02   PNFUL 115/07
   PNFUL 116/32   MOTHR 142/11   MOTHR 142/21   MOTHR 149/14
   GRACE 151/27   GRACE 169/30   GRACE 172/05   DEAD 179/02
   DEAD 182/25   DEAD 190/10   DEAD 192/15   DEAD 208/07
UNTO (1) .... GRACE 173/23
UNUSUAL (2) .... RACE 45/14
   PNFUL 111/31
UNUSUALLY (1) .... RACE 45/34
UNVEILING (1) .... GRACE 170/17
UNWORTHY (1) .... GRACE 164/16
UNYOKE (1) .... DEAD 199/12
UP (217)
UPHELD (1) .... DEAD 196/31
UPHOLD (1) .... PARTS 95/32
UPON (64) .... SISTR 9/15
   SISTR   13/21   SISTR   13/27   ENCTR   23/16   ENCTR   23/24
   ENCTR   24/21   ARABY   31/19   ARABY   31/23   ARABY   32/09
   ARABY   33/14   EVELN   41/04   RACE   46/02   RACE   46/10
   GALNT   49/01   GALNT   49/06   GALNT   51/23   HOUSE   68/03
   LITTL   71/09   LITTL   71/17   LITTL   71/31   LITTL   81/12
   LITTL   82/21   PARTS   87/24   PARTS   87/32   PARTS   88/03
   PARTS   89/06   PARTS   90/08   PARTS   91/12   PARTS   98/15
   PNFUL 111/19   IVY D 134/14   MOTHR 143/19   MOTHR 145/23
   MOTHR 145/25   MOTHR 149/33   GRACE 156/09   GRACE 160/29
   GRACE 165/23   GRACE 167/11   GRACE 167/11   GRACE 167/18
   GRACE 167/19   GRACE 167/19   GRACE 172/07   GRACE 173/03
   GRACE 173/10   DEAD 186/23   DEAD 187/29   DEAD 192/30
   DEAD 193/24   DEAD 201/27   DEAD 204/06   DEAD 204/11
   DEAD 213/16   DEAD 213/33   DEAD 218/02   DEAD 220/07
   DEAD 222/11   DEAD 222/20   DEAD 222/27   DEAD 223/23

DEAD	223/29	DEAD	223/31	DEAD	224/04	ARABY	33/06

UPPER (9) ....
GRACE 164/07

| ARABY | 35/30 | GALNT | 50/29 | GALNT | 53/03 | DEAD | 222/20 |
| GRACE | 173/07 | DEAD | 176/04 | DEAD | 176/10 | GRACE | 173/12 |

UPRIGHT (2) ....

| DEAD | 222/19 |

UPSET (2) ....
LITTL 80/22

| PARTS | 87/33 |

UPSTAIRS (8) ....
HOUSE 67/18

| PARTS | 86/07 | PARTS | 86/15 | PARTS | 89/24 | PARTS | 97/14 |
| GRACE | 151/08 | DEAD | 175/08 | DEAD | 177/15 | | |

UPTURNED (1) ....
DEAD 202/04

UPWARDS (6) ....
SISTR 14/08

| GALNT | 55/31 | HOUSE | 62/33 | PNFUL | 107/06 | PNFUL | 107/17 |
| DEAD | 178/16 | | | | | | |

URCHINS (1) ....
PARTS 93/08

URGED (4) ....
HOUSE 66/22

| PNFUL | 110/30 | PNFUL | 115/12 | DEAD | 211/33 | | |

US (77) ....
SISTR 10/10

SISTR	10/16	SISTR	14/06	SISTR	14/10	SISTR	14/12
SISTR	15/03	SISTR	15/05	SISTR	16/11	SISTR	16/22
SISTR	17/10	ENCTR	19/01	ENCTR	19/12	ENCTR	20/01
ENCTR	21/11	ENCTR	22/18	ENCTR	22/24	ENCTR	22/26
ENCTR	23/15	ENCTR	23/16	ENCTR	24/14	ENCTR	24/26
ENCTR	24/29	ENCTR	24/32	ENCTR	24/32	ENCTR	24/33
ENCTR	25/06	ENCTR	25/07	ENCTR	25/12	ENCTR	25/21
ENCTR	25/21	ENCTR	25/26	ENCTR	26/02	ENCTR	26/13
ENCTR	26/19	ENCTR	26/21	ENCTR	26/28	ENCTR	26/32
ARABY	30/03	ARABY	30/05	ARABY	30/07	ARABY	30/21
GALNT	60/26	LITTL	74/31	LITTL	75/26	LITTL	79/21
LITTL	80/10	PARTS	88/34	IVY D	121/06	IVY D	123/09
IVY D	123/34	IVY D	124/18	IVY D	128/24	IVY D	128/28
IVY D	132/06	IVY D	132/26	IVY D	132/29	IVY D	133/22
IVY D	133/24	IVY D	135/17	MOTHR	137/23	MOTHR	148/30
GRACE	163/16	GRACE	164/28	GRACE	166/03	DEAD	192/22
DEAD	192/25	DEAD	203/03	DEAD	203/06	DEAD	203/11
DEAD	203/12	DEAD	203/30	DEAD	204/08	DEAD	204/11
DEAD	204/34	DEAD	205/09	DEAD	205/09	DEAD	211/08

USE (8) ....
HOUSE 61/07

| PARTS | 92/06 | PARTS | 92/27 | PNFUL | 114/26 | GRACE | 160/20 |
| GRACE | 174/14 | DEAD | 203/22 | DEAD | 205/21 | | |

USED (53) ....
SISTR 10/05

SISTR	12/01	SISTR	13/21	SISTR	13/22	SISTR	13/24
SISTR	13/26	ENCTR	22/11	ENCTR	24/23	ARABY	33/18
EVELN	36/07	EVELN	36/08	EVELN	36/12	EVELN	36/15
EVELN	36/16	EVELN	37/16	EVELN	38/04	EVELN	38/13
EVELN	38/32	EVELN	39/01	EVELN	39/07	GALNT	51/03
GALNT	51/07	GALNT	52/25	GALNT	52/26	GALNT	52/29
HOUSE	63/03	HOUSE	67/18	HOUSE	67/20	LITTL	70/15
LITTL	72/25	LITTL	73/03	LITTL	76/06	CLAY	100/20
CLAY	100/24	CLAY	101/30	CLAY	102/10	IVY D	123/26
GRACE	165/34	DEAD	177/27	DEAD	186/25	DEAD	187/04
DEAD	188/13	DEAD	191/25	DEAD	199/05	DEAD	199/09
DEAD	207/09	DEAD	207/22	DEAD	218/28	DEAD	218/31
DEAD	219/04	DEAD	219/05	DEAD	219/13	DEAD	221/03

USEFUL (1) ....
GRACE 158/05

USELESS (7) ....
ARABY 29/10

| ARABY | 35/25 | LITTL | 71/14 | LITTL | 84/14 | LITTL | 84/16 |
| LITTL | 84/16 | DEAD | 223/02 | | | | |

'USHA (2) ....
IVY D 123/15

| IVY D | 124/17 |

USHER'S (1) ....
DEAD 176/04

```
USING (1) ........................................ HOUSE   62/18
USUAL (4) ........................................ SISTR   14/34
     HOUSE   68/14     PARTS   93/20     DEAD   191/01
USUALLY (5) ...................................... EVELN   36/16
     EVELN   38/16     HOUSE   62/18     GRACE  154/12  DEAD  189/13
USURIOUS (1) ..................................... GRACE  159/27
USURY (1) ........................................ GRACE  159/33
UTTER (2) ........................................ PARTS   91/19
     DEAD   179/19
UTTERANCE (1) .................................... SISTR   11/17
UTTERED (4) ...................................... PARTS   98/19
     IVY D  124/20     GRACE  163/03     GRACE  170/08
UTTERLY (1) ...................................... PNFUL  115/32


VACANT (3) ....................................... GALNT   51/28
     MOTHR  139/16     MOTHR  140/14
VACANTLY (2) ..................................... GALNT   58/21
     MOTHR  139/27
VACATED (1) ...................................... IVY D  122/29
VACATION (1) ..................................... SISTR    9/02
VAGRANT (2) ...................................... GALNT   50/23
     LITTL   80/21
VAGUE (5) ........................................ SISTR   11/33
     GRACE  160/02     DEAD   194/13     DEAD   220/19  DEAD  220/22
VAGUELY (4) ...................................... ENCTR   21/23
     ARABY   35/07     GALNT   50/26     GALNT   56/05
VAIN (1) ......................................... DEAD   220/14
VAINLY (1) ....................................... DEAD   204/19
VALISES (1) ...................................... GRACE  160/22
VALOROUS (1) ..................................... DEAD   213/10
VALUE (3) ........................................ LITTL   72/03
     PNFUL  116/12     MOTHR  141/26
VAMPED (1) ....................................... HOUSE   62/25
VANITY (1) ....................................... ARABY   35/33
VANQUISHED (1) ................................... GALNT   58/09
VARIANCE (1) ..................................... GRACE  173/29
VARIATIONS (1) ................................... GALNT   56/22
VARIOUS (1) ...................................... RACE    46/14
VARYING (1) ...................................... ENCTR   26/15
VASE (1) ......................................... DEAD   196/29
VASES (2) ........................................ ARABY   35/04
     ARABY   35/21
VASSALS (1) ...................................... CLAY   106/05
VAST (4) ......................................... GALNT   50/23
     GRACE  170/06     GRACE  174/04     DEAD   223/18
VATICAN (1) ...................................... GRACE  165/25
VEHEMENTLY (1) ................................... LITTL   81/26
VEIL (1) ......................................... ARABY   31/26
VEILED (2) ....................................... GALNT   53/05
     DEAD   220/13
VEIN (1) ......................................... DEAD   204/24
VEINS (3) ........................................ PARTS   96/15
     DEAD   213/08     DEAD   219/02
VELVET (1) ....................................... SISTR   13/32
VELVETY (1) ...................................... IVY D  126/07
VENAL (1) ........................................ PNFUL  117/13
VENIAL (1) ....................................... SISTR   13/09
VENTURE (1) ...................................... PNFUL  116/10
VERDICT (1) ...................................... PNFUL  115/08
VERGE (1) ........................................ GALNT   49/11
VERIFIED (1) ..................................... GRACE  174/26
```

VERITABLE (1) .... CLAY   99/16
VERMIN (1) .... IVY D 127/29
VERMIN-LIKE (1) .... LITTL   71/33
VERNACULAR (1) .... LITTL   80/11
VERSE (5) .... LITTL   73/29
    LITTL   74/08   LITTL   84/01   LITTL   84/03   CLAY   106/03
VERSION (2) .... LITTL   72/29
    PARTS   93/33
VERY (132)
VESSEL (1) .... ENCTR   23/23
VESTED (1) .... SISTR   14/28
VESTIBULE (1) .... MOTHR 139/09
VESTMENTS (1) .... SISTR   13/06
VETERAN'S (1) .... GRACE 157/02
VEXATION (2) .... PARTS   86/17
    CLAY   103/33
VIANDS (1) .... DEAD   182/34
VIBRATE (1) .... PARTS   91/31
VIBRATED (1) .... PNFUL 111/21
VICE (1) .... PNFUL 115/25
VICES (1) .... LITTL   78/16
VICIOUS (1) .... SISTR   11/25
VICIOUSLY (1) .... PARTS   98/17
VICTIM (2) .... GRACE 151/17
    GRACE 157/03
VICTIMISED (1) .... GRACE 160/25
VICTIMS (1) .... DEAD   202/26
VICTOR (1) .... PARTS   96/21
VICTORS (1) .... RACE   42/09
VICTORY (1) .... ENCTR   19/09
VIDOCQ (1) .... ARABY   29/13
VIEW (7) .... GALNT   56/14
    GALNT   60/04   LITTL   83/33   PNFUL 114/28   IVY D 120/33
    MOTHR 143/11   DEAD   204/29
VIEWS (1) .... RACE   43/16
VIGOROUS (1) .... DEAD   187/15
VIGOROUSLY (2) .... IVY D 124/19
    DEAD   177/14
VIGOUR (1) .... GALNT   50/11
VILLONA (12) .... RACE   43/02
    RACE   43/09   RACE   44/01   RACE   44/05   RACE   45/34
    RACE   46/15   RACE   47/06   RACE   47/21   RACE   47/24
    RACE   47/33   RACE   48/04   RACE   48/17
VILLONA'S (1) .... RACE   44/12
VINDICATE (1) .... LITTL   80/29
VINDICTIVE (1) .... DEAD   220/21
VINEGAR (1) .... GALNT   57/25
VIOLENCE (3) .... EVELN   38/02
    HOUSE   68/13   PARTS   90/31
VIOLENT (3) .... PARTS   91/11
    PARTS   96/27   GRACE 156/24
VIOLENTLY (2) .... PARTS   90/26
    PNFUL 112/09
VIOLET (1) .... ARABY   30/04
VIRTUAL (1) .... RACE   42/09
VIRTUE (1) .... RACE   45/29
VISIBLE (3) .... SISTR   12/02
    ARABY   32/10   HOUSE   68/28
VISION (2) .... EVELN   40/11
    GALNT   57/32
VISIONS (2) .... HOUSE   68/30
    HOUSE   68/31

VISIT (9) .... SISTR 14/03
   EVELN 38/32   LITTL 80/32   CLAY 100/29   PNFUL 111/34
   IVY D 132/11   DEAD 189/27   DEAD 190/20   DEAD 191/31
VISITED (1) .... DEAD 203/02
VISITING (4) .... ENCTR 24/10
   PNFUL 109/10   DEAD 189/16   DEAD 190/02
VISITOR (3) .... EVELN 37/15
   CLAY 100/29   GRACE 166/13
VISITS (1) .... PNFUL 110/18
VITRIOL (1) .... ENCTR 22/20
VIVACIOUS (1) .... DEAD 179/29
VIVACITY (1) .... PARTS 93/34
VIVID (2) .... LITTL 75/06
   GRACE 156/05
VOCATION (1) .... ENCTR 19/18
VOICE (69) .... SISTR 11/27
   ENCTR 26/12   ENCTR 26/16   ENCTR 27/29   ENCTR 28/07
   ARABY 35/15   ARABY 35/29   EVELN 40/14   RACE 46/19
   GALNT 50/11   GALNT 57/24   GALNT 57/31   GALNT 60/25
   HOUSE 66/05   LITTL 70/13   LITTL 85/01   PARTS 86/02
   PARTS 86/18   PARTS 98/20   CLAY 106/01   PNFUL 111/24
   PNFUL 111/27   PNFUL 117/05   PNFUL 117/31   IVY D 120/22
   IVY D 126/07   IVY D 132/34   MOTHR 144/32   MOTHR 145/29
   MOTHR 147/11   MOTHR 149/05   GRACE 150/18   GRACE 151/27
   GRACE 162/09   GRACE 163/04   GRACE 165/24   GRACE 165/24
   GRACE 169/33   GRACE 170/07   DEAD 184/12   DEAD 184/12
   DEAD 185/04   DEAD 190/15   DEAD 192/34   DEAD 193/02
   DEAD 193/05   DEAD 193/19   DEAD 193/22   DEAD 193/25
   DEAD 194/03   DEAD 194/07   DEAD 198/29   DEAD 198/32
   DEAD 199/34   DEAD 204/01   DEAD 206/08   DEAD 209/34
   DEAD 210/02   DEAD 210/17   DEAD 210/20   DEAD 210/20
   DEAD 212/15   DEAD 214/15   DEAD 217/03   DEAD 218/26
   DEAD 220/09   DEAD 220/13   DEAD 221/06   DEAD 221/13
VOICE' (1) .... MOTHR 142/30
VOICES (4) .... DEAD 194/07
   DEAD 198/09   DEAD 198/24   DEAD 199/16
VOLUBLY (2) .... RACE 46/08
   MOTHR 146/10
VOLUME (2) .... LITTL 83/28
   MOTHR 142/25
VOLUMES (2) .... HOUSE 63/33
   PNFUL 112/15
VOLUNTARIES (1) .... RACE 48/05
VOLUPTUOUS (1) .... LITTL 83/16
VOTE (3) .... IVY D 119/13
   IVY D 122/05   IVY D 123/03
VOTES (3) .... IVY D 130/17
   IVY D 130/18   IVY D 131/13
VOUCH (1) .... LITTL 78/18
VOWS (1) .... GRACE 171/18
VOYAGE (1) .... ENCTR 23/20
VRAIMENT (1) .... RACE 47/19
VULGAR (5) .... HOUSE 66/18
   LITTL 77/03   PNFUL 115/23   DEAD 198/07   DEAD 198/21
VULGARIANS (1) .... DEAD 220/03

WAD (1) .... GRACE 161/15
WAGES (2) .... EVELN 38/11
   PNFUL 111/04
WAILING (3) .... LITTL 84/09
   LITTL 84/15   MOTHR 147/15

```
WAIST (5) ...................................................... GALNT  50/05
      GALNT  55/25    MOTHR 146/26    GRACE 151/19    DEAD  216/17
WAISTCOAT (5) ................................................. HOUSE  67/28
      IVY D 123/27    DEAD  178/24    DEAD  179/07    DEAD  186/22
WAIT (12) ..................................................... ARABY  33/21
      GALNT  53/22    LITTL  81/31    LITTL  81/33    LITTL  82/03
      PARTS  88/06    PARTS  91/33    IVY D 122/07    IVY D 130/23
      IVY D 130/23    MOTHR 144/28    GRACE 155/13
WAITED (18) .................................................... SISTR  15/11
      SISTR  17/24    ENCTR  22/13    ENCTR  27/32    ARABY  30/18
      GALNT  56/08    GALNT  57/14    HOUSE  68/29    PNFUL 117/31
      IVY D 124/13    IVY D 127/14    MOTHR 140/15    MOTHR 149/13
      GRACE 162/24    DEAD  179/02    DEAD  187/10    DEAD  197/22
      DEAD  216/29
WAITERS (1) ................................................... LITTL  72/06
WAITING (18) .................................................. SISTR  11/26
      ENCTR  22/08    ARABY  30/20    EVELN  37/28    EVELN  38/30
      GALNT  56/08    HOUSE  62/01    HOUSE  68/33    HOUSE  69/06
      LITTL  73/16    LITTL  82/28    PARTS  88/05    PARTS  96/31
      MOTHR 136/15    MOTHR 146/03    GRACE 155/16    DEAD  196/13
      DEAD  197/01
WAITING-ROOM (1) .............................................. PNFUL 114/12
WAIVED (1) .................................................... ENCTR  20/03
WAKE (1) ...................................................... RACE   46/23
WAKEN (2) ..................................................... LITTL  82/20
      LITTL  83/30
WAKING (1) .................................................... ARABY  32/13
WALK (15) ..................................................... ENCTR  21/16
      ARABY  33/24    GALNT  50/32    GALNT  59/25    GALNT  60/06
      LITTL  72/13    LITTL  85/14    GRACE 152/22    GRACE 156/25
      DEAD  180/12    DEAD  188/14    DEAD  192/04    DEAD  207/07
      DEAD  208/10    DEAD  222/25
WALKED (44) ................................................... SISTR  12/27
      SISTR  13/30    ENCTR  22/19    ENCTR  22/26    ENCTR  24/20
      ENCTR  24/29    ARABY  30/20    ARABY  31/03    ARABY  33/01
      ARABY  34/32    ARABY  35/27    RACE   45/22    GALNT  49/11
      GALNT  51/20    GALNT  52/05    GALNT  54/06    GALNT  54/17
      GALNT  55/20    GALNT  56/07    GALNT  56/11    GALNT  56/24
      GALNT  58/05    GALNT  58/15    GALNT  58/30    LITTL  71/27
      LITTL  72/17    LITTL  84/21    PARTS  88/08    PARTS  88/28
      PARTS  93/14    PNFUL 108/29    PNFUL 112/08    PNFUL 112/25
      PNFUL 113/07    PNFUL 117/02    PNFUL 117/02    PNFUL 117/03
      IVY D 122/22    MOTHR 136/05    MOTHR 143/17    GRACE 172/04
      DEAD  178/28    DEAD  216/20    DEAD  222/02
WALKING (20) .................................................. ENCTR  22/34
      ENCTR  26/21    RACE   47/12    GALNT  51/30    GALNT  56/33
      GALNT  57/30    GALNT  58/18    GALNT  59/25    GALNT  60/15
      LITTL  72/06    IVY D 128/16    MOTHR 136/02    MOTHR 149/08
      DEAD  175/10    DEAD  197/33    DEAD  207/23    DEAD  213/04
      DEAD  213/11    DEAD  219/13    DEAD  221/03
WALKING-STICK (1) ............................................. PARTS  98/08
WALKS (2) ..................................................... LITTL  71/07
      PNFUL 110/15
WALL (14) ..................................................... ENCTR  27/02
      EVELN  37/12    EVELN  40/23    EVELN  40/28    LITTL  70/02
      PARTS  87/19    PARTS  97/11    PNFUL 117/12    PNFUL 117/18
      IVY D 118/05    IVY D 118/10    GRACE 161/11    DEAD  186/15
      DEAD  221/25
WALLS (6) ..................................................... ENCTR  23/01
      LITTL  84/24    CLAY  100/31    CLAY  106/06    PNFUL 107/07
      IVY D 120/34
WALTER (3) .................................................... ENCTR  25/08
```

```
                     ENCTR  25/14    ARABY  29/12
WALTZ (8) ...............................................  RACE    47/24
       DEAD   179/02    DEAD   182/02    DEAD   182/16    DEAD   183/26
       DEAD   191/05    DEAD   202/05    DEAD   202/08
WALTZES (1) .............................................  HOUSE   62/25
WALTZING (2) ............................................  GRACE  156/01
       DEAD   190/33
WANDER (3) ..............................................  ENCTR   27/03
       PNFUL  116/03    DEAD   188/13
WANDERED (8) ............................................  ENCTR   23/32
       ENCTR   24/02    PARTS   90/21    PARTS   95/11    PNFUL  112/05
       DEAD   181/28    DEAD   184/15    DEAD   186/15
WANDERING (5) ...........................................  SISTR   17/33
       ARABY   32/24    GALNT   58/14    LITTL   72/18    DEAD   180/22
WANDERS (1) .............................................  LITTL   83/32
WANE (2) ................................................  ENCTR   23/16
       DEAD   192/21
WANING (1) ..............................................  LITTL   71/28
WANT (20) ...............................................  SISTR   16/02
       GALNT   54/30    GALNT   54/31    LITTL   76/08    LITTL   77/11
       PARTS   87/22    PARTS   95/24    CLAY   101/11    IVY D  122/02
       IVY D  122/04    IVY D  124/16    IVY D  127/22    IVY D  131/27
       IVY D  131/33    MOTHR  144/06    GRACE  163/29    GRACE  170/33
       DEAD   183/21    DEAD   216/04    DEAD   221/23
WANTED (23) .............................................  SISTR   17/34
       ENCTR   21/04    ENCTR   27/14    EVELN   40/19    GALNT   54/02
       HOUSE   67/05    HOUSE   67/27    LITTL   73/10    LITTL   83/05
       LITTL   84/04    CLAY   100/16    CLAY   102/17    CLAY   102/25
       PNFUL  117/19    MOTHR  142/04    MOTHR  144/02    MOTHR  148/17
       GRACE  158/29    GRACE  161/05    DEAD   180/28    DEAD   188/17
       DEAD   191/13    DEAD   219/16
WANTS (5) ...............................................  HOUSE   69/05
       PARTS   86/07    IVY D  121/27    DEAD   190/34    DEAD   198/07
WAR (1) .................................................  ENCTR   19/08
WARD (6) ................................................  IVY D  119/11
       IVY D  119/14    IVY D  119/16    IVY D  131/16    IVY D  131/28
       GRACE  172/28
WARES (1) ...............................................  ARABY   35/26
WARFARE (1) .............................................  ENCTR   21/03
WARILY (1) ..............................................  GALNT   57/08
WARM (17) ...............................................  ENCTR   22/03
       ENCTR   27/15    GALNT   49/01    GALNT   49/02    GALNT   49/07
       GALNT   58/04    LITTL   80/15    PNFUL  111/18    IVY D  124/32
       GRACE  155/22    GRACE  156/33    DEAD   188/24    DEAD   189/07
       DEAD   192/02    DEAD   213/21    DEAD   213/31    DEAD   220/25
WARMED (1) ..............................................  HOUSE   67/12
WARM-HEARTED (1) ........................................  DEAD   203/09
WARMLY (6) ..............................................  HOUSE   66/03
       HOUSE   67/09    MOTHR  142/25    GRACE  166/10    DEAD   190/03
       DEAD   199/21
WARMTH (1) ..............................................  MOTHR  145/06
WARNED (1) ..............................................  HOUSE   67/23
WARNING (3) .............................................  GALNT   60/09
       PNFUL  110/08    DEAD   185/16
WARRIORS (1) ............................................  IVY D  134/21
WAS (1159)
WASH (4) ................................................  SISTR   15/25
       SISTR   16/08    GRACE  163/02    GRACE  163/10
WASHED (1) ..............................................  GRACE  151/25
WASHING (1) .............................................  DEAD   217/30
WASHSTAND (2) ...........................................  PNFUL  107/09
       PNFUL  107/15
```

WASN'T (8) .... SISTR 16/15
    EVELN 38/14   LITTL 78/34   CLAY 100/02   CLAY 101/22
    CLAY 104/10   MOTHR 144/13   GRACE 165/11
WASTE (2) .... ARABY 29/09
    ARABY 32/13
WATCH (3) .... RACE   42/04
    LITTL 80/06   PARTS 97/03
WATCH-CHAIN (1) .... PARTS 92/30
WATCHED (18) .... ENCTR 23/21
    ENCTR 24/18   ENCTR 26/34   ARABY 30/17   ARABY 32/22
    GALNT 52/08   GALNT 56/12   HOUSE 63/14   HOUSE 63/16
    HOUSE 64/03   LITTL 71/11   LITTL 81/19   PARTS 95/22
    IVY D 119/24   GRACE 155/29   DEAD 211/34   DEAD 222/09
    DEAD 223/24
WATCHING (7) .... ENCTR 21/32
    ENCTR 23/01   ARABY 30/25   EVELN 36/01   PARTS 92/03
    PNFUL 117/19   DEAD 216/17
WATER (8) .... ENCTR 22/02
    ARABY 31/24   HOUSE 68/22   LITTL 74/30   LITTL 75/18
    CLAY 105/03   PNFUL 112/33   GRACE 151/24
WATER-CARAFE (1) .... PNFUL 112/31
WATERHOUSE'S (1) .... GALNT 50/31
WATER-JUG (1) .... HOUSE 68/21
WATERPROOF (3) .... GALNT 50/02
    GALNT 50/04   GALNT 60/16
WATERS (3) .... EVELN 36/13
    EVELN 37/04   GRACE 157/22
WAVE (1) .... DEAD 213/30
WAVED (3) .... GRACE 159/09
    DEAD 185/22   DEAD 214/32
WAVES (3) .... GALNT 49/15
    GALNT 50/06   DEAD 223/31
WAVING (1) .... DEAD 178/32
WAX (1) .... DEAD 215/30
WAX-PLANTS (1) .... CLAY 100/28
WAY (60) .... SISTR   9/04
    SISTR 14/34   SISTR 17/09   ENCTR 24/26   EVELN 36/05
    EVELN 38/21   RACE   45/22   RACE   46/32   GALNT 51/08
    GALNT 52/15   GALNT 52/29   GALNT 54/03   GALNT 56/16
    GALNT 56/32   GALNT 58/32   GALNT 59/15   GALNT 59/21
    LITTL 71/32   LITTL 72/14   LITTL 75/30   LITTL 77/01
    LITTL 80/28   LITTL 80/29   LITTL 83/27   PARTS 89/34
    PARTS 92/10   PARTS 94/02   PARTS 98/14   CLAY 100/17
    CLAY 102/11   CLAY 104/12   CLAY 104/22   CLAY 104/27
    PNFUL 112/12   PNFUL 117/27   IVY D 119/27   IVY D 120/09
    IVY D 123/03   IVY D 129/07   IVY D 129/23   IVY D 130/16
    IVY D 131/24   IVY D 132/03   IVY D 133/05   IVY D 135/13
    MOTHR 141/23   MOTHR 148/30   MOTHR 148/31   GRACE 151/22
    GRACE 164/13   GRACE 165/04   GRACE 174/13   DEAD 179/31
    DEAD 180/06   DEAD 190/32   DEAD 191/21   DEAD 197/34
    DEAD 216/31   DEAD 218/18   DEAD 221/04
WAYS (3) .... ARABY 30/30
    HOUSE 64/34   PNFUL 110/16
WAYWARD (1) .... DEAD 223/19
WE (167)
WEAK (1) .... DEAD 216/26
WEAKENED (2) .... ARABY 33/10
    MOTHR 137/11
WEAKNESS (1) .... GRACE 174/19
WEALTH (3) .... RACE   42/05
    RACE   45/07   DEAD 205/10
WEAR (4) .... MOTHR 137/08

```
      DEAD  180/19    DEAD  181/03    DEAD  187/22
WEARILY (3) ...................................... GALNT  54/10
      IVY D 119/32    DEAD  214/21
WEARINESS (1) .................................... ENCTR  21/09
WEARING (3) ...................................... PARTS  87/03
      MOTHR 139/08    GRACE 152/12
WEARISOME (1) .................................... ENCTR  21/03
WEARS (1) ........................................ DEAD  181/06
WEARY (4) ........................................ EVELN  38/10
      GALNT  54/12    GALNT  58/09    DEAD  216/22
WEARY-LOOKING (1) ................................ ARABY  34/28
WEATHER (5) ...................................... ENCTR  24/34
      CLAY  103/04    PNFUL 112/04    IVY D 119/16  DEAD  211/19
WEATHERS (11) .................................... GALNT  51/22
      PARTS  94/19    PARTS  94/21    PARTS  94/26  PARTS  94/32
      PARTS  95/05    PARTS  95/09    PARTS  95/26  PARTS  95/30
      PARTS  96/06    PARTS  96/18
WEATHERS' (1) .................................... PARTS  96/16
WEB (2) .......................................... GALNT  52/08
      DEAD  213/19
WEBB'S (1) ....................................... DEAD  188/15
WE'D (4) ......................................... SISTR  16/10
      IVY D 122/15    MOTHR 139/28    GRACE 163/15
WEDDING (3) ...................................... GRACE 155/33
      GRACE 156/04    DEAD  178/06
WEDDING-CAKE (1) ................................. CLAY  102/24
WEDGE (1) ........................................ IVY D 129/24
WEDNESDAY (3) .................................... MOTHR 139/05
      MOTHR 139/07    DEAD  188/07
WEEK (12) ........................................ SISTR  12/24
      ENCTR  21/30    ARABY  32/04    EVELN  37/07  HOUSE  62/11
      HOUSE  66/11    PNFUL 111/34    IVY D 130/19  MOTHR 137/17
      MOTHR 146/22    DEAD  200/25    DEAD  221/27
WEEKS (4) ........................................ EVELN  38/33
      PNFUL 110/04    MOTHR 137/23    GRACE 156/10
WEIGH (2) ........................................ EVELN  37/19
      LITTL  73/30
WEIGHING (1) ..................................... GRACE 164/22
WEIGHT (3) ....................................... ARABY  33/30
      HOUSE  64/24    PARTS  96/11
WEIGHTED (1) ..................................... DEAD  202/10
WELCOME (8) ...................................... RACE  42/13
      RACE  42/14     IVY D 122/02    IVY D 122/16  IVY D 124/32
      IVY D 132/02    IVY D 132/25    DEAD  188/10
WELCOMED (1) ..................................... MOTHR 142/25
WELL (114)
WE'LL (14) ....................................... GALNT  55/09
      LITTL  80/04    PARTS  96/28    PARTS  96/29  IVY D 127/33
      GRACE 153/07    GRACE 155/18    GRACE 155/19  GRACE 155/27
      GRACE 171/10    DEAD  178/05    DEAD  191/05  DEAD  208/25
      DEAD  209/17
WELL-CUT (1) ..................................... LITTL  70/03
WELL-FED (1) ..................................... GRACE 156/07
WELL-FILLED (1) .................................. DEAD  218/19
WELLINGTON (2) ................................... DEAD  192/07
      DEAD  202/10
WELL-LADEN (1) ................................... DEAD  197/09
WELL-MEANING (1) ................................. DEAD  220/03
WENT (113)
WERE (274)
WE'RE (12) ....................................... LITTL  75/01
      IVY D 133/14    GRACE 162/28    GRACE 162/34  GRACE 163/02
```

GRACE 163/05	GRACE 163/10	GRACE 170/29	GRACE 170/32
DEAD 177/29	DEAD 184/07	DEAD 188/33	
WEREN'T (2)			CLAY 104/17
GRACE 168/19			
WEST (9)			SISTR 14/05
ENCTR 19/01	ENCTR 20/07	ENCTR 20/32	DEAD 188/05
DEAD 188/09	DEAD 190/12	DEAD 190/29	DEAD 191/13
WESTERN (1)			MOTHR 145/24
WESTLAND (2)			ARABY 34/18
RACE 47/10			
WESTMORELAND (4)			GALNT 58/23
GALNT 58/25	PARTS 93/06	GRACE 153/16	
WESTWARD (3)			DEAD 202/11
DEAD 223/26	DEAD 223/30		
WET (6)			HOUSE 67/15
CLAY 105/13	IVY D 119/17	MOTHR 142/11	DEAD 180/27
DEAD 221/17			
WETS (1)			DEAD 210/25
WHARF (2)			ENCTR 21/15
ENCTR 22/20			
WHAT (194)			
WHATEVER (5)			CLAY 106/15
IVY D 131/19	GRACE 169/20	GRACE 171/19	DEAD 190/26
WHAT'S (10)			LITTL 75/21
LITTL 75/30	PARTS 98/03	IVY D 120/08	IVY D 121/17
GRACE 151/21	GRACE 152/14	GRACE 159/12	GRACE 162/26
GRACE 169/06			
WHEELS (1)			SISTR 17/08
WHEEZING (1)			GALNT 49/17
WHEEZY (1)			DEAD 175/04
WHELP (1)			PARTS 98/18
WHEN (267)			
WHENEVER (13)			SISTR 16/32
EVELN 37/15	EVELN 37/26	RACE 47/33	GALNT 51/28
LITTL 72/13	CLAY 100/28	IVY D 120/08	IVY D 120/15
GRACE 156/04	GRACE 156/22	GRACE 159/30	DEAD 180/26
WHERE (71)			SISTR 13/34
SISTR 15/08	SISTR 17/05	ENCTR 21/28	ENCTR 24/02
ARABY 30/08	ARABY 30/10	ARABY 30/11	ARABY 33/11
ARABY 34/08	EVELN 37/08	EVELN 38/30	EVELN 38/32
GALNT 50/28	GALNT 55/06	GALNT 55/08	GALNT 56/07
HOUSE 68/01	LITTL 70/10	LITTL 78/26	LITTL 84/13
PARTS 86/16	PARTS 89/16	PARTS 91/01	CLAY 106/18
PNFUL 109/01	PNFUL 109/02	PNFUL 110/33	PNFUL 117/03
IVY D 123/29	IVY D 125/31	IVY D 130/12	MOTHR 136/10
MOTHR 136/13	MOTHR 137/20	MOTHR 143/21	MOTHR 145/19
MOTHR 146/13	GRACE 150/17	GRACE 151/10	GRACE 152/05
GRACE 152/09	GRACE 154/27	GRACE 159/23	GRACE 160/01
GRACE 161/09	GRACE 166/23	DEAD 178/16	DEAD 178/21
DEAD 179/28	DEAD 179/28	DEAD 181/30	DEAD 181/31
DEAD 189/09	DEAD 189/12	DEAD 190/14	DEAD 196/12
DEAD 196/12	DEAD 199/20	DEAD 202/10	DEAD 206/03
DEAD 206/21	DEAD 209/05	DEAD 209/17	DEAD 210/16
DEAD 212/19	DEAD 214/30	DEAD 221/25	DEAD 221/28
DEAD 223/17	DEAD 223/32		
WHEREAS (1)			HOUSE 65/16
WHERE'ER (1)			IVY D 134/16
WHEREFORE (1)			GRACE 173/23
WHERE'S (3)			LITTL 73/04
PARTS 97/25	IVY D 132/22		
WHETHER (18)			SISTR 13/09
ENCTR 25/07	ENCTR 26/31	ARABY 30/18	ARABY 31/16

ARABY 31/32   HOUSE 66/21   LITTL 73/18   PARTS 89/09
IVY D 122/07   IVY D 125/25   MOTHR 141/06   GRACE 162/24
DEAD 186/04   DEAD 190/18   DEAD 204/30   DEAD 208/08
DEAD 208/09
WHICH (196)
WHILE (73) .... SISTR 9/17
SISTR 10/25   SISTR 14/34   SISTR 16/03   ENCTR 19/06
ENCTR 22/07   ENCTR 25/05   ENCTR 26/18   ARABY 32/02
RACE 43/25   RACE 45/21   RACE 45/24   GALNT 54/14
GALNT 56/21   GALNT 57/06   GALNT 59/26   HOUSE 66/25
HOUSE 67/26   LITTL 76/18   LITTL 81/31   LITTL 82/30
LITTL 84/10   LITTL 85/20   PARTS 89/12   PARTS 93/23
PARTS 94/04   PARTS 94/12   PARTS 97/32   CLAY 101/15
CLAY 103/06   CLAY 103/11   CLAY 105/07   PNFUL 109/25
PNFUL 113/25   PNFUL 116/17   IVY D 119/26   IVY D 120/02
IVY D 127/13   IVY D 130/02   IVY D 133/28   MOTHR 138/29
MOTHR 139/19   MOTHR 144/03   MOTHR 145/27   MOTHR 145/33
MOTHR 146/08   GRACE 152/10   GRACE 153/12   GRACE 154/26
GRACE 154/31   GRACE 163/21   GRACE 163/22   GRACE 169/13
GRACE 173/05   DEAD 177/06   DEAD 177/14   DEAD 180/31
DEAD 183/09   DEAD 185/28   DEAD 186/01   DEAD 187/10
DEAD 190/24   DEAD 191/21   DEAD 192/17   DEAD 194/12
DEAD 196/06   DEAD 197/15   DEAD 202/21   DEAD 205/07
DEAD 205/24   DEAD 215/07   DEAD 219/31   DEAD 222/09
WHILST (1) .... LITTL 83/33
WHIMPERING (1) .... PARTS 98/12
WHINING (1) .... PARTS 94/17
WHIP (3) .... ENCTR 27/22
ENCTR 27/22   ENCTR 27/27
WHIPPED (5) .... ENCTR 27/05
ENCTR 27/07   ENCTR 27/11   ENCTR 27/12   DEAD 209/22
WHIPPER-SNAPPERS (1) .... DEAD 194/23
WHIPPING (3) .... ENCTR 27/13
ENCTR 27/15   ENCTR 27/24
WHISKIES (3) .... LITTL 80/16
PARTS 93/34   PARTS 95/25
WHISKY (14) .... LITTL 74/29
LITTL 74/32   LITTL 75/20   LITTL 76/25   LITTL 77/24
LITTL 77/32   LITTL 80/12   GRACE 166/29   GRACE 167/02
GRACE 167/26   GRACE 169/05   DEAD 183/08   DEAD 183/17
DEAD 185/28
WHISPER (1) .... GRACE 172/23
WHISPERED (3) .... DEAD 182/04
DEAD 190/11   DEAD 201/26
WHISPERING (1) .... CLAY 105/16
WHISTLE (2) .... EVELN 40/31
PNFUL 113/31
WHISTLED (1) .... GRACE 153/05
WHISTLING (2) .... MOTHR 146/32
DEAD 206/22
WHITE (36) .... SISTR 14/30
ENCTR 23/10   ENCTR 26/06   ARABY 32/07   ARABY 32/10
EVELN 39/22   EVELN 41/15   RACE 44/21   GALNT 50/03
GALNT 54/23   GALNT 55/27   GALNT 56/10   GALNT 57/04
HOUSE 61/16   HOUSE 61/16   HOUSE 61/17   HOUSE 67/08
HOUSE 68/32   LITTL 70/13   LITTL 70/18   LITTL 79/20
LITTL 82/21   PNFUL 107/12   PNFUL 107/17   PNFUL 107/17
PNFUL 113/03   MOTHR 139/16   GRACE 172/08   GRACE 173/08
DEAD 190/15   DEAD 197/04   DEAD 197/17   DEAD 202/12
DEAD 209/29   DEAD 214/28   DEAD 214/29
WHITENING (1) .... IVY D 118/02
WHITES (1) .... PARTS 86/12

WHITE-SHADED (1) .... PNFUL 107/15
WHITHER (1) .... DEAD   220/14
WHIT-MONDAY (1) .... CLAY   100/11
WHO (149)
WHO'D (1) .... IVY D 119/28
WHO'D (1) .... PARTS   90/29
WHOLE (7) ....⌒........ GRACE 169/13
    PARTS   94/10   PNFUL 115/19   GRACE 169/08
    DEAD   179/19   DEAD 188/33
WHOLLY (3) .... EVELN   38/26
    RACE   46/17   DEAD 218/08
WHOM (8) .... EVELN   37/20
    RACE   46/06   LITTL 71/02   PNFUL 115/27   IVY D 134/09
    MOTHR 136/17   MOTHR 142/03   DEAD 209/04
WHO'S (3) .... PARTS   96/13
    IVY D 120/21   DEAD 206/28
WHOSE (16) .... ENCTR   23/28
    EVELN   37/11   RACE   42/16   RACE   46/09   IVY D 118/12
    IVY D 130/04   GRACE 154/05   GRACE 173/32   DEAD 180/22
    DEAD   185/27   DEAD 193/18   DEAD 203/33   DEAD 204/30
    DEAD   204/31   DEAD 204/33   DEAD 218/20
WHY (47) .... SISTR   11/03
    SISTR   11/11   SISTR 11/27   SISTR 11/28   ENCTR   22/10
    ENCTR   25/17   ENCTR 25/34   ARABY 31/14   ARABY   32/01
    ARABY   35/03   EVELN 40/19   LITTL 81/26   LITTL   83/11
    LITTL   83/17   PARTS 87/07   PARTS 87/08   PARTS   92/32
    CLAY   104/07   PNFUL 111/09   PNFUL 117/06   PNFUL 117/06
    IVY D 120/12   IVY D 123/04   IVY D 127/12   IVY D 130/18
    IVY D 132/01   IVY D 132/24   IVY D 132/26   MOTHR 144/15
    GRACE 164/09   DEAD 188/01   DEAD 189/15   DEAD   189/32
    DEAD   190/01   DEAD 191/09   DEAD 198/32   DEAD   199/14
    DEAD   199/17   DEAD 201/07   DEAD 207/14   DEAD   212/11
    DEAD   214/05   DEAD 217/07   DEAD 218/03   DEAD   218/23
    DEAD   218/27   DEAD 219/16   *
WICKLOW (1) .... IVY D 119/18
WIDE (5) .... ENCTR   24/06
    EVELN   40/26   IVY D 125/33   GRACE 173/20   DEAD   184/28
WIDE-AWAKE (2) .... SISTR   18/08
    SISTR   18/14
WIDE-BRIMMED (1) .... IVY D 130/09
WIDELY (1) .... MOTHR 145/26
WIDOW (1) .... ARABY   33/18
WIFE (39) .... EVELN   38/29
    HOUSE   61/08   HOUSE 61/10   LITTL 71/21   LITTL   79/22
    PARTS   97/16   CLAY 100/17   CLAY 104/31   CLAY   104/34
    CLAY   106/17   PNFUL 110/20   PNFUL 114/33   PNFUL 115/02
    MOTHR 137/12   GRACE 154/25   GRACE 155/09   GRACE 158/18
    GRACE 170/14   GRACE 170/22   GRACE 171/28   GRACE 171/33
    GRACE 173/03   DEAD 176/26   DEAD 177/04   DEAD   177/06
    DEAD   177/10   DEAD 179/21   DEAD 180/03   DEAD   190/32
    DEAD   191/15   DEAD 195/13   DEAD 200/10   DEAD   209/29
    DEAD   210/02   DEAD 210/16   DEAD 211/01   DEAD   211/34
    DEAD   222/10   DEAD 223/06
WIFELY (1) .... DEAD   215/11
WIFE'S (1) .... GRACE 156/10
WIG (1) .... IVY D 127/30
WILD (11) .... ENCTR   19/01
    ENCTR   20/07   ENCTR 20/32   ENCTR 21/01   ARABY   29/14
    HOUSE   66/08   LITTL 72/25   PARTS 91/29   IVY D 132/09
    DEAD   215/17   DEAD 215/26
WILDLY (1) .... PARTS   98/14
WILFUL (1) .... MOTHR 145/10
WILKINS (1) .... IVY D 131/03

WILL (38) .... ARABY 29/18
    ARABY 32/12   RACE 47/28   GALNT 55/06   LITTL 74/29
    LITTL 78/04   LITTL 79/22   LITTL 81/10   IVY D 122/08
    IVY D 128/27   IVY D 131/19   IVY D 131/29   IVY D 131/30
    MOTHR 145/12   MOTHR 148/27   GRACE 166/34   GRACE 174/30
    GRACE 174/31   DEAD 180/29   DEAD 181/20   DEAD 182/15
    DEAD 184/01   DEAD 188/32   DEAD 189/01   DEAD 189/06
    DEAD 191/01   DEAD 195/29   DEAD 202/20   DEAD 203/05
    DEAD 203/24   DEAD 203/33   DEAD 204/03   DEAD 204/10
    DEAD 204/10   DEAD 204/26   DEAD 204/27   DEAD 206/05
    DEAD 206/23
WILLINGLY (1) .... DEAD 203/33
WIN (3) .... HOUSE 64/24
    HOUSE 65/08   LITTL 70/06
WIND (4) .... RACE 44/12
    GRACE 153/18   GRACE 162/26   DEAD 180/06
WINDING (3) .... PNFUL 117/21
    PNFUL 117/22   PNFUL 117/23
WINDOW (34) .... SISTR 9/03
    SISTR 9/10   SISTR 12/01   ARABY 31/25   ARABY 32/33
    ARABY 33/08   EVELN 36/01   EVELN 36/02   EVELN 39/33
    EVELN 39/33   RACE 46/28   GALNT 57/02   GALNT 57/04
    LITTL 71/05   PARTS 88/31   PNFUL 113/16   PNFUL 115/16
    GRACE 154/08   GRACE 154/11   DEAD 191/32   DEAD 192/03
    DEAD 209/04   DEAD 209/10   DEAD 213/23   DEAD 214/19
    DEAD 216/11   DEAD 216/12   DEAD 216/28   DEAD 217/22
    DEAD 219/24   DEAD 221/17   DEAD 221/17   DEAD 222/02
    DEAD 223/23
WINDOW-PANES (1) .... SISTR 14/04
WINDOWS (6) .... ENCTR 23/33
    ARABY 30/13   HOUSE 63/27   PNFUL 107/05   DEAD 180/05
    DEAD 202/08
WINDS (1) .... LITTL 83/31
WINDY (1) .... HOUSE 67/15
WINE (6) .... SISTR 15/03
    PARTS 88/32   CLAY 104/19   CLAY 105/23   DEAD 201/29
    DEAD 222/23
WINE-COLOURED (2) .... PARTS 86/10
    PARTS 96/08
WINE-GLASS (1) .... SISTR 15/14
WINE-GLASSES (2) .... SISTR 15/02
    LITTL 74/20
WINE-MERCHANT'S (1) .... HOUSE 65/14
WINETAVERN (1) .... DEAD 214/17
WING (1) .... DEAD 197/10
WINGS (1) .... DEAD 184/28
WINNING (2) .... RACE 42/11
    RACE 48/11
WINNOWED (1) .... GALNT 50/11
WINTER (4) .... SISTR 11/04
    ARABY 30/01   DEAD 220/28   DEAD 220/29
WINTRY (1) .... PNFUL 113/13
WIPED (2) .... SISTR 17/13
    IVY D 129/19
WIPING (2) .... CLAY 101/02
    MOTHR 142/27
WIRES (2) .... ARABY 31/19
    GALNT 54/09
WISDOM (1) .... LITTL 71/15
WISE (2) .... EVELN 37/19
    HOUSE 64/16
WISER (2) .... GRACE 171/02

```
          GRACE 173/22
WISH  (15) ..........................................  SISTR   10/23
     ENCTR   26/14     ARABY   35/15     GALNT   53/33     HOUSE   64/16
     LITTL   79/07     LITTL   79/09     PNFUL 112/02     IVY D 122/10
     GRACE 157/32     DEAD  176/28     DEAD  201/01     DEAD  203/08
     DEAD  219/07     DEAD  223/11
WISHA  (3) ...........................................  IVY D 128/10
     IVY D 128/10     IVY D 128/11
WISHED  (18) ........................................  SISTR   12/26
     ARABY   32/14     ARABY   32/28     RACE    48/14     GALNT   51/26
     HOUSE   65/07     LITTL   70/02     LITTL   73/21     LITTL   73/28
     LITTL   80/29     PNFUL 107/01     PNFUL 117/19     MOTHR 147/30
     GRACE 160/02     GRACE 160/03     GRACE 160/28     GRACE 173/33
     GRACE 174/15
WISHES  (1) .........................................  LITTL   79/03
WISHING  (3) ........................................  HOUSE   64/12
     LITTL   81/02     DEAD  217/31
WISTFUL  (1) ........................................  LITTL   74/08
WIT  (1) ............................................  RACE    48/09
WITH  (488)
WITHDRAWN  (1) ......................................  IVY D 131/04
WITHDREW  (1) .......................................  GRACE 155/30
WITHER  (1) .........................................  DEAD  223/08
WITHHELD  (1) .......................................  PNFUL 117/06
WITHIN  (12) ........................................  ARABY   29/05
     ARABY   30/26     RACE    44/28     RACE    46/24     LITTL   73/22
     LITTL   73/29     LITTL   83/23     LITTL   84/12     CLAY  106/06
     PNFUL 111/07     IVY D 129/28     DEAD  182/03
WITHOUT  (32) .......................................  SISTR   10/10
     SISTR   12/18     SISTR   17/15     ENCTR   24/17     ENCTR   26/20
     ENCTR   28/04     GALNT   51/32     GALNT   54/17     GALNT   55/14
     GALNT   60/21     HOUSE   68/29     LITTL   72/12     LITTL   82/16
     LITTL   84/28     CLAY  104/16     PNFUL 109/09     PNFUL 115/29
     PNFUL 116/16     MOTHR 146/18     GRACE 152/06     GRACE 154/02
     GRACE 160/12     GRACE 164/19     GRACE 166/27     DEAD  178/13
     DEAD  191/22     DEAD  193/05     DEAD  197/20     DEAD  197/29
     DEAD  200/31     DEAD  203/28     DEAD  214/27
WITNESS  (3) ........................................  PNFUL 112/13
     PNFUL 114/09     PNFUL 115/05
WITNESSED  (1) ......................................  MOTHR 147/26
WITS  (1) ...........................................  GRACE 158/21
WITS'  (1) ..........................................  LITTL   72/32
WITTICISM  (1) ......................................  PARTS   91/26
WIZENED  (1) ........................................  DEAD  183/11
WIZEN-FACED  (1) ....................................  DEAD  182/18
WOE  (3) ............................................  IVY D 134/08
     IVY D 134/17     GRACE 171/07
WOMAN  (41) .........................................  SISTR   14/08
     SISTR   14/14     SISTR   15/25     SISTR   16/07     ARABY   33/17
     GALNT   54/22     GALNT   55/14     GALNT   59/07     GALNT   59/26
     GALNT   59/33     GALNT   60/02     GALNT   60/10     HOUSE   61/01
     HOUSE   61/03     HOUSE   62/04     HOUSE   63/08     LITTL   77/26
     LITTL   81/28     LITTL   82/04     LITTL   84/30     PARTS   90/01
     PARTS   97/08     PARTS   97/16     CLAY  101/07     CLAY  101/21
     PNFUL 112/21     PNFUL 114/04     MOTHR 142/03     MOTHR 142/10
     MOTHR 143/17     MOTHR 143/25     GRACE 155/32     GRACE 157/15
     DEAD  179/27     DEAD  183/29     DEAD  190/15     DEAD  190/26
     DEAD  195/01     DEAD  209/25     DEAD  210/04     DEAD  223/13
WOMAN'S  (4) ........................................  SISTR   14/21
     GALNT   55/23     GALNT   56/13     GALNT   57/32
WOMEN  (16) .........................................  SISTR   12/04
     ARABY   31/05     GALNT   52/14     PARTS   93/08     PARTS   95/08
```

WORK-GIRLS (2) .... GALNT   57/13
    GALNT   57/23
WORKING (3) .... ENCTR   23/02
    CLAY 101/27   IVY D 121/27
WORKING-CLASSES (1) .... IVY D 121/28
WORKING-MAN (5) .... IVY D 121/17
    IVY D 121/19   IVY D 121/30   IVY D 121/31   IVY D 121/33
WORKING-MEN (1) .... PNFUL 116/11
WORKMEN (2) .... PNFUL 110/34
    GRACE 159/26
WORKMEN'S (1) .... PNFUL 111/03
WORKS (6) .... ENCTR   22/20
    ENCTR   25/08   ENCTR   25/14   ENCTR   25/15   ENCTR   25/16
    GRACE 171/11
WORLD (35) .... SISTR   9/08
    SISTR   15/12   ENCTR   27/25   ENCTR   27/26   ENCTR   27/29
    EVELN   41/06   RACE   43/32   RACE   44/22   GALNT   58/07
    HOUSE   64/30   LITTL   76/08   LITTL   77/07   LITTL   78/10
    LITTL   81/08   LITTL   85/18   PNFUL 108/21   IVY D 120/08
    IVY D 132/06   IVY D 134/22   GRACE 161/24   GRACE 164/13
    GRACE 164/19   GRACE 164/32   GRACE 173/22   GRACE 173/32
    GRACE 174/05   GRACE 174/05   GRACE 174/11   DEAD 201/12
    DEAD 203/33   DEAD 204/17   DEAD 220/22   DEAD 223/07
    DEAD 223/20   DEAD 223/21
WORLDLINGS (1) .... GRACE 173/33
WORLDS (1) .... DEAD 176/28
WORM (1) .... PNFUL 117/23
WORMS (1) .... SISTR   10/05
WORN (1) .... SISTR   13/06
WORSE (5) .... IVY D 120/15
    GRACE 156/23   DEAD 193/34   DEAD 197/21   DEAD 221/09
WORSHIP (1) .... GRACE 165/31
WORSHIPPERS (2) .... HOUSE   63/30
    GRACE 174/07
WORTH (3) .... RACE   43/34
    GALNT   58/06   IVY D 129/34
WOULD (223)
WOULDN'T (26) .... SISTR   9/19
    SISTR   10/29   SISTR   16/02   SISTR   16/23   LITTL   79/18
    PARTS   90/33   PARTS   94/30   CLAY 100/01   CLAY 100/14
    IVY D 123/02   MOTHR 148/10   MOTHR 148/12   GRACE 166/34
    GRACE 169/14   GRACE 170/05   DEAD 178/30   DEAD 180/28
    DEAD 191/14   DEAD 194/14   DEAD 195/01   DEAD 201/14
    DEAD 207/04   DEAD 210/28   DEAD 217/05   DEAD 220/31
    DEAD 221/10
WOUND (1) .... PARTS   95/13
WRAPPED (3) .... MOTHR 149/23
    DEAD 196/28   DEAD 197/17
WRAPS (1) .... LITTL   72/09
WRECKS (1) .... PNFUL 115/30
WRETCHED (2) .... ENCTR   20/25
    ENCTR   20/26
WRETCHES (1) .... PNFUL 115/27
WRINGING (1) .... DEAD 196/11
WRINKLED (1) .... DEAD 211/16
WRINKLES (1) .... DEAD 182/25
WRINKLING (1) .... DEAD 185/27
WRIST (1) .... ARABY   32/03
WRISTS (1) .... HOUSE   67/10
WRITE (11) .... ENCTR   21/13
    LITTL   73/18   LITTL   73/20   LITTL   83/26   LITTL   84/02
    PARTS   88/17   PARTS   90/24   PNFUL 111/09   MOTHR 145/12

```
      DEAD   187/33       DEAD   188/04
WRITES (1) .................................................  ENCTR   20/27
WRITING (7) ................................................  LITTL   71/05
      PARTS   86/06     PNFUL  108/03    IVY D  135/33       GRACE  161/19
      DEAD   188/22     DEAD   214/03
WRITTEN (11) ...............................................  SISTR   13/17
      ARABY   35/01     RACE    48/22    PARTS   88/15       PNFUL  108/06
      PNFUL  112/18     GRACE  154/08    DEAD   192/11       DEAD   214/05
      DEAD   214/08     DEAD   220/32
WRONG (10) .................................................  SISTR   18/16
      ENCTR   20/11     CLAY   104/12    CLAY   105/19       MOTHR  145/32
      GRACE  165/14     GRACE  167/13    GRACE  174/29       GRACE  174/30
      DEAD   179/18
WROTE (11) .................................................  SISTR   16/12
      ENCTR   20/26     PARTS   90/26    PNFUL  112/01       PNFUL  112/16
      IVY D  125/04     IVY D  133/23    GRACE  156/17       GRACE  167/24
      DEAD   188/07     DEAD   221/10
WROUGHT (1) ................................................  IVY D  134/18
WRY (1) ....................................................  LITTL   82/06


XIII. (1) ..................................................  GRACE  167/05


'Y (2) .....................................................  GRACE  153/08
      GRACE  153/21
YA (1) .....................................................  ENCTR   19/16
YACHT (3) ..................................................  RACE    47/21
      RACE    47/24     RACE    48/15
YACHTING (1) ...............................................  GALNT   49/14
YAHOOS (1) .................................................  GRACE  161/20
YAKA (3) ...................................................  ENCTR   19/16
      ENCTR   19/16     ENCTR   19/16
YARDS (2) ..................................................  IVY D  131/33
      GRACE  150/04
YAWNING (1) ................................................  PNFUL  116/20
YE (2) .....................................................  IVY D  133/05
      IVY D  133/05
YEAR (20) ..................................................  HOUSE   66/13
      LITTL   79/32     LITTL   80/02    LITTL   81/02       CLAY   105/25
      PNFUL  109/28     IVY D  122/03    MOTHR  137/07       MOTHR  137/21
      MOTHR  142/32     DEAD   176/10    DEAD   178/03       DEAD   180/04
      DEAD   186/21     DEAD   189/10    DEAD   190/20       DEAD   191/24
      DEAD   202/32     DEAD   203/09    DEAD   215/04
YEARS (35) .................................................  SISTR   12/08
      EVELN   37/07     EVELN   37/11    RACE    43/13       HOUSE   64/28
      HOUSE   65/14     HOUSE   66/06    LITTL   70/01       LITTL   71/02
      LITTL   72/23     LITTL   78/34    LITTL   80/19       CLAY   100/10
      CLAY   101/33     PNFUL  108/17    PNFUL  108/30       PNFUL  112/12
      PNFUL  113/23     PNFUL  113/30    PNFUL  115/01       PNFUL  115/02
      PNFUL  117/03     GRACE  156/13    GRACE  157/10       DEAD   175/18
      DEAD   175/18     DEAD   176/06    DEAD   194/07       DEAD   202/15
      DEAD   207/17     DEAD   211/23    DEAD   214/01       DEAD   214/02
      DEAD   214/08     DEAD   223/10
YEAR'S (1) .................................................  DEAD   185/13
YEARS' (1) .................................................  DEAD   188/18
YELLING (2) ................................................  ENCTR   19/14
      PARTS   93/09
YELLOW (9) .................................................  ENCTR   25/21
      ARABY   29/14     HOUSE   64/01    PARTS   95/15       IVY D  125/30
      GRACE  152/12     DEAD   196/23    DEAD   196/34       DEAD   212/31
YELLOWING (1) ..............................................  EVELN   37/11
```

YERRA (1) .... IVY D 127/16
YES (56) .... SISTR 15/29

SISTR 17/19	ARABY 31/33	ARABY 32/31	ARABY 35/12
HOUSE 69/04	LITTL 75/33	LITTL 79/02	LITTL 80/02
LITTL 80/09	PARTS 87/17	PARTS 87/23	PARTS 97/29
CLAY 99/12	PNFUL 114/09	IVY D 119/27	IVY D 120/24
IVY D 122/31	IVY D 123/25	IVY D 127/32	IVY D 129/32
MOTHR 140/31	MOTHR 143/06	GRACE 159/03	GRACE 159/03
GRACE 160/13	GRACE 160/13	GRACE 161/26	GRACE 162/15
GRACE 163/01	GRACE 164/09	GRACE 164/14	GRACE 164/34
GRACE 165/21	GRACE 165/22	GRACE 167/16	GRACE 167/24
GRACE 168/08	GRACE 168/30	GRACE 168/32	GRACE 171/22
DEAD 177/29	DEAD 181/05	DEAD 200/03	DEAD 200/03
DEAD 201/07	DEAD 208/26	DEAD 209/15	DEAD 209/19
DEAD 211/01	DEAD 211/20	DEAD 217/01	DEAD 221/27
DEAD 223/03	DEAD 223/03	DEAD 223/27	

YESTERDAY (2) .... PNFUL 113/24
    IVY D 127/19
YET (21) .... SISTR   9/14

ARABY 30/33	ARABY 33/03	EVELN 37/10	RACE 43/31
GALNT 58/10	GALNT 59/10	GALNT 59/16	HOUSE 68/02
PARTS 92/27	IVY D 121/04	IVY D 121/05	MOTHR 149/26
GRACE 165/11	GRACE 173/32	DEAD 176/25	DEAD 204/01
DEAD 206/26	DEAD 206/31	DEAD 213/30	DEAD 216/23

YIELD (1) .... DEAD 218/08
YIELDING (1) .... DEAD 218/01
YOU (420)
YOU'D (4) .... LITTL 76/08
    IVY D 127/34   MOTHR 144/18   DEAD 188/04
YOU'LL (13) .... SISTR 10/12

SISTR 16/25	GALNT 51/09	GALNT 52/10	LITTL 79/21
LITTL 81/14	PARTS 91/33	PARTS 92/01	PARTS 92/01
PARTS 92/02	PARTS 98/16	MOTHR 145/15	DEAD 180/19

YOUNG (111)
YOUNGER (6) .... ENCTR 19/12
    PNFUL 109/28   IVY D 130/07   GRACE 154/16   GRACE 168/34
    DEAD 191/04
YOUNGEST (1) .... DEAD 205/01
YOUNGSTER (1) .... SISTR 10/21
YOUNGSTERS (2) .... LITTL 79/12
    CLAY 103/06
YOUR (51) .... SISTR 10/12

SISTR 16/20	ENCTR 20/19	ENCTR 20/24	ENCTR 20/30
ARABY 33/26	GALNT 53/10	LITTL 75/14	LITTL 77/31
LITTL 79/04	LITTL 81/14	LITTL 81/21	PARTS 87/20
PARTS 88/07	PARTS 92/01	PARTS 96/11	PARTS 96/25
PARTS 97/25	CLAY 102/05	CLAY 102/06	IVY D 119/13
IVY D 127/31	IVY D 128/02	IVY D 130/18	IVY D 131/17
MOTHR 144/15	MOTHR 144/16	GRACE 157/27	GRACE 161/04
GRACE 161/17	GRACE 167/34	GRACE 170/29	GRACE 171/04
DEAD 178/06	DEAD 178/06	DEAD 181/03	DEAD 181/04
DEAD 182/16	DEAD 189/16	DEAD 189/19	DEAD 189/27
DEAD 189/28	DEAD 189/28	DEAD 193/22	DEAD 193/24
DEAD 195/19	DEAD 195/33	DEAD 198/29	DEAD 202/20
DEAD 207/04	DEAD 214/07		

YOU'RE (16) .... GALNT 52/17

LITTL 76/06	PARTS 96/11	IVY D 121/24	IVY D 121/27
IVY D 122/09	GRACE 151/32	GRACE 155/06	GRACE 164/17
GRACE 167/13	DEAD 180/01	DEAD 181/19	DEAD 184/06
DEAD 193/34	DEAD 194/30	DEAD 196/01	

YOURS (1) .... LITTL 79/07
YOURSELF (11) .... ENCTR 25/27

	LITTL	72/31	LITTL	77/11	LITTL	78/33	CLAY	99/04
	IVY D	120/15	MOTHR	138/28	MOTHR	144/16	GRACE	152/25
	DEAD	187/34	DEAD	195/22				
YOURSELVES (2)						....	GRACE	161/32
	GRACE	173/23						
YOUS (1)		....					MOTHR	142/29
YOUTH (8)		....					RACE	44/03
	RACE	46/10	GALNT	50/04	HOUSE	64/28	HOUSE	64/31
	PNFUL	109/02	DEAD	204/04	DEAD	204/33		
YOU'VE (4)		....					ARABY	34/04
	LITTL	78/28	DEAD	181/15	DEAD	190/04		

ZARATHUSTRA (1)	....	PNFUL	112/16
ZEAL (1)	....	RACE	46/23
ZEPHYR (1)	....	LITTL	83/32

```
1ST (1) ........................................... SISTR  12/06
1891 (1) .......................................... IVY D 134/04
1895 (1) .......................................... SISTR  12/06
57E (1) ........................................... PNFUL 114/14
6TH (1) ........................................... IVY D 134/04
65 (2) ...........................:................ GRACE 161/04
      GRACE 161/17
```

```
A (3) .............................................. LITTL  77/29
     GRACE 167/30     GRACE 167/31
ABSENT (1) ........................................ PARTS  89/14
AGED (1) .......................................... PARTS  90/01
ALL (1) ........................................... ARABY  31/07
ALONG (1) ......................................... LITTL  78/25
AN (1) ............................................ GALNT  59/17
AND (2) ........................................... CLAY  102/28
     GRACE 168/26
APPLE (1) ......................................... ARABY  29/15
ARM (3) ........................................... SISTR  12/13
     SISTR  14/33     HOUSE  64/03
ASHEN (1) ......................................... ENCTR  24/25
AWAKE (2) ......................................... SISTR  18/08
     SISTR  18/14


BACON (2) ......................................... HOUSE  64/02
     HOUSE  64/02
BANISTER (1) ...................................... SISTR  14/11
BANKS (1) ......................................... LITTL  73/15
BARREL (1) ........................................ MOTHR 138/12
BE (1) ............................................ DEAD  207/11
BED (3) ........................................... HOUSE  68/27
     PNFUL 107/13     DEAD  218/16
BEEF (2) .......................................... SISTR  16/27
     GRACE 156/20
BELLS (1) ......................................... DEAD  180/17
BETTER (1) ........................................ DEAD  176/12
BICYCLE (1) ....................................... ARABY  29/17
BISCUIT (1) ....................................... MOTHR 138/12
BITTERS (1) ....................................... DEAD  183/02
BLACK (1) ......................................... ENCTR  24/23
BLANK (1) ......................................... GRACE 162/33
BLOODY (1) ........................................ GRACE 157/33
BLUE (2) .......................................... LITTL  81/11
     PARTS  95/13
BLUSH (1) ......................................... MOTHR 138/32
BOARD (1) ......................................... DEAD  186/11
BOAT (1) .......................................... EVELN  38/29
BOILER (1) ........................................ DEAD  207/18
BONA (1) .......................................... GRACE 159/24
BONE (2) .......................................... MOTHR 143/30
     DEAD  176/19
BOOK (5) .......................................... CLAY  105/02
     CLAY  105/21     CLAY  105/26     PNFUL 107/11     DEAD  193/11
BOOTS (2) ......................................... CLAY  101/27
     CLAY  101/28
BOTTLE (1) ........................................ ENCTR  27/17
BOUND (1) ......................................... DEAD  193/11
BOX (3) ........................................... SISTR  12/17
     SISTR  18/07     MOTHR 139/22
BOYS (1) .......................................... ARABY  31/06
BREAD (1) ......................................... HOUSE  64/06
BREAK (1) ......................................... CLAY  100/22
BREAKFAST (3) ..................................... GALNT  57/12
     HOUSE  64/01     DEAD  213/17
BRIMMED (1) ....................................... IVY D 130/09
BROTHER (1) ....................................... GRACE 172/04
BROWN (1) ......................................... ARABY  33/13
BRUSH (1) ......................................... ARABY  32/30
BY (1) ............................................ DEAD  188/16
```

BYE (2) .... PNFUL 112/10
    MOTHR 138/02

CAKE (2) .... CLAY 102/12
    CLAY 102/24
CANDLE (1) .... RACE   46/08
CARAFE (1) .... PNFUL 112/31
CARD (2) .... LITTL 79/29
    DEAD 217/19
CASE (2) .... LITTL 78/05
    PNFUL 107/11
CATHOLICS (1) .... GRACE 159/30
CHAIN (1) .... PARTS 92/30
CHAIR (3) .... SISTR 12/13
    SISTR 14/33   HOUSE 64/03
CHANGING (1) .... ARABY 30/04
CHEVAL (1) .... DEAD 218/18
CHRISTMAS (4) .... DEAD 178/26
    DEAD 178/31   DEAD 178/31   DEAD 217/19
CIGAR (1) .... LITTL 78/05
CIGARETTE (1) .... IVY D 125/02
CLAD (1) .... ARABY 33/13
CLASS (4) .... ARABY 34/15
    MOTHR 136/10   GRACE 166/22   DEAD 176/12
CLASSES (1) .... IVY D 121/28
CLEAN (3) .... LITTL 75/04
    PARTS 87/03   IVY D 130/08
CLERKS (1) .... LITTL 71/25
CLOTHES (2) .... PNFUL 107/10
    PNFUL 107/13
COAL (1) .... PNFUL 107/10
COAT (5) .... SISTR 12/14
    PNFUL 113/10   IVY D 120/28   IVY D 125/27   GRACE 156/08
COCK (1) .... IVY D 125/13
COLLAR (1) .... MOTHR 143/30
COLLECTOR (1) .... RACE   47/12
COLONEL (1) .... CLAY 102/33
COLOUR (1) .... LITTL 75/05
COLOURED (3) .... PARTS 86/10
    PARTS 96/08   DEAD 177/25
COMBING (1) .... HOUSE 67/07
COME (1) .... ARABY 31/07
COMER (2) .... GALNT 54/10
    GRACE 152/16
COMMON (1) .... GRACE 165/04
COMPLEXIONED (2) .... ENCTR 22/28
    DEAD 198/18
CONFESSION (1) .... SISTR 18/07
CONTAINED (1) .... HOUSE 63/32
CORN (1) .... HOUSE 63/02
COSY (1) .... ENCTR 19/14
COUNTER (1) .... DEAD 197/26
COVERED (3) .... SISTR 12/02
    ARABY 29/11   DEAD 206/21
CRABBED (1) .... GRACE 170/19
CROSS (2) .... DEAD 189/23
    DEAD 209/07
CROWNS (1) .... CLAY 100/11
CUP (1) .... DEAD 213/17
CUT (2) .... LITTL 70/03
    DEAD 187/22

CYCLING (3) .... GRACE 151/22
    GRACE 151/33   GRACE 152/23

DARK (2) .... ENCTR 2?/28
    DEAD 198/18
DAY (7) .... ENCTR 24/32
    ENCTR 28/01   LITTL 75/29   PNFUL 113/21   IVY D 129/29
    IVY D 131/13   DEAD 199/19
DEAD (1) .... SISTR 14/13
DEEP (1) .... DEAD 222/06
DIAMOND (1) .... DEAD 176/19
DIDDLE (1) .... MOTHR 149/07
DIRECTIONS (1) .... DEAD 209/07
DISCLOSED (1) .... PNFUL 110/01
DISHES (1) .... DEAD 196/22
DO (3) .... IVY D 123/33
    IVY D 123/33   MOTHR 149/07
DOOR (15) .... SISTR 12/03
    GALNT 60/02   PARTS 97/13   CLAY 104/13   CLAY 104/32
    CLAY 105/01   CLAY 105/03   CLAY 105/18   GRACE 172/04
    DEAD 175/04   DEAD 196/07   DEAD 206/17   DEAD 208/20
    DEAD 210/11   DEAD 210/16
DOORS (1) .... DEAD 177/19
DOWN (2) .... IVY D 123/23
    MOTHR 137/15
DOZEN (1) .... LITTL 77/29
DRAWING (12) .... ARABY 29/08
    ARABY 31/20   HOUSE 62/24   MOTHR 138/11   DEAD 179/02
    DEAD 182/02   DEAD 185/14   DEAD 186/03   DEAD 191/34
    DEAD 195/12   DEAD 202/06   DEAD 222/29
DRAWN (1) .... DEAD 222/06
DRESS (1) .... CLAY 101/28
DRESSING (10) .... MOTHR 139/14
    MOTHR 139/21   MOTHR 142/15   MOTHR 143/24   MOTHR 144/23
    MOTHR 145/30   MOTHR 147/22   DEAD 175/08   DEAD 177/15
    DEAD 179/22
DRIVERS (1) .... RACE 45/15
DUMB (1) .... DEAD 180/17

EARNED (1) .... EVELN 38/15
EATING (1) .... PNFUL 108/34
EGG (1) .... PARTS 91/20
EIDER (1) .... MOTHR 137/15
EIGHT (1) .... ENCTR 19/09
ELECTRIC (1) .... DEAD 216/02
EMERGED (1) .... IVY D 118/06
ENTERED (1) .... PARTS 89/13
EVENING (2) .... DEAD 185/01
    DEAD 185/02
EVER (1) .... ARABY 30/04
EXAMINATION (1) .... DEAD 189/23
EYE (1) .... IVY D 125/13

FACED (4) .... PARTS 96/30
    PARTS 97/16   DEAD 182/18   DEAD 183/29
FACTOR'S (1) .... HOUSE 63/02
FAIR (1) .... MOTHR 142/31
FANGLED (1) .... SISTR 17/07
FASHIONED (3) .... MOTHR 147/11

```
        DEAD  179/31      DEAD  196/32
                                                        HOUSE   64/02
FAT (1) ..........................................      HOUSE   61/04
FATHER (1) .......................................      GRACE  170/30
FEARING (1) ......................................      PNFUL  111/05
FEATURED (1) .....................................      GRACE  156/07
FED (1) ..........................................      DEAD   192/15
FEELING (1) ......................................      LITTL   71/25
FELLOW (5) .......................................      GRACE  174/12
        MOTHR 143/07     GRACE 159/24     GRACE 159/30  DEAD   204/14
FELLOWSHIP (1) ...................................      GRACE  159/24
FIDE (1) .........................................      DEAD   218/19
FILLED (1) ...................✓...................      MOTHR  142/21
FIRST (1) ........................................      SISTR   12/08
FIVE (3) .........................................
        HOUSE  64/28     GRACE 156/13                   MOTHR  149/07
FOL (1) ..........................................      DEAD   207/11
FORGOTTEN (1) ....................................      DEAD   205/23
FORK (1) .........................................      PNFUL  113/23
FORTY (1) ........................................      HOUSE   64/27
FOUR (4) .........................................
        CLAY  102/28     MOTHR 137/19     GRACE 163/15  DEAD   187/20
FRANK (1) ........................................      HOUSE   66/08
FREE (1) .........................................      IVY D  125/27
FROCK (2) ........................................
        GRACE 156/08                                    DEAD   218/19
FRONT (1) ........................................      DEAD   196/31
FRUIT (1) ........................................

                                                        DEAD   218/21
GILT (1) .........................................      GALNT   57/13
GIRLS (3) ........................................
        GALNT  57/23     PARTS 93/12                    PNFUL  108/25
GLANCES (1) ......................................      SISTR   15/14
GLASS (5) ........................................      DEAD   218/18
        HOUSE  65/20     HOUSE  68/20     DEAD  197/27  SISTR   15/02
GLASSES (2) ......................................
        LITTL  74/20                                    DEAD   207/18
GLUE (1) .........................................      GRACE  170/30
GOD (1) ..........................................      PARTS   93/12
GOINGS (1) .......................................      PARTS   87/03
GOLD (1) .........................................      ENCTR   24/32
GOOD (31) ........................................      HOUSE   67/19
        ENCTR  28/01     GALNT  50/32     GALNT  58/33  DEAD   177/02
        PNFUL 112/10     MOTHR 138/02     GRACE 155/27  DEAD   206/13
        DEAD  185/01     DEAD  185/02     DEAD  204/14  DEAD   212/22
        DEAD  212/19     DEAD  212/20     DEAD  212/22  DEAD   212/26
        DEAD  212/23     DEAD  212/23     DEAD  212/25  DEAD   212/29
        DEAD  212/26     DEAD  212/27     DEAD  212/28  DEAD   215/08
        DEAD  212/30     DEAD  212/30     DEAD  214/33
        DEAD  216/08     DEAD  222/24                   PNFUL  110/09
GRANDFATHER (1) ..................................      SISTR   12/14
GREAT (3) ........................................
        PNFUL 110/09     PNFUL 110/09                   ENCTR   27/17
GREEN (2) ........................................
        CLAY  101/12                                    ENCTR   24/23
GREENISH (1) .....................................      ENCTR   24/25
GREY (4) .........................................
        CLAY  101/12     IVY D 118/12     MOTHR 144/32

                                                        IVY D  118/12
HAIRED (3) .......................................
        MOTHR 142/31     MOTHR 144/32
```

```
HALF   (15) ............................................... ARABY   30/21
       GALNT   59/17     HOUSE   65/19     LITTL   70/16     LITTL   75/24
       LITTL   77/29     PARTS   93/22     CLAY   100/11     PNFUL  110/01
       MOTHR  139/25     GRACE  153/17     GRACE  162/21     GRACE  162/23
       GRACE  166/28     DEAD   222/05
HALL   (10) ............................................... GALNT   60/02
       HOUSE   62/24     HOUSE   68/10     HOUSE   68/14     DEAD   175/04
       DEAD   196/07     DEAD   206/17     DEAD   208/20     DEAD   210/11
       DEAD   210/16
HAND   (3) ................................................ PNFUL  107/14
       IVY D  123/23     DEAD   188/13
HANDED (2) ................................................ PARTS   90/29
       GRACE  163/15
HANDKERCHIEF (1) .......................................... HOUSE   65/28
HARD   (3) ................................................ EVELN   38/15
       PNFUL  111/05     DEAD   205/01
HAT    (2) ................................................ ARABY   32/30
       PARTS   88/24
HAY    (1) ................................................ DEAD   177/25
HEARTED (2) ............................................... EVELN   38/28
       DEAD   203/09
HEARTEDLY (1) ............................................. LITTL   73/03
HEAVY  (1) ................................................ DEAD   184/30
HIGH   (2) ................................................ MOTHR  136/10
       DEAD   185/30
HOP    (2) ................................................ IVY D  127/16
       DEAD   183/02
HOUR   (2) ................................................ GALNT   59/17
       HOUSE   65/19
HOUSE  (9) ................................................ GALNT   50/17
       HOUSE   61/14     PARTS   90/22     PARTS   92/25     PARTS   97/05
       CLAY   101/27     PNFUL  108/34     PNFUL  116/08     GRACE  159/22
HOUSES (1) ................................................ HOUSE   66/09
HOW    (1) ................................................ IVY D  123/33
HUMOUREDLY (1) ............................................ DEAD   206/13
HUNKER (1) ................................................ IVY D  121/25


I      (1) ................................................ MOTHR  149/07
ILL    (1) ................................................ DEAD   192/15
IN     (3) ................................................ HOUSE   61/04
       DEAD   191/24     DEAD   191/25
INNOCENT (1) .............................................. RACE    43/14
IRISH  (1) ................................................ LITTL   74/10


JACKET (2) ................................................ HOUSE   67/07
       IVY D  120/28
JOG    (1) ................................................ LITTL   78/25
JUG    (1) ................................................ HOUSE   68/21


KEY    (1) ................................................ DEAD   186/11
KNOCKER (1) ............................................... SISTR   12/03


LACED  (1) ................................................ GRACE  160/21
LADEN  (1) ................................................ DEAD   197/09
LADY   (1) ................................................ LITTL   83/12
LAMP   (3) ................................................ GALNT   59/06
       GALNT   59/24     PNFUL  111/01
LAMPS  (1) ................................................ RACE    46/08
```

LANTERN (1) .... GRACE 171/31
LAUGHING (2) .... SISTR 18/08
    SISTR 18/14
LAW (3) .... HOUSE 61/04
    DEAD 191/24   DEAD 191/25
LAY (1) .... GRACE 172/04
LEAF (1) .... DEAD 196/24
LEATHER (2) .... DEAD 178/14
    DEAD 193/11
LIDDED (1) .... DEAD 184/30
LIFE (1) .... ENCTR 21/09
LIGHT (2) .... LITTL 73/03
    DEAD 216/02
LIKE (4) .... SISTR 18/08
    SISTR 18/14   LITTL 71/33   LITTL 83/12
LOOKING (8) .... ARABY 34/28
    RACE 43/14   GALNT 57/02   HOUSE 68/20   LITTL 74/10
    CLAY 102/33   GRACE 170/19   GRACE 173/07
LOUD (1) .... HOUSE 65/09
LOVING (1) .... MOTHR 141/17
LOW (1) .... DEAD 187/22
LUNCH (1) .... LITTL 70/08

MAGIC (1) .... GRACE 171/31
MAKER (1) .... CLAY 99/16
MAKING (1) .... DEAD 222/23
MAN (6) .... IVY D 121/17
    IVY D 121/19   IVY D 121/30   IVY D 121/31   IVY D 121/33
    DEAD 186/30
MANNERED (1) .... DEAD 187/20
MASTER (1) .... ENCTR 23/21
MATCH (1) .... PARTS 94/17
MATRON (1) .... CLAY 99/17
ME (1) .... IVY D 123/23
MEANING (1) .... DEAD 220/03
MEN (2) .... PNFUL 116/11
    GRACE 174/12
MERCHANT (1) .... GRACE 156/16
MERCHANT'S (1) .... HOUSE 65/14
MERRY (1) .... DEAD 222/23
MIDDLE (1) .... PARTS 90/01
MINDED (2) .... GALNT 58/12
    GRACE 157/33
MINDEDNESS (1) .... PARTS 89/14
MIRROR (1) .... PNFUL 107/14
MONDAY (1) .... CLAY 100/11
MOONS (1) .... LITTL 70/16
MORROW (5) .... ENCTR 21/25
    EVELN 40/32   LITTL 79/25   LITTL 81/27   IVY D 128/26
MOTHER (1) .... GALNT 55/28
MUSIC (6) .... HOUSE 62/24
    HOUSE 68/10   HOUSE 68/14   PNFUL 112/14   MOTHR 141/17
    DEAD 193/11
MY (1) .... IVY D 127/16

NAPKINS (1) .... DEAD 184/19
NEVER (1) .... DEAD 207/11
NEW (3) .... SISTR 17/07
    GALNT 34/10   GRACE 152/16
NEXT (5) .... CLAY 104/13

```
        CLAY   104/32    CLAY    105/01    CLAY    105/03    CLAY   105/18
NIGHT (38) ...........................................  EVELN   38/29
        GALNT   50/32    GALNT    58/33    LITTL   79/26    PNFUL  109/22
        IVY D  121/06    GRACE   155/10    GRACE  155/27    DEAD   177/02
        DEAD   180/02    DEAD    180/27    DEAD   184/07    DEAD   193/23
        DEAD   202/19    DEAD    203/26    DEAD   204/04    DEAD   204/11
        DEAD   204/26    DEAD    204/34    DEAD   212/15    DEAD   212/19
        DEAD   212/20    DEAD    212/22    DEAD   212/22    DEAD   212/23
        DEAD   212/23    DEAD    212/25    DEAD   212/26    DEAD   212/26
        DEAD   212/27    DEAD    212/28    DEAD   212/29    DEAD   212/30
        DEAD   212/30    DEAD    214/33    DEAD   215/08    DEAD   216/08
        DEAD   222/24
NIGHTS (1) .............................................  HOUSE   67/19
NINE (1) ...............................................  HOUSE   66/12
NOSED (1) ..............................................  SISTR   11/17

O' (2) .................................................  IVY D  127/16
        DEAD   186/30
O'CLOCK (1) ............................................  ENCTR   19/09
OF (2) .................................................  GALNT   55/28
        DEAD   177/19
OFFICE (4) .............................................  PARTS   92/31
        PARTS   93/05    PARTS    93/12    MOTHR  139/22
OIL (2) ................................................  PNFUL  111/01
        IVY D  128/04
OLD (3) ................................................  MOTHR  147/11
        DEAD   179/31    DEAD    196/32
ONE (3) ................................................  GALNT   58/01
        LITTL   75/24    PARTS    93/22
OPEN (2) ...............................................  EVELN   38/28
        DEAD   222/05
OPENED (1) .............................................  ARABY   30/21
ORDERS (1) .............................................  DEAD   197/26
ORGAN (1) ..............................................  EVELN   40/07
OUT (3) ................................................  GRACE  168/26
        GRACE  168/26    DEAD    177/19
OVER (2) ...............................................  PNFUL  108/12
        PNFUL  113/10

PANES (1) ..............................................  SISTR   14/04
PAPER (1) ..............................................  ARABY   29/11
PAPERS (1) .............................................  IVY D  125/02
PARTY (1) ..............................................  LITTL   79/29
PAST (2) ...............................................  MOTHR  139/25
        GRACE  153/17
PATENT (1) .............................................  DEAD   178/14
PAWN (2) ...............................................  PARTS   92/31
        PARTS   93/05
PEACE (1) ..............................................  CLAY    99/16
PEACOCK (1) ............................................  PARTS   95/13
PEARL (1) ..............................................  GALNT   55/28
PENNY (3) ..............................................  GRACE  167/30
        GRACE  167/31    DEAD    200/28
PIANO (1) ..............................................  DEAD   194/18
PIECE (1) ..............................................  DEAD   200/28
PIER (1) ...............................................  HOUSE   65/20
PILLOW (1) .............................................  SISTR   16/04
PINK (2) ...............................................  HOUSE   61/18
        MOTHR  138/32
PINT (1) ...............................................  GRACE  166/28
```

PITCHED (1) .... DEAD 185/**30**
PLANTS (1) .... CLAY 100/28
PLAYER (1) .... EVELN 40/07
PLUM (1) .... GALNT 57/07
POCKET (2) .... HOUSE 65/28
    PNFUL 113/09
POINT (1) .... GRACE 162/33
POOR (1) .... GALNT 57/02
POST (2) .... GALNT 59/06
    GALNT 59/24
POWERFUL (1) .... GRACE 173/07
PRAYER (3) .... CLAY 105/02
    CLAY 105/21   CLAY 105/26
PUBLIC (7) .... GALNT 50/17
    HOUSE 66/09   PARTS 90/22   PARTS 92/25   PARTS 97/05
    PNFUL 116/08   GRACE 159/22
PUDDING (3) .... GALNT 57/07
    HOUSE 64/06   DEAD 205/23
PUMP (1) .... ARABY 29/17

QUARTERS (1) .... MOTHR 141/30

RABBLE (1) .... IVY D 134/29
RACK (2) .... PARTS 88/24
    PNFUL 107/10
RAG (1) .... IVY D 128/04
RAIL (3) .... SISTR 14/11
    HOUSE 68/27   DEAD 218/16
RATE (1) .... MOTHR 142/21
RE (3) .... SISTR 12/02
    PARTS 89/13   IVY D 118/06
RED (2) .... SISTR 11/17
    DEAD 183/29
REFRESHMENT (2) .... DEAD 186/07
    DEAD 187/16
RETURN (1) .... HOUSE 68/09
RIMMED (2) .... PARTS 87/03
    DEAD 218/21
RIND (1) .... HOUSE 64/02
RIPE (1) .... PNFUL 108/12
RIVER (1) .... LITTL 73/15
ROOM (31) .... SISTR 14/13
    ARABY 29/08   ARABY 31/20   HOUSE 61/14   HOUSE 62/24
    HOUSE 64/01   HOUSE 68/09   PNFUL 114/12   MOTHR 138/11
    MOTHR 139/14   MOTHR 139/21   MOTHR 142/15   MOTHR 143/24
    MOTHR 144/23   MOTHR 145/30   MOTHR 147/22   DEAD 175/08
    DEAD 177/15   DEAD 179/02   DEAD 179/22   DEAD 182/02
    DEAD 185/14   DEAD 186/03   DEAD 186/07   DEAD 187/16
    DEAD 191/34   DEAD 195/12   DEAD 196/10   DEAD 202/06
    DEAD 205/33   DEAD 222/29
ROUT (1) .... IVY D 134/29

SAILING (1) .... ENCTR 23/10
SCHOOL (1) .... ENCTR 21/09
SCUTTLE (1) .... PNFUL 107/10
SECOND (2) .... GRACE 166/22
    DEAD 188/13
SELF (2) .... HOUSE 63/32
    DEAD 205/11

SELLERS (1) .... PARTS 94/17
SENSE (1) .... GRACE 165/04
SETS (1) .... ARABY 35/05
SEVEN (2) .... GRACE 162/21
    GRACE 162/23
SHADED (1) .... PNFUL 107/15
SHAPED (3) .... PARTS 91/20
    DEAD 196/24   DEAD 196/25
SHARP (1) .... PARTS 97/16
SHAVEN (3) .... LITTL 75/04
    PARTS 87/03   IVY D 130/08
SHERIFF (1) .... GRACE 158/25
SHILLING (2) .... MOTHR 139/01
    DEAD 176/20
SHIRT (2) .... IVY D 127/10
    DEAD 218/19
SHOP (3) .... SISTR 12/28
    ARABY 31/06   CLAY 102/12
SIDE (7) .... PARTS 97/13
    CLAY 99/05   PNFUL 108/25   PNFUL 113/09   GRACE 157/10
    GRACE 172/04   DEAD 196/22
SIMPLE (1) .... GALNT 58/12
SINGERS (1) .... ARABY 31/07
SINGLE (1) .... PARTS 90/29
SIX (1) .... RACE 43/13
SIXTY (1) .... SISTR 12/08
SLATE (2) .... LITTL 75/05
    LITTL 81/11
SLEEVES (1) .... IVY D 127/10
SLIDING (1) .... IVY D 121/25
SNAPPERS (1) .... DEAD 194/23
SNOW (2) .... DEAD 177/19
    DEAD 206/21
SNUFF (2) .... SISTR 12/17
    SISTR 12/24
SOFA (1) .... SISTR 16/04
SON (2) .... DEAD 191/24
    DEAD 191/25
SONG (1) .... DEAD 193/11
STAGE (1) .... MOTHR 147/14
STAINS (1) .... SISTR 12/24
STALK (1) .... DEAD 196/25
STAND (3) .... PNFUL 112/14
    DEAD 193/11   DEAD 196/31
STICK (1) .... PARTS 98/08
STIFFENED (1) .... DEAD 177/19
STILL (1) .... DEAD 218/16
STOCK (1) .... DEAD 218/16
STOOL (1) .... DEAD 194/18
STOPPERS (1) .... DEAD 197/27
STRAIGHT (1) .... GRACE 160/21
STREET (2) .... ARABY 31/07
    DEAD 188/16
SUB (2) .... CLAY 99/17
    GRACE 158/25
SUFFERER (1) .... MOTHR 143/07
SUIT (3) .... GRACE 151/22
    GRACE 151/33   GRACE 152/23
SULLEN (1) .... PARTS 96/30
SUPPER (5) .... DEAD 192/08
    DEAD 192/16   DEAD 193/09   DEAD 196/10   DEAD 205/33

TABLE (6) .... ARABY   33/19
      DEAD   184/19   DEAD   192/08   DEAD   192/16   DEAD   193/09
      DEAD   215/33
TABLES (1) .... CLAY   99/05
TEA (7) .... SISTR   16/27
      ENCTR   19/14   ARABY   33/19   ARABY   35/05   CLAY   101/24
      GRACE 156/16   GRACE 156/20
TENTHS (1) .... HOUSE   66/12
THE (1) .... MOTHR 149/07
THINGS (1) .... CLAY   101/24
THINKING (1) .... HOUSE   66/08
THIRD (1) .... ARABY   34/15
THIRDS (1) .... GRACE 173/12
THIRTY (4) .... GALNT   58/01
      HOUSE   64/27   HOUSE   64/28   LITTL   73/26
THOUGHT (2) .... DEAD   192/12
      DEAD   203/22
THREE (4) .... ENCTR   23/21
      PNFUL 113/23   MOTHR 141/30   DEAD   176/20
THRUSTS (1) .... GRACE 157/10
THUMB (1) .... IVY D 127/16
TICKET (1) .... RACE   47/12
TIME (5) .... GALNT   57/12
      LITTL   70/08   DEAD   178/26   DEAD   178/31   DEAD   178/31
TO (26) .... ENCTR   21/25
      EVELN   40/32   LITTL   75/29   LITTL   79/25   LITTL   79/26
      LITTL   81/27   PNFUL 109/22   PNFUL 113/21   IVY D 121/06
      IVY D 128/26   IVY D 129/29   IVY D 131/13   GRACE 155/10
      DEAD   180/02   DEAD   180/27   DEAD   184/07   DEAD   193/23
      DEAD   199/19   DEAD   202/19   DEAD   203/26   DEAD   204/04
      DEAD   204/11   DEAD   204/26   DEAD   204/34   DEAD   207/11
      DEAD   212/15
TOILET (1) .... DEAD   215/33
TORMENTED (2) .... DEAD   192/12
      DEAD   203/22
TRAM (2) .... RACE   45/15
      PARTS   93/12
TRAVELLERS (1) .... GRACE 159/24
TREE (1) .... ARABY   29/15
TWENTY (4) .... RACE   43/13
      PNFUL 115/01   MOTHR 137/19   GRACE 156/13
TWO (5) .... LITTL   73/26
      CLAY   102/28   PNFUL 115/01   MOTHR 139/01   GRACE 173/12

UP (1) .... CLAY   100/22

VEINED (1) .... HOUSE   61/18
VERMIN (1) .... LITTL   71/33
VESSEL (1) .... ENCTR   23/10
VOICED (1) .... HOUSE   65/09

WAITING (1) .... PNFUL 114/12
WALKING (1) .... PARTS   98/08
WAR (1) .... DEAD   186/30
WARDROBE (1) .... MOTHR 147/14
WARM (1) .... DEAD   203/09
WATCH (1) .... PARTS   92/30
WATER (2) .... HOUSE   68/21

```
      PNFUL  112/31
WAX  (1) ........................................... CLAY   100/28
WEARY  (1) ......................................... ARABY   34/28
WEDDING  (1) ....................................... CLAY   102/24
WEEK  (2) .......................................... GRACE  167/30
      GRACE  167/31
WELL  (5) .......................................... LITTL   70/03
      GRACE  156/07    DEAD   197/09    DEAD   218/19   DEAD   220/03
WHIPPER  (1) ....................................... DEAD   194/23
WHIT  (1) .......................................... CLAY   100/11
WHITE  (1) ......................................... PNFUL  107/15
WIDE  (3) .......................................... SISTR   18/08
      SISTR   18/14    IVY D  130/09
WINDOW  (1) ........................................ SISTR   14/04
WINDOWS  (1) ....................................... SISTR   12/28
WINE  (6) .......................................... SISTR   15/02
      SISTR   15/14    HOUSE   65/14    LITTL   74/20   PARTS   86/10
      PARTS   96/08
WIZEN  (1) ......................................... DEAD   182/18
WON  (1) ........................................... DEAD   205/11
WORK  (2) .......................................... GALNT   57/13
      GALNT   57/23
WORKING  (8) ....................................... PNFUL  116/11
      IVY D  121/17    IVY D  121/19    IVY D  121/28   IVY D  121/30
      IVY D  121/31    IVY D  121/33    DEAD   205/01


YOU  (2) ........................................... ARABY   31/07
      IVY D  123/33
```